Dictionary of Literary Biography® • Volume Seventy-nine

American Magazine Journalists, 1850-1900

Rathbun and Monica M. Grecu (1987)

60 *Canadian Writers Since 1960,* Second Series, edited by W. H. New (1987)

61 *American Writers for Children Since 1960: Poets, Illustrators, and Nonfiction Authors,* edited by Glenn E. Estes (1987)

62 *Elizabethan Dramatists,* edited by Fredson Bowers (1987)

63 *Modern American Critics, 1920-1955,* edited by Gregory S. Jay (1988)

64 *American Literary Critics and Scholars, 1850-1880,* edited by John W. Rathbun and Monica M. Grecu (1988)

65 *French Novelists, 1900-1930,* edited by Catharine Savage Brosman (1988)

66 *German Fiction Writers, 1885-1913,* 2 parts, edited by James Hardin (1988)

67 *Modern American Critics Since 1955,* edited by Gregory S. Jay (1988)

68 *Canadian Writers, 1920-1959,* First Series, edited by W. H. New (1988)

69 *Contemporary German Fiction Writers,* First Series, edited by Wolfgang D. Elfe and James Hardin (1988)

70 *British Mystery Writers, 1860-1919,* edited by Bernard Benstock and Thomas F. Staley (1988)

71 *American Literary Critics and Scholars, 1880-1900,* edited by John W. Rathbun and Monica M. Grecu (1988)

72 *French Novelists, 1930-1960,* edited by Catharine Savage Brosman (1988)

73 *American Magazine Journalists, 1741-1850,* edited by Sam G. Riley (1988)

74 *American Short-Story Writers Before 1880,* edited by Bobby Ellen Kimbel, with the assistance of William E. Grant (1988)

75 *Contemporary German Fiction Writers,* Second Series, edited by Wolfgang D. Elfe and James Hardin (1988)

76 *Afro-American Writers, 1940-1955,* edited by Trudier Harris (1988)

77 *British Mystery Writers, 1920-1939,* edited by Bernard Benstock and Thomas F. Staley (1988)

78 *American Short-Story Writers, 1880-1910,* edited by Bobby Ellen Kimbel, with the assistance of William E. Grant (1988)

79 *American Magazine Journalists, 1850-1900,* edited by Sam G. Riley (1988)

80 *Restoration and Eighteenth-Century Dramatists,* First Series, edited by Paula R. Backscheider (1989)

81 *Austrian Fiction Writers, 1875-1913,* edited by James Hardin and Donald G. Daviau (1989)

82 *Chicano Writers,* First Series, edited by Francisco A. Lomelí and Carl R. Shirley (1989)

83 *French Novelists Since 1960,* edited by Catharine Savage Brosman (1989)

84 *Restoration and Eighteenth-Century Dramatists,* Second Series, edited by Paula R. Backscheider (1989)

85 *Austrian Fiction Writers After 1914,* edited by James Hardin and Donald G. Daviau (1989)

86 *American Short-Story Writers, 1910-1945,* First Series, edited by Bobby Ellen Kimbel (1989)

87 *British Mystery and Thriller Writers Since 1940,* First Series, edited by Bernard Benstock and Thomas F. Staley (1989)

88 *Canadian Writers, 1920-1959,* Second Series, edited by W. H. New (1989)

89 *Restoration and Eighteenth-Century Dramatists,* Third Series, edited by Paula R. Backscheider (1989)

90 *German Writers in the Age of Goethe, 1789-1832,* edited by James Hardin and Christoph E. Schweitzer (1989)

91 *American Magazine Journalists, 1900-1960,* First Series, edited by Sam G. Riley (1990)

92 *Canadian Writers, 1890-1920,* edited by W. H. New (1990)

93 *British Romantic Poets, 1789-1832,* First Series, edited by John R. Greenfield (1990)

94 *German Writers in the Age of Goethe: Sturm und Drang to Classicism,* edited by James Hardin and Christoph E. Schweitzer (1990)

95 *Eighteenth-Century British Poets,* First Series, edited by John Sitter (1990)

96 *British Romantic Poets, 1789-1832,* Second Series, edited by John R. Greenfield (1990)

97 *German Writers from the Enlightenment to Sturm und Drang, 1720-1764,* edited by James Hardin and Christoph E. Schweitzer (1990)

98 *Modern British Essayists,* First Series, edited by Robert Beum (1990)

99 *Canadian Writers Before 1890,* edited by W. H. New (1990)

100 *Modern British Essayists,* Second Series, edited by Robert Beum (1990)

101 *British Prose Writers, 1660-1800,* First Series, edited by Donald T. Siebert (1991)

102 *American Short-Story Writers, 1910-1945,* Second Series, edited by Bobby Ellen Kimbel (1991)

103 *American Literary Biographers,* First Series, edited by Steven Serafin (1991)

104 *British Prose Writers, 1660-1800,* Second Series, edited by Donald T. Siebert (1991)

105 *American Poets Since World War II,* Second Series, edited by R. S. Gwynn (1991)

106 *British Literary Publishing Houses, 1820-1880,* edited by Patricia J. Anderson and Jonathan Rose (1991)

107 *British Romantic Prose Writers, 1789-1832,* First Series, edited by John R. Greenfield (1991)

108 *Twentieth-Century Spanish Poets,* First Series, edited by Michael L. Perna (1991)

109 *Eighteenth-Century British Poets,* Second Series, edited by John Sitter (1991)

110 *British Romantic Prose Writers, 1789-1832,* Second Series, edited by John R. Greenfield (1991)

111 *American Literary Biographers,* Second Series, edited by Steven Serafin (1991)

112 *British Literary Publishing Houses, 1881-1965,* edited by Jonathan Rose and Patricia J. Anderson (1991)

113 *Modern Latin-American Fiction Writers,* First Series, edited by William Luis (1992)

114 *Twentieth-Century Italian Poets,* First Series, edited by Giovanna Wedel De Stasio, Glauco Cambon, and Antonio Illiano (1992)

115 *Medieval Philosophers,* edited by Jeremiah Hackett (1992)

116 *British Romantic Novelists, 1789-1832,* edited by Bradford K. Mudge (1992)

117 *Twentieth-Century Caribbean and Black African Writers,* First Series, edited by Bernth Lindfors and Reinhard Sander (1992)

118 *Twentieth-Century German Dramatists, 1889-1918,* edited by Wolfgang D. Elfe and James Hardin (1992)

119 *Nineteenth-Century French Fiction Writers: Romanticism and Realism, 1800-1860,* edited by Catharine Savage Brosman (1992)

(Continued on back endsheets)

Dictionary of Literary Biography® • Volume Seventy-nine

American Magazine Journalists, 1850-1900

Edited by
Sam G. Riley
Virginia Polytechnic Institute & State University

A Bruccoli Clark Layman Book
Gale Research Inc.
Detroit • Washington, D.C. • London

Advisory Board for
DICTIONARY OF LITERARY BIOGRAPHY

Louis S. Auchincloss
John Baker
William Cagle
Jane Christensen
Patrick O'Connor
Peter S. Prescott

Matthew J. Bruccoli and Richard Layman, *Editorial Directors*
C. E. Frazer Clark, Jr., *Managing Editor*

The paper used in this publication meets the minimum requirements of American National Standard for Information Sciences—Permanence Paper for Printed Library Materials, ANSI Z39.48-1984.

This publication is a creative work copyrighted by Gale Research Inc. and fully protected by all applicable copyright laws, as well as by misappropriation, trade secret, unfair competition, and other applicable laws. The authors and editors of this work have added value to the underlying factual material herein through one or more of the following: unique and original selection, coordination, expression, arrangement, and classification of the information.
Gale Research Inc. will vigorously defend all of its rights in this publication.

Copyright © 1989 by Gale Research Inc.
835 Penobscot Building
Detroit, MI 48226-4094
All rights reserved including the right of reproduction in whole or in part in any form.

ISBN 0-8103-4557-9
88-31930 CIP

Printed in the United States of America.
Published simultaneously in the United Kingdom
by Gale Research International Limited
(An affiliated company of Gale Research Inc.)

10 9 8 7 6 5 4 3

*This volume is dedicated to
Heather Marie Riley,
Most delightful of daughters,
by her proud, admiring Dad*

Contents

Plan of the Series ix	Richard Harding Davis (1864-1916) 114
Foreword xi	*John C. Bromley*
Acknowledgments xvii	James Dunwoody Brownson De Bow (1820-1867) 123
Lyman Abbott (1835-1922) 3	*Whitney R. Mundt*
James Boylan	William Jennings Demorest (1822-1895) 132
Louisa May Alcott (1832-1888) 12	*Douglas S. Campbell*
Lee Jolliffe	Mary Mapes Dodge (1831?-1905) 136
Henry Mills Alden (1836-1919) 17	*Charles Egleston and Kathleen Kearney Keeshen*
Thomas B. Connery	Frederick Douglass (1817-1895) 139
Thomas Bailey Aldrich (1836-1907) 27	*Lloyd E. Chiasson*
J. Douglas Tarpley	Richard Kyle Fox (1846-1922) 143
Timothy Shay Arthur (1809-1885) 33	*Sam G. Riley*
Kathleen L. Endres	Jeannette L. Gilder (1849-1916) 149
Maturin Murray Ballou (Lieutenant Murray) (1820-1895) 43	*W. J. Hug*
George Everett	Richard Watson Gilder (1844-1909) 153
John Kendrick Bangs (1862-1922) 50	*Lloyd J. Graybar*
Jack A. Nelson	E. L. Godkin (1831-1902) 160
Walter Hilliard Bidwell (1798-1881) 55	*Terry Hynes*
Gary W. Selnow	Fletcher Harper (1806-1877) 174
Albert Taylor Bledsoe (1809-1877) 58	*James Glen Stovall*
Paula Cozort Renfro	Bret Harte (1836-1902) 181
Amelia Bloomer (1818-1894) 64	*Charles A. Fleming*
Linda Steiner	Paul Hamilton Hayne (1830-1886) 191
Mary L. Booth (1831-1889) 69	*Rayburn S. Moore*
Maurine H. Beasley	William Dean Howells (1837-1920) 196
Francis Fisher Browne (1843-1913) 74	*A. J. Kaul*
Roger Cameron Lips	John Foster Kirk (1824-1904) 204
H. C. Bunner (1855-1896) 84	*Janet E. Ramsey*
W. J. Hug	Frank Leslie (Henry Carter) (1821-1880) 209
Edward Livermore Burlingame (1848-1922) 90	*William E. Huntzicker*
Patt Foster Roberson	Eliakim Littell (1797-1870) and Robert S. Littell (1831-1896) 222
C. Chauncey Burr (1815?-1883) 94	*Cathy Packer*
Janet E. Ramsey	James Russell Lowell (1819-1891) 225
William Conant Church (1836-1917) and Francis Pharcellus Church (1839-1906) ... 102	*Bert Hitchcock*
Ralph Frasca	John Ames Mitchell (1845-1918) 232
Davis Wasgatt Clark (1812-1871) 107	*Therese L. Lueck*
Kathleen L. Endres	Charles Jacobs Peterson (1819-1887) 236
Rollin M. Daggett (1831-1901) 111	*Karen Nipps*
Jack A. Nelson	William Sydney Porter (O. Henry) (1862-1910) 242
	Carolyn Garrett Cline

George Palmer Putnam (1814-1872) 251
  Shirley M. Mundt

Henry J. Raymond (1820-1869) 258
  Nora Baker

Josephine St. Pierre Ruffin (1842-1924) 265
  Nora Hall

Edward I. Sears (1819?-1876) 269
  Donna Ullrich-Eaton

Roswell Smith (1829-1892) 273
  Frederic B. Farrar

Elizabeth Cady Stanton (1815-1902) 277
  Beth M. Waggenspack

Lucy Stone (1818-1893) 283
  Lee Jolliffe

Albion W. Tourgée (1838-1905) 286
  Kate Esary Russell

Joseph Addison Turner (1826-1868) 295
  Wallace B. Eberhard

John Brisben Walker (1847-1931) 298
  Erwin K. Thomas

George Wilkes (1817-1885) 302
  Sam G. Riley

Victoria C. Woodhull (1838-1927) 306
  John A. Lent

Checklist of Further Readings 315

Contributors 321

Plan of the Series

...Almost the most prodigious asset of a country, and perhaps its most precious possession, is its native literary product—when that product is fine and noble and enduring.

Mark Twain*

The advisory board, the editors, and the publisher of the *Dictionary of Literary Biography* are joined in endorsing Mark Twain's declaration. The literature of a nation provides an inexhaustible resource of permanent worth. We intend to make literature and its creators better understood and more accessible to students and the reading public, while satisfying the standards of teachers and scholars.

To meet these requirements, *literary biography* has been construed in terms of the author's achievement. The most important thing about a writer is his writing. Accordingly, the entries in *DLB* are career biographies, tracing the development of the author's canon and the evolution of his reputation.

The purpose of *DLB* is not only to provide reliable information in a convenient format but also to place the figures in the larger perspective of literary history and to offer appraisals of their accomplishments by qualified scholars.

The publication plan for *DLB* resulted from two years of preparation. The project was proposed to Bruccoli Clark by Frederick G. Ruffner, president of the Gale Research Company, in November 1975. After specimen entries were prepared and typeset, an advisory board was formed to refine the entry format and develop the series rationale. In meetings held during 1976, the publisher, series editors, and advisory board approved the scheme for a comprehensive biographical dictionary of persons who contributed to North American literature. Editorial work on the first volume began in January 1977, and it was published in 1978. In order to make *DLB* more than a reference tool and to compile volumes that individually have claim to status as literary history, it was decided to organize volumes by topic, period, or genre. Each of these freestanding volumes provides a biographical-bibliographical guide and overview for a particular area of literature. We are convinced that this organization—as opposed to a single alphabet method—constitutes a valuable innovation in the presentation of reference material. The volume plan necessarily requires many decisions for the placement and treatment of authors who might properly be included in two or three volumes. In some instances a major figure will be included in separate volumes, but with different entries emphasizing the aspect of his career appropriate to each volume. Ernest Hemingway, for example, is represented in *American Writers in Paris, 1920-1939* by an entry focusing on his expatriate apprenticeship; he is also in *American Novelists, 1910-1945* with an entry surveying his entire career. Each volume includes a cumulative index of subject authors and articles. Comprehensive indexes to the entire series are planned.

With volume ten in 1982 it was decided to enlarge the scope of *DLB*. By the end of 1986 twenty-one volumes treating British literature had been published, and volumes for Commonwealth and Modern European literature were in progress. The series has been further augmented by the *DLB Yearbooks* (since 1981) which update published entries and add new entries to keep the *DLB* current with contemporary activity. There have also been *DLB Documentary Series* volumes which provide biographical and critical source materials for figures whose work is judged to have particular interest for students. One of these companion volumes is entirely devoted to Tennessee Williams.

We define literature as the *intellectual commerce of a nation*: not merely as belles lettres but as that ample and complex process by which ideas are generated, shaped, and transmitted. *DLB* entries are not limited to "creative writers" but extend to other figures who in their time and in their way influenced the mind of a people. Thus the series encompasses historians, journalists, publishers, and screenwriters. By this means readers of *DLB* may be aided to perceive litera-

---

*From an unpublished section of Mark Twain's autobiography, copyright © by the Mark Twain Company.

ture not as cult scripture in the keeping of intellectual high priests but firmly positioned at the center of a nation's life.

DLB includes the major writers appropriate to each volume and those standing in the ranks immediately behind them. Scholarly and critical counsel has been sought in deciding which minor figures to include and how full their entries should be. Wherever possible, useful references are made to figures who do not warrant separate entries.

Each *DLB* volume has a volume editor responsible for planning the volume, selecting the figures for inclusion, and assigning the entries. Volume editors are also responsible for preparing, where appropriate, appendices surveying the major periodicals and literary and intellectual movements for their volumes, as well as lists of further readings. Work on the series as a whole is coordinated at the Bruccoli Clark Layman editorial center in Columbia, South Carolina, where the editorial staff is responsible for accuracy of the published volumes.

One feature that distinguishes *DLB* is the illustration policy–its concern with the iconography of literature. Just as an author is influenced by his surroundings, so is the reader's understanding of the author enhanced by a knowledge of his environment. Therefore *DLB* volumes include not only drawings, paintings, and photographs of authors, often depicting them at various stages in their careers, but also illustrations of their families and places where they lived. Title pages are regularly reproduced in facsimile along with dust jackets for modern authors. The dust jackets are a special feature of *DLB* because they often document better than anything else the way in which an author's work was perceived in its own time. Specimens of the writers' manuscripts are included when feasible.

Samuel Johnson rightly decreed that "The chief glory of every people arises from its authors." The purpose of the *Dictionary of Literary Biography* is to compile literary history in the surest way available to us–by accurate and comprehensive treatment of the lives and work of those who contributed to it.

The *DLB* Advisory Board

Foreword

The half century from 1850 to 1900 was one of tremendous upheaval and change in American life, and this turbulence was duly reflected in the magazines of the era. The Civil War was an enormous agent of change, and after it the increasing industrialization and urbanization of America occasioned still other changes.

As the nation edged toward war, the number of political periodicals grew, roughly doubling during the 1850s. The vast majority of magazines in the prewar period were either regional or local in circulation; a handful of general and women's magazines and a few journals of law, medicine, and religion had national circulations of any size. Even some magazines with *U.S.*, *American*, or *National* in their titles were unable to achieve substantial circulations outside their own locales. When war came, this localism was intensified.

By 1860 about one-third of all magazine circulation was accounted for by those published in New York City. After New York came Philadelphia, Baltimore, and Boston. The most important of the decade's new magazines, *Harper's New Monthly* and the *Atlantic Monthly*, soon raised the standard of popular reading. Other important monthlies were *Graham's* and *Sartain's* of Philadelphia, *Putnam's* (1853-1857) and *Knickerbocker* (1833-1865) of New York, and *Russell's Magazine* (1857-1860) of Charleston, South Carolina. Also achieving great popularity were the new illustrated weeklies, led by *Frank Leslie's Illustrated Newspaper*, which actually was more of a magazine; *Harper's Weekly* (1857-1916); and *Gleason's Pictorial Drawing-Room Companion*. These periodicals featured a combination of large wood engravings, light literature, and news. Other popular weeklies in the 1850s were the *Saturday Evening Post* (1821-1969), *Flag of Our Union* (1846-1870), and *Saturday Press* (1858-1866), the magazine in which Mark Twain and Josh Billings first reached a large and widespread audience. Still leader of the women's magazine field was *Godey's Lady's Book* (1830-1898). In the South, which had no really large cities, magazines were overwhelmingly regional in appeal; only *De Bow's Review* (1846-1880) and the *Southern Literary Messenger* (1834-1864) had much circulation outside the region. The West was founding a few magazines of its own, including the *Golden Era* and *Pioneer: or, California Monthly Magazine*. Quarterly reviews had lost their former importance; some had broadened their traditional content, making them resemble the more dignified general monthlies, while some of the general magazines began running book reviews.

The largest single genre in number of titles was the religious periodical–quarterlies, monthlies, and weeklies published by a wide array of faiths all over the nation. After religious periodicals, the most active category was the agricultural periodical. Prominent examples were *Country Gentleman* (1853-1955), *Southern Field and Fireside* (1859-1864), *Ohio Farmer* (1852-current), *Journal of Agriculture* (1856-1921), and *California Farmer* (1854-1884). As the Midwest and West became more developed agriculturally, the number of farm periodicals in these regions increased accordingly. Though their great growth period had not yet begun, there were specialized business periodicals in this period, including *Coach-Makers' Magazine* (1858-1871), *Harness and Carriage Journal* (1857-1883), and *American Telegraph Magazine* (1852-1853). Legal journals did not enjoy much growth in the 1850s, but insurance periodicals proliferated; outstanding in the latter field was *Tuckett's Insurance Journal* (1852-1861). The North and the South each had its own dominant magazine of general commerce: *Hunt's Merchant's Magazine* (1830-1870) in New York and *De Bow's Review* in New Orleans. The era's leading magazine of general science was the *American Journal of Science*. Other scientifically and technically oriented periodicals were *Inventor*, *Mathematical Monthly*, and *Mining Journal*. There were many periodicals devoted to rail travel, and medical journals increased in number.

In the prewar years the women's magazines for the most part kept clear of political controversy. Most Northern religious periodicals spoke out against slavery, while their opposite numbers in the South sought to rationalize their region's "peculiar institution." Representative antislavery magazines of the time were the venerable *Liberator* (1831-1865), the *National Era* (1847-1859), and the *Pittsburgh Saturday Visiter* (1848-1852). An immense outpouring of magazine comment on both sides followed publication of the era's bestselling book, *Uncle Tom's Cabin* (1852), which had just appeared serially in the *National Era*; also exciting much comment was John Brown's Harpers Ferry raid in 1859. In addition to abolition, temperance was a leading cause, supported by such periodicals as *Templar's Magazine* (1850-1874) and the *Old Oaken Bucket* (1849-1852).

Before the Civil War much magazine writing was still being done by "ladies and gentlemen" as a leisure pursuit. Most of the contributors neither expected nor received payment for their work, but a few of the better or larger magazines, such as the *Atlantic*, the *New York Ledger*, *Putnam's*, *Graham's*, and *Godey's* paid a few dollars a page. The magazine business was still largely a personal one, editor and publisher often being one and the same person. Advertising did not yet provide much of a magazine's income, and sales were mostly by subscription. The typical monthly of the 1850s sold for three dollars yearly, most weeklies for two dollars.

Whereas intensified demand for war news kept newspapers from declining during the Civil War, magazines–especially those that had previously enjoyed national circulation, such as *Harper's* and *Godey's*–suffered a major loss of subscribers. In the North the financial panic of 1857, followed by the war, which cut off Southern subscriptions, caused a decline in the number of magazines. In the South shortages of paper, ink, and printing equipment that had formerly come from the North; high postal rates; a shortage of labor; and, finally, the arrival of hostile troops caused most Southern periodicals either to discontinue publication until war's end or to fold permanently. On the other hand a surprising number of new magazines were founded during the conflict, including the *Southern Monthly* (1861-1862), *Countryman* (1862-1866), the *Southern Illustrated News* (1862-1865), the *Magnolia* (1862-1863), the *Bohemian* (1863), *Southern Punch* (1863-1864), the *Illustrated Mercury* (1863-1864), *Age: A Southern Eclectic Magazine* (1864-1865), and *Smith and Barrow's Monthly* (1864). In the North the illustrated weekly magazines provided good war coverage, giving newspapers heavy competition. Several Northern military periodicals were published during this period: the *Military Gazette* (1858-1861), *Army and Navy Gazette* (1862-1863), and *Army and Navy Official Gazette* (1863-1865). Copperhead in sentiment were the *Old Guard* (1862-1870), *Day Book* (1849-1863), and *Knickerbocker*.

At mid century American readers were still tied to the Mother Country due to the enormous popularity of English writers, especially Charles Dickens for fiction, Thomas Carlyle for nonfiction, and William Wordsworth and Alfred Tennyson for verse. Also heavily represented in American magazines were William Makepeace Thackeray, Henry Fielding, Jane Austen, and Elizabeth Barrett Browning. Among French writers, George Sand, Alexandre Dumas, Honoré de Balzac, and Victor Hugo were popular in mid-1800s America, as to a lesser extent were the Germans Johann Wolfgang von Goethe, Heinrich Heine, and Jean Paul Richter. Home-grown writers of note were James Fenimore Cooper, Washington Irving, Edgar Allan Poe, William Cullen Bryant, Ralph Waldo Emerson, Nathaniel Hawthorne, James Russell Lowell, Oliver Wendell Holmes, and Mrs. Lydia H. Sigourney. In the South, William Gilmore Simms's work was preeminent.

Novels were popular and were run serially in American magazines. The *Atlantic*, *Putnam's*, *Continental* (1862-1864), and the *Southern Literary Messenger* encouraged domestic novelists, while *Harper's New Monthly* and the eclectics, such as *Eclectic Magazine* (1844-1907) and *Living Age* (1844-1941), took advantage of the absence of international copyright agreements and predominantly used English material with neither permission nor payment. The short story had not yet come into its own; most short magazine fiction was sugary and sentimental, as was most verse. History and biography had become more in demand by this time, possibly in reaction to the politically charged times, and travel articles appeared everywhere, as they still do today. Humor writing was a staple by mid century; especially popular were the dialect humorists Artemus Ward, Bill Arp, Petroleum Vesuvius Nasby, and, of course, Mark Twain. Outstanding humor periodicals were *Vanity Fair* (1859-1863) and *Frank Leslie's Budget of Fun* (1859-1878). *Southern Punch* (1863-1865) commenced publication in Richmond, Virginia, after Lee's defeat at Gettysburg and obtained a sizable circulation.

Both wood and metal engraving were used for illustrations at mid century; the pictorial weeklies led the way with wood, while the older *Godey's*, *Peterson's*, *Sartain's*, and the *Eclectic Magazine* stayed mainly with steel and copper. Fashion plates were popular in women's magazines.

Prizefighting and horse racing were the sports that got the most magazine attention;

sports and games were not as popular as they would later become in America, yet such specialized periodicals as *Billard Cue* (1856-1874) and *Chess Monthly* (1857-1861) were published in the period. Spiritualism was an 1850s craze that resulted in magazines of its own, such as *Spiritual Telegraph* (1853-1857) and *Sacred Circle* (1854-1856). Secret societies were popular and had their own periodicals, including *Freemason's Monthly Magazine* (1841-1873), *American Quarterly Review of Freemasonry* (1857-1859), and *American Odd Fellow* (1862-1874).

The years following the Civil War were a period of pronounced growth in magazine publishing. Journalism historian Frank Luther Mott counts seven hundred periodicals in 1865 and thirty-three hundred by 1885; even in the Reconstruction South magazine activity was considerable. Magazines went after subscribers more aggressively, boosting circulation by using premiums such as books and pictures to reward new or renewed subscriptions. Advertising became more important during the poor economic years 1873 to 1878, when *Scribner's* (1870-1881) and the *Galaxy* (1866-1878) took the lead in attracting advertisers with their large circulations. The style of magazine writing lightened and became less didactic following the war. By this time most articles were signed instead of anonymous as the prudish manners of the prewar years began to fade; even so, many of the most popular "magazinists" of that era, such as Eugene Benson, Junius Browne, Frederick Perkins, Titas Coan, and David Wasson, have been all but forgotten.

The best and brightest of the monthlies were, as in the 1850s, *Harper's* and the less popular, more high-toned *Atlantic*. New general readership literary magazines, in addition to *Scribner's* and the *Galaxy* included *Beadle's Monthly* (1866-1867), *Lippincott's* (1868-1916), *Putnam's* (New Series, 1868-1870), and *Scribner's*. Of more humble literary quality was *Frank Leslie's Popular Monthly* (1876-1956). Even lower in literary worth but attaining an enormous circulation was the *People's Literary Companion* (1869-1907). The latter two magazines went after advertisers who sold their wares to the public by direct mail.

Thoughtful new journals of opinion were the *Nation* (1865-current) and the *Round Table* (1863-1869), and joining *Harper's* and *Frank Leslie's Illustrated Newspaper* in the news-oriented illustrated weekly field was *Appleton's Journal* (1869-1881). In the South the most active magazine cities were Atlanta, Baltimore, Louisville, Richmond, and New Orleans. Atlanta's *Sunny South* (1875-1907) and Louisville's *Home and Farm* (1876-1918) were the leaders in a region where a circulation of one hundred thousand was an enormous success. Reconstruction was a common topic in Northern magazines, and such Southern writers as George Cable, George Egbert Craddock, and Thomas Nelson Page found ready markets for their work in the North.

At the end of the 1870s a great westward population shift occurred, and Chicago, St. Louis, Cincinnati, Milwaukee, and Topeka became more active in magazine publishing. Noteworthy are the *Chicagoan* (1868-1869), *Lakeside Monthly* (1869-1874), *Current* (1883-1888), and *Dial* (1880-1929) of Chicago; *Whittaker's Milwaukee Magazine* (1871-1877); and *Kansas Magazine* (1872-1873) of Topeka. Easterners were fascinated by accounts of cowboys, Indians, outlaws, and the gold and silver camps.

The many religious newspapers which had become popular in the 1820s began withdrawing from the coverage of secular news in the 1870s. The coming of the big daily newspapers better equipped to handle hard news was probably responsible for this change. Overall, however, the total number of religious periodicals doubled between war's end and 1885. The religious magazines of this period became more competitive with one another.

Except for a few periodicals such as the *Atlantic*, magazines were against woman suffrage, despite the fact that far more women than men were magazine subscribers. Many journals emerged as spokesmen for woman's rights: *Revolution* (1868-1872), *Sorosis* (1868-1869), *Woman's Journal* (1870-1873), *Ballot Box* (1876-1881), *Woman's Words* (1877-1881), *Queen Bee* (1879-1896), *Aegis* (1880-1886), *Woman's Tribune* (1883-1909), and most outspoken of them all, *Woodhull and Claflin's Weekly* (1870-1876). Not all women joined the cause, as was evidenced by the antisuffrage *True Woman* (1870-1873).

At the same time, fashion magazines became more popular than ever; most were located in New York and Philadelphia. *Harper's Bazar* (1867-current) took the lead, competing with *Demorest's Monthly* (1865-1899), *Frank Leslie's Ladies' Journal* (1871-1881), and *Delineator* (1873-1937). Most home magazines of the era came out of New York, including *Hearth and Home* (1868-1875), *Fireside at Home* (1879-1918), and *Housewife* (1882-1917). Two especially successful Philadelphia titles were *Woman's Home Journal*

(1878-1909), and *Ladies' Home Journal* (1883-current).

The growth of specialized or "class" periodicals was enormous in the decades following the Civil War. Many new journals appeared in all the science fields, and as the nation industrialized, innumerable engineering, manufacturing, and mechanical periodicals were established. Literature seemed to be elbowed aside by science, commerce, and industrial progress. Professional journals, especially in medicine, also enjoyed considerable growth after the Civil War, and education journals published by teachers' organizations or by state government agencies were plentiful. The two major magazines of general commerce, *Hunt's* and *De Bow's*, fell to increased specialization, the former in 1870, the latter a decade later. "Booster magazines" began to appear and join newspapers in extolling the virtues of their regions to attract economic development. Examples are *Virginias* (1880-1885) and *Northwest Magazine* (1883-1903).

Interest in sports broadened and intensified, and each sport had its magazines. Hunting, fishing, boating, and bicycling had such periodicals as *Forest and Stream* (1873-1930), *American Angler* (1881-1900), and *American Canoeist* (1882-1891). The first bicycling periodical, *Velocipedist*, was published in New York City in 1869. Cycling suffered a decline in public interest until the solid rubber tire was introduced in the early 1870s; then *American Bicycling Journal* (1877-1879) and several similar periodicals capitalized on the craze. Of the spectator sports, horse racing was preeminent and was represented by several specialized periodicals. Second in popularity was baseball, the first periodical for which was *Ball Player's Chronicle* (1867) of New York. To further the farmers' interests, thousands of local granges were formed in the late 1860s and early 1870s; many created their own periodicals. The number of farm journals roughly tripled between 1870 and 1885.

More than any other nation, America published magazines for young readers. About half were Sunday school or other denomination-affiliated periodicals, though these did not match the circulation of the secular juveniles. *Youth's Companion* (1827-1936) and *Merry's Museum* (1841-1872) were still publishing; new titles included *Demorest's Young America* (1866-1875), *Frank Leslie's Boys and Girls Weekly* (1867-1883), *Burke's Weekly for Boys and Girls* (1867-1871), and the best of the lot, *St. Nicholas* (1873-1943).

The new process of electrotyping made wood a practical medium for long pressruns, and wood engraving began to replace steel and copper plate engraving in the late 1850s and early 1860s. Especially known for their wood-engraved illustrations were *Appleton's*, *Scribner's*, *St. Nicholas*, and *Harper's Weekly*. The overall amount of illustration in American magazines increased greatly, and critics began to worry that pictorial content had encroached too far into space that might better be occupied by written copy.

Nevertheless, fiction was in a strong position during the latter part of the nineteenth century. The importance of the serial novel continued to increase, thanks in large part to the popularity of the foreign novelists. The 1870s and 1880s were a time of growing importance for the short story, though most short fiction continued to be blighted by what *Harper's New Monthly* editor Henry Mills Alden characterized as the precious, the mock-heroic, and the morbid. Similarly saccharine was the poetry of these decades, though Walt Whitman, Sidney Lanier, and Lowell provided good verse for various magazines. After fiction, travel writing was next in popularity among magazine readers, who seemed to want fewer pretty descriptions, less sentiment, more historical treatment, and more attention to mores in their travel articles. Supplying these qualities were such writers as Bayard Taylor, Mark Twain, John Hay, William Dean Howells, Thomas Bailey Aldrich, and Charles Leland. Travel writing had to become more practical during these years because more Americans were beginning to travel abroad.

Supplying the South's need for historical accounts of how things used to be, and of the Lost Cause, were several magazines designed specifically for this purpose: Atlanta's *Scott's Monthly Magazine* (1865-1870), North Carolina's *The Land We Love* (1866-1869) and *Our Living and Our Dead* (1873-1876), and Louisville's *Southern Bivouac* (1882-1883).

The outstanding humor magazine of the 1870s was *Puck* (1877-1918). Shorter-lived offerings were *Punchinello* (1870) and *Carl Pretzel's Pook* (1872-1874), which became *Carl Pretzel's National Weekly* (1874-1893). In the 1880s came the estimable *Judge* (1881-1939) and *Life* (1883-1936). *Mascot* (1881-1900) was founded in New Orleans, *Texas Siftings* (1881-1897) in Austin, and *Arkansas Traveler* (1882-1916) in Little Rock.

England had served as the model for many American magazines: the *Atlantic* and *Putnam's* borrowed features from the English *Blackwood's*, the *Nation* owed much to the *Spectator*, the *Galaxy* to *Cornhill Magazine*, and *Harper's Weekly* to the *Illustrated London News*. But by the 1870s *Scribner's* and *Harper's* began selling well in England, their popularity due mainly to their voluminous illustration.

Politics was discussed in more of the general magazines than formerly, including *Harper's New Monthly*, *Scribner's*, *Putnam's*, *Galaxy*, and *Lippincott's*. The old prewar partisanship was breaking down, and most of the magazines that included political content were not tied to a particular party. Labor unions organized and became politically active after the war; by 1885 around four hundred labor periodicals were being published, most of them local in scope.

As the cities grew, so did their social problems–awful living conditions for the poor, prostitution, violent crime, corrupt government–but Victorian public reticence was still too strong for most magazines and newspapers to risk offending their readers with frank attention to these problems. In the celebrated fight against the Tweed Ring in New York City, the only magazine really to commit itself was *Harper's Weekly*. Still, the progress of science and technology, plus the democratization of politics, made more intense by great waves of immigration, served to weaken the hold of Puritanism on the American mind, causing a great deal of interest in changing manners and mores. Many travel articles of this era were in reality comparative glimpses at how other peoples lived.

In the late 1880s and the 1890s some of the larger national magazines set the stage for the era of low-priced, giant-circulation monthlies and weeklies of the early 1900s. *Lippincott's* and *Cosmopolitan* reduced their per-copy price from twenty-five cents to twenty cents in the 1880s. *Harper's Monthly*, selling at thirty-five cents, had tough competition from *Scribner's Magazine* (1887-1939) at twenty-five-cents. *Harper's* adopted a twenty-five-cent price in 1899, and *Munsey's*, *Peterson's*, and *Godey's* went to ten cents in the 1890s. The *Ladies' Home Journal* gained an enormous circulation in the 1890s at five cents a copy. These price cuts were made possible in part by cheaper paper, lower printing costs, and halftone photoengraving, which by the early 1890s was on its way to replacing the far more costly wood and metal engraving processes. The popular magazines of the 1890s were not sensational, but they were lavishly illustrated compared to earlier decades. Subject matter had gained in variety, and articles on the problems of the day were more common. Fiction was deemphasized in the 1890s in favor of history, politics, and economics. Even the *Atlantic Monthly* became less literary and more political in the 1890s, as did the *Century* and *Scribner's Magazine*.

Mail rates for magazines were reduced in 1885, and in 1897 rural free delivery was inaugurated. Magazine advertising headed up sharply the last decade of the century, and full-page ads became fairly common. During the last few years of the 1890s single-copy sales increased, as well.

By 1890 magazines were able to recruit new editing and writing talent from a fairly substantial pool of persons who had worked with other magazines, and the term *magazinist* came into use. Prior to that time most staffing had come from newspapers or from contributors who had little or no full-time experience with any kind of magazine. It had also become common for writers to prepare copy first for magazine publication, then collect their magazine work and try to have it published in book form. Even the best writers of the day were happy to use magazine publication as a means of prepromoting their books.

In general, illustrated weeklies were losing ground by the 1890s, though the finest of them all, *Harper's Weekly*, still enjoyed a solid position, as did the former *Frank Leslie's Illustrated Newspaper*, which became *Frank Leslie's Illustrated Weekly* in 1891 and *Leslie's Weekly* in 1895. *Collier's* began as *Once a Week* in 1888, gaining a larger circulation at seven cents a copy. By 1905 the abundantly illustrated *Collier's* had a circulation of roughly one million, almost as much as the *Saturday Evening Post*. By this time the *Post* cost five cents, *Collier's* ten cents.

Local and regional magazines became vastly more popular in the 1890s. One type of local periodical was the city weekly, which offered a mix of politics, commentary on the entertainment scene, humor, society chit-chat, and light literary fare. Examples of this genre were *M'lle New York* (1895-1899); *Reedy's Mirror* (1891-1920) of St. Louis; the *Kansas City Independent* (1895-1916); *Fetter's Southern Magazine* (1892-1895); the *South Illustrated* (1886-1889); *Tatler of Society in Florida* (1886-1889); *New England Magazine* (1884-1917); *Bostonian: An Illustrated Magazine of Local Interest* (1894-1896); *Brooklyn Life* (1890-1931); the *Washington* (D.C.) *Mirror* (1899-1905); Cleveland's *Town Topics* (1887-1916); Indianapolis's *Indianian* (1897-1900); Des Moines's *Midland Monthly*

(1894-1899); *Agora: A Kansas Magazine* (1891-1896) of Salina and Topeka; *St. Louis Life* (1889-1897); *Milwaukee Magazine* (1870-1876); Colorado's *Great Divide* (1889-1896); Portland's *Pacific Monthly* (1898-1911); Alaska's *North Star* (1887-1898); Honolulu's *Paradise of the Pacific* (1888-1966); and California's *Overland Monthly* (1868-1935), *Californian Illustrated Magazine* (1891-1894), *Sunset* (1898-current), and *Golden Era* (1852-1893). Students of magazine history should resist any temptation to think of city and regional magazines as inventions of the 1960s and 1970s, a more recent major growth era for this genre.

Sports got heavy attention from the magazine industry in the 1890s, both from general magazines and from such specialized periodicals as the *American Yachtsman* (1887-1908), *Horseman* (1881-1915), *Sporting News* (1886-current), *Sporting Life* (1883-1926), *Golfer* (1894-1906), *American Lawn Tennis* (1898-1901), *Bicycling World* (1879-1915), *Bowler's Journal* (1893-1934), *Sports Afield* (1887-current), and *Field and Stream* (1896-current).

In the literary magazines of the 1890s the short story had become an important staple, and by the later years of the decade writers were producing what was called the "short short story." The major literary debate of these years concerned the merits of realistic as opposed to romantic fiction. *Harper's* and *Dial* spoke for realism; most magazines that aimed at a mass circulation retained their faith in romanticism. By the end of the 1890s poetry was receiving far less space than it had previously.

During the 1880s and 1890s general magazines developed a more practical bent, decreasing their emphasis on literature, history, and travel in favor of politics, the economy, and social problems. Thus the content of magazines and newspapers became more similar during the period. Much attention was paid to monopolies and trusts, imperialism, protective tariffs, and socialism as the nation's magazines tried to deal with the ramifications of the country's burgeoning wealth.

Poised on the brink of a new century, the American magazine was a changed creature. It was already in the process of becoming a large industry led by national magazines of enormous circulation, and overall it informed, as opposed to entertained, more than it had been able to do in the mid 1800s. A far greater range of specialized periodicals existed, and even the general content magazines were placing more emphasis on providing their readers with practical factual matter. Journalism historian Agnes Repplier once described nineteenth-century magazines as being characterized by propriety-bound patronization, editors seeming to say to their readers: "We will help you. We will uplift and improve you." By century's end the tone was less gentle and polite, more frankly journalistic. Less literary in purpose than before, the American magazine was stronger and would soon be ready to enter an important period of investigative reporting.

–*Sam G. Riley*

Acknowledgments

This book was produced by Bruccoli Clark Layman, Inc. Karen L. Rood is senior editor for the *Dictionary of Literary Biography* series. Philip B. Dematteis was the in-house editor.

Production coordinator is Kimberly Casey. Art supervisor is Cheryl A. Crombie. Copyediting supervisor is Joan M. Prince. Typesetting supervisor is Kathleen M. Flanagan. William Adams, Laura Ingram, and Michael D. Senecal are editorial associates. The production staff includes Brandy H. Barefoot, Rowena Betts, Charles D. Brower, Joseph M. Bruccoli, Amanda Caulley, Teresa Chaney, Patricia Coate, Sarah A. Estes, Cynthia Hallman, Judith K. Ingle, Warren McInnis, Kathy S. Merlette, Sheri Beckett Neal, Virginia Smith, and Mark Van Gunten. Jean W. Ross is permissions editor. Susan Todd is photography editor. Penney L. Haughton did photographic copy work for the volume.

Walter W. Ross and Jennifer Toth did the library research with the assistance of the reference staff at the Thomas Cooper Library of the University of South Carolina: Daniel Boice, Cathy Eckman, Gary Geer, Cathie Gottlieb, David L. Haggard, Jens Holley, Dennis Isbell, Jackie Kinder, Marcia Martin, Jean Rhyne, Beverly Steele, Ellen Tillett, Carol Tobin, and Virginia Weathers.

Dictionary of Literary Biography® • Volume Seventy-nine

American Magazine Journalists, 1850-1900

Dictionary of Literary Biography

Lyman Abbott
(18 December 1835-22 October 1922)

James Boylan
University of Massachusetts, Amherst

MAJOR POSITIONS HELD: Editor, *Illustrated Christian Weekly* (1870-1876); associate editor (1876-1881), editor in chief (1881-1922), *Christian Union*, renamed *Outlook* in 1893.

BOOKS: *Cone Cut Corners*, by Abbott and others, as Benauly (New York: Mason, 1855);
Matthew Caraby, by Abbott and others, as Benauly (New York: Mason, 1859; Cincinnati: Rickey, Mallory, 1859);
Jesus of Nazareth: His Life and Teachings (New York: Harper, 1869); republished as *A Life of Christ* (New York: Harper, 1882);
Old Testament Shadows of New Testament Truths (New York: Harper, 1870);
Laicus; or, The Experiences of a Layman in a Country Parish (New York: Dodd & Mead, 1872);
The New Testament, with Notes and Comments: Volume I, Matthew and Mark (New York & Chicago: Barnes, 1875; London: Hodder & Stoughton, 1875);
Uncontradicted Testimony in the Beecher Case, Compiled from Official Records (New York: Appleton, 1876);
A Popular Commentary on the Gospels according to Matthew and Mark (New York, Chicago & New Orleans: Barnes, 1876);
The Acts of the Apostles: With Notes, Comments (New York, Chicago & New Orleans: Barnes, 1876; London: Hodder & Stoughton, 1876);
An Illustrated Commentary on the Gospels according to Mark and Luke (New York, Chicago & New Orleans: Barnes, 1878);

Lyman Abbott

The Gospel according to Luke: With Notes, Comments (New York, Chicago & New Orleans:

Barnes, 1878; London: Hodder & Stoughton, 1878);

An Illustrated Commentary on the Gospel according to St. John (New York, Chicago & New Orleans: Barnes, 1879);

Certain of Your Own Philosophers: An Appeal to Rationalists (New York: Winthrop Press, 1879);

A Study in Human Nature (New York: Chautauqua Press, 1884);

Restrictive Legislation: An Address (New York: Church Temperance Society, 1885);

In Aid of Faith (New York: Dutton, 1886);

The Epistle of Paul to the Romans, with Notes, Comments, Maps (New York & Chicago: Barnes, 1888);

Signs of Promise: Sermons Preached in Plymouth Pulpit, Brooklyn, 1887-9 (New York: Fords, Howard & Hulbert, 1889);

Ruth and Naomi: A Sermon. Printed in the Reporting Style of Phonography (London: Pitman, 1889);

That Unknown Country; or, What Living Men Believe Concerning Punishment after Death, Together with Recorded Views of Men of Former Times (Springfield, Mass.: Nicholas, 1890);

The Simplicity of Christianity (New York: Christian Union, 1891);

How to Become a Christian: Five Simple Talks to the Young (New York: Revell, 1891);

The Evolution of Christianity (Boston & New York: Houghton, Mifflin, 1892; London: Clarke, 1892);

The Roman Catholic Question (New York: Christian Union, 1893);

New Streams in Old Channels: Selected from the Writings of Lyman Abbott, D.D., edited by Mary Sorrs Haynes (Boston: Lothrop, 1894);

A Plea for Peace: A Sermon Preached in Plymouth Church, December 22nd, 1895 (Brooklyn, N.Y.: Collins & Day, 1895);

The Prophets of the Christian Faith, by Abbott and others (New York & London: Macmillan, 1896);

Jubilee Anniversary: Sermon Delivered at the Fiftieth Annual Meeting of the American Missionary Association, October 20th, 1896 (New York: American Missionary Association, 1896);

The Bible as Literature (Brooklyn, N.Y.: Miss L. L. Whitlock, 1896);

Christianity and Socialism (New York, 1896);

Armenian Question (New York, 1896);

Christianity and Social Problems (Boston & New York: Houghton, Mifflin, 1896; London: Clarke, 1897);

The Bible and the Child: The Higher Criticism and the Teaching of the Young, by Abbott and others (London: Clarke, 1897);

The Theology of an Evolutionist (Boston & New York: Houghton, Mifflin, 1897; London: Clarke, 1897);

The Soul's Quest after God (New York & Boston: Crowell, 1897; London: Bowden, 1898);

The Life and Letters of Paul and the Apostle (Boston & New York: Houghton, Mifflin, 1898);

The Message of the World's Religions: Reprinted from "The Outlook," by Abbott and others (New York: Longmans, Green, 1898);

The Duty and Destiny of America (Brooklyn, N.Y.: Brown, 1898);

The New Puritanism: Papers, by Abbott and others (New York: Fords, Howard & Hulbert, 1898; London: Clarke, 1898);

The Supernatural: An Address Delivered before the Alumni of Bangor Theological Seminary, May 18, 1898, on "The Relation of Nature and the Supernatural to the Christian Thought of To-day" (New York: Howland, 1899);

The Life That Really Is (New York: Ketcham, 1899);

Why I Am Not a Universalist (Boston, 1900);

Why Go to Church? (Boston: Page, 1900);

Salvation from Sin (New York: Crowell, 1900);

Problems of Life: Selections from the Writings of Rev. Lyman Abbott, D.D., edited by Sarah Truslow Dickinson (New York: Dodd, Mead, 1900);

The Kingdom of Heaven on Earth: A Sermon Preached at the Diamond Jubilee of the Congregational Home Missionary Society, Tremont Temple, Boston, Mass., May 14, 1901 (N.p., 1901);

The Life and Literature of the Ancient Hebrews (Boston & New York: Houghton, Mifflin, 1901; London: Clarke, 1901);

The Rights of Man: A Study in Twentieth Century Problems (Boston & New York: Houghton, Mifflin, 1901; London: Clarke, 1901);

Henry Ward Beecher (Boston & New York: Houghton, Mifflin, 1903);

The Other Room (New York: Outlook, 1903; London: Melrose, 1904);

Why Women Do Not Wish the Suffrage (New York, 1904);

The Religion of "Parsifal" (New York: Outlook, 1904);

The Great Companion (New York: Outlook, 1904; London: Macmillan, 1906);

One Who Loved His Fellow-men: An Appreciation (New York: Gilliss Press, 1904);

The Christian Ministry (Boston & New York: Houghton, Mifflin, 1905; London: Constable, 1905);

The Personality of God (New York: Crowell, 1905);

The Industrial Problem: Being the William Levi Bull Lectures for the Year 1905 (Philadelphia: Jacobs, 1905; London: Moring, 1907);

An Illustrated Commentary on the Gospels (New York: Barnes, 1906);

The Home Builder (Boston & New York: Houghton, Mifflin, 1906);

How to Study Shakespeare, with Articles on General Literature and Directions for Forming and Conducting Study Circles, by Abbott and others (New York: University Society, 1907);

Christ's Secret of Happiness (New York: Crowell, 1907);

Address at a Mass-meeting in Carnegie Hall, New York, March 4th, 1907, under the Auspices of the Friends of Russian Freedom (New York, 1907);

Impressions of a Careless Traveler (New York: Outlook, 1907);

William H. Taft, an Appreciation (New York, 1908);

The Temple (New York: Macmillan, 1909);

Seeking after God (New York: Crowell, 1910);

The Ethical Teachings of Jesus (Philadelphia: University of Pennsylvania, 1910);

The Spirit of Democracy (Boston & New York: Houghton Mifflin, 1910; London: Constable, 1911);

The Problem of Human Destiny as Conditioned by Free Will: Discussion, by Abbott, Rev. Eric Waterhouse, and Prof. William G. Tousey (Boston & Chicago: Murray Press, 1911);

My Four Anchors: What We Know in the Realm of Religion (Boston & New York: Pilgrim Press, 1911);

American in the Making (New Haven: Yale University Press, 1911);

Theodore Roosevelt as I See Him (New York, 1912);

A Living Immortality (New York: Dutton, 1912);

Letters to Unknown Friends (Garden City, N.Y.: Doubleday, Page, 1913);

Reminiscences (Boston & New York: Houghton Mifflin, 1915);

The Last Days of Jesus Christ (New York: Dutton, 1918);

The Twentieth Century Crusade (New York: Macmillan, 1918);

Inspiration for Daily Living: Selections from the Writings of Lyman Abbott, D.D., edited by O. E. P. S. (Boston & Chicago: Pilgrim Press, 1919);

Silhouettes of My Contemporaries (Garden City, N.Y.: Doubleday, Page, 1921; London: Allen & Unwin, 1922);

What Christianity Means to Me: A Spiritual Autobiography (New York: Macmillan, 1921);

The Crucifiers (New York: Woman's Press, 1923);

The Dignity and Worth of a Man as a Child of God: An Address Delivered at the Annual Meeting of the American Missionary Association (New York: American Missionary Association, Bible House, n.d.);

OTHER: Henry Ward Beecher, *Sermons*, edited by Abbott, 2 volumes (New York: Harper, 1868; London: Dickinson, 1890);

Beecher, *Morning and Evening Exercises*, edited by Abbott (New York: Harper, 1871);

A Dictionary of Religious Knowledge, for Popular and Professional Use: Comprising Full Information on Biblical, Theological, and Ecclesiastical Subjects, edited by Abbott and T. J. Conant (New York: Harper, 1875);

Hints for Home Reading: A Series of Chapters on Books and Their Use, edited with contributions by Abbott (New York: Putnam's, 1880);

How to Succeed: In Public Life, as a Minister, as a Physician, as a Musician, edited with contributions by Abbott (New York: Putnam's, 1882);

Edward Payson Roe, *Birthday Mottoes*, selected by Abbott (New York: Dodd, Mead, 1882);

Henry Ward Beecher: A Sketch of His Career. With Analyses of His Power as a Preacher, Lecturer, Orator and Journalist, and Incidents and Reminiscences of His Life, edited by Abbott (New York: Funk & Wagnalls, 1883); revised edition, edited by Abbott and S. B. Halliday (Hartford, Conn.: American Publishing/Chicago: Peale, 1887);

For Family Worship, edited by Abbott (New York: Dodd, Mead, 1883; London: Clarke, 1885);

John B. Gough, *Platform Echoes; or, Leaves from My Note-book of Forty Years: Comprising Living Truths for Head and Heart*, introduction and biographical sketch by Abbott (Hartford, Conn.: Worthington, 1885);

Best Thoughts of Henry Ward Beecher, compiled by Abbott (New York: Goodspeed, 1893);

The Plymouth Hymnal, for the Church, the Social Meeting and the Home, edited by Abbott, Charles H. Morse, and Herbert Vaughan Abbott (New York: Outlook, 1893);

"Jesus Christ as Missionary," in *The Life and Work of the Redeemer*, by Abbot and others (London: Cassell, 1901);

Jacob Abbott, *A Boy on a Farm, at Work and at Play*, edited by Clifton Johnson, introduction by Abbott (New York: American Book Co., 1903);

"An Interpreter of Life," in *The World's Best Poetry*, edited by Bliss Carman (Philadelphia: Morris, 1904), III: ix-xxv;

Charles Wagner, *My Appeal to America: Being My First Address to an American Audience*, edited by Abbott (New York: McClure, Phillips, 1905);

The Parables, edited by Abbott (New York: Appleton, 1907);

Alan Warner, ed., *The Real Roosevelt: His Forceful and Fearless Utterances on Various Subjects*, foreword by Abbott (New York & London: Putnam's, 1910);

The Guide to Reading, edited by Abbott (New York: Mentor Association & N. Doubleday, 1917);

"The Use and Misuse of the Bible," in *Evolution or Christianity God or Darwin?*, by William Marion Goldsmith (St. Louis & Winfield, Kans.: Anderson Press, 1924), pp. 117-121.

PERIODICAL PUBLICATIONS: "The Eternal City," *Harper's Monthly*, 44 (December 1871): 1-19;

"The City of the Saints," *Harper's Monthly*, 45 (July 1872): 168-186;

"The Revision of Creeds," *North American Review*, 136 (January 1883): 11-16;

"Danger Ahead," *Century*, 31 (November 1885): 51-59;

"The New Reformation," *Century*, 37 (November 1888): 71-80;

"Christianity versus Socialism," *North American Review*, 148 (April 1889): 447-453;

"Flaws in Ingersollism," *North American Review*, 150 (April 1890): 446-457;

"No Theology and New Theology," *Forum*, 9 (April 1890): 189-197;

"The Wages System," *Forum*, 9 (July 1890): 518-529;

"Industrial Democracy," *Forum*, 9 (August 1890): 658-669;

"Can a Nation Have a Religion?" *Century*, 41 (December 1890): 275-281;

"Modern Methods of Social Reform," *Chautauquan*, 13 (September 1891): 738-740;

"Compulsory Arbitration," *Arena*, 7 (December 1892): 30-36;

"The Personal Problem of Charity," *Forum*, 16 (February 1894): 663-669;

"The Son of a Carpenter," *Cosmopolitan*, 16 (March 1894): 515-528;

"Religious Teaching in Our Public Schools," *Century*, 49 (April 1895): 943-948;

"Postal Telegraphy," *Arena*, 15 (January 1896): 242-244;

"A Summing-Up of the Vital Issues of 1896," *Review of Reviews*, 14 (November 1896): 544-549;

"The Growth of Religious Tolerance in the United States," *Forum*, 23 (August 1897): 653-660;

"The Basis of an Anglo-American Understanding," *North American Review*, 166 (May 1898): 513-521;

"Our Indian Problem," *North American Review*, 167 (December 1898): 719-728;

"The Advance of Women," *World's Work*, 8 (July 1904): 5033-5038;

"Why I Believe We Do Not Die," *Ladies' Home Journal*, 22 (October 1905): 11-12;

"The Story of Christianity," *Munsey's*, 34 (December 1905): 259-274;

"The Nature of Prayer," *North American Review*, 167 (November 1907): 337-339;

"The Significance of the Present Moral Awakening in the Nation," *South Atlantic Quarterly*, 7 (July 1908): 205-209;

"What Money Is Really Good For," *Ladies' Home Journal*, 25 (September 1908): 17, 61;

"Why the Vote Would Be Injurious to Women," *Ladies' Home Journal*, 27 (February 1910): 21-22;

"Answer to the Arguments in Support of Woman Suffrage," *Supplement to the Annals of the American Academy of Political and Social Science* (May 1910): 28-35;

"Wanted–A Campaign for our Homes," *Chautaquan*, 59 (July 1910): 246-250;

"My Fifty Years as a Minister," *Ladies' Home Journal*, 30 (January 1913): 5-6.

In his career of nearly seventy years, Lyman Abbott divided his life between the roles of journalist and clergyman. As a Protestant minister, he was aligned with the activist movement that preached the reform-minded doctrines known collectively as the Social Gospel. As an editor, he shaped a religious magazine that competed on equal terms, both in substance and in audience,

Cover for an issue of the magazine Abbott edited from 1881 until his death in 1922. The title was changed from Christian Union *to* Outlook *in 1893.*

with the major public-affairs weeklies of the era. Known in journalism primarily as the editor of the *Outlook*, Abbott was also an industrious contributor to other magazines and the author of a shelfful of books popularizing religious issues. Although his critics concluded that neither his preaching nor his journalism often reached beyond the superficial, none could doubt his immense productiveness or his ability to sense and exploit popular trends.

Abbott was born on 18 December 1835 in Roxbury, Massachusetts, into a family of Congregationalist educators. His mother, Harriet Vaughan Abbott, died when he was seven; he was raised by his aunts in Farmington, Maine, in the absence of his father, Jacob Abbott, who ran a school in New York City. When he was thirteen, his father gave him the choice of two thousand dollars to get started in business or a college education, and he enrolled in 1849 at New York University, then a tiny institution in lower Manhattan. After receiving his bachelor's degree in June 1853 he read for the law and became an apprentice at a firm founded by his two older brothers. At the same time he gained his first experience as a journalist, reporting on legal matters for a new daily, the *New York Times*.

After being admitted to the bar in 1856 and marrying his second cousin Abby Frances Hamlin on 14 October 1857, Abbott became restless and began to seek a new career. He came under the influence of the nationally renowned Henry Ward Beecher, pastor of the Plymouth Congregational Church in Brooklyn, after Beecher's "great revival" of 1858. In July 1859 Abbott announced to his family that he intended to become a minister and returned to Maine to qualify himself through a self-supervised study program designed in collaboration with Beecher. He was ordained in March 1860 and was called the same month to a Congregational church in Terre Haute, Indiana, where he spent the Civil War years trying to keep peace among his deeply divided parishioners.

Near the end of the war Abbott moved into the realm of public affairs and journalism. In February 1865 he returned to New York to become executive secretary of the American Union Commission, a multidenominational organization formed to aid black and white war refugees. He went on to become general secretary of the commission's successor, the American Freedmen's Union Commission. For the latter he edited a small monthly publication, *American Freedman*, in which he advocated that the organization sponsor desegregated, nonsectarian schools in the South. The commission ended its work in 1869, having assisted marginally in black education.

In the same period Abbott became involved in commitments that brought him to the lowest point of his adult life. In 1866, while serving with the Union Commission, he also accepted the pastorate of a small Manhattan church. It prospered under his guidance, but he let himself become entangled in a bizarre mission to Paris that eventually entailed his returning to America with the body of a parishioner's daughter. Back in New York, he found dissension in the congregation and discovered that his wife was ill of tuberculosis. To aid his wife's recovery, he resigned in 1869 and moved up the Hudson River to Cornwall, New York. Unemployed, he turned to freelance writing and developed the ability to write speedily and voluminously. He had a fruitful relationship with Harper and Brothers, the New York publisher, not only writing monthly book reviews for *Harper's Monthly Magazine* (based on his wife's reading of the books) but in short order turning out two books on Bible study.

In 1871 the American Tract Society of New York, the leading religious publishing house, offered him the editorship of a new magazine, the *Illustrated Christian Weekly*. He accepted after obtaining a reluctantly yielded guarantee of editorial autonomy. One of his contributions to the publication was a weekly column titled "Outlook," a discussion of current events and religious issues; the column was conservative theologically but opposed racism and upheld public education. Abbot remarked in his *Reminiscences* (1915), "In its bearing on my life the editorship of the 'Illustrated Christian Weekly' was chiefly valuable as an apprenticeship for the larger work which, wholly unsuspected by me, lay before me."

That larger work began to take shape in August 1876, when Abbott agreed to a year's trial as associate editor of the *Christian Union*, a weekly edited since 1870 by Beecher. After initial popularity the publication had fallen on hard times, hurt not only by the panic of 1873 and a fire in the publishing plant, but by the Beecher-Tilton scandal of 1875, in which Beecher was taken to court on charges of committing adultery with a parishioner's wife. (The jury failed to reach a verdict.) Beecher's interest in recruiting Abbott stemmed not only from Abbott's success at the *Illustrated Christian Weekly* but from his loyalty to Beecher, as evidenced in an 1876 pamphlet Abbott wrote about the case.

When Abbott began work at the *Christian Union* in September 1876, its circulation had fallen from 132,000 to 15,000, and its publishing company, J. B. Ford and Company, had declared bankruptcy. Under a reorganized firm, the Christian Union Publishing Company, Abbott began a vigorous campaign to restore the periodical's solvency and reputation. In fact, his title of associate editor was largely a courtesy to Beecher; that Abbott was in charge from the start is shown by his immediate decision to stop sending prepublication page proofs to Beecher. He announced that the weekly would manifest "that spirit of honor, of equity, and of generosity toward those whom it opposes, which characterizes Christianity as distinguished from sectarianism." Abbott's unchallenged editorial control was formally recognized in 1881 with Beecher's retirement, Abbott's purchase of Beecher's interest in the weekly, and his assumption of the title of editor in chief.

Abbott built an organization at the *Christian Union* that was much like a family–and, indeed, included his own family. His wife ran a children's department and was a major adviser. A Cornwall friend and neighbor, Lawson Valentine, served as president of the Christian Union Company for a decade; when he died in 1891, Abbott's son Lawrence F. Abbott took over for the next thirty-two years. Another son, Ernest Hamlin Abbott, succeeded his father as editor. Hamilton W. Mabie, a lawyer, was hired in 1879 as editor of church news but soon branched out into literary essays; he became associate editor in 1884 and stayed until his death in 1916.

The long-term trend of Abbott's editorship was to make the *Christian Union* less specifically a religious publication; he consistently pushed it in the direction of a general magazine of social and political comment. He signaled this tendency when he transplanted from the *Illustrated Chris-*

tian Weekly a department called "The Outlook," providing "a systematic paragraph history of the week." Under Abbott's guidance the publication examined a broad range of issues, including temperance, the tariff, the rights of blacks and Indians, immigration, conservation, and coinage of silver.

In particular, the *Christian Union*, which was allied with the new social Christianity movement, came to focus in the 1880s on what was becoming known as "the industrial problem"–the welfare of the poor and working classes. Abbott's sympathies were engaged by his trips to the Wyoming Valley, the Pennsylvania coal fields, English slums, and public lodging houses in 1882. Editorially, he advocated a wide range of reforms, such as shorter working hours, industrial education, and colonization.

The *Christian Union* also published literature calling attention to inequality and poverty. One series was called "Our Neighbors–the Poor." The magazine also published Josephine Shaw Lowell's "The Bitter Cry of the Poor in New York," "Mrs. Herndon's Income" by the pioneering muckraker Helen Campbell, and "A Plain Talk with Employers" by a leading advocate of social Christianity Washington Gladden. An editorial in 1885 proclaimed: "We must heed the bitter outcry of our modern cities and set ourselves to still the crying. . . . " In the mid 1880s Abbott became active in the new American Economic Association and the *Christian Union* published a series on socialism by the association's president, Richard T. Ely. Yet Abbott was not a socialist himself and at critical points, such as the Pullman strike of 1894, did not side with labor. His role was primarily that of a publicist of issues.

His biographer, Ira V. Brown, points to Abbott's work on the "Indian question" as an example of the flawed character of his influence in public affairs. Abbott joined the Indian Rights Association in 1882 and was active in its meetings at Lake Mohonk, New York, for several years. He focused public interest on Indian issues by publishing Helen Hunt Jackson's novel *Ramona* serially in the *Christian Union* starting in May 1884. His proposals–dispersal of Indian tribes, abrogation of Indian treaties, reallocation of Indian lands, and a system of federal Indian schools–were influential in the writing of the Dawes Act, passed in February 1887. Assessing his influence, Brown says: "Never a profound student of any problem, his ideas were often superficial and his judgments hasty. His knowledge of Indian affairs was entirely secondhand, yet he played a significant role in molding and expressing public opinion in that field."

In issues related to religion, Abbott's most distinct influence was as an advocate of incorporating evolutionary theory into theology. He wrote in his *Reminiscences*: "I would as soon have a monkey as a mud man for an ancestor." He summed up his views in *The Theology of an Evolutionist* (1897), a book that thoroughly dismayed his Episcopalian brother, the Reverend Edward Abbott, and millions of like-minded believers.

Beecher died in March 1887, leaving vacant the best-known pulpit in the country, that of Plymouth Congregational Church. Abbott, Beecher's protégé, was engaged as a temporary replacement; a year later he was offered the permanent position, though not without opposition. His wife thought that the fifty-two-year-old editor should not add to his burdens; the congregation was divided over rumors that Abbott had been offered a huge salary, perhaps even in five figures (The actual amount was eight thousand dollars.)

Abbott was installed on 16 January 1890, along with an associate pastor who was engaged to lighten his work load. Even so, Abbott's time had to be carefully divided between the weekly and the church; he spent two mornings early in the week at the editorial offices and wrote his editorials over the following weekend. The consequence of this schedule was chronic indigestion. After being ordered to bed by his doctor in October 1898, Abbott reluctantly gave up his post at Plymouth Congregational.

In the meantime he had moved his weekly even further into the general-interest field. In 1891 the *Christian Union* changed from a newspaper to a magazine format. Two years later Abbott gave the magazine the name of its public-affairs column–*Outlook*–because, as he recalled later, nonchurch people "looked upon the 'Christian Union' with suspicion as an ecclesiastical journal; churchmen looked upon it with suspicion as not ecclesiastical enough."

The first issue under the new name, on 1 July 1893, carried a statement redefining the publication: "The Outlook is a weekly family newspaper. It is a running history of the year in fifty-two chapters. Its editorials, contributed articles, and departments deal with the things of today in the broadest and most dispassionate spirit." The change in emphasis even led to the abolition of the religion department in 1899. The response was encouraging: circulation in the 1890s rose from twenty thousand to thirty thousand and advertising revenue increased.

Before the decade ended there was a change in the publication's political temper as well, revealed in the *Outlook's* position on the Spanish-American war. Having resisted chauvinism through the increasingly imperial-minded 1890s, Abbott and the *Outlook* dismissed the destruction of the battleship *Maine* as merely an opportunity for the sensational press. But in a sermon on 13 March 1898 Abbott reversed himself, and he eventually supported the war in the name of what he called "the new imperialism–the imperialism of freedom." He heaped scorn upon the revolt by Filipinos seeking independence and concluded in 1901, "Barbarism has no rights which civilization is bound to respect." Civilization, he made clear, was the exclusive possession of the Anglo-Saxon race.

Abbott's new political tendencies soon found a responsive ally in the White House. Abbott had known Theodore Roosevelt since 1884, and the *Christian Union* and the *Outlook* had sympathetically followed his rise in New York City politics. Less than a month after Roosevelt succeeded the slain McKinley in 1901, Abbott was called to the White House and became a member of Roosevelt's kitchen cabinet. Abbott's agreement with Roosevelt extended beyond an assertive, imperialist foreign policy to the Bismarckian vision of regulatory, interventionist, centrist statesmanship that Roosevelt eventually dubbed "the new nationalism." The *Outlook* enthusiastically supported the administration and serialized Jacob Riis's flattering campaign biography when Roosevelt ran for reelection in 1904. Roosevelt in turn wrote that Abbott "combines a good natured evenness of temper with the power of flaming wrath against unrighteousness." Previously chary of political alliances, Abbott now hitched his wagon, and that of the *Outlook*, to Roosevelt's star.

One issue that helped cement their alliance was their common distaste for the journalistic exposures of the era, for which Roosevelt coined a term of opprobrium, *muckraking*, in a 1906 speech that the *Outlook* reprinted. Abbott's repulsion was enhanced by muckrakers' insinuations that the *Outlook* was under the control of John D. Rockefeller's Standard Oil Company, a favorite target of exposés. The charges stemmed from thirty years before, when James Stillman, later an associate of Rockefeller in the National City Bank, had bought a ten percent nonmanagerial interest in the *Christian Union*. Abbott, much aggrieved, complained that "journalistic prostitutes" had twisted the facts.

In 1906 Abbott proposed that the president accept an editorship on the *Outlook* when he left office. An agreement was completed in July 1908, and on the day after the national election Abbott announced that Roosevelt would join the staff on 5 March 1909–the day after the inauguration–as a "special contributing editor" and would write twelve articles a year at one thousand dollars apiece. The first of these, which appeared in the issue of 6 March, was titled: "Why I Believe in the Kind of American Journalism for Which the Outlook Stands."

Eventually the Roosevelt presence proved to be too robust for the *Outlook* and its elderly editor. When Roosevelt ran for president on the Progressive ticket in 1912, Abbott declared the *Outlook's* impartiality. But the editorials gradually bent in Roosevelt's direction; the magazine came to be considered Roosevelt's mouthpiece, and, according to Abbott's biographer, reporters "treated Roosevelt's *Outlook* office as the Progressive headquarters." The magazine lost thousands of subscribers who were offended by its partisanship.

Although Roosevelt resigned as an editor in June 1914, his influence hovered over the *Outlook* during World War I. Stridently anti-German from the start, the magazine also became strongly militaristic and interventionist after the German sinking of the *Lusitania* in 1915. The high point of Abbott's efforts was an address before a tumultuous prowar meeting in Carnegie Hall a month before American entry. He provided a religious rationale for war and victory in *The Twentieth Century Crusade* (1918).

Although he never resigned the editorship of the *Outlook*, Abbott worked on a reduced schedule after an illness in 1918. On 22 October 1922, after completing the last of his thirty-one books, he died in New York City.

The *Outlook*, already past its best years, declined after his death. In 1927 Abbott's heirs sold their interest in the magazine to Francis Rufus Bellamy, who in 1928 combined it with the *Independent*, an even older weekly with religious origins. In 1932 the combined magazine suspended publication; later that year it reemerged under changed ownership as the *New Outlook* under the editorship of Alfred E. Smith, the former governor of New York. It ceased publication permanently in 1935.

Tributes immediately after Abbott's death emphasized his longevity and the patriarchal role he had played in public life. His biographer, writing thirty years later, saw him as an editor and preacher without deep or fixed principles: "He had an unusual facility for seeing which way the wind was blowing, and he generally charted his course accordingly." He is remembered as the builder and preserver of a magazine that was almost unique in its time in successfully moving from the religious sphere into public affairs. The vigor of the *Outlook* lasted just as long as that of its creator.

Biography:

Ira V. Brown, *Lyman Abbott, Christian Evolutionist: A Study in Religious Liberalism* (Cambridge: Harvard University Press, 1953).

References:

Lawrence F. Abbott, *Impressions of Theodore Roosevelt* (Garden City, N.Y.: Doubleday, Page, 1919);

Van Wyck Brooks, *The Flowering of New England, 1815-1865* (New York: Dutton, 1936);

Brooks, *New England: Indian Summer, 1865-1915* (New York: Dutton, 1940);

Ira V. Brown, "Lyman Abbott and Freedmen's Aid," *Journal of Southern History*, 15 (February 1949): 22-38;

Brown, "Lyman Abbott: Christian Evolutionist," *New England Quarterly*, 23 (June 1950): 218-231;

Paul H. Buck, *The Road to Reunion, 1865-1900* (Boston: Little, Brown, 1937);

George Harvey, "From Journalism to Politics," *North American Review*, 200 (August 1914): 178-182;

Richard Hofstadter, *Social Darwinism in American Thought, 1860-1915* (Philadelphia: University of Pennsylvania Press, 1944);

Luther P. Jackson, "The Educational Efforts of the Freedmen's Bureau and Freedmen's Aid Societies in South Carolina, 1862-1872," *Journal of Negro History*, 8 (January 1923): 1-40;

Bert J. Loewenberg, "Darwinism Comes to America, 1859-1900," *Mississippi Valley Historical Review*, 28 (December 1941): 339-368;

Hamilton W. Mabie, "Doctor Lyman Abbott," *World's Work*, 3 (February 1902): 1772-1775;

Henry F. May, *Protestant Churches and Industrial America* (New York: Harper, 1949);

Edwin W. Morse, *The Life and Letters of Hamilton Wright Mabie* (New York: Dodd, Mead, 1920);

Frank Luther Mott, *A History of American Magazines, 1850-1865* (Cambridge: Harvard University Press, 1938), pp. 253, 273;

Mott, *A History of American Magazines, 1865-1885* (Cambridge: Harvard University Press, 1938), pp. 76n, 85, 304, 422n, 423n 426-435;

Henry F. Pringle, *Theodore Roosevelt, a Biography* (New York: Harcourt, Brace, 1931);

Albert Shaw, "Lyman Abbott at Eighty," *Review of Reviews*, 53 (January 1916): 76-78;

"Tatler: Notes from the Capital. Lyman Abbott," *Nation*, 105 (26 July 1917): 102.

Louisa May Alcott

(29 November 1832-6 March 1888)

Lee Jolliffe
Ohio University

See also the Alcott entries in *DLB 1: The American Renaissance in New England*, and *DLB 42: American Writers for Children Before 1900*.

MAJOR POSITION HELD: Editor, *Merry's Museum* (1867-1870).

BOOKS: *Flower Fables* (Boston: Briggs, 1855);
Hospital Sketches (Boston: Redpath, 1863); revised and enlarged as *Hospital Sketches and Camp and Fireside Stories* (Boston: Roberts, 1869);
The Rose Family: A Fairy Tale (Boston: Redpath, 1864);
On Picket Duty, and Other Tales (Boston: Redpath, 1864);
Moods (Boston: Loring, 1865; revised edition, Boston: Roberts, 1882);
The Mysterious Key, and What It Opened, anonymous (Boston: Elliott, Thomes & Talbot, 1867);
Morning-Glories, and Other Stories (New York: Carleton, 1867; enlarged, Boston: Fuller, 1868);
Kitty's Class Day (Boston: Loring, 1868);
Aunt Kipp (Boston: Loring, 1868);
Psyche's Art (Boston: Loring, 1868);
Three Proverb Stories (Boston: Loring, 1868);
Nelly's Hospital (Washington, D.C.: U.S. Sanitary Commission, 1868);
Little Women; or, Meg, Jo, Beth and Amy, 2 volumes (Boston: Roberts, 1868-1869; London: Low, 1868-1869);
Concord Sketches (Boston: 1869);
An Old-Fashioned Girl (Boston: Roberts, 1870; London: Low, 1870);
Will's Wonder Book (Boston: Fuller, 1870);
Little Men: Life at Plumfield with Jo's Boys (London: Low, Son & Marston, 1871; Boston: Roberts, 1871);
My Boys: Vol. I of Aunt Jo's Scrap-Bag (Boston: Roberts, 1872; London: Low, 1872);
Shawl-Straps: Vol. II of Aunt Jo's Scrap-Bag (Boston: Roberts, 1872; London: Low, 1872);

Louisa May Alcott

Work: A Story of Experience (1 volume, Boston: Roberts, 1873; 2 volumes, London: Low, 1873);
Something to Do (London: Ward, Lock & Tyler, 1873);
Cupid and Chow-Chow: Vol. III of Aunt Jo's Scrap-Bag (Boston: Roberts, 1874; London: Low, 1874);
Eight Cousins; or, The Aunt-Hill (Boston: Roberts, 1875; London: Low, 1875);
Beginning Again: Being a Continuation of "Work" (London: Low, 1875);
Silver Pitchers; And Independence, a Centennial Love Story (Boston: Roberts, 1876; London: Low, 1876);

Rose in Bloom: A Sequel to "Eight Cousins" (Boston: Roberts, 1876; London: Low, 1876);

A Modern Mephistopheles, anonymous (Boston: Roberts, 1877; London: Low, 1877);

Under the Lilacs (11 parts, London: Low, Marston, Searle & Rivington, 1878; 1 volume, Boston: Roberts, 1878);

My Girls, etc.: Vol. IV of Aunt Jo's Scrap-Bag (Boston: Roberts, 1878);

Water Cresses (New York: Crowell, 1879);

Jimmy's Cruise in the Pinafore, etc.: Vol. V of Aunt Jo's Scrap-Bag (Boston: Roberts, 1879; London: Low, 1879);

Meadow Blossoms (New York: Crowell, 1879);

Jack and Jill: A Village Story (Boston: Roberts, 1880; London: Low, 1880);

The Christmas Tree (London: Routledge, 1881);

Proverb Stories (Boston: Roberts, 1882);

An Old-Fashioned Thanksgiving: Vol. VI of Aunt Jo's Scrap-Bag (Boston: Roberts, 1882; London: Low, 1882);

Spinning-Wheel Stories (Boston: Roberts, 1884; London: Low, 1884);

Lulu's Library, 3 volumes (Boston: Roberts, 1886-1889; volume 1, London: Low, 1886); volume 3 republished as *Recollections of My Childhood Days* (London: Low, 1890);

Jo's Boys, and How They Turned Out: A Sequel to "Little Men" (Boston: Roberts, 1886; London: Low, 1886);

A Garland for Girls (London: Blackie, 1887; Boston: Roberts, 1888);

A Modern Mephistopheles and A Whisper in the Dark (Boston: Roberts, 1889; London: Low, 1889);

Comic Tragedies Written by "Jo" and "Meg" and Acted by the "Little Women" (Boston: Roberts, 1893; London: Low, 1893);

Thoreau's Flute (Detroit: Stylus Press, 1899);

Three Unpublished Poems (Boston: Sears, 1919);

Behind a Mask: The Unknown Thrillers of Louisa May Alcott, edited by Madeleine B. Stern (New York: Morrow, 1975);

Louisa's Wonder Book: An Unknown Alcott Juvenile, edited by Stern (Mount Pleasant, Mich.: Central Michigan University & Clark Historical Library, 1975);

Plots and Counterplots; More Unknown Thrillers of Louisa May Alcott, edited by Stern (New York: Morrow, 1976).

OTHER: "The Little Seed," in *Margaret Lyon; or, A Work for All* (Boston: Crosby, Nichols, 1854);

"The Skeleton in the Closet," in *The Foundling*, by Perley Parker (Boston: Elliott, Thomes & Talbot, 1867);

Theodore Parker, *Prayers*, preface by Alcott (Boston: Roberts, 1882);

"A Sermon without a Text," in *What Can a Woman Do; or, Her Position in the Business and Literary World*, by Mrs. M. L. Rayne (Detroit: Dickerson, 1887), pp. 435-437.

PERIODICAL PUBLICATIONS: "The Rival Painters: A Tale of Rome," anonymous, *Olive Branch*, 17 (8 May 1852);

"The Rival Prima Donnas," as Flora Fairfield, *Saturday Evening Gazette* (11 November 1854);

"The Lady and the Woman," *Saturday Evening Gazette* (4 October 1856);

"With a Rose, That Bloomed on the Day of John Brown's Martyrdom," *Liberator*, 30 (20 January 1860);

"Love and Self-Love," *Atlantic Monthly*, 5 (March 1860);

"Pauline's Passion and Punishment," 2 parts, *Frank Leslie's Illustrated Newspaper*, 15 (3 and 10 January 1863);

"M. L.," 5 parts, *Commonwealth*, 1 (24 and 31 January; 7, 14, 22 February 1863);

"Hospital Sketches," 4 parts, *Commonwealth*, 1 (22 and 29 May; 12 and 26 June 1863);

"Thoreau's Flute," *Atlantic Monthly*, 12 (September 1863);

"My Contraband; or, The Brothers," *Atlantic Monthly*, 12 (November 1863);

"The Hospital Lamp," 2 parts, *Daily Morning Drum Beat*, 24-25 February 1864;

"Enigmas," 2 parts, *Frank Leslie's Illustrated Newspaper*, 18 (14 and 21 May 1864);

"Love and Loyalty," 5 parts, *United States Service Magazine*, 2 (July, August, September, November, December 1864);

"An Hour," 2 parts, *Commonwealth*, 3 (26 November, 3 December 1864);

"V. V.: or, Plots and Counterplots," anonymous, 4 parts, *Flag of Our Union*, 20 (4, 11, 18, 25 February 1865);

"Nelly's Hospital," *Our Young Folks*, 12 (April 1865);

"A Marble Woman: or, The Mysterious Model," as A. M. Barnard, 4 parts, *Flag of Our Union*, 20 (20 and 27 May, 3 and 10 June 1865);

"Behind a Mask: or, A Woman's Power," *Flag of Our Union*, 21 (13 October-3 November 1866);

"The Abbot's Ghost: or, Maurice Traherne's Temptation," 4 parts, *Flag of Our Union*, 22 (5, 12, 19, 26 January 1867);

"Tilly's Christmas," *Merry's Museum*, new series 1 (January 1868);

"Wishes," *Merry's Museum*, new series 1 (January 1868);

"What Polly Found in Her Stocking," *Merry's Museum*, new series 1 (January 1868);

"My Little Friend," *Merry's Museum*, new series 1 (February 1868);

"Where Is Bennie?," *Merry's Museum*, new series 1 (February 1868);

"My May Day among Curious Birds and Beasts," *Merry's Museum*, new series 1 (March 1868);

"My Doves," *Merry's Museum*, new series 1 (March 1868);

"Our Little Newsboy," *Merry's Museum*, new series 1 (April 1868);

"Will's Wonder-Book," 8 parts, *Merry's Museum*, new series 1 (April-November 1868);

"Happy Women," *New York Ledger*, 11 April 1868;

"The Blue and the Gray: A Hospital Sketch," *Putnam's Magazine*, 1 (June 1868);

"Mr. Emerson's Third Lecture," *National Anti-Slavery Standard*, 29 (31 October 1868);

"My Polish Boy," 2 parts, *Youth's Companion*, 41 (26 November, 3 December 1868);

"Tessa's Surprises," *Merry's Museum*, new series 1 (December 1868);

"Sunshiny Sam," *Merry's Museum*, new series 1 (December 1868);

"Back Windows," *Merry's Museum*, new series 2 (January 1869);

"Dan's Dinner," *Merry's Museum*, new series 2 (February 1869);

"A Curious Call," *Merry's Museum*, new series 2 (February 1869);

"A Visit to the School-Ship," *Merry's Museum*, new series 2 (March 1869);

"The Little Boats," *Merry's Museum*, new series 2 (April 1869);

"Milly's Messenger," *Merry's Museum*, new series 2 (May 1869);

"A Little Gentleman," *Merry's Museum*, new series 2 (June 1869);

"My Fourth of July," *Merry's Museum*, new series 2 (July 1869);

"An Old-Fashioned Girl," 6 parts, *Merry's Museum*, new series 2 (July-December 1869);

"Madam Cluck, and Her Family," *Merry's Museum*, new series 2 (August 1869);

"A Marine Merry-Making," *Merry's Museum*, new series 2 (October 1869);

"Becky's Christmas Dream," *Merry's Museum*, new series 3 (January 1870);

"Ripple," *Merry's Museum*, new series 3 (May 1870);

"The Nautilus," *Merry's Museum*, new series 3 (August 1870);

"Women in Britanny," *Christian Register*, 51 (6 January 1872);

"Shawl Straps," 4 parts, *Christian Union*, 5 (13 March, 20 March, 27 March, 3 April 1872);

"Cupid and Chow-Chow," 2 parts, *Hearth and Home*, 4 (18 and 25 May 1872);

"Work; or, Christie's Experiment," 29 parts, *Christian Union*, 6 (18 and 25 December 1872); 7 (1, 8, 15, 22, 29 January; 5, 12, 19, 26 February; 5, 12, 19, 26 March; 2, 9, 16, 23, 30 April; 7, 14, 21, 28 May; 4, 11, 18 June 1873);

"Hope for Housekeepers," *Boston Transcript*, 14 November 1873;

"Transcendental Wild Oats," *Independent*, 18 December 1873;

"How I Went Out to Service: A Story," *Independent*, 4 June 1874;

"Letter of Miss Louisa Alcott," *Woman's Journal*, 6 (14 November 1874);

"Woman's Part in the Concord Celebration," *Woman's Journal*, 6 (1 May 1875);

"Silver Pitchers: A Temperance Tale," 6 parts, *Youth's Companion*, 48 (6, 13, 20, 27 May; 3, 10 June 1875);

"A New Way to Spend Christmas," *Youth's Companion*, 49 (9 March 1876);

"Only an Actress," *Demorest's Monthly Magazine*, 12 (April 1876);

"How It All Happened," *Harper's Young People*, 2 (21 December 1880);

"Victoria: A Woman's Statue," 3 parts, *Demorest's Monthly Magazine*, 17 (March, April, May 1881);

"Reminiscences of Ralph Waldo Emerson," *Youth's Companion*, 55 (25 May 1882);

"W.C.T.U. of Concord," *Concord Freeman*, 10 (30 June 1882);

"R. W. Emerson," *Demorest's Monthly Magazine*, 18 (July 1882);

"Mr. Alcott's True Condition," *Woman's Journal*, 14 (6 January 1883);

"In Memoriam Sophia Foord," *Woman's Journal*, 16 (11 April 1885);

"Miss Alcott on Mind-Cure," *Woman's Journal*, 16 (18 April 1885);

"Old Times at Old Concord," *Woman's Journal*, 16 (18 April 1886);

"When Shall Our Young Women Marry?" *Brooklyn Magazine*, 4 (April 1886);

"A Flower Fable," *Woman's Journal*, 18 (26 February 1887);

"Early Marriages," *Ladies' Home Journal*, 4 (September 1887);

"Recollections of My Childhood," *Youth's Companion*, 61 (24 May 1888).

Louisa May Alcott is an unexpected inhabitant in the world of magazine editing. Her name is better known as the author of *Little Women* (1868-1869) and other children's stories, and her novels are now as often scrutinized by social historians as they are read with tears and laughter by youngsters. Alcott did edit a magazine, however, in the course of her long and varied career.

The second of the four daughters of Amos Bronson and Abigail May Alcott, Louisa May Alcott was born on 29 November 1832 in Germantown, Pennsylvania, where her father kept a school. Bronson Alcott was a philosopher who rarely found remunerative employment, and Louisa's childhood was one of quiet poverty and hard work. Bronson's connection with the Transcendentalist movement in New England assured that Louisa and her sisters were immersed in literature and philosophy from youth, and he haphazardly taught them at home what other children learned at school.

Transcendentalism carried the Alcotts in 1843 to Fruitlands, a utopian community in Harvard, Massachusetts, for an uncomfortable experiment in vegetarianism and community living. Alcott later described this episode in her story "Transcendental Wild Oats" (1873). But her philosopher father also brought Ralph Waldo Emerson, Margaret Fuller, Henry David Thoreau, and other great minds of the period into Louisa's sphere. After the Alcotts left Fruitlands, they moved to Concord, where they lived near Emerson for many years. (Some biographers believe that Alcott's interest in Emerson, described in her journals as a teenager's crush, was more long lasting than she admits; certainly he was a life-long friend.)

Alcott's early life is familiar to most readers; she recounted it honestly in *Little Women*, changing only the character of the father: Bronson Alcott was more chilly and unapproachable than Mr. March. The loving Marmee, the plays in the barn, Jo's struggles to become a writer, and Beth's death all were real.

Alcott worked at any job open to women in her era; she sewed, "went out to service," minded children, taught school, and eventually managed to sell her short stories to the penny press. She describes her early struggles to support her family in *Work* (1873). During the Civil War she spent six weeks as a nurse at the Union Hospital in Georgetown, where she contracted typhoid fever; she also collected material for the stories in *Hospital Sketches* (1863), which attracted national attention and set her on the road to success as a writer.

An 1865 trip to Europe as companion to an invalid gave Alcott the necessary distance from her childhood to see it clearly. On her return, because her father had promised a publisher that she would provide "a book for girls," she wrote *Little Women*. In her journal for September 1867 she wrote: "[Thomas] Niles, partner of Roberts, asked me to write a girls' book. Said I'd try. F. [Horace B. Fuller] asked me to be the editor of 'Merry's Museum.' Said I'd try. Began at once on both new jobs; but didn't like either."

Published in Boston, *Merry's Museum* was a pedagogic children's magazine; text and illustrations alike were meant to teach. Boys were apparently the intended audience. (Alcott had always professed to prefer boys to girls; after writing *Little Women* she commented, "Never liked girls or knew many, except my sisters.") The magazine contained articles on topics such as ants, bees, costumes through the ages, reindeer, the source of cinnamon, Roman emperors, British philosophers, diamonds from Brazil, Inca sculpture, classification of birds, castes in India, Robin Hood, and Henry Morgan. There were also stories: Alcott wrote many of these herself, among them "Tilly's Christmas" (January 1868), "My Little Friend" (February 1868), "Our Little Newsboy" (April 1868), "Will's Wonder-Book" (serialized from April to November 1868), "Tessa's Surprises" (December 1868), and "Sunshiny Sam" (December 1868). She also wrote poetry for the magazine. She was not happy with the editorial post: in early January 1868 she wrote in her journal, "F. pays me $500 a year for my name and some editorial work on Merry's Museum," but by 18 January she was writing, "F. seems to expect me to write the whole magazine, which I did not bargain for."

The success of *Little Women* freed Alcott from financial need. In 1870 she resigned the editing position and went to Europe for a year in an effort to improve her health, which she had damaged by working fourteen-hour days. In later life she was a vocal supporter of the woman's rights movement. In a letter to her publisher in 1881 she wrote, "If it [Mrs. Harriet H. Robinson's *Massachusetts in the Woman Suffrage Movement* (1881)] only records the just and wise changes Suffrage has made in the laws for women, it will be worth printing; and it is time to keep account of these first steps, since they count most. I, for one, don't want to be ranked among idiots, felons, and minors any longer, for I am none of the three...."

Louisa May Alcott died in Boston on 6 March 1888, the day her father was buried. He had achieved the fame he sought: he was known as "the father of Little Women." Louisa, the sole support of her family, has often been called by a name he gave her: "Duty's faithful child."

Letters:

Alfred Whitman, "Letters to Her Laurie," *Ladies' Home Journal*, 18 (16 September 1901): 5-6, 18; (11 October 1901): 6;

Jessie Bonstelle and Marian DeForest, *Little Women: Letters from the House of Alcott* (Boston: Little, Brown, 1914);

Elizabeth Bancroft Schlesinger, "The Alcotts through Thirty Years: Letters to Alfred Whitman," *Harvard Library Bulletin*, 5 (11 August 1957): 363-385;

Madeleine B. Stern, "Louisa May Alcott's Feminist Letters," *Studies in the American Renaissance*, 2 (1978): 429-452.

Bibliographies:

Lucile Gulliver, *Louisa May Alcott: A Bibliography* (Boston: Little, Brown, 1932);

Leona Rostenberg, "Some Anonymous and Pseudonymous Thrillers of Louisa May Alcott," *Bibliographical Society of America Papers*, 37 (second quarter 1943): 131-140;

Madeleine B. Stern, "Louisa M. Alcott's Contributions to Periodicals, 1868-1888," *More Books*, 18 (1943): 411-420;

Judith C. Ullom, *Louisa May Alcott: A Centennial for "Little Women"* (Washington, D.C.: Rare Book Division, Library of Congress, 1969);

Alma J. Payne, *Louisa May Alcott: A Reference Guide* (Boston: Hall, 1980).

Biographies:

Ednah D. Cheney, *Louisa May Alcott: The Children's Friend* (Boston: Prang, 1888);

Cheney, *Louisa May Alcott: Her Life, Letters, and Journals* (Boston: Roberts, 1889);

Belle Moses, *Louisa May Alcott, Dreamer and Worker: A Story of Achievement* (New York: Appleton, 1909);

Edith Willis Linn and Henry Bazin, eds., *Alcott Memoirs Posthumously Compiled from Papers, Journals, and Memoranda of the Late Dr. Frederick L. H. Willis* (Boston: Badger, 1915);

Cornelia Meigs, *The Story of the Author of Little Women: Invincible Louisa* (Boston: Little, Brown, 1933);

Katharine S. Anthony, *Louisa May Alcott* (New York: Knopf, 1938);

Madeleine B. Stern, *Louisa May Alcott* (Norman: University of Oklahoma Press, 1950);

Marjorie Worthington, *Miss Alcott of Concord: A Biography* (New York: Doubleday, 1958);

Helen Waite Papashvily, *Louisa May Alcott* (Boston: Houghton Mifflin, 1965);

Martha Saxton, *Louisa May: A Modern Biography of Louisa May Alcott* (Boston: Houghton Mifflin 1977);

Madelon Bedell, *The Alcotts* (New York: Clarkson Potter, 1981).

References:

Jan Cohn, "The Negro Character in Northern Magazine Fiction of the 1860's," *New England Quarterly*, 43 (1970): 572-592;

Sarah Elbert, *A Hunger for Home: Louisa May Alcott and Little Women* (Philadelphia: Temple University Press, 1984);

Carol Gay, "The Philosopher and His Daughter: Amos Bronson Alcott and Louisa," *Essays in Literature*, 2 (1974): 181-191;

Katharine F. Gerould, "Miss Alcott's New England," *Atlantic Monthly*, 108 (August 1911): 180-186;

Abigail A. Hamblen, "Louisa May Alcott and the Racial Question," *University Review* (Kansas City), 37 (1971): 307-313;

Stephanie Harrington, "Does *Little Women* Belittle Women?," *New York Times*, 10 June 1973, Sec. 2, p. 19;

Henry James, Review of *Moods*, *North American Review*, 101 (September 1867): 276-281;

Joy A. Marsella, *The Promise of Destiny: Children and Women in the Short Stories of Louisa May Alcott* (Westport, Conn.: Greenwood Press, 1983);

Helen Waite Papashvily, *All the Happy Endings* (New York: Harper, 1956);

Alma J. Payne, "Duty's Child: Louisa May Alcott," *American Literary Realism*, 6 (Summer 1973): 260-261;

Madeleine B. Stern, *Critical Essays on Louisa May Alcott* (Boston: G. K. Hall, 1984);

Marion Talbot, "Glimpses of the Real Louisa May Alcott," *New England Quarterly*, 11 (December 1938): 731-738;

Lorenzo Dow Turner, "Louisa May Alcott's 'M.L.,'" *Journal of Negro History*, 14 (October 1929): 495-522.

Papers:
The primary collections of Louisa May Alcott's papers are at the Boston Public Library; the Fruitlands Museum, Harvard, Massachusetts; and the Houghton Library, Harvard University.

Henry Mills Alden
(11 November 1836-7 October 1919)

Thomas B. Connery
College of Saint Thomas

MAJOR POSITIONS HELD: Managing editor, *Harper's Weekly* (1863-1869); editor, *Harper's New Monthly Magazine*, renamed *Harper's Monthly Magazine* in 1900 (1869-1919).

BOOKS: *Harper's Pictorial History of the Great Rebellion*, by Alden and Alfred H. Guernsey (New York: Harper, 1868);
God in His World: An Interpretation, anonymous (New York: Harper, 1890);
A Study of Death (New York: Harper, 1895; London: Osgood, McIlvaine, 1895);
Magazine Writing and the New Literature (New York & London: Harper, 1908);
In After Days: Thoughts on the Future Life, by Alden, William Dean Howells, Henry James, John Bigelow, Thomas Wentworth Higginson, William Hanna Thomson, Guglielmo Ferrero, Julia Ward Howe, and Elizabeth Stuart Phelps (New York & London: Harper, 1910).

OTHER: *The Heart of Childhood*, edited by Alden and William Dean Howells (New York & London: Harper, 1906);
Quaint Courtships, edited by Alden and Howells (London & New York: Harper, 1906);
Their Husbands' Wives, edited by Alden and Howells (New York & London: Harper, 1906);
Under the Sunset, edited by Alden and Howells (New York & London: Harper, 1906);

Henry Mills Alden

Different Girls, edited by Alden and Howells (New York & London: Harper, 1906);
Life at High Tide, edited by Alden and Howells (New York & London: Harper, 1907);

Shapes That Haunt the Dusk, edited by Alden and Howells (New York & London: Harper, 1907);

Southern Lights and Shadows, edited by Alden and Howells (New York & London: Harper, 1907).

PERIODICAL PUBLICATIONS: "Fifty Years of Harper's Magazine," *Harper's Monthly Magazine*, 101 (May 1900): 947-960;

"William Dean Howells: Recollections of a Fellow-Worker," *Book News Monthly* (January 1908): 729-731;

"Mark Twain: Personal Impressions," *Book News Monthly* (April 1910): 579-582;

"Mark Twain–an Appreciation," *Bookman*, 31 (June 1910): 366-369;

"An Anniversary Retrospect," *Harper's Monthly Magazine*, 121 (June 1910): 38-45.

Henry Mills Alden was the editor of *Harper's New Monthly Magazine*–which became *Harper's Monthly Magazine* in 1900–from 1869 to 1919, a career remarkable for its length but equally remarkable for its vitality, vision, and achievement. During his fifty years at *Harper's* the magazine helped shape American culture and literature through its encouragement of literary realism, its support of traditional yet distinctly American values, and its discovery of a host of gifted writers and illustrators. Though he remained virtually anonymous to the public, including *Harper's* readers, he was highly regarded and respected throughout the literary and journalistic establishments. To William Dean Howells, his friend and colleague at *Harper's*, Alden was "the greatest editor of his time, or almost any time"; to J. Henry Harper, Alden was "the Nestor of magazine editors," one who "naturally stands at the head of the [*Harper's*] roster"; to the *Nation*, Alden was one of journalism's "most influential figures"; and to a newspaper that eulogized him he was "a conservator of literature and literary principles, an educator, a discoverer of literary talent and genius."

It is fitting that Alden oversaw *Harper's* editorial content at a time when the magazine mirrored the nation's establishment of its cultural identity, since his own development fit the American democratic belief that hard work and talent would be recognized and rewarded. He was born in 1836 in Mount Tabor, Vermont, to Ira Alden, who owned a small farm, and Elizabeth Packard Moore Alden. He was a direct descendant of John and Priscilla Alden, the *Mayflower* Pilgrims; his mother came from Wilmington, Vermont, and was the niece of Zephaniah Moore, second president of Williams College and first president of Amherst College. Alden would later remember Mount Tabor as "a typical American community" containing all the provincial village features sought by so many nineteenth-century American writers. The surrounding woods were inhabited by bears that frightened children walking to school, and religious revivals often ended with baptisms in the river.

When Alden was seven years old, his father, apparently tired of struggling to scrape out a living from the Green Mountains soil, moved his family to the industrial town of Hoosick Falls, New York. Alden's older brother and uncle had sent back favorable reports about Hoosick Falls, especially noting the opportunity for work in the cotton mills which lined both sides of the Hoosick River. The family arrived in town in the middle of the night, carrying all its possessions, and within days Alden found work as a "bobbin boy" in a cotton mill. Days at the mill began at dawn and lasted until eight in the evening, with a half hour for breakfast and a half hour for lunch.

Although conditions were difficult, Alden remembered Hoosick Falls as a place where labor was respected and class distinctions were not clearly marked. Alden occupied his mind during his factory work routine by thinking of the lessons of the previous Sunday school and by dreaming of someday going to college. His mother, who wanted him to enter the ministry, encouraged his dreams. At fourteen he entered Ball Seminary to prepare for college, paying his way by sweeping rooms and building fires. The school's young principal, the Reverend Charles J. Hill, believed in Alden's intellectual capability, and in 1852, two years after arriving at Ball, Alden delivered the valedictory address at graduation exercises.

Hill, who had just been graduated from Williams, insisted that Alden go on immediately to college. In 1853 Alden arrived on the Williams campus with Hill's letters of introduction to professors and friends who were still undergraduates there, and with a few dollars he had earned working as a surveyor. He supported himself and paid for part of his education by teaching in neighboring schools in the winter and by doing an assortment of jobs during the summer.

Under its president, Mark Hopkins, Williams was intellectually lively, and Alden thrived there, associating with such fellow students as James Garfield, Horace E. Scudder, and Washington Gladden. Alden studied language and philosophy, particularly the classics and Greek culture, with such intensity and was so introspective that he was called "Metaphysics" by his classmates. He later said that this book learning was nicely balanced by his contact with the rural families with whom he boarded while teaching. That experience, as well as his rural and working-class roots, would later enable Alden to gauge the literary needs of his readers.

When Alden went on to Andover Theological Seminary in 1857, he seemed to be pursuing his mother's wish for him to become a minister; but he seemed as attracted by the institution's library, which contained one of the largest collections of Greek literature in the country, as by the school's religious studies curriculum. Perhaps just as attractive as the intellectual possibilities was the seminary's benevolent fund that helped out the poorer students. Alden borrowed from the fund and consequently did not have to teach while at the seminary.

Once again, his potential caught the attention of someone in a position to help him. A poem he wrote while at Andover, "The Ancient Lady of Sorrows," impressed Harriet Beecher Stowe, whose husband, Calvin E. Stowe, was on the Andover faculty. Mrs. Stowe invited Alden to their house, Stone Cabin. Alden soon showed her an article he had written on the Eleusinian mysteries, and Mrs. Stowe, without telling Alden, sent the article to James Russell Lowell, editor of the *Atlantic Monthly*. Alden learned what Mrs. Stowe had done only when he received a letter of acceptance from Lowell. Another article on the same subject was published by the *Atlantic*, so that by the end of his studies at Andover, Alden was beginning to think of a literary rather than a religious career. Pursuit of either career, however, was delayed as he returned home to relieve his oldest brother in caring for their invalid father. He supported himself by filling in at churches without ministers, although he had not been ordained. Alden also continued to write articles on Greek culture that he sent to the *Atlantic*, although they were not immediately accepted.

In April 1861 his brother resumed care of their father, and Alden went to New York City, stepping off a Hudson River steamboat with two dollars in his pocket. He had been corresponding with his old college chum Scudder, who had urged Alden to join him in New York, where Scudder worked as a private tutor and wrote children's stories. Alden moved in with Scudder and soon found a job teaching history and literature at a girls' school. In July he married Susan Frye Foster, whom he had met in Andover; they had four children.

By the time his wife joined him in the fall in New York, he was teaching at a boys' school for about seven dollars a week. To supplement his income he contributed editorials to the *New York Times* and the *New York Evening Post*. Charles Nordhoff of the *Evening Post* recommended that Alden be appointed the paper's war correspondent in Virginia. Alden, however, had already attempted to enlist in the Union army but had been rejected due to a weak heart. So he declined the reporting assignment because he did not feel healthy enough to cover a war.

In the spring of 1862 he was commissioned to assemble a descriptive guidebook on the Central Railroad of New Jersey and its connections into the Pennsylvania coalfields. The small job proved to be a major turning point in his career: Harper and Brothers published the book, and in the summer of 1863 he joined the firm's editorial department. He would never have another employer.

Before joining Harper he finally heard from the *Atlantic* concerning the articles he had submitted while taking care of his father. James T. Fields, the Boston publisher, had become editor of the *Atlantic* when his company took over the magazine, and he had come across Alden's articles. On a trip to New York Fields invited Alden to dinner and was surprised to discover that the author of the articles on Greek culture was a young man; he had assumed that Alden was about sixty. Fields was impressed by the articles, as well as by an editorial Alden had written for that day's *Evening Post*, and told Alden that he had shown the articles to Ralph Waldo Emerson, Lowell, and Wendell Phillips, all of whom were similarly impressed. Although Fields said the articles were not right for the *Atlantic*, being too narrow in appeal, he invited Alden to present the material in a series of lectures at the Lowell Institute in Boston. In the winter of 1863-1864 Alden delivered the twelve lectures, titled "The Structure of Paganism," and was paid sixteen hundred dollars, enabling him at last to pay his tuition debt at Williams and Andover.

Alden's first job with Harper was assessing manuscripts submitted to *Harper's New Monthly Magazine*; but after a short time Fletcher Harper made him managing editor of *Harper's Weekly*, which featured large, abundant illustrations and was subtitled *A Journal of Civilization*. Alden's duties at the *Weekly* were combined with his work on *Harper's Pictorial History of the Great Rebellion* in collaboration with *Harper's New Monthly Magazine* editor Alfred H. Guernsey. The book was completed in 1868.

As managing editor of the *Weekly*, Alden essentially served as a high-level assistant to Fletcher Harper. The publisher played the role of editor in chief, keeping a close eye on every phase of the operation of both the *Weekly* and the monthly. While Alden was responsible for selecting the articles and writing the captions for the accompanying pictures, and for daily office management, Harper decided on policy and politics, determined the overall direction of the magazine, selected all serialized stories, and picked almost all of the illustrations.

Alden later called Harper his teacher. "He knew where to be bold and where to be cautious," Alden said. The pupil carefully absorbed the ways of his mentor, and that sense of when to plunge and when to step back would become an Alden characteristic as an editor. Alden also demonstrated to Harper that he was capable of subsuming his own personality within the magazine's. Alden's ability and his seemingly total lack of desire for fame convinced Harper that he would be an ideal successor to Guernsey when the latter stepped down as editor of the monthly in early 1869.

Prior to the Civil War the circulation of *Harper's New Monthly Magazine* had been the highest of any magazine to that time, almost hitting two hundred thousand. It had gained its popularity by printing works by English writers such as Dickens, Thackeray, Eliot, Bulwer, and Trollope. Circulation declined substantially during the war but climbed again afterward as the magazine increasingly turned to American authors. Much of what it published, however, both English and American, was overly sentimental, self-conscious, and distinctly mediocre at best, with some freshness coming from such writers as Herman Melville, Fitzhugh Ludlow, John T. Trowbridge, John W. DeForest, Elizabeth Stuart Phelps, and Rose Terry. Alden's task was to discover and cultivate American literary talent, while maintaining the Harper vision that the magazine reach "the great mass of the American people" as a family publication. Comfortable in the world of high culture yet strongly imbued with democratic principles,

Opening page from the magazine Alden edited from 1869 to 1919

Alden was uniquely suited to combine popularity with selectivity.

Alden saw his job as serving the public by presenting it with literature that was instructive without being didactic and enlightening while being entertaining. He had no problem subscribing to Fletcher Harper's chief editorial principle: to publish what was intelligible, interesting, and useful to the average American. In 1900 Alden would write that *Harper's* was the original of a specific type of magazine, one "addressed to all readers of average intelligence, having for its purpose their entertainment and illumination, meeting in a general way the varied claims of their human intellect and sensibility, and in this accommodation following the lines of their aspiration." Critics charged that the magazine tried too hard to reach a lower level of readers, but Alden thought that there was nothing intrinsically wrong with "the power of appeal." A first-class popular magazine could readily accommodate popular interest, he said, and at the same time could improve "in every essential respect as to substance and form, while constantly broadening its appeal." After Harper retired in 1875, Alden was given far more freedom by the new publishers, but he continued to base his editorial policy on maintaining high standards acceptable to a large audience.

For Alden the best way to inform and entertain a reader was in story form, and he sought writers who were particularly adept at storytelling. "The problems of our modern life–its complex texture, its lights and shadows–are best presented in a living, moving drama," he wrote. The imagination was necessary, according to Alden, to show "the atmosphere and conditions of our American life." But writing that had no basis in the facts of life or real emotional experience was "a waste of the divine faculty." *Harper's* preferred realistic fiction over essays and other types of articles because Alden believed that realistic fiction–what he called the "new realism"–produced the most faithful portrait of life. Alden's "new realism" brought literature "down to earth" in a way that exalted the common and ordinary; it did not merely mean photographic descriptions of the world but "the feeling of it." Such views were almost the same as Howells's, and Alden helped to persuade Howells to write a monthly column on literature called "The Editor's Study," beginning in January 1886.

He would later praise Howells's "Editor's Study" essays as "unwaveringly American" pieces of criticism addressed not "to the acute and exceptional intellect but to the common sense, where it has a ready entrance." Alden's appreciation of things democratic was not mere posturing. He believed his magazine served the "plain, thoughtful" people, of which he was one. As editor of a widely read, highly respected magazine, he associated with most of the great writers of his time, including Howells, Henry James, Mark Twain, Thomas Hardy, Sarah Orne Jewett, Mary E. Wilkins, Rebecca Harding Davis, Brander Matthews, Charles Dudley Warner, Hamlin Garland, Owen Wister, Henry Blake Fuller, Lafcadio Hearn, Thomas Nelson Page, Helen Hunt Jackson, and Bret Harte. Despite his position and connections, he shunned fashionable literary circles and exclusive clubs and treated unknown writers with the same care and courtesy accorded established authors. Regardless of their status, visitors asking to see the editor were pointed in the direction of Alden's office, which remained the same during all his years at the magazine–cramped and simple, with no trappings of authority or position; Alden staunchly resisted several attempts to move him to larger, plusher quarters. His office door was always open. Inside, much of the space was filled by an old, unattractive black walnut desk which was covered with papers and manuscripts. Shelves behind the desk were stacked with unpublished manuscripts, recent and old. Dust and cigar ashes covered everything. The elevated train noisily clattered by outside the large window, just a few feet from his head. Visitors sat in a chair just inside the door.

Visitors expecting an indifferent and condescending editor, too busy and full of himself and his magazine to be concerned with their meager affairs, found the opposite. The atmosphere in the office the size of a horse stall was tranquil rather than tense; a kind, patient man with a bearded, angular face warmly received them and gave them his time and advice. His voice was low, more like a husky whisper, and his speech slow and deliberate, but as he talked it flowed with certainty and confidence. James Lane Allen, a writer who had a long association with *Harper's*, remembered Alden as the editor who not only published his poetry and fiction for the first time but who commissioned him, an unknown, to write about the Kentucky bluegrass region where Allen lived. He recalled arriving from Kentucky, nervously seeking out Alden at the Harper offices, and Alden telling him, as he told all newcomers: "I see that you feel yourself a beginner and a stranger. We are used to beginners here: they are welcome. If there were no beginners, we should soon reach the end of our usefulness. And there are no strangers. Not here. Strangers are for the world of convention, of artifice, of distrust. Here reality is the only thing and reality is everything. What, then, in reality do you seek and what of reality do you bring?"

Visitors were often young unpublished writers who insisted on personally delivering a manuscript to the editor because they believed that was the only way to get it into his hands. But Alden opened *every* manuscript and read it first, carefully looking for signs of talent and clear depiction of American people, manners, and places, the "reality" he demanded and felt to be so vital to literature. Alden believed that any new writer presenting a manuscript to him deserved not just a rejection, if rejection were necessary, but gentle counsel as well. He said that in such matters he had "almost a paternal responsibility." Part of that responsibility meant not providing false encouragement or misleading writers in regard to their talent or a story's potential. Once he told a young woman that her work was not suitable for publication, and she wondered if she should rewrite it if it had promise. Rather than send her off with a false sense of hope, Alden suggested she not waste her time with that story, but if she felt compelled to write, to start over with something new, keeping in mind that it might be "a rough, uphill road, thronged with many competing travellers."

What pleased him the most, however, was discovering that such a visitor had talent. He took particular pride in such discoveries, and one of his proudest finds was Owen Wister. In 1892 *Harper's* wanted to do a series on the American cowboy before he passed into history and folklore. The magazine's first choice was Rudyard Kipling, but he had other commitments. Several other writers were considered before the assignment was given to Wister, who had submitted a short story that impressed Alden. With Alden's encouragement Wister established himself as the leading Western writer of his day.

Alden was also principally responsible for attracting Lafcadio Hearn to *Harper's*, which had serialized most of the writer's work by 1890. It was Alden who persuaded the sensitive and shy Hearn to attend a dinner whose guests included Howells and the Harpers. Hearn nearly backed out several times on the way; when he and Alden sat down at the table, the uncomfortable Hearn tried to slip away–only to have Alden grab him by the coattails and pull him back to his chair, where he remained until long after dinner.

Alden's instinct for literary trends and possibilities was as sharp as his instinct for potential literary talent. When George Du Maurier submitted his novel *Trilby* (1894) for serialization, many of the *Harper's* staff were opposed to its publication: they argued that the magazine had published Du Maurier's *Peter Ibbetson* (1891) to only mild success and that the lax morals depicted in the book would not be accepted by *Harper's* readers. Alden, however, decided to publish the novel because he had observed "the increasing tolerance of our moral judgments as a people" and because *Trilby* had novelty and "essential purity." *Trilby* became the greatest serial success of the decade. While the novel ran, *Harper's* circulation jumped by one hundred thousand, and Trilby dolls, shoes, and luncheons became the rage; clergymen used the story to illustrate moral judgment; nine acting companies toured the country dramatizing the story. The publishers even received "a pathetic letter from an afflicted mother telling us that her daughter was desperately ill and would probably survive but a few weeks, and that she was anxious to see the final chapters before she died." Her request was granted.

If an author's previous failure did not influence Alden's assessment of a novel, neither did previous success. Howells submitted *The Minister's Charge* (1886) to Alden in 1885, following the popular success of Howells's *The Rise of Silas Lapham* (1885), and Alden rejected it; the reasons are not clear. Alden also declined to publish James's *The Ambassadors* (1903) because he believed it would not be popular. Although Alden was correct, James's book today is considered an American classic.

While he was bold in the *Trilby* case, he was cautious in handling the serialization of Thomas Hardy's *Jude the Obscure* (1895), published in *Harper's* in 1894 as "Hearts Insurgent." Alden felt that Hardy's novel was a bit too explicit, so he made changes and even persuaded Hardy to rewrite a chapter that contained a pig-killing scene. When Hardy complained that the objections to his work were based on "purism," Alden agreed but pointed out that it was not his purism but that of *Harper's* readers; and he reminded Hardy that the rule at the magazine was to publish only that which could "be read aloud in any family circle." After praising Hardy's work at some length, he wrote: "It is a pity that you should touch a word of the story, but you have been very good to lend yourself so kindly and so promptly to our need, when the task is in itself so ungraceful." He then told Hardy that he was sensitive to the pig killing because readers had objected to cruelty to animals in a Wister story.

Four years earlier, in 1890, Alden had angered James when he omitted a chapter from the serialization of Alphonse Daudet's *Port Tarascon*. James had translated the book from the French and complained about the magazine's cutting of the "anti-Christ" episode. But Alden explained that passages in the chapter would have offended large numbers of the magazine's Christian readers. He said that the thoughtful reader would have appreciated the chapter, but he could not

Alden and guests celebrating his seventieth birthday in 1906. From left: Richard Watson Gilder, Woodrow Wilson, William Dean Howells, Alden, George M. Harvey, Thomas Bailey Aldrich, the Right Reverend Ethelbert Talbot, Edmund Clarence Stedman.

take the chance that many more would misunderstand it.

Alden never apologized for such censorship, and he explained his reasoning in 1910 in almost the same language he used to James. Such items should never be cut from a book, he said, because the buyer chooses his book. But a magazine goes to an audience which the magazine is pledged implicitly never to offend. Alden would reject or cut an item he thought offensive; he would also reject a submission he believed was too remote thematically from his readers.

Alden was quick to admit when he had misjudged a manuscript. He said that when he read in the *Atlantic* a story by Rose Terry Cooke that he had rejected, he knew immediately that he had made a mistake. When a short story by Amelie Rives that he had rejected was published in *Lippincott's Magazine*, he wrote to Rives that his mistake was the "most striking illustration of an editor's fallibility that has ever confronted me." He explained that he had thought most *Harper's* readers would be put off by the story's old-fashioned manners and speech. "But I was wrong," he wrote. "I should have had a boldness equal to my personal appreciation of the merits of your work. I stand convicted of a kind of cowardice. . . . " Alden told her that his job naturally led to overcaution but added that in almost every case the caution was valid.

Alden's skill and shrewdness in dealing with different personalities is shown by such letters as those to Rives and Hardy. Although he was generally conducting business in such correspondence, he had a way of individualizing those letters and even making them personal, adjusting his style and tone to suit the correspondent and the subject of discussion. He wrote to Congressman Samuel S. Cox, who was known for his wit, asking for a humorous piece: "We want from your pen a humorous, a downright funny article for our MAGAZINE. Will you let us have it? . . . You may choose your own subject, and if it is susceptible of illustration, so much the livelier. I need not add that the compensation will be satisfactory to you if the article is to us." He praised the poet Thomas Bailey Aldrich without being obsequious yet very specifically told Aldrich what he wanted from him: "Having been much impressed by your recent tribute to Tennyson, I am tempted to ask you for a poem on Booth (a sonnet, if you will) to go with this frontpiece. If you feel inclined toward this...." Aldrich did indeed feel inclined, and *Harper's* had its sonnet.

Friends, colleagues, and writers valued Alden's directness and honesty, and these characteristics were central to his having what Howells called an "unequaled fitness for his work." He could be just as direct and honest when taking on critics of *Harper's*. In an 1894 article in the *Evangelist*, a minister praised the *North American Review* and the *Forum* and accused *Harper's* and the *Century* of being decadent in their competition for the popular audience. Alden was blunt in his reply: "I have read your article.... The first part is good down to the paragraph in which you suggest the decadence of the popular magazines.... All of your article which suggests the decadence ... seems to me unfair and not based upon careful consideration of what these magazines (particularly Harper's) are doing.... Show me anything in our Reviews equal to Lowell's six articles on 'The Old English Dramatists,' recently published in Harper's. Make out a list of our best writers (from the highest literary point of view), and tell me where you are sure to find their contributions. It will be seldom in Reviews–often in both Harper's and the Century.... I feel that you are all wrong in this idea of decadence."

Harper's and the *Century* had been competing for the general literary audience since the 1880s, and from the mid 1880s to the mid 1890s *Harper's* was clearly the superior publication in terms of literary quality, variety, and physical appearance. Its circulation during this period has been estimated at a healthy two hundred thousand or better, with another thirty-five thousand to fifty thousand in England. One of *Harper's* successful ingredients was illustrations. The minister had cited the extensive use of illustrations as a sure sign of decadence, and the inclusion of more and larger illustrations from the 1870s onward drew criticism from those who felt that they trivialized and deemphasized prose. Writers often objected to how their articles were illustrated, and Hearn wrote one of the nastiest letters ever sent to *Harper's* after he discovered that the artist accompanying him for a series on Japan was being paid twice as much as he was. Alden, however, defended the use of illustrations and was at least partly responsible for their increased use, seeing them as another way to both better depict the actual in America and entertain his readers. He maintained that without the artists' work, *Harper's* would not have become "a continuous world-explosion." To a charge that the illustrations were "mere prettiness," Alden replied that *Harper's* pictures gave "the precise truth" and that even the magazine's lighter illustrations were "the result of careful study and will themselves be studied in years to come, but not for their prettiness." *Harper's* illustrators included Frederic Remington, Edwin Abbey, C. S. Reinhart, Howard Pyle, A. E. Sterner, and William T. Smedley.

Although Alden came down clearly on the side of realism in his artistic and literary preferences, and although he was highly practical and adaptable in responding to the demands of the reading public, he retained a philosophical, religious, and even mystical side. The office visits Alden cherished most came from friends who had no business with the magazine. On such occasions Alden would forget manuscripts and illustrations and correspondence and, Howells said, "launch himself in one of those psychological speculations dearer to him than anything else in the world.... he would dream aloud in a steady flow ... [speculating on] his question of the Soul, of God, of Life and Death."

His philosophical bent was exercised in the writing of two books. *God in His World* (1890), a declaration of Alden's faith in Christ and his reconciliation of that belief with modern science, was published anonymously and went through four printings. One minister declared it "very remarkable" and a "penetrating look into the 'mind of Christ,'" as well as "the interpretation of an oracle." Alden said that he had merely been a vehicle for a divine voice, that he had been "swept forward as by a torrent, a precipitation of the storage of thirty years during which I had been silent, so far as any expression of my intimate thought and feeling was concerned." He started the book on an all-night train trip from Washington to New York and feverishly finished it during free moments from the office. *A Study of Death* (1895), written about the time of his wife's death, was well received but was not nearly as popular as *God in His World;* the book considers life as an expression of a universal vital force. The *New York Times* called it "the profoundest essay in mysticism ever written by an American." Alden leavened his mysticism with humor in declaring alcohol civilization's most potent blessing because it killed off those too weak physically to endure it, as well as those too feeble mentally to use it moderately.

In February 1900 Alden married Ada Foster Murray, a poet from Virginia. The following January he became the author of the "Editor's Study" column, which he continued for the next eighteen years. For the most part the column concerned itself with literature, dealing with the magazine's accomplishments, considering its content and role, and looking at the place of realistic fiction in periodicals and in literary history. Alden viewed the column as a chance to interpret the magazine's literary content for the reader. Much of his 1908 book, *Magazine Writing and the New Literature*, consisted of selections from the "Editor's Study" columns.

From a twentieth-century perspective, *Magazine Writing and the New Literature* probably contains Alden's most interesting and valuable writing, although it was his least successful book. The book and the columns make it clear that Alden was very much aware of his magazine's role in the development of American literature in the second half of the nineteenth century. He was correct in claiming that *Harper's* and other such periodicals had given young writers an outlet as well as the financial means to continue to shape their art, although he erred in ignoring newspaper journalism's role in generating what he called "new literature" in America.

By the "new literature" Alden meant literature concerned with contemporary themes and actual emotions and behavior. It meant no longer depicting classic battles between heroes and villains; in the new literature good and evil were blended in a portrayal of human nature that better reflected reality. The essential role of *Harper's* during his years as editor was to be a vehicle for realism. Almost fifteen years before the publication of *Magazine Writing and the New Literature* he declared that if someone wanted to know what life was like in the 1890s, they would find it not in the personal essays written in the more upscale reviews "but in the immediate reflection of the life itself in such matter as makes up the whole texture of a magazine like *Harper's*." In *Magazine Writing and the New Literature* Alden sees realism as part of the evolution of the imagination and says that it was generated by new knowledge that made the "myth-making and speculative fancy" of earlier literature insufficient.

George Harvey, who became president of Harper after the house declared bankruptcy and was reorganized in 1900, relied on Alden's judgment and skill as previous publishers had. But changes were made. Harvey favored splashy magazine promotions and pushed for publishing only broadly popular fiction. It is conceivable that Alden's rejection of James's *The Ambassadors* was influenced by Harvey's preferences: James was becoming too highbrow for a magazine that was sliding past its prime in a publishing world dominated by the big general interest magazines, such as *Munsey's*, *McClure's*, and *Cosmopolitan*, and in a country that seemed hungry for facts, information, and public affairs. But one need not blame Harvey, for Alden was always willing to change with the times and his readers. The magazine remained a vehicle for the short story, but Alden endorsed running more articles on science, archaeology, sociology, and politics. He pointed out to readers that *Harper's* was not "a planned machine" but "a living organism, open to the main currents of the world's life and thought," and therefore was ready to change and grow with them. Alden always welcomed the new, seeing it as positive and progressive, and perhaps that characteristic was as important as any to his success as well as that of *Harper's*. When Harvey resigned in 1915, one of his last acts as president was to write Alden in appreciation of their years together; significantly, Alden replied that his brightest years at Harper had been during Harvey's presidency.

Those who knew Alden were struck by his combination of genuine graciousness with wisdom–or, if not wisdom, a native intelligence mixed with common sense. John Corbin, a young assistant who worked with Alden during the latter's last years at the magazine, described these qualities: "His kindness was as simple and frank as his pride, and pervaded every act of his daily life. I have never known . . . a being so genial, so beneficent. . . . Above everything was his unfailing wisdom. . . . It was the wisdom of a sage among men."

Although he was respected in those last years, he was no longer a vital force, because both Alden's day and *Harper's* had passed. In the wake of the Progressive era and the muckraking movement, and on the eve of the Wilsonian era in government and the country's participation in a world war, Alden's literary sensibility was less valued. He died in October 1919, a month short of his eighty-third birthday. Within ten years *Harper's* would no longer be a general literary magazine but would be devoted primarily to public affairs and social issues, and aspiring fiction writers would have to look elsewhere for support.

For fifty years Alden was the one constant at a magazine that was one of the nation's most important cultural forces. Yet his biography has not been written, and his impact as editor has not been properly assessed. It would seem that he has become a victim of his own modesty and unwillingness to publicize himself. Frank Luther Mott's *A History of American Magazines*, written in the 1930s, notes his influence at *Harper's*, but a major journalism history text of the 1980s does not even mention him. Nevertheless, *Harper's* would not have been the same publication without Alden, and Howells's succinct assessment remains appropriate: "He was a man of rare gifts, a poet, a philosopher, a scholar, an acute critic . . . an editor perfect in his time and place."

References:

James Lane Allen, "Henry Mills Alden," *The Bookman*, 50 (November-December 1919): 330-336;

John Corbin, "Henry Mills Alden: A Sketch," *New York Times Book Review*, 19 October 1919, p. 556;

Eugene Exman, *The House of Harper: One Hundred Fifty Years of Publishing* (New York, Evanston & London: Harper & Row, 1967);

J. Henry Harper, *The House of Harper* (New York: Harper, 1912);

Frank Luther Mott, *A History of American Magazines, 1850-1865* (Cambridge, Mass.: Harvard University Press, 1938), pp. 382-405;

William Dean Howells, "In Memoriam," *Harper's Monthly Magazine*, 140 (December 1919): 133-136;

"The Editor of Harper's," *Literary Digest*, 63 (25 October 1919): 32-33.

Thomas Bailey Aldrich

(11 November 1836-19 March 1907)

J. Douglas Tarpley
CBN University

See also the Aldrich entries in *DLB 42: American Writers for Children Before 1900; DLB 71: American Literary Critics and Scholars, 1880-1900;* and *DLB 74: American Short Story Writers Before 1880.*

MAJOR POSITIONS HELD: Junior literary critic, *Evening Mirror* (1855); subeditor, *Home Journal* (1855-1859); associate editor, *Saturday Press* (1858-1860); literary critic, *Rudd & Carleton Publishing Co.* (1862); managing editor, *Illustrated News* (1863); editor, *Every Saturday* (1866-1874); editor, *Atlantic Monthly* (1881-1890).

BOOKS: *The Bells: A Collection of Chimes* (New York: J. C. Derby/Boston: Phillips, Sampson/Cincinnati: H. W. Derby, 1855);
Daisy's Necklace and What Came of It: A Literary Episode (New York: Derby & Jackson/Cincinnati: H. W. Derby, 1857);
The Course of True Love Never Did Run Smooth (New York: Rudd & Carleton, 1858);
The Ballad of Babie Bell, and Other Poems (New York: Rudd & Carleton, 1859);
Pampinea, and Other Poems (New York: Rudd & Carleton, 1861);
Out of His Head: A Romance (New York: Carleton, 1862);
Poems (New York: Carleton, 1863);
The Poems of Thomas Bailey Aldrich (Boston: Ticknor & Fields, 1865; revised edition, Boston: Osgood, 1874; London: Routledge, 1874; revised again, Boston: Houghton, Mifflin, 1882; revised again, Boston: Houghton, Mifflin, 1885); revised as volumes one and two of *The Writings of Thomas Bailey Aldrich* (Boston & New York: Houghton, Mifflin, 1897);
Père Antoine's Date-Palm (Cambridge, Mass.: Privately printed, 1866);
The Story of a Bad Boy (Boston: Ticknor & Fields, 1869; London: Low, Son & Marston, 1869); republished as *Tom Bailey's Adventures; or, the Story of a Bad Boy* (Boston: Osgood, 1877);

Thomas Bailey Aldrich

Pansy's Wish: A Christmas Fantasy with a Moral (Boston: Marion, 1870);
Jubilee Days, 16 numbers (Boston: Osgood, 1872);
Marjorie Daw and Other People (Boston: Osgood, 1873; London: Routledge, 1873); enlarged as *Marjorie Daw and Other Tales* (Leipzig: Tauchnitz, 1879); and *Marjorie Daw and Other Stories* (Boston: Houghton, Mifflin, 1885; Edinburgh: Douglas, 1894);
Prudence Palfrey: A Novel (London: Routledge, 1874; Boston: Osgood, 1874);
Cloth of Gold, and Other Poems (Boston: Osgood, 1874; London: Routledge, 1874);
Flower and Thorn: Later Poems (London: Routledge, 1876; Boston: Osgood, 1877);
Miss Mehetabel's Son (Boston: Osgood, 1877);
A Rivermouth Romance (Boston: Osgood, 1877);

Opening page from an issue of the magazine Aldrich edited from 1881 to 1890

A Midnight Fantasy, and The Little Violinist (Boston: Osgood, 1877);

The Queen of Sheba (London: Routledge, 1877; Boston: Osgood, 1877; revised edition, Edinburgh: Douglas, 1885);

Baby Bell (Boston: Osgood, 1878; London: Routledge, 1878);

The Stillwater Tragedy (1 volume, Boston: Houghton, Mifflin, 1880; 2 volumes, Edinburgh: Douglas, 1886);

XXXVI Lyrics and XII Sonnets (Boston: Houghton, Mifflin, 1881);

Friar Jerome's Beautiful Book and Other Poems (Boston: Houghton, Mifflin, 1881; London: Low, 1881);

From Ponkapog to Pesth (Boston: Houghton, Mifflin, 1883);

Mercedes, and Later Lyrics (Boston: Houghton, Mifflin, 1884); revised in part as *Mercedes: A Drama in Two Acts* (Boston & New York: Houghton, Mifflin, 1894);

The Second Son: A Novel, by Aldrich and M.O.W. Oliphant (Boston & New York: Houghton, Mifflin, 1888);

Wyndham Towers (Edinburgh: Douglas, 1889; Boston & New York: Houghton, Mifflin, 1890);

The Sisters' Tragedy, with Other Poems, Lyrical and Dramatic (Boston & New York: Houghton, Mifflin, 1891; enlarged, London: Macmillan, 1891);

An Old Town by the Sea (Boston & New York: Houghton, Mifflin, 1893);

Two Bites at a Cherry, with Other Tales (Edinburgh: Douglas, 1893; Boston & New York: Houghton, Mifflin, 1894);

Unguarded Gates, and Other Poems (Boston & New York: Houghton, Mifflin, 1895);

Later Lyrics (Boston & New York: Houghton, Mifflin, 1896; London: Lane, 1896);

Judith and Holofernes: A Poem (Boston & New York: Houghton, Mifflin, 1896);

On Influence of Books (Boston: Hall & Locke, 1901);

A Sea Turn, and Other Matters (Boston & New York: Houghton, Mifflin, 1902; London: Watt, 1902);

Ponkapog Papers (Boston & New York: Houghton, Mifflin, 1904);

Judith of Bethulia: A Tragedy (Boston & New York: Houghton, Mifflin, 1904; revised edition, Boston & New York: Houghton, Mifflin, 1905);

Pauline Pavlovna: A Drama in One Act (Boston & New York: Houghton, Mifflin, 1907?).

Collection: *The Writings of Thomas Bailey Aldrich*, 9 volumes (volumes 1-8, Boston & New York: Houghton, Mifflin, 1897; volume 9, Boston & New York: Houghton, Mifflin, 1907).

Thomas Bailey Aldrich is of interest today for his contributions to American literature and journalism. As a literary figure he contributed to the development of realism in adolescent fiction; one of his novels introduced a character type that became the antecedent of the "bad boy" developed later by Mark Twain and others. As a journalist Aldrich held editorial positions with several publications in New York and Boston. His journalistic career reached its height during the time he served as editor of the *Atlantic Monthly*, a period some critics consider to be among the most successful in terms of quality in *Atlantic* history.

Thomas Bailey Aldrich was born in Portsmouth, New Hampshire, on 11 November 1836, the only child of Elias Taft Aldrich and Sarah Abba Bailey Aldrich. The family on both sides was of New England colonial stock. His father was a wanderer, and Aldrich later said that as a child he had traveled to virtually every state of the union. The family lived in New York from 1841 to 1844 and in New Orleans from 1844 to 1849, then returned to Portsmouth. Elias Aldrich died of cholera on a Mississippi River steamboat at Memphis on 6 October 1849. Since his father did not leave enough money to finance a college education, at age sixteen Aldrich accepted a position as a clerk in the New York Commission office of his uncle, Charles Frost.

Before his move to New York he had written verse, some of which had been published in the *Portsmouth Journal*. In New York he began to write poetry even more diligently, since the job of clerk did not keep him busy. He later said he wrote at least two lyrics daily under the "stimulus of the metropolis." He published a book of his poetry, *The Bells*, in 1855, the same year his sentimental poem "The Ballad of Babie Bell" appeared in the *Journal of Commerce* and was reprinted by newspapers across the country. Aldrich resigned his clerkship to devote himself to a literary career and was soon hired as junior literary critic of the *Evening Mirror*.

Within a few months he became a subeditor for Nathaniel Parker Willis and George Pope Morris's *Home Journal*, a post once held by Edgar Allan Poe. The *Home Journal* included essays, poetry, fiction, book reviews, and general comment about the New York cultural scene. The "Interesting to the Ladies" department commented on latest fashions, while "Little or Nothings" contained riddles, anecdotes, and instruction about etiquette and polite conduct.

At the *Home Journal* Aldrich worked under the guidance of Willis and Morris, gaining wide editorial experience. He wrote to a friend, "I had no idea of what *work* is till I became 'sub.' I have found that reading proof and writing articles on subjects, 'at sight,' is no joke. The cry for 'more copy' rings through my ears in dreams, and hosts of little phantom printer's devils walk on my body all night and prick me with sharp-pointed types." Aldrich's tenure on the publication also provided him with opportunities to enlarge his literary and journalistic network of acquaintances in the city. His new circle included the writers Bayard Taylor, E. C. Stedman, Henry Clapp, Jr., Ada Clare, Fitz Hugh Ludlow, George Arnold, William Winter, Fitz James O'Brien, and R. H. Stoddard; the dramatist Edwin Booth; and the sculptor Launt Thompson.

When Clapp established the *Saturday Press* in October 1858, Aldrich accepted an invitation to become an associate editor along with Winter and O'Brien. Whereas Aldrich's assignment at the *Home Journal* had been to chronicle the activities of New York society, his new job required him to satirize respectability in America. For a few months he retained his position at the *Home Journal*, but early in 1859 he decided to devote himself to the *Saturday Press* full-time. Expressing an epigrammatic view of "current pretenses," the publication was popular with young literary talents across the country; but financial difficulties forced it to cease publication in early 1860.

Aldrich actually enjoyed his newfound freedom from journalistic responsibilities. In April 1860, after trying for three years, he sold verse for the first time to the *Atlantic Monthly*, the leading literary magazine of the day. Leading New England literary figures who regularly contributed to the *Atlantic* included Ralph Waldo Emerson, Henry Wadsworth Longfellow, and Harriett Beecher Stowe.

When the Civil War broke out, Aldrich unsuccessfully sought a military appointment, then became a war correspondent in the fall of 1861 for the *New York Tribune*; he was attached to General Blenker's division of the Army of the Potomac in Virginia. Moved deeply by the horrors of war, expressed later in his literary work, he left the assignment in early 1862 and returned to Portsmouth. He traveled between Portsmouth, New York, and Boston for several years.

He continued to write and publish poetry and short stories and in 1862 was hired as a literary adviser to the New York publishing house Rudd and Carleton. In January 1863 he was named managing editor of the *Illustrated News*. This assignment lasted until the end of the year, when the periodical ceased publication. During the next two years he also continued to develop his contacts with New England writers.

On 28 November 1865 Aldrich married Lilian Woodman. Shortly thereafter he moved to Boston to become editor of a new magazine, *Every Saturday*, which first appeared on 1 January 1866. Published by Ticknor and Fields, which became Fields, Osgood and Company in 1868, the magazine was composed almost entirely of material pirated from contemporary English and French periodicals. In preparation for his responsibilities,

Aldrich at his summer home in Tenant's Harbor, Maine

Aldrich said, he read "hundreds and hundreds" of French and English novels.

Aldrich "took root" in Boston, claiming to be a Bostonian by temperament, philosophy, and adoption. As he said in later years, "Though I am not genuine Boston, I am Boston-plated." He and his wife lived on Pinckney Street from 1867 to 1870, then moved to a larger house on Charles Street. Most of their summers were spent in Portsmouth.

In 1869 Aldrich's "The Story of a Bad Boy" was serialized in *Our Young Folks*, a children's magazine published by Fields, Osgood and Company. It was begun in Portsmouth and completed in Boston on 16 September 1868, one day before his twin sons Frost and Talbot were born. The magazine's subscription list grew by several thousand because of the story, which was published as a book the same year. It remains Aldrich's most lasting literary contribution. It marked the beginning of a period in which adolescent literature began to look realistically at the "natural escapades" of boyhood. Mark Twain, a friend of Aldrich's, and J. D. Salinger would write in this genre with greater impact than Aldrich.

In 1870 Fields, Osgood and Company changed *Every Saturday* into a large illustrated weekly designed to compete with *Harper's Weekly*, then at the zenith of its success. Aldrich advised against the change but remained as editor. The magazine returned to its original format at the end of 1871, was sold to H. O. Houghton and Company at the end of 1873, and died in 1874. At that time Aldrich moved with his family to a

Aldrich's grave in Mount Auburn Cemetery

farm near the village of Ponkapog outside the city. For the next seven years he lived as a freelance writer. Between 1875 and 1880 the *Atlantic Monthly* published twenty-three of his poems, three novels, and many prose sketches. He fished and played with his sons, and he and his wife visited Europe in 1875 and 1879.

In February 1881 William Dean Howells resigned as editor of the *Atlantic*, and Aldrich accepted an invitation from the publisher, Houghton, Mifflin and Company, to fill the vacancy. In a letter to Stedman he said, "I have a very clear understanding of the responsibilities I have assumed in taking the editorship of the *Atlantic*. I accepted the post only after making a thorough examination of my nerve and backbone. I fancy I shall do very little writing in the magazine, at first. I intend to edit it." According to his biographer, Ferris Greenslet, "Aldrich made an excellent magazine for the lettered reader. Under his conduct the *Atlantic* attained a notable unity of tone and distinction of style. A little less accessible to new and unknown talent than Mr. Howells had been, he was yet quick to receive the note of distinction, and few of his swans turned out geese."

He was not interested in politics and current affairs but in literature, and he published more of it than any previous *Atlantic* editor: fiction by Henry James, Helen Hunt Jackson, Marion Crawford, Margaret Oliphant, and Thomas Hardy; poetry by Longfellow, James Russell Lowell, Oliver Wendell Holmes, and John Greenleaf Whittier; and historical papers by John Fiske and Francis Parkman, Jr. He assembled an excellent group of reviewers, including Horace E. Scudder, George Parsons Lathrop, Richard Grant White, and George E. Woodberry. Under Aldrich the *Atlantic* won an international reputation as, in the phrase of an English journal, "the best edited magazine in the English language." He became well known among contributors and would-be contributors for his succinct and insightful letters, whether of acceptance or rejection. As Greenslet says, "The books in which his correspondence was copied are fruitful reading for the magazine writer, professional or amateur."

Aldrich resigned as editor of the *Atlantic* in the spring of 1890; he was succeeded by

Scudder, who had occupied the position during Aldrich's summer vacations in Europe. Aldrich wrote in a letter to a friend, "What a blessed relief it is not to make a hundred bitter enemies per month by declining MSS. I am so happy these days that I sometimes half suspect some calamity lurking round the corner."

The Aldriches traveled abroad in the summers of 1890, 1891, 1892, 1900, and 1901 and went around the world in the winters of 1894-1895 and 1898-1899. After returning from his 1895 tour, he wrote: "I have returned to find everything precisely as I left it. I have just finished the pipe which I laid down half-smoked that morning long ago when the carriage came to take me to the railway station. Nothing has changed, excepting myself. I am blissfully ignorant of all things literary. I haven't looked into a single American magazine, or read more than a cablegram in a newspaper, since October 4, 1894. If you ever wish to refresh and strengthen your mind, steer clear of American literature for seven months and seven days! I am naturally intellectual, but editorial work and accidental reading of dialect poems and stories have come near to extinguishing the white light of reason." Aldrich moved among his farm in Ponkapog; the house at 59 Mount Vernon Street in Boston that he bought in 1883; and The Crags, a summer place he built in Tenant's Harbor, Maine, in 1893.

The calamity he had feared came in 1901 when his son Charles became ill with tuberculosis and was moved to the purer air of Saranac Lake. Aldrich and his wife moved into a house nearby. Charles's death on 6 March 1904 at the age of thirty-six, was a blow from which Aldrich never fully recovered. In January 1907 Aldrich suddenly fell ill and underwent surgery; he died on 19 March at his home in Boston. He was buried in Mount Auburn Cemetery, Cambridge, Massachusetts.

Although Aldrich was one of the most respected literary men of his time, ranked by contemporaries with Mark Twain as a novelist and Henry Wadsworth Longfellow and James Russell Lowell as a poet, he is remembered as a writer today almost solely for his contribution to adolescent literature. His seminal bad-boy character type was destined to become the Huck Finns and Holden Caulfields of the American novel. Within a few years after his death realism and naturalism came into vogue in American literature. Literary critics of the early twentieth century ignored or dismissed Aldrich's poetry and fiction. In 1965, however, Charles Samuels concluded that Aldrich's contemporaries were right. "Aldrich deserves to be remembered as a skillful writer of light verse and as the author of a small body of excellent lyric poetry.... He can favorably be compared with the revered Lowell, Longfellow, and Whittier."

Aldrich's reputation as a journalist has fared better. His editorship of various publications, the *Atlantic Monthly* in particular, is consistently assessed by critics as solid and influential. As editor of the *Atlantic*, Aldrich lived at the center of the late-nineteenth-century literary world. His editorial decisions guided many young writers and helped to define the artistic standards of the day. He was a conservative editor, preferring the classical American literary tradition and accepting few innovations. Although he published fewer new writers than did his predecessors, most of those he did publish were eventually recognized as outstanding talents, attesting to his sensitivity and judgment. Under his editorship the *Atlantic Monthly* set the standards of American literary taste. On the other hand, Aldrich's exclusion of articles on politics, economics, and social issues restricted the magazine's audience to sophisticated and cultivated readers, causing a decline in circulation. Nevertheless, his editorship of the *Atlantic Monthly* has earned him a permanent page in the annals of American magazine journalism.

Biographies:

Ferris Greenslet, *The Life of Thomas Bailey Aldrich* (Boston: Houghton Mifflin, 1908);

Lillian Aldrich, *Crowding Memories* (Boston & New York: Houghton Mifflin, 1920).

References:

William H. Bishop, "Authors at Home: T. B. Aldrich on Beacon Hill, and Round It," *Critic*, 7 (8 August 1885): 61-63;

Edith Baker Brown, "Thomas Bailey Aldrich," *North American Review*, 189 (January 1909): 130-135;

Mary Silva Cosgrave, "Life and Times of T. B. Aldrich," *Horn Book*, 42 (April-August 1966): 223-232, 350-355, 464-473;

Gilbert Donaldson, "Thomas Bailey Aldrich," *Reader*, 9 (May 1907): 657-665;

C. Hartly Grattan, "Thomas Bailey Aldrich," *American Mercury*, 10 (May 1925): 41-45;

Charles R. Mangum, "A Critical Biography of Thomas Bailey Aldrich," Ph.D. dissertation, Cornell University, 1950;

Paul Elmer More, "Thomas Bailey Aldrich," in his *Shelburne Essays, Seventh Series* (New York: Putnam's, 1910), pp. 138-152;

Vernon Louis Parrington, *Main Currents in American Thought*, 3 volumes (New York: Harcourt, Brace, 1927), III: 54-60;

William H. Rideing, *The Boyhood of Living Authors* (New York: Crowell, 1887), pp. 16-27;

Rideing, "Glimpse of T. B. Aldrich," *Putnam's Monthly and Critic*, 7 (January 1910): 398-406;

Charles E. Samuels, *Thomas Bailey Aldrich* (New York: Twayne, 1965);

Donald Tuttle, "Thomas Bailey Aldrich's Editorship of the Atlantic Monthly," Ph.D. dissertation, Western Reserve University, 1939.

Papers;
Aldrich's personal library is at the Thomas Bailey Aldrich Memorial Museum, Portsmouth, New Hampshire. The majority of his papers are at the Houghton Library, Harvard University, and the Olin Library, Cornell University.

Timothy Shay Arthur

(6 June 1809-6 March 1885)

Kathleen L. Endres
Bowling Green State University

See also the Arthur entries in *DLB 3: Antebellum Writers in New York and the South* and *DLB 42: American Writers for Children Before 1900.*

MAJOR POSITIONS HELD: Editor, *Baltimore Athenaeum and Young Men's Paper* (1833-1836); *Baltimore Literary Monument* (1836-1839); *Ladies' Magazine of Literature, Fashion and Fine Arts* (1844-1846); *Arthur's Home Gazette* (1850-1854); *Arthur's Home Magazine* renamed *Lady's Home Magazine* in 1857, renamed *Arthur's Home Magazine* in 1861, renamed *Arthur's Lady's Home Magazine* in 1871, renamed *Arthur's Illustrated Home Magazine* in 1874, renamed *Arthur's Home Magazine* in 1880 (1854-1885); *Children's Hour* (1866-1872); *Once a Month* (1869).

BOOKS: *The Young Wife's Book: A Manual of Moral, Religious and Domestic Duties* (Philadelphia: Carey, Lea & Blanchard, 1836);

Insubordination: An American Story of Real Life (New York: Colman/Baltimore: Knight & Colburn, 1841); republished as *Insubordination; or, The Shoemaker's Daughters* (Philadelphia: Berford, 1844);

The Widow Morrison: A Leaf from the Book of Human Life (Baltimore: Knight & Colburn/New York: Giffing, 1841); republished in *Alice; or, The Victim of One Indiscretion* (1844); republished with *Alice Mellville; or, The Indiscretion as Mary Ellis; or, The Runaway Match* (Philadelphia: Anners, 1850);

Six Nights with the Washingtonians: A Series of Original Temperance Tales (Philadelphia: Godey & McMichael, 1842); republished as *Temperance Tales; or, Six Nights With The Washingtonians* (Philadelphia: Anners, 1849); enlarged as *The Tavern-Keeper's Victims; or, Six Nights with the Washingtonians* (Philadelphia: Leary, Getz, 1860);

Tired of Housekeeping (New York: Appleton, 1842);

Bell Martin; or, The Heiress: An American Story of Real Life (Philadelphia: Burgess & Zieber, 1843); revised as *Bell Martin: An American Story of Real Life* (Philadelphia: Anners, 1849; London: Hodson, 1858);

Fanny Dale; or, The First Year after Marriage (Philadelphia: Berford, 1843); republished as *Fanny Dale; or, A Year after Marriage* (Philadelphia: Berford, 1843; London: Hodson, 1852);

The Ladies' Fair (Philadelphia: Godey & McMichael, 1843);

Timothy Shay Arthur (Engraving by William G. Armstrong, from the Dictionary of American Portraits, *edited by Hayward and Blanche Cirker [New York: Dover, 1967])*

The Tailor's Apprentice: A Story of Cruelty and Oppression (Philadelphia: Godey & McMichael, 1843);

The Little Pilgrims: A Sequel to The Tailor's Apprentice (Philadelphia: Godey & McMichael, 1843);

Married and Single; or, Marriage and Celibacy Contrasted, in a Series of Domestic Pictures (Philadelphia: Anners, 1843);

Lovers and Husbands: A Story of Married Life (Philadelphia: Anners, 1843; London: Hodson, 1848);

The Story Book (Philadelphia: Godey & McMichael, 1843);

Making a Sensation, and Other Tales (Philadelphia: Godey & McMichael, 1843);

Madeline; or, A Daughter's Love and Other Tales (Philadelphia: Anners, 1843);

The Ruined Family and Other Tales (Philadelphia: Godey & McMichael, 1843); republished as *Temperance Tales* (Philadelphia: Godey & McMichael, 1843);

The Seamstress: A Tale of the Times (Philadelphia: Berford, 1843);

The Stolen Wife: An American Romance (Philadelphia: Berford, 1843);

Sweethearts and Wives; or, Before and after Marriage (New York: Harper, 1843);

The Two Merchants; or, Solvent and Insolvent (Philadelphia: Burgess & Zieber, 1843);

The Village Doctors and Other Tales (Philadelphia: Godey & McMichael, 1843);

Alice; or, The Victim of One Indiscretion (New York: Allen, 1844);

Cecilia Howard; or, The Young Lady Who Had Finished Her Education (New York: Allen, 1844);

Family Pride; or, The Palace and the Poor House: A Romance of Real Life (Philadelphia: Berford, 1844);

Hints and Helps for the Home Circle; or, The Mother's Friend, as Mary Elmwood (New York: Allen, 1844);

Hiram Elwood, the Banker; or, "Like Father, Like Son" (New York: Allen, 1844);

The Martyr Wife: A Domestic Romance (New York: Allen, 1844);

Pride or Principle, Which Makes the Lady? (Philadelphia: Berford, 1844);

Prose Fictions: Written for the Illustrations of True Principles, in Their Bearing upon Every-day Life (Philadelphia: Zieber, 1844);

The Ruined Gamester; or, Two Eras in My Life (Philadelphia: Lindsay & Blakiston, 1844);

The Two Sisters; or, Life's Changes (Philadelphia: Zieber, 1844);

Anna Milnor: the Young Lady Who Was Not Punctual, and Other Tales (New York & Philadelphia: Ferrett, 1845);

The Club Room, and Other Temperance Tales (Philadelphia: Ferrett, 1845);

The Heiress: A Novel (New York & Philadelphia: Ferrett, 1845);

Lovers and Husbands: A Story of Married Life (New York: Harper, 1845);

The Maiden: A Story for My Young Countrywomen (Philadelphia: Ferrett, 1845);

The Two Husbands and Other Tales (Philadelphia: Ferrett, 1845);

The Wife: A Story for My Young Countrywomen (Philadelphia: Anners, 1845; London: Hodson, 1852);

The New Story Book for Girls and Boys (London: Darton & Clark, 1845);

Our Neighbors, in the Corner House: A Novel (New York: Carleton/London: Hotten, 1846);

The Mother (Philadelphia: Ferrett, 1846; London: Speirs, 1869);

Random Recollections of an Old Doctor (Baltimore: Taylor, 1846);

Advice to Young Ladies on Their Duties and Conduct in Life (Boston: Howe, 1847; London: Hodson, 1856);

The Lady at Home; or, Leaves from the Everyday Book of an American Woman (Philadelphia: Anners, 1847);

The Young Wife: A Manual of Moral, Religious and Domestic Duties (Philadelphia: Lindsay & Blakiston, 1847);

Advice to Young Men on Their Duties and Conduct in Life (Boston: Howe, 1847; London: Hodson, 1854);

The Beautiful Widow (Philadelphia: Carey & Hart, 1847);

A Christmas Box for the Sons and Daughters of Temperance (Philadelphia: Sloanaker, 1847);

Improving Stories for the Young (Philadelphia: Anners, 1847);

Keeping Up Appearances; or, A Tale for the Rich and Poor (New York: Baker & Scribner, 1847);

Retiring from Business; or, The Rich Man's Error (New York: Young, 1847; London: Blackwood, 1879);

Riches Have Wings; or, A Tale for the Rich and Poor (New York: Baker & Scribner, 1847; London: Hodson, 1848);

The Young Music Teacher, and Other Tales (Philadelphia: Anners, 1847);

The Young Lady at Home: A Series of Home Stories for American Women (Philadelphia: Potter, 1847);

Rising in the World: A Tale for the Rich and Poor (New York: Collins, 1847; London: Blackwood, 1879);

Stories for My Young Friends (Philadelphia: Gihon, 1848; London: Hodson, 1855);

Agnes; or, The Possessed: A Revelation of Mesmerism (Philadelphia: Peterson, 1848; London: Hodson, 1852);

Debtor and Creditor: A Tale of the Times (New York: Baker & Scribner, 1848; London: Blackwood, 1879);

The Lost Children: A Temperance Tale (New York: Oliver, 1848);

Love in a Cottage (Philadelphia: Peterson, 1848);

Lucy Sandford: A Story of the Heart, a Temperance Tale (Philadelphia: Peterson, 1848);

Making Haste to Be Rich; or, The Temptation and Fall (New York: Baker & Scribner, 1848; London: Blackwood, 1879);

Temptations: A Story for the Reformed with Other Tales (New York: Oliver, 1848);

Love in High Life: A Story of the "Upper Ten" (Philadelphia: Peterson, 1849);

Mary Moreton; or, The Broken Promise: A True Story of American Life (Philadelphia: Peterson, 1849);

Wreaths of Friendship: A Gift for the Young, by Arthur and F. C. Woodworth (New York: Baker & Scribner, 1849);

Our Children: How Shall We Save Them? Also, Keeping It Up, and The Problem, as James Nack (New York: Oliver, 1849);

Sketches of Life and Character (Philadelphia: Bradley, 1849);

Not at Home (Boston: Gleason, 1849);

I Knew How It Would Be (Boston: Gleason, 1849);

Alice Mellville; or, The Indiscretion, published with *Mary Ellis; or, The Runaway Match* (Philadelphia: Anners, 1850);

All for the Best; or, The Old Peppermint Man: A Moral Tale (Boston: Crosby & Nichols, 1850);

The Debtor's Daughter; or, Life and Its Changes (Philadelphia: Peterson, 1850);

The Divorced Wife (Philadelphia: Peterson, 1850);

Golden Grains from Life's Harvest Field (Philadelphia: Bradley, 1850);

True Riches, and Other Tales (Philadelphia: Potter, 1850);

Illustrated Temperance Tales (Philadelphia: Bradley, 1850); enlarged as *The Lights and Shadows of Real Life* (Philadelphia: Bradley, 1851);

The Orphan Children: A Tale of Cruelty and Oppression (Philadelphia: Peterson, 1850);

Pride and Prudence; or, The Married Sisters (Philadelphia: Peterson, 1850);

The Two Brides (Philadelphia: Peterson, 1850);

The Young Artist; or, The Dream of Italy (New York: Dodd, 1850);

Lessons in Life, for All Who Will Read Them (Philadelphia: Lippincott, Grambo, 1851; London & Edinburgh: Nelson, 1853);

Off-Hand Sketches, a Little Dashed with Humour (Philadelphia: Lippincott, Grambo, 1851);

Seed-Time and Harvest; or, Whatsoever a Man Soweth, That Shall He Also Reap (Philadelphia: Lippincott, Grambo, 1851);

Stories for Parents (Philadelphia: Lippincott, Grambo, 1851);

Stories for Young Housekeepers (Philadelphia: Lippincott, Grambo, 1851);

The Two Wives; or, Lost and Won (Philadelphia: Lippincott, Grambo, 1851);

The Way to Prosper; or, In Union There Is Strength, and Other Tales (Philadelphia: Bradley, 1851; London: Blackwood, 1884);

Woman's Trials; or, Tales and Sketches from the Life around Us (Philadelphia: Lippincott, Grambo, 1851; London: Partridge & Oakey, 1851);

Words for the Wise (Philadelphia: Lippincott, Grambo, 1851; Glasgow: Oliphant & White, 1853);

A Wheat-Sheaf, Gathered from Our Own Fields, by Arthur and Woodworth (New York: Dodd, 1851);

The Tried and the Tempted (Philadelphia: Lippincott, Grambo, 1851; Glasgow: Oliphant & White, 1853);

Home Scenes, and Home Influence: A Series of Tales and Sketches (Philadelphia: Lippincott, Grambo, 1851);

The Banker's Wife; or, Like Father Like Son (Philadelphia: Peterson, 1851);

True Riches; or, Wealth without Wings (Philadelphia: Bradley, 1852; London: Hodson, 1856);

Cedardale; or, The Peacemakers (Philadelphia: Lippincott, Grambo, 1852; Halifax, U. K.: Milner & Sowerby, 1864);

Haven't-Time and Don't-Be-In-A-Hurry, and Other Stories (Philadelphia: Lippincott, Grambo, 1852);

The History of Georgia, from Its Earliest Settlement to the Present Time, by Arthur and William Henry Carpenter (Philadelphia: Lippincott, Grambo, 1852);

The History of Kentucky, from Its Earliest Settlement to the Present Time, by Arthur and Carpenter (Philadelphia: Lippincott, Grambo, 1852);

The History of Virginia, from Its Earliest Settlement to the Present Time, by Arthur and Carpenter (Philadelphia: Lippincott, Grambo, 1852);

The Last Penny, and Other Stories (Philadelphia: Lippincott, Grambo, 1852);

The Lost Children, and Other Stories (Philadelphia: Lippincott, Grambo, 1852);

Maggy's Baby, and Other Stories (Philadelphia: Lippincott, Grambo, 1852; Halifax, U. K.: Milner & Sowerby, 1855);

Our Little Harry, and Other Poems and Stories (Philadelphia: Lippincott, Grambo, 1852);

Pierre, the Organ-Boy, and Other Stories (Philadelphia: Lippincott, Grambo, 1852);

The Poor Woodcutter, and Other Stories (Philadelphia: Lippincott, Grambo, 1852; Halifax, U.K.: Milner & Sowerby, 1855);

Uncle Ben's New-Year's Gift, and Other Stories (Philadelphia: Lippincott, Grambo, 1852); title story republished as *The New Year's Gift* (London: Partridge & Oakey, 1852);

Who Are Happiest? And Other Stories (Philadelphia: Lippincott, Grambo, 1852);

Who Is Greatest? And Other Stories (Philadelphia: Lippincott, Grambo, 1852);

The Wounded Boy and Other Stories (Philadelphia: Lippincott, Grambo, 1852);

Confessions of a Housekeeper, as Mrs. John Smith (Philadelphia: Lippincott, Grambo, 1852); enlarged as *Trials and Confessions of an American Housekeeper* (Philadelphia: Lippincott, Grambo, 1854); enlarged edition republished as *Ups and Downs; or, Trials of a Housekeeper* (Philadelphia: Lippincott, 1857); republished again as *Trials and Confessions of a Housekeeper* (Philadelphia: Evans, 1859);

Home Scenes and Home Influence (Philadelphia: Lippincott, Grambo, 1852);

Married Life: Its Shadows and Sunshine (Philadelphia: Lippincott, Grambo, 1852; London: Partridge & Oakey, 1852);

Jessie Hampton (London: Partridge & Oakey, 1852);

The Ways of Providence; or, "He Doeth All Things Well" (Philadelphia: Lippincott, Grambo, 1852);

The History of New Jersey, from Its Earliest Settlement to the Present Time, by Arthur and Carpenter (Philadelphia: Lippincott, Grambo, 1853);

The History of New York, from Its Earliest Settlement to the Present Time, by Arthur and Carpenter (Philadelphia: Lippincott, Grambo, 1853);

The Fireside Angel (Boston: Crown, 1853); republished as *Lily: The Fireside Angel* (London: Hodson, 1855); enlarged as *Fireside Angel, and Other Stories* (Boston: Lothrop, 1869);

The History of Ohio, from Its Earliest Settlement to the Present Time, by Arthur and Carpenter (Philadelphia: Lippincott, Grambo, 1853);

The History of Vermont, from Its Earliest Settlement to the Present Time, by Arthur and Carpenter (Philadelphia: Lippincott, Grambo, 1853);

The String of Pearls, for Boys and Girls, by Arthur and Woodworth (Auburn: Derby/Buffalo: Orton & Mulligan, 1853);

Before and after the Election; or, The Political Experiences of Mr. Patrick Murphy (Philadelphia: Bradley, 1853);

Finger Posts on the Way of Life (Philadelphia: Bradley, 1853);

Heart-Histories and Life-Pictures (New York: Scribner, 1853);
Home Lights and Shadows (New York: Scribner, 1853);
The Home Mission (Boston: Crown/Philadelphia: Bradley, 1853);
Iron Rule; or, Tyranny in the Household (Philadelphia: Peterson, 1853);
The Old Astrologer (Philadelphia: Peterson, 1853?);
The Old Man's Bride (New York: Scribner, 1853);
Sparing to Spend; or, The Loftons and Pinkertons (New York: Scribner, 1853);
The Angel of the Household (Philadelphia: Bradley, 1854); enlarged as *The Angel of the Household, and Other Tales* (Philadelphia: Evans, 1858)–adds *The Home Mission* (1853);
Shadows and Sunbeams (Boston: Crown/Philadelphia: Bradley, 1854);
The History of Connecticut, from Its Earliest Settlement to the Present Time, by Arthur and Carpenter (Philadelphia: Lippincott, Grambo, 1854);
The History of Pennsylvania, from Its Earliest Settlement to the Present Time, by Arthur and Carpenter (Philadelphia: Lippincott, Grambo, 1854);
The History of Tennessee, from Its Earliest Settlement to the Present Time, by Arthur and Carpenter (Philadelphia: Lippincott, Grambo, 1854);
Ten Nights in a Bar-Room and What I Saw There (Philadelphia: Lippincott, Grambo/Bradley, 1854; Glasgow: Scottish Temperance League, 1855);
The Good Time Coming (Philadelphia: Bradley, 1855; London: Hodson, 1856);
Leaves from the Book of Human Life (Boston: Crown, 1855);
Trial and Triumph; or, Firmness in the Household (Philadelphia: Peterson, 1855);
What Can Woman Do? (Boston: Crown/Philadelphia: Bradley, 1856);
The Young Male Music Teacher and Other Tales (New York: Derby & Jackson, 1856);
The History of Illinois, from Its Earliest Settlement to the Present Time, by Arthur and Carpenter (Philadelphia: Lippincott, Grambo, 1857);
The Withered Heart (Boston: Crown/Philadelphia: Bradley, 1857; republished as *Jane Hardy; or, The Withered Heart: Edited by an English Lady* (London: Knight, 1857);
The Little Bound-Boy (Philadelphia: Bradley, 1858);
The Angel and the Demon: A Tale of Modern Spiritualism (Philadelphia: Bradley, 1858);
The Hand but Not the Heart; or, The Life-Trials of Jessie Loring (New York: Derby & Jackson, 1858);
Steps towards Heaven; or, Religion in Common Life: A Series of Lay Sermons for Converts in the Great Awakening (New York: Derby & Jackson, 1858);
Lizzy Glenn; or, The Trials of a Seamstress (Philadelphia: Peterson, 1859);
The Allen House; or, Twenty Years Ago and Now (Philadelphia: Potter, 1860);
Aunt Mary's Preserving Kettle (London: Partridge, 1863);
Nancy Wimble; or, The Village Gossip (London: Partridge, 1863);
Light on Shadowed Paths (Philadelphia: Potter, 1863);
Growler's Income Tax (New York: Loyal Publication Society, 1864);
Sowing the Wind, and Other Stories (New York: Sheldon, 1864);
Sow Well and Reap Well (London: Nelson, 1864);
Hidden Wings, and Other Stories (New York: Sheldon, 1864);
Out in the World: A Novel (New York: Carleton, 1864);
Sunshine at Home, and Other Stories (New York: Sheldon, 1864);
Home-Heroes, Saints, and Martyrs (Philadelphia: Lippincott, 1865); republished as *Home Heroines: Tales for Girls* (Edinburgh: Nimmo, 1867);
Nothing but Money: A Novel (New York: Carleton, 1865; London: Milner, 1867);
Life's Crosses, and How to Meet Them (Edinburgh: Nimmo, 1865);
What Came Afterwards: Being a Sequel to "Nothing but Money" (New York: Carleton, 1865);
The Lost Bride; or, The Astrologer's Prophecy Fulfilled (Philadelphia: Peterson, 1866);
Words of Warning: A Series of Tales and Sketches (London: Nelson, 1866);
Blind Nelly's Boy and Other Stories (Philadelphia, 1867);
The Son of My Friend (Philadelphia: Arthur, 1867; London: Partridge, 1870);
After the Storm (Philadelphia: Potter, 1868);
After a Shadow, and Other Stories (New York: Sheldon, 1869);
Not Anything for Peace, and Other Stories (New York: Sheldon, 1869);
The Peacemaker, and Other Stories (New York: Sheldon, 1869);

Opening page of an issue of Arthur's magazine aimed at the middle-class female reader

The Seen and the Unseen (Philadelphia: Lippincott, 1869);

Heroes of the Household (Philadelphia: Lippincott, 1869);

Beacon Lights: Tales and Sketches for Girls (Edinburgh: Hislop, 1869);

All's for the Best (Philadelphia: Lippincott, 1869);

Rainy Day at Home (Boston: Lothrop, 1870);

The Unsteady Hand (London: Tweedie, 1870);

Talks with a Philosopher on the Ways of God with Man (Philadelphia: New Church Tract and Publication Society, 1870);

Tom Blinn's Temperance Society, and Other Tales (New York: National Temperance Society and Publication House, 1870);

Orange Blossoms, Fresh and Faded (Philadelphia: Stoddart/New York: Gibson/Boston: Maclean, 1871; Wakefield, U. K.: Nicholson, 1876);

Idle Hands, and Other Stories (Philadelphia: Porter & Coates, 1871);

The Wonderful Story of Gentle Hand, and Other Stories (Philadelphia: Stoddart, 1871);

Grace Myers' Sewing Machine, and Other Tales (Glasgow, Scottish Temperance League, 1872);

Three Years in a Man-Trap (Philadelphia: Stoddart, 1872; Glasgow: Scottish Temperance League, 1873);

Cast Adrift (Philadelphia: Stoddart/New York: Gibson/Boston: Maclean, 1873; London: Milner, 1878);

Choice Tales (London: Blackwood, 1873);

Comforted (Philadelphia: Lippincott, 1873);

Woman to the Rescue: A Story of the New Crusade (Philadelphia: Stoddart/Cincinatti: Queen City Publishing/Chicago: Goodman/New York: Douglass & Meyers/Boston: George M. Smith/San Francisco: Bancroft, 1874);

Danger; or, Wounded in the House of a Friend (Philadelphia: Stoddart/Chicago: Western Publishing House/Boston: George M. Smith, 1875);

The Power of Kindness, and Other Stories (London: Nelson, 1875);

The Two Savings Banks; or, "Laying-Up for a Rainy Day" (Philadelphia, 1876?);

The Bar-Rooms at Brantley; or, The Great Hotel Speculation (Philadelphia: Porter & Coates, 1877; London: Hamilton, Adams, 1879);

The Latimer Family; or, The Bottle and the Pledge, and Other Temperance Stories (Philadelphia: Peterson, 1877);

Strong Drink: The Curse and the Cure (Philadelphia, Cincinnati, Chicago & Springfield: Hubbard/St. Louis: Thompson/San Francisco: Bancroft, 1877); part two republished as *Grappling with the Monster; or, The Curse and Cure of Strong Drink* (New York: Lovell, 1877);

The Wife's Engagement Ring (New York: National Temperance Society and Publishing House, 1877);

Temperance Stories for the Young (London: Partridge, 1878);

The Mill and the Tavern (New York: National Temperance Society and Publishing House, 1878);

The Strike at Tivoli Mills, and What Came of It (Philadelphia: Garrigues, 1879);

Window Curtains (New York: Ogilvie, 1880);

Feet and Wings; or, Among the Beasts and Birds, as Uncle Herbert (Philadelphia: Lippincott, 1880);

Saved as by Fire: A Story Illustrating How One of Nature's Noblemen Was Saved from the Demon Drink (Philadelphia, Boston, New York, Hartford, Cincinnati, St. Louis, San Francisco, Kansas City & Atlanta: Cottage Library Publishing House, 1881);

Death-Dealing Gold; or, The Miser's Fate (Philadelphia: Columbian Publishing Co., 1890);

Adventures by Sea and Land; or, Perils and Hairbreadth Escapes of Travellers in Every Part of the World (New York: Worthington, 1890);

The Little Savoyard, and Other Stories: A Collection of Instructive and Entertaining Sketches for Young Readers (New York: Worthington, 1891);

Story Sermons (Philadelphia: Alden, 1893);

The Two Little Girls and What They Did (London: Partridge, 1899);

Leaves from the Book of Human Life (Philadelphia: Evans, 1899);

Talks with a Child on the Beatitudes (New York: Swinney, n.d.).

OTHER: *The Brilliant: A Gift Book for 1850*, edited by Arthur (New York: Baker & Scribner, 1850);

The Crystal Fount, for All Seasons, edited by Arthur (New York: Cornish, Lamport, 1850);

The Temperance Gift, edited by Arthur (New York: Leavitt & Allen, 1854);

The Temperance Offering, for All Seasons, edited by Arthur (New York: Lamport, Blakeman & Law, 1854);

Friends and Neighbors; or, Two Ways of Living in the World, edited by Arthur (Philadelphia: Peck & Bliss, 1856);

The Mother's Rule; or, The Right Way and the Wrong Way, edited by Arthur (Philadelphia: Peck & Bliss, 1856);

Our Homes: Their Cares and Duties, Joys and Sorrows, edited by Arthur (Philadelphia: Peck & Bliss, 1856);

The True Path, and How to Walk Therein, edited by Arthur (Philadelphia: Peck & Bliss, 1856);

The Wedding Guest: A Friend of the Bride and Bridegroom, edited by Arthur (Philadelphia: Peck & Bliss, 1856);

Words of Cheer for the Tempted, the Toiling, and the Sorrowing, edited by Arthur (Philadelphia: Peck & Bliss, 1856; London: Nelson, 1866);

Little Gems from the Children's Hour, edited by Arthur as Uncle Herbert (Chicago: Western Publishing House, 1875);

The Prattler: A Picture and Story Book for Boys and Girls, edited by Arthur as Uncle Herbert (Philadelphia: Lippincott, 1876);

The Budget: A Picture and Story Book for Boys and Girls, edited by Arthur as Uncle Herbert (Philadelphia: Lippincott/New York: Lovell, 1877);

My Own Book, edited by Arthur as Uncle Herbert (Philadelphia: Lippincott, 1877);

My Pet Book, edited by Arthur as Uncle Herbert (Philadelphia: Lippincott, 1877);

My Primer, edited by Arthur as Uncle Herbert (Philadelphia: Lippincott, 1877);

The Playmate: A Picture and Story Book for Boys and Girls, edited by Arthur as Uncle Herbert (Philadelphia: Lippincott, 1878);

The Boys' and Girls' Treasury: A Picture and Story Book for Young People, edited by Arthur as Uncle Herbert (Philadelphia: Lippincott, 1879);

Lucy Grey and Other Stories for Boys and Girls, edited by Arthur as Uncle Herbert (Philadelphia: Lippincott, 1880);

Pleasant Stories and Pictures, edited by Arthur as Uncle Herbert (Philadelphia, 1880);

Sophy and Prince, and Other Stories for the Young, edited by Arthur as Uncle Herbert (Philadelphia: Lippincott, 1881);

Uncle Herbert's Speaker and Autograph Album Verses, edited by Arthur as Uncle Herbert (Philadelphia: Ruth, 1886).

For the most part, Timothy Shay Arthur's success as a magazine journalist and editor rested on changes within America's reading public. The mid to late nineteenth century witnessed the emergence of the middle-class female reading public as a major magazine market. Arthur's writing style and editorial philosophy were ideally suited to appeal to that segment of society. His writing–whether editorials, essays, short stories, or novels–always contained a moral lesson. His most successful publishing ventures, *Arthur's Home Magazine* and the *Children's Hour,* incorporated a similar philosophy.

Arthur was born on 6 June 1809 on a farm near Newburgh in Orange County, New York, to William and Anna Shay Arthur. His father has been variously described as a miller and a laborer, but in either case, it is clear that the family's means were limited. As a result of their strained circumstances, Arthur's parents were unable to provide him with much education; he seems to have depended on home instruction. According to Arthur's own account in *The Lights and Shadows of Real Life* (1850), he was brought up with stories about his namesake, his maternal grandfather who served as an officer in the American army during the Revolutionary War, and with Bible readings and religious instruction at home. Not until the family moved to Baltimore in 1817 did Arthur attend school with any regularity, and it was not a pleasant experience. According to his teacher Arthur was a dull student, incapable of grasping fundamental skills. By the age of nine, he still had not mastered addition. As Arthur admitted, "As for Arithmetic, I did not master half the common rules, and Grammar was in my mind completely unintelligible." After several years of seemingly fruitless instruction, his teacher advised his father not to waste money on the education of his son but to put him out to learn a trade. At age thirteen Arthur left school and went to work in a mill. From fifteen to twenty he served as an apprentice to a tailor; poor eyesight, however, forced him to give up that trade. While working as a tailor the undereducated teenager began an undirected self-education program; he also began a lifelong involvement in the temperance movement by joining the first antidrinking society formed in Maryland.

Forced to give up tailoring and with little business training, Arthur found a job in a countinghouse. The post offered only a small salary, little opportunity for advancement, and no real chance to learn the business. Prospects seemed to improve three years later when he was hired as a western agent for a banking company. The institution soon failed, however, and in 1833 Arthur returned to Baltimore, jobless.

Throughout his apprenticeship and his days with the countinghouse, Arthur had written short stories and poetry and had sought out others with similar interests. By 1833 he was a member of a Baltimore literary group that included Dr. Nathan C. Brooks, Rufus Dawes, and W. H. Carpenter. With these men Arthur in 1833 launched the *Baltimore Athenaeum and Young Men's Paper,* a weekly literary publication that lasted three years. After achieving marginal success with the *Athenaeum,* Arthur founded the *Baltimore Literary Monument* in 1836. For another three years, this magazine had a reputation as a well-regarded literary periodical.

His success in publishing gave Arthur the financial stability he needed to marry Eliza Alden in 1836; they eventually had seven children. Also in 1836 he published his first book–*The Young Wife's Book: A Manual of Moral, Religious and Domestic Duties.* The next year he began to place domestic tales in *Godey's Lady's Book.* These submissions marked Arthur's entrance into a major magazine appealing to the middle-class female reader.

In this early phase of his career, however, Arthur was not yet ready to specialize in one kind of journalism. In 1840 he became involved in political journalism as editor of Duff Green's *Baltimore Merchant*, a campaign weekly for William Henry Harrison. At the *Merchant*, Arthur also covered early meetings of the Washington Temperance Society, a group of reformed alcoholics. The material he gathered at the meetings became the basis for a collection of stories entitled *Six Nights with the Washingtonians: A Series of Original Temperance Tales* (1842). The volume established Arthur's reputation as a spokesman in the crusade against drink.

In 1841 Arthur moved his family to Philadelphia. The city was the home of many large, successful monthlies, such as *Godey's* and *Graham's*, both of which published Arthur's stories. In the 1840s alone, *Godey's* published sixty of Arthur's works. Moreover, Philadelphia had many book publishers who found Arthur to be one of the most prolific writers of the period. By the 1850s his books, which included *Ten Nights in a Bar-Room and What I Saw There* (1854)–the largest selling temperance book of the period–were second in sales only to Harriet Beecher Stowe's *Uncle Tom's Cabin*. Arthur continued to produce books at an astonishing pace throughout the next two decades, and most were published by Philadelphia houses. Philadelphia also proved to be an ideal environment for Arthur's own magazine ventures. His first, the *Ladies' Magazine of Literature, Fashion and Fine Arts*, was launched in 1844. Although it had contributions from such well-known literary figures as Nathaniel P. Willis, Park Benjamin, J. G. Percival, and A. J. H. Duganne, the magazine met with only limited success; after two years it was merged with *Godey's*. His 1850 venture was much more successful. That year Arthur launched a weekly called *Arthur's Home Gazette*, which was incorporated into *Arthur's Home Magazine*, a monthly, in 1854. From 1853 until his death Arthur edited the *Home Magazine*, which went through several name changes. Between 1855 and 1872, when Arthur was busy with a variety of writing and publishing endeavors, Virginia F. Townsend, a popular short story writer, helped edit the *Home Magazine*.

Arthur's Home Magazine never matched the quality, circulation, success, or reputation of its major competitors, *Godey's* and *Peterson's*. Still, it represented an excellent example of the smaller women's publications that were produced in the mid to late nineteenth century. It also illustrated how Arthur was able to translate a highly successful literary formula into an editing philosophy that appealed to middle-class nineteenth-century women. The *Home Magazine* had a small, but loyal following; its circulation probably ranged from ten thousand to thirty thousand, a respectable readership by nineteenth-century standards, but low in comparison to *Godey's* and *Peterson's*, each of which exceeded one hundred thousand readers.

Arthur's readership functioned as a kind of family. Readers wrote the editor and contributed work to the magazine, a relationship cultivated both by the method of selling subscriptions and by Arthur's editorial tone. Like many other women's publications, *Arthur's Home Magazine* was sold primarily through clubs in the North and Midwest. If readers brought in more subscribers, all would benefit from the lower rate. The cost for subscribing to the magazine ranged between $2.00 and $3.50 over the years; through the clubs, however, the cost could be substantially lowered. For example, in 1861 a subscription cost $2.00, but if a reader could bring seven friends into the *Arthur's* circle of subscribers, the cost was only $1.20 a year for each in the club. Not only was such a method an effective means to increase circulation, but it also helped ensure reader loyalty because groups of subscribers knew each other and, presumably, discussed the magazine's content.

Reader loyalty was also cultivated by Arthur's editorial style. Readers were not just subscribers, they were friends and vital to the success of the magazine. As Arthur once wrote in his magazine, "Tried friends should not part when days of darkness come, but draw close together." That attitude was reciprocated. Subscribers frequently wrote Arthur, attesting to the magazine's importance in their lives.

The content of *Arthur's* encouraged a close relationship between the reader and the editor. Arthur wanted his magazine to be more than mere reading material; he wanted it to achieve a higher moral goal. Thus, Arthur made his *Home Magazine* an extension of his literary philosophy. With short stories, essays, and poetry, all written as moral lessons, his magazine was designed to be an ideal home companion. According to Arthur, the magazine was intended "to furnish a home literature, fully imbued with Christian sentiments–a home literature that comes to the earnest worker in life, and gives him strength for duty; comes to the mourner with words of comfort; to the thoughtless with suggestions of a life-purpose; to the weary one, fainting over her tasks, with a new incentive to action; to husband, father, wife, mother, child, brother, sister, maiden and young men–to all who have minds to think and hearts to feel, with the inspirations of a high purpose."

The *Home Magazine*'s departments reflect that commitment. The child had the "Boys and Girls Treasury," an array of letters, stories, science, and moral lessons. The wife and mother had practical advice in the "Health Department" and "Mother's Department." For inspiration, there were the "Lay Sermons," which frequently were written by Arthur; short stories; poetry; and essays. Husbands and young men could find out about current literature in the "New Publications" department.

Illustrations were also designed to be inspirational. While never as numerous or as grandly engraved as those in *Godey's* or *Peterson's*, *Arthur's* illustrations tried to capture the tranquillity and charm of idealized family life. Many showed doting parents and well-behaved children.

Arthur bought stories from some of the best-known writers in the women's literary market. Lucy Larcom, Helen Bostwick, Clara Augusta, J. Starr Holloway, Julia Dorr, Alice Cary, and Ella Wheeler contributed their own brands of moral tales, all of which showed the evils of vanity and the strength of women doing their traditional duties. Stories that illustrated the folly of drink, a favorite topic of the editor, were also common.

During the Civil War Arthur expanded the magazine's focus to include stories, poems, and essays designed to buoy the spirits of his female readers. But Arthur saw women expanding their roles during wartime. In November 1861 the editor told his readers what was expected: "No individual, however humble or apparently uninfluential, can, in this crisis, stand aloof from the conflict, and be innocent before God." The editorial content of the magazine reflected that philosophy. In short stories, poetry, essays, editorials, and departments, Arthur and his contributors urged readers never to lose heart and always to support President Lincoln. An unabashed advocate of the Union, Arthur implored his readers to involve themselves politically to assure correct opinion in their neighborhoods, and to apply pressure so that the war was vigorously pursued, and to see that slavery was eliminated. Because of such positions, *Arthur's Home Magazine* tended to be regarded as among the more radical women's periodicals published during the Civil War.

In 1867 Arthur started yet another magazine, the *Children's Hour*, one of the few periodicals of its era specifically aimed at children. Continuing Arthur's philosophy of providing strong moral lessons, the monthly contained warnings against the evils of disobedience, selfishness, drink, and breaking the Sabbath. Arthur himself wrote many of the tales. The magazine was absorbed by a competitor, *St. Nicholas*, in 1874.

A man of almost boundless energy, Arthur made time to contribute to many civic and church activities. He was a leading member of the Swedenborgian Church in Philadelphia. The temperance cause remained a lifelong commitment and in the late 1870s he helped establish the Franklin Home for Inebriates in Philadelphia. In 1876 he served as chairman of the executive committee of Philadelphia's Centennial Exhibition. Arthur died in Philadelphia on 6 March 1885 after an illness lasting several weeks.

Arthur edited six different magazines–frequently two at once–while at the same time writing and editing books and contributing stories and serials to other newspapers and magazines. The magazines he edited ranged in variety from political to literary and in quality from mediocre to fine. It was one of the latter–*Arthur's Home Magazine*, aimed at women and the home–that brought him his greatest fame as an editor. For thirty-two years Arthur brought his readers–or "friends," as he viewed them–moral tales and uplifting editorials and essays. While his magazine never matched the grandeur or popularity of *Godey's* or *Peterson's*, *Arthur's Home Magazine* nonetheless served its loyal readership well. Despite his productivity Arthur has been overlooked as an editor in most histories of journalism. But he never expected to be remembered. He was content believing that he had been guided by Providence to do good for his fellow man or woman through his inspirational stories and appealing periodicals.

Biographies:
T. S. Arthur: His Life and Works. By One Who Knows Him (Philadelphia: Stoddard, 1873);
Donald A. Koch, "The Life and Times of Timothy Shay Arthur," Ph. D. dissertation, Western Reserve University, 1954.

References:
Kathleen L. Endres, "The Women's Press Goes

for a Soldier: A Study in Propaganda, Patriotism and Public Image," *Civil War History*, 30 (March 1984): 31-53;

D. L. Milliken, "Methods of T. S. Arthur," *Writer*, 1 (October 1887): 141-142;

Edward Palen, "A Talk with T. S. Arthur," manuscript, dated 1882, Manuscript Department, University of North Carolina, Chapel Hill.

Maturin Murray Ballou
(Lieutenant Murray)
(14 April 1820-27 March 1895)

George Everett
University of Tennessee, Knoxville

See also the F. Gleason's Publishing Hall entry in *DLB 49: American Literary Publishing Houses, 1638-1899*.

MAJOR POSITIONS HELD: Editor, *Flag of Our Union* (1846-1854), *Gleason's Pictorial Drawing-Room Companion* (1851-1854), *Boston Globe* (1872-1874); editor and publisher, *Flag of Our Union* (1854-1863), *Ballou's Pictorial Drawing-Room Companion* (1854-1859), *Ballou's Dollar Monthly* (1855-1863), *Weekly Novelette* (1857), *Welcome Guest* (1860), *Boston Budget* (1879-1895), *Ballou's Magazine* (1879-1893).

BOOKS: *Fanny Campbell; or, The Female Pirate Captain*, as Murray (New York: Long, 1844);

Red Rupert, the American Bucanier, as Murray (Boston: Gleason, 1845);

The Protege of the Grand Duke: A Tale of Italy, as Frank Forester (Boston: Gleason, 1845);

The Naval Officer; or, The Pirate's Cave: A Tale of the Last War, as Murray (Boston: Gleason, 1845; London: Pratt, 1849);

Albert Simmons; or, The Midshipman's Revenge: A Tale of Land & Sea, as Forester (Boston: Gleason, 1845);

The Child of the Sea; or, The Smuggler of Colonial Times. And The Love Test (Boston: United States Publishing Co., 1846);

The Spanish Musketeer: A Tale of Military Life, as Murray (Boston: Gleason, 1847);

Roderick the Rover; or, The Spirit of the Wave, as Murray (Boston: Gleason, 1847);

Maturin Murray Ballou (Gale International Portrait Gallery)

The Gipsey; or, The Robbers of Naples, as Murray (Boston: Gleason, 1847);

Rosalette; or, The Flower Girl of Paris: A Romance of France, as Murray (New York: French, 1848);

The Duke's Prize: A Story of Art and Heart in Florence, as Murray (New York: French, 1848)–

also contains "The Prima Donna," by M. V. St. Leon; "The Artist of Florence," by James De Mille; "A Tale of a Crusader," by Charles E. Waite; "The Australian Footman," by De Mille; "The Corsair of Scio," by De Mille;

The Cabin Boy; or, Life on the Wing: A Story of Fortune's Freaks and Fancies, as Murray (Boston: Gleason, 1848);

The Adventurer; or, The Wreck on the Indian Ocean: A Land and Sea Tale, as Murray (Boston: Gleason, 1848);

The Belle of Madrid; or, The Unknown Mask: A Tale of Spain and the Spanish, as Murray (Boston: Gleason, 1849);

The Turkish Slave; or, The Mahometan and His Harem: A Story of the East, as Murray (Boston: Gleason, 1850);

The Magician of Naples; or, Love and Necromancy: A Story of Italy and the East, as Murray (New York: French, 1850)–also contains "The Black Avenger of the Spanish Main," by Edward Z. C. Judson;

The Circassian Slave; or, The Sultan's Favorite: A Story of Constantinople and the East, as Murray (Boston: Gleason, 1851);

The Heart's Secret; or, The Fortunes of a Soldier: A Story of Love and the Low Latitudes, as Murray (Boston: Gleason, 1852);

Life-Story of Hosea Ballou, for the Young (Boston: Tompkins, 1854);

History of Cuba; or, Notes of a Traveller in the Tropics: Being a Political, Historical, and Statistical Account of the Island, from Its First Discovery to the Present Time (Boston: Phillips, Sampson/Derby, 1854);

The Turkish Spies Ali Abubeker Kaled, and Zenobia Marrita Mustapha; or, The Mohammedan Prophet of 1854: A True History of the Russo-Turkish War, as Murray (Baltimore & Philadelphia: Orton, 1855);

The Sea-Witch; or, The African Quadroon: A Story of the Slave Coast, as Murray (New York: French, 1855)–also contains "La Tarantula," by Giddings H. Ballou; "The Goldsmith of Paris," by H. W. Loring; "Miss Henderson's Thanksgiving Day," by Horatio Alger, Jr.; "The Fireman," by Miss M. C. Montaigne;

Miralda; or, The Justice of Tacon: A Drama, in Three Acts (Boston: Spencer, 1858);

The Arkansas Ranger; or, Dingle the Backwoodsman: A Story of East and West, as Murray (Boston: Office of The Flag of Our Union, Ballou's Pictorial, and Ballou's Dollar Monthly, 1858);

The Pirate Smugglers; or, The Last Cruise of the Viper, as Murray (Boston: Elliott, Thomes & Talbot, 1861);

Captain Lovell; or, The Pirate's Cave: A Tale of the War of 1812, as Murray (New York: Brady, 1870);

The White Brave; or, The Flower of the Lenape Lodge, as Murray (New York: Beadle, 1872; Glasgow & London: Cameron & Ferguson, n. d.);

Due West; or, Round the World in Ten Months (Boston & New York: Houghton, Mifflin, 1884);

Due South; or, Cuba Past and Present (Boston & New York: Houghton, Mifflin, 1885);

Due North; or, Glimpses of Scandinavia and Russia (Boston: Ticknor, 1887);

Genius in Sunshine and Shadow (Boston: Ticknor, 1887);

Under the Southern Cross; or, Travels in Australia, Tasmania, New Zealand, Samoa, and Other Pacific Islands (Boston: Ticknor, 1887; London: Trübner, 1888);

The Outlaw; or, The Female Bandit: A Story of the Robbers of the Apennines, as Murray (Boston: Studley, 1887);

Foot-Prints of Travel; or, Journeyings in Many Lands (Boston: Ginn, 1888);

The Dog Detective and His Young Master, as Murray (New York: Street & Smith, 1888);

Mezzoni the Brigand; or, The King of the Mountains, as Murray (New York: Street & Smith, 1889);

The Masked Lady; or, The Fortunes of a Dragoon, as Murray (New York: Street & Smith, 1889);

The New Eldorado; A Summer Journey to Alaska (Boston & New York: Houghton, Mifflin, 1889);

Aztec Land: Central America, The West Indies and South America (Boston & New York: Houghton, Mifflin, 1890);

Equatorial America: Descriptive of a Visit to St. Thomas, Martinique, Barbadoes, and the Principal Capitals of South America (Boston & New York: Houghton, Mifflin, 1892);

The Story of Malta (Boston & New York: Houghton, Mifflin, 1893);

The Pearl of India (Boston & New York: Houghton, Mifflin, 1894).

OTHER: *Treasury of Thought: Forming an Encyclopaedia of Quotations from Ancient and Modern Authors*, compiled by Ballou (Boston: Osgood, 1872);

Pearls of Thought, compiled by Ballou (Boston: Houghton, Mifflin, 1881);

Notable Thoughts about Women: A Literary Mosaic, compiled by Ballou (Boston: Houghton, Mifflin, 1882);

Edge-Tools of Speech, compiled by Ballou (Boston: Ticknor, 1886).

For more than fifty years Maturin Murray Ballou wrote sensational novels for a growing American middle class that craved popular literature, and he prospered. A century later his prodigious literary efforts are forgotten, and posterity remembers him only for innovations early in his career. With a partner he established the first successful pictorial weekly in America; he appears to have been the first to market dime novels to the American public, preceding Beadle and Adams by three years; and he prescribed contributors' story lines in a way that anticipated Edward Stratemeyer by fifty years. But having opened new territory, Ballou proved unprepared to share it with others; he moved on to other things, leaving it to aggressive competitors to exploit his gains.

Ballou was born in Boston on 14 April 1820, the youngest of nine children of the Reverend Hosea Ballou and Ruth Washburn Ballou. He was a sixth-generation namesake of Maturin Ballou, a pioneer of Anglo-Norman stock who had shared ownership of the Providence Plantations with Roger Williams in 1646.

That he should be a moralistic and prolific writer seemed preordained. His father and two uncles were Universalist clergymen, and his grandfather was a Baptist minister. The Library of Congress held well over a hundred books in various editions written by his father, who founded three Universalist journals as well.

Ballou completed high school and passed the Harvard entrance examination but did not enter the university. In 1839 he became a clerk at the Boston post office; he married Mary Anne Roberts on 15 September of that year. Simultaneously he gained considerable experience with the religious journals edited by his father and a cousin, and he had his first secular piece published in a local miscellany called the *Olive Branch.*

For health reasons Ballou and his wife traveled extensively, especially in the West Indies, and Ballou began a lifelong practice of sending letters back to Boston for publication as travel pieces. When he returned he became deputy navy agent at the Boston Custom House. His knowledge of the sea and the navy would provide material for many adventure tales in decades to come.

In 1844 Ballou joined a Boston printer, Frederick Gleason, to form F. Gleason's Publishing Hall and the pretentiously named United States Publishing Company. Using the pen name Lieutenant Murray, Ballou wrote, and he and Gleason published, sensational stories such as *The Naval Officer; or, the Pirate's Cave* (1845) and *The Child of the Sea; or, The Smuggler of Colonial Times. And The Love Test* (1846).

Other authors also were published by Gleason's, and the partners soon saw a need for a regular outlet for the sensational stories that were so much in demand. In 1846 they inaugurated their first periodical, the *Flag of Our Union,* with Gleason serving as promoter and business manager and Ballou as chief writer and editor-manager. In 1847 the pair announced a "grand scheme" involving the payment of one hundred dollars for each of the fifty best manuscripts received. The quota may not have been filled, as later contests were scaled down; in 1848 only one prize of $150 for the best story was offered, and it did the publisher's image no good when the prize went to "Rosalette; or, the Flower Girl of Paris," by Lieutenant Murray. Some promising writers were published in the *Flag of Our Union*– Horatio Alger, Jr., Sylvanus Cobb, Jr., Mrs. Ann Stephens (author of Beadle and Company's first dime novel in 1860), Park Benjamin, and E. Z. C. Judson. If their stories seemed to resemble the sensational adventures of "Lieutenant Murray," small wonder; the editorial profile announced in the magazine seemed to describe Ballou's own work: "We wish for such contributions as shall be strictly moral in their tone, highly interesting in their plot, replete throughout with incident, well filled with exciting yet truthful description, and, in short, highly readable and entertaining. Domestic stories, so-called, are not exactly of the class we desire; but tales–of the sea and land–of the striving times of the revolution–of dates still farther back, are more in accordance with our wishes." These guidelines may have been too confining. Had Judson been left to choose his own plots and locales, he might have introduced in the *Flag of Our Union* his Ned Buntline series of Western stories which would prove so popular. Edgar Allan Poe seemed driven only by necessity to submit a few poems for five dollars each to a journal he considered "not very respectable."

But Ballou had made his decision: brought up in what was still the literary capital of the country, where small journals of quality were struggling under such editors as Ralph Waldo Emerson, Nathan Hale, Jr., Margaret Fuller, and James Russell Lowell, he cast his lot with the popular market in America. The decision was a lucrative one: Gleason later said that his share of the profits from the *Flag of Our Union* reached twenty-five thousand dollars a year.

In 1851 the latest journalistic novelty in England was the *London Illustrated News,* which was then ten years old; one of its woodcut engravers, Henry Carter, had immigrated to New York and set up shop as "Frank Leslie" and was available to work for Ballou. Ballou had seen the increasing role illustrations were playing in the sale of cheap popular novels, and he decided that the country was ready for a weekly picture paper. The decision not to make it a *news*paper may not have been a conscious one. Ballou's comment on the editorial page of the first issue of *Gleason's Pictorial Drawing-Room Companion,* 3 May 1851, implies that the distinction between news and editorial miscellany was not yet clear in America: "Let those who feel a pride in American art, and the excellence of native workmanship, compare our paper with a copy of the London *Illustrated News*, a journal which has heretofore taken the lead in illumined publications throughout the world. The London *News* may be found at the periodical depots, price *twenty-five cents* per single number, or *three dollars* per annum. The *Companion* may also be found at all the periodical depots, price *ten cents* per single number, or *three dollars* per annum. We ask our readers to compare these two publications minutely, and then judge for themselves which is the most beautiful and valuable paper." He went on to assure readers that the new pictorial would get better and better "as our various artists get more and more to understand exactly what is desired in the illustrated department." The comment is revealing: all of the improvement is to be in the illustrations; the reading material is to undergo no particular change.

The contents of the sixteen eleven-by-fifteen-inch pages in the 7 May 1853 issue are typical of the magazine. The top third of page 1 is dominated by the traditional *Gleason's* nameplate, a detailed engraving of Boston Harbor showing a dozen ships. The remainder of the page is given over to an elaborate woodcut of two goddesses framing a florid May Day scene; a few inches of type serve as a caption. More grandiose garlands, plus three-by-five-inch portraits of a French politician and a Hungarian baron, dominate the fourth and fifth pages. The eighth and ninth pages are given to five large woodcut views of the United States Military Academy at West Point. The twelfth page consists of a Berlin artist's painting (as copied by a woodcut engraver) of two children in a garden, and a picture of a perch with a paragraph on May fishing. The facing page has an elaborately illustrated masthead–Frederick Gleason, proprietor, and Maturin M. Ballou, editor–and a decorative house advertisement giving the subscription rates under an illustration of two angels bearing trumpets. The back page serves the leftovers–another picture of West Point, two more May Day drawings, and a five-by-five-inch woodcut illustrating a scene from a short story on one of the inside pages. The other pages consist entirely of type, and except for the large format, these pages could just as easily have appeared in the *Flag of Our Union*. The type pages include a serial story, "Hildebrand; or, The Buccaneer and the Cardinal"; short stories by Cobb, Benjamin Perley Poore, Miss Agnes Leslie, and Mrs. Caroline Orne; four poems, one of them by Alger; half a dozen one-paragraph fillers clipped from exchanges; a column of jokes and clever sayings; and eighteen column inches of news briefs, gossip, and editorial comment on current events under the headings "Editorial Melange," "Wayside Gatherings," and "Foreign Items."

In 1853 Ballou's star engraver, Leslie, with financial backing from P. T. Barnum and A. E. and H. D. Beach, started a news pictorial called the *Illustrated News* in New York. Despite a circulation of seventy thousand, his backers gave up and sold the new paper to Gleason's after a year; it was incorporated into *Gleason's Pictorial Drawing-Room Companion.* Leslie stayed in New York and laid plans for another illustrated newspaper.

In the early 1850s the Gleason enterprise was flourishing. Gleason claimed that the *Flag of Our Union* had the largest weekly circulation in the nation; the *Pictorial Drawing-Room Companion* jumped to a circulation of 50,000 within a few months of its first issue, and Gleason later said that it had reached 110,000 by 1854. Much of this success was attributable to Gleason's network of sales agents in New York, Philadelphia, Baltimore, Cincinnati, Detroit, and St. Louis. This sales network was Gleason's main contribution after the printing plant, and it was not insignificant. But his hardworking junior partner may have begun to brood about the share of the profits going to Gleason, who was off traveling in Eu-

Front page of an issue of the illustrated paper Ballou bought from Frederick Gleason in 1854 and renamed after himself

rope, while the editor got the papers out on time in the face of growing production problems. In 1854 Ballou threatened to start rival papers if Gleason did not sell out to him. The *Pictorial* of 18 November 1854 carried a statement from Gleason: "The undersigned, after ten years of unprecedented success as a publisher–years of uninterrupted and agreeable association with the reading public, and the army of subscribers whose names grace the list of 'The Flag of Our Union' and 'Gleason's Pictorial'–having realized an ample competency, fully commensurate with his desires, now retires from business altogether." In the same issue appeared installment twenty-three of Gleason's "Notes of Foreign Travel," recounting his European journeys.

On another page is the announcement of "Gleason's Dollar Monthly," a new publication to be started on 1 January 1855. Billed as the cheapest magazine in the world, it is to be "filled with entertaining and popular stories, by our best writers, with sketches, poems, scraps of wit and humor, and a miscellaneous compound of the notable events of the times in both hemispheres...." When the first issue appeared the name was *Ballou's Dollar Monthly;* the "Gleason's" in the announced title indicates the precipitous nature of the takeover. *Ballou's* also replaced *Gleason's* in the title of the *Pictorial Drawing-Room Companion*.

The *Dollar Monthly* was one hundred pages octavo, with each short story running several pages. Ballou took pride in its literary quality. He showed which material was paid for and which was not by running the unpaid pieces unleaded (no spacing between lines); he wrote much of the material himself. At a dollar a year or ten cents a copy, the magazine underpriced the other monthlies of the time, and within two years Ballou was claiming the second-highest circulation in the United States.

He moved serials, stories, and poems freely from one publication to another, and he published the longer pieces in book form as well. The *Flag of Our Union* began to run more stories about Indians and the West, but the *Dollar Monthly* generally held to the original formula calling for stories at sea or abroad, frequently with female protagonists.

Literary critics have little to say on behalf of Ballou's and his contributors' stories, except perhaps that he knew how to reach his market. Even his editorial judgment was expedient. In the *Pictorial Drawing-Room Companion* of 9 July 1853 he wrote concerning "strong-minded" or liberated women, "We tremble for their modesty, delicacy, and truthfulness to the sweet characteristics of their better natures." But in his sensational novelette *The Circassian Slave* (1851), the slave girl, a sixteen-year-old "of unsurpassed beauty," confronts a eunuch who has seen her slipping through the sultan's harem:

> "Torinda!" cried the eunuch, turning pale as death, for he knew well the consequence of suffering anyone to pass through his chamber at night.
> "Aye, Torinda," said our heroine, "Suffer me to pass without molestation, for well you know that whether I escape or not your doom is sealed."
> "I know it," said the eunuch sadly; "but I would rather fall beneath your sword than meet the sultan's wrath. Strike!"
> "I will," said Torinda–and drawing back her arm she motioned to the eunuch to hold his head up straight. With a sad smile he obeyed. The sword descended quickly but surely upon his neck, and the head rolled from the body to the ground. After wiping the blade of the sabre, Torinda turned to depart. It was then that the thought struck her that she had no horse to ride to the camp.

Story writers were familiar with Ballou works such as this one. When the editor said he wanted stories "replete throughout with incident," they knew by example what he had in mind.

Ballou's Dollar Monthly had a fairly long life, as story papers went, becoming *Ballou's Monthly* in 1866 and continuing under other owners into the 1890s.

The *Dollar Monthly* was Ballou's last major journalistic success. He had decided to stay in Boston to write and publish cheap literature for the masses, but the greatest masses were in New York. By 1856 Robert Bonner's *New York Mirror* surpassed 150,000 in circulation, twice that of the *Flag of Our Union*. Bonner soon would lead all literary journals with a circulation nearing half a million. Cobb accepted a lucrative offer by Bonner in 1856, and other writers soon followed the money trail to Manhattan.

Ballou countered with another innovation, the *Weekly Novelette*, in 1857. It specialized in four-part yarns in weekly installments, borrowing heavily from the columns of other Ballou publications. The idea is said to have inspired Erastus Beadle to start the dime novel in 1860; but Ballou could not seem to decide what to do with the new publication, and it lasted only thirteen weeks.

Ballou's Pictorial Drawing-Room Companion began to struggle. Not only had Bonner lured away some of its key writing talent, but Leslie's new *Illustrated Weekly Newspaper*, started in 1855, brought new competition for both subscribers and engravers. When a third illustrated weekly was started at Harper's in 1857, the demand for fast woodcutters tripled. In 1858 Ballou had to cut the yearly price of the *Pictorial* to $2.50 (it had been raised to $4.00 in 1852 and later dropped back to the original $3.00) to meet the competition, but the circulation figures did not respond. Finally, at the end of 1859, he announced his retirement from the field:

VALEDICTORY

Nearly nine years have elapsed since the undersigned commenced the editorship of this illustrated journal. Though at the outset it was under the proprietorship of another publisher, whose business interest we afterward purchased, yet the undersigned *prepared the first, last and every intervening number of the paper for the press.* . . . We were the pioneer of illustrated papers in the country, and the success of the work has been all and more than could have been anticipated, until so many competitors have entered the field, and competition has so lowered the price of illustrated journals, that it is no longer possible to give such engravings as should ornament a pictorial sheet and leave the least margin for profit.

He announced that *Pictorial* subscriptions would be transferred to a new literary journal, the *Welcome Guest*, to commence 1 January 1860. Thus Ballou, "the pioneer of illustrated papers," withdrew just as the woodcut weeklies were entering what would be their most prosperous decade thanks to the insatiable public demand for pictures of the Civil War.

The *Welcome Guest* did not succeed. The public did not want more sea stories or Turkish spy tales at a time when battle lines were forming across the country. Ballou sold his publications to a new Boston publishing house, Elliott, Thomes and Talbot, in 1863. He traveled, turned to civic affairs, and built the St. James Hotel in south Boston.

In 1872 Ballou and other Boston leaders established the *Boston Globe*. The paper was capitalized at $150,000 with Ballou as editor, but most of the money was gone by early 1874. The introspective writer of adventures was not suited to the scramble of metropolitan daily newspaper journalism, and the enterprise was turned over to twenty-seven-year-old Charles H. Taylor, who was destined to bring the paper to greatness.

Ballou was more successful with two other ventures. In 1879 he started the *Boston Budget*, a Sunday paper which lasted into the twentieth century, and *Ballou's Magazine*, a fifteen-cent miscellany which ran until 1893. Each claimed a circulation of about eighteen thousand in the mid 1880s, but their editor did not let himself become tied down as he had been with the *Pictorial* in those hardworking years of the 1850s. He lectured, wrote plays (none were ever staged), and cranked out travel books as he continued to crisscross his beloved seas. He took a trip around the world in 1882 and visited the polar regions in 1886. He died in Cairo, Egypt, in 1895, still on the road a few weeks short of his seventy-fifth birthday.

As a journalist, Ballou deserves minimal credit. He did not hesitate to write fanciful tales and present them to a gullible public as fact. His *Turkish Spies* (1855) was subtitled *A True History of the Russo-Turkish War*, by "Lieutenant Murray, of the Allied Armies Now in Turkey." Neither is he due much credit as a writer: a novelist who must end his final chapter with "Reader, our story is finished" (*The Circassian Slave*) lacks a certain narrative skill. His travel books were better written but tended to be collections of surface observations and first impressions.

As an instrument of popular culture, he made a significant contribution. In his pictorials he brought early, and appealing, glimpses of the world to a public incapable of imagining faraway places on the basis of the printed word. Though his novelettes were sensational and often violent, his pictorials were refined, restrained, and full of optimism. The pictorials established a tradition of informing by image rather than by word; they began a progression which would take the American people through photoengravings, movies, television, holograms, and forms as yet unseen. This development from verbal to pictorial mass communication has been one of the most important trends in media history, and Maturin Ballou was largely responsible for starting it.

References:

Peter Benson, "Maturin Murray Ballou" and "Gleason's Publishing Hall," in *Publishers for Mass Entertainment in Nineteenth Century Amer-*

ica, edited by Madeleine B. Stern (Boston: Hall, 1980), pp. 27-34, 137-145;

Louis M. Lyons, *Newspaper Story: One Hundred Years of the Boston Globe* (Cambridge, Mass.: Belknap Press, 1971), pp. 3-13;

Madeleine B. Stern, *Imprints on History* (Bloomington: Indiana University Press, 1956), pp. 209-218.

John Kendrick Bangs

(27 May 1862-21 January 1922)

Jack A. Nelson
Brigham Young University

See also the Bangs entry in *DLB 11: American Humorists, 1800-1950*.

MAJOR POSITIONS HELD: Literary editor, *Life* (1884-1888); columnist, *New York Sun* (1888-1889); editor, *Munsey's Weekly* (1889); humor editor, *Harper's New Monthly Magazine*, *Harper's Bazar*, *Harper's Young People*, and *Harper's Weekly* (1889-1900); editorial writer, *Daily Continent* (1891); editor, *Literature* (1899), *Harper's Weekly* (1899-1901), *Metropolitan Magazine* (1903); drama critic, *Sporting News* (1903); editor, *Puck* (1904-1905).

SELECTED BOOKS: *The Lorgnette* (New York: Coombes, 1886);

Roger Camerden: A Strange Story, anonymous (New York: Coombes, 1887);

Katharine: A Travesty (New York: Gilliss Brothers & Turnure, Art Age Press, 1887);

New Waggings of Old Tales, by Bangs, Frank Dempster Sherman, and Oliver Herford (Boston: Ticknor, 1887);

Mephistopheles: A Profanation (New York: Gilliss Brothers & Turnure, Art Age Press, 1889);

Tiddleywink Tales (New York: Russell, 1891);

The Tiddleywink's Poetry Book (New York: Russell, 1892);

In Camp with a Tin Soldier (New York: Russell, 1892);

Half-Hours with Jimmieboy (New York: Russell, 1893);

John Kendrick Bangs

Toppleton's Client; or, A Spirit in Exile (London: Osgood, McIlvaine, 1893; New York: Webster, 1893);

Coffee and Repartee (New York: Harper, 1893);

The Water Ghost and Others (New York: Harper, 1894);

Three Weeks in Politics (New York: Harper, 1894);
The Idiot (New York: Harper, 1895);
Mr. Bonaparte of Corsica (New York: Harper, 1895);
A Chafing-Dish Party (New York: Harper, 1896);
The Mantel-Piece Minstrels (New York: Russell, 1896);
A House-Boat on the Styx (New York: Harper, 1896);
The Bicyclers, and Three Other Farces (New York: Harper, 1896);
The Battle of College Point (New York: Harper, 1897);
The Pursuit of the House-Boat (New York: Harper, 1897);
Paste Jewels (New York: Harper, 1897);
Ghosts I Have Met, and Some Others (New York & London: Harper, 1898);
Peeps At People: Being Certain Papers from the Writings of Anne Warrington Witherup (New York: Harper, 1898);
The Dreamers: A Club (New York & London: Harper, 1899);
The Enchanted Typewriter (New York & London: Harper, 1899);
Cobwebs from a Literary Corner (New York & London: Harper, 1899);
The Idiot at Home (New York & London: Harper, 1900);
The Booming of Acre Hill (New York: Harper, 1900);
Over the Plum Pudding (New York & London: Harper, 1901);
Mr. Munchausen: Being a True Account of Some of the Recent Adventures Beyond the Styx of the Late Hieronymous . . . Baron Munchausen (Boston: Noyes, Platt, 1901);
Uncle Sam, Trustee (New York: Riggs, 1902);
Olympian Nights (New York & London: Harper, 1902);
Bikey the Skicycle & Other Tales of Jimmieboy (New York: Riggs, 1902);
Mollie and the Unwiseman (Philadelphia: Coates, 1902);
Emblemland (New York: Russell, 1902);
The Inventions of the Idiot (New York & London: Harper, 1904);
Mrs. Raffles: Being the Adventures of an Amateur Cracks-Woman Narrated by Bunny (New York & London: Harper, 1905);
The Worsted Man: A Musical Play for Amateurs (New York & London, 1905);
R. Holmes & Co.: Being the Remarkable Adventures of Raffles Holmes Esq., Detective and Amateur Cracksman by Birth (New York & London: Harper, 1906);
Andiron Tales (Philadelphia: Winston, 1906);
Alice in Blunderland, An Iridescent Dream (New York: Doubleday, Page, 1907);
Potted Fiction, Being a Series of Extracts from the World's Best Sellers Put Up in Thin Slices for Hurried Consumers (New York: Doubleday, Page, 1908);
The Genial Idiot: His Views and Reviews (New York & London: Harper, 1908);
The Real Thing and Three Other Farces (New York & London: Harper, 1909);
The Autobiography of Methusaleh (New York: Dodge, 1909);
A Christmas Toast (Boston: Davis, 1910);
Songs of Cheer (Boston: French, 1910);
Mollie and the Unwiseman Abroad (Philadelphia & London: Lippincott, 1910);
Jack and the Check Book (New York & London: Harper, 1911);
Echoes of Cheer (Boston: French, 1912);
A Little Book of Christmas (Boston: Little, Brown, 1912);
A Line o' Cheer for Each Day o' the Year (Boston: Little, Brown, 1913);
The Foothills of Parnassus (New York: Macmillan, 1914);
From Pillar to Post: Leaves from a Lecturer's Notebook (New York: Century, 1916);
Half Hours with the Idiot (Boston: Little, Brown, 1917);
The Cheery Way: A Bit of Verse for Every Day (New York & London: Harper, 1920).

During the 1890s and into the twentieth century John Kendrick Bangs was one of the major humorists in the United States. As humor editor of *Harper's New Monthly Magazine, Harper's Bazar, Harper's Weekly,* and *Harper's Young People* for over a decade, he had a wide influence on the development of humorous journalism in the United States. Besides his association with the Harper brothers, Bangs's earlier tenure with the humor magazine *Life*, his editorship of *Puck* in 1904 and 1905, his own contributions to various magazines, and his wide impact as a lecturer and as a writer of humorous books give him a place as a leading figure in the history of magazine journalism in America. Known as one of the "University Wits" prominent in magazines during the 1890s, Bangs poked fun at American life, particularly upper-class life, in genial and genteel prose and verse.

Portrait of Bangs drawn on a fungus by Peter Newell (Francis Hyde Bangs, John Kendrick Bangs: Humorist of the Nineties *[New York: Knopf, 1941])*

Born on 27 May 1862, the son of a prosperous lawyer in New York City, Bangs first came to the attention of editors while a student at Columbia University, where he edited and wrote much of the student literary magazine, *Acta Columbiana*. Frank Luther Mott, in his *A History of American Magazines* (1957), wrote that "the *Acta* should have a niche of its own in the hall of fame for collegiate journalism.... especially under John Kendrick Bangs in 1882-83, it was a gem of purest ray serene. Here Bangs won his first reputation as a humorous author, and under the names of Shakespeare Jones and T. Carlyle Smith ('The Great Collegiate Vituperator') he wrote pieces that not only gave flavor and charm to one of the best of college magazines, but were widely quoted in the general press."

Before leaving Columbia Bangs accomplished the task of writing and editing an entire issue of *Acta* by himself under various pen names. H. C. Bunner, the young editor of *Puck*, a national humor magazine, attacked the issue and the irresponsibility and lack of experience of the writers, all of whom, of course, were Bangs. Although he had never heard of Bangs, wrote Bunner, "It is our duty to tell him that he is making a mistake in trying to edit a paper before he has served an apprenticeship to the profession of journalism." Actually, Bangs had already appeared in the pages of *Puck* with a limerick. In addition, he had been instrumental in founding the College Press Association in 1882 and had served as the group's first president.

In January 1883, while visiting Gilliss Brothers, the firm which printed the *Acta*, Bangs met John Ames Mitchell, a young Harvard graduate who that month was producing the first issue of a humor magazine called *Life*. Since Mitchell had no publishing experience, Bangs helped him with that first issue, and the two developed a deep friendship.

In spring 1884 Bangs joined *Life* as literary editor. He had studied at Columbia Law School for a few months but had spent most of his energies writing for several periodicals, including *Life* and *Puck*. For four years Bangs controlled the literary content of *Life*, bringing a brilliance and

Bangs, circa 1899, with J. Henry Harper and David A. Munro, editor of the North American Review

spriteliness to those pages that helped lift the humor magazine to prominence.

Editors often complain about humorists that they are either brilliant or reliable, but not both. Mitchell said that Bangs combined both virtues. He was an enormously energetic worker, and throughout his life he was a prolific writer. During his years with *Life* he was its most voluminous contributor, and the magazine bore the heavy imprint of his talents. The prime target of the satirical and lampooning style of *Life* was America's upper classes, a subject of which the magazine's readers never seemed to tire. Bangs, under the pseudonym "Antical Manhattaner," poked fun at the newly designated four hundred of New York society.

As Carlyle T. Smith, "Foreign Correspondent and Chum to Potentates," Bangs kept readers informed about the higher life of Europe. Bangs's "By the Way" column, which developed to page length, became the most quoted section of *Life*. When the antiobscenity crusader Anthony Comstock objected to the dancing naked cupids commonly found on the covers of *Life*, Bangs and the editors had a heyday. They printed pictures of zoo animals wearing trousers and even of petticoats covering the limbs of trees.

After his marriage to Agnes Hyde in 1886 Bangs invested five thousand dollars with the publisher George J. Coombes, who in December 1886 published Bangs's first book. *The Lorgnette*, a series of jests aimed at society, was pronounced a failure by Bangs himself. The following year Bangs produced another book, *Roger Camerden: A Strange Story*. The short novel is a study in overwrought imagination and double delusion, reflecting Bangs's interest in the occult. *Roger Camerden* was published anonymously in its first edition, but Bangs added his name in later editions. In late 1887 Bangs contributed to *New Waggings of Old Tales*, a well-received volume of burlesque stories and verse in which popular authors such as James Russell Lowell were satirized.

Bangs resigned from *Life* in March 1888 and wrote a column for the *New York Sun* during that year and into the next. At the same time Henry Mills Alden, editor of *Harper's New Monthly Magazine*, invited Bangs to take over its humor department. "The Editor's Drawer" was already the most famous department at *Harper's*, which had been around since 1850. But in 1889, with the rise of *Life*, *Judge*, and *Puck* as successful comic weeklies, the anecdotal approach of the column had become dated. Only twenty-six years old, Bangs soon made his mark in the column. Mott wrote that Bangs changed the column to a "really distinguished collection of pictorial and literary satire."

In 1889 Frank A. Munsey, who was already publishing the *Golden Argosy*, a magazine for juveniles, entered the adult field with *Munsey's Weekly*, which he hoped to turn into a cross between *Harper's* and *Life*. To accomplish this goal Munsey turned to Bangs, who was only working part-time for *Harper's*. Munsey had written a novel, *A Tragedy of Errors*, which he wanted to publish serially in the magazine. For the sake of the readers, Bangs rejected the book. The result was that Bangs left the magazine after six months. Nevertheless, Bangs continued to be a frequent contributor to *Munsey's*.

By 1890 Bangs had taken over the humor sections of *Harper's Bazar* and *Harper's Young People*. In addition he contributed miscellaneous matter to *Harper's Weekly*. For a decade he was in charge of humor at the four Harper magazines, stamping his idea of humor not only on those magazines but on a generation of writers to follow.

It was mainly in his role as editor of "The Editor's Drawer" in *Harper's Monthly* that Bangs achieved his place in magazine history. As presiding genius of what was generally considered the most distinguished department of humor of any magazine in the English-speaking world, Bangs made his influence widely felt. Bangs used the department to publish most of the leading light versifiers and short-prose humorists of the day. Even after he gave up editing "The Editor's Drawer" in 1900, many of the changes Bangs instituted endured until the department was discontinued in 1924.

Bangs's own introductory matter frequently took the shape of satirical farces such as the four playlets that he later published in book form in 1896 as *The Bicyclers*. In the same way, his introductory sketches of the humor department in *Harper's Bazar* later found their way into books such as *Coffee and Repartee* (1893), *Peeps At People* (1898), and *The Dreamers: A Club* (1899).

In the early 1890s Bangs wrote a series of children's books, many of which were first published in the pages of *Harper's Young People*. Several featured a three-and-a-half-year-old named Jimmieboy and his talking tiddleywinks, along with a series of grotesque creatures with such names as Whimperjam, the Mangatoo, and Anniroony Bird. The father of three sons, Bangs wrote juvenile literature throughout his career, but never so much as during this period.

Although he was less well known as a man of letters during the late 1890s, Bangs produced the literary criticism published in the "Literary Notes" section of *Harper's New Monthly Magazine*. In addition, in January 1899 Harper's took over the publication of an American edition of *Literature*, a periodical of critical journalism that had been published in England since 1897. Bangs served as that journal's editor during its brief life, which lasted less than a year because of financial problems at Harper Brothers. Mark Twain was negotiating with Bangs for inclusion of an article he was preparing on copyright when *Literature* ceased publication.

In the 1899 reorganization of the Harper Brothers publishing empire Bangs relinquished his various positions on the company's magazines and concentrated his efforts as editor of *Harper's Weekly*. Because of his background in humor, there were some misgivings expressed when he took over the direction of the "Journal of Civilization," as the weekly subtitled itself. In a short time, however, those misgivings were put to rest as Bangs took complete charge of the periodical, working at his customary hectic pace to improve and extend the magazine's already excellent coverage.

Since *Harper's Weekly* also published a limited amount of fiction, Bangs worked with such writers as Emile Zola, Jack London, Theodore Dreiser, and Rudyard Kipling. Some idea of the regard in which Bangs was held may be gained from the fact that when Mark Twain returned to America at the end of a five-year absence in Europe he announced that he was going to run for the presidency with Bangs as his vice-president.

In September 1901 Bangs's position in favor of the American presence in Cuba, voiced in several pieces published in the magazine, ran afoul of the wishes of George Harvey, then manager of the Harper properties. The result was that Bangs left *Harper's Weekly*, although he continued to contribute to it for years.

In 1904 Bangs served as editor of *Puck*, a major national humor magazine, but he apparently felt confined in the job and bowed out after a year. At age forty-five Bangs retired from New York and moved to Maine, determined to make a living through the lecture circuit and his books. He continued to lecture and to write voluminously under dozens of pen names. A ledger for the years 1909 to 1910 shows more than a thousand acceptances from periodicals around the country. Bangs continued his prolific output until his death of intestinal cancer on 21 January 1922.

Much of the gentle humor of this American wit wears thin after all these years, reflecting perhaps too much of the upper-class point of view. Yet Bangs's satirical peeps at the bloated egos of celebrities, including literary figures, hold up well. The influence of Bangs's style is evident in the *New Yorker* of the 1920s, a magazine based on the notions that urbanity, subtle social satire, and gentle humor might succeed. Bangs's three decades of popularity with American readers stands as testimony to the validity of that style.

Biography:
Frances Hyde Bangs, *John Kendrick Bangs: Humorist of the Nineties* (New York: Knopf, 1941).

References:

Thomas L. Masson, *Our American Humorists* (Freeport, N.Y.: Books for Libraries Press, 1966);

Frank Luther Mott, *A History of American Magazines, 1850-1865* (Cambridge: Harvard University Press, 1957), p. 166;

Mott, *A History of American Magazines, 1865-1885* (Cambridge: Harvard University Press, 1957), pp. 399-400;

Norris W. Yates, *The American Humorist: Conscience of the Twentieth Century* (Ames: Iowa State University Press, 1964).

Walter Hilliard Bidwell
(21 June 1798-11 September 1881)

Gary W. Selnow
Virginia Polytechnic Institute and State University

MAJOR POSITIONS HELD: Editor, *American National Preacher and Village Pulpit* (1841-1867); owner and editor, *New York Evangelist* (1843-1855); owner and editor, *Eclectic Magazine of Foreign Literature, Science, and Art* (1846-1868), *American Biblical Repository* (1846-1849); publisher and owner, *American Theological Review* (1860-1862).

Walter Hilliard Bidwell must figure prominently in any serious review of scholarly nineteenth century theological periodicals produced in the United States. During his eighty-three years Bidwell published, owned, or edited four such publications, mostly in Pennsylvania and New York. His academic training at Yale University and the Yale Divinity School and his experience as a pastor of a Congregational Church in Massachusetts prepared him well in the content area of his publications.

The *Eclectic Magazine of Foreign Literature* was the only nontheological periodical with which Bidwell was associated. Although religious and theological themes occasionally could be found in its pages, the *Eclectic* lived up to its name and presented an assortment of articles, poems, and commentaries, generally of a semischolarly nature, dealing with a wide variety of secular topics. Partly as a remedy for poor health and partly in pursuit of material for the *Eclectic*, Bidwell spent a good deal of time traveling throughout Europe. Indeed, his excursions abroad were so frequent and lengthy that he was as well known for his sojourns as for his publishing work.

Bidwell was born on 21 June 1798 in Farmington, Connecticut, to William Bidwell, a farmer, and Mary Pelton Bidwell. Bidwell worked on the farm with his parents until his early twenties. Although the records are sketchy, it appears that he received some formal schooling during these years and in the three years after leaving home before entering Yale in 1824.

He completed his undergraduate studies at Yale in 1827 and soon after married Susan M. Duryea of New York. Bidwell spent much of his time during this period working at inconsequential jobs to earn funds necessary to repay debts incurred during his studies. In 1830 his wife's poor health necessitated that the couple spend a full year in England and France. From this point on Bidwell eagerly sought foreign travel and demonstrated a keen interest in foreign literature. Work on theological publications may have utilized his original vocation and paid the bills, but it seems that foreign travel and a study of foreign literature became Bidwell's primary passion.

Shortly after returning from Europe Bidwell enrolled at the Yale Divinity School. He was granted a license to preach in spring 1833. In September Bidwell was ordained as pastor of the Congregational Church in Medfield, Massachusetts. The tasks of the pulpit damaged Bidwell's voice, and in 1837 he quit the ministry. Medfield's weather was incompatible with the prescribed remedy for Bidwell's failed voice and general weakened health; in search of a milder climate he moved to Philadelphia.

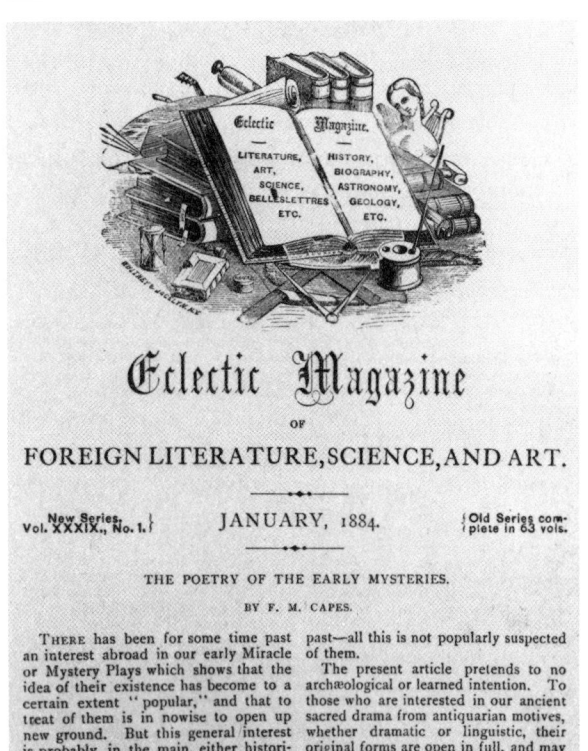

Opening page from the magazine Bidwell edited from 1846 to 1868. It was the only nontheological publication with which he was associated.

It is unclear how Bidwell spent the next four years. All available records take up the account of his life in 1841 when he accepted editorship of the *American National Preacher and Village Pulpit*, a monthly collection of sermons provided by nearly five hundred ministers of all evangelical denominations. During the nineteen years of Bidwell's stewardship the *American National Preacher* is estimated to have published more than 170,000 sermons. This vast repository of manuscripts served largely as a data base for the preparation of sermons by line preachers and as research material for theology students.

In 1843 Bidwell became the proprietor and nominal editor of the *New York Evangelist*, a weekly religious journal. It is unclear how involved he became in the day-to-day operation of the *Evangelist*, although it is likely he was more concerned with the business and production aspects of the publication than with the editorial function. With the responsibilities of two publications already begging his time and attention, in 1846 Bidwell assumed control of two more major periodicals: the *American Biblical Repository*, one of the oldest and most esteemed religious quarterlies of the day and the *Eclectic Magazine of Foreign Literature, Science, and Art*.

The *Eclectic* truly was eclectic, with a format and style approaching a meld of today's *Reader's Digest*, *New Yorker*, and *Atlantic Monthly*. It carried some original articles and translations but mainly reprinted pieces from other magazines and journals. It drew routinely from several dozen publications, mainly English, including *Bentley's Miscellany*, the *London Quarterly*, the *Contemporary Review*, *Tait's Magazine*, *Westminster and Foreign Quarterly Review*, *Cornhill Magazine*, *Temple Bar*, *Macmillan's Magazine*, *Chambers' Journal*, *British Quarterly*, the *Edinburgh Review*, *People's Journal*, *Dublin University Magazine*, *Mrs. Ellis's Morning Call*, the *Standard of Freedom*, and *Hogg's Instructor*. The *Eclectic* carried commentary, biographical sketches, poetry, stories, book reviews, and obituaries of famous people. It covered such topics as history, humor, diplomacy, politics, philosophy, and, of course, literature. Its reviews of science and art were rarely technical in nature and dealt mostly with the literature of science and art. For instance, the *Eclectic* carried such articles as "Poetry of Science" and "Gifts of Science to Art." Occasionally the magazine provided information on the latest scientific discoveries in mechanics, geography, climatology, and biology, all written with the technical limitations of the lay reader in mind.

Bidwell's affection for theological and foreign subjects was evident in the *Eclectic*'s selection of articles. The magazine often carried pieces on the theological implications of contemporary events; the reasoning was nearly always analytical and dispassionate, reflecting Bidwell's intellectual approach to theological matters. Almost all editions of the magazine had at least one article on a foreign country, with a particular concentration on Great Britain, from which Bidwell drew much of his reprinted material.

A final noteworthy feature of the *Eclectic* was its superb engravings. Each edition of the magazine carried one plate depicting some element of a feature article. These full-page pictures, generally engraved by J. Sartain and always created expressly for the *Eclectic*, were magnificent productions even by today's standards.

For the next few years Bidwell was fully occupied in coordinating, managing, or editing a weekly, a monthly, and two quarterly publications. Then, in 1849, he relinquished control of the *American Biblical Repository*. It may have been that the journal was failing or at least not maintaining the standards audiences had come to expect, or it may have been that Bidwell finally realized his own physical limitations. Soon afterward he embarked on a four-month tour of England, France, Switzerland, and Italy to relieve the stress and exhaustion brought about by the intense schedule of the previous half-dozen years. In 1851 he toured England, Holland, Germany, Austria, Switzerland, and France, and in 1853 he visited France, Spain, Portugal, and Morocco.

In 1853 Bidwell appears to have settled into the routine of running his theological journals and the *Eclectic*. Throughout this period, however, his health is reported to have declined, a condition which contributed to a gradual reduction in the scope of his responsibilities. In 1855 he gave up the *New York Evangelist* which, because of its busy weekly production schedule, was the most taxing publication under his control. In 1860, however, he took on another journal, the *American Theological Review*, of which he became publisher and proprietor. Bidwell's contributions to this production did not include the daily editorial functions, which were executed by Prof. Henry B. Smith, but were limited to a general operational oversight. His association with the *American Theological Review* ended in 1862 when the publication was merged with the *Presbyterian Quarterly Review*. Ownership and control of the consolidated journal was assumed by the Reverend J. M. Sherwood.

Finally, Bidwell's intensive labors during the previous ten years took their toll, and in 1863 he was described as having a violent brain inflammation. At the direction of his physicians Bidwell once again sought the salubrious effects of foreign travel, this time for two years in England, France, Switzerland, Germany, Russia, Finland, Sweden, and Denmark. Bidwell returned in restored health to New York, where he devoted most of his time to production of the *Eclectic Magazine*. Records indicate that his affiliation with the *American National Preacher* continued until 1867, although there is no information on the level of his input to that publication.

In 1867, at the behest of Secretary of State William Henry Seward, Bidwell accepted an appointment as special commissioner of the United States to various foreign countries. This time possessing diplomatic rank, Bidwell engaged once again in his beloved foreign travel, sojourning to western Asia, Greece, Egypt and Palestine, Syria, and Turkey, in a tour that lasted eight months.

On his return Bidwell discontinued his affiliation with the *Eclectic*. He made several more trips abroad for pleasure; there is no evidence that his journeys contributed to the production of articles. Bidwell's final years were spent mostly in Oberlin, Ohio, where he had relatives. He traveled occasionally to New York and Chicago, but even these visits became less frequent and of shorter duration as he advanced into his eighties. Despite his many ailments and periods of depression, he was a vigorous man to the end. He died unexpectedly at Saratoga Springs, New York, on 11 September 1881.

The relevance of Walter Bidwell's work to American periodical publishing must be viewed in the context of the two areas in which he made major contributions. First, his demonstrated interest in scholarly theological matters was evident early with his training at Yale Divinity School and his subsequent ministry. It is likely that his formal education in theology and philosophy contributed much to his intellectual outlook on religious topics, which, no doubt, was influential in his stewardship of journals of this genre. He favored logic and reason over emotion in his approach to theological questions.

Bidwell's second contribution arose from his interest in foreign countries, their people, and literature. Most of the population of the United States during this period was first or second generation, so there was a natural affinity among readers for information from abroad. Bidwell went beyond current news accounts, however, and provided a blend of information from foreign philosophers, writers, and scholars. His selection of articles provided a representation not only of foreign events but of foreign thought. Moreover, he did not confine his survey of foreign topics to primary western European countries from which most immigrants came but expanded the scope to include, among others, Asia, the Middle East, Latin America, and Africa. He sought thereby not only to satisfy his readers' immediate interests but to expand their perspective on the world as well.

Bidwell was a bridge between the religious and the secular. His credentials and reputation provided him considerable standing among mainstream religious leaders of the day, enabling him to maintain on the agenda an intellectual and analytical approach to theology. Also, few editors at the time had such a renaissance view of the world. He recognized and appreciated the growing importance of science to a developing nation, the aesthetic value of art and music, and the potential contributions of humanistic thought. He was able to retain the confidence of religious leaders, while appealing to the intellectual curiosity of secular audiences. His value to periodical publishing, therefore, must be viewed from the larger perspective of his abilities to see a unity in the eclectic approach.

References:

Obituary Records of Graduates of Yale College (June 1882): 78-79;

Eclectic Magazine, 63 (September 1864): 121-122.

Albert Taylor Bledsoe

(9 November 1809-8 December 1877)

Paula Cozort Renfro
Southwest Texas State University

See also the Bledsoe entry in *DLB 3: Antebellum Writers in New York and the South.*

MAJOR POSITIONS HELD: Coeditor (1867-1870, 1876-1877), editor (1871-1875), *Southern Review.*

BOOKS: *An Examination of President Edwards' Inquiry into the Freedom of the Will* (Philadelphia: Hooker, 1845);

A Theodicy; or, Vindication of the Divine Glory, as Manifested in the Constitution and Government of the Moral World (New York: Carlton & Phillips, 1853; London: Otley, 1864);

An Essay on Liberty and Slavery (Philadelphia: Lippincott, 1856);

Is Davis a Traitor; or, Was Secession a Constitutional Right Previous to the War of 1861? (Baltimore: Innes, 1866); republished as *The War between the States; or, Was Secession a Constitutional Right Previous to the War of 1861-65?* (Lynchburg, Va.: Bell, 1915);

The Philosophy of Mathematics, with Special Reference to the Elements of Geometry and the Infinitesimal Method (Philadelphia: Lippincott, 1868).

Chief among the intellectual defenders of the South on the subject of slavery and secession was Albert Taylor Bledsoe, a man who wrote the most brilliant, concise Southern apologia after the Civil War and who for ten years published the *Southern Review*, a quarterly magazine whose

Albert Taylor Bledsoe (Dictionary of American Portraits, edited by Hayward and Blanche Cirker [New York: Dover, 1967])

purpose was to vindicate the South. The most versatile of the early Southern philosophers, Bledsoe was a soldier, minister, lawyer, teacher, and head of a bureau in the Confederate War Department before he became an editor. His life brought him into close relationship with many of the intellectual leaders of the South and with some of the most prominent military and political figures of both North and South.

Bledsoe was born in 1809 in Frankfort, Kentucky, to Moses Bledsoe, a newspaper publisher, and Sophia Childress Taylor Bledsoe, a relative of President Zachary Taylor. As a child he was educated at home and in a private academy. When he was fifteen, with only the rudiments of an education, he was sent to the Unites States Military Academy, where he studied math, physics, civil and military engineering, French, drawing, and chemistry. Difficulty with math and French in his first year at West Point forced Bledsoe to repeat the entire year of study. He was shaken by his failure and applied himself to math and French with new vigor. At the end of the year he was ranked eighth in general merit in a class of sixty-three.

His promise in mathematics was indicated by an incident in this second year. His mathematics professor presented the class a geometry problem that had remained unsolved with pure geometry from the time of Archimedes, though many famous mathematicians had worked on a solution. Bledsoe, at sixteen, was fascinated by the intellectual challenge, and he worked at it until he produced a solution his professor deemed perfect. Bledsoe's distaste for routine, which would plague him in his work for the rest of his life, is indicated by his initial failure in math and his subsequent determination to meet the intellectual challenge of the unsolved problem.

In 1830 Bledsoe graduated from West Point, sixteenth in a class of forty-two. There he was acquainted with Jefferson Davis and Robert E. Lee. He was also converted to Christianity, thus beginning the interest in religious questions to which he devoted so much attention throughout his life. Upon graduation he was commissioned second lieutenant and assigned to Fort Gibson, Indian Territory, one of the most remote frontier stations in what is now Oklahoma. He found military life tedious, felt temperamentally unsuited for a military career, and resigned his commission on 31 August 1832.

Bledsoe then took up the study of law with his uncle Samuel Taylor in Virginia. While he was occupied with the study of law, the president of Kenyon College in Gambier, Ohio, offered Bledsoe a position as tutor in mathematics, which he accepted. The death of Bledsoe's younger brother William in a cholera epidemic in 1833 sharpened Bledsoe's interest in philosophical and religious problems, and he began to study theology at the Episcopal seminary located on the Kenyon campus. There he came under the influence of Dr. William Sparrow, a member of the theological faculty who recognized Bledsoe's metaphysical bent and encouraged him to refute Jonathan Edwards's (1754) tract on freedom of the will. While Bledsoe was at Kenyon, he met the woman he would marry, Harriet Coxe, and became a deacon in the Episcopal Church. From the time he left Kenyon, whether he was teaching, serving as a minister, practicing law, serving as a government official, or editing a magazine, Bledsoe's main interest was in philosophical inquiry.

In 1835 Bledsoe moved to Miami University in Oxford, Ohio, to teach mathematics, and on 15 April 1836 he married Harriet Coxe, with whom he had seven children, only four surviving childhood. Throughout their forty-year marriage Harriet provided encouragement and support, sometimes financial, for her husband. Her children described her as pious, reserved, and self-restrained, though her husband was genial and impulsive and became irascible as he grew older. At Miami Bledsoe became involved in disagreements with the university over the issues of slavery, church doctrine, and discipline of students. On the subjects of slavery and discipline, Bledsoe found his own position to be more conservative than that of the administration. In doctrine, he found the university, which was closely identified with the Presbyterian church, to be populated by those who took a stance on free will he himself found distasteful. The university's lax student discipline seems to have led to his resignation from the faculty on 25 July 1836.

Later that year he was appointed rector of Grace Church, Sandusky, Ohio, where he remained only a short time before becoming rector of Christ Church in Cincinnati, Ohio. While at Christ Church Bledsoe also preached in Kentucky, in Hamilton, Ohio, and in Cuyahoga Falls, Ohio. He found himself in conflict, however, with two points of Episcopalian doctrine–original sin and predestination–and in September 1839 he officially left the ministry.

Bledsoe had already begun to practice law several months before he departed from the ministry, and he took up the practice of law in Illinois, first in Carrollton and then in Springfield. From 1838 to 1848 he practiced before the Illinois Supreme Court, where Abraham Lincoln and Stephen A. Douglas were fellow members of the bar. In fact, the Bledsoes lived in the same boarding house as Abraham and Mary Todd Lincoln, and Harriet helped Mrs. Lincoln care for her newborn son, Robert Todd. Bledsoe was a successful lawyer and was praised for his remarkable memory and his logical mind. He was particularly successful before the Supreme Court, which required careful preparation of cases, and more than once received a basket of champagne in recognition of having won the largest number of suits in a year. But he found mundane business affairs tedious. In fact, he was restless, and in fall 1844 he left Springfield for Cincinnati and then Washington, D. C., where he entered into a law partnership with his brother-in-law, Richard Coxe. The partnership lasted only a few months, and he and Harriet returned to Springfield.

Bledsoe became an editorial writer for Whig newspapers, the *Sangamo Journal* and the *Illinois Journal*. Then, in 1845, he published his refutation of Jonathan Edwards, *An Examination of President Edwards' Inquiry into the Freedom of the Will*. The essay refutes Edwards's Calvinist determinism, the doctrine of the elect, and predestination. The critical reception of the piece was generally good, but the sale of the publication was small, and its influence was limited. He followed this publication with essays and editorials for the *Methodist Quarterly Review*, the *Biblical Repository*, and the *Sangamo Journal*, early statements of the arguments he later made concerning the nature of liberty, slavery, and secession of the Southern states. The years in Springfield were productive. The *Illinois Journal* editorials and the essay on Edwards can be said to contain the essence of Bledsoe's thought.

The law, like the military and the ministry, had lost its appeal to Bledsoe, and he sought a position in mathematics at the new University of Mississippi in Oxford in 1848. He was awarded the position over sixty other applicants and, along with it, positions as acting president and librarian as well as membership on many committees. Divisions between North and South were already becoming evident, and Bledsoe's opening day address to his eighty students acknowledged a sectional consciousness, saying that Southerners should trust "the education of their sons to a Southern Institution." In Oxford the Bledsoes were among the minority not having slaves, but during this period Bledsoe came to approve of slavery as a practical matter, as necessary for social order. Despite the demands of his duties, Bledsoe continued his theological inquiries, and his second book, *A Theodicy; or, Vindication of the Divine Glory, as Manifested in the Constitution and Government of the Moral World*, was published in 1853. This book was Bledsoe's most successful financially, selling approximately thirty thousand copies in eleven editions. He considered it his best book, and his argument for free will set forth there still enjoys wide currency.

Bledsoe was awarded an honorary doctor of laws degree when he left the University of Mississippi in 1854 to become a professor of mathematics at the University of Virginia, the most prestigious school in the South. He had letters of recommendation from both Robert E. Lee and Jefferson Davis for the position, and is described as a genial, jovial teacher at Virginia. In 1856 he published *An Essay on Liberty and Slavery*, in which he uses several of the standard defenses of slavery, including an appeal to scripture and the presumption of the inferiority of the Negro race. He argues that the Negro, by nature, is unindustrious and that society has an obligation to compel its members to live, not as they please, but as they ought to live–to work. He concludes that slavery has harmed no one and has done a great deal of good for society. The essay, which received considerable notice and praise in the Southern periodicals, represents the hardening of opinion that was bringing North and South to the brink of war.

At the beginning of the Civil War the University of Virginia organized a School of Military Science and Civil Engineering and offered its professorship to Bledsoe, giving him thirty days to accept. By the time Bledsoe received the offer, he was already a colonel in the Confederate army, so he refused. In 1861 he was given a year leave from the University of Virginia and made chief of the War Bureau. Faced again with tedious work, he was again dissatisfied. He served in the War Bureau for a year, then resigned and conceived a plan to write the definitive justification of secession. His plans required him to do research in London, and the university granted him a second year's leave of absence; his wife provided the money for the trip. In September 1863 he departed for London, where he became friendly with Confederate sympathizers and wrote articles for the *Index*, a pro-Confederate

Opening page from the magazine Bledsoe cofounded in 1867 and edited until 1877. Its principal purpose was to vindicate the South.

newspaper, in which he explained the causes of the war. From London he wrote to President Davis: "After reading all the speeches in Congress, on both sides, I was profoundly ignorant of the transcendent merits of our cause; so little research had been done by our politicians. No cause, in my humble opinion, so great and so glorious, has ever been so feebly advocated by the pen, or so nobly advocated by the sword."

The war was over by the time he returned to the United States in 1866, and he took the oath of allegiance, but he remained unreconstructed. Bledsoe always claimed that Robert E. Lee asked him to prepare a defense of the South. *Is Davis a Traitor; or, Was Secession a Constitutional Right Previous to the War of 1861?*, published in 1866, was Bledsoe's vindication of the Southern cause. Bledsoe's first concern was to show that secession was a constitutional right rather than a revolutionary act. He admitted that the war had settled the issue of the right to secede for the future but argued that the leaders of the South should not be judged ex post facto, arguing that the right of secession existed before the war. He based his case on the traditional position on states' rights expounded by Jefferson, Madison, and other founding fathers. The states, which were originally independent, had voluntarily agreed to the Constitution. Since agreement was voluntary, secession was possible. Though the story may be apocryphal in that the book influenced the decision not to prosecute Jefferson Davis as a traitor, it is considered the most successful of the Southern apologias. It is concise and closely reasoned.

Because Bledsoe's affiliation with the University of Virginia had been terminated while he was in London, he was forced upon his return to cast about for a source of income. In 1868 he published *The Philosophy of Mathematics, with Special Reference to the Elements of Geometry and the Infinitesimal Method*, a manuscript he had written several years earlier dealing with the theoretical foundations of calculus and geometry. But, most important, in 1867 he and William Hand Browne, a scholar and literary critic who later taught at Johns Hopkins University, founded the *Southern Review* in Baltimore, which after the war became the center of Southern literary life. The quarterly was introduced with the January 1867 issue and was dominated by Bledsoe from the beginning. It was one of many Southern periodicals which sprang up after the war, and its principal purpose was to vindicate the South.

The *Southern Review* carried eight or nine long articles per issue, twenty to fifty pages each, and a section of brief book notices. Articles were unsigned, numbered by roman numerals, and each was headed by a list of books or articles that bore some relation to the subject of the article. The journal carried no fiction and little poetry. Subject matter included political, historical, theological, philosophical, and scientific topics, biographical sketches, and literary and art criticism.

Browne left the *Southern Review* after only two years. The reasons are unclear, though letters from Browne to a friend indicate that he held no great affection for Bledsoe. Two associate editors followed Browne, Maj. Richard M. Venable in 1869 and the Rev. Edward J. Stearns in 1870. Neither provided significant editorial influence. From 1871 to 1875 Bledsoe was sole editor.

The most burdensome and disagreeable part of his job was financial management. The people of the South were not able to support the many publications which sprang up after the war; most died after only a few years, many after only a few issues. The *Southern Review* experienced financial difficulties, never having more than three thousand subscribers. In 1868 Bledsoe was forced to supplement his income by becoming principal of a school for girls and taking some private pupils. Two of his daughters became teachers to lend support to the family. Financial headaches led him to seek endorsement from the Methodist General Conference. The endorsement was given, and the conference recommended the quarterly to the ministers and laymen of the church but offered no financial support. In 1871 the Southwestern Book and Publishing Company of St. Louis became publishers of the *Southern Review*. Editorial offices remained in Baltimore. But Bledsoe had so much difficulty with the publishers that he sought to be released from the arrangement. Thus in 1875 one of Bledsoe's daughters, Sophia Bledsoe Herrick, became associate editor and copublisher and took over the business department. In an arrangement that took effect with the October 1877 issue, the Methodist Conference took over the business operation and paid Bledsoe a salary as editor. Bledsoe had refused to exclude politics from the quarterly, but some subscribers did not want a Methodist organ and did not renew. Moreover, segments of the Methodist conference were unhappy with the content of the *Southern Review*.

The magazine was the perfect forum for Bledsoe to exercise his intellectual capacities in defense of the South. Though Lee had urged Bledsoe to exercise moderation and forbearance in his work, these were qualities that Bledsoe lacked. He portrayed heroes of the Confederacy as noble and gallant and Northern society as coarse. Northern influence, he argued, debased the South, as manifested in the corruption of the Grant administration. He complained that the very people who had denounced Southern heroes were now involved in a scandal. Bledsoe also defended Southern writers against slights and railed against historical writing, particularly about the Civil War, by Northern writers. Even textbooks written by Northerners were subjects of his tirades. He encouraged teachers to support projects such as the Southern University Series of textbooks and parents to exercise care to assure that their children were not exposed to biased Northern texts.

As time went on, Bledsoe came to see democracy itself as the root of the country's problems, particularly the idea that man is inherently good, on which the doctrine of popular sovereignty is based. In a long article in the *Southern Review* in 1869, he called democracy "the great error of the eighteenth century." He argued that men are ruled by their passions and that when a majority is given power they oppress a minority. The South, he argued, fell victim to this rule of democracy. Bledsoe recognized his argument undermined the moral superiority of the Southern cause, in that there was no reason to believe that the South, given superior power, would have proved less despotic than the North. Though it did not lessen his venom for the North, he concluded, in a 1870 article, that the depravity of man is the problem: "All are alike, if not equally, incapable of self-government.... Even our own beloved people of the South, we fearlessly assert, are not so much better than all the rest of the world, as to be capable of the enjoyment of such a boon."

Sophia Bledsoe Herrick may have exerted an influence on Bledsoe to tone down the sectional differences reflected in the magazine. A few articles contributed by Northerners appeared in the magazine by the late 1860s. By then Bledsoe was capable of making light of his own vehemence against the North. He wrote that he was not "disposed to deny that our sins of temper have been real as well as numerous." As Bledsoe became more reflective, he finally offered the South the consolation that it was "better to be the victims than the authors of oppression": "Be thankful, that you see, at last, the real nature of self-government by the people, and know it by its fruits, which you have tasted. Rejoice that your once blind faith in that monstrous of all monstrous tyrants, 'the numerical majority,' is no more. Cease to curse the Yankees, and reserve your wrath for that monstrous tyrant, under whose dominion they found themselves, and to whom many of their most atrocious deeds may be fairly imputed. Thank God that it has been, and is, your sublime privilege to suffer wrong with the weak, rather than to enjoy the vulgar triumph of wickedness with the strong."

Bledsoe produced a huge volume of work for the *Southern Review*, but his most creative period was over by 1870. In his last years he wrote as much as three-fourths of the 250 pages in an issue, but the articles tended to be repetitious, and some were reprints or adaptations from earlier works.

From 1867 until his death on 8 December 1877 after a stroke, Bledsoe devoted almost all of his time to the *Southern Review,* a quarterly for which there had never been a real demand, which made no concessions to popular taste, and which estranged itself from readers outside the South. Kept alive by Bledsoe's own determination "to keep up the *Review* as long as we live, or can wield a pen," the quarterly maintained high standards of literary quality, though it showed some decline during the 1870s as the religious emphasis became more pronounced. It published an able group of contributors. Bledsoe's own writing was vigorous, passionate, erudite, earnest, sometimes profound, and almost always opinionated. He wrote of anything that struck his fancy and was vitriolic in attacking other men's ideas. Bledsoe bridged the gap between the puritan influence of Jonathan Edwards and the philosophic orientation of John Stuart Mill. He had a wide knowledge of European philosophy and mathematics as well as of the history of science. His religious commitment, however, caused him to reject out of hand the work of Charles Darwin because he believed it conflicted with the teachings of revealed religion, thus shutting himself off from modern thinkers.

In many respects, Bledsoe's *Southern Review* was the best and easily the most interesting of the Southern periodicals founded after the Civil War. Bledsoe liked a good fight and remained embroiled in controversy until the time of his death. He battled for conservative, even ultraconservative, political views against forces of change. His defense of secession after the war and his continuing hostility toward the North represent the unreconstructed Southern mind. He occupies a minor position in American letters and in histories of American thought.

References:
John Boyce Bennett, "Albert Taylor Bledsoe: Social and Religious Controversialist of the Old South," Ph.D. dissertation, Duke University, 1942;

Bennett, "Albert Taylor Bledsoe: Transitional Philosopher of the Old South," *Methodist History,* 11 (October 1972): 3-14;

J. W. Cooke, "Albert Taylor Bledsoe: An American Philosopher and Theologian of Liberty," *Southern Humanities Review,* 8 (Spring 1974): 215-228;

Willard Murrell Hays, "Polemics and Philosophy: A Biography of Albert Taylor Bledsoe," Ph.D. dissertation, University of Tennessee, 1971;

Sophia Herrick, "Albert Taylor Bledsoe," *Alumni Bulletin of the University of Virginia,* 6 (May 1899): 1-6;

Herrick, "Albert Taylor Bledsoe," in *Library of Southern Literature,* edited by Edwin Anderson Alderman and Joel Chandler Harris (Atlanta: Martin & Holt, 1908-1913), I: 395-399;

Herrick, "Personal Recollection of My Father and Mr. Lincoln and Mr. Davis," *Methodist Review,* third series, 41 (April 1915): 665-679;

R. M. Weaver, "Albert Taylor Bledsoe," *Sewanee Review,* 52 (January-March 1944): 34-45.

Papers:
Many of Bledsoe's papers were lost or destroyed during the Civil War. The largest collection of his postwar letters is at the University of Virginia. The Dinwiddie Papers at the Virginia Historical Society contain material collected by a granddaughter for a proposed biography.

Amelia Bloomer
(27 May 1818-30 December 1894)

Linda Steiner
Governors State University

MAJOR POSITIONS HELD: Editor and publisher, *Lily* (1849-1855); assistant editor, *Western Home Visitor* (1853-1855).

Even in her own lifetime Amelia Bloomer was best known for wearing, as well as editorially defending and popularizing, "bifurcated trowsers"; although the costume was not her own invention, she was deluged with requests for patterns for and information about the pantaloons soon internationally known as "bloomers." But Bloomer made much more substantial contributions to both the nineteenth-century temperance and woman suffrage movements as editor and publisher of the *Lily*. Although the *Lily* was initially established as a temperance organ, Bloomer included articles on woman's rights from the outset, and the *Lily* can be considered the first American woman suffrage periodical.

The youngest child of Ananias Jenks, a clothier, and Lucy Jenks, Amelia Jenks was born in 1818 in Homer, New York, where she attended the district school. Her earliest memory was of playing a childish prank on some Indians who had come to sell her father a knife. Despite her lack of higher education, at age seventeen she was hired to teach in a district school in Clyde, New York. After one term she moved to Waterloo, where she took a job as tutor and governess for the children of Oren Chamberlain. There she met Dexter Chamberlain Bloomer, a former schoolteacher who was studying law and copublishing and editing the *Seneca County Courier*, a Whig weekly newspaper. They were married on 15 April 1840 without the bride officially promising to "obey." Amelia had been brought up as a Presbyterian and her husband as a Quaker; but in 1843 they both joined the Episcopal church, and she became active in its parish work.

Soon after the marriage Amelia Bloomer began writing under both male and female pseudonyms for area newspapers such as the *Water Bucket*, the organ of the Seneca Falls temperance society; the *Free Soil Union*; and the *Temperance*

Amelia Bloomer

Star of Rochester. Her columns have the earnest but dramatic language typical of reform-minded editorial writing of the era. She also served as deputy to her husband, who was the town postmaster. In 1848 she attended the first woman's rights convention, organized in Seneca Falls, New York, by Lucretia Mott and Elizabeth Cady Stanton.

Shortly after the convention the Seneca Falls temperance women, bitter that they were never allowed to do more than financially support male temperance leaders, decided to put out their own "little temperance paper," with Bloomer as editor. Dexter Bloomer argued

Front page of the first issue of Bloomer's paper, which advocated temperance and woman's rights

against the idea, predicting that the women would run themselves "into debt, get into trouble and make a failure of it." Indeed, the temperance society eventually abandoned its plans, although not until it had issued a prospectus and made arrangements with a local printer. So Bloomer, fearing that otherwise people would say it was "just like women . . . what more could you expect of them," continued with the project "to save the credit of our sex and preserve our own honor." The eight-page quarto monthly first appeared in January 1849, with the motto "Devoted to the interests of woman." Bloomer commented in her debut editorial that "It is WOMAN that speaks through The Lily. . . . Surely she may, without throwing aside the modest retirement which so much becomes her sex, use her influence to lead her fellow-mortals away from the destroyer's path."

After the second issue the associate editor, Anna C. Mattison, resigned, leaving Bloomer to do everything except typesetting and printing. Articles were contributed by other reform-minded women, including Mary Vaughan, Frances Gage (writing as "Aunt Fanny"), and Stanton, who signed her woman's rights columns "Sunflower." Bloomer also published articles, fiction, and poetry by lesser-known writers, including some rank, if zealous, amateurs. As the *Lily* grew, however, she became more selective and less patient with badly written submissions. She responded to one contributor: "You need much practice before you write for the public. . . . We cannot give it an insertion in its present state, and have no time to rewrite it."

Although in her own articles Bloomer at first stuck fairly closely to the temperance issue, she soon plunged into woman's rights much more vigorously than the magazine's delicate name–which Bloomer never liked–would suggest. Her October 1849 lead editorial was titled "Women's Rights." In March 1850 she asserted: "We see and hear so much that is calculated to keep our sex down and impress us with a conviction of our inferiority and helplessness, that we feel compelled to act on the defensive and stand for what we consider our just rights."

Eventually Bloomer even took the position that women should be allowed to vote, although she argued that they should prepare for suffrage "by showing that [they are] worthy of receiving and capable of exercising it." Even in the context of the temperance movement Bloomer's editorial target shifted from the evils of liquor to the evils of ineffective organization by women; she praised the Daughters of Temperance less for their work in promoting abstinence than for giving women the opportunity to work together, to think, and to develop business skills.

The *Lily* articulated and dramatized a new kind of middle-class woman, a "sensible woman"; this ideal is expressed, for example, in an article which called on popular magazines to feature "active, healthy, sensibly dressed women, in place of the waxen-faced, wasp-like beflowered and befurbelowed caricatures of women." Bloomer's advocacy of pantaloons symbolized her commitment to the new sensible woman, just as the costume itself symbolized that new woman's interest in being allowed natural and convenient movement and serious activities. On occasion nearly an entire issue was devoted to "Our dress," with daguerreotypes of Bloomer wearing the "trowsers," instructions for making them, and advertisements for ready-made ones. Bloomer reprinted letters and newspaper clippings critical of the costume, and her snappy rebuttals served to teach converts how to defend themselves. Bloomer eventually abandoned the cause and returned to a more conventional dress style; but meanwhile, national controversy and agitation over Bloomerism certainly did not hurt the circulation of the *Lily*, which rose from five hundred to four thousand at fifty cents a year.

Bloomer frequently lectured around the state; as newspapers often noted, although her topic was officially temperance, she discussed woman's rights as well. Indeed, Bloomer commented that one could not speak about temperance and intemperance without also speaking of woman's rights and wrongs. Woman's rights advocates were, however, divided among themselves both philosophically and strategically. At the 1853 meeting of the Woman's State Temperance Society participants split over the issue of whether men should be admitted as members. Stanton and Susan B. Anthony argued for admitting men on the grounds of equal rights and equal duties; when their position was voted down, they declined reelection as officers. Bloomer agreed with the majority that the time had not come for a radical change, and she accepted election as corresponding secretary. When the suffrage movement itself split into two factions in 1869, Bloomer joined the more conservative organization, the American Equal Rights Association.

In December 1853 the Bloomers moved to Mount Vernon, Ohio, where Dexter Bloomer had bought a part interest in the *Western Home Visitor*, a reform weekly. The *Lily* was transplanted and changed to a four-page folio semimonthly. Amelia Bloomer also served as assistant editor of the *Visitor*, declaring in her first editorial that since she had her own organ, she was not likely to introduce into the *Visitor* anything particularly "obnoxious" on reform topics; at the same time, she announced herself as an "uncompromising opponent of wrong and oppression . . . and a sustainer of the right and the true." She wrote one to three pages each week for the *Lily*, which grew to a circulation of six thousand. When male printers refused to work with a woman compositor hired by Bloomer, she accepted their resignations and cheerfully replaced them with women, commenting that the "moral atmosphere has been purified." The delay of two issues of the *Lily* was "nothing compared with what has been gained on the side of justice and right," she wrote. In a February 1854 editorial published in both the *Lily* and in her husband's paper, Bloomer denounced as "twaddle" and "nonsense" the notions that women must obey their husbands and that men who cannot dominate their wives are unmanly.

After a year in Ohio the Bloomers moved to Council Bluffs, Iowa, where they adopted a boy and, later, his sister. Dexter Bloomer eventually became mayor of the city. Since Council Bluffs lacked facilities for printing the *Lily* and good rail connections for distributing it, in early 1855 Bloomer sold the periodical to Mary E. Birdsall of Richmond, Indiana; Birdsall had been editor of the ladies' department of the *Indiana Farmer*, and Bloomer pronounced her "sound" on woman suffrage and temperance. Bloomer continued as corresponding editor until January 1856. But the journal, by then an eight-page quarto semimonthly, lost its verve; it combined routine convention reports with pedantic moralizing. In the spring of 1856 the *Lily* purchased the subscription list of a defunct suffrage

Engraving from an 1851 daguerreotype of Bloomer in the "trowsers" which became named for her

Bloomer's husband, Dexter C. Bloomer (Council Bluffs, Iowa, Public Library)

paper, the *Una*, but ceased publication late in the year. With the exception of one small paper, the *Mayflower*, published in Indiana during the Civil War, the woman's rights movement had no periodical after the death of the *Lily* until Stanton and Anthony began their *Revolution* in 1868.

In 1890, in response to a comment that the paper had died of "fun poked at it," Bloomer insisted that it had outlived ridicule and was highly respected: "It had done its work, it had scattered seed that had sprung up and borne fruit a thousandfold."

Bloomer continued to be active in temperance and suffrage organizations, to lecture on reform, and to contribute frequent articles and editorials to newspapers and reform periodicals. She represented Iowa at the 1869 meeting in New York of the American Equal Rights Association, was elected in 1871 as president of the newly formed Iowa Woman Suffrage Society, and in 1873 worked for legislation equalizing the property rights of husbands and wives in Iowa. She was chosen to write the chapter about the suffrage movement in Iowa for the three-volume *History of Woman Suffrage* (1881-1886) edited by Stanton and others. An invalid in her last years, Bloomer died of heart failure in 1894 at age seventy-six.

Biography:
Dexter C. Bloomer, *Life and Writings of Amelia Bloomer* (Boston: Arena, 1895).

References:
Paul Fatout, "Amelia Bloomer and Bloomerism," *New York Historical Society Quarterly*, 36 (October 1952): 360-374;

Philip D. Jordan, "The Bloomers in Iowa," *Palimpsest*, 20 (September 1939): 295-309;

Linda Steiner, "Finding Community in Nineteenth Century Suffrage Periodicals," *American Journalism*, 1 (Summer 1983): 1-16;

Margaret Farrand Thorp, *Female Persuasion* (New Haven: Yale University Press, 1949).

Papers:
A complete run of the *Lily* on microfilm is in the Sophia Smith collection at Smith College, the New York State Library at Albany, and the University of Illinois at Urbana. The New York State Library has Bloomer's own files of the *Lily*, with notes in her handwriting. Letters and papers concerning Bloomer are located at the Seneca Falls Historical Society and the Council Bluffs Free Public Library.

Mary L. Booth
(19 April 1831-5 March 1889)

Maurine H. Beasley
University of Maryland

MAJOR POSITION HELD: Editor, *Harper's Bazar* (1867-1889).

BOOK: *History of the City of New York from its Earliest Settlement to the Present* (New York: Clark & Meeker, 1859).

TRANSLATIONS: *The Marble-Workers' Manual* (New York: Sheldon, Blakeman, 1856);
Victor Cousin, *Secret History of the French Court under Richelieu and Mazarin* (New York: Delisser & Procter, 1859);
New and Complete Clock and Watchmakers' Manual, compiled and translated by Booth (New York: Wiley, 1860);
Edmond François Valentin About, *Germaine* (Boston: Tilton, 1860);
About, *The King of the Mountains* (Boston: Tilton, 1861);
Agénor Étienne de Gasparin, *The Uprising of a Great People: The United States in 1861* (New York: Scribners, 1862);
Gasparin, *America before Europe: Principles and Interest* (New York: Scribners, 1862; London: Low, 1862);
Augustin Cochin, *The Results of Emancipation* (Boston: Walker, Wise, 1863);
Cochin, *The Results of Slavery* (Boston: Walker, Wise, 1863);
Édouard de Laboulaye, *Paris in America* (New York: Scribners, 1863);
Gasparin, *Reconstruction: A Letter to President Johnson* (New York, 1865);
Gasparin, *Letter from Messieurs de Gasparin, Martin, Cochin, and Laboulaye, to the Loyal Publication Society of New York* (New York: Westcott, 1866);
Laboulaye, *Laboulaye's Fairy Book: Fairy Tales of All Nations* (New York: Harper, 1866);
Eugène Sue, *Mysteries of the People* (New York: Clark, 1867);
Jean Macé, *Home Fairy Tales*, translated by Booth (New York: Harper, 1867);

Mary L. Booth (Dictionary of American Portraits, edited by Hayward and Blanche Cirker [New York: Dover, 1967])

Laboulaye, *Abdallah, or, The Four-Leaved Shamrock* (London: Low, Son & Marston, 1868);
Henri Martin, *A Popular History of France from the First Revolution to the Present Time*, translated by Booth and A. L. Adger, 3 volumes (Boston: Estes & Lauriat, 1877-1882);
Blaise Pascal, *Thoughts*, translated by W. F. Trotter, includes letters translated by Booth (New York: Collier, 1910).

Mary Louise Booth, one of the most celebrated literary women of the nineteenth century, edited *Harper's Bazar* from its founding on 2 November 1867 until her death in 1889. Under her meticulous guidance the magazine, subtitled "A Repository of Fashion, Pleasure and Instruction," prospered from the first as a weekly aimed at a family audience. An individual of commanding personal presence with a keen grasp of business, Booth presided over a publication that by 1880 boasted a readership of half a million drawn by both its excellent fashion illustrations and clever fiction.

A bookish child, Booth was the eldest of four children of Nancy Monsell and William Chatfield Booth. Born in Millville (later Yaphank), Long Island, New York, she moved with her family to Brooklyn when she was thirteen. She received her education in Yaphank and Brooklyn, where her father was the principal of a public school. (She later taught in his school.) Yet for the most part she was autodidactic, reading the entire Bible at age five and exhibiting exceptional ability at French, completing Racine in the original at seven.

Booth moved into Manhattan at about the age of eighteen and worked as a vest maker, sewing during the day and studying and writing at night. Initially she contributed articles without being paid to educational and literary journals and newspapers and eventually was hired on a piece-rate basis to cover educational and women's topics for the *New York Times*. She also began to translate French works since relatively few persons were engaged in this field. Starting with *The Marble-Workers' Manual* in 1856, she proceeded to translate nearly forty volumes, mostly on literary and historical subjects.

Meanwhile, she wrote her one major work, the *History of the City of New York* (1859), the first complete history of the city from its Dutch origins to its growth as a financial center. The first comprehensive history of the city, the book went through four editions, the last in 1880, and won praise from historians. The success of the book led her publisher to propose that she go abroad and write popular histories of European cities, but the advent of the Civil War ended this plan.

A fervent antislavery advocate, Booth aided the Union cause by translating Gasparin's *The Uprising of a Great People: The United States in 1861* (1862) in only one week, a work she felt would hearten the Union cause. She had to work rapidly because her publisher feared the war would end before the book could be published. Subsequently, she translated other pro-North French works, winning praise from Abraham Lincoln and other statesmen.

Because of her acclaim as an author and translator, Fletcher Harper selected Booth as editor of his new periodical aimed mainly at women and patterned after *Der Bazar*, a Berlin magazine. A family version of *Harper's Weekly*, the new publication featured the same kind of serials, double-page pictures, miscellany, and humor as the *Weekly*, with fashions and patterns taking the place of politics and public affairs. Fashion plates came from Berlin in the form of duplicate electrotypes made by *Der Bazar* along with advance proofs describing the continental modes. Later, tracing patterns were enclosed with each issue.

Initially reluctant to assume the post at *Harper's Bazar*, Booth soon proved her fitness for the editorship, laboring at her desk daily from nine to four. After its first six weeks, the magazine had gained a circulation of one hundred thousand. Features included serials by well-known British writers like Wilkie Collins and Mary Elizabeth Braddon, short stories by American writers (among them George W. Curtis, who used the pseudonym of "An Old Bachelor," Harriet Prescott Spofford, and Mary Wilkins Freeman), and columns with titles such as "Diets for Invalids" and "Women and Men," the latter written by Thomas W. Higginson, a popular essayist.

Booth aimed the contents at a middle-class audience, whom she counted on to be churchgoers (mostly Protestant) committed to a conventional moral code and eager to improve themselves. Attention was given to household management (the readers were assumed to have servants), etiquette, interior decoration, recipes, and health. Although the magazine promoted the cumbersome, restrictive garments considered fashionable for women, it never objected to women going to bathing beaches. Winslow Homer, one of its chief illustrators, pictured women in seashore costumes, including stockings.

According to its first editorial, the aim of *Harper's Bazar* under Booth's direction was to combine the useful with the beautiful. It assured readers that they would receive the news on fashions from Europe at the same time it appeared in Paris and Berlin, along with directions for fancy work and dressmaking. In this respect the *Bazar* differed from existing periodicals, including *Godey's Lady's Book*, *Peterson's Magazine*, *Frank Leslie's Gazette of Fashion*, and lesser-known magazines, which often ran fashion plates redrawn from French publications a year or more after they first appeared.

Herself a strong advocate of woman suffrage, Booth maintained a close friendship with Susan B. Anthony and served as a secretary at woman's rights conventions in Saratoga, New York, and New York City in 1855 and 1860 respectively. Even so, she had no intention of publishing articles favorable to suffrage in the *Bazar*. She explained her editorial philosophy in a letter to Higginson in 1884 in which she outlined topics she considered appropriate for his "Women and Men" column: "It has always been thought inexpedient to advocate woman suffrage therein, either explicitly or implicitly. It has been a cardinal principle with the *Bazar*, as a home journal, conservedly to abstain from the discussion of vexed questions of religion, politics, and kindred topics, and, while maintaining a firm and progressive attitude, to endeavor to promote harmony at the fireside for which it was designed–to bring peace, and not a sword. In a word, it has sought to carry out the Emersonian doctrine of always affirming and never denying." Urging Higginson to follow the pattern of George William Curtis, who wrote on the moralities of home and social life, she continued, "It surely involves no sacrifice of principle to be silent on a topic specially adapted to aggressive reform journals in writing for a paper with a wholly different purpose, especially as there is so much else to be said therein of the most vital importance to women that you will find noble work to do."

Booth gave her views on the editor's role in an interview with Charles F. Wingate in 1875. Asked to name the qualifications needed to be a capable editor, she answered, "An editor's first qualifications are sagacity to discover what the public wants, and knowledge how to supply the demand. A good editor must have quick and sure perception, coolness in emergencies, the habit of ready decision, correct taste, and a judicial mind. To be fully equipped, he or she must also have the acquired qualities of thorough culture, extensive reading and wide literary experience." Asked if women were fitted for journalism, she replied, "Eminently so; especially in those departments of newspaper discussion which pertain to the family and to the needs of their own sex.... political journalism proper, in the present state of society, seems to me so essentially masculine, that it is best managed by men, though in the golden age which we are all looking forward to, I dare say women will also take part in it."

In the office Booth was described by her close friend Harriet Prescott Spofford as entirely "the business woman, firm and masterly, courageous, faithful, patient, sagacious." But at home she lived the life of an upper-class Victorian woman, changing to "lovely gowns and laces" and putting on expensive jewels. She shared a house near Central Park with Annie Wright, a childhood friend, who was the widow of a sea captain. Each Saturday night during the winter months the two women entertained a variety of literary figures and other notables.

Booth took immense pride in her publication, telling Wingate that "financially, the *Bazar* is reputed to be the most rapid success ever known in journalism." Contrary to most other publications, she said, the *Bazar* "has paid handsomely from the very first number, a thing almost unprecedented in journalistic annals." She attributed its success to "the need that existed for just such a journal" as well as to her own efforts and those of the Harper Brothers. She understood that the *Bazar*, which sold by subscription for four dollars a year, appealed to readers almost desperately eager to keep up with–or slightly ahead of–the styles of the day. Yet she insisted to Wingate that the publication "endeavored to discourage extravagance and folly, and to commend only what is sensible." She pointed out that fashions "form ... but a fraction of the *Bazar*, which is filled with fine art illustrations, numerous humorous cuts and other engravings, together with stories, poems, essays, miscellany, juvenile literature, etc., from the best pens, both of Europe and America."

Ultimately earning a salary of four thousand dollars annually, Booth received a handsome reward for her services as editor by the standards of the day. She personally read every line of manuscript and proof and scrutinized every illustration. "It is not what the editor writes, but what he chooses for his paper, that makes or mars his success," she once stated. "It is the judicial capacity that marks the true editor."

Certainly Booth herself believed that women had innate attributes that fitted them to be writers and editors, among them "acute and subtle intuition, and habits of keen observation, readiness of thought, and refined taste," as she told Wingate. She urged that women get literary training on a par with men. Too many women, she said, thought that journalism would be easy work. "The trouble is that women who have not education enough to be teachers, or practical ability enough to be anything else, turn to literature as a last resort, and expect to earn fortunes by

Cover for an issue of the magazine Booth edited from its founding in 1867 until her death in 1889

their crude pen-product, when, perhaps, they don't even know how to write a letter correctly. Journalism seems to be regarded by a large class as a sort of refuge for those who have failed in every other avocation."

As an editor Booth held to high standards, seeking material of merit regardless of whether the authors were well-known. She also advocated an end to the insertion of items in return for favors given to journalists. "Nothing degrades journalism more than the editorial bribery and 'dead headism,' great and small, which cannot be too strongly deprecated by respectable editors," she said in the Wingate interview.

In a letter to Susan B. Anthony, Booth expressed her views on woman's place in society. She did not believe in fomenting discontent between the sexes and thought that a better understanding would emerge in time: "As you know, I have always felt the deepest interest in the elevation of women, which is synonymous with that of humanity, for man must be always on the plane of his wife, sister and mother.... The antagonism to political equality is rapidly disappearing, as it is beginning to be recognized that in politics, as in everything else, woman's help is needed, and the republic can not afford to have her stand aloof.... But this phase of the subject has been so much misunderstood, both by men and women, that time is needed to clear away the mists of misconceptions...."

For herself she chose to pursue literary endeavors that had little to do with woman's rights. She continued translating in spite of her busy schedule as *Bazar* editor, gaining unqualified praise from Henri Martin for translating his three-volume *A Popular History of France from the First Revolution to the Present Time* (1877-1882). Elizabeth Cady Stanton credited her with "great service" to suffrage "by showing that a woman can work as earnestly and persistently at a closely confining business as a man, and can hold for years a place at the head of a profession so difficult and so arduous."

Although Booth's life revolved around her work and her place in the New York literary world, on a trip to Venice in 1887 she became engaged to a suitor whom she had refused previously. The attachment, however, did not endure after she left Italy. As a child she had suffered from rheumatic fever, but she enjoyed good health until the winter of 1889, when she was stricken with a heart condition. She died in New York City in 1889, a few weeks before her fifty-eighth birthday, of fibroid phthisis and degeneration of the heart.

Booth's importance in journalism lies in part in her encouragement to other women and in her ability to merge ideas of proper Victorian behavior with the demands of an exacting editorial position. Her contemporary Sarah Bolton, author of an 1888 book on *Successful Women*, noted, in a chapter on Booth, "To show other women that a woman may have consummate ability, and yet be gentle and refined and warm-hearted,... and that if one woman can stand at the head of a great journal it must be logically true that other trained women may come to stand at the head of the business they select—these, too, are public lessons of a life and a character worthy of study by our noblest girls."

As well, her achievements as an editor exclusive of her interest in woman's rights merit recognition. Employing a combination of modesty and personal power, she built up a magazine still in existence today (the spelling of *Bazar* was changed to the present *Bazaar* in 1929). She gathered together a corps of talented contributors and improved the magazine consistently, both in its physical appearance and literary quality. Working from a small office fitted only with a desk, sofa, and two chairs, she had neither a typewriter nor a secretary. Fletcher Harper and his brothers, who ran what was then one of the strongest publishing houses in the United States, treated her with great deference and respect. This stemmed not only from the success of her magazine but from their recognition that she had a masculine grasp of business and could not be shoved aside. She represented a new type of American career woman—one who wrote for women and shared many of their domestic interests but was also able to move surely and successfully, if somewhat circumspectly, in the masculine world of power and influence.

Interview:
Charles F. Wingate, ed., *Views and Interviews on Journalism* (New York: Patterson, 1875), pp. 253-259.

References:
Stella Blum, ed., *Victorian Fashions & Costumes From Harper's Bazar: 1867-1898* (New York: Dover, 1974);

Sarah Knowles Bolton, "Mary Louise Booth," in her *Successful Women* (Boston: Lothrop, 1888), pp. 34-50;

Eugene Exman, *The House of Harper: One Hundred and Fifty Years of Publishing* (New York: Harper & Row, 1967);

Ida H. Harper, *The Life and Work of Susan B. Anthony*, 3 volumes (Indianapolis: Hollenbeck Press, 1898-1908), pp. 146, 155, 316, 458, 615;

Joseph H. Harper, *The House of Harper: A Century of Publishing in Franklin Square* (New York: Harper, 1912), pp. 250-251;

Harriet Prescott Spofford, "Mary Louise Booth," in *A Little Book of Friends* (Boston: Little, Brown, 1916), pp. 117-130;

Elizabeth Cady Stanton, Susan B. Anthony, and Matilda Joslyn Gage, eds., *History of Woman Suffrage*, 3 volumes (Rochester, N.Y.: Susan B. Anthony, 1887);

Marie E. Zakrzewska, "Mary L. Booth," *Woman's Journal* (6 April 1889): 105-106.

Papers:
There are twenty-nine letters by Mary L. Booth in the New York Public Library, twenty-eight in miscellaneous papers and one, which contains autobiographical material, in the Duyckinck Collection. There also are nine letters in the New York Historical Society archives in New York City.

Francis Fisher Browne
(1 December 1843-11 May 1913)

Roger Cameron Lips
University of Minnesota at Duluth

MAJOR POSITIONS HELD: Editor and part owner (1869-1871), editor and owner (1871-1874), *Western Monthly*, renamed *Lakeside Monthly* in 1871; managing editor, *Chicago Alliance* (1877-1878); founder, editor, and part owner (1880-1892), owner and editor, *Dial* (1892-1913).

BOOK: *Volunteer Grain* (Chicago: Way & Williams, 1895).

OTHER: *Golden Poems by British and American Authors*, edited by Browne (Chicago: McClurg, 1881; revised and enlarged, 1906);
The Golden Treasury of Poetry and Prose: Choice Selections from the Works of Leading British and American Authors for a Period of Five Hundred Years (New York & St. Louis: Thompson, 1883);
Bugle-Echoes: A Collection of Poems of the Civil War, Northern and Southern, edited by Browne (New York: White, Stokes & Allen, 1886);
The Every-Day Life of Abraham Lincoln: A Biography of the Great American President from an Entirely New Standpoint, with Fresh and Invaluable Material, edited by Browne (New York & St. Louis: Thompson, 1886); revised and enlarged as *The Every-Day Life of Abraham Lincoln: A Narrative and Descriptive Biography with Pen-Pictures and Personal Recollections by Those Who Knew Him* (Chicago: Browne & Howell, 1913; London: Murray, 1914);
Holger Drachmann, *Paul and Virginia of a Northern Zone*, translated by Browne and Thorkild A. Schovelin (Chicago: Way & Williams, 1895); republished as *Nanna: A Story of Danish Love* (Chicago: McClurg, 1901);
"John P. Altgeld: A Character Study," in *Dedicatory Exercises at the Unveiling of Bronze Tablets in Memory of John P. Altgeld* (Chicago: John P. Altgeld Memorial Association of Chicago, 1910), pp. 23-38.

PERIODICAL PUBLICATIONS: "Mr. Dobson's Poems," *Dial*, 1 (May 1880): 6-8;
"Our Intent," *Dial*, 1 (May 1880): 17-18;

Francis Fisher Browne

"The Mechanism of Poetry," *Dial*, 1 (July 1880): 55-58;
"Lord Byron," *Dial*, 1 (October 1880): 112-114;
"A Popular Novel," *Dial*, 1 (November 1880): 131-133;
"The Indian 'Song of Songs,'" *Dial*, 1 (November 1880): 133-135;
"Wordsworth," *Dial*, 1 (February 1881): 211-213;
"A Later Lake Poet," *Dial*, 1 (February 1881): 214-216;
"Mr. Whittier's New Volume," *Dial*, 1 (March 1881): 236-237;

"Carlyle's Philosophy," *Dial*, 2 (July 1881): 63-64;

"The Poetry of an Aesthete," *Dial*, 2 (August 1881): 82-85;

"Swinburne's 'Mary Stuart,'" *Dial*, 2 (February 1882): 237-238;

"Longfellow," *Dial*, 2 (April 1882): 275-277;

"Sidney Lanier," *Dial*, 5 (January 1885): 244-246;

"Matthew Arnold," *Dial*, 9 (May 1888): 5;

"The New Dial," *Dial*, 13 (1 September 1892): 127-128;

"The Presidential Contest. I.–Altgeld of Illinois," *National Review*, 28 (December 1896): 452-473;

"American Publishing and Publishers," *Dial*, 28 (1 May 1900): 340-343;

"The Dial's Quarter-Century," *Dial*, 38 (1 May 1905): 305-307;

"The 'Eternal Or' of the Librarian," *Public Libraries*, 16 (June 1911): 233-237.

In nearly forty years as an editor of literary journals, Francis Fisher Browne sought constantly to advance ideas and to increase the knowledge of the reading masses. His first love was poetry, and the naturalist John Muir said that Browne "knew almost every poet, and could quote their finest pieces as if reading from their books." His major accomplishment was the *Dial*, which he founded and edited. Based in Chicago, it quickly gained a national readership and held its audience for thirty-three years under Browne. In a letter among Browne's papers John Greenleaf Whittier described the *Dial* as "the best purely literary journal in America." Browne was tenacious in overcoming obstacles to create his magazine, and he kept the *Dial* alive by insuring that it remained excellent in content, style, format, and critical standards. Browne's words about the magazine on its twenty-fifth anniversary could be applied to the editor himself: "Its effort has been to achieve distinction through consistency and persistency; to be itself, with its own standards and character; to have its ideals, and live up to them." He never sacrificed the integrity of his magazine for financial gain; consequently, he was always poor and was even short of cash during the final months of his life. Nor did he use the magazine to publicize himself, and so he was quickly forgotten after his death.

Browne was born at South Halifax, Vermont, on 1 December 1843 to William Goldsmith and Eunice Fisher Browne. He was descended on both sides from New England Puritans. Charles Lummis, a good friend of Browne's, called him "a Puritan thawed, not spoiled" and said that "'austere' is the precise word for his intellectual and moral attitude; but not the word for his humanity." His father taught in schools in Vermont and Massachusetts but later became an editor for the *Vermont Telegraph* and the *Voice of Freedom*, antislavery papers published in Brandon, Vermont. When Browne was still quite young the family moved to western Massachusetts, where Browne irregularly attended various public schools. From 1856 to 1858 he learned much about printing and journalism by helping his father, who was then editor of the *Chicopee Journal*.

In the summer of 1862 Browne enlisted in the Forty-sixth Massachusetts Regiment, serving for one year in North Carolina. Though his service time was short, camp fevers led to recurrent bouts of poor health throughout his life. When his regiment was discharged he went to Rochester, New York, to study law in a law office. He entered the law department of the University of Michigan on 1 October 1866 but left on 27 March 1867, returned to Rochester to work as a printer, and married Susan Seaman Brooks, who gave him six sons and three daughters. Immediately after the wedding he took his new wife by lake steamer from Buffalo to Chicago.

Browne dreamed of giving the West its first nationally respected literary magazine. His task seemed formidable because of the youthfulness of the city and the rawness of the surrounding region. As his obituary in the *Dial* said, he came to a city in which "zeal in commercial activity was its only rule of action, pride in commercial success its only ideal." The first Chicago weekly that was predominantly literary in character was the *Gem of the Prairie*, established in 1844; almost every succeeding year in the 1840s and 1850s a new publication was started. The first monthly literary magazine to be published in Chicago was the *Western Magazine*, established by William R. Rounseville in October 1845. That so many magazines were attempted would seem to indicate considerable interest in literature in Chicago in the late nineteenth century, but most of the men who created these magazines were soon discouraged by difficulties. Browne succeeded where others failed because of his tenacity and capacity for self-sacrifice.

He started as a printer and became part owner and manager of a printing shop on Dearborn Street while looking for an opportunity to work at a literary magazine. He soon found an opening with the *Western Monthly*, established by H. V. Reed and E. C. Tuttle in December 1868. During the first year its issues usually included about sixty-five pages and cost two dollars per year; then it expanded to eighty pages at three dollars per year. Browne sold his interest in his print shop to buy Tuttle's share of the magazine, and the April 1869 issue announced Francis Fisher Browne as a new partner and editor. In an 1869 stock issue organized by Reed and Browne, about fifty prominent Chicagoans helped the new partners raise capital of one hundred thousand dollars. Browne quickly showed that he wanted a magazine with integrity more than he wanted money by eliminating "boosting," the practice of printing articles about businessmen willing to pay for publicity. He gave the magazine a more pronounced literary character and improved its style, its typography, and the intellectual quality of its articles. He sought writing expressing the experiences and thoughts of the Midwest region.

An 1870 prospectus of the *Western Monthly* announces its intention to "produce a Magazine which should properly represent the growing Literature of the great Mississippi Valley" and claims that the owners "will spare no pains or expense to insure the future excellence of their Magazine." The prospectus describes the magazine's regular contributors as authors of books, university professors, leading newspaper journalists, and prominent clergymen. Browne expanded the magazine ambitiously. In November 1870 an advertisement inside the cover announced that the magazine would soon become ninety-six pages at a cost of four dollars per year and that it would be part of the Lakeside Publishing and Printing Company, "which has just been organized in Chicago, with a Capital Stock of half a million dollars, and which already owns the finest and most extensive printing office in the West." Lakeside also published other magazines and provided general printing service; its owners hoped eventually to play the role in Chicago that Harper and Brothers played in New York and that Fields, Osgood and Company played in Boston. They wanted to make Chicago a major book and periodical publishing center, not just a wholesale distribution center for publications from the East. In the November 1870 *Western Monthly* Browne wrote that Chicago was destined to be "a great literary and publishing, no less than a commercial, centre" and described major improvements between 1860 and 1870 in the city's printing facilities: the manufacture of presses, the increasing numbers of electrotype and stereotype foundries, the improvement of the quality of the bookbinding services. He noted also that increasing numbers of talented writers had become available to write for the *Western Monthly*. Soon, he predicted, "Western books will find a sale in the Eastern market."

The *Western Monthly* rapidly gained readers, reputation, and influence, but it remained a sectional periodical in that it tended to speak somewhat defensively for the West against the East. The magazine published poetry and fiction, including translations. While it had a distinctively literary emphasis and tone, it also printed general-information articles about a variety of topics, such as "Parks and Boulevards in Cities," "In the California Redwoods," "Darwinism and Christianity," "Greater Britain," "Henry Ward Beecher and His Church," "Up the Nile with Cook's Tourists," "The United States' North Pole Expedition," and "When Did the Human Race Begin?" The magazine also serialized novels such as *Twenty Years Ago: A Story of Real Life on the Prairies* and nonfiction books such as *Some California Savages*. Each issue reviewed at least one book and included a list of "Books Received."

Browne sought authors who were experts in their subjects, gradually raising his standards for the acceptance of manuscripts. He worked hard to attract capable contributors, but the magazine did not make enough money to enable him to pay them. Most of the contributors were residents of Chicago or the Midwest, and many placed their first publications with the magazine.

Soon the *Western Monthly* was serving the Midwest in the way that the *Atlantic Monthly* served New England and the *Overland Monthly* served California. Browne, however, was not satisfied with a regional magazine, and in 1871 he changed its name to the *Lakeside Monthly*. The magazine did gradually gain eastern readers and even achieved a small audience in London and Paris. It was praised by publications in New York, Boston, and Philadelphia, and by foreign journals such as *La Revue des deux Mondes*, the *Spectator*, the *Saturday Review of London*, and the *Canadian Illustrated News*.

Browne's editorial and business skills were no match for the major misfortunes which killed the magazine. In 1870 a fire destroyed the magazine office, the entire October issue, all manuscripts, all plates, and even the type. Next came the great Chicago fire of 1871, which consumed the new building housing Lakeside Publishing

Company, destroying its presses and other physical assets; not even the subscription lists were saved. Browne's partner, Reed, withdrew, but the magazine missed only two issues and even published an outstanding January 1872 number containing vivid accounts of the fire. Circulation grew from nine thousand at the time of the fire to fourteen thousand by May 1872. By this time the magazine had lost about fifty thousand dollars of its investors' money. Ironically, only in its last year did it fully pay its expenses.

Readers could learn little about Browne from the *Lakeside Monthly;* he thought it bad taste for an editor to publicize himself and did not print editorials or articles signed with his name or display his name prominently as editor. Always struggling for funds to keep the magazine alive and to improve it, he never let any word of his personal difficulties appear in the columns. After the 1871 fire Browne printed this understated and unsigned note: "We would be glad to receive a few sets of *The Lakeside Monthly* from January to October, 1871 (inclusive) in exchange for *The Lakeside* for the year 1872."

In September 1872 Jay Cooke's bank failed, precipitating the panic of 1873. The ensuing depression resulted in a loss of subscribers and advertisers, destroying the magazine's hard-won financial stability. Browne almost died of cholera and could not work at all for months. The *Lakeside Monthly* ceased with the February 1874 issue; the announcement suspending publication indicates Browne's intention to revive the magazine in September 1874, but he failed. *Scribner's Monthly,* which admired the magazine enough to propose a merger, assigned John Binckley to compose a history of the *Lakeside Monthly* to be published as part of a merger announcement. A glowing tribute to Browne's editorial ability, the article said that "for that healthful conservatism which spurns the taint of sensationalism, and for typographical taste, [the *Lakeside Monthly*] probably deserves the palm amongst all." For a while Browne contemplated some sort of combination with *Scribner's,* but eventually he declined the offer. He even insisted that the Binckley article remain unprinted, even though it would have spread his fame and helped him to find new employment. He wrote that the *Lakeside Monthly,* "which had been at least *bona fide* in its motives, should have a *bona fide* ending, rather than a make-believe Pythagorean continuance." Remembering the magazine in 1892, a writer for the *Inland Printer* called it one of the five best monthlies that ever existed in America. In 1938 the journalism historian Frank Luther Mott described *Lakeside* as "the most important general literary magazine of a consistently high class ever published in Chicago."

In January 1875 Browne, still too ill to work, wrote to his father asking for money. His father sent him twenty-five dollars and advised him to change careers because "literary matters require the hardest work and afford the poorest pay of any kind of business." Not much is known about Browne's life from 1874 to 1877 except that he wrote editorials for various Chicago newspapers and did publicity work for several railroads. His fortunes improved in 1877 when he became managing editor of the *Chicago Alliance,* an influential weekly religious journal which initially hired him as literary editor. In May 1878 Browne left the *Alliance* to become literary adviser and editor for Jansen, McClurg and Company, one of the two principal Chicago publishers. This work acquainted Browne with many authors who were eventually to contribute to his next magazine. He hoped to establish a journal of literary criticism modeled after English monthly reviews he admired, such as the *Athenaeum* and the *Academy.* The job also provided an ideal business partner for the next magazine: A. C. McClurg shared with Browne the beliefs that a book publishing company and a companion magazine could help each other, and that books helped to civilize a nation.

In May 1880, with Jansen, McClurg and Company listed as publisher, the *Dial: A Monthly Review and Index of Current Literature* appeared. In some features it seems to have imitated Boston's *Literary World,* but it soon surpassed it in quality. Throughout the magazine's life the text was printed in two columns, each about three inches wide. The *Dial* did not carry illustrations at a time when popular magazines used them lavishly. It averaged about twenty pages, exclusive of advertising pages. It featured excellent printing on heavy paper and cost $1.00 a year until October 1881, when it went up to $1.50. The price rose to $2.00 in 1892 and stayed there for the next twenty years. Twenty-five years after the magazine's founding Browne noted the consistency of appearance of the issues filling the bound volumes on library shelves: "Fluctuations in a journal's character and standards, a lack of fixed ideals and clearly defined aims, the indecision and instability that lead to trying first one tack and then another in the hope of catching the winds of popular favor, are usually typified in capricious changes of external form." For thirty-three years the magazine showed remarkable consistency in its length, layout, typeface, the length and style of reviews, and its continuing features, such as "Briefs on New Books" and "Literary Notes & News."

Linking itself to the short-lived journal of the New England Transcendentalists, the first issue carried an article on the earlier *Dial*. It said that the magazine's intended audience was "the book-lover and book-buyer" and promised to avoid destructive literary criticism: "It will endeavor to distinguish between literary criticism and literary cynicism." The *Dial* reviewed the books its editor thought most important and also printed long lists of new book titles. The first issue noted the journal's desire to serve those of "literary tastes or habits" who "wish to keep themselves informed of the character of this vast literary current which flows constantly by" and who desire "some general knowledge of the progress of events in other fields of thought." Most of the books reviewed were fiction, poetry, or books about authors and literature. Next in importance were books about American history and politics. But books on many other subject areas were covered, including foreign countries, philosophy, economics, religion, art, English language, classical studies, geography, gardening, and science.

The editorial offices of the *Dial* were first located in the Jansen, McClurg and Company building at 117-119 State Street. In 1882 the publishing company and the magazine moved to the Rutter Building at 117-121 Wabash Avenue. With the publisher's backing, the magazine's early years were free of debt. The connection helped Browne sell advertising space to eastern publishers eager to sell books to Jansen, McClurg's wholesale distribution division. The ads were printed on extra pages in the front and back, and the magazine text was free of commercial clutter. Browne refused to sell space advertising a book favorably reviewed within the same issue because he did not want the public to suspect that the purchase of an advertisement could influence the magazine to provide a favorable review.

Many of the contributors in the early years of the *Dial* were authors, editors, or translators of books published by McClurg. Browne was able to solicit reviews from the best writers submitting book manuscripts to McClurg and to encourage the best of those submitting essays to the magazine to submit manuscripts to the publisher. De-

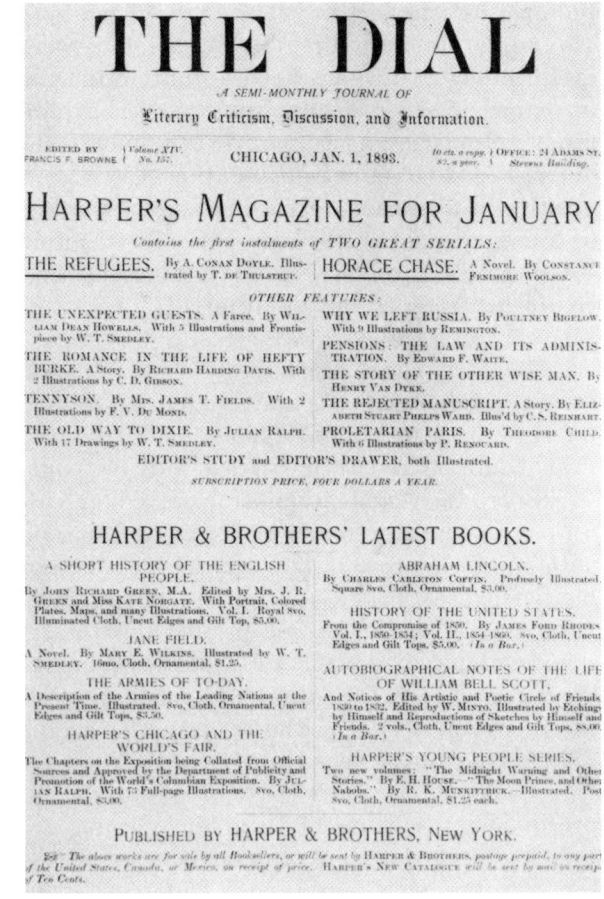

Opening page from an issue of the Chicago literary magazine Browne founded in 1880

spite the partnership, some McClurg books were unfavorably reviewed in the *Dial*. Most reviews and articles in the *Dial* were signed, and the magazine rarely printed reviews under pseudonyms. Browne believed that anonymous reviewers were more likely to be petty and malicious; also, he thought that signatures of reviewers helped to guarantee the magazine's claim to use of "specialists of recognized standing." The magazine did carry some unsigned features: "Literary Notes & News" filled half a page with news related to books and the publishing business; several pages were devoted to one-paragraph reviews under the heading "Briefs on New Books"; the "Personal Mention" section provided biographical notes about writers, scholars, and editors. Browne said that these brief anonymous notices were written by the same authorities who wrote the signed reviews.

Browne's health was too weak for the Chicago winters, so he began to travel to California starting in the winter of 1887-1888. The frequency of his visits increased until 1902, when Pasadena became his winter home. Substituting for his father during his absences was his eldest son, Francis G. Browne, who became business manager in 1888. William Morton Payne, a Chicago high school teacher, was the principal writer for the magazine while Browne was editor and was chief literary critic from 1884 to 1915.

Young scholars often received their first opportunities to get into print in the *Dial* because established scholars expected pay and would not write for the magazine. Browne worked hard to assemble a core of authorities who wrote well and held beliefs and values similar to his own. In 1905 he wrote about his contributors: "In entire sympathy with the ideals and motives of the journal, all have labored zealously ... to uphold its standard and enhance its interest and value." For thirty-three years the magazine displayed remarkable consistency of opinion and tone, even though Browne never tampered with the contents of the reviews. *Dial* writers comprised a narrow spectrum of opinion: for example, almost no contributions were written by southerners, and few were written by women; the magazine used many articles by Protestant ministers but none by Catholic priests. Moreover, if a review presented Browne's viewpoint on a topic such as protective tariffs, he did not feel obliged to present opposing viewpoints.

Browne's method of building his unpaid staff was to ask for more reviews when he received one he liked. Philosopher and theologian John Bascom and classicist Paul Shorey sent contributions for decades. A small group produced more than half the magazine. By 1892 Payne had written fifty-one articles or reviews, University of Iowa professor Melville Best Anderson forty-six, and Chicago librarian and historian William Frederick Poole thirty-three. At first the *Dial* depended heavily on Chicago writers; later it increased the numbers of reviewers from outside Chicago, but most were still midwesterners. Browne insured that his reviewers did not express a sectionalist viewpoint, however, for his goal was always to create a national audience for his magazine. In addition to professional writers and scholars, contributors to the *Dial* included clergymen, lawyers, bankers, stockbrokers, wholesale grocers, manufacturers, real estate agents, physicians, soldiers, and housewives. Promising young writers Browne encouraged include Frederick Jackson Turner, Woodrow Wilson, Norman Foerster, Henry Seidel Canby, Frederic Ives Carpenter, Albert Shaw, Eugene Field, and Edward E. Hale, Jr.

After twelve years McClurg and Browne agreed to a friendly separation of the magazine from the publishing company. The published notice from "Messrs. A. C. McClurg & Co." (the firm's name had changed in 1886) states that while the *Dial* is "the foremost American critical journal," the publisher fears that the public might misunderstand its connection with a bookselling house and wishes the magazine to be perceived as a "high-grade and wholly independent journal of literary criticism" displaying "freedom from constraint through publishers' or booksellers' influence."

On 1 September 1892 the magazine became independent and began to appear on the first and sixteenth of every month. The masthead carried a new subtitle signaling expansion of the old format: *A Semi-Monthly Journal of Literary Criticism, Discussion and Information*. The lead essay, "The New Dial," said that the magazine would "assume a distinct voice upon questions of general intellectual concern." Browne had decided that merely reviewing books limited the magazine's opportunities for discussion. The *Dial* began carrying editorials on the first page and used more short, general essays which were not reviews. The general articles often related to literature or education: "The Chicago University," "Whittier and Slavery," "Of the Justification of Learning in a Democracy," "English at Harvard," "Education of Women in England." Also at this time the *Dial* began to include letters from readers under the heading "Communications."

When Browne became sole owner of the *Dial*, he named Payne and Edward Gilpin Johnson as associate editors. Johnson's main responsibility for the next nine years was the leading review of "the most important book of the fortnight," a feature of the new *Dial*. It was supposed to be "descriptive and extractive rather than critical." The last significant addition to the *Dial* under Browne's management was the "Casual Comment" section, which started in the 16 October 1906 issue. This feature consisted of several pages of unsigned paragraphs covering a variety of topics and written in a personal style reminiscent of eighteenth-century British essayists.

The *Dial* ran about six major reviews in each issue. To deal with the flood of American fiction and poetry, Payne occasionally wrote "Recent Poetry" and "Recent Fiction" essays which would review fifteen or more books at once. Translated fiction was reviewed annually in "A Year of Continental Literature." Travel books were also reviewed in groups. The major reviews both evaluated the book at hand and provided a general discussion of the topic covered by the book. Since Browne liked to give the magazine's attention only to worthy books and avoided harsh attacks, most books were praised, but with varying degrees of enthusiasm. Books that were considered bad were simply ignored.

The *Dial* announced in 1892 that it stood "preeminently for objective and scientific criticism" based on universal canons. Critics were to evaluate books not according to their subjective responses but on the basis of ethical, aesthetic, rhetorical, or linguistic principles. Browne's own reviews of poetry books show that he expected poets to be learned, to write with moral purpose, and to show mastery of conventional devices of form. Qualities Browne wanted in reviewers included expert knowledge, an agreeable manner free of flippancy, morality, a readable style free of technical language which might confuse the general reader, and appreciative rather than destructive impulses. Speaking to librarians about reviewing books, Browne said near the end of his life that he had "always been glad to praise them when he could, sorry to blame them when he must, and anxious chiefly to arrive . . . at a just and fair appraisal of their worth." He also spoke about his lifelong aversion to "log-rolling," the practice of reviewers using their writing to help their author friends. He considered such reviews unethical and thought that a magazine that used them would quickly lose its reputation.

In accordance with Browne's preference, the personalities of contributors do not stand out in *Dial* reviews. Most display the same courteous and good-tempered formality of tone. Their assertions are likely to be understated. Sentences are usually clear but seldom short. Writers use active verbs and avoid slang. They avoid flippancy and facetiousness. Browne never wanted his writers to be sensationalistic or trendy.

The *Dial* reviews reflected Browne's conservative canons: that poetry is the highest genre; that literature should aim to create beauty; that it should instruct while it delights; that it must address life's great issues; that it should display humanity at its best. *Dial* reviewers revered established late-nineteenth-century authors of England–Arnold, Tennyson, Swinburne, Browning, Eliot, Scott, and Dickens–and New England–Emerson, Lowell, Longfellow, Whittier, and Hawthorne. They considered English writers superior to American writers. Reviews praised the romantic fiction of Tolstoy, Turgenev, Balzac, Hugo, and Flaubert since the *Dial* opposed books portraying human nature at its worst. The *Dial* ignored Zola until 1892 when the fight for critical acceptance in America had been won by Zola's supporters. Most *Dial* reviewers did not wish to read of the ugly, the indecent, the mundane, the indelicate, the immoral. The *Dial* scorned Melville and James and virtually ignored Twain and Crane. Realistic local detail and dialect were not valued assets of fiction to *Dial* reviewers, but realists with less bite than Twain, such as Harte, Jewett, and Foote, were approved. Fiction reviewers were also conservative about form, preferring unity of action and chronological development of plot. The *Dial* thought Henry James's novels were spoiled by lack of definite plot outline. Obviously, the *Dial* did not discuss naturalistic or muckraking fiction. The *Dial* did not like to see poets defy traditional rules of versification, and among living nineteenth-century poets, Alfred Tennyson was most admired by *Dial* writers. American poets who were approved had to resemble the favored English poets. The *Dial* called Carl Sandburg's poetry "inchoate observation" which was "not even doggerel." Surprisingly, Walt Whitman was mildly praised in the *Dial*, but not until 1886, and his verse was described as badly flawed, filled with "indefensible rhythmic and verbal vagaries." When Hamlin Garland complained angrily about the conservative standards of the *Dial*, which were unfavorable to western realistic fiction, Browne wrote to Garland denying the charge that he was unsympathetic to western authors. On 18 October 1893 he wrote that he believed western literature could not be helped by lowering critical standards: "It is no longer a baby, to be coddled and flattered and pap-suckled. . . . We must show that we are willing to have it tried by the standards of world literature, rather than by the standards of the back settlement." That Browne was recognized in the city as the chief arbiter of Chicago literary taste and the leader of its literary circle is demonstrated by his appointment as chairman of the Committee on the Congress of Authors for the 1893 Columbian Exposition.

Before 1892 the *Dial* had editorialized on only one subject: it often advocated international copyright. The regular editorials which began in 1892 usually avoided politics and controversial subjects such as labor strife. Payne, who agreed with Browne about almost everything, wrote more editorials than anyone else. Representative titles were "Reading and Education," "Touchstones of Criticisms," "The Carnegie Foundation," "The Teaching of Literature," "The Prices of Books," "Literary Censorship," "The Future of Library Science," and "The Neglected Art of Translation." The magazine's quiet voice suggests that Browne thought his readers did not wish to confront in the *Dial* the controversies they found in newspaper stories and editorials.

Browne was a powerful force on his magazine but remained relatively invisible to readers. He made many strong friendships among the literati, yet in 1910, when the *Dial* printed portions of many letters congratulating the magazine on its thirty years of continuous publication, almost none of the selections even mentioned Browne. An editorial note preceding the letters brags that the *Dial* "has not been given to self-glorification or the exploitation of personality." Browne's ideas and values can be discerned in the *Dial*, but he usually did not state them above his name. He did express controversial political opinions in print, not in his own magazine but in letters to newspapers. For example, he opposed American imperialism in letters to the *New York Evening Post* published on 31 July and 12 November 1900.

Browne was proud of his Puritan heritage, and *Dial* reviews of books on colonial history praised the Puritans, but Browne was an extremely liberal Unitarian who approved all forms of Protestantism and opposed religious intolerance. *Dial* reviews advocated acceptance of evolution theory. Browne believed in a moral universe controlled by a benevolent deity, a universe in which human material and intellectual progress are inevitable. Browne quoted poets rather than scriptural texts when he discussed his faith in the design of the universe. He approved of the way Ralph Waldo Emerson and Matthew Arnold associated the functions of religion and poetry. Arnold's poetry was his favorite, and Browne's son said that his father's character and habits of thought were "in many ways closely akin to Arnold's." The only one of his own poems Browne ever published in the *Dial* was a sonnet he wrote in response to the death of Arnold in 1888.

An editorial of 1900 promises that the *Dial* will ignore "narrower issues of politics" but will speak about questions that "touch the very principles upon which our civilization is based." The *Dial* tried to be politically neutral and never expressed a presidential preference or discussed results of elections, but Browne's ideas about government can be discerned in his magazine. He brought with him from New England a passionate love of moral and democratic government. He viewed the Civil War as a holy war to preserve the union and to free the slaves, and *Dial* reviews of books about the war reflected that attitude. But Browne strongly opposed the use of war to settle international disputes and printed editorials criticizing presidential actions that seemed to lead toward war. An editorial in the number for 1 January 1896 denounced the confrontation with England that resulted from President Cleveland's message on the Venezuela boundary controversy. The editorial apologizes for introducing political controversy into the magazine: "That so monstrous a thing as a war with England about the disputed boundary line of a South American state should even have been hinted at by irresponsible politicians and journalists was sufficiently discouraging; that it should have received the sanction implied by the recent message of the President and its reception by the national legislature, and that the popular response to these official acts should have been what it has been, is saddening.... The field of The Dial is not that of political discussion.... But we feel it our duty, as an organ of serious thought, to protest against the spirit of recklessness that has taken possession of the public mind...." Browne vehemently opposed American imperialism and the Spanish-American War, and he became a vice president of the Anti-imperialist League. Though he admired Grant, he turned against Grant's party because of the corruption in his administration.

Dial reviews criticized machine politics, the spoils system, and party bosses; but Browne usually sided with the Democratic party, voting seven out of nine times for its presidential candidates and agreeing with its positions on major issues. He saw the 1896 Democratic convention as "the birth of a new party–a party devoted in spirit, whatever its mistakes of method, to human rights and human progress, to the welfare of the common people, to the promulgation of a newer and truer Democracy." Browne thought that the Republican party was the advocate of the wealthy and privileged. He supported free trade and opposed protective tariffs, which he thought enriched the rich at the expense of the poor. Books reviewed and reviewers were generally antitariff.

He also supported the income tax and opposed the use of court injunctions in labor disputes because he favored the redistribution of wealth. But the *Dial* consistently opposed socialist schemes, whether advocated in nonfiction books or in novels. Instead of socialism, *Dial* writers supported the concept of profit sharing.

That he was concerned about woman's rights was demonstrated in 1905 when he wrote a letter to the *Los Angeles Record* objecting because the woman director of the Los Angeles Public Library was being replaced by a man. She had written to Browne asking for help since he was a prominent winter resident of the area. His letter in her behalf is especially revealing because the man chosen to replace the librarian was Browne's longtime personal friend Charles Lummis. Lummis was offended by Browne's letter, but their friendship survived.

Though fiercely democratic, Browne was sufficiently elitist to believe that the uneducated masses were potentially dangerous to civilized society. Thus, the *Dial* strongly favored free public education. After 1892 public education was a frequent topic in editorials and reviews. *Dial* editorials disapproved of curriculum changes in the direction of "practical" education that taught students how to make a living rather than how to live. An editorial in 1895 criticizes "the study of man in his character as tool-making and tool-using animal, mainly intent upon material comfort and progress." The magazine favored improved science instruction, but not at the expense of the humanities, and took the view that new scientific truths demonstrably proved should quickly be accepted and taught. The *Dial* disapproved of the increase in experimentation with instruction which the theories of John Dewey encouraged, objected to interference with the academic freedom of teachers by politicians and businessmen, and opposed the introduction into public schools of military training and military dress.

In addition to his magazine work, Browne edited several books. *Golden Poems by British and American Authors* (1881) was reprinted nine times before a revised edition was published in 1906. *The Golden Treasury of Poetry and Prose* (1883) contains samples of the best work of five hundred authors representing the cream of English literature, five hundred engravings, and biographies of authors. *Bugle-Echoes* (1886) is a book of poems related to the Civil War; only a few of the poets included are much read today. For the most part, arrangement of the selections was chronological according to subjects.

His most significant book was *The Every-Day Life of Abraham Lincoln* (1886), a biography based on recollections of more than five hundred people personally acquainted with Lincoln. Browne collected accounts of Lincoln from published sources and corresponded with many individuals to solicit original reminiscences. The book sets out in chronological order the facts of Lincoln's life and blends the recollections with the biographical outline. Browne sought to "avoid mere opinions and eulogies" and to give "actual experiences, incidents, anecdotes, and reminiscences." Four large editions were sold out within three months, and an expanded, revised version was published after his death in 1913.

Browne published some of his own poems in a slim volume, *Volunteer Grain*, brought out by the short-lived Chicago publisher Way and Williams in 1895. He wrote poetry all his adult life; he published some short poems in newspapers, in his magazines, and in magazines edited by others; many others remained only in his handwritten drafts. They are sentimental poems in conventional metrical verse, without originality of thought or imagery. Their interest today is that they provide some insight into a man who declined so many other opportunities to show himself personally to his readers. Some poems reveal a few of the men he admired, such as President Grant, Longfellow, and Lowell; some reveal that Browne the city dweller loved natural places such as Santa Barbara; some reveal how public events such as the treatment of the so-called anarchists of the Haymarket riot stirred him. Contemporary editors reprinted some of Browne's poems in anthologies.

Trying to capitalize on the *Dial* name and staff expertise, Browne tried several related business ventures. The *Dial* for 1 November 1893 carried an announcement offering to undertake the publication of works by authors unable to interest commercial publishers in their manuscripts. Little is known about the success of this venture, except that the advertisements disappeared from the magazine after a few years.

Browne also used the Dial Company to publish the *Trade Book List*, a monthly bulletin of new books for the use of booksellers. Begun in 1895, it was successful from the start; later it became *Books of the Month* and was distributed by booksellers to help advertise books. After Browne's death, his son Herbert S. Browne continued the publication and eventually sold it to the R. R. Bowker Company. Less successful was the monthly *What's in the Magazines: A Guide and Index to the Contents of the Current Periodicals*, which was issued from January 1906 through January 1908. It was not intended for professional use by librarians but for the general reader.

The venture that excited Browne most was a bookstore he established in November 1907. The store was in the Fine Arts Building, which also housed studios of painters, architects, sculptors, cartoonists, and musicians; literary clubs; art galleries; publishers' offices; working quarters for foreign language teachers; and dancing and dramatic schools. Frank Lloyd Wright designed the interior, which included handsome oak woodwork; beautiful lighting fixtures illuminating the bookshelves; quiet alcoves with long tables; sculptures; ornamental vases filled with striking arrangements of leaves and flowers; and a fireplace surrounded by easy chairs, where teas and informal lectures were given to bring book lovers together. The store was intended to combine features of a bookstore and a library. The store was successful for a time, but later it began losing money, and it closed in 1912. The store was undoubtedly hurt by the practice of department stores selling popular books at discount prices. As early as 1900 *Dial* articles had opposed that practice for its danger to bookstores.

Disappointed by the failure of the bookstore and in poor health, Browne spent his final months revising his Lincoln biography for a new edition which he finished shortly before his death in the Miradero Sanitarium in Santa Barbara on 11 May 1913. Letters from across the country flowed to the magazine office paying tribute to Browne and the magazine he had created. In 1914 his sons sold the *Dial* to the Henry O. Shepard Company, publishers of the *Inland Printer*, who moved it to New York in 1918.

References:

John M. Binckley, "The Life Story of a Magazine," *Dial*, 54 (16 June 1913): 489-492;

Waldo Ralph Browne, "Francis Fisher Browne, 1843-1913," *Dial*, 54 (1 June 1913): 437-441;

John Vance Cheney, "Francis Fisher Browne," *Book Buyer*, 20 (May 1900): 301-303;

"The 'Dial' and Its Editor," *Inland Printer*, 10 (October 1892): 33-35;

"The 'Dial's' Puritan Editor," *American Review of Reviews* (July 1913): 115-116;

Herbert E. Fleming, "The Literary Interests of Chicago," *American Journal of Sociology*, 11 (November 1905): 377-408, 499-531, 784-816; 12 (July 1906): 68-118; later reprinted as a dissertation under the title "Magazines of a Market-Metropolis, Being a History of the Literary Periodicals and Literary Interests of Chicago," Ph.D. dissertation, University of Chicago, 1906;

Llewellyn Jones, "Culture and Democracy," *Public*, 16 (30 May 1913): 506-508;

Lloyd Lewis, "Francis Fisher Browne," *Newberry Library Bulletin*, 1 (September 1945): 23-36;

Charles F. Lummis, "In Western Letters," *Land of Sunshine*, 12 (April 1900): 296-302;

Frederic John Mosher, "Chicago's 'Saving Remnant': Francis Fisher Browne, William Morton Payne, and The Dial (1880-1892)," Ph.D. dissertation, University of Illinois, 1950;

Frank Luther Mott, *A History of American Magazines, 1865-1885* (Cambridge, Mass.: Harvard University Press, 1938), pp. 413-416, 539-543;

John Muir, "Browne the Beloved," *Dial*, 54 (16 June 1913): 492.

Papers:

Browne's papers are at the Newberry Library, Chicago. They include documents related to his magazines; letters, poems, and essays by Browne; clippings about Browne from periodicals; photographs; and letters to him.

H. C. Bunner
(3 August 1855-11 May 1896)

W. J. Hug
Auburn University

See also the Bunner entry in *DLB 78: American Short Story Writers, 1880-1910.*

MAJOR POSITION HELD: Editor, *Puck* (1878-1896).

BOOKS: *A Woman of Honor* (Boston: Osgood, 1883);

Airs from Arcady and Elsewhere (New York: Scribners, 1884; London: Hutt, 1885);

In Partnership: Studies in Story-Telling, by Bunner and Brander Matthews (New York: Scribners, 1884; Edinburgh: Douglas/London: Hamilton, Adams, 1885);

The Midge (New York: Scribners, 1886);

The Story of a New York House (New York: Scribners, 1887);

"Short Sixes": Stories to Be Read While the Candle Burns (New York: Keppler & Schwarzmann, 1891; London: Brentano's, 1891);

Zadoc Pine and Other Stories (New York: Scribners, 1891; London: Gay & Bird, 1891);

The Runaway Browns: A Story of Small Stories (New York: Keppler & Schwarzmann, 1892; London: Brentano's, 1892);

Rowen: "Second Crop" Songs (New York: Scribners, 1892);

"Made in France": French Tales Retold with a United States Twist (New York: Keppler & Schwarzmann, 1893);

More "Short Sixes" (New York: Keppler & Schwarzmann, 1894);

Jersey Street and Jersey Lane: Urban and Suburban Sketches (New York: Scribners, 1896);

The Suburban Sage: Stray Notes and Comments on His Simple Life (New York: Keppler & Schwarzmann, 1896);

Love in Old Cloathes and Other Stories (New York: Scribners, 1896; London: Downey, 1897);

The Poems of H. C. Bunner (New York: Scribners, 1896; enlarged, 1897, enlarged again, 1917);

Three Operettas, Librettos by Bunner, music by Oscar Weil (New York: Harper, 1897);

H. C. Bunner

Our Girls: Poems in Praise of the American Girl (New York: Moffatt, Yard, 1907).

Collections: *The Stories of H. C. Bunner, First Series* (New York: Scribners, 1916);

The Stories of H. C. Bunner, Second Series (New York: Scribners, 1916);

The Stories of H. C. Bunner, "Short Sixes" (New York: Scribners, 1917);

The Stories of H. C. Bunner: More "Short Sixes," The Runaway Browns (New York: Scribners, 1917).

PLAY PRODUCTION: *The Tower of Babel*, by Bunner and Julian Magnus, Philadelphia, Chesnut Street Theatre, 17 February 1879.

PERIODICAL PUBLICATIONS: "Cheating at Letters," *Century*, 27 (March 1895): 716;
"Living Critics: Brander Matthews," *Bookman*, 3 (March 1896): 40-42.

Throughout the 1880s and early 1890s, H. C. Bunner edited the most successful comic magazine in America–*Puck*. With Bunner as editor, *Puck* evolved from the English-language offshoot of a struggling comic weekly in German to a literary and satirical magazine wielding substantial social and political influence nationwide. None of the writing in *Puck* was more crucial in developing and maintaining its popularity than the material the editor himself provided. Readers appreciated the urbanity and wit of Bunner's poems, parodies, and short stories as subtler complements to the journal's biting, sometimes vicious, caricatures and editorials lampooning the social and political foolishness of the Gilded Age. Bunner's contributions to *Puck* and to other magazines were so popular that he published collections of his verse and fiction throughout his life. The most notable are his selection of poems titled *Airs from Arcady and Elsewhere* (1884), a volume of short fiction, "*Short Sixes*," (1891), and his adaptations of several Maupassant stories, "*Made in France*" (1893).

Henry Cuyler Bunner was born on 3 August 1855, the first of two sons of Ruth Tuckerman Bunner and Rudolph Bunner of Oswego, New York. His father, a former lawyer, edited the local newspaper, the *Oswego Palladium*, until the family moved to New York City in 1865; Rudolph Bunner's occupation from then until his death ten years later has not been recorded.

In New York City, Henry–or "H. C.," as he preferred to be called throughout his life–frequently visited the home of his uncle Henry Tuckerman, a free-lance contributor to the local press and magazines. As he sampled Tuckerman's library of more than seventeen hundred volumes, Bunner first developed the interest in literature that would dominate his life. After a stint in public grammar school he was admitted to a private secondary school through his uncle's influence. Here he edited a short-lived student monthly called the *Essay*, for which he provided poems and stories. However, it expired after the third number because of poor financial management–one of the contributors recalled that the *Essay* cost its staff twenty dollars an issue to print but sold for a nickel a copy. Nevertheless, the schoolboy's enthusiasm with writing and editing intensified; he was particularly drawn to continental authors, some of whom would later influence him heavily.

Bunner's formal education ended in 1871, when he was sixteen. Though his schoolmaster thought highly of his abilities and even offered to pay for his education at Columbia University, Rudolph Bunner was financially straitened and chose instead to place his son in business with a firm of German wine importers on Wall Street. To Bunner the work was "beastly," and he sought to escape it during his off-hours through literary endeavor. His letters from this period reflect his wide reading–John Keats, William Wordsworth, Thomas Carlyle, Johann Wolfgang von Goethe, Friedrich von Schiller, Heinrich Heine. He finally was fired after about two years for refusing the owners' demands that he come to work on George Washington's birthday.

From 1873 until 1877 Bunner worked a variety of jobs while serving his literary apprenticeship. He continued to read widely, mostly French and German literature, and became a consistent contributor to various short-lived New York weeklies, particularly Louis Engel's *Arcadian*. His association with this "musical and dramatic sheet" furthered his development in several important ways. A series of poems entitled "Some Translations from the French" in the *New York Arcadian* introduced him to vers de société, a light but intricate style of poetry often based upon French metrical forms. It would provide the pattern for some of Bunner's best poetry, and the series' author, Brander Matthews, would become his closest friend and literary collaborator. Bunner's *Arcadian* poems and parodies gave him many opportunities to sharpen the poetic facility and the wit that would characterize his writing in *Puck*. In one of the most entertaining *Arcadian* pieces, "Quatrains Imitated from Sir Thomas Bailey," he dons the guise of the "Special Bull-Dozer," a parodical and zany poet-editor.

The comic cleverness and seeming spontaneity of Bunner's *Arcadian* pieces caught the attention of fellow writer Sydney Rosenfeld, to whose short-lived theatrical weekly *Figaro* Bunner had also contributed. In the spring of 1877 Rosenfeld was asked to edit the English counterpart of a German comic weekly called *Puck*, and he immediately took on Bunner as his assistant. The two men and whatever other writers they could hire at modest wages were to provide the text for the English edition, while the cartoons would be adapted from the German original. Unfortunately, *Puck* operated on such a shoestring that Rosenfeld and (particularly) Bunner were forced to write much of the text themselves–Brander Matthews later recalled his own amazement at discovering that his three favorite pieces in an early issue of *Puck* had all been Bunner's. The heavy work load soon became too much for Rosenfeld; after only a year he resigned the editorial post to devote himself to writing plays. Bunner, at the age of twenty-two, became the magazine's second editor, a position he would hold until his death.

The arrangement was fortunate for him and for *Puck*. To become established, the weekly needed an energetic and witty editor not only to supervise its material and publication, but to grind out quality copy whenever needed. Bunner effectively handled both responsibilities; Matthews was intrigued by Bunner's ability to generate diverse sorts of writing on demand: "Whatever might be wanted he stood ready to supply–rimes of the times, humorous ballads, *vers de société*, verses to go with a cartoon, dialogues to go under a drawing, paragraphs pertinent and impertinent ... comicalities of all kinds." Bunner, on the other hand, had found an eager publisher for his writing. Though the bulk of it was now light topical material produced to fill the pages of one or another of the issues, his own artistic integrity demanded that the quality of all his work be relatively high. His position also offered him opportunities for serious journalism. Bunner now wrote editorials on a broad variety of issues: the evils of high tariffs, the political immoralities of presidential candidate James G. Blaine, the polygamy of the Mormons, the foolishness of the suffragettes. The social concerns he addressed in his editorials would emerge in the fiction he wrote in the late 1880s and the 1890s; for example, "The Zadoc Pine Labor Union" sharply criticizes labor excesses, and "As One Having Authority" decries the fanaticism of camp meetings in the South.

Under the direction of Bunner, *Puck* soon began to flourish. Week after week, Bunner cleverly combined the invective of the journal's cartoons and his own editorials with the subtler wit of its articles, poetry, and fiction–which he often wrote as well. His editorial recipe produced a consistently zesty mixture that attracted a growing and loyal readership. The English-language *Puck* soon outstripped its German original. By 1882 it had a circulation of eighty thousand. In 1884 its strident advocacy of Grover Cleveland over Blaine in the presidential election brought *Puck* into national prominence: Cleveland himself acknowledged the editorials as among the most potent influences in the campaign. By 1890 *Puck* had garnered ninety thousand readers, a circulation it would maintain until after Bunner's death in 1896. The editor's satisfaction at his magazine's satiric wit and popularity permeates his waggish poetical retrospective published on 4 March 1885 for the eighth birthday of *Puck*. Bunner recalls the evils plaguing the world in 1877, the year *Puck* appeared, then characterizes the magazine's typically saucy response to them.

For a comic weekly like *Puck*, occasional material was in constant demand, as were weekly series. One of the most popular was Bunner's 1880 series of articles and poems signed "V. Hugo Dusenbury." As Matthews described him, Dusenbury was "the professional poet, prepared to ply for hire, to fill all orders promptly, to give you verse while you wait, and write poems in every style, satisfaction guaranteed." In the Dusenbury pieces, Bunner parodied the works of familiar literary figures from Dante Gabriel Rossetti to John Greenleaf Whittier and satirized current fads and pretensions. One of Dusenbury's most popular offerings, "Shake, Mulleary, and Goethe" (Shakespeare, Molière, and Goethe), burlesques the widespread desire among the Gilded Age nouveau riche for the fashionable appearances of culture despite their obvious lack of it:

> I have a bookcase, which is what
> Many much better men have not.
> There are no books inside, for books,
> I am afraid, might spoil its looks.
> But I've three busts, all second-hand,
> Upon the top. You understand
> I could not put them underneath–
> Shake, Mulleary and Go-ethe.

Despite the popularity of material like the Dusenbury pieces, Bunner knew that *Puck* was an inappropriate forum for the stylistic and tonal refinement of his more carefully prepared work, so he submitted his more serious poems and stories to such formal literary periodicals as *Scribner's Magazine*, *Harper's New Monthly Magazine*, *Century*, and *Atlantic Monthly*. But the irony of the situation rankled him, as he admitted in a letter to Walter Learned, a *Puck* contributor who would become his brother-in-law: "The average reader of *Puck* wants to guffaw. Delicate work is wasted on him. When I do anything which I consider delicate (Heaven alone knows how other people regard it) I look out for a magazine audience. If I put it in *Puck*, my readers want to know what I am giving them. This is disheartening to the poet— beastly disheartening." Nevertheless, Bunner accepted circumstances, and throughout his career as editor of *Puck*, he published his best work, particularly his poetry, elsewhere. He encouraged others to do so as well when he felt that the quality of their writing would go unnoticed in his comic weekly. The owners of *Puck* were astute literary and businessmen: they not only accepted Bunner's judgments about what readers would and would not like, but they knew that the appearance of their editor's work in the country's best literary magazines would only enhance the periodical's reputation and improve circulation.

In 1880 Bunner became friends with a new *Puck* contributor, Walter Learned, and met his youngest sister, Alice. Over the next several years, Bunner often visited the Learned family's Connecticut home, and his acquaintance with Alice developed gradually into affection, then courtship. By 1884 their relationship had warmed sufficiently for Bunner to title the final poem in *Airs from Arcady and Elsewhere* discreetly "To Her." However, it was not until a year later that he wrote Alice his first love letter. On 6 January 1886, the couple were wed. In their ten years of marriage they would have five children; two would die in infancy. Despite his family obligations, Bunner hardly slackened the pace of his literary work. He continued to handle all editorial responsibilities for *Puck* and to provide whatever material was needed from issue to issue. But by 1887, with the standing and circulation of *Puck* established, Bunner's reputation as a talented contributor to the nation's leading magazines was more valuable to the owners of *Puck* than his skills as editor. To allow him more time for his own writing, they hired H. G. Paine to manage day-to-day operation. From then until his death nine years later, Bunner spent more time working on his own projects in the suburban Nutley, New Jersey, home to which he and Alice moved in their first year of marriage and far less time in the offices of *Puck*.

In the early 1890s Bunner prepared a good deal of fiction for *Puck*. Much of it, like "The Runaway Browns" and "Mavericks: Short Stories Rounded Up," was competent but routine

Cover for an issue of the humorous weekly of which Bunner was the second editor

hackwork calculated to give the readers of *Puck* a comfortable laugh. In one series, however, Bunner wanted to do more. "Short Sixes: Stories to be Read While the Candle Burns" were written at the particular request of the journal's owners, who asked Bunner for a group of light, comic pieces, each no more than twenty-five hundred words—that is, short enough to be read by the brief span of light provided by one of the small candles that came twelve to a pound but were called, for unknown reasons, "short sixes." In the thirteen stories of the series Bunner sought to reproduce in a modest way that conciseness and humor of the French storyteller Guy de Maupassant, whose fiction he much admired—but he revealed this intention only to his friends. "Short Sixes" appeared in *Puck* throughout the Summer and Fall of 1890, then were released in book form in a single volume in 1891. *"Short Sixes": Stories to Be Read While the Candle Burns* immediately became the most popular of Bunner's books, going through five printings in five months, as well as publication in Britain and frequent reprintings after the author's death. Reviews were consistently favorable; most praised the stories' simplicity and jovial humor. The *Critic* detected the French influence but asserted that "the color and feeling of Mr. Bunner's tales is [sic] as American as those of Maupassant are French."

Despite his growing preoccupation with fiction, Bunner had not sworn off poetry entirely. Though by this time he published little in the way of vers de société, he maintained his name as a poet with parodies and occasional verse, written mostly for *Puck*. These were so popular among the weekly's readers that in 1892 Bunner decided to publish a selection of them. He knew, however, that a volume of poetry would be examined much more critically than individual poems included in his comic weekly, and he admitted to Matthews the difficulty in "scar[ing] up" enough quality work for the book. When the volume, titled *Rowen: "Second Crop" Songs* appeared in late 1892, reviewers politely confirmed its lack of substance: most spoke favorably of the book but often in qualified terms. In a typically ambiguous notice, the reviewer for the *Atlantic Monthly* discreetly complimented Bunner's avoidance of "that ambitious quality which takes so many singers beyond their depth."

After the appearance of *Rowen*, Bunner again devoted himself primarily to short fiction. He still published poems occasionally in *Puck*, *Scribner's*, or *Century*, but in the four remaining years of his life, he wrote four volumes of fiction. He became especially concerned about whether his writing had actually represented his best efforts. In an 1893 letter to *Puck* illustrator A. B. Frost, he confessed that "the older I grow, the more I worry about my work–not whether it is *good* or not; that is according as the Lord has dealt out faculty to me;–but I am troubled to know whether I am doing the best I can, or whether I might put in harder licks. God knows I wouldn't spare myself if I thought I could better the job." Perhaps this desire to produce the best work of which he was capable spurred Bunner to do his second, more ambitious adaptation of Guy de Maupassant.

"*Made in France: French Tales Retold with a United States Twist* (1893) are not translations of the Frenchman's fiction. At the very opening of "Tony," the first story of the collection, Bunner admits that "I can no more translate the charm of [Maupassant's] French than those little machines with rolls of perforated paper can grind out a tune in the way that Mr. Paderewski plays it." Nor are they original pieces in imitation of Maupassant, as are "*Short Sixes*." In "*Made in France*" Bunner attempts to retell Maupassant's stories in the American idiom while maintaining the French writer's characteristic qualities: the deceptive simplicity of structure and style in his stories and their wry, though often poignant irony. In choosing among Maupassant's works for adaptation, Bunner carefully avoided those that genteel American readers would consider risqué. His brief preface assures his audience that the stories are based solely on Maupassant's "ethical situations," though one story, "The Prize of Propriety," ironically recounts the rapid dissolution of a demure young man once his sterling morality is rewarded. Another, "The Joke on M. Peptonneau," is in fact a joke on most readers as well. The story is not a Maupassant adaptation, but a Bunner original, recounting shenanigans that occurred in the offices of *Puck*. The ten stories comprising the collection appeared in *Puck* throughout the spring of 1893, then were published in a single volume during September 1893. The few reviews that appeared praised Bunner's Americanization of Maupassant, but none caught "The Joke on M. Peptonneau."

In December 1893 Bunner arranged a banquet to honor his longtime confidante Matthews, who was by then a professor at Columbia. Mark Twain, W. D. Howells, and Bunner himself were among those who paid tribute to Matthews as friend and writer. During 1894 Bunner sought to capitalize on the popularity of "*Short Sixes*" with a sequel series in *Puck*, called "More Short Sixes." However, he adhered less closely to the manner of Maupassant in these than in the originals: subject matter and plot are often more eccentric, less lifelike, as titles like "Mr. Vincent Egg and the Wages of Sin" and "The Ghoolah" suggest. When ten of the thirteen stories were reprinted in book form, reviewers responded favorably. But *More "Short Sixes"* (1894) never generated the popular acclaim or the sales of their namesakes.

The year 1895 saw still another series of Bunner stories in *Puck*: "The Suburban Sage." Based upon the Bunner family's years in Nutley, these light sketches gently satirize the follies endemic to fashionable suburban life, from "The Suburbanite and His Golf" to "The Suburban Dog" to "The Society Church." During March, Bunner published in the *Century* a summary expression of his theory of fiction, the essay entitled "Cheating at Letters." He emerges here as a literary iconoclast independent of any school of fiction. Bunner criticizes the genteel preachiness of the romanticists as well as the stilted literalism of the realists. In his view, every story, whether romantic or realist, proffers its own illusion of reality, and the "realism" of this illusion dictates the quality of the story: "If I can write a story which will make you believe, *while you are reading it*, that when my hero was strolling down Fifth Avenue ... he met a green dragon forty-seven feet long, with eighteen legs and three tails, and that the dragon wept bitterly, and enquired the way to a cheese-shop—why, that's realism."

Soon after his literary credo appeared Bunner's accomplishments as storyteller, poet, and editor were acknowledged: in June 1895 he received an honorary M.A. from Yale University. It was his highest accolade, and the final one while he lived. In the fall he was stricken with tuberculosis. Though he continued to serve as editor of *Puck*, he rarely was able to come from Nutley into New York City. When his condition worsened in early 1896, he briefly visited a California sanitarium. Bunner died at his home in Nutley on 11 May 1896.

In the flurry of interest in Bunner's work that immediately followed his death four new Bunner collections were published: *The Suburban Sage: Stray Notes and Comments on His Simple Life* (1896), his last series of *Puck* stories; *Jersey Street and Jersey Lane: Urban and Suburban Sketches* (1896), a selection of New York City sketches also from *Puck*; *Love in Old Cloathes and Other Stories* (1896); and *The Poems of H. C. Bunner* (1896), selected by Matthews. Reviews of all four were favorable; virtually every notice praised Bunner's humor and craftsmanship and pondered what he might have produced had he lived.

During the first quarter of the twentieth century, Bunner's literary standing remained relatively high. Critics and educated readers considered him a significant if minor artist whose stories and poems were light but skillfully done. In his 1925 anthology of *Modern American Verse*, Louis Untermeyer includes Bunner's parodic ballad "Behold the Deeds!" as "a splendid example of [the poet's] wit and technical ingenuity." In later years, his literary reputation has steadily diminished; those who recall him at all remember him only as editor of *Puck* or author of *"Short Sixes."* To contemporary readers, Bunner's work does not seem inferior so much as obsolete. His poetical forte, vers de société, was out of fashion by 1890; his occasional verse is, by nature, tied to specific events mostly long forgotten. And although Bunner disliked the didacticism and sentimentality prevalent in genteel fiction, many of his own stories now seem to reflect these same qualities.

Yet a careful reading of Bunner uncovers pieces that deserve to be remembered. His apparent ease in sustaining the delicate pathos of "The Way to Arcady" and "To A. L. B." is masterful. The ironic doggerel of "Shake, Mulleary, and Goethe" delightfully lampoons the bourgeois speaker's flimsy pretensions. Psychology of character subtly and suspensefully emerges in "A Letter and A Paragraph." And the adaptations of Maupassant in *"Made in France"* represent a provocative literary experiment. A minor literary artist H. C. Bunner may have been, but these and others of his works confirm that he was an artist, nevertheless.

Biography:

Gerard E. Jensen, *The Life and Letters of Henry Cuyler Bunner* (Durham: Duke University Press, 1939).

References:

Brander Matthews, "H. C. Bunner," in his *The Historical Novel and Other Essays* (New York: Scribners, 1901), pp. 165-189;

Matthews, "The Uncollected Poems of H. C. Bunner," *Bookman*, 43 (July 1916): 474-480;

Benjamin W. Wells, "Henry Cuyler Bunner," *Sewanee Review*, 5 (January 1897): 17-32.

Papers:

Collections of Bunner's letters and manuscripts are housed in the libraries of Columbia and Princeton universities; the Huntington Library, San Marino, California; the University of Virginia; and the public library in New London, Connecticut. The libraries of Yale and Harvard universities each have several Bunner letters.

Edward Livermore Burlingame

(30 May 1848-15 November 1922)

Patt Foster Roberson
Southern University

MAJOR POSITION HELD: Editor, *Scribner's Magazine*, 1887-1914.

OTHER: *Art Life and Theories of Richard Wagner*, selected and translated by Burlingame (New York: Holt, 1875);

Current Discussion: A Collection from the Chief English Essays on Questions of the Time, edited by Burlingame, 2 volumes (New York: Putnam's, 1878);

"The Plains and the Sierra," in *Picturesque America*, 2 volumes, edited by William Cullen Bryant (New York: Appleton, 1872 and 1874; revised, 1894);

Stories by American Authors, edited by Burlingame, 10 volumes (New York: Scribners, 1884-1885).

Edward Livermore Burlingame

Edward Livermore Burlingame was the first editor of *Scribner's Magazine*, an illustrated monthly which began publication in January 1887. His goal was to produce "a magazine of good literature in the widest sense." He sought out literary and artistic works that were original, intellectually stimulating, and of lasting literary value. He was among the first editors to recognize the literary importance of travel narratives, collections of letters, autobiographical accounts, reminiscences of historically significant moments, and unpublished diaries.

A prospectus of the new magazine was issued in 1886 to give a general idea of its aims and scope, stating, in part, that "Scribner's, it is promised, will be, in the widest sense, a magazine of general literature, its purpose being to bring together, not only good reading, but literature of permanent value. Each number will be illustrated, and the artistic work will be spirited and original." On its debut, a *New York Times* reviewer wrote, "The periodical will at once take its place far forward in the magazine ranks, and it will command intelligent attention from readers everywhere.... It has no doubt come to make a stay among us at once amusing, instructive, and protracted." Of the second number, the reviewer wrote, "Scribner has arrived and settled itself permanently in this town of able and prosperous magazines."

Burlingame was fond of expressing his editorial orientation by saying that his "geese were not all swans." Nevertheless, his high standards of excellence and association with eminent scholars established a distinguished reputation for the magazine and attracted major writers and artists in America and abroad. Among these were Sir James Matthew Barrie, Joel Chandler Harris, Bret Harte, Henry James, Rudyard Kipling, Brander Matthews, Maxfield Parrish, Howard

Pyle, Robert Louis Stevenson, and Edith Wharton. He had the ability to recognize literature of permanent value and possessed the editorial judgment and authority to publish it.

Edward Livermore Burlingame was born on 30 May 1848 in Boston to Anson and Jane Cornelia Livermore Burlingame. He went to Harvard University, leaving in 1861 to become private secretary to his father, who had been appointed United States minister to China. He became fluent in French and German and resumed his studies in Berlin, Paris, and St. Petersburg, earning a Ph.D. in economics from the University of Heidelberg in 1869. By traveling and working with his father, Burlingame was exposed not only to world diplomats but also to prominent artists and writers. This cosmopolitan experience, which ended in 1870 when Anson Burlingame died suddenly, would form a foundation for his later work.

He married Ella Frances Badger of San Francisco in 1871. They had four children: Jean, Frederic Anson, Constance, and William Roger. For the first few years after his marriage Burlingame held several short-lived literary positions. In 1871 he worked on the editorial staff of the *New York Tribune*, and from 1872 to 1876 he assisted with the revision of Appleton's *American Cyclopaedia*. He spent several months translating a volume of writings, selected from the work of the composer Richard Wagner, which appeared in 1875 under the title *Art Life and Theories of Richard Wagner*.

Charles Scribner's Sons hired Burlingame in 1879 as a book editor, and in 1886, when plans were made for *Scribner's Magazine*, he accepted the position of editor for the new periodical. He filled this post from January 1887, when the first issue appeared, to 1914, when he retired.

During his editorship Burlingame worked closely with Charles Scribner, consulting with him almost every day, either in person or by mail. Their offices at 743-745 Broadway, opposite Astor Place, were comfortable, convenient, and thoroughly unpretentious, with Brussels carpets, oak woodwork, solid and substantial desks, and large, leather-covered revolving chairs. Scribner's private office had a fireplace, kept roaring in cold weather. Next to Scribner's office, Burlingame had "a little cubby hole partitioned off" with similar furniture and a black walnut bookcase.

At first *Scribner's Magazine* was confused with *Scribner's Monthly*. The Century Company had bought the *Monthly*, and Scribner had agreed not to publish another magazine for at least five years. He waited six and tried to make it clear that *Scribner's Magazine* was a new magazine. He told the *New York Times* that Burlingame would be the editor and that "the proposed magazine is an entirely new enterprise, and in no way an outgrowth or revival of the old *Scribner's Monthly*." The new magazine was 9 1/2 by 6 1/2 inches and printed with black ink on heavily coated paper. The yellow cover, designed by architect Stanford White, was illustrated with a simple laurel border around the edge and a lamp of learning within a laurel wreath in the center. The lamp became the Scribners trademark. On the magazine's demise, *Time* magazine mentioned the "ugly yellow cover."

Each monthly issue carried 128 pages of text, including essays, fiction, seasonal articles, poetry, and serials, all illustrated, at first in black and white, later in four colors. The December number carried the annual index by author and subject.

Atlantic Monthly, *Century*, and *Harper's*, already established as quality magazines and backed by major publishing houses, sold for thirty-five cents a copy or four dollars a year. Burlingame deliberately underpriced *Scribner's Magazine*, at twenty-five cents a copy or three dollars a year, as a selling point.

The first issue grossed seventy-four hundred dollars and sold 140,000 copies, causing one critic to comment that *Scribner's Magazine* had been born full grown. By 1900 circulation was 200,000 with a subscription list at 19,000.

Although Burlingame's initial budget was five hundred thousand dollars, *Scribner's Magazine* was one of the first to solicit advertising. The first issue carried sixty-four advertisements, display and classified, for a great variety of items, including artificial limbs, breakfast cereal, furs, jewelry, perfume, typewriters, and wire bustles. Advertising peaked at about one hundred pages per number at three hundred dollars a page.

Burlingame was discriminating but considerate in his search for potential contributors, and as critical to established writers as to promising newcomers. Each issue of the magazine was made up nearly three months ahead of the publication date to allow time to proofread everything, obtain illustrations, lay out pages, and allow authors to make any changes they wished. Lead articles in the first issues show Burlingame's interest in a diversity of literary appeal. "Reminiscences of the Siege and Commune of Paris," first in a four-part series by E. B. Washburne, a former minister to France with whom Burlingame corresponded extensively, was given "the place of honor in the magazine, opening the first number." "A Collection of Unpublished Letters of Thackeray," first in a seven-part series introduced and selected by Jane Octavia Brookfield, was a source of excitement for Burlingame, who called the letters "among the most important purely literary material that could be thought of." Other early features included "The Likenesses of Julius Caesar" by John Codman Ropes; "The Stability of the Earth" by N. S. Shaler; "The Development of the Steamship, and the Liverpool Exhibition of 1886" by Commander F. E. Chatwick, U.S. Navy; "Some Illustrations of Napoleon and His Times," first in a two-part series by Ropes; and "The Physical Proportions of the Typical Man" by D. A. Sargent, M.D. Some nonfiction topics for serials were American summer resorts, men's occupations, contemporary painting, and the art of living, which included segments on income, dwellings, furnishings, education, use of time, and the conduct of life.

Burlingame was not willing to print a piece after it had been brought out by another publisher in book form, and he made no exceptions to the rule. But when Charles Scribner's Sons had an appropriate book in the works, efforts would be made to arrange with the author for excerpts to be published first in *Scribner's Magazine*. Or when the magazine published works by relative unknowns and their reputations began to grow, a book might follow. Sometimes whole books (several chapters at a time) were serialized in the magazine before appearing in book form. The final installment in the magazine would appear immediately prior to the book, and this number also would contain appropriate advertising for the book.

In 1890 Burlingame began writing a column titled "The Point of View" that ended each number. In it he commented editorially on a wide variety of subjects. On the vanity of authors he wrote that modesty is the rarest and lowest virtue, and on the signing of editorials he commented that identification of the author is a "temptation to writers to make their work of the kind to attract remark." He thought the editor who discovered plagiarism dreaded less that offenders go unpublished, but that his own skill in detecting go unrecognized. He scolded newspaper editors for the manner in which they presented the

Cover for the first issue of the magazine of which Burlingame was the first editor

news and considered newspaper book reviews "singularly inadequate, and often inept."

In May 1893 he published a special Exhibition Number in honor of the opening of the World's Fair, "not only to show the literary, artistic and mechanical resources" of *Scribner's* but also to recognize the contributors to this number as "an important representation not merely of what is ephemeral, but of actual contemporary literature at its best, if in its briefest forms." In soliciting manuscripts he wrote a letter explaining that he expected to use twenty writers from the United States, England, and France, and thirty or forty artists. In most cases he offered payment "at somewhat more than our customary rates, or perhaps you would prefer to name some terms that would be satisfactory to you." Among those included were Robert Blum, Henry Cuyler Bunner, Arthur Burdett Frost, Thomas Hardy, Sarah Orne Jewett, Bret Harte, Henry James, and Robert Louis Stevenson.

For the series "The Great Streets of the World" (May-October 1891) he looked for "articles which used the text of some 'great street' rather for a little sketching of national and local characteristics and types than for mere description." Authors included Francisque Sarcey on the boulevards of Paris, Andrew Lang on Piccadilly, Paul Lindau on Berlin's Unter den Linden, and Richard Harding Davis on Broadway. He paid Henry James $250 for an article on the Grand Canal in Venice. Zazzos, a well-known Venetian artist, was already busy making illustrations.

In October 1893 he began a correspondence with Joel Chandler Harris of the *Atlanta Constitution*, commissioning him to tour the Southeast and Gulf seaboards following several devastating storms. The Red Cross estimated thirty thousand people faced winter without food or shelter. Burlingame was dissatisfied with the sketchy newspaper accounts and thought Harris could tell the story because Harris knew the "Negro, region and civilization." He saw the destruction as a matter of national interest but felt that it was impractical to treat the matter as news and preferred to publish the article after the fact. Burlingame offered to pay all expenses and five hundred dollars for fourteen thousand to fifteen thousand words to be divided into two articles which would be illustrated by Daniel Smith, a sketch artist and photographer who carried a "travelling camera." The main portion of the article would be expeditionary, setting forth conditions and impressions on the Atlantic, where the situation was growing worse daily. In February 1894 "The Sea Island Hurricanes, Part I: The Devastation" appeared, followed in March by "Part II: The Relief."

When the magazine was in its prime, Burlingame went to Europe nearly every summer on Scribners business, which included the solicitation of manuscripts. The amount of money paid for manuscripts was considered competitive by U.S. standards and high by foreign standards. Consequently, writers abroad found the magazine's reputation and Burlingame's proposals attractive. He also assisted in obtaining U.S. rights on works published abroad and worked on international rights of unpublished works. By combining payment on articles with advances and percentages on book rights, Burlingame was able to secure some of the best writers of the time.

After twenty-eight years Burlingame resigned as editor but continued to work as editorial adviser to the publishing house until his death in 1922. From 1904 he was a member of the Scribners board of directors. Burlingame received an honorary A.M. degree from Harvard in 1901 and an honorary Litt.D. from Columbia in 1914. He held membership in the Century Club of New York City. His nickname, used only by his closest friends, was Ned. He died suddenly in 1922 at his home, 440 West End Avenue, New York City, and was buried at Mount Auburn Cemetery, Cambridge, Massachusetts.

Robert Bridges, who had been Burlingame's assistant almost from the beginning of the magazine, assumed the editorship after Burlingame's resignation in 1914. From its founding number to its demise, Burlingame and *Scribner's Magazine* were noted for the writers and artists published. Malcolm Cowley wrote an epitaph in *New Republic*: "It was a distinction to be printed in *Scribner's*, and something of a distinction even to read it." In England, the Sheffield *Daily Telegraph* called it "the most readable of all the magazines. The conductors never fail to achieve one great essential of success–variety." Roger Burlingame wrote of his father, "He was committed, first to his own understanding of literature which had set high levels. But he was committed, too, to a business which must live. He knew that art might please even when it failed, in its entirety, to please him but he refused to let it degrade, whatever the pleasure.... my father wanted what was good printed."

Biography:
Roger Burlingame, *Of Making Many Books: A Hundred Years of Reading, Writing and Publishing* (New York: Scribners, 1946).

References:
Frederick Lewis Allen, "Fifty Years of Scribner's Magazine," *Scribner's Magazine*, 101 (January 1937): 19-24;

John Delaney, "The Archives of Charles Scribner's Sons," *Princeton University Library Chronicle*, 46 (Winter 1985): 137-177;

Robert Grant, "Edward Livermore Burlingame," *Harvard Graduates' Magazine* (March 1923): 368-369.

Papers:
The major collection of Burlingame correspondence and editorial materials is at the archives of Charles Scribner's Sons, housed at the Firestone Library, Princeton University.

C. Chauncey Burr

(1815?-1 May 1883)

Janet E. Ramsey
State University College at Buffalo

MAJOR POSITIONS HELD: Coeditor, *Gavel* (1844-1845); editor, *Nineteenth Century* (1848-1849?), *New York Daily National Democrat* (1849-?), *Nation* (1855), *Old Guard* (1862-1869).

BOOKS: *Discourse on Revivals in the Universalist Church Portland Apr. 5* (Portland, Maine, 1840);
A Review of Rev. Mr. Lane's Lectures Against Universalism (Troy, N.Y., 1844);
Substance of an Extemporaneous Oration, on Irish Repeal, Delivered in Troy, Oct. 23, 1844 (Albany, N.Y.: Munsell & Tanner, 1844);
A Review of Rev. Dr. Berg's Three Discourses in Favor of Capital Punishment (Philadelphia, 1845);
The History of the Union and of the Constitution (Hackensack, N.J.: Dawley, 1862);
Notes on the Constitution of the United States (New York: Feeks, 1864).

OTHER: *Social Melodies: A Collection of Hymns, for the Use of Prayer-meetings, Sabbath-schools, Bible-classes and Families*, edited by Burr (Portland, Maine: Colesworthy, 1841);
George Lippard, *Washington and His Generals*, introductory essay by Burr (Philadelphia: Zieber, 1847);
The Lectures of Lola Montez; with a Full and Complete Autobiography of Her Life, edited by Burr (New York: Rudd & Carleton, 1858);
Abel P. Upshur, ed., *The Federal Government: Its True Nature and Character*, introduction and notes by Burr (New York: Van Evrie, Horton, 1868).

Charles Chauncey Burr was one of the most enigmatic and colorful characters of American magazine journalism. His fame derives from his editing of the Civil War journal the *Old Guard*; Burr was consistently outrageous, argumentative, and controversial. He championed the "political principles which date from the foundation of the Government (that is, 1776)," the Confederacy and the South, and the supremacy of the Caucasian race, all the while urging cessation of the war and violently attacking, from New York City, President Lincoln and "the blundering stupidity and intolerant fanaticism of [his] Administration."

While today many of Burr's views seem outlandish and absurd, his apparent erudition, his dexterity with language and logic, and his fervent emotion still strike the reader of his publications as powerful and persuasive–even if, as Frank L. Mott says, it is hard to imagine Burr's surviving without capital letters and exclamation points. If Burr's anti-Lincoln hysteria seems hopelessly at odds with history's estimation of that president, Burr's championing of the Southern writer Edgar Allan Poe, at a time when his reputation was being severely discredited, makes him one of Poe's earliest defenders.

Those in the North who sympathized with the South during the Civil War were called Copperheads, after the poisonous snake with a copper-colored head that strikes without warning (traitorously); but Burr, in a typically clever twist of words, responded to critics of his politics and his Copperhead journal by claiming that the nickname derived from "the copper head of Liberty on the old coin of the United States."

Burr's editing of the *Old Guard* was not the only controversial element of his life. Like most strong-minded, vociferous political figures, he seems to have created many enemies, who accused him of all sorts of unsavory behavior– accusations which Burr mentions, but fails specifically to address, in the editor's column (called "The Editor's Table") of his magazine. Biographers are forced to puzzle over the reliability of contemporary references to Burr as an "ex-abolitionist," "ex-preacher," and "ex-agent" for a notorious dancer, as well as the story that he deserted a wife and three children in Ohio. Even Burr's title is an enigma, for he is cited as "the Rev. C. Chauncey Burr" on the title page of an 1847 book for which he wrote an introduction,

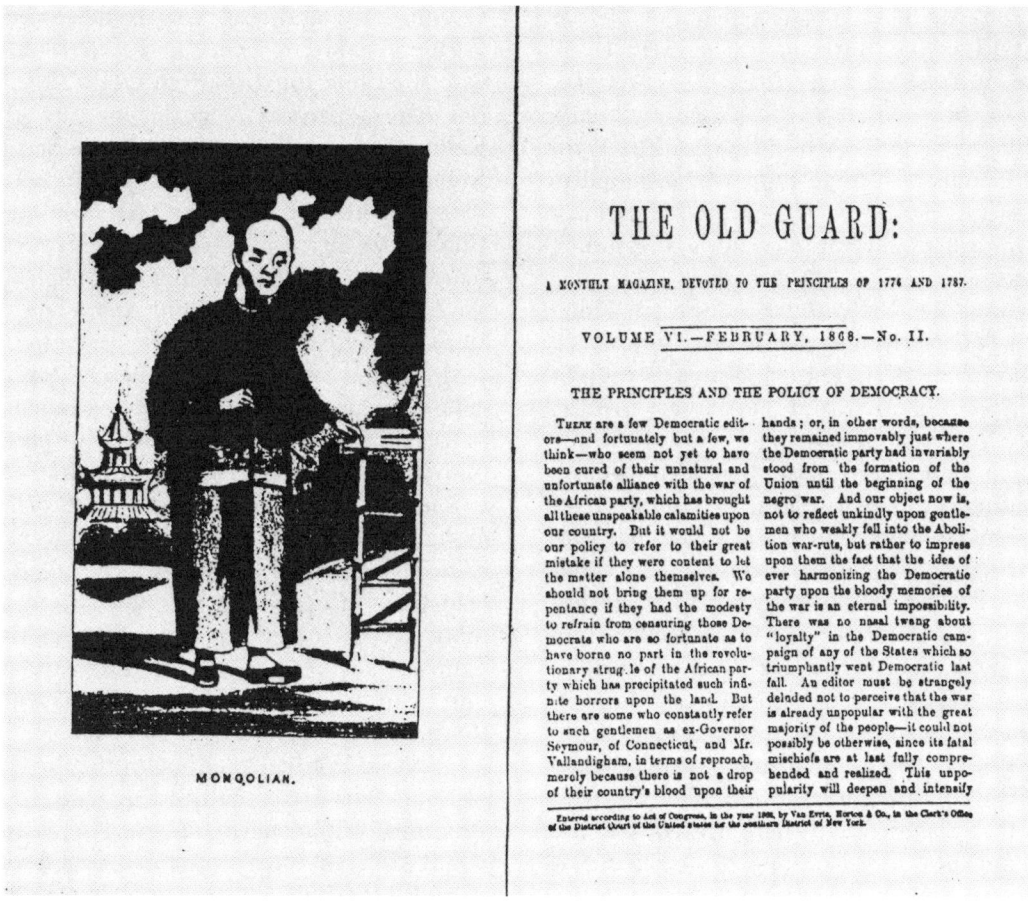

Opening pages from an issue of the pro-Confederacy journal Burr edited from 1862 to 1869. The illustration is related to the series of articles in which he claimed to prove the intellectual superiority of the Caucasian race.

but in a May 1866 column in the *Old Guard*, Burr asserts that, although "we are right, and in these profane times very reverend ... we never belonged to any church." Since his religious affiliation was apparently with the Universalist church, Burr's biographers must assume that he did not define Universalist membership as a typical religious affiliation.

The *New York Times* obituary for Burr (3 May 1883) asserts that he was born in 1815, although at least two sources give 1817 as his year of birth. He apparently was born and grew up in Maine and wrote in one edition of the *Old Guard* (May 1867) that he and "Artemus Ward" (Charles F. Browne) were born in neighboring towns. The *New York Times* obituary says Burr, after graduating from Bowdoin College, taught school in Portland. Historian Joseph George, Jr., however, notes that the Bowdoin College archives contain "no record that Burr ever attended that school." The same scholar produces evidence from the *Maine Universalist Convention Record Book, 1830-1870* that Burr was in Portland in 1840–accused of abusing in print the reputation of a fellow clergyman, although the "dispute was apparently settled amicably." Burr's presence in Portland about this time is supported by the publication in Maine of a text (*Discourse on Revivals in the Universalist Church Portland Apr. 5*, 1840) and a hymnal (*Social Melodies*, 1841).

The *New York Times* obituary asserts that Burr "qualified himself for the Bar" and began practice in Philadelphia. They add that "he afterward went to Troy, where he preached in a Universalist church with marked success." Publication evidence, however, seems to suggest that Burr went to Troy before going to Philadelphia, or at least was frequently a visitor in New York. In 1844 Burr published in Troy, New York, *A Review of Rev. Mr. Lane's Lectures Against Universalism* and in Albany, *Substance of an Extemporaneous Oration, on Irish Repeal, Delivered in Troy, Oct. 23, 1844*. Burr is also listed as editor of the *Gavel: A Monthly Magazine Devoted to Odd-fellowship and Gen-

eral Literature, an 1844 Albany publication. It was not until 1845 that Burr published in Philadelphia the forty-seven-page *Review of Rev. Dr. Berg's Three Discourses in Favor of Capital Punishment*, followed in 1847 by his "Essay on the Writings and Genius of George Lippard," included in Lippard's *Washington and His Generals*. Lippard's text was reprinted several times, always including Burr's essay.

In the late 1840s Burr edited in Philadelphia a "quarterly miscellany" magazine titled the *Nineteenth Century*. Rather than a precursor to Burr's conservative and antiabolitionist *Old Guard*, the *Nineteenth Century* was a reformist magazine, which denounced slavery and the South, and published in its first volume of January 1847 John Greenleaf Whittier's poem "The Reformer." What happened later to change Burr's abolitionist views to his proslavery position is not entirely clear; he describes his transformation in the July 1866 issue of the *Old Guard*. "Born in Maine, we inherited all the ignorance and prejudice of New England on the subject of the negro 'slavery.' But in 1849, when a young man, we traveled extensively through the South, and saw with a glance that 'slavery,' as it there existed, was the happiest and best possible thing for the negro as well as for the white people who have a large population of negroes in their midst–that it was indeed the only thing for the best good of both races. From that time to the present moment we have combatted Abolitionism in every shape which it has assumed. We have fought it, unsparingly, for almost twenty years, and we shall fight it for twenty years to come, if we live so long."

According to the *New York Times* obituary, Burr moved to New York in 1849 and established the *New York Daily National Democrat* (later the *Daily News*), a fact which Burr's writing verifies in the same 1866 *Old Guard* column, where he boasts that in the *New York Daily National Democrat* "we never gave Abolitionism, or its bastard Freesoilism, a single half-hour's rest, so far as our circulation went." According to the *New York Times*, his advocacy of the right of secession "with all the powers of his tongue and pen" led Franklin Pierce to offer Burr the position of minister to the court at Berlin, but he declined.

Burr's change of politics may have influenced his marital status, although not enough material on his personal life exists to know definitely. George writes that "his [Burr's] hostile critics during the Civil War accused him of deserting a wife and three children in Ohio in 1856. Coming east, so the story went, he settled in New York and married again. Later, in 1863, his first wife sued him for divorce in Ohio." *Appleton's Cyclopaedia of American Biography* indicates that Celia Kellum, a New York reformer married to C. B. Kellum and living with him in Cincinnati, "was divorced from him, and in 1851 married Charles Chauncey Burr; was again divorced, and in 1865 married Mr. (William Henry) Burleigh," an antislavery journalist. They add that Celia Burleigh "took an active part in advocating woman suffrage and other reform movements." It is not difficult to imagine a divorce either contributing to or resulting from Burr's intense hostility toward both abolitionism and woman's rights, expressed so bluntly and forcefully later in the *Old Guard*. Certainly his response in the April 1869 issue to a "woman's rights paper" which called him an "old fogie" rings with bitter invective that seems motivated by something more personal than what name-calling would warrant. "From the depth of our heart we pity the husband and children of these strong-tongued and fiery-passioned women, who cannot be content with the angelic duties of home. For the benefit of the State, such fierce Amazons ought never to have children. Nor ought they to have husbands, unless the State should inflict such women upon its criminals as a punishment more to be dreaded than hard work in the State Prison for life."

An enigmatic three-line article in the 26 November 1851 issue of the *New York Times* notes that "The Elmira *Karlon*, a paper edited by C. C. Burr and 'my brother HEMAN,' has ceased to exist, the spirit having departed from it," and a *New York Times* front-page article from 23 September 1853 quotes at considerable length a speech made in New York City by Burr, newly elected chair of the European Democrats, to five thousand people at a demonstration in Metropolitan Hall. Generally, however, Burr's movements throughout the late 1840s and 1850s are impossible to trace precisely. Continuing publication of the *Nineteenth Century* seems to have occurred in New York, and Library of Congress records suggest Burr was there editing a new publication, the *Nation*, in September of 1855. Also during these years, however, according to Wood Grey, Burr was an "abolitionist newspaperman in Ohio" and "served as press-agent for the American tour of the notorious Lola Montez." Why Burr should be involved with a European dancer known for her involvement in Bavarian politics and Parisian duels is unclear; but he is widely recognized as the ghostwriter of her lectures, published in 1858 after her American tour.

In a February 1864 edition of the *Old Guard*, Burr talks of his travels "five years ago" to the "Lakes of Killarney," and in other editions of the magazine describes the portraits at Hampton Court, so it is likely he spent some time in the late 1850s traveling in Europe. Indeed, if anything is clear about Burr, it is that he never stayed very long in a single place.

Whatever his wanderings and intellectual flirtations with such issues as capital punishment, universalism, Revolutionary War legends, and abolitionism, Burr found his creative focus with the beginning of the Civil War and the election of Abraham Lincoln. In 1861 he contributed to the *Day Book* (renamed the *Caucasian* during that year) a pro-Southern New York weekly newspaper. In June 1862 he began publishing the *Old Guard* as a pamphlet of twenty-four pages. The subtitle originally described the monthly journal as "devoted to the principles of 1776 and 1787"; in 1865 the subtitle was changed to "devoted to literature, science and art, and the political principles of 1776 and 1787." The first three numbers of the journal, both edited and published by Burr, were issued under a warning from the federal government concerning treasonable utterances–a fact which made Burr ever after a vehemently staunch defender of freedom of the press. In his habitually melodramatic style Burr recalls in December 1863 that he began publishing the *Old Guard* "under the perpetual threat of the Bastile [*sic*]," and he rejoices that the press is "now liberated from the shackles which the besotted tyrants at Washington had imposed upon it."

At least the first two volumes of the journal (the June 1862 issue was volume 1, but the sequence began again with volume 1 in January 1863) were written, according to his own testimony, almost entirely by Burr. In January of 1863, following problems with mailing, Burr turned over the business of publication of the journal to Van Evrie, Horton and Co., in New York, in order, he said, to concern himself solely with editorial affairs.

During the Civil War years, Burr claimed that his magazine was the only Democratic monthly magazine then issued, and he bitterly attacked the Republicans, calling them the "mongrel," "African," and "negro" party, and labeling their president, Abraham Lincoln, as the tyrant "Abraham I." Burr had a string of objections to Lincoln, many of them to his personal demeanor: "Personally he is a Satyr; socially, a goul [*sic*]," Burr writes in December 1864; he calls Lincoln "a laugher and joker" (March 1867), tells how he played with his toes in the presence of company, and accuses Lincoln of being part Negro. His political objection to Lincoln was primarily that he was a tool and an instrument of the men around him. In an open letter to the president, "Military Coercion," published in the April 1863 *Old Guard*, Burr warns Lincoln that the people believe him to be guided by men who "are not saving the Union, and do not wish to save it"–men who, Burr says, have formed a conspiracy, "a fixed plan and determination to destroy the very form of our Government, and to substitute a centralized despotism in its place." In a March 1867 assessment of "Abraham Lincoln's Place in History," Burr categorizes Lincoln as a "tool rather than the plotter of wrong," who was basically "only the embodiment of the souls of Garrison and Sumner, and Wade and Thaddeus Stevens."

Through the war years Burr's journal continually harangued Lincoln for his suspension of habeas corpus and for his issuing the Emancipation Proclamation, which Burr saw as Lincoln's reversal of his own judgment on slavery in order to appease his political party and win the war. To Burr, Lincoln's efforts to restore the Union were nothing short of a violation of his oath of office, for Burr strongly believed that the intention of the framers of the Constitution was that states should have the right to secede. Lincoln's oath to uphold the Constitution meant that the president should uphold the right of any state to withdraw from the Union. "The Constitution must be the President's guide in dealing with rebellion," Burr writes in April 1863. "If he allows himself to be pushed outside of that, does he not become a rebel too? There is no necessity binding him but the Constitution and the laws. If he attempts more he is an unnecessary usurper and tyrant."

So strongly did he believe in the constitutional right of the states to join or leave the Union, that Burr delivered in 1862 a series of three lectures on "The History of the Union and the Constitution," which were then published and reprinted in several editions from 1862 to 1866. He repeated essentially his arguments in the April 1863 *Old Guard*: "While the framers of the Constitution refused to clothe the Federal Government with any power to make war upon a State, they were careful to make it its duty to assist the State authorities in suppressing insurrections within their jurisdiction, if duly called

Cover for a book ghostwritten by Burr

upon. Beyond this the General Government cannot go without violating the Constitution."

As the war progressed, Burr became more vitriolic in his accusations against the president, convinced that his reelection would mean the ruin of the country. In a New Jersey speech which Burr delivered the day before the election and subsequently published in the December 1864 *Old Guard*, he condemns Lincoln for creating a bureaucratic corruption that has "made places for five hundred thousand more office-holders than this government ever knew before," as well as an indebtedness of up to eighty percent of "all the real and personal property of the North." Not stopping there, however, he reckons that Lincoln "has sacrificed a life" for "every man that voted for him in 1860" and accuses him of sending "a corpse into almost every family in the land." In short, Lincoln was responsible for the demise of American civilization: "Public virtue and private honor have fallen together under his de-

moralizing sway. American civilization itself lies besmeared with blood and filth, under his feet."

Burr's despair at Lincoln's reelection was summed up by his April 1865 description of the weather of the Inaugural Day: "the bleakest, wettest, and altogether the most disagreeable day of the whole year. As if nature shuddered at the calamity of a second inauguration of Abraham Lincoln, the heavens above wept and the earth beneath groaned under depths of filth. For a short time towards noon, the clouds lifted a little, but, at the precise hour of the inauguration, they settled down again with a density and bleakness truly terrible. It would seem that God's own hand had drawn a wet pall over the face of the land, at the moment when the perjured usurper was to go through the daring mockery of again taking an oath to support a Constitution he is striving to destroy."

Lincoln's assassination brought some mitigation of Burr's hostility; he was able to write in Lincoln's death notice in the June 1865 *Old Guard* that "it is generally believed that he [Lincoln] had finally settled upon a policy which would speedily end our civil strife, and find rest to our bleeding land." Nonetheless, Burr's final assessment of Lincoln in the March 1867 *Old Guard* was uncompromisingly harsh–"Quick and keen in all the lower attributes, such as cunning, perception, and imitation, but obtuse in the regions of judgment, reflection and conscience"–and in November of the same year, Burr attacked not only husband, but wife: "Mrs. Lincoln was a worthy enough companion of her husband. They were a vulgar pair; if we speak of culture and refinement, an indecent pair."

But if Burr, in the *Old Guard*, saw Lincoln as a figure he could compare to Maximilien Robespierre, he found all abolitionists equally loathsome. Burr simply could not comprehend why America should tear itself in two over what he believed was the naive, "naturally ignorant" European notion that all races were "all the same beings, save in color." In the March 1865 *Old Guard* he asks his readers: "In the impious and monstrous attempt to practice the European theory of a single race, shall we strive to 'abolish' the distinctions that separate us from these races, and ruin our republican institutions, and indeed debauch and destroy American civilization for centuries?" and he answers himself: "but we cannot destroy ourselves if we would and shall therefore finally come back to common sense, and restore civilization south of us, instead of destroying it in our midst."

According to the *New York Times* obituary, Burr styled himself as an expert in ethnology, and insisted the Negro "had never been destined by nature for a 'man and a brother.' " The views Burr espouses in the *Old Guard* seem, in the light of the twentieth century, simple racism, but he expresses his ideas as seriously and passionately as the best scientific theory of his time. Mott makes it clear that the "controversy over the theory of the unity of mankind" was by no means settled during the Civil War period; in fact, according to Mott, the question was debated so enthusiastically and endlessly in publications of that time, that it was nearly "thrashed threadbare" with "denial of the descent of man from one parent stock by Professors J. C. Nott and Louis Agassiz, replies on the basis of the Scripture, and rejoinders galore in *De Bow's*, the *North American Review*, *Putnam's*, and other periodicals."

Burr's "studies" of the races of man, he tells his readers in March 1865 (and again in December 1869), were submitted ten years earlier to the Smithsonian Institution for publication, but unfortunately for the general well-being of the country, the institution preferred to publish a work on snakes. Nonetheless, in February 1868 Burr presents a hierarchal theory of race in the *Old Guard*, in a series dealing with the "Caucasian," "Mongolian," "Oceanic (Malay)," "Indian," "Equimaux," and "Negro"–the Negro representing the lowest of that order, and the Caucasian the highest. Burr is quite sanguine with the assertion that the white race is superior to all others, even when it means arguing, for example, that the Mongolian race has no real history or culture: "it is sufficient to say that not only is there no such thing as Chinese history proper, but in the nature and necessity of things there can be none." The presence of language and culture in ancient races shows only that "many and continuous invasions [of Caucasians] must have occurred."

For Burr, "all races . . . save our own, are adapted to certain centres of existence, and left to their tendencies and capabilities, they never transcend climatic and industrial laws." The Negro, he believed, was climatically and temperamentally adjusted to being a slave in the South, as other races were created by God to exist in their particular environments, performing preordained types of labor. Southerners were wise enough to know this truth; abolitionists were not. Abolitionists were "fanatics" who "have been teaching the Northern people to despise the South," Burr writes in an *Old Guard* open letter to the Reverend Henry Ward Beecher in June 1863. Burr had no hesitation in translating current polygenetic theories into his own social and political diatribe, as represented typically in a September 1866 article on the "Apelike Tribes of Men": "we do not deny that the negro is a man, but he is the lowest of the human species, as the great ape is the highest of the brute creation. And he is so low in the human scale that he can lay no claims to a companionship, on any terms of equality, with the white family of mankind."

In later editions of the *Old Guard* after the war ended, Burr continued his antiabolitionist, pro-Confederacy campaigns, decorating his 1866 numbers with steel-plate portraits of Robert E. Lee, Thomas ("Stonewall") Jackson, Wade Hampton, J. E. B. Stuart, and eight other Southern generals. During that time the size of the magazine was enlarged and literary subjects included. Burr added more poetry (there had always been a number of his own poems), as well as serial novels by William Gilmore Simms and Thomas Dunn English; he included as well "Our Book Table," an editorial column of book reviews. Jay B. Hubbell writes that in the late 1860s the *Old Guard* was almost "the only magazine in the North that would print anything written by a Southerner unless he was prepared to admit that the North was right on all controversial issues." Burr published Paul Hamilton Hayne, John Esten Cooke, Helen Rich, John R. Thompson, and James W. Wall. Publisher J. H. Van Evrie also contributed to the magazine.

Most intriguing of Burr's literary articles were those that he apparently wrote concerning Edgar Allan Poe. One, appearing in January 1866 and entitled "Poe and Coleridge," is interesting because it relates firsthand the experience of witnessing Poe lecture. The second defends Poe against a critical article by Edmund Clarence Stedman. The third and most significant *Old Guard* article disputes negative accounts of Poe's life told by his biographer Dr. R. W. Griswold, using as evidence a letter to Burr by Sarah Helen Whitman, once engaged to Poe, and another letter by Dr. John H. B. Latrobe, one of three judges in an 1883 Baltimore *Saturday Visiter* [sic] contest. Poe had won a prize, but his enemies suggested he won merely because he had the most artistic and legible handwriting. In all three articles, Burr is effusive in his praise of Poe, claiming that "we now enter the name of . . .

Edgar Allan Poe, upon our fameroll as that of the greatest genius to whom America has given birth–as that of a critic, a philosopher, and a poet . . . and, besides, as a gentleman." If imitation indicates sincere praise, Burr's imitation of Poe's poem "The Raven" reveals the editor's enthusiasm for the genius of the poet's style, which Burr quite clearly duplicates (without assigning specific credit) in "The Republican Raven," a poem he declares was "written Nov. 7th, 1861, amid the shoutings of the Republicans over their political victory."

John Tebbel writes that the *Old Guard* was a magazine that "choked to death on its own passion," but it seems more accurate to say that the *Old Guard* died more slowly as the end of the war changed the focus of the journal and its editor from political matters to literary and scientific ones. There is no indisputable indication why the *Old Guard* eventually failed, but its many yearlong serializations of various novels and essays create a repetitiveness in later volumes; the content becomes fairly predictable.

Burr ended his editorship of the magazine after December 1869, saying simply in that issue that he was going to a "new and more extended field of editorial duties." He hastened to reassure his readers that "it must not be imagined that we have grown weary of the advocacy of those grand foundation doctrines of State Sovereignty and White Supremacy on which the Republic was reared." Library of Congress records, however, indicate no later publications under Burr's name except an 1868 introduction and notes to a text on the Constitution edited by Abel Parker Upshur. Burr's farewell to his readers seems to indicate that he expected Van Evrie and Horton to continue publishing the *Old Guard*, but when Thomas Dunn English became editor in January 1870, publication was by English and Company in New York. Under English's editorship, the magazine lasted one year.

Burr's activities after 1869 remain virtually unknown. The *New York Times* obituary says he died in 1883 at his home in West Hoboken Heights, New Jersey. Two or three days before his death, the paper relates, "he was attacked by a congestion to the brain."

In many ways it is difficult to assess the significance of Burr's life and the impact of his magazine. Mott, while stressing Burr's sincerity, argues that "the whole file [of the *Old Guard*] displays too much ill-nature to win sympathy for its cause." Mott assumes that the publication's primary aim was to enlist new believers, but rather it may have been to encourage and support existing believers in Burr's theories and politics. Burr frequently printed letters from sympathizers, particularly Southerners, who declared their appreciation for the support of such a publication and their gratitude to its editor for encouraging them to carry on with their minority views.

Burr seemed to enjoy both reprinting critical comments which his adversaries said about him and collecting tidbits of opposition editorial argument from a variety of far-flung publications. In one page alone of the October 1865 "The Editor's Table" in the *Old Guard*, Burr cites the remarks of five opposition editors–four of whom he identifies as being from Chicago, San Jose, Lancaster, and Indiana. Such widespread interest in political commentary would seem to indicate Burr's commitment to influencing contemporary public opinion, but Burr's general refusal to name specific editors or publications suggests that he was not in fact interested in engaging with any of them in continuing argument which would lead to consensus and resolution. Mott's term "ill-nature" seems to describe appropriately the manner in which Burr deflected all the criticism he printed; Burr frequently dismissed opposition arguments with an ad hominem attack or a non sequitur. The following flippant response is illustrative:

> The Lancaster *Intelligencer* has a pungent editorial, entitled "The Republican Party Gone Up!" Has not our contemporary mistaken the direction in which that party has gone? We confess that we should never look after such sinners in that direction.

It may have been this sort of sneering together at a common enemy that won readers for Burr's magazine among those who already shared his political and racial views. As a spokesman for this outvoted but undaunted segment of the Northern population, Burr might perhaps be easily dismissed as a somewhat egotistical, pompous extremist, who momentarily earned a select readership because he voiced the baser fears and prejudices of a threatening, turbulent time.

It would be wrong, however, to dismiss Burr quite so readily. In his outspoken, direct way, he persisted in raising at least a few critical questions which have subsequently continued to provoke scholars and historians: What did the framers of the Constitution intend regarding states' rights? When does national security make it necessary to suspend the writ of habeas corpus and freedom of the press? What was Lincoln's true motivation in proclaiming emancipation? What were Northerners fighting for—abolition or the Union? Was keeping the South in the Union ever worth dying for?

At his worst, Burr may have been a flim-flam journalist, one who capitalized on the issues and emotions of his times in order to have the power to needle presidents and influence politics. At his best, however, Burr asked some unpopular but common-sense questions that were appropriate to the inflated warmongering on both sides of the Mason-Dixon line. In their essential sympathy for the dignity and humanity of the people of the South, Burr and his enemy Lincoln would probably equally agree with the ideas expressed in the March 1863 article in the *Old Guard* on "The Rights and Wrongs of Secession":

> Many of us have fathers, and brothers, and sisters, and all of us have friends there [in the South]–shall we believe that all these have suddenly become totally depraved?–Does not reason rather tell us that they are men like ourselves, and that it is only a difference of locality, and the natural attachment to the scenes and institutions of home which have separated us? . . . Why have we made his beautiful fields a Golgotha? Why have we filled all his blooming valleys with blood?

References:

Joseph George, Jr., " 'Abraham Africanus I': President Lincoln Through the Eyes of a Copperhead Editor," *Civil War History*, 14 (September 1968): 226-239;

Wood Grey, *The Hidden Way: The Story of the Copperheads* (New York, 1942);

Jay B. Hubbell, "Charles Chauncey Burr: Friend of Poe," *PMLA*, 69 (September 1954): 833-840;

Charles M. Knapp, *New Jersey Politics During the Period of the Civil War and Reconstruction* (Geneva, N.Y., 1924);

Frank Luther Mott, "*The Old Guard*," in his *A History of American Magazines, 1850-1865* (Cambridge: Harvard University Press, 1938), pp. 137-140, 544-546;

William Warren Rogers, "C. Chauncey Burr and *The Old Guard*," *Proceedings of the New Jersey Historical Society*, 73 (July 1955): 170;

John Tebbel, *The American Magazine: A Compact History* (New York: Hawthorn, 1968), p. 97.

William Conant Church
(11 August 1836-23 May 1917)

and

Francis Pharcellus Church
(22 February 1839-11 April 1906)

Ralph Frasca
University of Iowa

William Conant Church

MAJOR POSITIONS HELD: Assistant editor, *New-York Chronicle* (1855-1860); editor, *New York Sun* (1860-1861); war correspondent, *New York Evening Post* (1861-1862), *New York Sun* (1862), *New-York Times* (1862); coeditor and copublisher (1863-1865), editor and copublisher (1865-1917), *Army and Navy Journal*; copublisher (1866-1868), coeditor (1866-1878), *Galaxy*; editor and copublisher, *Internal Revenue Record and Customs Journal* (1870-1895).

BOOKS: *The Life of John Ericsson*, 2 volumes (New York: Scribners, 1890; London: Low, 1890);
Ulysses S. Grant and the Period of National Preservation and Reconstruction (New York & London: Putnam's, 1897);
Reconstruction (New York & London: Putnam's, 1897);
"Militarism" and "The Emperor": Two Articles Reprinted from the American Army and Navy Journal and from the New York Times (Chicago: Germanistic Society of Chicago, 1914?).

OTHER: *Retirements in the Military Services of the United States, 1903-1946*, compiled by Church (New York: Army and Navy Journal, 1903).

Francis Pharcellus Church

MAJOR POSITIONS HELD: Assistant editor, *New-York Chronicle* (1860-1862); war correspondent, *New-York Times* (1862); coeditor and copublisher (1863-1865), copublisher (1863-1874), *Army and Navy Journal*; coeditor and copublisher, *Galaxy* (1866-1868); coeditor, *Galaxy* (1868-1878); copublisher, *Internal Revenue Record and Customs Journal* (1870-1895); editor, *New York Sun* (1874-1906).

Opening page from an issue of the literary magazine founded by William C. and Francis P. Church

BOOK: *Is There a Santa Claus?* (Boston: Privately printed, 1921; enlarged edition, New York: Grosset & Dunlap, 1934).

Lt. Col. William Conant Church and his younger brother Francis Pharcellus (Frank) Church–whose immortal editorial containing the line "Yes, Virginia, there is a Santa Claus" has stirred children and adults since it appeared in the *New York Sun* in 1897–edited and published the *Army and Navy Journal* and the *Internal Revenue Record and Customs Journal*. Their major contribution to literature, however, was the *Galaxy*, founded in 1866 as a New York counterpart to Boston's *Atlantic Monthly*. Virtually ignoring the luminaries of the New England literary set, the *Galaxy* printed history, fiction, science, and topical comment by some of the most prominent authors of the day.

The Church brothers seemed an unlikely duo to hold the editorial reins of a literary magazine. They were born in Rochester, New York, in 1836 and 1839 to the Baptist minister Pharcellus Church and Chara Emily Conant Church. They received little schooling in literature or the arts, being educated with emphases on mathematics and foreign languages. William attended the Rochester Collegiate Institute and Boston's Mayhew School and Boston Latin School, while Francis studied at Charles Anthon's Latin School in New York.

William terminated his formal education at age fifteen to support his mother and four siblings when his father fell ill. Four years later he joined the *New-York Chronicle*, a weekly religious newspaper established on 18 December 1854 by his father and J. S. Backus. William acquired twenty-five percent interest in the newspaper on Christmas Day 1855 by paying Backus $610 and turning over a deed to forty acres of land. William assisted his father in editing and publishing the newspaper for five years before departing for the *New York Sun* and its short-lived conversion to religious journalism.

Since its 1833 inception under Benjamin Day, the *Sun* had dwelt on the scandalous and the sensational. That policy changed in August 1860 when the pietistic newspaperman W. C. Conant and the wealthy Episcopal minister Archibald Morrison purchased the paper from Moses Beach for $100,000 and hired William Church as a figurehead editor and publisher. In reality Conant functioned as editor and publisher, but desiring anonymity, he cast Church in the dual role; Church actually served as Conant's assistant.

The twenty-four-year-old Church had made the leap from serving as his father's assistant on a small religious weekly to the prominent and powerful–in title, at least–helm of a major metropolitan daily. His enjoyment of his new position, however, quickly paled before the reality of Conant's control. In Church's opinion, Conant was moving too fast in converting the *Sun* from sensationalism to religious fervor. Church was ordered to discard advertisements for liquor, cigars, and theater productions and at the same time to enlarge the newspaper, giving chief prominence to religious news. Although he attempted to show Conant and Morrison that this plan would result in financial disaster, they remained unswerving in their course. Church, Conant, and Morrison soon decided that it would be best for all concerned if the former left New York and toured Europe as a foreign correspondent while earning his full salary of four thousand dollars for the remainder of his contract. He set sail for England on 11 December 1860. While he was abroad, his prophecy of doom came true. Within a year, the proprietors defaulted on their payments and lost control of the *Sun* to its former owner, Beach.

Church returned from Europe in July 1861 and in the next fifteen months served as a Civil War correspondent for three New York newspapers–the *Evening Post*, the *Sun*, and the *New York Times*. His strong belief in the righteousness of the North's cause prompted him to ask Gen. Silas Casey for a military commission, and Casey appointed him captain of volunteers and provisional brigades on 4 October 1862. He participated in the battles of Fair Oaks and Williamsburg, in the latter sustaining a slight injury. After his recuperation he was promoted to major and then to lieutenant colonel of volunteers. On 18 June 1863 he resigned his commission to participate in the founding of the *Army and Navy Journal*. The same year he married Mary Elizabeth Metcalf of Baltimore.

Meanwhile, Francis Church graduated with honors in 1859 from Columbia College (later Columbia University). He studied law briefly in the office of New York judge Hooper C. Van Vorst, then joined his father and William at the *New-York Chronicle*. He became his father's chief assistant when William went to the *Sun*. In 1862 he again followed his brother's lead and commenced part-time work as a war correspondent for the *New-York Times*, leaving in 1863 to join William at the *Army and Navy Journal*.

The *Army and Navy Journal* was established by a group of New York men who were alarmed at the growing criticism of the federal government by newspaper men and pamphleteers and at what they felt was the resulting posture of disloyalty taken by many in the North during the Civil War. The group, which called itself the Loyal Publication Society, founded the *Army and Navy Journal* in the belief that "tracts, papers and journals of unquestionable loyalty" were needed to counter "the enemies of the Government and the advocates of a disgraceful PEACE." They desired to establish a publication which would "commend itself to the public and to the Army and Navy, and become a necessity in every tent, barrack, hospital and wardroom," according to the founders' announcement in the journal's first issue.

William Church, one of the most eager members of the Loyal Publication Society, became editor and quickly plotted the course which was to make the *Army and Navy Journal* the foremost unofficial spokesman for the United States militia. The first issue appeared on 29 August 1863, billing itself as "a weekly newspaper, devoted to the interests of the Army and Navy, and to the dissemination of correct military information." In the first issue of the second year, Church noted that he had "labored to make the journal worthy of the pride of military men and truly representative of the honor and dignity of the profession of arms."

Francis Church shared editorial and publishing responsibilities for the first two years of the journal's existence; afterward he devoted most of his time to other pursuits. William Church remained as the editor of the *Army and Navy Journal* until his death in 1917.

With the *Army and Navy Journal* growing in circulation and prestige, the brothers took on a new challenge in 1866 when they started the *Galaxy*, a literary magazine which presented itself as New York's answer to Boston's *Atlantic Monthly*. The New York poet and literary critic Edmund Clarence Stedman was one of the magazine's earliest and most ardent supporters. Spurred by his friend Henry A. Blood's exhortation "If Boston can support a literary journal cannot New York? Your wealthy men must be made to feel that the literary honor of the great city is at stake," Stedman urged his cohorts in the intelligentsia to contribute to the new publication. Stedman wrote that the Church brothers "are doing their bravest to establish a New York magazine, and ought to be helped and encouraged by New York authors."

During the magazine's life more than six hundred writers contributed to it; it might be said that the *Galaxy* was the chief repository in the post-Civil War years for the work of literary figures outside of New England. Such old-guard New England authors as Ralph Waldo Emerson, Henry Wadsworth Longfellow, John Greenleaf Whittier, Oliver Wendell Holmes, Harriet Beecher Stowe, Edward Everett Hale, and James Russell Lowell were seldom represented in the pages of the *Galaxy*.

The magazine made its debut on 1 May 1866 with the subtitle *An Illustrated Magazine of Entertaining Reading*. In its first year it was published as a fortnightly, afterward as a monthly. The Church brothers served as editors and publishers during the first two years but relinquished the role of publisher in 1868 to Sheldon and Company. The Churches continued as editors throughout the magazine's life, with Francis doing most of the editorial work.

Born within a few years of the *Galaxy* were *Lippincott's Magazine* (1868) and *Scribner's Monthly* (1870). The competition among these magazines for the most prominent contributors became as fierce as the competition for subscribers. The *Galaxy* fared admirably, attracting such writers as Walt Whitman, Henry James, Eugene Benson, Justin McCarthy, Bret Harte, Richard Harding Davis, and Charles Astor Bristed. The Church brothers borrowed George E. Pond from the *Army and Navy Journal* staff to write an editorial column of primarily political matter titled "Drift-Wood." Prof. E. L. Youmans edited the "Scientific Miscellany" department for four years before being replaced by John Adams Church, the editors' younger brother, who had taught mineralogy at the Columbia School of Mines and edited the *Engineering and Mining Journal*. Chef Pierre Blot wrote a column on the art of dining. Former Secretary of the Navy Gideon Welles wrote several series about Abraham Lincoln's role in the Civil War. Richard Grant White was perhaps the most prolific contributor, producing the bulk of the "Nebulae," the magazine's editorial section, as well as writing extensively about language, culture, and manners in America, particularly in New York. The *Nation* commented that White "really talks as much about 'cultivation' as if he were not in full possession of it." Mark Twain's ten-page "Memoranda" column ran only from May 1870 until March 1871 but was probably the most popular feature the magazine ever contained. Twain provided liberal doses of his extravagant style of humor in such sketches as "How I Edited an Agricultural Paper," "Burlesque Map of Paris," "To Raise Poultry," and a farcical review of his own book *The Innocents Abroad* (1869). Twain abandoned the column because of the stress produced by the deaths of his father-in-law and a family friend and the illnesses of his wife and newborn son.

During Twain's brief association with the *Galaxy* the magazine attained its highest circulation, about twenty-three thousand in early 1871. Other features running in the magazine at that time included such serial stories as Justin McCarthy's "Lady Judith," Col. J. W. DeForest's "Overland," and Thurlow Weed's autobiography. Serials formed an integral part of the magazine's content. Noting the first birthday of the *Galaxy*, the *Nation* commented: "Hitherto its strong point has apparently been its serial stories, which have generally been of more than average goodness" and christened the magazine "the second-best literary magazine in the country," presumably trailing the *Atlantic Monthly*. Among the most popular serials printed in the *Galaxy* were Anthony Trollope's "Claverings," "The Eustace Diamonds," and "An Editor's Tales"; H. H. Boyesen's "A Norseman's Pilgrimage"; Rebecca Harding Davis's "Waiting for the Verdict"; and Gen. George Custer's "Life on the Plains," which was cut short by Custer's death at the Little Bighorn.

The *Galaxy* was usually 144 pages long. For the first six years it bore illustrations which varied widely in quality, but it carried none after March 1872. During its life it was praised as a landmark of literature. The *New York Graphic* commented on the *Galaxy*: "It is more in accordance with the spirit and feelings of the reading public of America than any other magazine that is published." Critical acclaim, however, could not sustain the *Galaxy*. Insufficient advertising revenue, competition from the growing number of literary magazines, and the gradual movement of the *Atlantic Monthly* away from sectionalism caused the demise of the *Galaxy* in 1878. From its peak in 1871 circulation plummeted to about seven thousand during its final year.

After the January issue was printed, the principals of the *Galaxy* sold its subscriber list to the *Atlantic Monthly*. In welcoming readers of the *Galaxy* in the February issue, the *Atlantic Monthly* commented that the publications "more than any other two American magazines have appealed to kindred tastes." The editorial note claimed that "the freshness, the brightness, the alertness, that gave tone to 'The Galaxy' will not cease, we hope, in the alliance which makes 'The Galaxy' and 'The Atlantic' one." It added that "we shall aim to perpetuate the finest characteristics of a magazine which for eleven years has been a presence in our periodical literature so distinctly agreeable and useful that it could not wholly pass away without great public regret."

With the end of the *Galaxy*, William and Frank Church, by this time forty-one and thirty-nine years old, respectively, were left with two magazines: the *Army and Navy Journal*, an assured success virtually devoid of competition and with a weekly circulation of between three thousand and thirty-five hundred; and the *Internal Revenue Record and Customs Journal*, a small trade publication they had started in 1870. Although the circulation of the latter magazine never exceeded one thousand, it was a profitable venture for the brothers. As with the *Army and Navy Journal*, William was the editor and shared publishing and ownership responsibilities with Frank.

Acting on his belief in the need for increased reliance on the rifle in the nation's military defense, William Church used the *Army and Navy Journal* to campaign for improved rifle training and the establishment of rifle ranges. With Capt. George W. Wingate, a member of the New York National Guard whom Church enlisted to write a series of six articles on rifle practice for the journal, Church founded the National Rifle Association (NRA) in 1871. Gen. Ambrose Burnside was elected the group's first president but failed to attend any meetings. Church took over as acting head and then became the organization's second president. With Church and the *Army and Navy Journal* leading the way, the NRA was ultimately successful in introducing systematic rifle instruction to the United States Army and the National Guard.

While serving as editor of the literary magazine, Frank had written editorials for several newspapers and had become a part-time staff member of the *New York Sun* in 1874. When the *Galaxy* folded he became a full-time editor and editorial writer at the *Sun*. *Sun* editor in chief Edward P. Mitchell recalled in his memoirs a Church editorial discussing other newspapers in New York, "We Survey Our Esteemed Contemporaries," as "displaying in pleasant conversational tone a knowledge of journalistic history and an insight into journalistic character that could hardly be expected of any but a major figure in the profession."

During his thirty-two years at the *Sun* Church wrote thousands of editorials. All but one have since been forgotten. That piece was printed on 21 September 1897 and titled "Is There a Santa Claus?" Mitchell recalled handing Church a letter from an eight-year-old girl named Virginia O'Hanlon, who wrote, "Please tell me the truth, is there a Santa Claus?" Her friends had told her that there was not. Church initially balked at Mitchell's suggestion of writing a reply but eventually acceded. Mitchell remembered: "He took the letter and turned with an air of resignation to his desk. In a short time he had produced the article which has probably been reprinted ... as the classic expression of Christmas sentiment, more millions of times than any other newspaper article ever written by any newspaperwriter in any language." Church had written in part: "Virginia, your little friends are wrong. They have been affected by the skepticism of a skeptical age. They do not believe except they see.... Yes, Virginia, there is a Santa Claus. He exists as certainly as love and generosity and devotion exist.... No Santa Claus! Thank God! he lives, and he lives forever. A thousand years from now, Virginia, nay, ten times ten thousand years from now, he will continue to make glad the heart of childhood."

William also had the opportunity to write lasting encomiums, although his subjects were not as universally adored. Shortly before naval engineer John Ericsson died in 1889, he commissioned his longtime friend Church to write his biography. Published in 1890, Church's eulogistic two-volume work remains the definitive source on the builder of the Civil War ironclad *Monitor*. Seven years later Church wrote a biography of his personal hero and ardent *Army and Navy Journal* patron, Ulysses S. Grant.

Both brothers were active in various societies until their deaths. Frank was a member of the Sons of the Revolution, the National Sculptor Society, and the Century Club. He died on 11 April 1906. William was a life member and director of the New York Zoological Society, a fellow in perpetuity of the Metropolitan Museum of Art, and a member of the executive committee of the National Security League. He died on 23 May 1917.

The *New York Times* honored William Church as "among the foremost journalists" of the era. Edward P. Mitchell wrote of Frank Church that "there was never a more delightful associate. Quick of perception of the interesting in every phase of human activity except politics (for which he cared little, bless his soul!), there was in his features something of that gentlemanly pugnacity ... a latent aggressiveness that marred neither the delicacy of his fancy nor the warmth of his sympathies."

References:

Donald N. Bigelow, "A 'Journal of Unquestionable Loyalty' Is Founded To Meet the Nation's Needs," *Army Navy Air Force Journal and Register*, 100 (31 August 1963): 42, 44, 46;

Bigelow, *William Conant Church and The Army and Navy Journal* (New York: AMS Press, 1968);

"The Magazines for June," *Nation*, 4 (30 May 1867): 432-433;

Edward P. Mitchell, *Memoirs of an Editor* (New York: Scribners, 1924): 42, 111, 115, 187, 214, 361;

"The New Magazine," *Nation*, 2 (26 April 1866): 534-535;

Albert Bigelow Paine, *Mark Twain: A Biography*, 3 volumes (New York & London: Harper, 1912), I: p. 347;

Laura Stedman and George M. Gould, *The Life and Letters of Edmund Clarence Stedman*, 2 volumes (New York: Moffat, Yard, 1910), I: pp. 207, 349, 380, 413;

"To Old Friends and New," *Atlantic Monthly*, 41 (March 1878): 272.

Papers:

Papers of William Conant Church are at the Library of Congress and the New York Public Library.

Davis Wasgatt Clark

(25 February 1812-23 May 1871)

Kathleen L. Endres
Bowling Green State University

MAJOR POSITION HELD: Editor, *Ladies' Repository* (1853-1864).

BOOKS: *Elements of Algebra: Embracing also the Theory and Application of Logarithms; Together with an Appendix, Containing Infinite Series, the General Theory of Equations, and the Most Approved Methods of Resolving the Higher Equations* (New York: Harper, 1843);
Mental Discipline, with Reference to the Acquisition and Communication of Knowledge, and to Education Generally; to Which is Appended a Topical Course of Theological Study (New York: Lane & Tippett, 1847);
Life and Times of Rev. Elijah Hedding (New York: Carlton & Phillips, 1855);
Sermons (Cincinnati: Poe & Hitchcock, 1856);
Portraits of Celebrated Women, with Brief Biographies (Cincinnati: 1863);
Man All Immortal; or, The Nature and Destination of Man as Taught by Reason and Revelation (Cincinnati: Poe & Hitchcock, 1864);
Sermons, by Rev. D. W. Clark . . . First Series (Cincinnati: Poe & Hitchcock, 1868);
The Ingham Lectures: A Course of Lectures on the Evidences of Natural and Revealed Religion; Delivered before the Ohio Wesleyan University, Delaware, Ohio (Cleveland: Ingham, Clarke/New York: Nelson & Phillips, 1872).

OTHER: *Death-Bed Scenes; or, Dying with and Without Religion: Designed to Illustrate the Truth and Power of Christianity*, edited by Clark (New York: Lane & Scott, 1851);
Historical Sketches; or, Narratives of Striking Events in the Course of Human Affairs, edited by Clark (Cincinnati: Swormstedt & Poe, 1856);
John Hannah and Frederick J. Jobson, *The Method of Man's Reconciliation with God; and, The Fullness of Christian Privilege: Two Sermons Preached before the General Conference of the Methodist Episcopal Church, United States of America, May 14, 1856*, edited by Clark (Cincinnati: Swormstedt & Poe, 1857);
Joseph M. Trimble, *Memoirs of Mrs. Jane Trimble: A Tribute of Affection from Her Grandson*, introduction by Clark (Cincinnati: Methodist Book Concern, 1861).

The Reverend Davis Wasgatt Clark was neither the first nor the last editor of the Methodist Episcopal *Ladies' Repository*. Yet, by virtue of his ten-year tenure with the magazine, he became the most pivotal to its success. Drawing on what he sensed nineteenth-century churchwomen wanted, Clark brought many innovations to the publication. As a result the *Ladies' Repository* became a monthly for the whole family and the second largest periodical issued by the Methodist church in the United States.

Neither Clark's involvement in journalism nor his career as a Methodist minister had been assured by his upbringing. He was born on Mount Desert Island, Maine, on 25 February 1812. His parents, John and Sarah Clark, were of Massachusetts stock. Clark was named after his maternal grandfather, Davis Wasgatt, who had been a Revolutionary soldier, a town leader on the island, and a clerk with the Congregational church.

But Wasgatt did not retain his ties to Congregationalism. Both he and the Clarks were soon swayed by an itinerant Freewill Baptist preacher and, like many others on the island, converted in 1815.

Because no Baptist church existed on the island, John and Sarah Clark gave their son his early religious training at home. Clark's home life was important in other regards as well. His fondness for books and learning was apparently nurtured at home, because the island educational system was only rudimentary. Clark attended school only two to three months a year. The remainder of his education was provided at home. The Clarks, farmers by occupation and better educated than many on the island, made books available to their son.

For much of his youth Clark aspired to be a seaman, the trade of many on his island home.

But at sixteen, he gave up that idea and planned for a career in the ministry. In 1828 Davis Wasgatt Clark and his mother joined the new Methodist Episcopal Church on Mount Desert. The next year he started on a course leading to the ministry by becoming a teacher in his native town. In 1831 Clark left for the seminary, returning to Mount Desert in the winter to teach school. By 1834 Clark entered Wesleyan University, where he was graduated with honors two years later. A few weeks later he became a mathematics teacher at Amenia Seminary, Dutchess County, New York, where he married and began contributing to a Methodist newspaper.

While he enjoyed his time at Amenia, Clark longed to minister, and in 1843 he achieved that goal. Clark tended a virulently antislavery flock in Winested, Connecticut. While he was aligned with the antislavery forces in the church, he was not radical enough to suit these Methodists and subsequently was transferred to a less strident New York City congregation. Throughout this period, Clark continued to contribute letters to such publications as the Pittsburgh *Christian Advocate*, the *Northern Christian Advocate*, and the *Christian Advocate and Journal*.

By 1851 Clark was a well-regarded member of the New York Methodist Conference. He played a pivotal role in a meeting where the New York ministers had to come to terms with the slavery issue, an issue that threatened to rip apart the state's congregation. The crisis came about because Congress had adopted a compromise package with the South, designed to keep the political balance nationally and admit California as a free state. In addition Congress passed a stringent new Fugitive Slave Act which denied blacks accused of being slaves a trial by jury and the right to testify on their own behalf. Clark wrote the compromise paper that eventually was accepted by the ministers. In his paper he called the Fugitive Slave Act contrary to the law of God and the principles of natural justice. While the compromise made Clark the target of proslavery abuse, it focused even greater attention on him as a standard-bearer of moderate Methodist antislavery sentiment.

Clark's reputation, coupled with his many contributions to Methodist newspapers throughout the United States and his ministry work, made him an ideal candidate for the editorship of the Methodist *Ladies' Repository* in 1852. Although he had never sought the position, he was elected by the General Conference of the Methodist Church and moved his family to Cincinnati, Ohio, where the magazine was published by the Western Book Concern. From the beginning, Clark had a clear idea of what he and the church wanted in a women's magazine. Echoing the sentiments that had guided Samuel Williams when he first suggested the idea of the *Ladies' Repository* to the Methodist General Conference in 1840 that Methodist women, and all Christian women, needed an alternative to the worldly *Godey's Lady's Book* or *Snowden's Lady's Companion*, Clark said that "The work is designed to impart solid intelligence, to beget habits of thought, to improve the taste, to refine and invoke the heart; but more than all, to cultivate the expansive virtues of the Christian faith. To accomplish all this it must be at once attractive, lively, chaste, and instructive.... Strong and muscular thought must be combined with the charms of a chaste literature, and the whole must be permeated with the spirit of a pure and holy faith."

The pre-Clark *Ladies' Repository* was a small, struggling monthly. Publishing a collection of inspirational essays, sermons, biblical instruction, poetry, and mission reports, the magazine had never achieved great popularity among the women of the Methodist Church. In 1852, the year before Clark became editor, the *Ladies' Repository* had a circulation of only thirteen thousand mostly in the Midwest and Northeast, where Methodism was strongest.

From the first, Clark determined that readers of the *Ladies' Repository* wanted more than sermons and biblical instruction written by ministers. They craved something they could use and something they could enjoy reading. As Clark explained, if the magazine were to grow it had to be "intrinsically valuable, worth being sought after, adapted to the want it was designed to supply in the literature of the Church." Arguing that the quality of the writing had to be improved significantly, Clark said, "Something more racy, lifelike, attractive, is demanded. An essay, to be desirable, must have originality, piquancy, force, attractiveness, and, therefore, can rarely originate from an unpracticed hand." Clark's *Ladies' Repository* was going to become a "moving panorama of life...."

To achieve increased circulation Clark instituted three principal changes. First, he started using fiction; previous editors of the *Ladies' Repository* had assiduously avoided short stories and serials. Second, Clark sought experienced writers to contribute to the *Ladies' Repository*. Third, he spent much time and money improving the quality of engravings in the book. Each innovation was tailored to the special interests of Christian women. At the same time, however, each was designed to improve the overall marketability of the magazine.

In fiction, for example, not every short story or serial would do. Each piece of fiction had to have a moral lesson. By the conclusion, female characters had to be more successful in their roles in life. Not only did each short story have to be morally uplifting, but it also had to be original to the *Ladies' Repository*. Before Clark the editors of *Ladies' Repository* frequently reprinted essays or poetry from other magazines. Clark wanted to give his readers what they could not find elsewhere, a policy that probably helped explain why the magazine's circulation increased rapidly. Clark used fiction to supplement the inspirational readings, biblical lessons, poetry, and nonfiction that remained the largest part of the *Ladies' Repository* and that was best suited to further the Christian, morally uplifting tone the magazine was designed to provide.

The new emphasis on fiction and original material meant that Clark needed more contributors. He actively sought men and women with writing experience and established reputations such as well-known writers Lydia H. Sigourney, Virginia F. Townsend, and William T. Coggeshall, who regularly contributed fiction, poetry, and nonfiction. In addition, Clark cultivated new talent such as Alice Cary, Emily C. Huntington, and Augusta Moore, who would soon publish their work in other women's magazines.

While much of his time was spent improving the editorial content of the magazine, Clark also concentrated on improving illustrations. From the beginning the *Ladies' Repository* carried engravings, although never as many as *Godey's Lady's Book* or *Peterson's Ladies' National Magazine*, its more popular and more worldly competitors. Yet, this was understandable, for the aim of the *Repository* was to show its readers that peace and tranquillity were part of God's plan. Typical were serene scenes of the countryside, the playful innocence of children, the love and warmth of a family gathered at the hearth, or portraits of clergymen or famous women. Clark improved the technical quality of the engravings. At various times he retained John Smilie and F. E. Jones, two Cincinnati engravers, to provide original illustrations for the magazine. Illustrations, like the written material, were done expressly for the *Ladies' Repository*. This emphasis on originality was not lost on newspaper editors, who frequently complimented the magazine for its high-quality illustrations.

The Western Book Concern, which published the *Ladies' Repository*, also was willing to make improvements to enhance the editorial and graphic changes. By 1855 an average issue was sixty-four pages, up from forty pages in 1850. Clark also used better paper than before, which further improved the quality of the illustrations. All these improvements came at no extra cost to the subscriber. The yearly subscription rate remained two dollars until the Civil War.

These improvements prompted more Methodist—and non-Methodist—women to subscribe, and the *Ladies' Repository* became more profitable. By 1855 circulation of *Ladies' Repository* had topped 20,000. By April 1856, two months before Clark was reelected editor, the number of subscribers reached 29,580 with the number "rapidly increasing." So quickly and unexpectedly did the circulation increase that Clark frequently had to apologize for delayed issues because the printer had not run enough copies. By the eve of the Civil War, the subscription list exceeded 40,000.

Unlike many women's publications issued in the North, the *Ladies' Repository* did not lose a substantial portion of its readership during the Civil War. The church had long before formally split over the slavery issue, and the *Ladies' Repository* was never able to make many inroads among members of the Methodist Church South. The journal did lose some readers, primarily Southern sympathizers in the Midwest and the border states, but the losses did not significantly hurt the magazine.

During the Civil War Clark continued his editorial policy of tailoring the *Ladies' Repository* to the wants and needs of the modern Christian woman. In wartime, the Christian woman needed events to be explained and discussed. Accordingly, Clark used the war—and war themes—in various parts of the magazine. The war became the backdrop for many short stories, poetry, and essays provided by contributors. The war even intervened in the "Sideboard for Children," a department for young readers.

Similarly, Clark had much to say about the war—and President Lincoln's handling of it—in his column, "The Editor's Table." In his editorials Clark used religion and morality as the framework for explaining the Civil War; but as the war dragged on, he came up with many ways for his readers to help the Union cause. Clark wanted his readers to do more than stay home and pray for victory.

During the war the Methodist *Ladies' Repository* was a consistent supporter of the Union. According to Clark and other contributors to the magazine, the *Ladies' Repository* had to be a Union supporter because Lincoln and the Northern forces were fighting not only for national survival but also for religious freedom. Given this orientation, it was natural for Clark to provide a highly moral look at the Northern soldiers. Into battle they went with a prayer on their lips and God in their hearts. If they fell in battle, they were promised eternal salvation. To a Christian female audience, such observations were comforting. For Clark, just the opposite was true of the Southern soldiers, who fought for sin, heresy, and decadence, which could be found in every aspect of Southern life, including the Methodist Church South, whose ministers had perverted God's teaching–"They have sought to sanctify treason, robbery and bloodshed."

Given the moral aspect of the war, women had many things to do to ensure a Northern victory. They should be frugal and patriotic, of course; but they had a larger role to play. They should mold public opinion on a grassroots level by being always on the lookout for "covert traitors." Similarly, Christian women should become involved politically. In a departure from prewar editorial sentiment, where women were urged to remain within their traditional spheres, Clark wanted his Christian readers to exert pressure on the government to vigorously pursue the war and to quickly free the slaves, two positions commonly associated with the more radical voices within the press during the Civil War. When Lincoln delayed and the Union Army suffered defeats, Clark questioned the president's motives and the ability of his generals.

Thus, Clark, through his editorials and his interpretation of the war as a Holy Crusade, wanted his female readers to influence the political arena, an area not traditionally open to women. Yet, by viewing the war in moral and religious terms, Clark argued that such behavior was acceptable if it succeeded in achieving the higher good of a Union victory. His opinion apparently was shared by the 124 delegates to the 1864 General Conference of the Methodist Church, who voted for Clark for bishop. He and Edward Thomson, editor of the *New York Christian Advocate and Journal*, were elected on the first ballot. In all, three editors of Methodist journals were elected to the episcopate that year, a reflection of the General Conference's approval of how these editors ran their magazines and newspapers during the Civil War.

The July 1864 issue of the *Ladies' Repository* was Clark's last. His place was taken by Rev. Isaac Wiley. After his election by the church, he worked in the South, concentrating on setting up a united Methodist Church. He also labored in the Pacific Coast and Rocky Mountain states, strengthening the church there. Clark died in Cincinnati on 23 May 1871 after a short illness.

Clark was an innovative editor who transformed the *Ladies' Repository* from a conservative example of church journalism into a modern, vital magazine appealing to Christian women. By bringing fiction, new contributors, and better illustrations to the book, Clark showed that church journalism could be dynamic and appealing to a wide range of readers, even those outside a particular denomination. In the process, the *Ladies' Repository* became one of the largest circulating magazines published in the Midwest and one of the largest circulating women's publications in the nation. While it paled in popularity to the more commercial *Godey's Lady's Book* and *Peterson's Ladies' National Magazine*, the *Repository* still exceeded the circulation of many of the other women's publications issued during the same period in the North. Unfortunately, these lessons were lost on many of the editors who followed Clark. Without his guidance, the magazine slipped in quality and readership. By 1876 the General Conference decided something had to be done to curb the financial losses of the *Ladies' Repository*. That year the ministers decided to change the name, scope, and character of the magazine to appeal to the church at large and not women in particular. The *Ladies' Repository*, the "jewel" of Methodist Episcopal journalism under Clark, had effectively died.

Biography:
Daniel Curry, *Life-Story of Rev. Davis Wasgatt Clark, D.D., Bishop of the Methodist Episcopal Church* (New York: Nelson & Phillips, 1874).

References:
Kathleen L. Endres, "The Women's Press Goes for a Soldier: A Study in Propaganda, Patriotism, and Public Image," *Civil War History*, 30 (March 1984): 31-53;

William W. Sweet, *The Methodist Episcopal Church and the Civil War* (Cincinnati: Methodist Book Concern Press, 1912).

Papers:
The Clark Collection is located at the Cincinnati Historical Society, Cincinnati, Ohio.

Rollin M. Daggett

(22 February 1831-12 November 1901)

Jack A. Nelson
Brigham Young University

MAJOR POSITIONS HELD: Cofounder and editor, *Golden Era* (1852-1860), *San Francisco Daily Evening Mirror* (1860-1862); editor, *Virginia City* (Nevada) *Territorial Enterprise* (1862-1875, 1877-1878).

BOOKS: *The Watch on the Heights: A Decoration Poem, Delivered at Arlington Heights, May 30, 1879* (Virginia City?, Nevada, 1879?);
Railroad Wrongs in Nevada (Washington, D.C., 1881);
Braxton's Bar: A Tale of Pioneer Years in California (New York: Carleton, 1882);
The Psychoscope: A Sensational Drama in Five Acts, by Daggett and Joseph T. Goodman (Virginia City, Nev.: Privately printed, 1871).

OTHER: David Kalakaua, *The Legends and Myths of Hawaii: The Fables and Folk-Lore of a Strange People*, edited by Daggett (New York: Webster, 1888).

PERIODICAL PUBLICATIONS: "Daggett's Recollections," *San Francisco Examiner*, 22 January 1893;
"Brisk Days on the Comstock," *San Francisco Morning Call*, 10 September 1893;
"Some of the California Writers of the Early Fifties," *San Francisco Chronicle*, 24 October 1897.

As a young miner in the California gold rush, Rollin M. Daggett settled in San Francisco and in 1852 was cofounder of the *Golden Era*, a literary journal that for half a century was a powerful force on the West Coast. In *San Francisco's Literary Frontier* (1969), Franklin Walker called the *Golden Era* "the most important journal ever published on the Pacific Coast." The *Golden Era* helped launch such writers as Bret Harte, Mark Twain, Joaquin Miller, Charles Warren Stoddard, Fitz Hugh Ludlow, Orpheus C. Kerr, and Ada Clare. Later Daggett moved to Virginia City, Nevada, where he joined former friends from the *Golden Era* as an editor of the West's most famous newspaper, the *Territorial Enterprise*.

Born in 1831 in Defiance, Ohio, Rollin Mallory Daggett was orphaned at age eleven and was reared by a sister. He worked as a printer's devil on the *Defiance Democrat* until 1849, when he was caught up by the gold fever that swept the nation and set off with a party to walk to California. Daggett later claimed that he left the party near Scott's Bluff, Nebraska, and made his way to California alone. His adventures included being taken in by Moqui Indians along the Colorado River, narrowly escaping from wild cattle, joining a cholera-ridden wagon train, and burying a man and wife and taking their two children on to Sacramento. After mediocre success as a miner he settled in San Francisco, where he worked for a time as a printer.

In 1852 he and J. Macdonough Foard decided to publish a literary paper to serve the California settlements. Daggett was then twenty-one and Foard nineteen. On 19 December they brought out the first issue of the *Golden Era*. To get subscriptions, Daggett donned his miner's boots and red flannel shirt and trudged through one mining camp after another, signing up homesick miners with a promise of "a Good Family Paper calculated for circulation in every parlor and miner's cabin." In one month he enrolled eleven hundred subscribers at five dollars a year.

The *Golden Era*, with its emphasis on literature by California writers, gained acceptance, as the miners found it a touch of home that romanticized their own experiences. The *Golden Era* reflected the life around it, and did so with an emphasis on sympathy for the characters involved in the drama of the frontier. Under such pseudonyms as "Blunderbuss" and "Korn Kob," Daggett wrote sketches based on his own travel and mining adventures. The stories were apparently a blend of fact and fiction, but had the ring of authenticity with vivid details of place and character. Although the *Golden Era* called itself a weekly family newspaper, its columns were filled chiefly with literary material. It was really a magazine; only in size and typography did it resemble a newspaper.

The vigor of the *Golden Era* attracted fledgling writers from around the West. Bret Harte's first prose work of consequence, "A Trip up the Coast," as well as his first published work to be preserved, a poem called "The Valentine," appeared in the *Golden Era*. John R. Ridge, who was half Cherokee, wrote under the name "Yellow Bird," and E. G. Paide's "Patent Sermons" under the name of "Don Jr." were copied across the nation. A. Delano, known as "Old Block," was a popular California humorist. Charles Warren Stoddard wrote in the *Golden Era* under the name "Pip Pepperwood" until he began using his real name.

With the burgeoning of San Francisco theater the *Golden Era* turned to spirited drama criticism; it was the first publication in the state with a dramatic department. Its reviews soon wielded such influence that its favor was sought by visiting artists and its offices became a center for the celebrities of the day.

Although the *Golden Era* was to continue as a force in California literature for another thirty years, Daggett sold his interest in it in April 1860 and, with Foard once more his partner, began publication of the *San Francisco Daily Evening Mirror*. A Republican organ in the crowded newspaper field of San Francisco, the *Mirror* attacked secessionist sentiment in the city; competition grew intense. After two years of struggle, Daggett announced his retirement from the *Mirror*; his career as a San Francisco editor was over.

Daggett once more headed for the mining fields–this time the fabulous silver strike known as the Comstock Lode near Virginia City, Nevada. There he became an editor of the *Territorial Enterprise*, which was owned by Joseph T. Goodman and Dennis E. McCarthy, both of whom had worked with him on the *Golden Era*.

In an 1893 reminiscence in the *San Francisco Examiner* Daggett tells of a day in August 1862 when a dusty, disreputable-looking young man came into the office of the *Territorial Enterprise* and announced that he was Samuel Clemens, the new reporter. "He had been living on alkali water and whang leather, with only a sufficient supply of the former for drinking purposes, for several months, and you may imagine his appearance," Daggett wrote. Clemens, who had been sending sketches of camp life in the Esmeralda mining district to the *Territorial Enterprise*, was hired to fill in for William Wright; the latter, better known by his pseudonym Dan De Quille, had returned to Iowa to visit his family. Before long, Clemens adopted the pen name by which he is now best known: Mark Twain. In his autobiography, published sixty years after his Virginia City days, Twain said that his 1864 departure from Nevada was caused by Daggett's spurring him to challenge a rival editor to a duel; this action was a violation of the law that prohibited dueling. Scholars doubt that such a duel was even proposed, attributing the story to Twain's penchant for telling tall tales. In any event, Twain went on to San Francisco, where he became a reporter for the *Morning Call* and a regular contributor to the *Golden Era*. His later success apparently brought a certain jealousy from his former colleagues at the *Territorial Enterprise*; the paper's review of Twain's *Roughing It* (1872) calls the work a "ridiculous hodge podge."

In 1864 the *Territorial Enterprise* staff started a literary journal titled the *Weekly Occidental*, patterned after the *Golden Era*. Daggett was represented in the first issue of March 1865, but only four issues appeared. No copies survive; if one can judge by Twain's account in *Roughing It*, much of the problem came from a serialized novel whose authors ran out of ideas after three issues.

Goodman, who was part owner of the *Territorial Enterprise* from 1861 to 1874, was a handsome bon vivant, a charming bohemian. He was the editorial writer for the paper and, along with Daggett, its resident poet. Daggett and Goodman had a good-natured rivalry as to the quality of their poetry. On one occasion they had a contest in which they were each to write a poem in twenty minutes; Goodman won handily, composing half a column of verse while Daggett was barely getting started.

In 1867, while retaining his position at the *Territorial Enterprise*, Daggett became clerk of the United States Circuit and District Courts for Nevada. In 1868 he married seventeen-year-old Maggie Curry of Philadelphia. They lived in a spacious home he had built on Mount Davidson. Two daughters were born to the Daggetts.

In 1872 the *Territorial Enterprise* opposed William Sharon, one of the silver kings of the Comstock, in his bid for the office of United States senator; in an editorial Goodman accused Sharon of "feeding on the vitals of the state like a hyena." Sharon spent half a million dollars to buy out Goodman's interest in the *Territorial Enterprise*, and Daggett was put in charge of writing editorials backing Sharon. Sharon became senator in an election tainted with charges of fraud and vote-buying.

The following year Daggett left the *Territorial Enterprise* to devote himself to business interests. In 1876 he was a Republican elector for Rutherford B. Hayes and was chosen as messenger to take Nevada's electoral votes to Washington. After the election Daggett returned to Nevada, where he again assumed the editorship of the *Territorial Enterprise*.

In 1877 Mr. and Mrs. Frank Leslie, publishers of *Frank Leslie's Illustrated Newspaper*, came to Virginia City with a staff of artists and reporters as part of a highly publicized transcontinental train trip. Later Mrs. Leslie wrote in their paper that the town was dreary, desolate, and "God-forsaken," and cast considerable doubt as to whether any virtuous women existed there. Daggett and his fellow editor Charles C. Goodwin were outraged, and on 14 July 1878 the *Territorial Enterprise* devoted its entire front page to a documented exposé of the backgrounds, business affairs, sex habits, and disreputable characters of Leslie and his wife. Daggett and Goodwin had hired a private detective in New York City to dig out the information.

An orator as well as a journalist and poet, Daggett often presented speeches to mark special occasions in Virginia City. With Goodman he occasionally wrote plays, such as *The Psychoscope: A Sensational Drama in Five Acts* (1871), which was presented at Piper's Opera House in 1872.

Daggett won election to the United States House of Representatives on the Republican ticket in 1878. His jocular nature and storytelling abilities made him popular with his fellow congressmen. His major accomplishment during his term was probably a speech on 25 February 1881 that was published as *Railroad Wrongs in Nevada* (1881). In the speech he detailed, with all his rhetorical powers, the subjugation of Nevada interests by the powerful California railroad barons.

By then Daggett had lost the 1880 election. He remained in Washington for some time maneuvering for a political appointment; failing to obtain one, he returned to Virginia City and renewed his literary efforts. The result was the publication in 1882 of a novel, *Braxton's Bar*. Based on his own experiences as a gold seeker, it recounts encounters with Indians and the vicissitudes of mining camp life. Although the book was favorably reviewed and is today considered one of the best accounts of early mining life written by a participant, Daggett could not resist using some cheap fictional devices. For example, much of the plot depends on coincidence: the protagonist, Mark Briggs, tries to rescue a miner from a burning cabin in California, but all he salvages is a Bible which, by chance, contains half of a map leading to hidden gold; later, the miner turns out to have been Briggs's uncle from Ohio, and the other half of the map appears and leads the hero to riches.

Appointed minister to Hawaii by President Chester A. Arthur in 1882, Daggett found himself perfectly at home with the leisurely island lifestyle. In fact, his unconventional actions brought letters of complaint to Washington from the missionaries about his dissolute behavior. Daggett became friends with King David Kalakaua and is supposed to have taught him to play stud poker. He also assisted Kalakaua in writing down the history and folklore of the Hawaiian Islands. When his term as minister ended in 1885, he went east and convinced Mark Twain that the book should be brought out by Twain's publishing company. The result was *The Legends and Myths of Hawaii: The Fables and Folk-Lore of a Strange People* (1888). Although it was well received, it was not a financial success and contributed to the difficulties of Twain's firm.

Retiring to Vacaville a small community between San Francisco and Sacramento, Daggett continued to contribute to California literary journals. He died in San Francisco on 12 November 1901.

Biography:

Francis Phelps Weisenberger, *Idol of the West: The Fabulous Career of Rollin Mallory Daggett* (Syracuse, N.Y.: Syracuse University Press, 1965).

References:

Ivan Benson, *Mark Twain's Western Years* (Palo Alto, Calif.: Stanford University Press, 1938), pp. 48-51, 66-68, 170-174;

John Walton Caughey, "Shaping a Literary Tradition," *Pacific Historical Review*, 8 (June 1939): 201-214;

Samuel L. Clemens, *Mark Twain's Autobiography*, edited by Albert Bigelow Paine, 2 volumes (New York & London: Harper, 1924), I: pp. 271, 273, 350; II: p. 262;

Clemens, *Roughing It* (Hartford, Conn.: American Publishing Co., 1872), pp. 347-349, 360-361, 368-369;

Ella Sterling Cummins, *Story of the Files* (San Francisco: World's Fair Commission of California, 1893), pp. 13-22, 23-33, 287-293;

Franklin R. Rogers, "Washoe's First Literary Journal," *California Historical Society Quarterly*, 36 (December 1957): 365-370;

Franklin Walker, *San Francisco's Literary Frontier* (Seattle: University of Washington Press, 1969), pp. 93, 94-95, 211-213;

Dixon Wecter, "Mark Twain and the West," *Huntington Library Quarterly*, 8 (August 1945): 359-377.

Richard Harding Davis

(18 April 1864-11 April 1916)

John C. Bromley
University of Northern Colorado

See also the Davis entries in *DLB 12: American Realists and Naturalists*; *DLB 23: American Newspaper Journalists, 1873-1900*; and *DLB 78: American Short Story Writers, 1880-1910*.

MAJOR POSITIONS HELD: Reporter, *Philadelphia Record* (1886), *Philadelphia Press* (1886-1889), *New York Evening Sun* (1889-1890); managing editor (1890-1893), associate editor (1893-1895), *Harper's Weekly*.

BOOKS: *The Adventures of My Freshman* (Bethlehem, Pa.: Privately printed, 1883);
Gallegher and Other Stories (New York: Scribners, 1891; London: Osgood, McIlvaine, 1891);
Stories for Boys (New York: Scribners, 1891; London: Osgood, McIlvaine, 1891);
Van Bibber and Others (New York: Harper, 1892; London: Osgood, McIlvaine, 1892);
The West from a Car-Window (New York: Harper, 1892);
The Rulers of the Mediterranean (New York: Harper, 1894; London: Gay & Bird, 1894);
Our English Cousins (New York: Harper, 1894; London: Low, Marston, 1894);
The Exiles and Other Stories (New York: Harper, 1894; London: Osgood, McIlvaine, 1894);
The Princess Aline (New York: Harper, 1895; London: Macmillan, 1895);
About Paris (New York: Harper, 1895; London: Gay & Bird, 1896);
Three Gringos in Venezuela and Central America (New York: Harper, 1896; London: Gay & Bird, 1896);
Cinderella and Other Stories (New York: Scribners, 1896);
Dr. Jameson's Raiders vs. the Johannesburg Reformers (New York: Russell, 1897);
Cuba in War Time (New York: Russell, 1897; London: Heinemann, 1897);
Soldiers of Fortune (New York: Scribners, 1897; London: Heinemann, 1897);
A Year from a Reporter's Notebook (New York & London: Harper, 1897); republished as *A Year from a Correspondent's Notebook* (London & New York: Harper, 1898);
The King's Jackal (New York: Scribners, 1898; London: Heinemann, 1898);

Richard Harding Davis

The Cuban and Porto Rican Campaigns (New York: Scribners, 1898; London: Heinemann, 1899);

The Lion and the Unicorn (New York: Scribners, 1899; London: Heinemann, 1899);

With Both Armies in South Africa (New York: Scribners, 1900);

In the Fog (New York: Russell, 1901);

Ranson's Folly (New York: Scribners, 1902; London: Heinemann, 1903);

Captain Macklin: His Memoirs (New York: Scribners, 1902; London: Heinemann, 1902);

"Miss Civilization": A Comedy in One Act (New York: Scribners, 1905);

Farces: The Dictator, The Galloper, "Miss Civilization" (New York: Scribners, 1906; London: Bird, 1906);

Real Soldiers of Fortune (New York: Scribners, 1906; London: Heinemann, 1907);

The Scarlet Car (New York: Scribners, 1907);

The Congo and Coasts of Africa (New York: Scribners, 1907; London: Unwin, 1908);

Vera, the Medium (New York: Scribners, 1908);

The White Mice (New York: Scribners, 1909);

Once upon a Time (New York: Scribners, 1910; London: Duckworth, 1911);

Notes of a War Correspondent (New York: Scribners, 1910);

The Consul (New York: Scribners, 1911);

The Man Who Could Not Lose (New York: Scribners, 1911; London: Duckworth, 1912);

The Red Cross Girl (New York: Scribners, 1912; London: Duckworth, 1913);

The Lost Road (New York: Scribners, 1913; London: Duckworth, 1914);

Who's Who: A Farce in Three Acts (London: Bickers, 1913);

Peace Manoeuvres: A Play in One Act (New York & London: French, 1914);

The Zone Police: A Play in One Act (New York & London: French, 1914);

The Boy Scout (New York: Scribners, 1914);

With the Allies (New York: Scribners, 1914; London: Duckworth, 1914);

"Somewhere in France" (New York: Scribners, 1915; London: Duckworth, 1916);

The New Sing Sing (New York: National Committee on Prisons and Prison Labor, 1915);

With the French in France and Salonika (New York: Scribners, 1916; London: Duckworth, 1916);

The Boy Scout and Other Stories for Boys (New York: Scribners, 1917);

The Deserter (New York: Scribners, 1917);

Adventures and Letters of Richard Harding Davis, edited by Charles Belmont Davis (New York: Scribners, 1917).

Collection: *The Novels and Stories of Richard Harding Davis*, Crossroads Edition, 12 volumes (New York: Scribners, 1916).

PLAY PRODUCTIONS: *The Other Woman*, New York, Theatre of Arts and Letters, 1893;

The Disreputable Mr. Raegen, Philadelphia, Broad Street Theatre, 4 March 1895;

The Taming of Helen, Toronto, Princess Theatre, 5 January 1903; New York, Savoy Theatre, 30 March 1903;

Ranson's Folly, Providence, R.I., Providence Opera House, 11 January 1904; New York, Hudson Theatre, 18 January 1904;

The Dictator, New York, Criterion Theatre, 4 April 1904;

The Galloper, Baltimore, Ford's Theatre, 18 December 1905; New York, Garden Theatre, 22 January 1906;

"Miss Civilization," New York, Broadway Theatre, 26 January 1906;

The Yankee Tourist, book by Davis, lyrics by Wallace Irwin, and music by Alfred G. Robyn, New York, Astor Theatre, 12 August 1907;

Vera, the Medium, Albany, N. Y., Bleecker Hall, 2 November 1908; revised as *The Seventh Daughter*, Cleveland, Colonial Theatre, 10 November 1910;

Blackmail, New York, Union Square Theatre, 17 March 1913;

Who's Who, New Haven, Conn., Hyperion Theatre, 28 August 1913; New York, Criterion Theatre, 11 September 1913;

The Trap, by Davis and Jules Eckert Goodman, Boston, Majestic Theatre, September 1914; New York, Booth Theatre, 19 February 1915;

The Zone Police, Tunkhannock, Pa., Piatt's Opera House, 11 August 1916;

Peace Manoeuvres, Bernardsville, N. J., Sommerset Hills Dramatic Association, 13 September 1917.

PERIODICAL PUBLICATIONS: "To the Ladies of the Chorus," *Stage*, no. 5 (27 October 1888): 7;

"A Summer Night on the Battery," *Harper's Weekly*, 34 (2 August 1890): 594;

"The Other Woman," *Scribner's Magazine*, 9 (March 1891): 385-392;

"Edward Harrigan and the East Side," *Harper's Weekly*, 35 (21 March 1891): 210;

"Lieutenant Grant's Chance," *Harper's Weekly*, 35 (16 May 1891): 563;

"The Story of Two Collegians," *Harper's Weekly*, 35 (4 July 1891): 495;

"Minister Patrick Egan," *Harper's Weekly*, 35 (12 September 1891): 696;

"Out of the Game," *Harper's Weekly*, 35 (31 October 1891): 843;

"The Crew of the Baltimore," *Harper's Weekly*, 35 (14 November 1891): 891-892;

"The Dynamite Explosion," *Harper's Weekly*, 35 (12 December 1891): 991;

"The Christmas Society," *Harper's Weekly*, 35 (19 December 1891): 1020-1021;

"The Circus in Midwinter," *Harper's Weekly*, 36 (16 January 1892): 66;

"An Unofficial Log," *Harper's Weekly*, 36 (20 August 1892): 796, 798-799;

"A Newspaper Man's Man," *Harper's Weekly*, 36 (3 September 1892): 856;

"E. H. Sothern," *Harper's Weekly*, 36 (24 September 1892): 918-919;

"The Dedication Ceremonies," *Harper's Weekly*, 36 (29 October 1892): 1038-1039;

"Albert Chevalier," *Harper's Weekly*, 36 (10 December 1892): 1194-1195;

"An American in Africa," *Harper's New Monthly Magazine*, 86 (March 1893): 632-635;

"The Last Days of the Fair," *Harper's Weekly*, 37 (21 October 1893): 1002;

"Mrs. Kendal *vs.* the Public," *Harper's Weekly*, 37 (28 October 1893): 1024;

"A Day With the Yale Team," *Harper's Weekly*, 37 (18 November 1893): 1110;

"The Story of the Horse Show," *Harper's Weekly*, 37 (25 November 1893): 1120-1122;

"The Thanksgiving Game," *Harper's Weekly*, 37 (9 December 1893): 1170;

"Our Suburban Friends," *Harper's New Monthly Magazine*, 89 (June 1894): 155-157;

"The Yale Oxford Meeting," *Harper's Weekly*, 38 (4 August 1894): 740;

"Banderium of Hungary," *Scribner's Magazine*, 21 (March 1897): 267-276;

"Our War Correspondents in Cuba and Puerto Rico," *Harper's New Monthly Magazine*, 98 (May 1899): 938-948;

"The Coronation of Alfonso XIII," *Collier's Weekly*, 29 (21 June 1902): 4-5;

"Echoes of the Coronation," *Collier's Weekly*, 29 (28 June 1902): 15;

"England's Tragedy," *Collier's Weekly*, 29 (5 July 1902): 15;

"The Revolution in Venezuela," *Harper's Weekly*, 46 (4 October 1902): 1421-1422;

"The Gentle Art of Bull Fighting," *Scribner's Magazine*, 32 (December 1902): 641-652;

"The Venezuela Question," *Collier's Weekly*, 30 (3 January 1903): 6-7;

"The Capture of Coamo," *Collier's Weekly*, 30 (28 February 1903): 10-11;

"King Edward in Paris," *Collier's Weekly*, 31 (30 May 1903): 12;

"Marking Time in Tokyo: The War Dogs Dine Out," *Collier's Weekly*, 33 (7 May 1904): 9;

"Marking Time in Tokyo: A War Drama," *Collier's Weekly*, 33 (14 May 1904): 11-12;

"Marking Time in Tokyo: The Forty-Eighth Ronin," *Collier's Weekly*, 33 (21 May 1904): 8;

"Marking Time in Tokyo: The Wrestlers of Japan," *Collier's Weekly*, 33 (4 June 1904): 6-7;

"Kits and Outfits," *Scribner's Magazine*, 37 (April 1905): 385-395;

"A Campaigner Under Many Skies," *Outing*, 46 (May 1905): 183-187;

"Cuba's Suicide," *Collier's Weekly*, 38 (27 October 1906): 21;

"The Capture of Boston," *Collier's Weekly*, 43 (4 September 1909): 10-11;

"Going to the Play in London," *Collier's Weekly*, 44 (23 October 1909): 15;

"The New World," *Collier's Weekly*, 47 (16 September 1911): 19-20;

"The War Correspondent," *Collier's Weekly*, 48 (7 October 1911): 21-22, 30;

"The Dirt Diggers," *Collier's Weekly*, 49 (29 June 1912): 14-15;

"The Men at Armageddon," *Collier's Weekly*, 49 (24 August 1912): 10-11;

"The Defeat of the Underworld: Some Impressions of the Becker Trial," *Collier's Weekly*, 50 (9 November 1912): 10-11, 28-29;

"Why Leave Home?," *Metropolitan Magazine*, 38 (August 1913): 31-32;

"Breaking into the Movies," *Scribner's Magazine*, 55 (March 1914): 275-293;

"When a War Is Not a War," *Scribner's Magazine*, 56 (July 1914): 41-52;

"Rheims during the Bombardment," *Scribner's Magazine*, 57 (January 1915): 70-76;

"Not Too Proud–But Unprepared," *Metropolitan Magazine*, 42 (July 1915): 9;

"The New Idea at Sing Sing," *New York Times Magazine*, 18 July 1915, pp. 1-3;

"The Log of the Jolly Polly," *Metropolitan Magazine*, 42 (October 1915): 15;

"The Plattsburg Idea," *Collier's Weekly*, 56 (9 October 1915): 7-9;

"Our Eagle without Wings," *Metropolitan Magazine*, 43 (November 1915): 7-8, 76-77, 79;

"France Makes Quick Recovery from Invasion," *New York Times Magazine*, 19 December 1915, pp. 4;

"From Paris to Salonika while the War Rages," *New York Times Magazine*, 16 January 1916, pp. 4-5;

"A Peep at the Famous St. Mihiel Salient," *New York Times Magazine*, 6 February 1916, pp. 3-4;

"The War That Lurks in Forest of the Vosges," *New York Times Magazine*, 13 February 1916, pp. 6-7;

"Following a King's Messenger," *New York Times Magazine*, 20 February 1916, pp. 3-4;

"Blinded in Battle, But Not Made Useless," *New York Times Magazine*, 27 February 1916, pp. 10-11;

"Verdun's Traps and Mazes," *New York Times Magazine*, 5 March 1916, p. 1;

"The Last Message of Richard Harding Davis," *Collier's Weekly*, 57 (5 August 1916): 19.

Richard Harding Davis, managing editor of *Harper's Weekly* from 1890 to 1893 and for all his writing career a steady contributor to the evolving literature of the American magazine, was the first native American to gain international fame both as a war correspondent and as a chronicler of world affairs. Equally at home in Delmonico's restaurant, in the palaces of Europe, and on the world's battlefields, he was at once the mirror of fashion–he is the man escorting the Gibson girls in Charles Dana Gibson's drawings–and a model of rectitude.

A relentless self-promoter and a flamboyant man who was dismissed by his first newspaper editor for trying to write with his gloves on, Davis was the first American reporter to cultivate and to enjoy the peculiar but fleeting fame this country lavishes upon writers more popular than profound. Departing only once from the orthodoxies of his day, when, in late middle age, he fell in love with a theatrical dancer and divorced his first wife to marry her, Davis was otherwise a paragon of the Gay Nineties. He was conservative in his politics, chauvinistic in his patriotism, imperialist in his world view, and carelessly, unthinkingly bigoted in his notions of caste and race. Yet he was also, in his late-blooming maturity, a horrified spectator at the slaughter of World War I. He discovered in the trenches new reverence for human life, new regard for the sufferings of his fellow creatures, and a great, if unsophisticated, regard for beauty. His compassion in the period from 1914 to his death in 1916 is all the more rare for having been previously undetectable.

Richard Harding Davis was born on 18 April 1864, son of the famous novelist and short-story writer Rebecca Blaine Harding Davis, who only narrowly missed founding a new, realistic school of American fiction with her grim 1861 *Atlantic* tale "Life in the Iron Mills." Davis's father, Lemuel Clarke Davis, by all accounts a gentle and successful man, was a lawyer who became a newsman and served as editor of the *Philadelphia Public Ledger*.

Davis had an ordinary childhood and studied first at a private school, then with a family tutor, and finally at Lehigh University. At college he refused to join a fraternity, but he founded two clubs at least as exclusive as the fraternities he scorned. He wore gloves to class, wrote for the *Lehigh Burr*, and enlisted his doting mother

Davis (right) editor of the Lehigh University newspaper, the Burr, *which he edited with W. W. Mills (left) and Charles Clapp*

as the publisher of a slim volume of unremarkable stories, *The Adventures of My Freshman* (1883), in his sophomore year. He was Lehigh's first halfback in football and made that university's first touchdown in 1883. He was asked to leave Lehigh University when it was noticed that his studies were not going nearly as well as his football.

After working as a reporter for the *Philadelphia Record* in 1886 and the *Philadelphia Press* from 1886 to 1889, he acquired a job with Arthur Brisbane on the *New York Evening Sun*. On his second day at the *Sun* Davis won the favor of managing editor Brisbane, and the New York reading public as well, with his tale of the flying tackle by which he had captured a swindler. In August 1890 he published his first and best short story, "Gallegher," which won him a large measure of fame. As a reporter he raided dens of vice with Anthony Comstock, learned about the New York police from Police Commissioner Theodore Roosevelt, and covered abortion, suicide, and execution with great melodramatic flare. His talents in great demand, Davis refused an offer from S. S. McClure, toyed briefly with the idea of succeeding his contemporary Brisbane as managing editor of the *Evening Sun*, and instead, in February of 1891, accepted the managing editor's position at *Harper's Weekly* at the age of twenty-six.

Davis was prepared for this new position neither by talent nor by disposition, and while he improved the *Harper's Weekly* coverage of theater and sports–topics of which he was fond–he soon preferred the romance of the traveler's life to the confines of the editor's chair. He spent more than half of 1892 outside New York, first in the American West and then in England; he spent the next year traveling the Mediterranean basin. When the owners of *Harper's Weekly* decided that their magazine needed the services of a less traveled, if also less famous, managing editor, Davis become an advisory associate editor before he left in early 1895 to be a full-time free-lance writer.

His editorship was one of his most prolific periods. Davis had produced three volumes of short stories, *Gallegher and Other Stories* (1891), *Stories for Boys* (1891), and *Van Bibber and Others* (1892). He had also written enough *Harper's Weekly* articles to serve as the basis for three travel books, *The West from a Car-Window* (1892), *Our English Cousins* (1894), and *The Rulers of the Mediterreanean* (1894). He wrote his first novel, *The Princess Aline*, which was serialized in *Harper's*

Magazine beginning in 1895 and published in book form later that year, at this time as well.

When Davis left *Harper's Weekly*, he was an established young man of great fame and modest fortune who was eager to conquer the world. Sent by William Randolph Hearst and by *Harper's Magazine* to Russia for the coronation of the czar, Davis inveigled his way into the ceremony, where he watched the last of the Romanovs assume his ill-fated throne. The fame of Davis, who was just thirty-one years old, may be attested by the fact that Hearst's *New York Journal* ran above Davis's account of the coronation a photograph not of the Czar but of Davis. Davis also went to Cuba for Hearst and for *Harper's Magazine* and produced there one of his most memorable melodramatic portraits, his picture in words of the execution of a young Cuban rebel: "He had a handsome, gentle face of the peasant type, a light, pointed beard, great wistful eyes, and a mass of curly black hair. He was shockingly young for such a sacrifice.... It seems a petty thing to have been pleased with at such a time, but I confess to have felt a thrill of satisfaction when I saw, as the Cuban passed me, that he held a cigarette between his lips, not arrogantly nor with bravado, but with the nonchalance of a man who meets his punishment fearlessly, and who will let his enemies see that they can kill but cannot frighten him."

Davis did not stay at the *Journal* long. Angered by a provocative illustration based on a misinterpretation of his copy from Cuba, Davis resigned in a manner most wounding to Hearst: he sent a telegram to Hearst's rival, Pulitzer, and accused Hearst and the *Journal* of what the *World* called "deliberate falsehood." Not a forgiving man, Davis did not, even two decades later, relent sufficiently to let his syndicate supply his World War I stories to the Hearst newspapers.

After leaving Hearst, Davis began a series of assignments which included covering the aged Queen Victoria's Jubilee and the first inaugural of President William McKinley. At last he saw his first battle, between Greek and Turkish soldiers at Velestinos, which he covered for the London *Times*.

In 1898 Davis covered the Spanish-American War for the *New York Herald*, *Scribner's Magazine*, and the London *Times*. Wholly untroubled by doubt, serene in his patriotic faith, Davis in Cuba was as much propagandist as reporter. There he was able to work with his old friend, the former police commissioner of New York, Lt. Col. Theodore Roosevelt, who was in Cuba as the leader, if not senior officer, of the fabled Rough Riders. Davis had declined a captain's commission to cover the Spanish-American War, a decision that he later regretted. By no means secure in his own decision not to fight, Davis's view of the war was tinged with intense patriotism.

The Spanish-American War was a lark for Davis, who scampered after Roosevelt with an entire lack of perspective; Davis did as much as any man to make Roosevelt a hero, and then president. Critical at times of U.S. leadership, Davis was never critical of his country's cause in Cuba. Davis was not a man of great complexity, and in him simple faith ran both deep and pure. He did not always mix easily or well with other writers and was antagonistic toward the daring few who did not share his enthusiasms. Of the reporters who made fun of the Rough Riders and who suggested that some of these "college swells" had brought golf clubs and valets to war, Davis wrote that they "ought in decency to go out and hang themselves with remorse." His distaste for his colleagues was evident in his contemptuous characterization of some of the correspondents covering the Rough Riders as receiving "their information from the wounded when they were carried to the rear, and from an officer who stampeded before the fight had fairly begun." His colleagues called Davis, with equal disdain, "Richard the Lion Harding."

On 4 May 1899 Davis married a wealthy Chicago woman, Cecil Clark. The marriage, which remained chaste, had its basis in companionship rather than romantic love; ultimately their mutual interests, including a love of travel, were not enough to sustain their union.

In January 1900 Davis was commissioned to cover the Boer War both by Bennett's *Herald* and by the London *Daily Mail*. That an American had been asked to cover a British war for a British paper was a tangible mark of the high esteem in which Davis was held in the English-speaking world. His new wife accompanied him to South Africa.

In this war Davis sided passionately with the Boers. In his first book about South Africa, *Dr. Jameson's Raiders vs. the Johannesburg Reformers* (1897) he had told the tale of the attempted creation of British South Africa. By late 1899 the forces of the British Empire were once more ready to move, and the army of conquest sent abroad by Great Britain was struggling against magnificent Boer cavalry for control of the land

Davis's second wife, Elizabeth McEvoy Davis, with their daughter, Hope

and wealth of South Africa. Davis threw his earlier pro-British preferences aside for the rugged Boer. He visited Pretoria just before the British took it, and there he saw the Boer leader Kruger, of whom he painted one of his most exotic pictures: "His eyes held no expression, but were like those in a jade idol.... in his ears he wore little gold rings, and his eyes, which were red and seared with some disease, were protected from the light by some great gold rim spectacles of dark glass with wire screens."

While he carefully covered both Briton and Boer, his pro-Boer sympathies increased steadily. Shown, while in Pretoria, the prison camp for officers from which the young Winston Churchill had lately escaped, Davis was offended by the conduct of the captured British officers. They had called out, as lonely men will, to passing women, and some of the women had petitioned that the shouting be stopped. In what one of his biographers, Fairfax Downey, once called "the most unlucky dispatch Davis ever wrote," Davis raged at the officers who had offended the Boer women:

"Personally I cannot see why being a prisoner would make me think I might speak to women I do not know; but some of the English officers apparently thought their new condition carried that privilege with it...." He contrasted them unfavorably to their foes: "I have never met," he wrote pointedly, "an uncivil Boer." For his venomous pro-Boer partisanship he was for a time made much less welcome in Great Britain.

He had failed to see the Boer War as a white man's struggle over land and riches properly belonging to blacks, and, with the war still unsettled, he left South Africa to return to America. There he resumed his career as a novelist, publishing in 1902 his most ambitious, if least rewarding novel, *Captain Macklin*, a thin tale of Central America which relates the hero's tiresome rise from disgrace at West Point to military glory. His earlier romantic novels had been criticized for his lack of character development; for Davis told stories about perfect people perfectly united at the book's end. In contrast the hero of *Captain Macklin* was a vain and rigid hero-worshiping adventurer–very much, in fact, like his creator. This failure and a frustrating trip to the Far East for *Collier's*–Davis could not get close enough to the Russo-Japanese War for his usual, very personal, dispatches–caused him to turn to drama. The theater had been for Davis a lifelong interest, and he quickly mastered farce. Two of his 1904 plays, *Ranson's Folly* and *The Dictator*, combined with *The Galloper* and *Miss Civilization* in 1905, made Davis's fortune. At one point he earned three thousand dollars a week from his plays. His interest in drama for the moment spent and his way of life for the moment assured, he took up his travels again, revisiting Cuba for *Scribner's* and investigating the Congo for *Collier's*.

In 1908 he happened to go to a New York show which featured a young actress who sang a song called "The Yama Yama Man." Elizabeth G. McEvoy, whose stage name was Bessie McCoy, captured the heart of Richard Harding Davis. His infatuation complete, he went to hear her sing night after night, and soon sought a divorce. His affairs, at this time painfully complex for so orthodox a man, were complicated by the fact that New York allowed divorce only upon a showing of adultery; hoping to avoid such scandal he continued to see Bessie while arranging a separation from Cecil, his first wife. Finally, in 1910, Cecil Davis agreed to file charges against Davis for desertion, and a friendly divorce ended their relationship. In the same year his mother, to whom he had been exceptionally close all his life, died, and after her death his energy was much depleted by a struggle against severe depression. At last, in the summer of 1912, he married Bessie McCoy, whose matron of honor was the old Davis friend, actress Ethel Barrymore. His new wife was twenty-four years old, just half his age.

Davis's health had been partially restored earlier in 1912 by the joyous energy of the Republican convention of that year, in which Davis helped his old friend Theodore Roosevelt struggle against William Howard Taft within the Republican party. Davis relished his role as a star of the Roosevelt effort, in which he also acquired a distaste for the Democrat Woodrow Wilson that lasted the rest of his life.

From the Bull Moose barricades he went to film, seeing his most popular novel, *Soldiers of Fortune* (1897), made into a feature film. The new Mrs. Davis, who had fallen ill shortly after their marriage with a series of nervous ailments which were no doubt the result of her rigid new husband's many demands, recovered as she learned to cope with Davis, who had forbidden her to work, and whose situation as a man divorced and remarried cost her also the sacraments of the Catholic church.

By now Davis was worried about money; for he had become accustomed to living lavishly on a scale partially supported by the wealth of his first wife. Bessie had no money, and Davis's earnings, while great, barely covered his expenses. President Wilson's brief martial fling against Mexico served as a tonic for Davis, and despite Bessie's pregnancy Davis left for Mexico in April 1914. Later in 1914, after World War I began, he applied to Secretary of State William Jennings Bryan for nomination as the sole American press representative permitted by the British with their army on the Continent. Bryan added to Davis's grievances against the Wilson administration by refusing to nominate him. Little deterred, Davis went to France, where he became a strident advocate of the strategy which insisted upon a fresh flow of men, munitions, and material to the stalemated western front.

His powers of description remained peerless, and his description of the passage of the German army through Brussels is much admired. "It was not of this earth, ghostlike," he wrote of the German army; "it carried all the mystery and menace of a fog rolling toward you across the sea."

In the destruction of the cathedral at Reims, he found new Christian metaphors, as orthodox in conception as the lapsed faith of his new wife: "There were other features of this fire and bombardment that the Catholic Church will not allow to be forgotten. The leaden roofs were destroyed, the oak timbers that for several hundred years had supported them were destroyed, stone statues and flying buttresses weighing many tons were smashed into atoms but not a single crucifix was touched, not one waxen or wooden image of the Virgin disturbed, not one painting of the Holy Family marred."

World War I was the last of Davis's wars, dwarfing in its horror all other conflicts of his age, and he had changed: slaughter now dismayed him and he no longer found romance in the deeds of daring men he had so cherished.

As he traveled through fresh scenes of havoc he found a symbol, as he had in all his previous travels, of what he felt: an extended metaphor of blindness. He saw in Europe many sightless soldiers, reduced in circumstances and in hope, and in their slow, difficult recovery he found an image of hope and new life. However greatly these scarred veterans were changed, they had survived the horrors through which they had passed. About these men Davis wrote with a calm eloquence unmatched in his other writing about war, made even more impressive by the fact that his symbols here seemed, and no doubt were, wholly unself-conscious.

His World War I coverage, which no longer romanticized either the war or the soldier, was complemented, and perhaps in some measure inspired, by the great pleasure he took in the birth in 1915 of his only child, Hope Harding. Wracked by the angina that had killed his father and weakened by frequent spells of dizziness, Davis nonetheless returned to action after his daughter's birth, visiting Salonika and, on his return to France, seeing again the slaughter on the western front. At last, sated with the sights and sounds of war, he returned to the United States, where he died at his home at Mt. Kisco, New York, on 11 April 1916, only a week before his fifty-third birthday.

His importance was not as a writer of romance or of farce, which were to him only lucrative amusements. He was, first and last, an observer of people and scenes, a chronicler of the passing moment. He stamped his own colorful, vibrant impressions upon the time in which he lived, and what is known of the era of Richard

Harding Davis is largely known through him. Much of the disregard for Davis's writing that surfaced in the years just after his death was a reaction both to his remarkable fame and to the disgust of the postwar generation for all that had seemed to give pleasure and light to the innocent days before 1914.

It is true that Davis did remarkable things to win and to keep his remarkable fame, but a part of the critical recoil from the canon of his work has been the feeling that no one who wrote as much as he did could possibly have written well. This judgment, while not unfair to his very perishable novels and farces, tends to ignore the real value of his powers of observation, which still illuminate the fascinating time in which he lived.

Bibliographies:
Henry Cole Quinby, *Richard Harding Davis: A Bibliography* (New York: Dutton, 1924);
Fanny Mae Elliott and Lucy Clark, *The Barrett Library Richard Harding Davis: A Checklist of Printed and Manuscript Works of Richard Harding Davis in the Library of University of Virginia* (Charlottesville: University Press of Virginia, 1963);
John M. Solensten, *Richard Harding Davis (1861-1916)* (Arlington: University of Texas Press, 1970);
Clayton L. Eichelberger and Ann McDonald, *Richard Harding Davis (1864-1916): A Checklist of Secondary Comment* (Arlington: University of Texas Press, 1971).

Biographies:
Fairfax Downey, *Richard Harding Davis: His Day* (New York & London: Scribners, 1933);

Gerald Langford, *The Richard Harding Davis Years: A Biography of Mother and Son* (New York: Holt, Rinehart & Winston, 1961).

References:
Phillip Knightley, *The First Casualty: From the Crimea to Vietnam. The War Correspondent as Hero, Propagandist, and Myth Maker* (New York: Harcourt Brace Jovanovich, 1975);
Mary S. Mander, "Pen and Sword: Problems of Reporting the Spanish-American War," *Journalism History*, 9 (Spring 1982): 2-9, 28;
Scott C. Osborn and Robert L. Phillips, Jr., *Richard Harding Davis* (Boston: Twayne, 1978);
"Portrait," *Saturday Evening Post*, 194 (17 September 1921): 10;
"Portrait," *Saturday Review of Literature*, 27 (16 December 1944): 7;
"Richard Harding Davis as Revealed by His Letters," *New Republic*, 14 (2 March 1918): 149-150;
John M. Solensten, "The Gibson Boy: A Reassessment," *American Literary Realism*, 4 (1971): 303-312;
Robert Waldron, "Around the World with Swash and Buckle," *American Heritage*, 18 (August 1967): 56-59, 71-74;
"War Correspondent," *Collier's Weekly*, 48 (7 October 1911): 21-22;
Larzer Ziff, *The American 1890s: Life and Times of a Lost Generation* (New York: Viking Press, 1966).

Papers:
The principal collection of Richard Harding Davis's papers is at the library of the University of Virginia in Charlottesville.

James Dunwoody Brownson De Bow

(10 July 1820-27 February 1867)

Whitney R. Mundt
Louisiana State University

MAJOR POSITIONS HELD: Owner, editor, and contributor, *Commercial Review of the South and West*, renamed *De Bow's Review of the Southern and Western States* in 1850, renamed *De Bow's Review and Industrial Resources, Statistics, Etc.* in 1861, renamed *De Bow's Review, Industrial Resources, Etc.* in 1862, renamed *De Bow's Review* in 1866 (1846-1867).

SELECTED BOOKS: *The Political Annals of South Carolina* (Charleston: Burges & James, 1845); also published as "Carolina Political Annals," *Southern Quarterly Review*, 7 (April 1845): 479-526;

Introductory to the First Report of the Bureau of Statistics, of the State of Louisiana (New Orleans, 1850);

The Industrial Resources, Etc., of the Southern and Western States; Embracing a View of Their Commerce, Agriculture, Manufactures, Internal Improvements, Slave and Free Labor, Slavery Institutions, Products, Etc., of the South, Together with Historical and Statistical Sketches of the Different States and Cities of the Union—Statistics of the United States Commerce and Manufactures, from the Earliest Periods, Compared with Other Leading Powers—the Results of the Different Census Returns since 1790, and Returns of the Census of 1850, on Population, Agriculture, and General Industry, Etc., 3 volumes (New Orleans: Office of *De Bow's Review*, 1852-1853, 1854); enlarged, 4 volumes (New Orleans & New York: Office of *De Bow's Review*, 1852-1853); republished as *The Industrial Resources, Statistics, Etc., of the United States, and More Particularly of the Southern and Western States; Embracing a View of Their Commerce, Agriculture, Manufactures, Internal Improvements, Slave and Free Labor, Slavery Institutions, Products, Etc., of the South,* (New York: Appleton, 1854); republished as *Encyclopedia of the Trade and Commerce of the United States, More Particularly of the Southern and Western States; Giving a View of the Commerce, Agriculture, Manufactures, Internal Improvements, Slave and Free Labor, Slavery Institutions, Products, Etc., of the South,* 2 volumes (Washington, D.C., 1853; London: Trübner, 1854); republished as *The Southern States, Embracing a Series of Papers Condensed from the Earlier Volumes of De Bow's Review, Upon Slavery and the Slave Institutions of the South, Internal Improvements, Etc., Together with Historical and Statistical Sketches of Several of the Southern and Southwestern States; Their Agriculture, Commerce, Etc.,* 1 volume (Washington & New Orleans, 1856);

The Seventh Census of the United States: 1850. Embracing a Statistical View of Each of the States and Ter-

James Dunwoody Brownson De Bow

ritories, Arranged by Counties, Towns, Etc., (Washington: R. Armstrong, printer, 1853);

Statistical View of the United States, Embracing Its Territory, Population—White, Free Colored, and Slave—Moral and Social Condition, Industry, Property, and Revenue; the Detailed Statistics of Cities, Towns and Counties; Being a Compendium of the Seventh Census, to Which are Added the Results of Every Previous Census, Beginning with 1790, in Comparative Tables, with Explanatory and Illustrative Notes Based upon the Schedules and Other Official Sources of Information (Washington: A.O.P. Nicholson, printer, 1854);

Mortality Statistics of the Seventh Census of the United States, 1850 (Washington: A.O.P. Nicholson, printer, 1855);

Introductory Remarks on Taking the Chair as President of the Southern Convention, at Knoxville, Tennessee, on the Tenth of August, 1857 (Washington: Lem Towers, printer, 1857);

The Interest in Slavery of the Southern Non-Slaveholder. The Right of Peaceful Secession. Slavery in the Bible (Charleston: Evans & Cogswell, 1860);

Tennessee Central or Pacific Railroad: Letters from J. D. B. De Bow, President of the Road, to the Public of Tennessee and the Capitalists of the Country Generally (Nashville, 1866).

PERIODICAL PUBLICATIONS: "Colonial Era of South Carolina," *Southern Quarterly Review*, 6 (July 1844): 30-63;

"Characteristics of Statesmen," *Southern Quarterly Review*, 6 (July 1844): 95-129;

"Conquest of Mexico," *Southern Quarterly Review*, 6 (July 1844): 163-227;

"Law and Lawyers," *Southern Quarterly Review*, 6 (October 1844): 370-427;

"The Life of Robert, Cavalier de la Salle, by Jared Sparks," *Southern Quarterly Review*, 7 (January 1845): 75-103;

"The Northern Pacific: California, Oregon and the Oregon Question," *Southern Quarterly Review*, 8 (July 1845): 191-243;

"International Rights of Peace and War," *Commercial Review of the South and West*, 1 (March 1846): 193-227;

"The Cotton Plant," *Commercial Review of the South and West*, 1 (May 1846): 289-319;

"Louisiana," *Commercial Review of the South and West*, 1 (May 1846): 385-443;

"The Importance of Correct Statistical Information in Relation to the Agricultural Interests of the Country, Illustrated in the Case of the Indian Corn of the Present Season," *Commercial Review of the South and West*, 1 (June 1846): 465-497;

"American Legislation, Science, Art and Agriculture," *Commercial Review of the South and West*, 2 (September 1846): 76-116;

"Progress of American Commerce," *Commercial Review of the South and West*, 2 (December 1846): 368-426;

"Progress of the Great West in Population, Agriculture, Arts and Commerce," *Commercial Review of the South and West*, 4 (September 1847): 31-85;

"Direct Trade of Southern States with Europe," *Commercial Review of the South and West*, 4 (October, November, December 1847): 208-225, 337-356, 493-502;

"Southern and Western Agricultural and Mechanic Associations, South Carolina and Louisiana Agricultural Societies: Proceedings," *Commercial Review of the South and West*, 4 (December 1847): 419-450;

"The West India Islands," *Commercial Review of the South and West*, 5 (May-June 1848): 455-499;

"Communication between the Atlantic and Pacific Oceans," *Commercial Review of the South and West*, 7 (July 1849): 1-37;

"La Salle and the Mississippi," *De Bow's Review and Industrial Resources, Statistics, Etc.*, 22 (January 1857): 13-37;

"Texas—a Province, Republic, and State," *De Bow's Review and Industrial Resources, Statistics, Etc.*, 23 (September 1857): 239-262;

"The Empire of Brazil," *De Bow's Review and Industrial Resources, Statistics, Etc.*, 24 (January 1858): 1-27;

"Southern Scenery, Watering Places, Resources, Etc.," *De Bow's Review and Industrial Resources, Statistics, Etc.*, 31 (August 1861): 170-196;

"Editorial (Upon History of De Bow's Review from Time of Issuance of Prospectus at Charleston in Fall of 1845 to Its Revival at Columbia in July-August Issue, 1864; Effect of War on Publishing at the South; and Progress of the War)," *De Bow's Review, Industrial Resources, Etc.*, 34 (July-August 1864): 97-104;

"Journal of the War—Entered Up Daily in the Confederacy," *De Bow's Review*, 1 (June 1866): 646-656, 2 (July 1866): 57-70, 2 (August 1866): 189-201, 2 (September 1866): 322-331, 2 (October 1866): 430-446, 2 (November 1866): 537-557, 2 (December 1866): 649-661;

"Memories of the War," *De Bow's Review*, 3 (January 1867): 1-12, 3 (February 1867): 138-145, 3 (March 1867): 225-233, 4 (October 1867): 286-289, 4 (November 1867): 434-436, 4 (December 1867): 530-532, 5 (February 1868): 160-162, 5 (April 1868): 357-360;

"Journal of the War," *De Bow's Review*, 3 (January 1867): 95-108, 3 (February 1867): 199-213, 3 (March 1867): 319-331;

"The Southern Pacific Railroad," *De Bow's Review*, 3 (March 1867): 247-268.

"*De Bow's Review* is the greatest remnant of the Old South, the greatest exponent of the spirit that informed its people, the greatest exemplar of the hopes that filled its prophets and its seers." These are the extravagant words used by a writer for the *New Orleans Times Democrat* to describe the magazine founded in 1846 by James Dunwoody Brownson De Bow and edited by him until his death in 1867. But these words reflect, accurately enough, the regard Southerners felt for the magazine and its owner, who had spoken out for the region of his birth in its most difficult moments.

De Bow achieved his fame through that magazine, which he described as "the most flourishing periodical in the South" from 1849 to 1862. He was willing, he wrote in 1864, "to take his place in the history of the times upon the record of those fifteen years of toil and labor in which the heyday and prime of manhood were spent. The one controlling and dominant idea of his life, now rapidly running into the yellow leaf, was the elevation, morally, physically, and politically, of his native South."

De Bow's intelligence and energy and skill in writing turned his magazine into the South's most influential journal. But he could have succeeded at almost anything else he chose to do: he studied law and was admitted to the bar; his skills as a statistician earned him a post as head of the Louisiana Bureau of Statistics; he was appointed to the chair of political economy at the University of Louisiana; and in 1853 President Franklin Pierce named De Bow superintendent of the seventh census, a duty which he carried out with distinction. But it is his achievement as "Magazinist of the Old South"–a title conferred by his biographer Ottis Clark Skipper–which has earned James Dunwoody Brownson De Bow his place in literary history.

De Bow was born in Charleston, South Carolina, on 10 July 1820 to Garrett and Mary Bridget Norton De Bow. He enjoyed what he was to describe as an "idyllic" life in Charleston until he was six, when his father died. The family's circumstances then became somewhat less prosperous, and young De Bow helped out by working in a grocery story. When he was sixteen, his mother and oldest brother died of cholera. He and a sister were sent to live with another sister, while his older brother was placed with relatives. About a year after their deaths, De Bow quit his job, visited his mother's relatives in their respective communities, and taught school briefly. In 1839 he attended a school in Cokesbury, achieving some distinction in debate and oratory.

He entered the College of Charleston in spring 1840 and excelled in public speaking and composition. He graduated three years later as valedictorian, but his success there had not prepared him for a profession. De Bow began reading law, and in May 1844 he was admitted to the bar of South Carolina. He began a practice in Charleston, but without immediate success. As politics had always interested him, he submitted an article, "Characteristics of the Statesman," to the *Southern Quarterly Review*. It appeared in July 1844 and De Bow's career in magazine journalism was under way.

The *Southern Quarterly Review* had been founded in January 1842 by Daniel K. Whitaker as an organ through which the South and Southwest might be heard. Its first number was published in New Orleans, but from 1843 to 1855 it was produced in Charleston. In 1856 the magazine was moved to Columbia, where the final four issues were published before the magazine expired in 1857.

But in 1843 it was beginning its career in Charleston, as was "James D. B. De Bow, Attorney at Law and Solicitor in Equity." De Bow's contributions to the new journal in 1844 must have been appreciated, for he was made the acting, or "junior," editor in the same year. At least De Bow regarded himself as a junior editor. Whitaker had left De Bow temporarily in charge of the magazine but later denied that he had created a title for him; De Bow simply assumed the title in his correspondence. Perhaps it was this little rift which encouraged De Bow to strike out on his own.

In late 1845 De Bow published a prospectus for a new journal, to be called the *Commercial Review of the South and West*. He intended it to be published in Charleston, but when the first number appeared in January 1846 it was issued from New Orleans, where De Bow had rented an office at Number 22, Exchange Place, in November 1845. He enlisted the aid of Stephen Franks Miller, a North Carolina lawyer, to prepare the first issues. De Bow's brother, Benjamin Franklin De Bow, joined him from Charleston to serve as business manager. The first months were difficult ones for the young editor. His friend Charles Gayarré described those times in a memorial to De Bow, published in the *Review* of June 1867: "Many a night he and a friend who assisted him toiled until nearly dawn in a small office in Exchange alley, No. 22. At that critical time they both slept in a room which had been given them by J. C. Morgan, the well known bookseller of the epoch. The bare walls of that room above the bookstore looked on no other furniture than a modest mattress lying on the floor, and on which the two companions rested at night. They literally lived on bread alone, with a little butter, however, to soften its dryness. Never did two persons exist on so small an expenditure; their daily outlays rarely exceeding twenty cents–that is, ten cents for each. They certainly deserved success, and they obtained it."

The identity of the "friend" has not been established with certainty. Edward Reinhold Rogers believes him to have been Gayarré himself, but Frank Luther Mott dismisses this speculation and proposes the name of R. G. Barnwell. However, Diffee William Standard writes that Barnwell did not join the enterprise until 1851, and Barnwell himself does not mention any such incident in his sketch of De Bow's life. Ottis Clark Skipper suggests obliquely that the friend was Edwin Q. Bell, brother-in-law to Frank De Bow. But whoever this person might have been, his willingness to assist in such circumstances was providential at a time when De Bow's journal was on the verge of failure.

De Bow's problems seem to have included poor compositors, few advertisers, lack of subscribers, and an inability to collect from the subscribers he had. The *Review* suspended publication from January through June 1849 and would not have survived without the financial intervention of Maunsel White, a wealthy sugar planter who advanced the funds for its resumption and promised additional support if needed.

De Bow also obtained the help of two agents, Foster and Price, who solicited subscriptions and helped return the magazine to solvency. Gayarré describes their efforts: "Price scoured plantations on rivers and bayous and in the most retired parts of the country through swamps, morasses and interminable piney woods. Foster swooped over cities and villages, knocking at every door, and, with an address which admitted of no refusal, subdued reluctance, cajoled opposition, warmed up indifference into giving tokens of approbation, and goaded avarice itself into liberality. The consequence was, that the lists of subscription began to lengthen, and the revenues to increase."

In 1848, about the time the *Review* suspended publication, its circulation numbered 825 subscribers. By late 1851 circulation had increased to more than 4,000, and in 1853 there were about 4,500 subscribers, making it the leading southern magazine. Advertising also increased, and after 1856 the magazine became a major source of income for De Bow. Between 1853 and 1861 he was earning two thousand to four thousand dollars yearly as owner and editor of the *Review*.

De Bow had built the *Review* into a widely circulated journal, and while most of his customers were in the South in 1855, there were 111 in free states and another 66 in foreign nations among his 4,656 subscribers. Demand for back issues led De Bow to offer a three-volume reprint of the best articles from back issues of the magazine. This set was published in 1852-1853 under the title *Industrial Resources, Etc., of the Southern and Western States* in one thousand copies and was offered for sale at ten dollars. This edition was republished in 1853, and a second edition was published that same year in one volume, supplemented by a second volume, which was a reprint of volume 14 of the *Review*. This second edition appeared under the title *Encyclopedia of Trade and Commerce of the United States*. Subsequent editions were printed under variant titles and in varied formats, and, according to Diffee William Standard, by 1860 "The set had gone through at least seven printings in its various editions."

De Bow was also able to attract well-known contributors, among them Duff Green, Samuel Kneeland, Horace Greeley, George Palmer Putnam, and William Gilmore Simms. Others included Edmund Ruffin, Joseph Addison Turner, and George Fitzhugh. De Bow was his own best contributor, of course. Early in the life of the *Review* he wrote much of the copy himself, and in 1866, while planning a book to be called *The South-*

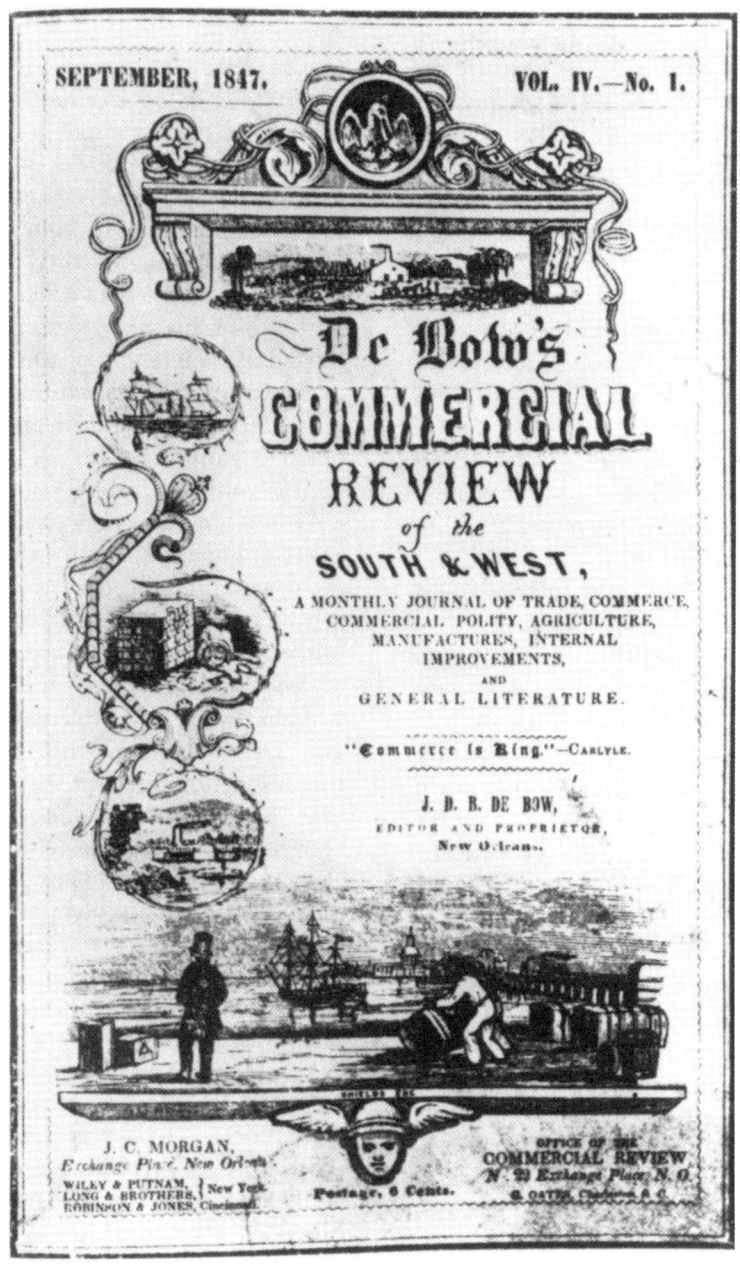

Cover for an issue of De Bow's journal

ern Confederacy, he selected 102 articles to be reprinted from among those he had published in his magazine.

As busy as he must have been with editing the *Review* and writing for it, he was pursuing other activities as well. In 1848, after the Louisiana legislature created the bureau of statistics, De Bow was appointed superintendent through the good offices of his friend Charles Gayarré, who was then Louisiana's secretary of state. With characteristic energy he set about to collect data on the state's resources and expenditures, banks, charities, the press, and intellectual societies such as the Louisiana Historical Society, which he had helped found in 1846 and still served as secretary. He sent questionnaires to the parishes, but the response was initially poor. Nevertheless, he submitted his introductory report to the legislature in 1850, and it apparently attracted interest throughout the United States. The U.S. Census Board, with which De Bow had been in communication, commented favorably on his work, and

De Bow printed the remarks of the Census Board in his *Review*, along with the data he had collected. The Louisiana legislature apparently did not appropriate funds for independent publication of his report, and its support of the bureau it had created was not commensurate with De Bow's ambitions for that agency. Consequently, he recommended to the legislature in 1852 that it abolish the office.

In spring 1848, at almost the same time De Bow was offered his post in the newly created bureau of statistics, his friend Maunsel White was attempting to raise funds to endow a "Chair of Commerce, Public Economy and Statistics" at the University of Louisiana in New Orleans. He wrote to the university board of administrators with his proposal for the professorship, attaching a synopsis of the plan of instruction, which had been drawn up by De Bow at White's request. The ambitious program called for theoretical studies into society and government, as well as practical and statistical studies into population and wealth in their application to commerce, agriculture, and manufacture. A list of twelve textbooks was appended, along with a list of forty-five volumes on economics, ninety-eight on commerce, and sixty-four on agriculture, manufacture, statistics, and other subjects. The university was expected to acquire the books on the longer list for the library. De Bow proposed that the professor would be required to prepare twelve public lectures.

The board of administration accepted White's offer to endow the professorship and in turn invited De Bow to occupy the chair. He accepted and began composing twenty-four lectures. He was ready to accept students by fall 1849, and he advertised the program in the August *Review*. Similar advertisements appeared in September, October, November, and December, but to no avail. The professorship turned out to be a "barren honor," as Gayarré describes it in his 1867 memorial to De Bow. "It was a professorship without students, and no ability could have commanded an audience," Gayarré writes. "The time had not yet come when any interest could have been taken in such subjects."

De Bow's professorship may have been a barren honor, but his efforts as superintendent of Louisiana's Bureau of Statistics were not entirely without fruition; besides enabling him to obtain data for publication in the *Review*, those efforts led to a request in 1853 that he accept the position of superintendent of the seventh census of the United States by appointment of newly elected President Franklin Pierce. He accepted, and in March he moved to Washington, D.C. He announced in the *Review* that there would be no change in the editorial policy of the magazine, but that the editor could be reached in Washington. The imprint of volume 4 of the magazine reads (rather proudly, one suspects): "New Orleans and Washington City."

Much of the data collection had been accomplished by his predecessor, and De Bow dismissed 125 members of the staff, leaving only 35 to accomplish the tasks remaining–namely, tabulation of the data, follow-up queries and corrections, organization of the report, proofing the galleys, and completing publication. De Bow supplied the introduction, notes, and appendix to the volume of 1,022 pages. De Bow's appointment was announced in March 1853, and by November the report was at the printer. To accomplish this task De Bow required his staff to work occasionally at night and on weekends. His brother Frank once refused to work on Sunday, and De Bow summarily fired him–reinstating him only after the intercession of friends.

The completed work was submitted to the secretary of the interior, who had been given charge of the new office of the census, and it must have met with favor, for in early 1854 Congress authorized the publication of a condensed version of the *Seventh Census of the United States*. In this volume De Bow was free to follow his own plan, although the content was essentially drawn from the larger version. The four-hundred-page compendium was titled *Statistical View of the United States*, and it was completed and published that same year. De Bow thereupon tendered his resignation, effective 31 December, but Congress called him back to publish still another volume, this one to summarize the mortality data which had been collected in the census but left unpublished. In 1855 *Mortality Statistics of the Seventh Census of the United States, 1850* appeared in 303 pages. De Bow continued in office until the close of the year, when he concluded his tenure as superintendent of the seventh census.

His three-year residence in Washington had gained him national recognition, as well as a great deal of copy for the *Review*. It also provided the opportunity for him to meet the young woman who was to become his wife. On 5 August 1854, De Bow, then thirty-four, married twenty-one-year-old Caroline Poe of Georgetown, D.C., who was a distant cousin of Edgar Allan

Poe. A daughter, Mary Emma, was born 23 May 1855; a son, James, was born the following fall. James died on 10 September 1857, before he had reached his first birthday, and De Bow's wife died five months later. De Bow renamed his daughter Caroline Mary in memory of his wife. Friends of De Bow wanted to take "Carrie," as she was also called, into their homes, but he preferred to rear her with the aid of a governess.

Before long his friends were introducing him to various young women, no doubt thinking of remedying his loneliness. De Bow's law partner, V. H. Ivy, invited Martha E. Johns of Nashville for a visit to New Orleans in 1859. Introductions were arranged, and before long De Bow was determined to marry her. While she seemed willing enough, her mother was cautious. But on 4 September 1860 De Bow and Johns married; they became the parents of four children: James Dunwoody Brownson, Benjamin Franklin, William Neal, and Evalina Johns. Carrie also lived with them.

De Bow was financially able to care for his growing family. In the five years before the beginning of the War between the States, his *Review* had become profitable, and by 1861 he had invested about thirty thousand dollars in securities and owned about 1,000 acres in Louisiana, 160 acres in Texas, and other parcels in Minnesota, Kansas, Iowa, Missouri, and Mississippi, along with houses in Richmond, Virginia; Columbus, Mississippi; and New Orleans.

De Bow was well known as a spokesman for Southern causes through his journal, but he had other leadership roles as well; in 1857 he was elected president of the Southern Commercial Convention at its meeting in Knoxville. In his address to the delegates he promoted means of improving the economy of the South through increased manufacture and trade, and he advocated reopening the slave trade. He declared his support for the Union only if rights of all its members were protected, by which he meant that the federal government was obligated to protect slaveholders. He believed that secession was preferable to submission to the antislavery fervor of the North, and he became president of the African Labor Supply Association when the Southern Commercial Convention met at Vicksburg in 1859.

But war reversed the fortunes of the *Review* and its editor. For example, between November 1860, when Abraham Lincoln was elected president, and April 1861, when war began, payments were received from only about six hundred of the four thousand subscribers. The number of these subscribers was to be cut in half, particularly in territory held by federal forces. Advertising income declined even more radically than subscriptions, as De Bow refused to accept orders from northern businesses. Then, in February 1862 Commodore David Farragut brought his naval force from the Gulf of Mexico up the Mississippi River to begin the military campaign against New Orleans. De Bow, faced with shortages in subscribers and in income, as well as paper, managed to issue a double number in March-April before suspending publication. By 25 April, Farragut was in New Orleans–or, rather, above New Orleans, as his ships looked down upon the city from the vantage point of the river, which was higher than ground level and prevented from flooding the land only by the levee system. De Bow left the city for Columbia, South Carolina, from which the May-August issue of the *Review* was published. During the remainder of the war only one other issue appeared: the July-August issue of 1864. Further publication was suspended until January 1866, when De Bow began the After the War Series.

De Bow was not left idle during the war because he had suspended the *Review*. He offered his services to the Confederate government, and in August 1861 he was appointed produce loan agent, charged with helping finance the Confederacy by exchanging bonds for supplies, primarily cotton. His salary was set at three thousand dollars per annum, but by fall 1863 it had risen to six thousand dollars. He and his family were able to survive the war without destitution, although they were separated much of the time and forced to move from city to city as the progress of the war dictated.

Shortly after war's end De Bow applied for and received a presidential pardon. He began immediately to search for ways to accelerate the reconstruction process, and he urged construction of railroads to facilitate commerce. De Bow was instrumental in persuading the City of Cincinnati to build a railroad to Chattanooga. He also urged construction of a line from Nashville to Knoxville and was elected president of the Tennessee & Pacific Railroad in 1866 to oversee this project. He published a number of letters in support of this project and obtained pledges from the governor of Tennessee.

Meanwhile, De Bow made plans to resurrect the *Review*. He returned to New Orleans, where he found his books and papers intact, and set about to collect old debts. Being moderately successful in this effort, De Bow announced that publication of the journal would resume, and that offices would be established in Nashville and Charleston as well as in New Orleans, and that other offices would be set up in the northern cities of New York, Boston, Washington, and Cincinnati. By the end of 1865 he had obtained enough subscribers to justify printing the first issue of the "After the War" Series.

The first number of volume 1 was issued with a date of January 1866. This was the thirty-fifth volume of the *Review* published since its inception, counting the thirty-two volumes published until the time of its suspension in early 1862; the single-issue volume published as volume 33, no. 1, with the May-August date; the double number published as volume 34, no. 1-2, with the July-August date; and volume 1 of the After the War Series, including six numbers published monthly from January through June 1866. Volume 1 of the new series refers on its covers to the "Complete series, 32 vols.," ignoring the two volumes published during the war years and thus confusing generations of librarians and bibliophiles. The second volume of the new series was published in six numbers from July through December 1866. In the April-May issue of 1867 (volume 3, no. 4-5), the death of J. D. B. De Bow was announced: "To friends at the South, a brief recountal of the circumstances attending the death of the Editor will possess a melancholy interest. Mr. De Bow had arrived in Elizabeth, N.J., but a short week prior to his decease, on a mission of love, to attend at the bedside of his brother. On the 22nd of February he complained of what seemed to be merely a cold; and not until the 26th were there any indications of serious illness. On that day symptoms of an alarming character were manifested, and his attending physician called a consultation. A careful diagnosis revealed an aggravated case of peritonitis, and the relatives and friends of the patient were at once advised of his condition and danger. Every resource of science, and every care and attention from willing hands and loving hearts, were at once employed, but fruitlessly, and at noon of the 27th–within twenty hours of the development of his disease, his spirit passed from time into eternity."

The brief obituary was written by Edwin Q. Bell, the brother-in-law of De Bow's brother Frank, who, with Bell, had worked on the *Review* since its inception. A little more than three weeks later, Bell had the sad duty of writing Frank's obituary for the *Review*. He noted that the brothers had been orphans in childhood and that De Bow had cared for the younger brother Frank as a father would. He wrote that Frank had so completely identified himself with the fortunes of his elder brother that De Bow's fame satisfied Frank's ambition.

De Bow's widow continued to publish the *Review* for a year after the editor's death, with his friends R. G. Barnwell and Edwin Q. Bell as editors. De Bow had moved his headquarters to Nashville in 1866, but the magazine was moved back to New Orleans when it was sold in March 1868 to William M. Burwell. It was suspended after the issue dated October 1870. Nine years later it was resurrected, and four numbers were issued (volume 43 of the complete series) between October 1879 and June 1880, when it expired forever.

De Bow's Review was one of the most important periodicals published in the South, and its influence was felt in the North as well. Its importance lay in its role as a voice of Southern regionalism and its tireless promotion of Southern causes, including slavery and secession. But the *Review* was important also because of its weighty substance–its careful record of the South's culture, geography, economy, and people. Sometimes its seriousness deterred potential subscribers, who shied away from its "severe didacticism." This quality was a reflection of De Bow's personality.

Ottis Clark Skipper states the case well for De Bow's place in history when he writes, "De Bow was one of the leading statisticians of his time, the most successful magazinist of the antibellum South, an enlightened champion of agriculture and manufactures, and, save when the prevailing sectional bitterness misled him, a worthy proponent of commerce, railroads and intellectual culture. If historians and economists have found him appallingly dull, they have learned more about the Old South from him than from any other authority."

The magazine was his alter ego. As historians Paul Paskoff and Daniel Wilson view it, the *Review* expresses De Bow's vision of Southern society–"a commercial and industrial, indeed a bourgeois, conception somewhat at odds with the dominant southern culture of mid-century." They believe the *Review* reflects "the dynamism and self-confidence of the cotton South." For most of the magazine's existence, Paskoff and Wilson write, "*De Bow's Review*, like the South itself, felt compelled to champion uniquely southern interests, even to the point of secession and war. In this, *De Bow's Review* was at its best and made the cause of the South its own."

Surely, one would think, De Bow's place in journalistic history is secure, and his final resting place is memorialized in some significant fashion. But in fact, De Bow's reputation has not survived beyond the memories of scholars. And his gravesite is unknown. In a fascinating piece of detective work, two scholars sought to locate his place of burial. Daniel E. Sutherland and Lisa Roberts were preparing a biographical sketch of De Bow for inclusion in an encyclopedia but were unable to find the location of his gravesite in standard sources. Even *De Bow's Review*, which published a lengthy appreciation of its founder as a "consolation to our grief," failed to mention his final resting place. The researchers wrote to the South Carolina Historical Society, only to find that there was no record of De Bow's interment in that state. A search of Louisiana histories and cemetery records turned up nothing. A request to New Jersey authorities for a copy of his death certificate revealed that the state did not even have a record of any James De Bow dying there between 1848 and 1868. The cemetery in Elizabeth had no tombstone for James De Bow. And the New Jersey *Journal* failed to mention his place of burial.

Sutherland and Roberts then turned to Nashville, where his widow had lived with her mother. The Nashville *Republican Banner* of 7 March 1867 carried a story which said that the body of James D. B. De Bow had arrived from New Jersey for burial on the farm of his mother-in-law, Mrs. John Johns. Consulting the records of land transactions in the state archives turned up the deed to John Johns's property on Richland Creek, purchased in 1836. An 1871 map of Davidson County, however, showed John Johns's property clearly delineated–but it was not on Richland Creek. Returning to the state archives, Sutherland and Roberts discovered that John Johns had sold land on Granny White Pike to J. D. B. De Bow in 1866. The deed included a surveyor's map which identified adjacent landowners, all of whom were shown on the 1871 map of Davidson County. A drive to the site revealed expensive homes, lawns, gardens, and swimming pools but no cemetery plots or tombstones. After a year's search they had found James Dunwoody Brownson De Bow–"sort of."

Sutherland and Roberts concluded that "De Bow is out there somewhere, under an asphalt driveway, or a mailbox, or, if lucky, under one of the manicured lawns. We had found De Bow, sort of, but with bittersweet success. Perhaps some things best remain undiscovered."

Bibliographies:
Selma Nachman, "A Collation of De Bow's Review," *Bulletin of the Bibliographical Society of America*, 4 (January-April 1912): 27-32;

James A. McMillen, *The Works of James D. B. De Bow* (Hattiesburg, Miss.: Book Farm, 1940).

Biographies:
W. D. Weatherford, *James Dunwoody Brownson De Bow* (Charlottesville, Va.: Historical Publishing, 1935);

Ottis Clark Skipper, "J. D. B. De Bow, the Man," *Journal of Southern History*, 10 (November 1944): 404-423;

Skipper, *J. D. B. De Bow: Magazinist of the Old South* (Athens: University of Georgia Press, 1958).

References:
R. G. Barnwell, "The Late J. D. B. De Bow," *De Bow's Review*, 4 (July-August 1867): 1-10;

Lillian Viola Doty, "*De Bow's Review*," M.A. thesis, University of South Carolina, 1930;

Robert F. Durden, "J. D. B. De Bow: Convolutions of a Slavery Expansionist," *Journal of Southern History*, 17 (November 1951): 441-461;

Charles Gayarré, "James Dunwoody Brownson De Bow," *De Bow's Review*, After the War Series 3 (June 1867): 497-506;

Herman Clarence Nixon, "De Bow's Review," *Sewanee Review Quarterly*, 39 (January-March 1931): 54-61;

Paul F. Paskoff and Daniel J. Wilson, eds., *The Cause of the South: Selections from De Bow's Review, 1846-1867* (Baton Rouge: Louisiana State University Press, 1982);

Sam G. Riley, *Magazines of the American South* (New York: Greenwood Press, 1986);

Edward Reinhold Rogers, *Four Southern Magazines* (Charlottesville: University of Virginia Press, 1902);

Ottis C. Skipper, "'De Bow's Review' after the Civil War," *Louisiana Historical Quarterly*, 29 (April 1946): 2-40;

Skipper, "J. D. B. De Bow and the Seventh Census," *Louisiana Historical Quarterly*, 22 (April 1939): 3-15;

Diffee William Standard, "De Bow's Review, 1846-1880: A Magazine of Southern Opinion," Ph.D. dissertation, University of North Carolina, 1970;

Daniel E. Sutherland and Lisa Roberts, "Looking for De Bow," *Louisiana History*, 27 (Winter 1986): 69-75;

Willis Duke Weatherford and Don L. Moore, *Analytical Index of De Bow's Review* (N.p., 1952).

William Jennings Demorest

(10 June 1822-9 April 1895)

Douglas S. Campbell
Lock Haven University

MAJOR POSITIONS HELD: Editor and publisher, *Mme. Demorest's Mirror of Fashions* (1860-1864), *New York Illustrated News* (1864), *Demorest's Illustrated Monthly and Mme. Demorest's Mirror of Fashions*, renamed *Demorest's Monthly Magazine* in 1878 (1864-1885), *Young America* (1866-1875); publisher, *Phunniest of Phun* (1865-1867).

A man with a passionate belief in the value of family life, William Jennings Demorest championed, within and outside his magazines, a number of causes, most notably prohibition of liquor. His second wife, Ellen Curtis Demorest, shared his values and energy, focusing her attention on the working woman. Their most famous joint effort, *Demorest's Monthly Magazine*, was an expression of their shared conviction that women should be financially free to pursue their interests in fashions, literature, art, music, health, and especially lofty moral causes. In addition to his publishing business, Demorest found time to patent several inventions, make a fortune in New York City real estate, run for political office, and participate in the founding of several philanthropic and reform organizations.

Born on 10 June 1822 in Brighton, New York, a suburb of Rochester, Demorest moved to New York City in his late teens. There he worked in a dry-goods store while studying for the ministry under his Presbyterian pastor. After marrying Margaret Willamina Poole in 1845, he accepted the advice of his pastor and his employer to turn his attentions to the financial support of his family and became a merchant. They had four children: Vienna (1847), Henry (1850), William (1859), and Evelyn (1865). Demorest's wife died in 1857; he married the daughter of a prosperous hat manufacturer the next year.

Ellen Curtis was an established businesswoman and talented designer of women's fashions when she married. Born on 15 November 1825 in Saratoga Springs, New York, as a teenager she had worked as a milliner to the resort trade in her hometown. She had left Saratoga Springs for New York when she was confident of her business skills.

During a sabbatical from her New York business after her marriage, Mrs. Demorest watched her maid cut out a dress using pieces of wrapping paper as a guide. This gave her the idea of designing paper patterns based on the latest fashions so that women could reproduce them accurately at home. When she mentioned the idea to her husband, he realized that an immense market could be tapped by mass-producing the patterns.

Demorest's plan had two parts. One was the creation in the autumn of 1860 of the first pattern magazine: *Mme. Demorest's Mirror of Fashions*. It carried a long but descriptive subtitle: *Mme. Demorest's Illustrated Quarterly Report and Mirror of Paris and New York Fashions for Ladies' and Children's Dress. In Style, the Parisian Beau Ideal of Beauty and Elegance. In Accuracy, the Perfection of Artistic Excellence.* The magazine at first resembled a catalog with printed pictures of dresses that women could make using Mme. Demorest's original paper designs. These designs were particularly appealing in part because Mme. Demorest was able to modify the extravagant European fashions to reflect a more practical American conservatism. To encourage home sewing, the *Mirror* included in each issue a sample copy of one pattern, a highly popular feature that eventually became the trademark of the magazine.

The other part of Demorest's plan was to establish a network of local distribution agencies to sell the patterns. The agents were encouraged to form clubs and were given premiums for new members. Both ideas were immensely successful. The distribution agencies grew at a phenomenal rate even during the Civil War, numbering three hundred at its end. The number of clubs reached fifteen hundred at the height of the movement. Many were located in Canada, Cuba, and several capitals of Europe. The privilege of organizing a club was given, whenever possible, to widows or spinsters, and the agencies were provided with packaged lots of patterns to set up in showroom displays. Growing with the clubs was the circulation of the magazine, which reached sixty thousand by the end of the war. The workroom in New York, where the patterns were manufactured, clearly revealed the commitment of the Demorests to the rights of women and minorities: black women worked alongside whites, received the same wages, and attended company parties. Customers who objected were told to take their business elsewhere.

The most important factor in the magazine's initial success was Mrs. Demorest's talent for fashion design. Two events were seized upon by Demorest to create publicity for her work. The first was the crinoline craze, which struck at about the same time the Civil War started. Crinolines were difficult to manage: they dragged on the sidewalks, popped open at inopportune times, and kept walking partners at an arm's distance. Still, they attracted devoted followers. Mrs. Demorest, at first cool to the fad, later turned out spectacularly billowing garments. Her most popular crinoline-related design, though, was the smallish Quaker hoopskirt that took up little room and was easy to walk in. Complementing this skirt was the equally popular Imperial Dress Elevator, which had weighted strings that enabled the wearer to raise or lower the skirt at will to keep it clear of the sidewalk. Women would ask each other, "Are you wearing your Imperial today?" (Demorest, an inveterate tinkerer, often designed inventions that were first conceived by Mrs. Demorest. Their collaboration produced a series of patented inventions of which the Imperial Dress Elevator was only one. Another was a gentle hair curler. According to an announcement in the magazine, "The invention consists of a hollow tube, with a small fountain attached, which is filled with boiling water." The announcement claimed that the advantage of this curler over previous ones is that it "produces the most soft, silky, and beautiful curls, without scorching or parching.")

The second event Demorest used to attract attention to his magazine was the 1863 marriage of tiny Mercy Lavinia Warren Bumpus to P. T. Barnum's famous midget, Tom Thumb. Lavinia joined the crowd of wartime brides who visited Mme. Demorest's Emporium to have their trousseaux made. Demorest was as aware as Barnum of the publicity value of the marriage, and he saw to it that each new subscriber to the *Mirror of Fashions* received a *carte de visite* of Mr. and Mrs. Tom Thumb.

The Demorests found a kindred soul in Mrs. Jane C. Croly, who, as editor and writer under the pen name "Jennie June," was the voice of the magazine's support for the social and economic independence of women. Her tenure began with the first issue of the *Mirror* in 1860 and continued until 1887. While her voice was strong and unequivocal, it was not always consistent. Within a single year, for example, she wrote in one issue, "You are only a woman, and must stay in the house and obey your father until you are married"; in another she wrote, "It is a crime in parents to compel their daughters to look forward to marriage as their only prospect for occupation, position, or livelihood." Yet it was within "Jennie June's" columns, especially "Talks with Women," that the Demorest philosophy was expressed most vividly and fully, summarized succinctly in these words: "The duty of parents consists of something more than merely endowing children with life; they ought also to insure to them as far as possible the means of happiness—a sound mind, a healthy body, and the methods by which to secure the best development of both."

It was with the purchase in January 1864 of the *New York Illustrated News*, however, that the Demorests entered the world of general magazine publishing. This magazine was combined with the *Mirror of Fashions* in August to form *Demorest's Illustrated Monthly and Mme. Demorest's*

Mirror of Fashions. The title was shortened in 1878 to *Demorest's Monthly Magazine*.

A typical issue of *Demorest's Monthly* might contain a poem by William Cullen Bryant or Edgar Allan Poe; musical scores from operas, perhaps with words provided by Demorest himself; tips on healthy life-styles, architectural designs of Victorian houses, advice on how to hold a conversation, book reviews; and in later issues, a "What Women Are Doing" section. This section featured such diverse accomplishments of women as a patent for a rotary engine and the first woman physician to be admitted as a member of the International Medical Congress.

Demorest had been active in the abolitionist movement before the Civil War, and he made another entry into the publishing field in 1865 with a magazine called *Phunniest of Phun*. For two years the magazine published cartoons by such artists as Frank Bellew and Thomas Nast that satirized those who asserted that the Civil War was fought to preserve the Constitution and not to free the slaves.

The founding in 1866 of *Young America*, a magazine for children, was perhaps an inevitable outgrowth of the reformist inclinations that fueled Demorest's early attempt to study for the ministry. An announcement in the September 1866 issue of *Demorest's Monthly* asserted that the new magazine "shall lead the minds of children 'from nature up to nature's God.' " Instead of stories imitating the then popular "Deadwood Dick" series, *Young America* ran fiction about pet dogs and the pleasures of the outdoors. There were maps, games, puzzles, and riddles, as well as articles on history, biography, astronomy, chemistry, and foreign countries. A popular feature was the how-to-make-it section, which gave instructions on building such items as a coaster sled or a brush. Subscription premiums included Bibles, harmonicas, and spyglasses. When the magazine folded in 1875, its epitaph read in part: "They [children] today imbibe a taste for the horrible, the exaggerated, and marvelous, which is catered to by unscrupulous persons, and which makes all else seem insipid and namby-pamby to them."

As the years went by, Mrs. Demorest's fashions occupied a smaller fraction of the pages of *Demorest's Monthly*. Still, she always took great pride in the originality of her designs, writing that those of her rivals were "copies of old and stale foreign pictures." Her designs were lavishly illustrated, and the descriptions were highly detailed. For the most part her contributions consisted of giving fashion advice and selecting illustrations of the latest fashions in women's and children's clothing. She said, for example, that a new "English breakfast cap" was "excessively ugly." She advised her readers to "stick to the pretty Neopolitan and Maltese styles, until something more becoming than these are designed for a novelty." An illustration of a pair of gloves was accompanied by the description, "Fine cloth gloves, with a soft reversible side, are fashionable this winter, stitched or embroidered in the same color as the cloth, and trimmed with a very narrow band of fur upon the wrists." The bicycle fad was strongly supported by *Demorest's Monthly*, and Demorest invented a bicycle that could be ridden easily by women in dresses. *Demorest's* also took note of the anxieties women expressed about how to lose weight. A scientific approach was suggested because obesity was considered by the editors to be a disease, not an indulgence.

The outlook of both Demorests is epitomized in the magazine's encomium of Mrs. Demorest: "She has been instrumental in placing many [other women] on the path of prosperous trade which leads to independence." At bottom, the Demorests and Croly saw in the holding of a vocation the foundation of all other forms of independence for women.

A variety of premiums encouraged subscriptions and subscription clubs. In addition to the regular premiums of a free pattern or a historical or sentimental engraving, Demorest sometimes offered special premiums. "A lady who furnished 30 subscribers," for example, received a Wheeler and Wilson Sewing Machine priced at fifty-five dollars.

In the 1870s temperance issues began to appear more frequently in *Demorest's Monthly*, along with Demorest's editorials about divorce, stock market manipulations, wars, lynchings in Tennessee, and an antidiscrimination law in New York State. One editorial uses nautical terms to illustrate Demorest's objections to government licensing of the sale of intoxicating beverages. The editorial begins with a reference to the "Ocean of Politics" upon which the "old hulk, Expediency" is drifting. The "life boats of law" are tossed about by "the angry waves of perverted appetite" for alcohol in the "sea of vile abuse." The solution is for responsible Christians to ride "on the crest of each breaker, shouting, 'Down with the saloon and up with the home.' " Another editorial calls for the enactment of prohibition: "To save our homes from the blighting, withering use of alcohol, to remedy the evils of the liquor traffic and escape the final results of this demoralization and degradation, we ought to be startled into an active and enthusiastic determination to throttle this monster with our votes at the ballot-box, and thus save our Christian institutions and civilization from the vortex of destruction that now threatens to engulf our whole country."

Although fond of such purple prose, Demorest was also capable of turning a catchy phrase on occasion. Of liquor licensing, he writes: "We license schools of vice and crime, and then imprison the pupils for learning the lessons." Paraphrasing Mark 8:36, he asks, "What can it profit a people if they gain a large revenue and lose all in life that is worth living for?"

By 1885 Demorest was so involved in reform movements, especially the temperance cause, that he turned the magazine over to sons Henry Clay and William C. Demorest, who renamed it *Demorest's Family Magazine* in November 1889. Two years later Mrs. Demorest retired from the pattern-making business, in part because of competition from the copyrighted Butterick patterns. Although the Demorests had taken out patents on many inventions, for some reason, they had failed to patent the paper patterns.

In 1884 Demorest had supported Kansas Gov. John St. John for president on the Prohibition party ticket. The next year Demorest himself was nominated as the party's candidate for lieutenant governor of New York. His slogan was "Up with the Home; down with the Saloon." Defeated, he ran, again unsuccessfully, for mayor of New York City in 1890.

In 1885 Demorest founded the National Prohibition Bureau, later called the Constitution League, to test the constitutionality of liquor licensing and taxation laws. Demorest also wrote temperance tracts, called "Prohibition Bombs," which were sent by the National Prohibition Bureau to anyone who requested them. Or, for a token sum, a person could ask the bureau to send a different tract each week to a specific name and address. Demorest's goal was to distribute one hundred million leaflets. A marketing genius, he was not satisfied to rely on the usual methods of distribution for his tracts: rather than merely give them away to people who might never read them, he encouraged youths under the age of twenty-one to memorize and recite them at Sunday school competitions. Winners were given medals of silver, gold, and gold set with diamonds. The first competition was held in 1887 at the Bedford Street United Methodist Church in New York; and missionaries soon spread the idea around the world. Demorest is said to have given away forty thousand medals at a cost of fifty thousand dollars. The number of youths who entered the contests has been estimated at 250,000 and the audience at 15,000,000.

In 1891 Demorest organized the National Anti-Nuisance League in an attempt to prevent the sale of liquor at hotels. The league's lawyers sought to enforce a United States Supreme Court ruling that "no legislature can bargain away the public health or the public morals." The group's position was that "it therefore remains for the people to demand the immediate enforcement of Prohibition of the atrocious liquor traffic by common law as a common nuisance."

By this time the drive for instituting mandatory prohibition was an all-consuming activity. He told one reporter, "Prohibition is the most significant word in the English tongue." Before Demorest could achieve his goal, however, he died of pneumonia on 9 April 1895 at age seventy-two, leaving real estate holdings worth one million dollars. Mrs. Demorest lived until 10 August 1898. That year *Demorest's Family Magazine* was sold to Arkell Publishing Company, printers of *Puck* and *Judge*. The next year it folded.

Biography:

Ishbel Ross, *Crusades and Crinolines: The Life and Times of Ellen Curtis Demorest and William Jennings Demorest* (New York: Harper & Row, 1963).

References:

Margaret La Forge, "Fashions for Everyone: Ellen Demorest," in *Enterprising Women*, by Caroline Bird (New York: Norton, 1976), pp. 73-81;

"W. Jennings Demorest," *Our Day* (1985): 8-12.

Mary Mapes Dodge

(26 January 1831?-21 August 1905)

Charles Egleston

and

Kathleen Kearney Keeshen

See also the Dodge entry in *DLB 42: American Writers for Children Before 1900*.

MAJOR POSITIONS HELD: Associate editor, *Hearth and Home* (1870-1873); editor, *St. Nicholas: Scribner's Illustrated Magazine for Girls and Boys*, renamed *St. Nicholas: An Illustrated Magazine for Young Folks*, in 1881 (1873-1905).

BOOKS: *The Irvington Stories* (New York: O'Kane, 1865; revised, New York: O'Kane, 1867; revised and enlarged edition, New York: Allison, 1898);

Hans Brinker; or, The Silver Skates: A Story of Life in Holland (New York: O'Kane, 1866; London: Low, 1867); revised as *Hans Brinker; or, The Silver Skates* (London: Sampson Low, Marston, Low & Searle, 1875; New York: Scribner, Armstrong, 1876);

A Few Friends and How They Amused Themselves: A Tale in Nine Chapters Containing Descriptions of Twenty Pastimes and Games, and a Fancy-Dress Party (Philadelphia: Lippincott, 1869);

Rhymes and Jingles (New York: Scribner, Armstrong, 1874; enlarged, New York: Scribners, 1881; enlarged again, New York: Scribners, 1904; London: Gay & Bird, 1904);

Theophilus and Others (New York: Scribner, Armstrong, 1876; London: Low, 1876);

Along the Way (New York: Scribners, 1879); enlarged and republished as *Poems and Verses* (New York: Century, 1904);

Donald and Dorothy (Boston: Roberts, 1883; London: Warne, 1883);

What American Authors Think about International Copyright (New York: American Copyright League, 1888);

The Land of Pluck: Stories and Sketches for Young Folk (New York: Century, 1894; London: Unwin, 1894);

Mary Mapes Dodge

When Life is Young: A Collection of Verse for Boys and Girls (New York: Century, 1894; London: Unwin, 1894).

OTHER: "Children's Magazines," *Scribner's Monthly*, 6 (July 1873): 352-354;

Baby Days: A Selection of Songs, Stories, and Pictures for Very Little Folks, compiled by Dodge (New York: Scribners, 1877); republished as *Baby World: Stories, Rhymes, and Pictures for Little Folks* (New York: Century, 1884); revised as

A New Baby World: Stories, Rhymes, and Pictures for Little Folks (New York: Century, 1897);

The Children's Book of Recitations Approved by Mrs. Mary Mapes Dodge, compiled by Dodge (New York: DeWitt, 1898).

The finest American children's magazine of the nineteenth century was *St. Nicholas: Scribner's Illustrated Magazine for Girls and Boys,* edited from its beginning in 1873 until 1905 by Mary Mapes Dodge. Dodge enlisted America's finest children's illustrators and writers to create original work maintaining throughout her tenure a high quality of production and a circulation of about seventy thousand.

Mary Elizabeth Mapes was born on 26 January 1830, 1831, or 1838 in New York City to James Jay Mapes and Sophia Furman Mapes. Called Lizzie by her family, she had three sisters and a brother. The Mapes home was frequented by many of the leading scientific and literary figures in New York City, such as Horace Greeley, William Cullen Bryant, and John Ericsson, and had a well-stocked library. The children were educated by their father and by tutors and governesses.

Mary Mapes married William Dodge, a New York lawyer, in 1851 and had two sons. She was widowed in 1858 and began writing to support her family. Her first published work, *The Irvington Stories* (1865), was designed to appeal to boys. Dodge's next book, *Hans Brinker; or, The Silver Skates: A Story of Life in Holland* (1866) had immediate success. In December 1868 she became an associate editor for *Hearth and Home,* a children's magazine edited by Harriet Beecher Stowe and Donald Grant Mitchell (who used the pseudonym Ik Marvel).

In 1870 Dodge's friend Roswell Smith, who had been one of the founders of *Scribner's Monthly: An Illustrated Magazine for the People* asked her to submit her ideas for a children's magazine to be sponsored by Scribners. Her response, published anonymously in *Scribner's Monthly* in July 1873, set forth the philosophy that was to undergird *St. Nicholas.* She proposed an entirely new format: a children's magazine, she said, should not "be a milk-and-water variety of the adults' periodical. But, in fact, the child's magazine needs to be stronger, truer, bolder, more uncompromising than the other...." It should not moralize: "Let there be no sermonizing either, no wearisome spinning out of facts,

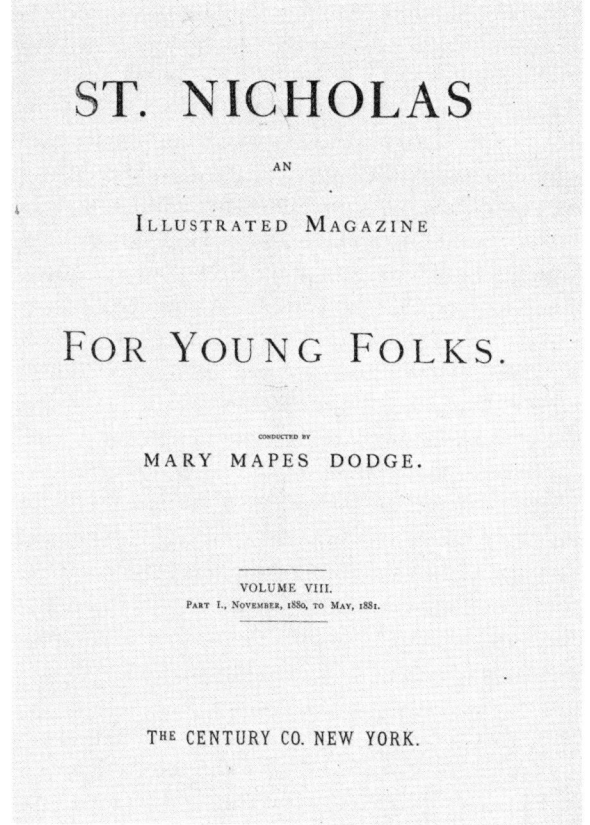

Title page for a bound volume of the children's magazine Dodge edited from 1873 until her death in 1905

no rattling of the dry bones of history." She said that the main focus of a children's magazine was to entertain: "Its cheer must be the cheer of the bird-song, not of condescending editorial babble.... Most children of the present civilization attend school. Their little heads are strained and taxed with the day's lessons. They do not want to be bothered nor amused nor taught nor petted. A child's magazine is its pleasure-ground."

Frank Stockton, who had worked with Dodge at *Hearth and Home,* joined her as assistant editor, and the first issue of *St. Nicholas* was published in November 1873. *St. Nicholas* was such an immediate success that it absorbed *Our Young Folks,* one of the best of its rivals, in January 1874. With it came its editor, John T. Trowbridge, who became a leading contributor to *St. Nicholas. St. Nicholas* absorbed the *Children's Hour* in July 1874 and *Schoolday Magazine* and *Little Corporal,* a Chicago publication widely distributed in the Midwest, in May 1875.

Because Scribners owned *St. Nicholas,* the magazine was able to use the high quality printing equipment of De Vinne press and the writers, artists, and engravers employed by *Scribner's Monthly*. Dodge required originality in writing. Such well-known authors as Noah Brooks, Rebecca Harding Davis, and Lucretia Peabody Hale contributed to the first issue, and the first volume included the work of Louisa May Alcott, Thomas Bailey Aldrich, William Cullen Bryant, Helen Hunt, Bret Harte, John Hay, Sarah Orne Jewett, Elizabeth Stuart Phelps, Olive Thorne, and Charles Dudley Warner. Alcott wrote three novels for *St. Nicholas*: *Eight Cousins* (1875), *Under the Lilacs* (1878), and *Jack and Jill* (1902). Margaret Oliphant and Susan Coolidge also wrote for the magazine. Stockton left the magazine in 1878 to devote more time to his writing, much of which first was published in *St. Nicholas*. His duties were taken over by William Fayal Clarke, who was appointed assistant editor. In 1881 the Century Company took over ownership of the magazine and renamed it *St. Nicholas: An Illustrated Magazine for Young Folks* but allowed Dodge to continue in control.

In the 1880s Dodge used more serials and natural history features, and she selected poetry which de-emphasized duty and encouraged fun. First published in *St. Nicholas* in the 1880s were Frances Hodgson Burnett's *Little Lord Fauntleroy* (1886), illustrated by R. B. Birch; Dodge's *Donald and Dorothy* (1883); Charles E. Carryl's *Davy and the Goblin* (1885); Edward Eggleston's *The Hoosier School-Boy* (1882); Mayne Reid's *The Land of Fire* (1884); Brander Matthews's *Tom Paulding* (1892); and Thomas Nelson Page's *Two Little Confederates* (1888). Poet and illustrator Palmer Cox contributed thirty pieces to *St. Nicholas* during the decade, including his first published work about the Brownies in February 1883. Novelist Julia Magruder's adapted selections from five of George Eliot's novels appeared in 1887 and 1888. In 1887 Tudor Jenks became an assistant editor and a major contributor. Ernest E. Thompson and John Burroughs were the most significant writers of natural history for *St. Nicholas* in the 1880s. The Agassiz Association, sponsored by the magazine, grew to ten thousand members by 1886.

During the last fifteen years of her editorship Dodge was able to increase the length of *St. Nicholas* and add more illustrations per issue. In September 1893 the magazine absorbed *Wide Awake*, the most popular New England periodical. Mark Twain contributed the serial *Tom Sawyer Abroad, by Huck Finn* (1894). Jack London's *The Cruise of the Dazzler* was published in the magazine in July 1902. Between November 1904 and October 1905 *St. Nicholas* published L. Frank Baum's *Queen Zixi of Ix*. Rudyard Kipling contributed three pieces in the 1890s, including "Rikki-Tikki-Tavi" (November 1893), later included in *The Jungle Book* (1894). Theodore Roosevelt's *Hero Tales from American History* (1895) was serialized in the 1890s, as was Howard Pyle's *The Story of Jack Ballister's Fortunes* (1895). Illustrations continued to be excellent, with Dodge adding color and photographs. The *Quarterly Illustrator* (December 1893) said that "nearly every illustrator of talent and note has got his handiwork between the covers of *St. Nicholas*." In 1893 Clarke was promoted to associate editor. He held this position until 1905, when he was promoted to editor on the death of Dodge.

References:

Roger Burlingame, *Of Making Many Books* (New York: Scribners, 1946);

Samuel Chew, *Fruit among the Leaves* (New York: Appleton Century Crofts, 1950);

Harriet Goss and Gertrude A. Baker, *Index to St. Nicholas* (Cleveland: Cumulative Index, 1901);

Martin I. J. Griffin, *Frank R. Stockton: A Critical Biography* (Philadelphia: University of Pennsylvania Press, 1939);

Anna Lorraine Guthrie, *Index to St. Nicholas* (New York: Wilson, 1920);

Jennie L. Keith, "Selected Illustrators of Children's Literature in *St. Nicholas* Magazine, 1873-1900," Master's thesis, Kent State University, 1964;

Mary J. Roggenbuck, "*St. Nicholas* Magazine: A Study of the Impact and Historical Influence of the Editorship of Mary Mapes Dodge," Ph.D. dissertation, University of Michigan, 1976;

Florence S. Sturges, "The *St. Nicholas* Years," in *The Hewins Lectures, 1947-1962*, edited by Siri Andrews (Boston: Horn Book, 1963), pp. 267-295.

Papers:

Most of Dodge's letters are at Columbia University; the Henry E. Huntington Library, San Marino, California; and in the archives of the Century Company in the New York Public Library.

Frederick Douglass

(February 1817-20 February 1895)

Lloyd E. Chiasson
University of Southwestern Louisiana

and

Philip B. Dematteis

See also the Douglass entries in *DLB 1: The American Renaissance in New England; DLB 43: American Newspaper Journalists, 1690-1872;* and *DLB 50: Afro-American Writers Before the Harlem Renaissance.*

MAJOR POSITIONS HELD: Editor and publisher, *North Star*, renamed *Frederick Douglass's Paper* in 1851 (1847-1860), *Douglass' Monthly* (1858-1863); corresponding editor (1870-1871), editor and publisher, *New National Era* (1871-1874).

BOOKS: *Narrative of the Life of Frederick Douglass, an American Slave* (Boston: Anti-Slavery Office, 1845; Dublin: Webb & Chapman, 1845); enlarged as *My Bondage and My Freedom* (New York: Miller, Orton & Mulligan, 1855); enlarged as *Life and Times of Frederick Douglass* (Hartfort, Conn.: Park, 1881; London: Christian Age Office, 1882; revised edition, Boston: De Wolfe, Fiske, 1892);

Farewell Speech of Mr. Frederick Douglass, Previously to Embarking on Board the Cambria, *upon His Return to America, Delivered at the Valedictory Soiree Given to Him at the London Tavern, on March 30, 1847: Published, by Order of the Council of the Anti-Slavery League, from the Shorthand Notes of Mr. W. Farmer* (London: Ward, 1847);

Abolition Fanaticism in New York: Speech of a Runaway Slave from Baltimore, at an Abolition Meeting in New York, Held May 11, 1847 (Baltimore, 1847);

Letter from Frederick Douglass to His Old Master . . . Thomas Auld (Edinburgh: Printed by H. Armour, 1848?);

Lectures on American Slavery (Buffalo, N.Y.: Reese & Co.'s Power Press, 1851);

Frederick Douglass

Oration, Delivered in Corinthian Hall, Rochester, by Frederick Douglass, July 5th, 1852 (Rochester, N.Y.: Printed by Lee, Mann, 1852);

The Claims of the Negro Ethnologically Considered. An Address before the Literary Societies of Western Reserve College, at Commencement, July 12, 1854 (Rochester, N.Y.: Printed by Lee, Mann, 1854);

Arguments: Pro and Con, on the Case for a National Emigration Convention, by Douglass, W. J. Watkins, and J. M. Whitfield (Detroit: Pomeroy, 1854);

The Anti-Slavery Movement: A Lecture by Frederick Douglass, before the Rochester Ladies' Anti-

Slavery Society (Rochester, N.Y.: Press of Lee, Mann, 1855); republished as *The Nature, Character, and History of the Anti-Slavery Movement: A Lecture* (Glasgow, 1855);

Address by Frederick Douglass, and Poem by A. C. Hills Delivered at the Erection of the Wing Monument, at Mexico, Oswego Co., N.Y., September 11th, 1855 (Syracuse, N.Y.: J. G. K. Truair, 1855);

Two Speeches by Frederick Douglass: One on West India Emancipation, Delivered at Canadaigua, Aug. 4th, and the Other on the Dred Scott Decision, Delivered in New York, on the Occasion of the Aniversary of the American Abolition Society, May 1857 (Rochester, N.Y.: C. P. Dewey, printer, 1857);

Eulogy of the Late Hon. Wm. Jay, by Frederick Douglass, Delivered on the Invitation of the Colored Citizens of New York City in Shiloh Presbyterian Church, New York, May 12, 1859 (Rochester, N.Y.: Press of A. Strong & Co., 1859);

The Constitution of the United States: Is It Pro-Slavery or Anti-Slavery?: A Speech Delivered in Glasgow, March 26, 1860, in Reply to an Attack Made upon His View by Mr. George Thompson (Halifax, U.K.: T. & W. Birtwhistle, printers, 1860?);

Addresses of the Hon. W. D. Kelley, Miss Anna E. Dickinson, and Mr. Frederick Douglass, at a Mass Meeting, Philadelphia, July 6, 1863, for the Promotion of Colored Enlistments (Philadelphia, 1863);

What the Black Man Wants: Speech of Frederick Douglass at the Annual Meeting of the Massachusetts Anti-Slavery Society at Boston (Boston?, 1865?);

The Equality of All Men before the Law Claimed and Defended: In Speeches by Hon. William D. Kelley, Wendell Phillips, and Frederick Douglass, and Letters from Elizur Wright and Wm. Heighton (Boston: Rand & Avery, 1865);

U. S. Grant and the Colored People: His Wise, Just, Practical, and Effective Friendship Thoroughly Vindicated by Incontestable Facts in His Record from 1862 to 1872. Words of Truth and Soberness! He Who Runs May Read and Understand!! Be Not Deceived, Only Truth Can Endure!!! (Washington, D.C., 1872);

Address Delivered by Hon. Frederick Douglass, at the Third Annual Fair of the Tennessee Colored Agricultural Association on Thursday, September 18, 1873, at Nashville, Tennessee (Washington, D.C.: New National Era and Citizen Print., 1873);

Oration by Frederick Douglass, Delivered on Occasion of the Unveiling of the Freedmen's Monument in Memory of Abraham Lincoln, in Lincoln Park, Washington, D.C., April 14th, 1876: With an Appendix (Washington, D.C.: Gibson Brothers, printers, 1876);

Speech on the Death of William Lloyd Garrison, at the Garrison Memorial Meeting in the 15th Street Presbyterian Church, Monday, June 2, 1879 (Washington, D.C.?, 1879?);

John Brown: An Address by Frederick Douglass, at the Fourteenth Anniversary of Storer College, Harper's Ferry, West Virginia, May 30, 1881 (Dover, N.H.: Morning Star Job Printing House, 1881);

The 21st Anniversary of the Emancipation of Slavery in the District of Columbia: An Address (Washington, D.C.: National Republican, 1883);

Proceedings of the Civil Rights Mass-Meeting Held at Lincoln Hall, Oct. 22, 1883: Speeches of Hon. Frederick Douglass and Robert G. Ingersoll (Washington, D.C.: Farrell, 1883);

National Convention of Colored Men, at Louisville, Ky., September 24, 1883 (Louisville, Ky.: Courier-Journal Job Printing Co., 1883);

Address by Hon. Frederick Douglass, Delivered in the Congregational Church, Washington, D.C., April 16, 1883: On the Twenty-first Anniversary of Emancipation in the District of Columbia (Washington, D.C., 1883);

Three Addresses on the Relations Subsisting between the White and Colored People of the United States (Washington, D.C.: Gibson Brothers, printers, 1886);

The Nation's Problem: A Speech, Delivered before the Bethel Literary and Historical Society in Washington, D.C., April 16, 1889 (Washington, D.C.?, 1889);

The Race Problem: Great Speech of Frederick Douglass, Delivered before the Bethel Literary and Historical Association in the Metropolitan A.M.E. Church, Washington, D.C., October 21, 1890 (Washington, D.C.?, 1890?);

The Reason Why: The Colored American Is Not in the World's Columbian Exposition. The Afro-American's Contribution to Columbian Literature (Chicago, 1893);

Lecture on Haiti: The Haitian Pavilion Dedication Ceremonies Delivered at the World's Fair, in Jackson Park, Chicago, Jan. 2d, 1893 (Chicago, 1893);

Address by Hon. Frederick Douglass, Delivered in the Metropolitan A.M.E. Church, Washington, D.C., Tuesday, January 9th, 1894, on the Lessons of the Hour: In Which He Discusses the Various As-

pects of the So-Called, but Mis-Called, Negro Problem (Baltimore: Press of Thomas & Evans, 1894);

A Defense of the Negro Race: An Address Delivered at the Annual Meeting of the American Missionary Association in Lowell, Mass., 1894 (New York: American Missionary Association Bible House, 1894);

Why Is the Negro Lynched? By the Late Frederick Douglass (Bridgewater: Printed by J. Whitby & Sons, 1895);

Negroes and the National War Effort: An Address by Frederick Douglass (New York: Workers Library Publishers, 1942);

Frederick Douglass: Selections from His Writings, edited by Philip S. Foner (New York: International Publishers, 1945);

Frederick Douglass, John Brown and West Virginia: "John Brown," an Address by Frederick Douglass and Delivered at Harpers Ferry, May 30, 1881 on the Occasion of the Fourteenth Anniversary of the Storer College, edited by John Reuben Sheeler (Institute: West Virginia State College, Department of History, 1953);

Frederick Douglass on Women's Rights, edited by Foner (Westport, Conn.: Greenwood Press, 1976);

A Black Diplomat in Haiti: The Diplomatic Correspondence of U.S. Minister Frederick Douglass from Haiti, 1889-1891, edited by Norma Brown (Salisbury, N.C.: Documentary Publications, 1977);

The Frederick Douglass Papers: Series One: Speeches, Debates, and Interviews. Volume I: Eighteen-Forty-One to Eighteen-Forty-Six, edited by John W. Blassingame (New Haven: Yale University Press, 1979).

OTHER: "The Heroic Slave," in *Autographs for Freedom*, edited by Julia Griffiths (Boston: Jewett, 1859).

PERIODICAL PUBLICATION: "An Appeal to Congress for Impartial Suffrage," *Atlantic Monthly*, 19 (January 1867): 112-117.

As a journalist, Frederick Douglass is mainly remembered for establishing the *North Star*, one of the most highly acclaimed abolitionist newspapers. He also founded and edited *Douglass' Monthly*, one of the few abolitionist magazines.

Frederick Augustus Washington Bailey was born in Tuckahoe, Talbot County, Maryland, probably in 1817. His mother, Harriet Bailey,

Douglass shortly before he founded his abolitionist newspaper, the North Star

could read–an unusual skill for a slave. His father may have been his white master. As a child he escaped the rigors of field labor for a time when he was sent from Lloyd Plantation in Talbot County to Fell Point in Baltimore, where he served as companion to the son of Hugh Auld, the younger brother of the overseer at Lloyd Plantation. Auld's kindhearted wife, Sophia Auld, taught him to read and write. He lived a remarkably unconfined life in Baltimore, cultivating white friends and, to a degree, moving freely in both white and black circles. One result was that he became more aware of the magnitude of social injustice in the United States. By the time he was sent back to Lloyd Plantation he had developed a keen social awareness. At age sixteen he helped establish two black Sabbath schools in Talbot County. Returned to Baltimore to work in a shipyard, he escaped his enslavement in 1838 by impersonating a free black sailor. He immediately went to Philadelphia and then to New York City, where he married a freedwoman, Anna Murray. Adopting the name Douglass to elude pursuers, the couple moved to Massachusetts, where Douglass worked at a series of menial jobs.

By 1839 Douglass was publicly speaking to black groups against the proposed "recolonization" of American blacks in Africa. In 1841 he attended a convention of the Massachusetts Anti-Slavery Society in Nantucket; after impressing the audience with his eloquent speaking and formidable intellect, he was asked to become a spokesman for the society. Douglass agreed and immediately went on tour.

Douglass's autobiography, *Narrative of the Life of Frederick Douglass, an American Slave* (1845), sold more than thirty thousand copies; the book made him a folk hero to many free northern blacks as well as a prominent figure in the abolitionist cause. In August 1847 he left for a speaking tour of Ireland, Scotland, and England. When he returned to the United States in 1847 he moved to Rochester, New York, and established the *North Star*. The newspaper's motto was "Right is of no Sex—Truth is of no Color—God is the Father of us all, and we are all Brethren." Although the weekly was an abolitionist journal, Douglass wrote in the first issue that it would be open to discussion of all topics of a "moral and humane character, which may serve to enlighten, improve and elevate mankind." Besides advocating the abolition of slavery, he diligently supported the women's movement.

The *North Star* was not a financial success, but it was a unique and powerful force in the antislavery movement. Its greatest asset was Douglass, who continually validated his cause through the quality of his work. The *North Star* was a constant reminder to the white public that the black race was not congenitally inferior. Douglass always insisted on high editorial and stylistic standards; the abolitionist editor William Lloyd Garrison praised the newspaper as one of the best literary journals, antislavery or proslavery, in the country.

Largely because of high illiteracy rates among blacks, five of every six readers of the *North Star* were white. The paper was well received by women because of its progressive stance concerning the women's movement. Douglass attended the first Women's Rights Convention in 1848 and was a lifelong supporter of woman suffrage. In fact, at one point he thought of changing the name of the newspaper to "The Brotherhood" but rejected the idea because it "implied the exclusion of the sisterhood."

In 1851 Douglass merged the *North Star* with the floundering *Liberty Party Paper* and renamed it *Frederick Douglass's Paper* in hopes that his fame might spark circulation growth, but the paper continued to struggle with financial difficulties. To raise funds for the journal, in 1859 a giftbook of essays, stories, and letters by various abolitionists titled *Autographs for Freedom* was published by Julia Griffiths, Douglass's business manager. One of the contributions was a short story by Douglass, "The Heroic Slave," about an uprising on a slave ship. The story suggests Douglass was moving away from his earlier stance that abolition might be attained without violence.

In 1858 Douglass established *Douglass' Monthly*, an abolitionist magazine published both in Great Britain and the United States, but primarily aimed at a British audience in the hope of garnering financial support for the Union. *Frederick Douglass's Paper* ceased publication in 1860. *Douglass' Monthly* followed in 1863.

In 1870 Douglass became corresponding editor of the *New National Era*, a weekly based in Washington, D.C. One year later he purchased the magazine and continued to publish it until 1874. In 1872 he was nominated for vice-president on the Equal Rights party ticket; he was to have run with Victoria C. Woodhull, another noted journalist and women's rights advocate, but he opted instead to campaign for the reelection of President Grant. In 1877 he was appointed United States marshal for the District of Columbia. His first wife died in 1882; in 1884 he married his white secretary, Helen Pitts.

In 1889 Douglass was named consul general to Haiti. He returned to private life two years later. He died of a heart attack on 20 February 1895 and was buried in Rochester, New York.

References:

Charles W. Chesnutt, *Frederick Douglass* (Boston: Small, Maynard, 1899);

Philip S. Foner, *The Life and Writings of Frederick Douglass*, 5 volumes (New York: International Publishers, 1950-1955, 1975);

Frederick May Holland, *Frederick Douglass: The Colored Orator* (New York & London: Funk & Wagnalls, 1891);

Waldo Martin, Jr., *The Mind of Frederick Douglass* (Chapel Hill & London: University of North Carolina Press, 1984);

Dickson Preston, *Young Frederick Douglass* (Baltimore & London: Johns Hopkins University Press, 1980);

Benjamin Quarles, *Frederick Douglass* (Washington, D.C.: Associated Publishers, 1948);

J. White, "Black Papers," *Journal of American Studies*, 19 (April 1985): 105-110.

Papers:
Frederick Douglass's papers are held at Howard University, the University of Southern California, and the Library of Congress.

Richard Kyle Fox

(12 August 1846-14 November 1922)

Sam G. Riley
Virginia Polytechnic Institute & State University

MAJOR POSITION HELD: Editor and publisher, *National Police Gazette* (1877-1922).

BOOKS: *Edward Hanlan, America's Champion Oarsman, with History and Portrait: Also, History and Portrait of Edward A. Trickett, the Great Australian Oarsman* (New York: Fox, 1880);

Slang Dictionary of New York, London and Paris: A Collection of Strange Figures of Speech, Expressive Terms and Odd Phrases Used in the Leading Cities of the World (New York: National Police Gazette, 1880);

John C. Heenan, Champion Pugilist of the World (New York: Fox, 1881);

Adventuress Eva; or, The Wiles of a Wicked Woman: Pages from the Life History of Mrs. Robert Ray Hamilton (New York: Fox, 1889);

Boxing, with Hints on the Art of Attack and Defense and How to Train for the Prize Ring . . . By an Expert (New York: Fox, 1889);

Devil Anse; or, The Hatfield-McCoy Outlaws . . . Trujillo; or Bob Montclair, the Terror of Eldorado (New York: Fox, 1889);

The Disaster Which Eclipsed History. The Johnstown Flood (New York: Fox, 1889);

The Great Battle Between John L. Sullivan and Jake Kilrain (New York: Fox, 1889);

Prize Ring Champions of England from 1719 to 1889 (New York: Fox, 1889);

Prize Ring Heroes: Life and Battles of Tom Hyer, Yankee Sullivan, John Morrissey, John C. Heenan, Tom King (New York: Fox, 1889);

Tom Sayers, England's Great Pugilist: His Life and Battles (New York: Fox, 1889);

Richard Kyle Fox (photo from the Albert Davis Collection)

The Black Champions of the Prize Ring From Molineaux to Jackson (New York: Fox, 1890);

Detective Secrets: Showing the Methods Pursued by Trustworthy Men, and Exposing the Tricks,

Schemes and Devices of a Certain Class of "Private" Detectives (New York: Fox, 1890);

Rube Burrow's Raids. Historic Highwaymen. Night Riders of Ozark; or, The Bald Knobbers of Missouri (New York: Fox, 1891);

Life and Battles of James J. Corbett, the Champion Pugilist of the World (New York: Fox, 1892);

The Life and Battles of Jack Johnson, Champion Pugilist of the World (New York: Fox, 1909);

The Cocker's Guide; How to Breed, Train, and Feed Game Birds for the Pit (New York: Fox, 1909);

Prof. Attila's Five Pound Dumb Bell Exercise (New York: Fox, 1913);

The New Book of Rules, Official and Standard. Together With the Rules of the Amateur Athletic Union (New York: Fox, 1913).

Richard Kyle Fox achieved considerable financial success as a magazine publisher but has been ignored in journalistic histories, especially by those historians who are inclined to put a good face on periodical publishing's history. Fox is seldom included in historical accounts of American magazines due to the base level of reading taste to which his *National Police Gazette* appealed. Writers of history too often forget that not all readers have had the luxury of educations calculated to attract them to a more dignified, intellectual class of reading matter.

Richard Fox was born in Belfast, Ireland, in 1846 to carpenter and mason James Fox and his wife Mary, the daughter of a Presbyterian minister. While a boy of twelve, Fox was employed by the *Banner of Ulster*, a Presbyterian paper with which he remained for four years. For an additional twelve years he worked for the leading Irish newspaper, the *Belfast News Letter*. He married Annie Scott of Belfast in 1869 and in 1874 immigrated to America, arriving in New York City on 12 July of that year aboard the ship *Tuscarora*. Within three days after his arrival, Fox was employed by the *New York Commercial Bulletin* as an advertising salesman. By the end of the same year he had become business manager of the *National Police Gazette*, a financially troubled periodical that had been founded in September of 1845 by journalist George Wilkes and lawyer Enoch E. Camp. The *Gazette*, which had been fashioned after such earlier English periodicals as *Bell's Penny Dispatch, Sporting and Police Gazette*, and the *Penny Sunday Times and People's Police Gazette*, had a few stormy but moderately successful years until Wilkes also signed on as an assistant editor of the *Spirit of the Times*, a sporting journal, and gradually lost interest in the *Gazette*.

Following the financial panic of 1857, the *Gazette* was sold to former New York police chief George Matsell, who did poorly with it and in turn sold it to his engravers, Mooney & Lederer. Herbert Mooney's editorial leadership was no more successful than Matsell's, and in 1878 Fox acquired full control of the moribund *Gazette* in lieu of salary and commissions owed him.

To make his periodical stand out, Fox began printing it on pink paper stock. Though an early Fox editorial piously promised that under his management nothing of "immoral tendency" would appear in the *Gazette*, the new owner must have soon repented of this attitude, for the periodical made its sensational way with accounts of vile seductions, fatal assignations, lynchings, druggings, prostitution, perversion, gory catastrophies, midnight revelry, gambling, and brawling. The *Gazette* was altogether a picture of New York City from the underside, a chronicle of events that were too rough or too undignified to be chronicled elsewhere. It was not a periodical for the squeamish or the prudish.

The *Police Gazette* was not quite a magazine and not quite a newspaper, much like today's *National Enquirer* and its several competitors. Such periodicals are produced on newsprint in tabloid format, yet they certainly do not report news in the manner of an ordinary newspaper. They are, therefore, often classified as nonnewspaper periodicals.

Like the owners of today's supermarket tabloids and pulps, Fox filled his periodical with sensationalism, carving out a market niche at or near the subbasement level of reading taste. Writer Gene Smith has described Fox as "a good hater," pointing out his distaste for minorities, the privileged class, the clergy, and politicians. Persons of the Jewish faith became, in Fox's terminology, those "of the sheeny persuasion." Indians were brutal "red devils," the best of whom were the dead ones. The position of the *Gazette* was that America's Chinese immigrants were "moral lepers," "opium eaters," and "despoilers of female virtue," and should be deported en masse. Mixed marriages especially roused Fox's ire. An 1889 woodcut pictured a black man strolling arm in arm with his white wife, the caption reading, "A Pretty White Girl of Xenia, Ohio, Marries a Hunk of Charcoal and Parades the Streets With Him."

Fox's distaste for organized religion and the clergy and the hypocrisy that sometimes accompanied them resulted in articles under such headlines as "Crooked Clergymen" or simply "Religious Notes." One example was an account of a Methodist minister in Illinois, a "sanctimonious villain" who tried to have his way with an innocent choir girl, another the saga of a New Hampshire Salvation Army evangelist who had been convicted of child abuse. Fox evidently saw no inconsistency in profiting from sexual titillation in his own pages while condemning "the foul stain of Mormonism" and its practice of polygamy.

When religious groups struck back at the *Gazette* instead of turning the other cheek, Fox gleefully gave space in his periodical to their remarks, as when in 1884 the Iowa Conference of the Methodist Episcopal Church passed a resolution denouncing the *Gazette* as "a crime against innocence and purity which cries to heaven for correction" and as "an insidious and deadly poison, debasing the morality of the youth of our commonwealth."

Under "Noose Notes" appeared lurid accounts of lynchings and hangings, and crimes that were bizarre or brutal enough were described in detail. In the 1880s Fox showed an increasing interest in the stage, particularly in actresses who disported themselves in tights and décolleté. Fox's ace writer Samuel Mackeever covered the New York stage scene for the *Gazette*, writing under the pen name "The Marquis of Largnette," following up on his earlier success as "Paul Prowler," a series of observations of life as lived in New York. Bylines did not appear on *Gazette* articles. Apparently a great deal of the periodical's copy was free-lanced by members of New York's newspaper press in their off-hours. Some of it was done on weekends when Fox would lock a number of hard-drinking journalists in a room with four bottles of whisky, food supplies, and couches for napping. When they were released on Sunday, Fox paid each of them ten dollars.

By contrast, most of the woodcut artists at the *Gazette* were full-time staffers. Among these were Paul Cusacha, Charles Kendrick, George E. McEvoy, Matt Morgan, and George G. White. The quality of *Gazette* woodcuts varied from crude to very fine, but always they were sensational, suggestive, or action-packed. Murders, brawls, disasters, and scenes of debauchery were to be expected in *Gazette* illustrations. Scenes of fist-fighting, hair-pulling females were a Fox favorite. Both the front and back cover pages were dom-

Offices of the National Police Gazette, *183 William Street at the corner of Spruce Street, New York*

inated by large woodcuts, and most of the inside contents were lavishly and luridly illustrated, as well. In this present day of angular *Vogue* models one is struck by the voluptuousness of the women presented in Fox's illustrations. By the early 1900s, halftones had largely supplanted linecuts in the *Gazette*.

After the first year of the *Gazette* with Fox in command, sports articles became far more common. Perhaps as much as any other media figure of the late 1800s, Fox ballyhooed sport and laid the foundation for making it the all-consuming fascination it has become in contemporary America. Though baseball, football, horse racing, sculling, and other sporting competitions received attention, Fox's real passion was boxing, not so much because of personal attachment to it, but because he saw this most savage of sports as the greatest possible circulation builder. One of the first major bare-knuckle fights covered by the *Gazette* was an eighty-seven-round match between American Paddy Ryan and Englishman Joe Goss. As this form of sport was illegal, the newspaper press of the day paid it only limited attention, which gave Fox a clear opening. Circulation for his fight issue reached an astonishing four hundred thousand. With an eye toward further profit, Fox became Ryan's primary backer.

Up-and-coming boxer John L. Sullivan came to New York and tried to arrange a match with Ryan. The "Boston Strong Boy" was unsuccessful in doing so until he snubbed Fox in a New York restaurant by refusing to come to Fox's table when invited. The match with Paddy Ryan was soon arranged, Fox counting on Ryan to avenge his wounded pride. Sullivan won instead, and in a mere eight minutes. Thereafter Fox brought in a series of challengers to humble the great Sullivan. All were defeated, yet the *Gazette* now enjoyed a steady 150,000 circulation, making Fox a wealthy man. Though he did not originate the idea of giving championship belts, Fox popularized the practice in America. The heavyweight belt, first held by Jake Kilrain, then taken away by Sullivan, cost Fox four thousand dollars and was studded with gold, diamonds, emeralds, rubies, and sapphires.

Fox can also be given at least partial credit for having boxing recognized in the United States as a legal sport. After his promotion of an 1883 match at New York's Madison Square Garden between Sullivan and Herbert Slade of New Zealand, a warrant was issued for Fox's arrest. Fox and his legal team went on the offensive, arguing that the event had been a "sparring exhibition" with gloves rather than an actual combat. His lawyers were able to point to a number of distinguished ministers, doctors, and other respectable personages, including Henry Ward Beecher, who boxed. The judge decided in Fox's favor, and the *Gazette* owner received a great deal of very pleasing publicity.

Many notables attended the fights that Fox promoted. Among them were Roscoe Conkling, William K. Vanderbilt, the Reverend Beecher, the Reverend DeWitt Talmage, Charles Tiffany, Cyrus Field, Elihu Root, James Colgate, and Henry Flagler. Their presence at ringside probably made boxing more socially acceptable and perhaps influenced the court in 1884 when next Fox went before a judge to defend boxing following the Sullivan-Alf Greenfield bout. Again Fox won.

Finally in 1892 the *Gazette* was able to report the knockout of John L. Sullivan by Jim Corbett.

Though Fox was not known to participate personally in any sport, he was an enthusiastic sponsor of all sorts of sporting events. He awarded belts and gold medals to winners in a wide variety of competitions–not just ordinary sports, but also the likes of horseback wrestling, teeth lifting, and walking marathons. In addition, the *Gazette* reported other bizarre contests: the exploits of a boxing kangaroo, a sleeping marathon, and a gory battle to the death between two bulls. Stories on dogfighting, cockfighting, rat baiting, and badger baiting abounded. Presaging today's *Guinness Book of World Records,* Fox also sponsored awards for championship hog butcherers, oyster openers, drink mixers, pea shuckers, pie eaters, whistlers, barbers, doughnut makers, steeple climbers, and the like.

Fox's fascination with the sensational introduced *Gazette* readers to strongmen Louis Cyr and Louis Kuhne ("Polydore, the Man of Iron"), and even a strongwoman, an imposing person calling herself "Minerva." Equally daunting were Hattie Leslie, champion woman pugilist; female wrestling champion Alice Williams; Jaguarina, the Spanish fencing sensation; and the more familiar Annie Oakley, who in 1883 received a *Gazette* medal from Fox for her incredible marksmanship. One of the most unusual of Fox's belted champions was amputee T. F. Grant, world champion one-legged clog dancer. One of the zaniest was Brooklyn newsboy Steve Brodie, whom the *Gazette* described as an "aerial jumper" and whose claim to fame was jumping off bridges.

The no-holds-barred content of the *Gazette* resulted in numerous libel suits, including one in which actress Lillian Russell asked twenty thousand dollars, but Fox was treated leniently by the courts. That the content of his advertising columns was the cause of Fox's arrest on at least four occasions was due to the zealous efforts of the New York Society for the Suppression of Vice, though his worst punishment was a five-hundred-dollar fine. The weekly *Gazette* carried two pages of advertising, mostly for items too disreputable to be advertised in more respectable periodicals. Included were a whole array of products for "weak manhood," cures for venereal diseases, body odor, drug addiction, piles, and tapeworms; decks of marked cards, surefire betting systems, and methods of enlarging "certain parts of the body."

Woodcut from the National Police Gazette, *showing Fox's predilection for illustrations featuring scantily clad women*

Fox's considerable revenue from circulation and advertising was increased by special picture supplements, "cabinet-size photographs," often of actresses–the buyer could specify whether he wanted shots showing them in tights, showing their busts, or in costume–and a sporting annual filled with rules and records. Also swelling his coffers were short, cheap books published under his own imprint. Some attributed authorship to Fox himself; others were done by writers who worked for the *Gazette*. The first of these attributed to Fox appeared in 1880: *Edward Hanlan, America's Champion Oarsman*. Several others were about boxing or famous pugilists: Sullivan, Kilrain, Tom Sayers, Jim Corbett, and others. All were profusely illustrated and brief enough to satisfy the shortest attention span.

It has been said that no one ever lost money by underestimating the taste of the American public. Fox must have agreed, as his net worth escalated most satisfactorily. In 1883 elaborate new seven-story quarters for the *Gazette* were completed on Franklin Square near the base of the new Brooklyn Bridge. One room was open to the public as a sort of museum of sport.

The *Gazette* circulation held at roughly 150,000 through most of the 1890s, then began to decline due to the competition of yellow journalism in general, and in particular to increased sports coverage and Sunday magazine sections in New York's newspapers. By World War I it had fallen to 60,000. The *Gazette* was too racy to be sold at ordinary newsstands and had long been found instead in bars and barbershops. With the adoption of the Eighteenth Amendment, the barroom circulation was lost; and in 1922, the year of Fox's demise, women began going to barbershops to have their hair bobbed, making it unseemly to have the *Gazette* lying around in view of lady customers.

In 1890 Fox's first wife died, and in 1913 he was married to Emma Louise (Raven) Robinson, who, like his sons Charles, Richard Jr., and Frederick, and one daughter, Mary Kyle, survived him.

At one time in his most prosperous years, Fox turned reformer, if only briefly. He purchased a row of run-down tenements in the Chinatown section of New York and renovated them for low-income renters, putting in marble stairways, hot water, gas heat, and bathrooms, and even decorating their public areas with bronze statues. Rent was set at ten to fifteen dollars monthly. His reformatory inclinations suffered when he received word that Fox Flats residents had sold his statues, bathroom fixtures, and even some of the marble from the stairways for rent and beer money.

The Foxes enjoyed the good life, making annual trips to Europe and collecting fine furniture and carpets. Some of Fox's time was spent at his California ranch at Arcadia in Los Angeles County. Fox died at his home in Red Bank, New Jersey, on 14 November 1922, leaving an estate of three million dollars and son Charles J. Fox in charge of the declining *Police Gazette*. Under editor Ralph D. Robinson, the periodical made a brief comeback, partly because of the popularity of boxer Jack Dempsey, and in 1926 circulation peaked at two hundred thousand. Then its fortunes sank again, largely because of competition from a new crop of confession magazines and other forms of pulp literature. In 1932 the *Gazette* was bankrupt and was sold for $545. It was revived by Mrs. Merle Williams Hersey in 1934 and limped on for some years in various formats.

In a sympathetic reflection on Fox that appeared in the Répétition Générale section of their magazine *Smart Set,* George Jean Nathan and H. L. Mencken noted that Fox had been of the editorial generation that included such eminences as Richard Watson Gilder, Henry Mills Alden, Walter Hines Page, and Lyman Abbott; yet of them all, only Fox had achieved "broad international fame." Only Charles Anderson Dana and William Randolph Hearst, they added, had had so profound an influence on American journalism. Fox's *Gazette* had been the first large-circulation periodical to treat sport as a serious, worthy topic and had anticipated the sports sections that eventually appeared in U.S. newspapers. Nathan and Mencken remarked that many other publishers had imitated Fox's use of tinted paper stock: Bennett in his *New York Telegram,* Hearst in his *Journal,* Pulitzer in the sporting edition of his *Evening World,* plus papers and periodicals in London, Paris, Rome, Venice, and Berlin. They reminded their readers that Fox originated the prize contest as a circulation builder, as well as the idea of holding competitions under the sponsorship of a periodical, and they heartily approved of Fox's editorial dictum: "1. Be interesting. 2. And be quick about it."

References:

Walter Davenport, "The Dirt Disher," *Collier's,* 81 (24 March 1928): 26, 30, 52-53;

Davenport, "The Nickel Shocker," *Collier's,* 81 (10 March 1928): 26-28, 38, 40;

Frank Luther Mott, *A History of American Magazines,* volume 2 (Cambridge, Mass.: Harvard University Press, 1930), pp. 325-337;

George Jean Nathan and H. L. Mencken, "Répétition Générale," *Smart Set,* 70 (February 1923): 33-35;

Gene Smith and Jane Barry Smith, eds., *The Police Gazette* (New York: Simon & Schuster, 1972);

Edward Van Every, *Sins of New York as "Exposed" by the Police Gazette* (New York: Blom, 1972).

Jeannette L. Gilder
(3 October 1849-17 January 1916)

W. J. Hug
Auburn University

MAJOR POSITIONS HELD: Review editor, *New York Herald* (1875-1881); coeditor (1881-1901), editor (1901-1906), *Critic*.

BOOKS: *Taken by Siege: A Novel* (Philadelphia: Lippincott, 1887);
The Autobiography of a Tom-Boy (New York: Doubleday, Page, 1900);
The Tom-Boy at Work (New York: Doubleday, Page, 1904).

OTHER: *The Homes and Haunts of Our Elder Poets*, edited by Gilder (New York: Appleton, 1881);
Essays from "The Critic," edited by Jeannette and Joseph Gilder (Boston: Osgood, 1882);
Representative Poems of Living Poets, American and English, Selected by the Poets Themselves, edited by Gilder (New York: Cassell, 1886);
Pen Portraits of Literary Women, by Themselves and Others, edited by Gilder and Helen Gray Cone (New York: Cassell, 1887);
Authors at Home: Personal and Biographical Sketches of Well-Known American Writers, edited by Jeannette and Joseph Gilder (New York: Cassell, 1888);
Masterpieces of the World's Best Literature, 8 volumes, edited by Gilder (New York: The Christian Herald, 1905);
The Heart of Youth: Young People's Poems, Gay and Grave, edited by Gilder (New York: Sturgis & Walton, 1911).

PLAY PRODUCTIONS: *Quits,* Philadelphia, Chestnut Street Theatre, 1876;
Sevenoaks, adapted from the novel by Josiah G. Holland, John T. Raymond's traveling theatre company, 1878.

Jeannette L. Gilder

From January 1881 until September 1906 Jeannette Gilder edited the *Critic*, one of America's more influential literary magazines. She and her brother Joseph began the project in a tiny second-story office at New York City's Eighth Street and Broadway and shared editorial duties until 1901, when Joseph retired to take a position as a London representative of a major publishing house. Though the *Critic*'s circulation was never much above five thousand, it became highly respected for its incisive reviews of literature, music, and drama, and for its publication of essays, poetry, and fiction by some of America's most talented writers, such as Walt Whitman, Thomas Bailey Aldrich, and Joel Chandler Harris. In fact, when the magazine was merged with *Putnam's Monthly* in 1906, *Putnam's* noted that "the list of its contributors during the quarter century of its existence includes the best known names of recent ... literature." Its achievement was due in large measure to the energy and enthusiasm of Jeannette Gilder.

Jeannette Leonard Gilder was born 3 October 1849 in Flushing, New York, one of seven children of William Gilder, the principal of a Long Island "female seminary," and Jane Nutt Gilder. But Gilder would never have become one of her father's model pupils. In her self-portrayals, *The Autobiography of a Tom-Boy* (1900) and *The Tom-Boy at Work* (1904), she proudly acknowledges that she was a rebel from the outset. Her childhood was a series of unfeminine exploits: she ran away from home at four, chose to ride horses backwards so she could slide off more easily, and sheared her hair because it was always in her way. Her love of books prompted her to rig a candle and piece of tin for a reflector, so she could read secretly after bedtime. Even as a girl, she disliked the occupations traditionally open to women: "I didn't want to be a dressmaker," she proclaims in *The Autobiography of a Tom-Boy*, "though I would not have minded being a cabinetmaker." After considering careers as soldier or doctor, she hit upon the notion of becoming a newspaper editor and at age twelve printed a newspaper written entirely by herself and one of her brothers. It was a childhood prelude to her literary career, which began far sooner than she or anyone else expected.

When William Gilder died of smallpox contracted while nursing federal troops late in the Civil War, his son Richard came out of the army and took work as a newspaper reporter to support the family. Though only fifteen, Jeanette was determined to help him. She first found a job doing research for a historical account of the troops in New Jersey during the Civil War. After that, she worked as a seamstress making gold bags at the Philadelphia mint, then as a clerk in an accountant's office. When Richard Gilder and a partner started a morning paper, the *Newark* (New Jersey) *Register*, she became a reporter for it and for Whitelaw Reid's *New York Tribune*. Though Richard Gilder soon left the *Register* to embark on a series of editorial jobs that brought him to the editor's chair at *Scribner's* and its successor, the *Century*, Jeannette remained with the paper, reviewing plays and books and writing editorials whenever the managing editor drank too much. She, too, departed, however, when one of the *Register*'s owners requisitioned her complementary tickets to an operatic concert. Soon after, she was fired as Newark reporter for the *Tribune* when Reid discovered that "J. L. Gilder" was a woman and became anxious that she might not be able to cover the beat–although she had done so for three years.

Through her friendship with the noted New York journalist Kate Field, she was hired by James Gordon Bennett of the *New York Herald* to write book reviews on the condition that she be innovative. At Field's suggestion, Gilder couched her reviews in the dramatic framework of a family conversation, with the various members taking different opinions in the discussion. "Chats about Books" became one of the *Herald*'s most popular features. Eventually, Gilder was promoted to the paper's review editor for literature, drama, and music. During her six years in this position she established herself as one of the most insightful interpreters of New York's artistic and intellectual scenes. Finally, with $750 she received for editing an Appleton giftbook, *The Homes and Haunts of Our Elder Poets* (1881), she and Joseph, who had been night editor for the *Herald*, embarked on the *Critic* project. Her concern for its quality and success would dominate her life for the next quarter century.

Though the *Critic*'s ownership, format, and publication schedule changed several times during its twenty-five years, the magazine always relied heavily upon the literary trade Jeannette Gilder knew best–reviewing. In fact, when the *Critic* first appeared, she and Joseph were obliged to write most of the reviews themselves, until they could build a knowledgeable and reliable staff. Early issues categorized reviews under four rubrics–"Literary Notes," "Music," "The Drama," "The Fine Arts"–and included a single essay on a literary topic; occasionally, poetry and fiction appeared as well. Over the years, the magazine became more diverse as greater emphasis was given to reviews of books and literary magazines and to essays, fiction, and poetry; less emphasis was given to reviews of drama, music, and the fine arts. But from the *Critic*'s beginning until its end, its notices were always incisive, high-toned, and conservative. Its literary reviews reflected a bias toward American writers: Henry James's novels were praised as epitomes of cool, analytic craftsmanship, while William Dean Howells's were described as less meticulous but expressive of greater feeling.

With the more liberal English and Continental authors, the *Critic*'s reviewers were not always as generous. Though inclined to be favorable to George Eliot and Ivan Turgenev, they complained that Thomas Hardy's *Jude the Obscure* (1895) reflected grave departures from morality

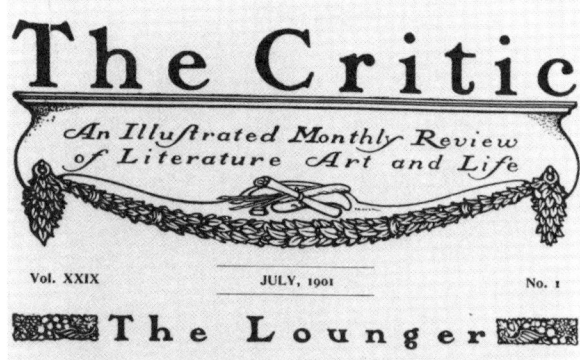

Opening page from a bound volume of the influential literary magazine edited by Gilder

and good taste. A review of Oscar Wilde's *Poems* (1881), asserted that "never in recent times has a book of so much and so carefully studied foppery been given to the public." But the Gilders and their staff reserved their true spleen for reviews of the risqué novels by the French naturalist Émile Zola. In discussing his *Au Bonheur des Dames* (1883), the *Critic* likened Zola to the Marquis de Sade. A later review decried Zola's *Pot-Bouille* (1882) as "a filthy book" and proclaimed that "no book so foul and vile has ever been issued by reputable French publishers."

In assessing current music, drama, and painting, the *Critic*'s conservatism and American bias were less apparent. Its liberality in these areas probably stemmed from Jeannette Gilder's awareness, acquired over her years as reviewer and editor for the *Tribune*, that these art forms were more mature abroad than in America. She and her staff consistently defended Wagner and his operas and gave their New York performances favorable notices. Her signed 1906 review of Henrik Ibsen's translated letters praised the Norwegian's sensitivity as a playwright and as a person. On the other hand, the *Critic* panned an 1883 exhibition of James M. Whistler's etchings as "slovenly," "careless," and inferior to his earlier work; the notice describing a 1904 exhibit by American portrait painters was decidedly mixed.

To complement the *Critic*'s reviews, Jeannette and Joseph Gilder provided essays, fiction, and poetry by an impressive array of both rising and established American writers. The magazine's first number featured E. C. Stedman on "William Blake, Poet and Painter"; its second included Walt Whitman's "How I Get around at 60 and Take Notes" and Edward Eggleston's "George Eliot and the Novel." Joel Chandler Harris's *Nights with Uncle Remus* (1883) was first published as a serial in the *Critic*. Its contributors and their material were so impressive that in the magazine's second year the Gilders published *Essays from "The Critic."* Nor did the magazine's quality slacken. The volumes published after the turn of the century include works by Thomas Wentworth Higginson, Henry Blake Fuller, Theodore Roosevelt, Julian Hawthorne, and Henry Cabot Lodge.

In these later years, after Gilder had taken over all editorial responsibilities, she continued to write "The Lounger," a popular column she had begun in the 1880s. Though sometimes devoted to a particular artistic issue, it was usually a grab bag of literary and intellectual small talk. For instance, "The Lounger" of January 1904 notes that Julian Hawthorne had left his job as a Philadelphia newspaper editor to write free-lance in Yonkers, New York; marks the death of the English philosopher Herbert Spencer; and reviews Jacob Riis's *Outlook* articles on Theodore Roosevelt and the University of Chicago's translation of *The Code of Hammurabi*. Gilder remarks in passing that Hammurabi's code is "interesting, but not perhaps . . . so worldly wise as the code of our own 'Poor Richard.'" "The Lounger" became so characteristic of the *Critic* that, when the magazine merged with *Putnam's Monthly* in 1906, *Putnam's* asked her to continue the feature. She did so until 1910, when *Putnam's* was taken over by the *Atlantic*.

Besides her responsibilities at the *Critic*, Gilder was constantly involved in a variety of journalistic, literary, and dramatic pursuits. For eighteen years she served as New York correspondent for the *Boston Saturday Evening Gazette* and later

Gilder in old age with her dog

the *Boston Evening Transcript*; for both she wrote under the pen name "Brunswick." At different times she was also New York correspondent for the *Philadelphia Press* and *Record* and the first American correspondent for the London *Academy*. In addition, she was a regular contributor to the *New York World,* the *Chicago Tribune,* the London *Daily Mail,* and to *Harper's* and *McClure's* magazines. Gilder edited several books in addition to *Essays from "The Critic."* She and her brother compiled *Authors at Home* (1888). With Helen Gray Cone she edited the two-volume *Pen Portraits of Literary Women* (1887). She served as sole editor of *Representative Poems of Living Poets* (1886) and the eight-volume *Masterpieces of the World's Best Literature* (1905). Her books include *Taken by Siege* (1887), a light novel about New York's newspaper and artistic life, and her two thinly veiled autobiographical volumes. Her years of reviewing for the *New York Herald* prompted Gilder to try her hand at playwriting as well, with moderate success. Her first drama, *Quits,* was produced by Philadelphia's Chestnut Street Theatre in 1876. In 1878 she dramatized Josiah G. Holland's 1875 best-seller *Sevenoaks,* which was performed by John T. Raymond's traveling company. With her insider's knowledge of theater and books, she established in 1895 a literary brokerage known as Miss Gilder's Syndicate. As New York agent for writers from around the country, she negotiated publication and dramatic rights to novels and performance rights to plays. The brokerage prospered until Gilder's death from a stroke on 17 January 1916. She was buried in Bordentown, New Jersey, her family's home during the Civil War.

Though Jeannette Gilder will not be remembered as an author in her own right, she merits a niche in the history of American magazines for her work as editor of the *Critic.* Her efforts and those of Joseph Gilder made it a consistent source of keen commentary on literature and the other arts, as well as an important vehicle for some of the best essayists, poets, and storytellers in the nation. E. C.. Stedman's appraisal of the *Critic* in its sixth year held just as true in its twenty-fifth: as he told Jeannette Gilder and her brother in 1887, "You maintain a high and impartial standard of criticism, and have brought out the talent of new and excellent writers."

Biography:

Julia R. Tutwiler, "Jeannette L. Gilder," in *Women Authors of Our Day in Their Homes,* edited by

Francis Whiting Halsey (New York: Pott, 1903), pp. 231-240.

References:

Leonard Butts, "The Critic," in *American Literary Magazines: The Eighteenth and Nineteenth Centuries*, edited by Edward E. Chielens (New York: Greenwood Press, 1986), pp. 121-125;

Frank Luther Mott, "The Critic," in his *A History of American Magazines, 1865-1885* (Cambridge: Harvard University Press, 1938), pp. 548-551.

Papers:

Collections of Jeannette L. Gilder's manuscripts are housed in the New York Public Library; the American Academy of Arts and Letters in New York; and the Schlesinger Library, Radcliffe College.

Richard Watson Gilder
(8 February 1844-18 November 1909)

Lloyd J. Graybar
Eastern Kentucky University

See also the Gilder entry in *DLB 64: American Literary Critics and Scholars, 1850-1880*.

MAJOR POSITIONS HELD: Editor, *Hours at Home* (1869-1870); managing editor, *Scribner's Monthly Magazine* (1870-1881); editor, *Century Illustrated Monthly Magazine* (1881-1909).

BOOKS: *The New Day: A Poem in Songs and Sonnets* (New York: Scribner, Armstrong, 1876; revised edition, New York: Scribners, 1880);

The Poet and His Master and Other Poems (New York: Scribners, 1878);

Lyrics and Other Poems (New York: Scribners, 1885; London: Hutt, 1886; revised edition, New York: Century, 1887); enlarged as *Five Books of Song* (New York: Century, 1894; London: Unwin, 1894; revised edition, New York: Century, 1900);

The Celestial Passion (New York: Century, 1887);

Ode: Read before the Society of the Phi Beta Kappa, Harvard University, June 26th, 1890 (Cambridge, Mass., 1890);

Two Worlds and Other Poems (New York: Century, 1891; London: Unwin, 1891);

The Great Remembrance and Other Poems (New York: Century, 1893);

Civic Patriotism: An Address at the Dinner of the New York Board of Trade and Transportation February Third, MDCCCXCIV (New York, 1894);

The University Settlement and Good Citizenship: An Address at the Annual Meeting of the University Settlement Society of New York January Twenty-ninth, MDCCCXCVII (New York, 1897);

"For the Country" (New York: Century, 1897);

The Real Question at Issue in the Municipal Campaign: A Speech at the Citizens' Union Headquarters of the 20th District, 256 E. 33d Street, on Monday Night, October 25 (New York, 1897);

In Palestine and Other Poems (New York: Century, 1898);

Poems and Inscriptions (New York: Century, 1901);

Commencement Address at Wellesley College June XXIII MDCCCCIII (Cambridge, Mass.: Riverside Press, 1903);

The Kindergarten: An Uplifting Social Influence in the Home and the District. An Address before the National Education Association, Boston, July 10, 1903. Also a Poem Entitled "The Child-Garden" (New York, 1904);

"In the Heights" (New York: Century, 1905);

A Book of Music (New York: Century, 1906);

The Fire Divine (New York: Century, 1907);

Poems of Richard Watson Gilder (Boston & New York: Houghton Mifflin, 1908);

Lincoln the Leader and Lincoln's Genius for Expression (Boston & New York: Houghton Mifflin, 1909);

Grover Cleveland: A Record of Friendship (New York: Century, 1910).

Richard Watson Gilder (portrait by Cecilia Beaux, in Letters of Richard Watson Gilder, *edited by Rosamond Gilder [Boston: Houghton Mifflin, 1916])*

OTHER: Ellen Clementine Howarth, *Poems*, edited by Gilder (Newark, N.J.: Denis, 1868);

"John Carman," in *A Masque of Poets: Including Guy Vernon, a Novelette in Verse* (Boston: Roberts, 1878), pp. 131-134;

"The Washington Memorial Arch," in *The History of the Centennial Celebration of the Inauguration of George Washington as First President of the United States*, edited by Clarence Winthrop Bowen (New York: Appleton, 1892), pp. 407-416;

Lincoln: Passages from His Speeches and Letters, introduction by Gilder (New York: Century, 1901);

Sonnets from the Portuguese and Other Poems by Elizabeth Barrett Browning; One Word More . . . by Robert Browning, introduction by Gilder (New York: Century, 1905);

Ralph Waldo Emerson, *Power, Success and Greatness*, introduction by Gilder (New York: Century, 1908);

"Live Thou in Nature," in *Roosevelt as the Poets Saw Him*, edited by Charles Hanson Towne (New York: Scribners, 1923), pp. 55-56.

PERIODICAL PUBLICATIONS: "Certain Tendencies in Current Literature," *New Princeton Review*, 4 (July 1887): 1-20;

"Journalism and American Literature," *Critic*, new series 15 (7 February 1891): 71;

"An 'Open Letter' about Editing," *Independent*, 48 (10 December 1896): 1669-1670;

"The Newspaper, the Magazine, and the Public," *Outlook*, 61 (4 February 1899): 317-321.

Although Richard Watson Gilder said that he would prefer to be remembered as a poet, his chief claim to fame, even during his own lifetime, came through his long tenure as managing editor and then editor of the *Century Illustrated Monthly Magazine*. Founded in 1870 as *Scribner's Monthly*, the magazine, which was renamed the *Century* after a change in management in 1881, ranked along with *Harper's* and the *Atlantic Monthly* as one of the late-nineteenth century's most esteemed general periodicals. Each issue of the *Century*, running to 140 or more pages, contained a mix of artistic features, serialized biography, essays on current issues, verse, and fiction. Considered by Hamlin Garland to be second only to William Dean Howells among editors in literary judgment, Gilder became through his position on the *Century* one of the most influential names in American letters. Gilder's most sympathetic biographer, Herbert Smith, has remarked that the 1880s might even be called "the Gilder Age."

Gilder was born on 8 February 1844 in Bordentown, New Jersey, the son of William Henry Gilder, a Methodist minister and schoolmaster, and Jane Nutt Gilder. Most of his youth was spent in Flushing, Long Island, New York, where his father was proprietor and headmaster of the Flushing Female Academy. Gilder once thought of preparing for a legal career, but his real enthusiasm was for writing and editing. At the age of twelve he began to frequent the office of the (Flushing) *Long Island Times*, where he learned the routines of publishing. He subsequently produced two amateur papers of his own, the *St. Thomas Register* and the *Leaflet*.

Gilder's service during the Civil War consisted of a brief term as a private in the Philadelphia Artillery, a militia company called up in 1863 to defend Harrisburg in the event of a Confederate breakthrough of Union defenses at Gettysburg. In retrospect the whole adventure seemed something of a lark, for Confederate troops never appeared at Harrisburg and the inexperienced outfit to which Gilder belonged suffered the embarrassment of loading their artillery only to realize they did not know how to unload it. Nevertheless, in later years Gilder took great pride in his membership in the Grand Army of the Republic, the organization of Union veterans.

The Civil War, however, did have a serious impact on the Gilder family; William Henry Gilder contracted smallpox and died while serving as a chaplain in the federal army. The death of his father forced Gilder to help support his family, and he was never able to attend college, something he always regretted. After a period as a paymaster on the Camden & Amboy Railroad in New Jersey, Gilder turned to a career in journalism, working briefly as a reporter on the *Newark Advertiser* in 1868 and subsequently becoming a cofounder of the *Newark Morning Register*. He took a second job in 1869 as editor of *Hours at Home*, a modest literary magazine operated by the publishers Charles Scribner and Company to advertise books by authors under contract to Scribner and to provide an outlet for the firm's shorter works.

The magazine, which was operated on a low budget, was distinctly mediocre as a result of its financial constraints and other limitations, primarily its complete subordination to the needs of Scribner. The publishers, however, hoped a prominent writer might be able to enliven the journal, and they asked Josiah G. Holland to take over the editorship. Holland, perhaps best known as the author of *Titcomb's Letters to Young People, Single and Married* (1858), was one of the era's favorite writers; his works identified with the themes of moral uplift and self-improvement. Holland and a recent acquaintance, Roswell C. Smith, a prosperous businessman who had shortly before retired at age thirty-nine, accepted Scribner's proposition on the condition that each of the two were to own thirty percent of the periodical, Scribner retaining the other forty percent. Rather than refashion *Hours at Home*, Holland and Smith planned to commence the publication of a new periodical, *Scribner's Monthly*, with the first issue to appear in November 1870.

For a year Gilder functioned as the lame-duck editor of *Hours at Home*, while assisting Holland in planning *Scribner's Monthly*. After the changeover Gilder shifted to the new periodical as associate editor. Holland, a man of pronounced moral and social views, impressed his strong personality upon *Scribner's Monthly* from the start. He wrote editorials and provided much serial fiction to the periodical as well. Other frequent contributors in the periodical's early years were Frank Stockton, Frances Hodgson Burnett, and Helen Hunt (Jackson). Also featured in the magazine were poetry, serialized biography, and articles on such diverse topics as the arts, the European scene, and nature studies. Throughout the decades *Scribner's Monthly* and the *Century* gave frequent attention to such topics of contemporary concern as conservation, education, municipal reform, abolition of the corrupt Louisiana lottery, and new developments in science.

From the beginning of his association with the magazine, Gilder, a slight man with a drooping, walruslike mustache, played a key role in *Scribner's Monthly*. In general he performed the duties of a managing editor, while contributing for several years to an opinion department, "The Old Cabinet," and collaborating with Alexander Drake, head of the art department, in developing illustrated articles. These illustrated pieces were a noteworthy feature of *Scribner's Monthly* and received even more emphasis in the *Century*. A series on the Old Masters and another on the cathedrals of England and France were but two of the illustrated features which earned the *Century* much distinction.

Gilder himself was intensely interested in the arts, in part through his wife, Helena de Kay, whom he had met while she was an art student in New York City. They were married in 1874 and had five children. Wherever the Gilders resided, whether in New York on East Fifteenth Street or off Washington Square, or in their summer homes on Cape Cod and, later, in the Berkshires, the creative elite gathered. Many of the leading writers of the time were friends of the Gilders, and these included establishment figures as well as outsiders such as Walt Whitman. Other regulars were such luminaries as artist John La Farge, sculptor Augustus Saint-Gaudens, architect Stanford White, and actor Joseph Jefferson.

As a writer as well as an editor, Gilder was very much at home in such an environment. A prolific poet who was skilled at rhyme and meter, but who lacked the gift to rise much above the ordinary, he was probably at his creative best in the 1870s. The collection of poetry *The New Day* (1876) stemmed from this time of his life. More

Cover, designed by Stanford White, for the magazine Gilder edited from 1870 until 1909. The magazine was renamed the Century in 1881.

than half of his published verse, however, came during Gilder's last twenty years, when he wrote many short pieces to commemorate public events and the famous persons of his day.

Although Gilder's poetic output showed no discernible slackening, circumstances directed his attention increasingly to his editorial work. As Holland was in declining health, and preferring to concentrate on his own literary efforts, he allowed Gilder more and more autonomy until by the mid 1870s Gilder was functioning as the de facto editor of *Scribner's Monthly*. In his characteristically gentle way Gilder, while committed to the concept of *Scribner's Monthly* as a family magazine, worked to change the emphasis in the periodical's fiction. He deemphasized the didactic tone that Holland had preferred, and cultivated new contributors while keeping on good terms with the old. Incoming manuscripts were screened by Sophie Bledsoe Herrick, the surviving ones then passing to an assistant editor. Gilder made the final determination, at least until the mid 1890s when his own waning health led him to defer more to Robert Underwood Johnson, his associate editor. Gilder took his responsibility with utmost seriousness, believing, he said, that "the care of manuscripts is the care of literature." He was adept both at consoling a rejected author and working with those fortunate enough to have a manuscript accepted. So numerous were the submissions–four thousand a year by the 1890s–that he fretted the best way of "killing an article for a generation is to have it accepted by the *Century Magazine*."

Two major changes came to the magazine at the start of the 1880s. Holland died in October 1881, having already sold most of his shares to Smith and establishing him as majority owner. The remainder of Holland's holdings went to Gilder, to younger editors such as Johnson and Clarence Buel, to Drake, and to several others in the business department. The second change was the 1881 termination of the agreement between *Scribner's Monthly* and the publishing house. In five years the publishing firm would start a new magazine named simply *Scribner's*, but the successor to the original *Scribner's Monthly* was the *Century Illustrated Monthly Magazine*, a title recommended by Gilder. The chance to purchase stock and to share in profits, as well as top salaries–Gilder's was ten thousand dollars a year by the 1890s–helped to assure continuity among key personnel. Little thought was given to altering what was clearly a successful format, and from the first issue in November 1881 the *Century* retained the place already attained by *Scribner's Monthly* as one of the era's finest general periodicals. Even better days were to come, for the *Century* soon achieved new peaks in circulation, advertising, and quality.

In its prose contributions *Scribner's Monthly* had once emphasized English authors, but as more Americans took to writing, Holland and especially Gilder relied increasingly on them. Henry James contributed several short pieces in the 1870s, and in the following decade *The Bostonians* (1886) was serialized in the *Century*. It was not one of Gilder's more popular choices, for the large and essentially middle-class readership of the *Century*, the majority of them women, failed to respond to James's prose style. Gilder had far greater luck with two other distinguished writers. He excerpted Mark Twain's *Adventures of Huckleberry Finn* (1884) and *A Connecticut Yankee in King Arthur's Court* (1889) and serialized *Puddn'head Wil-

son (1894). For much of the time the third great American author of the period, William Dean Howells, was associated with rival periodicals, first the *Atlantic Monthly* and later *Harper's*. But during the few years Howells was free from these commitments, the *Century* serialized *A Modern Instance* (1882), *A Woman's Reason* (1883), and *The Rise of Silas Lapham* (1885). Over a two-year span Howells appeared in all but two issues of the *Century*, and Gilder, reluctant to force too much Howells upon the *Century* readers, chose to serialize *Silas Lapham* but not *Indian Summer*, a decision that hindsight would show to be astute.

In fiction the apogee of the *Century* seems to have come in the February 1885 issue when chapters from *The Bostonians* and *Silas Lapham* both appeared, in addition to an excerpt from *Huckleberry Finn*. "No single number of any magazine has ever offered enduring literature more generously," Robert Berkelman has observed. The magazine also had considerable success in its short stories, publishing many that proved popular with readers if not with critics. Gilder early recognized talent and helped to develop the appeal of Thomas Nelson Page, George Washington Cable, Joel Chandler Harris, Hamlin Garland, and Edward Eggleston. It was Gilder, in fact, who helped persuade Eggleston, already popular as a writer of children's stories, to try his hand at fiction for adults.

The greatest continuing success enjoyed by the *Century* was a series of participants' recollections of the Civil War that appeared in its pages from 1884 to 1887 under the overall title "Battles and Leaders of the Civil War." The series had its genesis in the favorable public reception of two articles on John Brown's Harper's Ferry raid. One treated it from a Southern point of view; the other, from an antislavery stand, was written by one of the abolitionists who had helped finance Brown's undertaking. Assistant editor Clarence Buel thought of asking participants from both sides to recall some of the memorable battles of the Civil War. Gilder, proud to have participated in the Civil War in his own small way, and mindful of his father's service as a chaplain, was receptive, but the magazine initially encountered great difficulty in getting high-ranking officers to recount their experiences.

Nonetheless, an account of the first battle of Bull Run appeared in the November 1884 issue, written by former Confederate general P. G. T. Beauregard. The breakthrough with potential contributors came shortly, when Ulysses S. Grant agreed to write the first of four pieces for the *Century;* Grant's commitment helped make the idea of writing for the *Century* respectable to other generals, and Grant in turn attempted to persuade William Tecumseh Sherman to undertake an article. At length Sherman did, and in the end virtually every surviving general of note on both sides participated, as did many naval officers. The series progressed in a generally chronological fashion, sometimes offering contrasting views on such topics as the battle of Shiloh or the naval engagement between the *Monitor* and *Merrimac*, and including accounts by ordinary soldiers and some noncombatants. Superb maps and illustrations enhanced the narratives.

During the three years the series ran, *Century* circulation jumped from a healthy 130,000 or so to nearly 250,000, as Americans both North and South showed an eagerness to read about the Civil War in firsthand accounts. Over twenty years the memories of postwar bitterness had receded sufficiently to make this success possible. Only in Great Britain, where an edition of the *Century* was published by Unwin, did the series fail to win acclaim.

Gilder attempted to follow up this series by paying John Hay and John Nicolay the then phenomenal sum of fifty thousand dollars for the serial rights to their massive biography of Abraham Lincoln, but the response to it was not as favorable. Another series of note was George Kennan's on the exile system in Czarist Russia. An effort to duplicate the success of the Civil War narratives with a series on the Spanish-American War was unsuccessful and came when the *Century* was already facing hard times.

Although its advertising continued to rise for a time, the *Century* began encountering difficulties in the 1890s. Smith, whose business judgment was unsurpassed, died in 1892. Under the new management Gilder retained firm editorial control–his relationship with Smith had been such that he never showed Smith a manuscript in advance. Gilder's health, however, was beginning to decline; and prolonged bouts of nervous exhaustion caused him to yield increased responsibility to Johnson.

The *Century* was also facing problems from the competition. The appearance of newspaper syndicates hurt the *Century* by competing for serial rights. Competition from *Ladies' Home Journal* also hurt, for middle-class women had always been numerous among subscribers to the *Century* and its predecessor. Also, the new, ten-cent month-

Gilder in his Century *office in 1894*

lies, *Munsey's* and *McClure's*, with their mass circulations, were able to outbid Gilder for popular authors. The new periodicals were also opening new directions in magazine journalism. *McClure's*, for instance, was livelier, used a more personality-oriented approach in many of its features, and by employing photoengraving rather than the woodcuts Gilder had always preferred, surpassed the *Century* in its handling of illustrated articles. Ironically, the founder of *McClure's*, S. S. McClure, had once been employed in the *Century* business office. McClure spent so much time thinking of new approaches to suggest to Gilder and the other editors that Smith had discharged him with the admonition that he should start his own magazine.

Like many other once successful publications faced with problems, the *Century* was unable to select a new course. Gilder and Johnson had become unreceptive to the newest trends in American letters, although a short story of high quality would appear occasionally. The *Century* did publish Jack London's *The Sea Wolf* (1904) and in the early 1900s provided space to such young poets as Edwin Arlington Robinson, Harriet Monroe, and Paul Laurence Dunbar. But in general the *Century* became more committed to the sentimental and romantic at a time when these literary styles were becoming quite dated. Thus the *Century* rejected Joseph Conrad's *Typhoon* (1903) and on Johnson's urging shied away from an Edith Wharton novel just as she was achieving eminence.

Gilder had welcomed realism in the early years and regarded *Silas Lapham* as everything he hoped for in this new development in literature. He was particularly comfortable with that novel's use of a man of ideals as its protagonist. Realism's emphasis shifted thereafter to an increasingly bleak portrayal of life that Gilder was unable to accept. Still less could he accept the naturalism of Stephen Crane and Frank Norris. Crane had first offered *Maggie: A Girl of the Streets* (1903) to the *Century*, but Gilder, like every other editor, had rejected it out of hand, believing, in the words of the disappointed Crane, that the book was "too honest." Gilder also rejected *The Red Badge of Courage* (1895), the work that established Crane's place in American prose.

Gilder seems to have welcomed the chance to divest himself of the responsibility for fiction, preferring to devote his time to his poetry, to his work for honest government, tenement reform, and other civic causes, and to writing biographies of Abraham Lincoln and former president Grover Cleveland, a close friend. As always, he took time to celebrate the arts. He died on 18 November 1909 of angina pectoris, thus missing the final decades of the decline of the *Century* and its absorption in 1930 by the *Forum*.

A leader in New York City civic and cultural affairs, Richard Watson Gilder was one of the most distinguished and successful editors of his day. For nearly a generation he helped keep *Scribner's Monthly* and then the *Century* among the very best of American magazines, using his influence as editor and critic to elevate taste in the arts and letters. By all accounts Gilder was a gentle man and a superb editor in the technical sense. He was a personal friend of many authors and an ally of all through his long advocacy of international copyright protection that was crowned with success in 1891. However, his position also placed him among the leaders of what was America's cultural establishment in the late decades of the nineteenth century, an establishment whose tastes would be ridiculed as prudish by a later generation.

Perhaps Gilder made a convenient target for subsequent critics such as Malcolm Cowley and Van Wyck Brooks. Certainly in his later years Gilder did retreat to the sentimental and escapist and in turning over more of the responsibilities for fiction to his associate Johnson, a man of more pronounced prejudices, ended up imposing those tastes on readers of the *Century*. For the most part, many of these readers did indeed expect it to uphold the genteel standards which had come to dominate the literary expression of the times. However, for perhaps twenty years in its prime, *Scribner's Monthly*, and its successor the *Century*, welcomed established authors such as Howells but also helped to popularize newer writers such as Cable and Garland. Whatever he might have been in his later years, the Gilder of the 1870s and 1880s was open-minded and in his own day condemned by some for his daring. Although success, then as now, can inhibit innovation, he was willing to take an occasional chance, but not to make the *Century* into a "battleground of opinion." He rejected Cable's "Posson Jone'" and Crane's later naturalistic works, but the constraints of his dual responsibilities to authors and subscribers also led him to avoid James after the unhappy experience with *The Bostonians*, whose main offense was not its daring but its dullness. Gilder presided over the *Century* at a time when American literature was in ferment and, argues his most admiring biographer, helped to make the magazine "the vehicle for the most significant statements of the renaissance, to develop new young writers from the South and West . . . , and to create the esthetic for the masterpieces written around 1885."

Letters:

Letters of Richard Watson Gilder, edited by Rosamond Gilder (Boston & New York: Houghton Mifflin, 1916).

References:

Robert Berkelman, "Mrs. Grundy and Richard Watson Gilder," *American Quarterly*, 4 (Spring 1952): 66-72;

Samuel C. Chew, ed., *Fruit among the Leaves: An Anniversary Anthology* (New York: Appleton-Century-Crofts, 1950), pp. 81-131;

William Webster Ellsworth, *A Golden Age of Authors: A Publisher's Recollection* (Boston & New York: Houghton Mifflin, 1919);

Sister Martha Ann Fitzpatrick, C.S.J., "Richard Watson Gilder, Genteel Reformer," Ph.D. dissertation, Catholic University of America, 1966;

Arthur John, *The Best Years of the Century: Richard Watson Gilder, Scribner's Monthly, and the Century Magazine, 1870-1909* (Urbana, Chicago & London: University of Illinois Press, 1981);

Robert Underwood Johnson, *Remembered Yesterdays* (Boston: Little, Brown, 1923), pp. 88-96;

Michael G. Kammen, "Richard Watson Gilder and the New York Tenement House Commission of 1894," in *Moralists or Pragmatists? The Mugwumps, 1884-1900*, edited by Gerald W. McFarland (New York: Simon & Schuster, 1975), pp. 100-119;

Herbert F. Smith, *Richard Watson Gilder* (New York: Twayne, 1970);

John Tomsich, *A Genteel Endeavor: American Culture and Politics in the Gilded Age* (Stanford: Stanford University Press, 1971);

L. Frank Tooker, *The Joys and Tribulations of an Editor* (New York & London: Century, 1923);

Edward Wagenknecht, "Richard Watson Gilder: Poet and Editor of the Transition," *Boston University Studies in English*, 1 (1955): 84-95.

Papers:
The Manuscript Division of the New York Public Library holds Richard Watson Gilder's personal papers as well as the "Gilder Letterbooks," letterpress copies of letters sent by Gilder from the Century Company offices, and the "Century Papers," the archives of the Century Company. However, these files are incomplete, as many of the letters received were separated from the archives and sold at an auction held by the Anderson Galleries, New York, 3 and 4 December 1928. The MLA *American Literary Manuscripts: A Checklist of Holdings in ... Libraries ... in the United States* lists forty-six libraries with holdings of manuscripts relating to Gilder.

E. L. Godkin
(2 October 1831-21 May 1902)

Terry Hynes
California State University, Fullerton

MAJOR POSITIONS HELD: Subeditor, *Workingmen's Friend* (1851-1853); correspondent, London *Daily News* (1853-1855, 1856-1857, 1859-1860, 1862-1866); contributing editor, *Northern Whig* (1856); contributor, *New York Times* (1859-1860, 1862-1865); editor, *Sanitary Commission Bulletin* (1864), *Nation* (1865-1899); associate editor (1881-1883), editor in chief (1883-1899), *New York Evening Post*.

BOOKS: *The History of Hungary and the Magyars: From the Earliest Times to the Close of the Late War* (London: Cassell, 1853; New York: Montgomery, 1853);

The Morals and Manners of the Kitchen, and Baby Suffrage (New York: Tompkins, 1875);

The Question of Elections, and of the Separation of Municipal Elections: Read January, 1876 (New York: Hamilton Steam Printers, 1876);

The Danger of an Office-Holding Aristocracy (New York: Putnam's, 1882);

Henry G. Pearson: A Memorial Address Delivered June 21, 1894 (New York: Privately printed, 1894);

The Triumph of Reform: A History of the Great Political Revolution, November Sixth, Eighteen Hundred and Ninety-four (New York: Souvenir Publishing Co., 1895);

E. L. Godkin

Reflections and Comments, 1865-1895 (New York: Scribners, 1895; London: Constable, 1896);

Problems of Modern Democracy: Political and Economic Essays (New York: Scribners, 1896; London: Constable, 1899);

Unforeseen Tendencies of Democracy (Boston & New York: Houghton, Mifflin, 1898; London: Constable, 1898);

A Letter on Lincoln (Riverside, Conn.: Hillacre Bookhouse, 1913).

PERIODICAL PUBLICATIONS: "The Constitution and Its Defects," *North American Review*, 99 (July 1864): 117-145;

"Aristocratic Opinions of Democracy," *North American Review*, 100 (January 1865): 194-232;

"The Democratic View of Democracy," *North American Review*, 101 (July 1865): 103-133;

"The Tyranny of the Majority," *North American Review*, 104 (January 1867): 205-230;

"The Labor Crisis," *North American Review*, 105 (July 1867): 177-213;

"Commercial Immorality and Political Corruption," *North American Review*, 107 (July 1868): 248-266;

"The Prospects of the Political Art," *North American Review*, 110 (April 1870): 398-418;

"The Political Outlook," *Century Magazine*, 19 (February 1880): 613-620;

"Libel and Its Legal Remedy," *Atlantic Monthly*, 46 (December 1880): 729-738;

"The Civil Service Reform Controversy," *North American Review*, 134 (April 1882): 379-394;

"The Republican Party and the Negro," *Forum*, 7 (May 1889): 246-257;

"Public Opinion and the Civil Service," *Forum*, 8 (November 1889): 237-247;

"Money Interests in Political Affairs," *Forum*, 10 (September 1890);

"'The Economic Man,'" *North American Review*, 153 (October 1891): 491-503;

"Diplomacy and the Newspaper," *North American Review*, 160 (May 1895);

"The Real Problems of Democracy," *Atlantic Monthly*, 78 (July 1896): 1-13;

"The Conditions of Good Colonial Government," *Forum*, 27 (April 1899): 190-203.

As a founder of the *Nation* and its first editor, holding the post from 1865 until 1899, E. L. Godkin was a central force in the growth of the magazine's prestige as a vehicle for nineteenth-century American liberalism. Under Godkin the *Nation* became a shaper of American political thought whose influence far surpassed what might have been expected from its small circulation.

Although he seldom acknowledged his Irish heritage and even attempted to conceal it, preferring instead to be thought of as an Englishman, Edwin Lawrence Godkin was born in County Wicklow, Ireland, on 2 October 1831, the oldest of five children and one of two sons of James and Sarah Lawrence Godkin. During his childhood the family moved frequently as his father, a Protestant minister, assumed a succession of Irish pulpits and editorial positions.

Godkin learned to read at home, and at age seven began grammar school at Armagh in northern Ireland, where his father had a post as a Congregational minister. At age nine he was enrolled in one of Ireland's better schools, Belfast's Royal Academical Institution. Within a year, however, his parents transferred him to Silcoates, near Leeds in Yorkshire, England, a classically oriented school for the sons of Congregational ministers; then, in the spring of 1845 they withdrew him from school. For the next year he seems to have been tutored by a maternal uncle and may have attended Belfast Academy. In 1846 he enrolled in Queen's College at Belfast, which had recently been established by Parliament in opposition to the views of Irish nationalists. In 1850 he was elected president of the college literary and scientific society. At Queen's he found a congenial philosophy in utilitarianism. "John Stuart Mill was our prophet," Godkin later recalled, "and Grote and Bentham were our daily food.... but America was our promised land." For Godkin, laissez-faire satisfied the utilitarian definition of expediency.

After he graduated from Queen's College in 1851, Godkin moved to London and began studying law at the Middle Temple. Shortly afterwards, however, he gave up the study of law and sought a job in journalism from the radical publisher John Cassell, an acquaintance of his father's. Cassell hired him as a subeditor on one of his new magazines, *Workingmen's Friend*, an unpretentious penny weekly filled with travel sketches, tales, verse, home instruction, and contributions by authors such as Jules Verne and Harriet Beecher Stowe that reflected Cassell's interests in pacifism and the working classes.

Godkin wrote for Cassell's magazine a series of historical sketches of Hungary that ran from November 1851 to February 1852 and became the basis for his first book, *The History of Hungary and the Magyars*, which was published by Cassell

Godkin as a Crimean War correspondent for the London Daily News

in 1853. The book focuses on the tyranny exercised by the Austrians over the Magyars and exhibits the forceful writing style that was a hallmark of Godkin's later work. He rails against "the grinding tyranny ... the ferocious insolence of the police, the unchecked brutality of the soldiery, the crowded state of the dungeons–crammed with wretches who had lingered in agony for months and years ... the torturings, the beatings with sticks, the daily fusillades on the glacis, and all the other horrors and enormities by which tyranny heaps outrage on humanity, and blasphemes God." Probably because of the attention being paid at the time to the Hungarian revolutionary Louis Kossuth, the book went through several printings, including an American edition; but Godkin later repudiated both Kossuth's version of democracy and the book's glorification of it and regretted the popular success the book had achieved.

In late 1853 Godkin was hired as a special correspondent to cover the Crimean War for the London *Daily News*. Godkin was one of the first English correspondents to enter the war zone, arriving in Constantinople two months before the most famous of the Crimean War journalists, William Howard Russell of the London *Times*, left London in February 1854. In the typical style of nineteenth-century journalism, Godkin wrote his reports as a series of letters which were published as such in the newspaper. His early letters were somewhat sophomoric in their enthusiasm for the integrity and professionalism of the Turkish soldiers and their diatribes against the Russian cossacks; later letters reflected more moderate judgments, although they also evidenced Godkin's anti-Semitism in some of his descriptions of Russian military ineptitude. By April 1854 Godkin had joined in the growing disapproval of the Turks and was also criticizing the western press coverage of the war (his own coverage had its shortcomings, including inaccuracies and the fitting of evidence to his opinions). During the summer he complained of the failure of the British and French expeditionary forces to take the offensive against the Russians before the onset of winter. His disillusionment with allied leadership grew stronger in the ensuing months, and by the spring of 1855 his disgruntlement again included the Turkish leaders. He returned to England in October 1855.

Near the end of his life Godkin assessed his experience during this period: "If I were asked now what I thought the most important result of the Crimean war, I should say the creation and development of the 'special correspondents' of newspapers. . . . My letters excited some attention in England mainly owing to their novelty. I do not think they had much other merit. The real beginning of newspaper correspondence was the arrival of 'Billy' Russell with the English army in the Crimea. . . . I therefore cannot help thinking that the appearance of the special correspondent in the Crimea, to whatever evils and abuses it may afterwards have led, was a troubling of the waters which was a good thing both for the British army and people. It led to a real awakening of the official mind. It brought home to the War Office the fact that the public has something to say about the conduct of wars, and that they are not the concern exclusively, as that delightful old charlatan, Lord Beaconsfield said, of 'sovereigns and statesmen.'"

Godkin stayed only briefly in London, where he seems to have been discouraged by the class bias that kept him outside influential political and social circles. He then went to Dublin, where his father was editor of the *Daily Express*, and shortly afterward to Belfast, where by March 1856 he was giving public lectures about the Crimean War. In April he accepted a job as contributing editor to the *Northern Whig*, a liberal triweekly newspaper that critized some aspects of the established rule in Ireland but supported conservative views about property rights and social revolution. Six months later he resigned and set sail for the United States, where he planned to make a tour of the South and write a series of reports on it for the London *Daily News*.

Godkin arrived in New York near the end of the presidential election contest between Democrat James Buchanan and the first Republican presidential candidate, John C. Frémont. Godkin later wrote that he was "astounded" by the "heat and extravagance" of the speeches he heard during the campaign, and his early observations confirmed his view that the United States was democratic more in theory than in practice. Before leaving on his trip to the South, Godkin stayed for about two weeks with Frederick Law Olmsted, who subsequently made his reputation as a landscape architect and as the designer of New York's Central Park and whom Godkin had met in Belfast in 1850. Olmsted was in the process of revising for publication in book form a series of letters he had written for the *New York Times* about his own two southern journeys in 1852 and 1853.

Godkin found southerners generally inhospitable but civil. He reached Mississippi in late November 1856 and returned to New York in early January 1857 after a brief sojourn in New Orleans, a city he judged unattractive and disorderly and described as "the finest example of mob government in the world." He rode swamp roads on horseback, endured stagecoaches in the rainy season, and was repelled by what he perceived as the hypocrisy of rural religious fundamentalists who assured him that they would kill anyone who attacked them, even if the attack was merely verbal.

Godkin's views about slavery were mixed. He thought that any "mental or moral rise" in slaves' conditions would lead to their unhappiness; his letter in the *Daily News* of 29 January 1857 says: "Their [slaves'] only refuge or consolation in this world is in their own stupidity and grossness. The nearer they are to the beast, the happier they are likely to be." But in the 25 March 1857 issue he wrote, "I have never passed them [slaves],–staggering along in the rear of the wagons, at the close of a long day's march, the weakest furthest in the rear, the strongest already utterly spent,–without wondering how Christendom . . . can so long look calmly on at so foul and monstrous a wrong as this American slavery."

Some of Godkin's newspaper correspondence of this period also reflects the ambivalence about American democracy which marked his later writings. He praised the ability of ordinary people to be treated equally with the well known and wealthy in public places but also expressed concerns about the tyranny of the majority: in the 20 January 1857 issue of the *Daily News* he wrote that Americans were "so long accustomed to look upon a democracy as affording the largest measure of liberty, that they cannot as yet bring themselves to see that a man's neighbours

Godkin in 1863

and friends may prove much more troublesome and vexatious tyrants than any king or emperor."

After returning to New York Godkin read law in the office of an attorney, passed the bar in 1858, and was in practice by 1859. But he quickly realized that the routines of the courtroom and office did not satisfy his need for action, and he returned to journalism. For a while he operated on a free-lance basis as the *Daily News* New York correspondent and as a contributor to the *New York Times*, the *New York Evening Post*, and a literary monthly, the *Knickerbocker*. During this period he developed his lifelong habit of allotting four hours each day to writing.

On a visit to the home of Yale University president Theodore Woolsey in 1857, he had met Frances Elizabeth Foote, the daughter of Samuel E. Foote, the wealthy retired president of the Ohio Life Insurance and Trust Company. Born in 1835, Frances was a cousin of Harriet Beecher Stowe and Henry Ward Beecher. Godkin and Frances were married in New Haven, Connecticut, on 27 July 1859.

Family responsibilities and the uncertainty of his professional direction weighed increasingly on Godkin. Convinced that he was having an emotional breakdown as well as a recurrence of a fever he had experienced when he covered the Crimean War, he sailed alone for Ireland shortly after the birth of his first child, Lawrence, in May 1860. His family joined him in the fall, and for the next two years they lived a life of leisure–spending the winter in Paris, the spring in London, and the summer in Switzerland. During his stay abroad, Godkin's sole literary output was a series of unsolicited letters to the *Daily News* responding to British and European newspaper attacks against the United States after Federal captain Charles Wilkes stopped the British merchant ship *Trent* and seized the Confederate ambassadors to England and France as political prisoners. Godkin's letters expressed support for Wilkes's action.

In the fall of 1862 he returned to New York with his family, having agreed again to serve as the *Daily News* special correspondent. By late October his letters to the newspaper were complaining of Lincoln's lack of firmness and discretion as well as poor judgment in his selection of military leaders. Godkin's criticisms of the president grew increasingly strident. On 1 January 1863 the *Daily News* published Godkin's assessment of the administration written just after the Union disaster at Fredericksburg: "That Mr. Lincoln is utterly unequal to the responsibility the crisis has imposed on him is now demonstrated beyond question in the opinion of everybody of all parties."

Godkin's racial prejudice also surfaced again in a letter to the *Daily News* in which he expressed his fears about the consequences of emancipation: "But every one feels that their [blacks'] exclusion [from the vote] could not last very long, in an atmosphere so charged with democracy; and then timid men not unnaturally ask, what would be the effect of the addition of this mass of ignorance, passion, and credulity to our electoral body? We have already suffered severely from the influx of Irish and Germans, unfitted by previous training for the exercise of the suffrage.... Would not four or five millions of citizens, with the marks of the whip still on their backs, who are impulsive beyond any civilized race, and whom we cannot absorb, furnish demagogues with a most tremendous weapon for the destruction or degradation of the nation?" During Reconstruction Godkin continued to express reservations about extending the political franchise to the Negro. He did argue that it would provide freedmen a defense against their former masters and would elevate the condition of blacks, but he advocated qualifications–including literacy, residency, and evidence of an independent income–that would have excluded most blacks from being able to vote. Ultimately, Godkin converted even Charles Eliot Norton and James Russell Lowell, co-editors of the *North American Review*, to his position. As late as 1877 Godkin expressed his prejudice in a letter he wrote to Norton after a stay in the South: "I do not see, in short, how the negro is ever to be worked into a system of government for which you and I would have much respect." Godkin also opposed most of the efforts of the woman's rights movement, objecting not only to woman suffrage but also to equal employment and coeducation.

In addition to the *Daily News* correspondence, which appeared twice each week, Godkin also resumed writing for the *New York Times* as, he later noted, "a contributor of two articles a week, on topics selected by myself." In the spring of 1863 Olmsted wrote to him about the possibility of starting a national weekly newspaper, but Godkin, who had shortly before given up an opportunity to buy into the *New York Times*, was reluctant to risk his money in publishing at this time. Later that year, however, Godkin started trying to raise funding for the newspaper, which he planned to call the *Week*. Unable to secure financial backing, however, in early 1864 Godkin accepted a position as editor of the fortnightly *Sanitary Commission Bulletin* at a salary of one hundred dollars a month. Together with his earnings from the columns he continued to write for the *Daily News* and the *New York Times*, Godkin's income was then about three thousand dollars a year, not including the return on investments which his wife had brought to their marriage. In addition, his family's home had been provided by his mother-in-law, so that his living expenses were relatively small.

The *Bulletin* editorship was short-lived: the publication was moved to Philadelphia later in 1864 and placed under a new editor. Meanwhile, however, Godkin had begun to write for the *North American Review*. His article on the defects of the United States Constitution, which appeared in July 1864, was the first of fifteen he eventually wrote for the *Review*. "Aristocratic Opinions of Democracy," which appeared in the January 1865 issue, argued for the influence of the frontier in shaping American democracy, a thesis Frederick Jackson Turner would make popular a generation later: "If we inquire what are those phenomena of American society which it is

Opening page from a bound volume of the influential weekly Godkin edited from 1865 until 1899

generally agreed distinguish it from that of older countries, we shall find, we are satisfied, that by far the larger number of them may be attributed in a great measure to what, for want of a better name, we shall call 'the frontier life' led by a large proportion of the inhabitants, and to the influence of this portion on manners and legislation, rather than to political institutions, or even to the equality of conditions. In fact, we think that these phenomena, and particularly those of them which excite most odium in Europe, instead of being the effect of democracy, are partly its cause, and that it has been to their agency more than to aught else, that the democratic tide in America has owed most of its force and violence."

In late April 1865 Norton and Maj. George Stearns offered Godkin the editorship of a new weekly they were planning, to be called the *Nation*. Stearns was an abolitionist who had supplied John Brown with weapons Brown used at Harpers Ferry, had helped recruit black troops during the war, and had been a founder in 1862 of the Boston antislavery weekly, the *Commonwealth*. Other backers of the *Nation* included the wealthy Philadelphia abolitionist and former clergyman James Miller McKim; McKim's soon-to-be son-in-law, Wendell Phillips Garrison, the son of the abolitionist William Lloyd Garrison; Joseph Richards, who was to be the publisher of the magazine; and various persons connected with the freedmen's associations of the Northeast. Norton, who knew that Godkin's views about blacks did not coincide with those of Stearns and McKim, apparently neglected to mention this discrepancy in basic philosophies when he persuaded them to offer the editorship to Godkin.

Godkin's condition for accepting the position was that he have complete editorial freedom. Stearns met several times with Godkin and finally, having heard no dissent from Godkin on key issues, agreed that his editorial power would be absolute. The backers required that Godkin raise in New York twenty-five thousand dollars of the total capital needed; they would raise the other seventy-five thousand in Boston, Philadelphia, and Baltimore. Godkin's salary was to be five thousand dollars a year; in addition, he would receive twelve percent of the profits after a six-percent annual dividend was paid to stockholders.

Dissension among the backers began almost immediately upon Godkin's confirmation. Ralph Waldo Emerson's support, which had been lukewarm, chilled when he heard that a foreigner had been named editor in chief. George Bancroft and abolitionist leaders Charles Sumner and William Lloyd Garrison were similarly cool toward Godkin. There were also disagreements between protectionists such as McKim and supporters of free trade. In the hope of defusing the situation and retaining Philadelphia support, Godkin promised McKim, who spoke for Philadelphia manufacturers, that the *Nation* would avoid the tariff issue altogether. Because of the demands on his time, Godkin gave up writing for the *New York Times*, but he continued for the next eighteen months to contribute regularly to the *Daily News*.

One of the tasks which fell to Godkin in the months prior to publication was the establishment of the legal organization to represent the nearly forty investors in the magazine. In setting up *The Nation* Association, Godkin followed New York law, which required that companies chartered in the state had to be controlled by state citizens. Godkin proposed that five of the nine trustees be from New York, with two each from Philadelphia and Boston. Thus Boston, the residence of the largest group of the *Nation*'s backers and the source of the majority of its capital, had disproportionately small control of the governing body. The inequity was compounded at the first meeting of the board of trustees in late May when Norton, McKim, and New Yorker Christian Detmold were elected as an executive committee to run the company. Thus Stearns, who had contributed twelve thousand dollars of his own money, whose reputation had persuaded others in Boston to contribute and who was one of the two Boston trustees, was eliminated from direct control of the publication. In addition, the trustees decided to call in all pledges immediately and in cash, upsetting backers who had subscribed with the understanding that they could pay in installments. When the first issue of the *Nation* went to press in late June, most of the Boston funds and all of the Philadelphia funds had been turned over to the association's treasurer; but Godkin was less successful in his home territory of New York, and more than fifteen thousand dollars was still outstanding.

After the *Nation* debuted on 6 July 1865, the dissension among the backers developed into internecine warfare. Wendell Garrison, Norton, and McKim continued to support Godkin, but Stearns tried to stir up opposition among other stockholders because of Godkin's equivocation regarding equal rights for blacks. The radicals lost the fight for editorial control of the magazine and Stearns removed himself from its operations, but rumblings of disagreement continued among the stockholders. When Godkin's conciliatory measure of hiring Olmsted as associate editor failed to relieve the tensions, he fired Richards, liquidated *The Nation* Association, and, with money left by some of the stockholders, took principal control of the magazine under the title E. L. Godkin and Company in 1866.

The *Nation*'s prospectus promised seven main objectives, three of which were concerned with improving conditions for the freedmen in the South. The other goals were accurate discussion of public affairs, the diffusion of democratic principles, emphasis on the importance of public education, and criticism of literature and art. Under Godkin's direction the magazine focused chiefly on current affairs and literature, art, and music criticism. Literary reviews in the *Nation*, however, were conceived broadly and took the form of general essays on the topics covered by the books reviewed. The magazine's thirty-six

1898 caricature of Godkin by J. Campbell Cory

pages began with three or four pages of paragraphs of commentary under the heading "The Week," followed by major editorials, correspondence from abroad, sometimes poetry, letters to the editor, several pages of literary notes and book reviews, two to four pages of commentary on art and music, a science department, and a financial review. The subscription rate was three dollars a year initially, increasing to six dollars in October 1865. The magazine appeared as a semiweekly in May and June 1866 while the ownership was unsettled.

A list of staff members and contributors to the *Nation* under Godkin reads like a Who's Who of American scholars and writers of the late nineteenth century: Norton, who wrote on a variety of subjects, especially art, poetry, and education, until his death in 1908; James Russell Lowell; Henry and William James; William Dean Howells, who was an assistant editor for some months in 1865-1866; William Francis Allen, history professor at the University of Wisconsin; Daniel Gilman, founder of Johns Hopkins University; Yale president Noah Porter; Arthur G. Sedgwick, Norton's brother-in-law, who in 1865, at age twenty, began a forty-year career writing on political issues for the *Nation* and who became a staff member in 1872; historian Francis Parkman; economist Charles Francis Adams, Jr.; ornithologist Elliott Coues; philosopher Charles Sanders Peirce; British correspondents James Viscount Bryce, Leslie Stephen, and Professor A. V. Dicey; Paris correspondent August Laugel; and Italian correspondent Jesse White Mario. Less well known today but quite important during the early years of the *Nation* was John R. Dennett, whose first assignment was to travel through the South in 1865 and describe conditions there. His series, "The South as It Is," remains one of the most insightful contemporary discussions of the South in the immediate aftermath of the Civil War. He remained a staff member, writing literature reviews, sections of "The Week," and political editorials, until he died of tuberculosis in 1874.

Godkin earned a reputation as an exacting, even ruthless, editor. He encouraged the *Nation* contributors to write with a straightforwardness and wit similar to his own style and, in the process, showed that serious writing could be lively and readable as well as informative and profound. All contributions appeared without bylines, Godkin's way of giving the magazine a unified voice and maintaining high standards. He wrote to a contributor in 1867: "The publication of names, of writers, by shifting the responsibility as to quality from the editor's shoulders makes him careless as to quality, and in part converts his paper into a dumping ground in which 'celebrities' shuck their rubbish. Moreover, it makes writers careless, too, because 'names,' have acquired such a potency, that in the existing state of culture in America, a good many men, are enabled under cover of them to palm off trash on the reader.... Then also, if you publish one man's name, you have to publish all, and publishing all, any week you are not able to get some distinguished body to 'scratch off' something for you, people think the number a poor one."

The *Nation* achieved a circulation of five thousand by its third issue; by 1870 circulation was approximately six thousand and grew steadily to about double that figure by the mid 1870s. Godkin claimed, however, that his primary aim was not for the *Nation* to be a commercial success. He wrote to Norton in April 1866: "I, on my part, undertook not to produce a paper that would be certain to sell well, but to produce a good paper, one that good and intelligent men would say *ought* to sell, and whose influence on those who read it, and on the country papers, would be enlightening, elevating, and refining.... The Nation, I am led to believe, is a good paper. Its influence is, I know, growing, and from this influence I expect pecuniary success ultimately to come." During Godkin's lifetime, however, the magazine's circulation did not increase significantly above twelve thousand. By 1870 Godkin's salary was two thousand dollars, a precipitous drop from the original, optimistic arrangement of 1865. As journalism historian Frank Luther Mott has noted, "Thus the power of the Nation came not from the number of its readers, but from their station and influence and from the frequency with which it was quoted."

That the Nation sometimes lacked a well-defined editorial position on issues was perhaps due to Godkin's mercurial nature, which was reflected in opinion shifts throughout his editorial career. For example, he at first vehemently opposed President Johnson's impeachment, then just as vehemently supported it, and finally declared Johnson's acquittal to be a vindication of the law. In 1867 he criticized Secretary of State William Seward's purchase of Alaska from Russia, but by 1874 he viewed the purchase as almost a stroke of good luck for the United States and likely to be regarded eventually as a sign of Seward's astuteness as a statesman.

Although Godkin's opinions shifted unpredictably and were occasionally based on insufficient or inaccurate information, among his chief assets were his ability to perceive issues and events that were shaping the direction of the United States and his willingness to take a firm stand on them. He dealt with issues while they were crucial and alive and, at times, his views had an immediate effect on government policy. His bold and thoughtful editorials endeared him to a generation of upper-class leaders who came of age in the late nineteenth century as loyal readers of the Nation.

In 1868 Godkin and the Nation supported the election of Ulysses S. Grant, but Godkin was sorely disappointed by the corruption of Grant's administration. The magazine opposed both Horace Greeley's and Grant's candidacies in 1872–to paraphrase another journal of the era, it despised one candidate and hated the other most fervently. In the 1876 Hayes-Tilden stalemate, it reluctantly favored Hayes in the hope of ending discord between the Republican and Democratic parties. In the 1880s the magazine supported Grover Cleveland, except for his jingoistic stance on the Venezuelan dispute with England. In the early 1890s Godkin vigorously unmasked the Tammany ring's leaders in a series of critical biographical sketches; according to some critics, the four-year battle Godkin conducted was an important contribution to the defeat of Tammany in the 1894 mayoral election. In the 1896 presidential campaign the magazine supported William McKinley as the lesser of two evils, although Godkin himself voted for John Palmer of Illinois, candidate of the gold Democrats.

The tenets of upper-middle-class liberalism that Godkin had imbibed at Queen's remained one of the unbroken threads in the fabric of his writings throughout his tenure at the Nation and, later, at the Evening Post. In Godkin's view, representative government should be placed in the hands of society's entrepreneurs. Extension of suffrage, even revolution, would be acceptable if they did not threaten private property or if they freed society from intrusions by the state. Expediency, not justice or morality, was the essential consideration. His loyalty to these views was reflected as late as 1891 in his essay " 'The Economic Man' " in the North American Review. The essay defended the economist David Ricardo's concept of the "Economic Man" and criticized what Godkin saw as the political, versus scientific, analysis offered by the "new school" of political economy. His defense of Ricardo's view was expressed in his typically straightforward manner: "Moral considerations do not, in any degree, affect [the "economic man's"] business transactions. There is no place in his system for brotherly kindness or charity. It is inexpedient for the state to attempt to regulate him in any way, either by keeping him out of the cheapest market or impeding his access to the dearest. All he asks of it is to be left alone to deal with his fellowmen in such manner as his own natural acuteness or his command of capital may permit. His one desire is to make all the money he can by every means not illegal. *Laissez faire, laissez passer*, comprises the sole and whole duty of the state toward him."

Godkin supported business against labor, opposing strikes because he believed that the basic interests of labor and capital were the same and because he saw strikes as inhibitors of progress,

Carl Schurz, who resigned as associate editor of the New York Evening Post *in 1883 after a series of quarrels with Godkin*

threats to social stability, and as leading to property destruction. He labeled the eight-hour day "pernicious nonsense" and opposed Chinese exclusion not on the grounds of equal rights but because the immigrants provided cheap, productive labor. He denounced protective tariffs as antagonistic to the interests of both capital and labor because they stifled competition, encouraged corruption, and resulted in higher prices. The *Nation* under Godkin also criticized the railroads, opposed economic inflation, and supported the principle of minority representation. In his later years, however, Godkin expressed concern about the effects on society of the unbridled growth of corporate power. As he said in his 1896 essay "The Real Problems of Democracy," published in the *Atlantic Monthly*, "Another new phenomenon which has greatly affected the development of democratic government, and has received no attention, is the growth of corporations. These aggregations of capital in a few hands have created a new power in the State, whose influence on government has been very grave. They employ a vast number of voters, over whom their influence is paramount; a single railroad company has in its service thousands of men. They own immense sums of money, which they think it but right to use freely for their own protection.... How to bring these corporations under the law, and at the same time protect them from unjust attacks, is one of the most serious problems of democratic government."

Criticism of the magazine was mixed. In an 1875 letter Richard Henry Dana, Jr., promised to send his son, who was preparing to travel abroad, issues of the *Nation* because "They will keep you well up in American affairs." Parkman wrote: "I owe too much to the *Nation* ... though I now and then dissent from its views, and have occasionally regretted what seemed to me a needless asperity, I regard it as the most valuable of American journals and feel that the best interests of the country are doubly involved in its success. I have always regarded the *Nation* as the most valuable of all American journals...." Lord Bryce believed that the *Nation* was "the best weekly not only in America, but in the world. It was read by the two classes which in America have most to do with forming political and economic opinion–I mean editors and University teachers." On the other hand, Theodore Roosevelt wrote in 1892: "It fairly make me writhe to think of the incalculable harm to decency that scoundrelly paper, edited by its scoundrelly chief, Godkin, has done." Samuel Bowles of the *Springfield Republican* captured the mixture well in 1869: "Often conceited and priggish, coldly critical to a degree sometimes amusing and often provoking, and singularly lacking not only in a generous enthusiasm of its own but in any sympathy with that generous American quality ... the paper yet shows such vigor and integrity of thought, such moral independence of party, such elevation of tone, and such wide culture, as to demand our respect and secure our hearty praise.... The *Nation* may not ever be popular in the common American sense; ... as a sort of moral policeman of our politics, our society and our art, it can hardly expect to be; but it assuredly has been and will be most useful."

In 1881 the railroad promoter and former journalist Henry Villard quietly purchased the *New York Evening Post* and gave control of the paper to its editor in chief, Carl Schurz; its associate editor, Horace White; and Godkin, who also became an associate editor. At the same time, Godkin sold the *Nation* to the *Evening Post* for forty thousand dollars. Because Villard wished to keep his ownership of the newspaper secret, the public understanding was that the editor and two associate editors were in fact the owners. It was agreed that Schurz and Godkin would receive annual salaries of eight thousand dollars each plus a guaranteed four percent annual dividend on the one hundred thousand dollar investment each was expected to make in the newspaper. White was to be president of the company and in charge of the newspaper's financial pages in order to represent Villard's interests and perspective.

Godkin and Schurz had become acquainted in 1870, and Schurz had contributed political articles to the *Nation*. Commentators disagree about the working relationship between the two at the *Evening Post*, some arguing that there was no animosity between them and others contending that Schurz's sentimental nature inevitably generated conflict in his relationship with the brusque, insensitive, and sometimes tactless Godkin. Godkin's biographer William Armstrong suggests that Godkin may have engineered dissension from the beginning in order to gain control of the paper. The rift between Godkin and Schurz also may have derived, in part at least, from their different perceptions about the appropriate style for the *Evening Post*: Schurz preferred a thoughtful and faithful adherence to evidence and a sometimes labored approach in dealing with issues; Godkin aimed at making the *Evening Post* readable and attractive, even if doing so meant sacrificing accuracy, treating issues superficially, or substituting irony, exaggeration, ridicule, and personal invective for argument when the evidence did not fit his conclusions. In the summer of 1882 Schurz went on vacation, and Godkin editorially attacked Republican leader James Blaine as one who had enjoyed the spoils of corruption before his belated embrace of civil service reform. The backlash from Blaine's supporters fell on Schurz's, not Godkin's, head. In late July 1883, when the railway telegraphers began a nationwide strike, Schurz's editorials attempted to present a neutral perspective while Godkin's were vitriolic attacks on the strikers. In early August, when Schurz left on vacation, Godkin took over as editor in chief. Further acrimonious exchanges between the two men made the breach irreparable, and in December Schurz published a formal announcement of his separation from the newspaper in which, referring to himself in the third person, he stated that he was withdrawing "in consequence of serious differences of opinion between himself and his associates concerning the treatment of important public questions in the editorial columns." The following summer, when Villard was financially vulnerable, Godkin tried to extend his power by persuading Villard to sell him his controlling interest in the newspaper. The effort ultimately failed, and Villard retained control of the *Evening Post*.

During the years of struggle between Godkin and Schurz the *Nation* had become in effect the newspaper's weekly edition; generally, the political articles that appeared in the magazine had previously appeared in the *Evening Post*. Wendell Garrison, who was Villard's brother-in-law, had become treasurer of the newspaper and nominal editor of the *Nation*. Although Godkin continued to write many of the articles that appeared in the magazine after he became associate editor of the *Evening Post*, some commentators believe that the vitality of the *Nation* began to decline under Garrison's control. Even Oswald Garrison Villard, Henry Villard's son and editor of the *Nation* from 1918 to 1932, wrote that the magazine became less polemical and more a vehicle of "an intense scholarship" under Garrison's direction. But Garrison's somewhat pedantic attention to details provided a valuable counterpoint to Godkin's volatility. Had it not been for Garrison's effectiveness in restraining Godkin's pen, the number of libel suits lodged against the magazine might well have been considerably higher.

Godkin led the *Evening Post*'s 1884 revolt against Blaine, arguing that Blaine had used his official position for private gain, and White and Godkin joined forces with Schurz and other independents to support the Democratic presidential candidate, Grover Cleveland. According to tradition, it was Godkin whom Charles A. Dana, editor of the *New York Sun*, had in mind when he applied the term *mugwump*, from an Algonquin word meaning chief, to those who deserted the Republican party and became political independents in the 1880s. The Mugwumps gained sufficient strength to determine Cleveland's election by a narrow margin. On the whole, Cleveland's first term was satisfactory to Godkin: Cleveland opposed high tariffs and supported civil service reform, a hard money policy, and government economy–all favorite Godkin positions. During the 1892 presidential campaign Godkin temporarily halted his attacks on Tammany Hall politicians so as not to detract from his support of Cleveland and the rest of the Democratic ticket, a

Godkin in 1899 (courtesy Cornelia Godkin)

tactic which subjected Godkin to the criticism of his opponents.

A policy which Godkin found particularly gratifying in Cleveland's second term was the president's opposition to expansionism, especially his refusal to support the annexation of the Hawaiian Islands. Throughout his editorial career Godkin almost always opposed imperialistic ventures (a major exception was his support of the annexation of Canada to the United States), although, in the liberal tradition, he had no qualms about exploiting the commercial possibilities of such situations. As early as 1866 he had expressed his views in the *Nation* by warning against adding to the western territory of the continental United States: "Our government and society are now suffering greatly from the too rapid and too wide diffusion of our population. Civilization, religion, education, and manners are all injured by the inordinate increase of 'frontier life' amongst us. Every interest of our society calls for more condensation of our people and less expansion of our territory." His anti-expansionism continued into the late 1890s. He disliked the jingoism of the "yellow journalism" of that era and, although not a pacifist, he saw the Spanish-American War as wasteful, unnecessary, and, because it undermined economic stability, a threat to the American entrepreneur.

In his later years Godkin grew increasingly pessimistic about the possibility of accommodating his early liberal ideals to an industrial age, particularly with regard to the potential of democratic government to improve society. In a letter to Norton in January 1895 he wrote: "I know of no good influence now which is acting on the masses, and the practice of reading trivial newspapers begets, even among men of some education, a puerile habit of mind.... You see I am not sanguine about the future of democracy. I think we shall have a long period of decline like that which followed the fall of the Roman Empire, and then a recrudescence under some other form of society. Our present tendencies in that direction are concealed by great national progress." Sharper still was Godkin's reply to Francis E. Leupp, longtime Washington correspondent for the *Evening Post,* in 1899: "Our present political condition is repulsive to me. I came here fifty years ago with high and fond ideals about America, for I was brought up in the Mill-Grote school of radicals. They are now all shattered, and I have apparently to look elsewhere to keep even moderate hopes about the human race alive."

Godkin and his wife had two children, in addition to their son Lawrence: Elizabeth, born in 1865, and Ralph, who died in infancy in 1868. Elizabeth died in 1873 after a brief illness; Frances Godkin never wholly recovered from the shock and on 11 April 1875 she, too, died. Godkin then moved to Cambridge, Massachusetts, and edited the *Nation* from a distance until he returned to New York in late 1877. (According to several critics, the declining fortunes of the *Nation* during these years may be credited in part to Godkin's absentee editorship.) On 14 June 1884 he married thirty-eight-year-old Katharine Sands, a member of a wealthy family prominent in New York and London society. They shared their home with Lawrence Godkin, a graduate of Harvard Law School and, by the late 1890s, attorney for the *Evening Post.*

After he began taking annual trips to England and Europe in 1889 (except for the presidential campaign summer of 1896, when he did not go abroad), Godkin insisted on longer and longer paid vacations from the *Evening Post,* a habit which irritated his colleagues at the newspaper. By 1892 his vacation was four months long; in 1897 he stretched it to five months. In 1897 also, Godkin received his second honorary degree, a doctorate of civil laws from Oxford; the first had been an honorary master of arts from Harvard in 1871. When his friend Norton received a D. C. L. in 1900 Godkin wrote in his congratulatory letter, "The degree is still the blue ribbon of literature." By 1898 Godkin's long absences had diminished his influence at the *Evening Post.* He returned from Europe in the fall of 1899 in ill health, suffering particularly from rheumatism, which had bothered him intermittently at least since the early 1870s. His son and Garrison engineered his "retirement," effective immediately with respect to his editorial responsibilities, although he was allowed to retain the title of editor in chief until 1 January 1900. In February 1900 he suffered a stroke while working on his memoirs and was incapacitated for six months. He lived briefly in Dublin, New Hampshire, and Lenox, Massachusetts, before moving to England in late May 1901. After suffering another stroke, he died on 21 May 1902 at Greenway House, Brixham, and was buried in Hazelbeach Churchyard, Northampton, England. His friends established a lecture series in his name at Harvard with an endowment of twelve thousand dollars. The lectures began in 1904 and, according to the terms of the endowment, were required to focus on some aspect of "the essentials of free government and the duties of the citizen."

When Godkin died his old friend and colleague Norton wrote of him: "He did more than any other writer of his generation to clarify the intelligence and to quicken the conscience of the thoughtful part of the community in regard to every important political question of the time." William James spoke even more directly of the editor's influence: "To my generation, his was certainly the towering influence in all thought concerning public affairs, and indirectly his influence has certainly been more pervasive than that of any other writer of the generation, for he influenced other writers who never quoted him, and determined the whole current of discussion." Within a generation after his death, however, commentators began to give a more moderate assessment of his contributions. Vernon Parrington wrote in *The Beginnings of Critical Realism in America, 1860-1920* (1930): "Throughout the Gilded Age this transplanted English liberal was the high priest of criticism in America.... his native aristocracy of temperament closed his mind to the virtues of certain homely American liberalisms.... Godkin's mind was keenly critical, but his sympathies were narrow and his prejudices great.... It is difficult today to understand his great influence with cultivated readers of his generation. In part perhaps it was due to his crisp assurance. He put things so plumply, he wrote so brilliantly, that his readers were persuaded he must think as neatly. Yet his trenchant prose style cannot hide a certain slightness of matter. His later comments tended to become ever thinner and shriller–not criticism at all, but the sharp expression of aging prejudice.... Unlike his great master [Mill] he did not go forward to meet new times ... but by standing still he did liberalism a real disservice."

This temperate view continues to be reflected in late-twentieth-century scholarship. As Armstrong expressed it, "When he was at his best, he could not be matched for the logic, clarity, and incisive humor of his editorials. At the same time the narrow conservatism in which he wrapped himself in his later years cannot be accounted a force for good.... The achievements of late-nineteenth-century science and technology created a host of social problems that cried out for solution, and Godkin, to whom compassion–like sentimentality–denoted frailty, lacked the intellectual outlook the times demanded."

Letters:
The Gilded Age Letters of E. L. Godkin, edited by William M. Armstrong (Albany: State University of New York Press, 1974).

Biographies:
Rollo Ogden, ed., *Life and Letters of Edwin Lawrence Godkin,* 2 volumes (New York & London: Macmillan, 1907);

William M. Armstrong, *E. L. Godkin: A Biography* (Albany: State University of New York, 1978).

References:
William M. Armstrong, "Additions to the *Nation* Index," *Bulletin of the New York Public Library,* 73 (April 1969): 4;

Armstrong, *E. L. Godkin and American Foreign Policy, 1865-1900* (New York: Bookman Associates, 1957);

Armstrong, "Godkin's *Nation* as a Source of Gilded Age History: How Valuable?," *South Atlantic Quarterly*, 72 (Autumn 1973): 476-493;

R. L. Beisner, "Thirty Years Before Manila: E. L. Godkin, Carl Schurz and Anti-Imperialism in the Gilded Age," *Historian*, 30 (August 1968): 561-577;

Henry M. Christman, ed., *One Hundred Years of The Nation* (New York: Macmillan, 1965);

Louis Filler, "The Early Godkin," *Historian*, 17 (Autumn 1954): 43-66;

Robert Fridlington, "Two *Nation* Portraits: Frederick Law Olmsted: Launching *The Nation*," *Nation*, 202 (3 January 1966): 10-12;

Alan P. Grimes, *The Political Liberalism of The New York* Nation, *1865-1932* (Chapel Hill: University of North Carolina Press, 1953);

Daniel C. Haskell, The Nation: *Indexes of Titles and Contributors*, 2 volumes (New York: New York Public Library, 1951-1953);

David S. Keene, "The Political Thought of E. L. Godkin," Ph.D. dissertation, Princeton University, 1961;

Joseph H. Killian, Jr., "Edwin Lawrence Godkin: A Study in the Liberal-Democratic Mind and the Entrepreneurial Tradition," Ph.D. dissertation, University of North Carolina at Chapel Hill, 1972;

Diana Klebanow, "Edwin L. Godkin and the American City," Ph.D. dissertation, New York University, 1965;

Phillip Knightley, *The First Casualty* (New York: Harcourt Brace Jovanovich, 1975), pp. 3-17;

Richard W. Lee, "A Thematic Analysis of Edwin L. Godkin's Editorials in *The Nation*, 1865-1899," Ph.D. dissertation, University of Iowa, 1972;

Mara N. Mayor, "Norton, Lowell and Godkin: A Study of American Attitudes Toward England, 1865-1885," Ph.D. dissertation, Yale University, 1969;

Frank Luther Mott, "*The Nation*," in his *A History of American Magazines, 1865-1885* (Cambridge: Harvard University Press, 1938), pp. 331-356;

Randall L. Murray, "Edwin Lawrence Godkin: Unbending Editor in Times of Change," *Journalism History*, 1 (Autumn 1974): 77-81, 89;

Allan Nevins, "Edwin Lawrence Godkin: Victorian Liberal," *Nation*, 171 (22 July 1950): 76-79;

Nevins, The Evening Post: *A Century of Journalism* (New York: Boni & Liveright, 1922);

Mary P. Norman, "The Reform Thought of Edwin Lawrence Godkin," Ph.D. dissertation, St. Louis University, 1967;

Vernon L. Parrington, "English Liberalism and Politics–Edwin Lawrence Godkin and *The Nation*," in his *Main Currents in American Thought*, volume 3: *The Beginnings of Critical Realism in America, 1860-1920* (New York: Harcourt, Brace, 1930), pp. 154-168;

Gustav Pollak, *Fifty Years of American Idealism: The New York* Nation, *1865-1915* (Boston: Houghton Mifflin, 1915);

Harold W. Stoke, "Edwin Lawrence Godkin, Defender of Democracy," *South Atlantic Quarterly*, 30 (October 1931): 339-349;

Kermit Vanderbilt, "Norton and Godkin: Launching *The Nation*," *Nation*, 200 (15 February 1965): 165-169;

Oswald Garrison Villard, "Edwin Lawrence Godkin: A Great American Editor," *South Atlantic Quarterly*, 6 (July 1907): 288-299.

Papers:

The most important of E. L Godkin's papers are in the Houghton Library at Harvard University and in the manuscript division of the New York Public Library.

Fletcher Harper

(31 January 1806-29 May 1877)

James Glen Stovall
University of Alabama

See also the Harper and Brothers entry in *DLB 49: American Literary Publishing Houses, 1638-1899.*

MAJOR POSITIONS HELD: Co-owner, Harper and Brothers, New York (1825-1877); publisher, *Harper's New Monthly Magazine* (1850-1875), *Harper's Weekly* (1857-1875), *Harper's Bazar* (1867-1875).

No name is more closely identified with the American publishing industry than that of Harper. From the early days of the Republic to the late twentieth century, that name has attached itself—in one form or another—to one of the nation's major publishing houses. There is scarcely an American who has not read a Harper-produced book or bought a Harper-edited magazine, or who has not been influenced by one of its many publications.

The single person most responsible for the widespread influence of the name Harper was Fletcher Harper, the youngest of the four Harper brothers. It was Fletcher Harper who was the guiding light in the expansion of the company's book business, who took the idea of a monthly and a weekly magazine and made them the dominant publications of the day, who opened and exploited the market for women's magazines, who encouraged editorial diversity within the ranks of the magazine staffs, and who stood solidly against the threats of powerful politicians when the magazines railed against their corruption.

Yet for all of his influence and success, Fletcher Harper was possibly the least "colorful" of the giants of nineteenth-century journalism. He had a quiet, calm nature that often placed him in the background of the great dramas of his time. He never ran for public office nor allowed his name to be attached to political causes. He rarely, if ever, wrote for any of his publications, although his skill as an editor was widely acknowledged. He lived the life of a devout Method-

Fletcher Harper (portrait by Charles Loring Elliott, 1862, in Eugene Exman, The House of Harper *[New York: Harper & Row, 1967])*

ist and a family man, shunning publicity without being a recluse. He had a keen sense of what his large mass of readers wanted, however, and he was skillful in guiding the editors, reporters, and artists of his publications toward that audience. Harper often let others speak for him, but there was little doubt that their words were also his.

Fletcher Harper was born on 31 January 1806, the fourth son of Elizabeth Kolyer and Joseph Harper, at Newtown, Long Island. His grandfather, James Harper, had emigrated from England in the mid 1700s, and his father was a home carpenter and jack-of-all-trades. His mother was the daughter of a well-to-do Dutch Lutheran family in Newtown, and her falling in love with the Methodist Harper caused much consternation in her family. Her father finally consented to the marriage, however, and Elizabeth Harper became a devoted Methodist and raised her children in an atmosphere of loyalty to the church. Elizabeth and Joseph Harper had four sons who survived to manhood: James, John, Joseph Wesley, and Fletcher.

When they were of age, James and John left home for New York City, where they were apprenticed to printers, and when they were free of their apprenticeship, they formed the publishing firm of J. & J. Harper in 1817. The two younger brothers followed in their footsteps, and Joseph Wesley (known as Wesley) joined the firm in 1823. Fletcher came into the company two years later. That same year, at the age of nineteen, he married Jane Freelove Lyon, with whom he had two sons. The division of labor within the firm followed the natural inclinations and skills of the brothers. James superintended the mechanical departments; John made most of the purchases and was put in charge of the finances; Wesley acted as a proofreader and secretary, handling much of the firm's correspondence; and Fletcher began as foreman of the composing room and grew to be in charge of the literary department. In the early years, each of the brothers had a hand in all parts of the business so that in 1833, the name of the firm was changed to Harper and Brothers. As to which brother was the "Harper" and which were the "Brothers," none could or would say. They worked harmoniously together, each placing mutual trust and confidence in the skills and opinions of the others.

As the business grew, however, it was Fletcher who became the first among the equals. More and more he exerted his influence on what the company produced and how it was produced. Even in its early years the business was a substantial one. Before 1825 the firm employed fifty people and kept ten large handpresses constantly in use. It seemed to be always expanding, particularly to accommodate new equipment. Harper and Brothers began stereotyping their works in 1830 and probably used steam-powered presses in 1833. In 1839 Fletcher pulled off one of the company's major business coups by securing an order from New York state to supply school libraries with books.

The lack of a copyright agreement between England and the United States presented Harper and Brothers with an opportunity for profitable exploitation, as it did to other publishers. While American writers had yet to achieve broad fame and popularity, English writers were well liked by American audiences, and their works were demanded by an expanding mass of readers. American printers and publishers often simply lifted the proof sheets of works by English authors and published them with no compensation whatsoever. The competition for such works was fierce. Messengers met packet ships before they had docked, and compositors and presses were readied for quick reproduction. The Harpers produced one of Sir Walter Scott's Waverly novels in twenty-one hours in order to have it at the booksellers first.

This theft of material–a common practice among most major American publishers–was a constant irritant to the English. The irritation was often focused on Harper and Brothers because that firm was the most successful at it. London's *Punch* said of Harper: "The house of book-taker and book-seller, Harper, of New York, is a house built of the skulls of English authors.... Harper makes his daily four meals of the bones of English penmen." To their credit, Harper began to pay handsome sums for advance sheets of English novels in the 1850s, but the practice of literary theft continued among other publishers.

In 1850 Harper and Brothers brought out the first of their periodical publications, *Harper's New Monthly Magazine*. The reason for its existence was simply explained by Fletcher Harper. "If we were asked why we first started a monthly magazine," he said, "we would have to say frankly that it was as a tender to our business." Harper could well justify his statement. Publishing a magazine seemed the next logical step for the brothers' growing business. They were at this point the producers of many books, including novels, travel and exploration narratives, school texts, histories, and biographies. Harper's Library of Select Novels had reached 615 volumes, and Harper's Family Library brought out one work each month.

The magazine, in fact, was produced in part to expand the book business. It was to be the advertising medium for other Harper publications, and for the first three decades of its existence, it accepted no outside advertising despite many offers to buy its space. Nor did it diverge significantly in its content from the direction that the publishing house had taken. In its first issue, it said, "The magazine will transfer to its pages as rapidly as they may be issued all the continuous tales of Dickens, Bulwer, Croly, Lever, Warren and other distinguished contributors to British Periodicals.... The design is ... to place within the reach of the great mass of the American people the unbounded treasures of the Periodical Literature of the present day." American writers had long been irritated that the Harpers had ignored their works in favor of more popular British authors, and the appearance of the magazine caused further consternation. One of the magazine's rivals called it a "good foreign magazine." It was excoriated as a worshipper of all things British and as a conduit of the British point of view.

Much of the content did come from Great Britain, but its largest single contribution in its first decade came from an American and was about a Frenchman. It was John S. C. Abbott's *History of Napoleon Bonaparte* (1855), an adoring biography that took the un-English view that Napoleon was a hero. The series was a great favorite of readers, not only for its content but also for its massive illustrations. The editors used woodcuts liberally to illustrate many of their articles so that by 1860 the magazine was averaging about fifty cuts per issue. By 1865 the company claimed that the magazine had included more than ten thousand engravings (at a cost of about thirty dollars each) during its first fifteen years of publication. The many illustrations, interesting content, and good writing took the magazine from a circulation of seventy-five hundred six months after its birth to a phenomenal two hundred thousand by 1860.

The magazine's guiding hand was Fletcher Harper, although the idea of the magazine was originally James Harper's. Fletcher Harper set the tone of the publication and saw to it, by gentle guidance of the editors, that it followed the course he had set for it. Its first managing editor was Henry J. Raymond, later the founder of the *New York Times*, and he was succeeded by Alfred H. Guernsey, a man who "possessed the exceptional ability to make a readable article of eight to twelve pages out of a two-volume historical or biographical work," wrote J. Henry Harper, Fletcher's grandson, in his 1912 history *The House of Harper*. It was exactly that kind of talent upon which the magazine depended to satisfy its growing readership.

A massive fire in December 1853 destroyed most of the Harper and Brothers physical plant and all of the January issue of the magazine, but it failed to interrupt the success of the company. Although the fire cost the company more than a million dollars, there were more than enough reserves to absorb this loss. The brothers quickly regrouped, and the January issue of the magazine was delayed for only about ten days. A new building was built, fronting on Franklin Square, and the Harpers resumed their preeminence in American publishing.

Fletcher Harper's influence could be seen in every phase of the Harper and Brothers operation, but it was *Harper's Weekly*, begun in 1857, to which he devoted most of his attention. Unlike the earlier magazine, the idea for this publication was Fletcher's. The *Weekly* emphasized news and opinion, which the *Monthly* had meticulously avoided. It was subtitled *A Journal of Civilization* and looked something like the *London Illustrated News*. Its real competition, however, was *Frank Leslie's Illustrated Newspaper*, which had begun two years earlier. Both publications took advantage of advances in printing technology that made illustrations more available and timely, and of the public's hunger for news. The nation was gripped by the dramatic debate over slavery and states' rights, and the publication that could deliver news in a speedy and attractive manner was bound to be successful.

Harper's Weekly, like just about everything else that Fletcher Harper touched, was certainly successful. Within two years ninety thousand copies of each issue were being produced. The first "editor" of the weekly was Theodore Sedgwick, the American ambassador to The Hague, who did much of the political writing for the paper from that post for a year. He was succeeded by John Bonner, already an employee of the Harper company, who served as managing editor for the next five years. Although one of the stated objectives of the magazine was to be a journal of opinion, the opinions expressed in the early editions were remarkably restrained. Harper refused to be drawn into a fight by those who violently objected to slavery or by those who violently defended it. The periodical continually called for compromise, saying at one point that slavery was a "matter that concerns the southern states exclusively," but that sentiment was drowned out by the increasing shrillness on both sides. The weekly supported the Republican nomination of William Seward for the presidency but paid little attention to the campaign of 1860 when Abraham Lincoln received the nomination.

The withdrawal of the Southern states from the Union provoked the editors of *Harper's Weekly* to become Unionists, but they admitted that Lincoln's success in holding the Union together would depend on the Northern willingness to fight. The editorial direction of the weekly was soft and uncertain until the appointment of George William Curtis as editor in 1862. Curtis had written for the publication for five years, was an admirer of Lincoln, and had been active in Republican Party politics. Fletcher Harper rightly perceived that now was the time to take a strong stand on the war and on Abraham Lincoln, and that Curtis was the man to do it.

Another addition to the staff was also to have a long-term impact on *Harper's Weekly*. Thomas Nast, a twenty-two-year-old artist who had worked at *Frank Leslie's Illustrated Newspaper* and the *Illustrated News*, had been let go by Frank Leslie in a budget-cutting move. Nast sent some of his illustrations to *Harper's*, and they were immediately bought and paid for handsomely. That arrangement continued until Nast was invited to join the staff. He did so but did not find the working conditions at the office suitable, so he was allowed to work out of his home. Fletcher Harper took particular interest in this young and greatly talented artist, and Nast responded with a devotion that lasted for many years. A measure of what Harper's patronage meant to Nast is found in the 1904 Albert Bigelow Paine biography of Thomas Nast, which the author dedicated to Fletcher Harper, "whose unfailing honesty and unfaltering courage made possible the great triumphs of Thomas Nast."

Nast's illustrations for *Harper's Weekly* were brilliant not only in their technical execution but also in their ability to capture the mood of the country and touch the emotions of the readers. Typical of these was his "Christmas Eve" illustration that ran on two inside pages of the 1862 Christmas edition; on one side was the picture of a mother kneeling beside a window in a bedroom where two children slept; on the other was a soldier seated at a lonely campfire. The two large pictures were surrounded by several other smaller scenes from the war. That picture evoked thousands of responses to the magazine and allowed Nast to continue drawing the large, detailed illustrations that would establish his fame.

Nast was as ardent a supporter of President Lincoln as Curtis, and together they pulled the weekly into his fold. Nast had met Lincoln briefly before his inauguration in 1861 and always held him in high regard. During the next four years, Lincoln came to recognize Nast's work and at one point expressed an appreciation for it by saying, "Thomas Nast has been our best recruiting sergeant. His emblematic cartoons have never failed to arouse enthusiasm and patriotism, and have always seemed to come just when these articles were getting scarce."

Before *Harper's Weekly* entered the Lincoln ranks, however, it had a serious brush with the War Department that almost cost it the right to publish. The publication's army of artists and writers had been active in the field, traveling with armies and observing what they could. At one point, one artist observed too much, in the eyes of Gen. George McClellan, and the Harpers received a telegram from Secretary of War Edwin Stanton suspending the publication. Fletcher Harper traveled to Washington and met with the ill-tempered secretary; his diplomatic handling of the matter allowed him to come away from the meeting not only with permission to resume publication but with the thanks of the secretary for other services rendered.

Harper's Weekly eventually became not only a supporter of Lincoln but a proponent of the war itself. "When you fight, fight," Harper said simply. Nast particularly was hard on those who would make peace before the South had been fully conquered. His 1864 "Compromise with the South" illustration was a powerful drawing that showed a large and healthy Confederate soldier, with his foot on the grave of a Union casualty, clasping hands with a broken and defeated Union soldier. The inscription on the gravestone read, "In Memory of Union Heroes in a Useless War." The picture covered a full page of the weekly and was later made into a campaign poster during the presidential campaign. Nast and *Harper's Weekly* continued their assault on the Copperheads and all those who would make peace with the South, and it increasingly pictured Lincoln as a statesman who could bring an honorable end to the conflict. "The profound confidence of the great mass of the people in the President is unshaken," the weekly editorialized. "It is simply impossible to make them believe ... that he is a monstrous despot or a political gambler." After Lincoln's reelection the weekly published a cartoon of him that made him seem twenty feet tall.

The Civil War offered *Harper's Weekly* and the other similar publications a golden opportunity. The public's demand for news and information about the war was insatiable, and the fact that these publications could deliver that plus pictures enabled their circulation figures to soar. By the end of 1861, 120,000 copies of *Harper's Weekly* were being distributed every week, and circulation stayed above the 120,000 mark for the rest of the war. By contrast, the circulation of *Frank Leslie's Illustrated News*, its closest competition, had declined to 50,000 by 1865. *Harper's* maintained this circulation figure with the high quality of its writing and illustration, which were clearly superior to similar publications of the time.

The end of the war signaled a decrease in the circulations of most periodicals, and both the *Monthly Magazine* and the *Weekly* were not immune. In fact, the monthly magazine declined so much that some thought was given to discontinuing it. Fletcher Harper decided to retain the publication, however, and it revived and flourished under the editorship of Henry Mills Alden, who succeeded Alfred Guernsey in 1869. (The two had collaborated in producing an illustrated history of the Civil War for Harper's in 1868.) There were also changes in the art department, and the magazine came to depend on illustrations even more heavily than before. This dependence was due to the emphasis that the magazine's competition, particularly *Scribner's* (later *Century*), had been placing on quality illustration. Alden's editorship would last for another fifty years and would keep the publication preeminent in its field.

The story of the birth of Harper and Brothers' third major publication is an illustration of the close relationship and high regard the brothers had for each other and especially for Fletcher. The youngest brother had conceived the idea for a women's magazine shortly after the war, but when he presented it to his partners they were reluctant. After all, they were running the most successful publishing company in the nation and saw little reason to extend themselves in another risky venture. Fletcher thought the idea was too good to let go, however, and he finally told them, "Well, I wish we could go into it as a firm, but if we cannot, I will publish it myself." At which John was reported to have said, "No, you will not. We'll defer to your judgment, and you shall have your *Bazar*." Thus was born *Harper's Bazar*.

The first issue appeared on 2 November 1867 and was subtitled "A Repository of Fashion, Pleasure and Instruction." The editor was Mary L. Booth, who had been a translator and a historian of the city of New York, and she remained with *Harper's Bazar* for more than twenty years. Typical issues contained English serials, pictures by Thomas Nast and other artists, humor, and public affairs. Fashion plates came from Berlin. The magazine was an immediate and continuing success. Within ten years, it had obtained a circulation of eighty thousand. (The spelling of the name was changed to *Bazaar* in 1929.)

Fletcher Harper kept a close watch on all of his publications, supervising their production, reading proofs, and offering gentle suggestions to editors, writers, and artists, but his special imprint was on the *Weekly*. It was the most vital of the Harper line, and it had the most impact on the day-to-day affairs of the city, state, and nation. The end of the Civil War did not mean a decrease in news or controversy. The assassination of President Lincoln and the subsequent capture and trial of the conspirators riveted the public's attention and kept subscriptions high.

The presidency of Andrew Johnson was also a matter of great interest to the public. At *Harper's Weekly*, opinion on Johnson was split. Curtis was a supporter of the president and was against his impeachment. "We believe that he is faithful to what he conceives to be the best interest of the country," he wrote. Nast disliked the president and cartooned him unmercifully as a bully, a Klansman, and a would-be king. When Johnson won his impeachment trial, Nast drew him as a dancing character with kingly robes, a crown on his head, and a bottle in his hand. That divergence of opinion was tolerated by Fletcher Harper, and it compelled him to explain that the publication "is an independent forum. There are many contributors. It is not necessary that all should agree."

The editor and the illustrator joined in their good opinions of Ulysses S. Grant, but the seeds of antagonism grew between them. Curtis was a high-toned gentleman who valued courtesy and the goodwill even of those whom he opposed. Nast was a brash and direct young man on whom subtlety was often wasted. "When he attacks a man with his pen, it seems as if he were apologizing for the act," Nast once said of Curtis. "I try to hit the enemy between the eyes and knock him down."

Cover, with an illustration by Thomas Nast, for an issue of the news and opinion magazine founded by Harper in 1857

The battle that was to bring *Harper's Weekly* and Thomas Nast lasting fame lay just ahead. The opening shots had been fired in the late 1860s when Nast had drawn cartoons exposing the supposed corruption of New York City. Those attacks were largely unfocused and dealt with the breakdown of city services. In 1869 Nast drew a cartoon entitled "The Economical Council, Albany, New York," in which he identified the members of the corrupt ring of politicians that held sway in New York City. From then on Nast had no inhibitions about his drawings or his accusations. The city of New York and much of the state legislature were controlled by four men, and their leader was William Marcy Tweed. Together they stole enormous sums from the public treasury; one later estimate said that they had robbed the city of some two hundred million dollars. The Tweed Ring's power was widespread. It used money and fear to buy off judges, bondsmen, contractors, merchants, and ministers. Its actions were generally known, or suspected, but proof was unavailable, because the city's financial records were not open to the public.

When Nast first aimed his pen at this corruption, he was advised to give up the fight because of its futility, and indeed a number of his drawings had Tweed saying, "What are you going to do about it?" It was an apt question. Few felt that anything *could* be done. Newspapers in the city either stood silent or rose to the defense of the ring. In 1871, however, George Jones took over the *New York Times* and joined with Nast and *Harper's Weekly* in the fight against the ring. Nast's cartoons were unsettling, but they had as yet caused little damage. Nast's parting shot of the year, however, provoked Tweed to retaliate. In a cartoon entitled "Tweedledee and Sweedledum," Tweed and his confederate William Sweeney were shown giving liberally from the public treasury to the "neediest" of their cohorts. It was subtitled, "A New Christmas Pantomime at the Tammany Hall." Tweed gave orders to the New York Board of Education to reject all bids from Harper and Brothers for schoolbooks and to cancel the contracts already in place. The board destroyed fifty thousand dollars worth of books and replaced them from a company closely identified with the ring.

A meeting of the board at Harper and Brothers was held, and it was quickly decided that a majority favored discontinuing the fight against Tammany. Fletcher Harper disagreed. He started to walk out of the meeting, saying, "Gentlemen, you know where I live. When you are ready to continue the fight against these scoundrels, send for me. Meantime, I shall find a way to continue it alone." The board quickly changed its mind, and the fight went on.

The ring had begun to overreach itself. Although the thefts were gigantic, there was not enough money or power to go around, and enemies developed from within. Finally, a disgruntled member of the ring smuggled financial figures out of the city controller's office and turned them over to the *New York Times*. The paper published them and challenged the ring to disprove them. This detailing of the ring's corruption turned many supporters against city officials. Nast continued hammering away, more confident than ever that he would be vindicated. He was even offered a bribe–an all-expenses-paid trip to Europe to study art–if he would cease his relentless attacks. Week after week, Nast produced scathing indictments of Tweed and his associates, and the *Times* continued to raise unanswerable questions about the city's finances. Charges were brought against Tweed, and the election in November 1871 turned many of his cronies out of office. Tweed went to jail, escaped, and was recaptured in Spain by a man who recognized him from the pictures that Nast had drawn. He died in the Ludlow Street Jail in 1878.

The victorious fight against the Tweed Ring brought much deserved praise to the *Times*, Nast, and *Harper's Weekly*. Together, they had fought a battle that few had thought winnable. Nast was hailed as a hero, invited to Washington, and entertained by President Grant and others. *Harper's Weekly*, too, was at the height of its powers. It had more subscribers than at any time in its history, and its influence was enormous. Nast next turned his pen toward Horace Greeley, the *New York Tribune* editor who became the Democratic presidential nominee in 1872. Greeley's appearance–his small glasses, bald head, and flowing white beard–lent itself to lampooning, and Nast made the most of it. Nast's campaign against Greeley opened old wounds with editor Curtis, some of whose friends found themselves the targets of Nast's cartoons. On several occasions, Curtis asked Nast to spare some of his friends, but Nast only continued to fling his arrows.

In all of these disputes, Fletcher Harper characteristically stayed in the background, content to give support to both Curtis and Nast and to allow the credit for the successes of the *Weekly* to go elsewhere. During these times, he was called upon to play the peacemaker between his two strong-willed employees, and he did so while maintaining the affection of both.

Harper retired quietly in 1875 and died on 29 May 1877. He was the last survivor of the original four brothers, and his death was followed by many eulogies to the gentleness and strength of his character and the scope of his professional vision. Harper, without making a great display, had changed the look and reach of American magazines. He had taken advantage of technical innovations to set the standard for quality production of publications. He had envisioned a more massive reading public than most of his peers, and he had worked to deliver material to that audience. When courage had been called for, he exhibited it in standing up to the corrupt politicians of New York. In all that he had done during the half century of his professional career, he had achieved a remarkable success and had established the name of Harper as an enduring imprimatur of American publishing.

Biography:
J. Henry Harper, *The House of Harper* (New York: Harper, 1912).

References:
"Fletcher Harper," *Harper's Weekly* (16 June 1877): 457-458;

"Fletcher Harper: A Memorial," *Harper's Weekly* (23 June 1877): 486;

Albert Bigelow Paine, *Thomas Nast, His Period and His Pictures* (New York: Harper, 1904), pp. 158-159, 305-306, 338-348, 491-493;

Carl Sandburg, *Abraham Lincoln: The War Years*, 4 volumes (New York: Harcourt, Brace, 1939), II: 387-388, 487-488, 617-618; III: 57-58, 382-384;

Algernon Tassin, *The Magazine in America* (New York: Dodd, Mead, 1916), pp. 209-211, 232-255.

Bret Harte
(25 August 1836-5 May 1902)

Charles A. Fleming
Oklahoma State University

See also the Harte entries in *DLB 12: American Realists and Naturalists; DLB 64: American Literary Critics and Scholars, 1850-1880;* and *DLB 74: American Short-Story Writers Before 1880.*

MAJOR POSITIONS HELD: Reporter, *Northern Californian* (1857-1860); writer and acting editor, *Californian* (1864-1866); editor, *Overland Monthly* (1868-1870).

BOOKS: *Condensed Novels, and Other Papers* (New York: Carlton/London: Low, 1867; enlarged edition, Boston: Osgood, 1871);

The Lost Galleon and Other Tales (San Francisco: Towne & Bacon, 1867);

The Luck of Roaring Camp, and Other Sketches (Boston: Fields, Osgood, 1870; enlarged, 1870);

The Heathen Chinee (Chicago: Western News Company, 1870);

Poems (Boston: Fields, Osgood, 1871);

East and West Poems (Boston: Osgood, 1871; London: Hotten, 1871);

Mrs. Skaggs's Husbands, and Other Sketches (London: Hotten, 1872; Boston: Osgood, 1873);

An Episode of Fiddletown and Other Sketches (London: Routledge, 1873);

M'liss. An Idyl of Red Mountain (New York: DeWitt, 1873);

Idyls of the Foothills (Boston: Osgood, 1875);

Echoes of the Foot-hills (Boston: Osgood, 1875);

Tales of the Argonauts, and Other Sketches (Boston: Osgood, 1875);

Gabriel Conroy (3 volumes, London: Warne, 1876; 1 volume, Hartford, Conn.: American Publishing Company, 1876);

Bret Harte

Two Men of Sandy Bar: A Drama (Boston: Osgood, 1876);

Thankful Blossom, a Romance of the Jerseys, 1779 (Boston: Osgood, 1877; London & New York: Routledge, 1877);

The Story of a Mine (London: Routledge, 1877; Boston: Osgood, 1878);

The Man on the Beach (London: Routledge, 1878);

"Jinny" (London: Routledge, 1878);

Drift from Two Shores (Boston: Houghton, Osgood, 1878);

The Twins of Table Mountain (London: Chatto & Windus, 1879);

The Twins of Table Mountain and Other Stories (Boston: Houghton, Osgood, 1879);

Jeff Briggs's Love Story and Other Tales (London: Chatto & Windus, 1880);

Flip and Other Stories (London: Chatto & Windus, 1882);

Flip and Found at Blazing Star (Boston: Houghton, Mifflin, 1882);

In the Carquinez Woods (London: Longmans, Green, 1883; Boston: Houghton, Mifflin, 1884);

On the Frontier (London: Longmans, Green, 1884; Boston: Houghton, Mifflin, 1884);

By Shore and Sedge (Boston: Houghton, Mifflin, 1885; London: Longmans, Green, 1885);

Maruja (London: Chatto & Windus, 1885; Boston & New York: Houghton, Mifflin, 1885);

Snow-Bound at Eagle's (Boston & New York: Houghton, Mifflin, 1886; London: Ward & Downey, 1886);

The Queen of the Pirate Isle (London: Chatto & Windus, 1886; Boston & New York: Houghton, Mifflin, 1887);

A Millionaire of Rough-and-Ready and *Devil's Ford* (Boston & New York: Houghton, Mifflin, 1887);

Devil's Ford (London: White, 1887);

A Millionaire of Rough-and-Ready (London: White, 1887);

The Crusade of the Excelsior (Boston & New York: Houghton, Mifflin, 1887; London: White, 1887);

A Phyllis of the Sierras and A Drift from Redwood Camp (Boston & New York: Houghton, Mifflin, 1888; London: Chatto & Windus, 1888);

The Argonauts of North Liberty (Boston & New York: Houghton, Mifflin, 1888; London: Blackett, 1888);

Cressy (2 volumes, London & New York: Macmillan, 1889; 1 volume, Boston & New York: Houghton, Mifflin, 1889; London: Macmillan, 1889);

The Heritage of Dedlow Marsh and Other Tales (1 volume, Boston & New York: Houghton, Mifflin, 1889; 2 volumes, London & New York: Macmillan, 1889);

A Waif of the Plains (London: Chatto & Windus, 1890; Boston & New York: Houghton, Mifflin, 1890);

A Ward of the Golden Gate (London: Chatto & Windus, 1890; Boston & New York: Houghton, Mifflin, 1890);

A Sappho of Green Springs and Other Stories (London: Chatto & Windus, 1891; Boston & New York: Houghton, Mifflin, 1891);

A First Family of Tasajara (2 volumes, London & New York: Macmillan, 1891; 1 volume, Boston & New York: Houghton, Mifflin, 1892);

Colonel Starbottle's Client and Some Other People (London: Chatto & Windus, 1892; Boston & New York: Houghton, Mifflin, 1892);

Susy: A Story of the Plains (Boston & New York: Houghton, Mifflin, 1893; London: Chatto & Windus, 1893);

Sally Dows, Etc. (London: Chatto & Windus, 1893); republished as *Sally Dows and Other Stories* (Boston & New York: Houghton, Mifflin, 1893);

A Protégée of Jack Hamlin's and Other Stories (Boston & New York: Houghton, Mifflin, 1894; enlarged edition, London: Chatto & Windus, 1894);

The Bell-Ringer of Angel's and Other Stories (Boston & New York: Houghton, Mifflin, 1894; abridged edition, London: Chatto & Windus, 1894);

Clarence (London: Chatto & Windus, 1895; Boston & New York: Houghton, Mifflin, 1895);

In a Hollow of the Hills (London: Chapman & Hall, 1895; Boston: Houghton, Mifflin, 1895);

Barker's Luck and Other Stories (Boston & New York: Houghton, Mifflin, 1896; London: Chatto & Windus, 1896);

Three Partners or The Big Strike on Heavy Tree Hill (Boston & New York: Houghton, Mifflin, 1897; London: Chatto & Windus, 1897);

Tales of Trail and Town (Boston & New York: Houghton, Mifflin, 1898; London: Chatto & Windus, 1898);

Stories in Light and Shadow (London: Pearson, 1898; Boston & New York: Houghton, Mifflin, 1898);

Mr. Jack Hamlin's Mediation and Other Stories (Boston & New York: Houghton, Mifflin, 1899; London: Pearson, 1899);

From Sand Hill to Pine (Boston & New York: Houghton, Mifflin, 1900; London: Pearson, 1900);

Under the Redwoods (Boston & New York: Houghton, Mifflin, 1901; London: Pearson, 1901);

On the Old Trail (London: Pearson, 1902); republished as *Openings in the Old Trail* (Boston & New York: Houghton, Mifflin, 1902);

Condensed Novels, Second Series: New Burlesques (Boston & New York: Houghton, Mifflin, 1902; London: Chatto & Windus, 1902);

Sue: A Play in Three Acts, by Harte and T. Edgar Pemberton (London: Greening, 1902);

Her Letter, His Answer and Her Last Letter (Boston: Houghton, Mifflin, 1905; London: Gay & Bird, 1905);

Trent's Trust and Other Stories (London: Nash, 1903; Boston & New York: Houghton, Mifflin, 1903);

The Lectures of Bret Harte, edited by Charles Meeker Kozlay (Brooklyn: Kozlay, 1909);

Stories and Poems and Other Uncollected Writings, compiled by Kozlay (Boston & New York: Houghton Mifflin, 1914);

Sketches of the Sixties, by Harte & Mark Twain (San Francisco: John Howell, 1926).

Collections: *The Writings of Bret Harte,* 20 volumes (Boston: Houghton, Mifflin, 1896-1914);

Bret Harte's Collected Works, Argonaut edition, 25 volumes (New York: Collier, 1906).

OTHER: *Outcroppings: Being Selections of California Verse,* edited by Harte (San Francisco: Roman/New York: Widdleton, 1865).

A growling California grizzly bear crossing railroad tracks was the emblem for the *Overland Monthly* magazine that appeared 1 July 1868 on San Francisco's newsstands. The editor, Bret Harte, had added the railroad tracks to the California state symbol to depict the conflict between California's savage vigor and encroaching civilization. Selection of this symbol was ironic. The *Overland Monthly* was to be a western alternative to the highly successful *Atlantic Monthly* and bore a striking physical resemblance to its East Coast counterpart. The goals of the *Overland Monthly* were to promote California, to make San Francisco the cultural center for the West, and to attract immigrants. The railroads played an important role in this, but when the East Coast and the West Coast became connected by a pair of steel rails, eastern culture–and eastern magazines–spread west on the heels of the immigrants. Bret Harte's emblem for his new magazine was prophetic. The same railroads that were to bring more people and business to California carried his *Overland Monthly* to eastern audiences and brought him literary recognition and international fame. The railroads did not bring success to the *Overland Monthly,* but they helped make Francis Bret Harte famous.

Francis Bret Harte was born on 25 August 1836 in Albany, New York, to Henry and Elizabeth Rebecca Ostrander Harte. He may have acquired a love of books and literature from his father, a teacher and school administrator, and he succeeded in having some poetry published as early as age eleven. He left school at age thirteen to help support his family after his father's death. His mother remarried and left for California in 1853, and Harte took passage for San Francisco the following year. In California he taught school for a short time and spent a brief period in the gold-mining camps. He also worked in and around San Francisco as a private tutor, a Wells Fargo Express messenger, a druggist's assistant, a typesetter for the *Humboldt Times* in Union, and as an assistant editor for the weekly *Northern Californian* in Eureka. All the while he submitted occasional poems and short stories to eastern magazines.

His job in 1857 with the *Northern Californian* provided his first major opportunity to use his literary skills. For more than two years he honed his writing skills and championed a variety of unpopular causes–especially those involving Mexicans and Indians. After writing a critical editorial about the killing of Indians at Mad River in February 1860, Harte thought it prudent to leave the newspaper and return to San Francisco. There he found work as a typesetter for the *Golden Era,* a small literary magazine, and began writing occasional columns for the magazine at one dollar each. Before long he was promoted to the editorial room and his literary career was underway.

While at the *Golden Era* he married Anna Griswold in 1862 and took a position with the California Mint in 1864–a job he kept for nearly a year after becoming editor of the *Overland Monthly.* The position with the mint provided a steady income and allowed Harte to pursue literary interests that had a less dependable return.

With some modest success and a regular job to fall back on, Harte joined forces with another writer, Charles Webb, and began publishing a

Front page for the first issue of the literary weekly Harte edited for two years. The two articles on the page were written by Harte.

weekly literary magazine, the *Californian,* in May of 1864. Samuel Clemens, who wrote under the name Mark Twain, was a reporter for the *Morning Call* in San Francisco, and was hired as one of the principal writers for the *Californian.* Harte and Twain had a close friendship that later deteriorated into antagonism. Twain learned much from Harte at the *Californian* and wrote that Harte "trimmed and trained and schooled me patiently until he changed me from an awkward utterer of coarse grotesquenesses to a writer of paragraphs and chapters that have found a certain favor in the eyes of even some of the very decentest people in the land."

Their stormy friendship lasted until 1877, when the two collaborated on a play, *Ah Sin.* The play was a flop both in New York and on tour, and Harte and Twain never saw or communicated with each other again. Over the next twenty-five years, Twain made many derogatory remarks about Harte and his work. Harte was far less critical of Twain, and while it is known that Harte owed Twain considerable sums of money which he never repaid, other reasons for the demise of their friendship remain unclear.

Harte contributed articles, fiction, book reviews, and poetry to the *Californian,* and served as editor during Webb's frequent absences. Within a year Harte's writing, his poetry in particular, caught the eye of a bookseller and collector of poems who had made some money in the gold fields and wanted to begin a career as a publisher. Anton Roman approached Harte with the idea of editing a volume of California poetry, and *Outcroppings: Being Selections of California Verse* was printed in time for Christmas 1865.

Publication of the book provided a flood of criticism about which poets had been included and which had been left out. Reviews were highly critical, some calling the book trash and others insisting that Harte had insulted all of California by his failure to include some poets.

While *Outcroppings* sold widely because of the controversy it had caused, the *Californian* was having financial problems. Webb, the publication's business manager, had lost most of his money in stock speculation and left for the East Coast in 1866. Harte left the magazine soon after and sought some other literary outlet.

Harte's partner in the *Outcroppings* venture was to provide that outlet. Despite an unsuccessful follow-on to *Outcroppings,* Roman had not given up his dream of being a publisher, and as the *Californian* floundered because of poor business management, he decided the time was right to publish a new magazine. His plan was to glorify California's past and promote its future instead of poking fun at Californians as did many existing publications. A positive and enthusiastic attitude would attract readers and advertisers, he believed. The magazine was to be the cultural centerpiece of the state's finest city.

Bret Harte had been recommended as a candidate for editor of the new magazine, but Roman had reservations at first. The basic strategy behind his proposed magazine was promotion and development of California to a national audience, and it was not to be a purely literary journal. Harte, Roman feared, might make it too literary, and Harte had earned a reputation with the *Californian* for criticizing almost everything about the area, from climate to treatment of minorities. This was not the editorial stance Roman was planning.

A mutual friend, however, convinced Roman that Harte was one of the few local people who had the potential for attracting national attention, and the offer was made. Harte was reluctant to accept at first. He had doubts about the magazine's financial backing and specific demands concerning his rights and responsibilities as editor. An agreement with Roman was finally reached in March 1868, and Harte became the first editor of the *Overland Monthly.* The first issue was planned for that July.

According to Roman, the magazine had to focus on the California pioneers and paint a more idealistic picture of them and their exploits. In particular, Roman was concerned with material development of California; promotion of the state's bright future would attract local advertisers and immigrants from the East. With the railroads snaking their way toward each other from the East and from the West, it was only a matter of time before they linked up and thousands of easterners poured into California, Roman argued. (The Central Pacific and Union Pacific linked up on 10 May 1869, ten months after the new magazine began publication.) Even the title of the magazine supported this promotional theme because it reached out toward the East and embraced an audience that was gradually moving westward. The word *overland* also referred to the railroad, the people, and trade that would soon be riding the rails to California. Harte explained: "Will the trains be freighted only with merchandise, and shall we exchange nothing but goods? Will not our civilization gain by the subtle inflowing current of Eastern refinement, and shall we not, by the same channel, throw into Eastern exclusiveness something of our own breadth and liberality? And if so, what could be more appropriate for the title of a literary magazine than to call it after this broad highway?"

Harte began work on a short story, "The Luck of Roaring Camp," which was to lead off the first issue of the new magazine. Harte's insistence on perfection, however, delayed its completion, and it missed the deadline for the first issue.

The first edition of the *Overland Monthly* received good reviews but contained no memorable writing. Harte himself contributed only a couple of poems to the periodical's first issue. The magazine looked much like the *Atlantic Monthly*–same size, same color cover, and similar typography–and was criticized for not containing "romantic" stories of robust California. Harte made up for this omission by completing "The Luck of Roaring Camp" for the second issue.

"The Luck of Roaring Camp" dealt with the activities of a California mining camp and was a parable of sorts, focusing on the basic good in all human beings and the triumph of faith, optimism, and civilization. The story concerns the illegitimate birth of a baby to a mining camp prostitute, Cherokee Sal, who dies in childbirth. The

Montgomery Street, San Francisco, in the 1860s. The water wagon stands in front of the offices of the Californian.

baby, Tommy Luck, becomes the son of the entire camp and changes the rowdy miners into decent, caring people until a flood wipes out most of the camp.

The story brought on the first of many differences of opinion between Harte and his publishers. A woman proofreader took offense at the story's profanity, at the prostitute character, and at the illegitimate birth of a main character. When the proof sheets reached Roman, he hesitated to give his approval to the story until Harte threatened to resign, and the story went to the printer unchanged.

"The Luck of Roaring Camp" has been soundly criticized for its stereotypes, clichés, lack of realism, and romanticism, but it made Harte famous. While the San Francisco press criticized it on grounds of morality, it got the attention of the eastern press and was very favorably reviewed. It even earned him an offer from the editor of the *Atlantic Monthly* to write something similar for that magazine.

Six months after the appearance of "The Luck of Roaring Camp," Harte published another soon-to-be-famous story, "The Outcasts of Poker Flat." This story also dealt with brotherly love and the transformation of "evil" people to good in the face of a crisis.

"The Outcasts of Poker Flat" concerns a gambler, two prostitutes, and a drunkard who are asked by the more proper citizens to leave the town of Poker Flat. En route to another town they are joined by a couple running away to get married, and the whole group gets snowed in. In the face of death, the outcasts are regenerated by the innocent young couple, and their goodness shines through only to end in tragedy.

These two stories–considered by many to be his best works of fiction–brought Harte national literary recognition, but his poem "Plain Language from Truthful James," popularly known as "The Heathen Chinee," which appeared in the September 1870 edition of the *Overland,* brought him worldwide fame. The poem had to do with the price Chinese people had to pay for success, and within a short time of publication, had been set to music several times and was published in Europe and Australia. In the poem, an innocent Chinese man, Ah Sin, is persuaded to play cards with gambler Bill Nye. Nye cheats Ah Sin but becomes indignant and violent when his victim cheats him. The narrator, Truthful James, also participates in the card game but sits back and moralizes as Ah Sin is set upon.

To Harte, who always championed minority groups and criticized white men for the way they treated Chinese and Mexicans, the poem represented the state of relations between Chinese laborers in California and their Occidental hosts. Chinese suffered at the hands of white people for trying to do the same things white people did, Harte believed, while too many Californians did nothing to correct the situation. Harte himself reportedly never liked the poem nor understood why it had become so popular.

Perhaps one of the reasons Harte disliked the poem was that it was often misunderstood. While Harte was sympathetic to the Chinese and deplored their treatment at the hands of his fellow Californians, the final lines of the poem have been misinterpreted as being critical of the Chinese. What Harte meant as irony was erroneously taken as authority by some to mistreat the Chinese. The poem concludes with these words:

> Which I wish to remark,
>   And my language is plain,
> That for ways that are dark,
>   And for tricks that are vain,
> The heathen Chinee is peculiar,
>   Which the same I would rise to explain.

The high quality of these pieces was maintained throughout Harte's stint as editor of the *Overland Monthly*, which lasted nearly two years. While the magazine's primary focus was on local people and activities–travel articles, features, and short fiction–it also carried articles about other locations in the United States as well as Europe, Asia, and South America. Harte made it a point to pare down articles and stories to make them as brief as possible and was thus able to include more pieces than other magazines of similar size. Plus, his fervor for cutting out unnecessary verbiage added to the quality of the magazine's content. While many magazines of the day were characterized by wordy Victorian romanticism, the *Overland Monthly* was more journalistic in style.

As a critic, Harte demanded realism and good, solid, succinct writing. He deplored symbolism, sentimentality, and moralizing–some of the faults attributed to his own writing by other critics. He was especially critical of women writers who, he believed, used too much sentimentality and melodrama. Harte also emphasized the need for strong, striking characterization and for realistic, appropriate dialogue. These were areas in which his writing was particularly strong.

Aside from occasionally contributing articles, stories, and poetry to the *Overland Monthly*, Harte wrote a regular column, "Etc." The column resembled a newspaper editorial and was a vehicle for social commentary. Although the column was often used to support the promotional theme of the magazine, it often contained reviews of literature and art as well as comments about literary figures. The column frequently dealt with controversial topics as well. Local government, provincialism, poor business practices, censorship, and even the local press were among the victims of Harte's eloquence.

Even outside of his column, Harte did not shy away from controversy. Articles dealing with the plight of women in California, with the problems faced by ranchers and farmers, with overpopulation, and even articles critical of the railroads were printed.

While Harte thrived on controversy, his publisher, Roman, suffered a nervous breakdown and the *Overland Monthly* was sold to John Carmany, a more demanding, organized businessman who was determined to show a profit. There were many conflicts between the two men, with Harte fervently supporting the literary quality and scope of the magazine and Carmany looking for ways to reduce costs and make money.

Harte's editorship of the *Overland Monthly* and personal contributions to the magazine's pages skyrocketed him to local and national fame. In San Francisco Harte was a celebrity. He lived well, dressed elegantly and associated with only the best of San Francisco society. Autograph collectors sought him out, and tourists included him on their lists of attractions.

Most of the applause for Harte's work came from the East, however, and it was that recognition that he valued more. To him the East represented the real seat of culture and literary genius in the United States, and offers from several Midwest and East Coast journals turned his head. Even the *Atlantic Monthly*–the chief model and competition for the *Overland Monthly*–sought his talents. The temptation to go in the direction of the loudest applause was too much for Harte to resist. Plus, by mid 1870 the financial difficulties the *Overland Monthly* was having (the periodical was often operating in the red–an omen not lost on its editor) provided more incentive for Harte to seek a position elsewhere.

The *Overland Monthly* did a far better job of promoting Harte than either itself or California and earned for him, among other honors, an offer of a professorship at the new University of California. He rejected that offer, along with substantial offers to remain with the *Overland Monthly*, and went east to glory in his newfound fame. In early February 1871 Harte left San Francisco with his wife and two children, never to return. Seventeen years after arriving in California as a penniless boy, he left as one of California's most distinguished citizens and one of the most famous writers in the country. Harte's departure from California marks the high point in his literary career. While he wrote much after leaving the West Coast, his best work was done prior to 1871.

On his way east, Harte made a brief stop in Chicago to consider editing a magazine there and visited relatives in New York for a few days, but the recognition he really sought was in Boston. Within a month of leaving San Francisco he had a contract with the *Atlantic Monthly*.

The *Atlantic Monthly* offered him ten thousand dollars for twelve monthly contributions–the highest amount offered an American writer at that time. But Harte did not handle his fame well, and his contract with the *Atlantic Monthly* was not renewed. In fact he had considerable difficulty fulfilling the initial agreement. The parties, special appearances, and social obligations took their toll, and the quality and volume of Harte's writing plummeted. He tried the lecture circuit for several years without notable success. Although he made some money writing and lecturing, he spent it faster than he earned it and incurred huge debts from his high living. Despite his problems, Harte would not return to California and even turned down an 1877 appeal from the dying *Overland Monthly* to become the magazine's editor again. Harte wrote publisher Carmany: "I can make here, by my pen, with less drudgery, with more security, honor and respect thrice as much as I can make in California at the head of the *Overland*–taking the peak as the estimate. As far as I can see the tastes, habits, and ideas of you people have not changed since you and I were forced to part company, because I could better myself here...."

Finally, in 1878 friends convinced him to accept a government consulship in Germany and leave his financial problems and family behind in America. He did not find Germany to his liking, and, prompted by several enjoyable visits to

Title page for the bound first volume of the literary magazine Harte intended as the western counterpart of the Atlantic Monthly. *Harte designed the logo of the bear crossing the railroad track.*

Great Britain, he managed a transfer to Glasgow, Scotland, two years later. He felt comfortable in Great Britain, and some of his literary fame lingered on. He found a niche in English society and an adoring audience still willing to listen to fanciful tales of California's long-past gold rush days. The demands of English social life and of his writing and lecturing were so great, however, that he had little time for his official duties, and after five years as a consul in Scotland he was "invited" to leave government service. In 1885 he retired and moved to London. He continued his writing during his seventeen years in London and found among the English a receptive audience. Despite quality stories such as "A Protégée of Jack Hamlin's" and "An Ingénue of the Sierras," he achieved little fame and died in 1902 at the country villa of a former diplomat. He was buried in a village churchyard southwest of London.

Harte became famous primarily because of his short stories and poetry published during his tenure as editor of the *Overland Monthly*. This is not to say that he produced nothing of quality before or after that period; he did. But nothing before or after achieved the same recognition. His writings were produced over more than forty years and fill twenty volumes. Only a few works, though, are remembered. As a writer, Harte was a talented humorist who could take fairly routine story formulas and give them new vigor and settings. His background as a journalist gave him a brisk style and a special skill for describing people, their mannerisms and dialogue. He is noted for his "local color" stories, although he was not the first humorist to use this technique. Heavily influenced by Charles Dickens, Harte was a storyteller, a reporter with wit and a flair for sentiment and romance. As an editor, Harte reached the two-year pinnacle of his literary career at the *Overland Monthly*. He had worked hard to reach that point and began a long slide downhill the moment he left. He is far better known for the short stories, insightful reviews, and poetry he produced in that position than he is for what he accomplished with the magazine itself.

Still, the *Overland Monthly* set new standards in those Victorian times for clear, solid writing, a succinct journalistic magazine style and logical argumentation. He was successful in his fight against censorship and for editorial freedom, and he sought to improve his readers' tastes in writing. Harte and his magazine broke new ground with the "local color" story and raised it to new literary heights. As the editor of the *Overland Monthly*, Harte did much to promote and romanticize the people and places of the Golden West–which is what he had set out to do in the first place.

Letters:

Bradford A. Booth, "Unpublished Letters of Bret Harte," *American Literature*, 16 (May 1944): 131-142;

Booth, "Bret Harte Goes East: Some Unpublished Letters," *American Literature*, 19 (January 1948): 318-335;

San Francisco in 1866 by Bret Harte, Being Letters to the Springfield Republican, edited by George R. Stewart and Edwin S. Fussell (San Francisco: Book Club of California, 1951).

Bibliographies:

George R. Stewart, Jr., *A Bibliography of the Writings of Bret Harte in the Magazines and Newspapers of California, 1857-1871*, University of California Publications in English, volume 3, number 3 (Berkeley: University of California Press, 1933);

Joseph Gaer, ed., *Bret Harte: Bibliography and Biographical Data* (San Francisco: State Emergency Relief Administration, California Press, 1935; New York: Franklin, 1967).

Biographies:

T. Edgar Pemberton, *Bret Harte: A Treatise and a Tribute* (London: Greening, 1900);

Pemberton, *The Life of Bret Harte* (New York: Dodd, Mead, 1903);

Henry W. Boynton, *Bret Harte* (New York: McClure, Phillips, 1903);

Henry Childs Merwin, *The Life of Bret Harte* (Boston & New York: Houghton Mifflin, 1911);

George R. Stewart, Jr., *Bret Harte: Argonaut and Exile* (Boston & New York: Houghton Mifflin, 1931);

Alvin F. Harlow, *Bret Harte of the Old West* (New York: Messner, 1943);

Richard O'Connor, *Bret Harte: A Biography* (Boston & Toronto: Little, Brown, 1966).

References:

Thomas Dykes Beasley, *A Tramp through Bret Harte Country* (San Francisco: Elder, 1914);

Walter Blair, *Native American Humor, 1800-1900* (New York: American Book Co., 1931);

Bradford A. Booth, "Mark Twain's Comments on Bret Harte's Stories," *American Literature*, 25 (January 1954): 492-495;

Noah Brooks, "Bret Harte: A Biographical and Critical Sketch," *Overland Monthly*, Bret Harte memorial number, 40 (September 1902): 201-207;

Brooks, "Bret Harte in California," *Century Magazine*, 58 (July 1899): 447-451;

Henry Seidel Canby, "The Luck of Bret Harte," *Saturday Review of Literature*, 2 (17 April 1926): 717-718;

George Pierce Clark, "Mark Twain on Bret Harte," *Mark Twain Journal* (Spring/Summer 1958): 12-13;

Margaret Duckett, "Bret Harte and the Indians of Northern California," *Huntington Library Quarterly*, 18 (November 1954): 59-83;

Duckett, "The 'Crusade' of a Nineteenth-Century Liberal," *Tennessee Studies in Literature*, 4 (1959): 109-120;

Duckett, *Mark Twain and Bret Harte* (Norman: University of Oklahoma Press, 1964);

Duckett, "Plain Language from Bret Harte," *Nineteenth-Century Fiction,* 11 (March 1957): 241-260;

Mrs. James T. Fields, "Bret Harte and Mark Twain in the 'Seventies': Passages from the Diaries of Mrs. James T. Fields," edited by M. A. DeWolfe Howe, *Atlantic Monthly,* 130 (September 1922): 342-348;

Patrick D. Morrow, *Bret Harte: Literary Critic* (Bowling Green, Ohio: Bowling Green State University Popular Press, 1979);

James Herbert Morse, "The Native Element in American Fiction," *Century Magazine,* 26 (July 1883): 362-375;

George R. Stewart, "Bret Harte upon Mark Twain in 1866," *American Literature,* 13 (November 1941): 264;

Stewart, "Some Bret Harte Satires," *Frontier,* 13 (January 1922): 93-101;

W. P. Trent and John Erskine, *Great American Writers* (New York: Holt, 1912);

Franklin Walker, *San Francisco's Literary Frontier* (New York: Knopf, 1939);

Roger R. Walterhouse, *Bret Harte, Joaquin Miller, and the Western Local Color Story* (Chicago: University of Chicago Libraries, 1939);

James H. Young, "Anna Dickinson, Mark Twain, and Bret Harte," *Pennsylvania Magazine of History and Biography,* 76 (January 1952): 39-45.

Papers:
The major repositories of Bret Harte's manuscripts are the Beinecke Library at Yale University and the Kozlay Collection at the Huntington Library.

Paul Hamilton Hayne

(1 January 1830-6 July 1886)

Rayburn S. Moore
University of Georgia

See also the Hayne entries in *DLB 3: Antebellum Writers in New York and the South* and *DLB 64: American Literary Critics and Scholars, 1850-1880*.

MAJOR POSITIONS HELD: Assistant editor (1852, 1854-1855), editor (1853-1854), *Southern Literary Gazette*, renamed *Weekly News and Southern Literary Gazette* in 1853; editor, *Russell's Magazine* (1857-1860); literary editor, *Southern Opinion* (1867-1868).

BOOKS: *Poems* (Boston: Ticknor & Fields, 1855);
Sonnets, and Other Poems (Charleston, S.C.: Harper & Calvo, 1857);
Avolio: A Legend of the Island of Cos. With Poems, Lyrical, Miscellaneous, and Dramatic (Boston: Ticknor & Fields, 1860);
Legends and Lyrics (Philadelphia: Lippincott, 1872);
Address of Col. Paul H. Hayne, of South Carolina before the Ladies of the Memorial Association of Alabama, Wednesday Evening, May 1st, 1872 (Montgomery, Ala.: Barrett & Brown, 1872);
The Mountain of the Lovers: With Poems of Nature and Tradition (New York: Hale, 1875);
W. Gilmore Simms: A Poem Delivered on the Night of the 13th of December, 1877, at "The Charleston Academy of Music," as a Prologue to the "Dramatic Entertainment" in Aid of the "Simms Memorial Fund" (Charleston, S.C.?, 1877?);
Lives of Robert Young Hayne and Hugh Swinton Legaré (Charleston, S.C.: Walker, Evans & Cogswell, 1878);
The Yorktown Ceremonial Ode (Charleston, S.C.: Walker, Evans & Cogswell, 1881);
Poems of Paul Hamilton Hayne: Complete Edition (Boston: Lothrop, 1882);
The Broken Battalions (Baltimore, 1885).

OTHER: *The Poems of Henry Timrod*, edited by Hayne (New York: Hale, 1873).

Paul Hamilton Hayne (from the Collection of South Caroliniana Library)

PERIODICAL PUBLICATIONS: "The North British Review Upon American Poetry," *Southern Literary Gazette*, new series 2 (2 October 1852): 151-152; (9 October 1852): 163; (16 October 1852): 175-176;
"A Word of Explanation," *Southern Literary Gazette*, new series 2 (23 October 1852): 187;
"William Gilmore Simms," *Appletons' Journal*, 4 (30 July 1870): 136-140;
"Southern Country Life," *Appletons' Journal*, 7 (16 March 1872): 285-289;
"Poe's Method of Writing," *Appletons' Journal*, 7 (4 May 1872): 490-491;
"Ante-Bellum Charleston," *Southern Bivouac*, new series 1 (September 1885): 193-202; (October 1885): 257-268; (November 1885): 327-336;

"Charles Gayarré," *Southern Bivouac*, new series 2 (June 1886): 28-37; (July 1886): 108-113; (August 1886): 172-176.

Paul Hamilton Hayne was a magazinist in the mold of Edgar Allan Poe and William Gilmore Simms. He spent much of his career editing magazines and contributing poems, essays, critical articles, editorials, and stories to them. As did Poe and Simms, he earned much of his livelihood from such journals, and his best work, as did theirs, usually appeared first in magazines. Much of his early reputation was based on his editorial experience with two prominent Southern journals, the *Southern Literary Gazette* and *Russell's Magazine*. After the Civil War his standing was firmly established through poems, reviews, essays, and editorial work for many Southern journals, including *Southern Opinion*, *Southern Society*, and *Southern Bivouac*, and through contributions, mostly of poems, to such important Northern literary monthlies as *Lippincott's*, *Scribner's* (later the *Century*), *Harper's*, and the *Atlantic*.

Hayne was born in 1830 in Charleston, South Carolina, to Paul Hamilton Hayne, naval officer and member of a family which produced a Revolutionary martyr and two United States senators, and Emily McElhenny Hayne, daughter of a Presbyterian minister. After his father's death in 1831 Hayne was reared by his mother and his uncle, Robert Y. Hayne, who had been Daniel Webster's opponent in the famous Senate debate on Foote's Resolution in 1830. He attended a local private school and the College of Charleston, graduating in February 1850. He then studied law and was admitted to the bar; but he had literary ambitions, and in May 1852 he became assistant editor of the *Southern Literary Gazette*, a local weekly that published fiction, verse, essays, reviews, and editorials and considered "literature" to be its "staple." The same year he married Mary Middleton Michel; they had one son.

Hayne immediately began to seek contributions from Simms and Henry Timrod and to write editorials on literary topics. Simms's *The Sword and the Distaff* (republished in 1854 as *Woodcraft; or, Hawks about the Dovecote*) was appearing in installments, and his play *Norman Maurice* (1851) and an extract from *As Good as a Comedy* (1852) both came out in the 19 June issue, shortly after Hayne took over the "chief editorial management" of the magazine in the editor's absence. Timrod contributed several poems, usually over his pen name, "Aglaus." Hayne also published or reprinted work by such Northern authors as Richard Henry Stoddard, John T. Trowbridge, William Cullen Bryant, Park Benjamin, N. P. Willis, and Fredrika Bremer.

In his editorials Hayne espoused the cause of writing in both South and North, an approach he pursued consistently throughout his career, even during and after the Civil War, despite his avid Confederate views and subsequent unreconstructed political opinions. "Literature has no sections," he wrote John Greenleaf Whittier in 1870. On 23 October 1852, for example, he reprinted John R. Thompson's long critical essay on *Uncle Tom's Cabin* from the *Southern Literary Messenger* because, as he observed, it was "important" that "the slanderous North's publication ... should meet with a clear and complete refutation at the South." A week earlier, however, he had as readily defended Henry Wadsworth Longfellow and Bryant against unfavorable criticism in an article on American poetry in the *North British Review*. Still, Hayne was interested in local writers and encouraged their work. Essie B. Cheesborough, a Charlestonian, praised him many years later for his "charming" treatment of contributors as well as for his reluctance to tamper with their work: "He gave us no advice," she observes in "Recollections of Paul Hamilton Hayne," a manuscript among the Hayne papers at Duke University, "how we ought or ought not, to write. He was exceedingly tolerant of our opinions, and the language in which they were clothed. He never gave himself what may be termed 'editorial airs.'"

In December 1852 Hayne took full control of the *Southern Literary Gazette* for a debt owed him by the owner, W. C. Richards, and renamed the magazine the *Weekly News and Southern Literary Gazette*. Fifteen months later he sold his interest in the journal and returned for a year to his old position of assistant editor, but the *Gazette* became more and more political in its outlook, and Hayne resigned in March 1855.

In April 1857 Hayne, Simms, and other South Carolina writers brought out *Russell's Magazine*, a monthly along the lines of the British *Blackwood's*. The magazine was named for John Russell, the proprietor of a Charleston bookstore that was a gathering place for the city's literati. Hayne was appointed one of the two editors, but after two issues assumed full editorial supervision of the magazine. Though Carolinian in origin and Southern in sympathy, "Maga," as Hayne frequently referred to it, was similar to the *Gazette* in that it was open to Northern contribu-

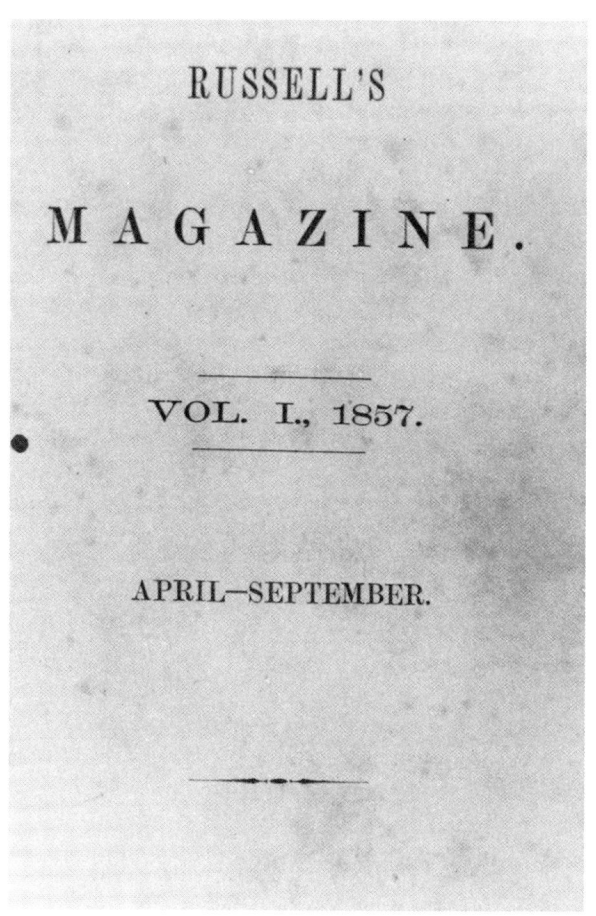

Cover for an issue of the Southern literary magazine edited by Hayne from its founding in 1857 until its demise in 1860 (from the Collection of South Caroliniana Library)

tions and, despite the strong political views of those who founded it, owed "no allegiance to cliques, sects, or parties." Neither Hayne nor anyone else, of course, could have separated politics from literature in the climate of opinion prevailing during this period–certainly the *Atlantic* and *Putnam's Monthly*, the journal's Northern contemporaries, made no effort to keep the two apart–but Hayne tried to do so, though with indifferent success. In the first number of *Russell's* he felt compelled "to pitch into" *Putnam's* for its unfair criticism of "Southern men and matters generally" and of Southern literature particularly. On the other hand, as late as January 1860, Hayne was still maintaining that the magazine's "province" was the "peaceful realms of literature" and not the "grand national or sectional issues of the day." On occasion he commended the proabolition *Atlantic* for its literary qualities. And, as in the *Gazette*, he defended American authors from all sections against British criticism: in March 1859 he criticized certain English journals for attacking Longfellow and Oliver Wendell Holmes and asserted that "the shameful antagonism so long characteristic of the English Reviews in regard to American writers and their works must give place to a cordial recognition of the ability of our authors whenever it is fairly and unquestionably manifested." A year later Hayne wrote in favor of Bryant when the author of "Thanatopsis" was censured for his politics in an editorial in the *Richmond Enquirer*. There was no reason to excoriate Bryant "the poet," he contended, when the editorial writer's "sole business" was with "Bryant the Black Republican." Such "narrow-minded arrogance and folly" gave, he concluded, "some colour to the charge of the intellectual blindness or inferiority (especially in matters of ART) of the Southern States."

Hayne's own aesthetic principles combined a preference for romantic poetry and Elizabethan drama with an interest in contemporary criticism and fascination with old-fashioned fiction by Daniel Defoe, Sir Walter Scott, James Fenimore Cooper, and Simms. He published essays on poetry by Timrod and William J. Grayson and on fiction by Simms and himself, as well as lengthy reviews of Alfred, Lord Tennyson, Percy Bysshe Shelley, Poe, and Simms. Timrod contributed his discerning consideration of Southern writing, "Literature in the South." Hayne printed over sixty of Simms's poems and six contributions in prose, including "The Asphodel," "Lamia–The Beautiful Sin," "Volans Video," a two-part piece on Francis Marion, and a chapter from *The Cassique of Kiawah* (1859). From Timrod he accepted thirty-seven poems, including "The Arctic Voyager," "Praeceptor Amat," and "Hark to the Shouting Wind." He published more than fifty of his own poems, among them "Avolio–A Legend of the Island of Cos," "After the Storm," and "The Sylph in the Laurel Tree." He also included such important contributions as Stoddard's "Herod Agrippa and the Owl," John W. De Forest's "The Smartville Ram Speculation," and John Esten Cooke's "Estcourt," a serial published from April to October 1857.

Hayne struggled throughout the journal's lifespan with the financial problems all Southern editors faced; he could pay few writers for their work–neither Stoddard nor Cooke received the sum promised for their main contribution, and Hayne received nothing for his own work. The magazine ceased publication in March 1860.

Poor health prevented Hayne from fighting in the Civil War and even cut short his service as

Copse Hill, the home near Grovetown, Georgia, that Hayne built and lived in after his Charleston estate was destroyed in the Civil War (courtesy of William Hamilton Hayne)

an aide to South Carolina governor Francis W. Pickens. His home destroyed during the war, he moved his family to Grovetown, Georgia, where he built a shanty called "Copse Hill" on some land he owned.

After the demise of *Russell's* Hayne contributed poems and prose to *Southern Field and Fireside*, the *Southern Illustrated News*, and other Confederate journals, and to the Charleston and Columbia papers. He did not return to editing until the Civil War was over, serving in various editorial capacities on such weeklies as *Southern Opinion* of Richmond and *Southern Society* of Baltimore and contributing columns and departments to the *Banner of the South* of Augusta, Georgia, *Scott's Monthly* of Atlanta, the *South Atlantic* of Wilmington, North Carolina, and newspapers in Georgia, South and North Carolina, and Kentucky.

Most of his magazine work in the postwar period, however, was for Northern journals, whose remuneration and audience were attractive to poverty-stricken Southern authors. After Appomattox he began to send poems to the *Round Table*, the *Old Guard*, the *Galaxy*, and *Appletons' Journal* in New York, and when *Lippincott's* appeared in Philadelphia in 1868, he submitted work there. All of these magazines published his poems in the late 1860s. By the 1870s he was contributing to the *Atlantic*, to all the Harper periodicals (the *New Monthly*, the *Weekly*, and the *Bazar*), and to the newly established *Scribner's Monthly*. His series of "Copse Hill" nature poems, including "Aspects of the Pines" and "The Voice in the Pines," appeared in the *Atlantic*; "Unveiled," a long irregular ode, was published in *Scribner's*; and "Muscadines," "The Snow Messengers," "In Harbor," and "Face to Face" were printed by *Harper's Monthly*. He published no prose in the major Northern monthlies, but *Appletons'* accepted short pieces from time to time, among them essays on Simms in 1870 and on Poe in 1872, and stories in 1871 and 1872.

By the 1870s Hayne had succeeded Simms as the leading literary spokesman for the South, and he was usually asked to celebrate important occasions with a poem. He wrote lyrics for the centennials of King's Mountain in 1880, of Yorktown in 1881, and of Charleston in 1883; for the sesquicentennial of Georgia in 1883, for the International Cotton Exposition in Atlanta in 1881, for the graduation of the class of 1883 at Smith College, and for the relief of Confederate veterans in Baltimore in 1885 (for which he composed *The*

Broken Battalions). Most of these poems were too long for magazine publication, but the ode on King's Mountain appeared in *Harper's Monthly*, and the other occasional lyrics were published separately in pamphlet form.

In the 1880s Hayne became the chief contributor to two Louisville journals: *Home and Farm* and *Southern Bivouac*. The first, a biweekly with a large circulation, was aimed at a rural audience; Hayne accordingly turned to natural settings and produced some of his most memorable poems of this type, including "In the Wheat Field," "The Last Patch (of Cotton)," and "Midsummer. (On the Farm.)." The *Southern Bivouac* was originally a magazine for Confederate veterans, but its focus changed to literature in 1885. Edited by Basil W. Duke and Richard W. Knott, who was also editor of *Home and Farm*, the *Bivouac* paid Hayne well, usually five dollars a page for prose and varying rates for poems. He responded by contributing a fine sonnet on Robert E. Lee and two of the best essays he ever published: "Ante-Bellum Charleston" and "Charles Gayarré." The first of these essays deals nostalgically with Hugh Swinton Legaré, Robert Y. Hayne, Simms, and *Russell's Magazine*; the section on Simms is the most discerning general estimate by a contemporary. The article on Gayarré is a challenge, especially to Louisianans, to give the old historian his due. At the end of the third installment of the essay appears Hayne's sonnet to his friend, an advance in sonnet technique and structure for Hayne. For these contributions and others Hayne received almost four hundred dollars.

For over thirty years Paul Hamilton Hayne contributed poems, essays, letters, stories, and critical articles to magazines and also served in various editorial capacities on journals. Magazines were central to his literary life and to his career as a man of letters. He died in 1886.

Letters:
A Collection of Hayne Letters, edited by Daniel Morley McKeithan (Austin: University of Texas Press, 1944);

The Correspondence of Bayard Taylor and Paul Hamilton Hayne, edited by Charles Duffy (Baton Rouge: Louisiana State University Press, 1945);

"A Southern Genteelist: Letters of Paul Hamilton Hayne to Julia C. R. Dorr," edited by Charles Duffy, *South Carolina Historical and Genealogical Magazine*, 52 (April 1951): 65-73; (July 1951): 154-165; (October 1951): 207-217; 53 (January 1952): 19-30;

A Man of Letters in the Nineteenth-Century South: Selected Letters of Paul Hamilton Hayne, edited by Rayburn S. Moore (Baton Rouge: Louisiana State University Press, 1982).

References:
Charles Anderson, "Charles Gayarré and Paul Hayne: The Last Literary Cavaliers," in *American Studies in Honor of William Kenneth Boyd*, edited by David K. Jackson (Durham, N.C.: Duke University Press, 1940), pp. 221-281;

Jack DeBellis, ed., *Sidney Lanier, Henry Timrod, and Paul Hamilton Hayne: A Reference Guide* (Boston: Hall, 1978), pp. 141-177;

Jay B. Hubbell, *The South in American Literature, 1607-1900* (Durham, N.C.: Duke University Press, 1954), pp. 655-657, 743-757, 773-777;

Ludwig Lewisohn, "Paul Hamilton Hayne," *Charleston* (South Carolina) *Sunday News*, 20 September 1903, p. 20;

Alton Taylor Loftis, "A Study of *Russell's Magazine*: Ante-Bellum Charleston's Last Literary Periodical," Ph.D. dissertation, Duke University, 1973;

Daniel M. McKeithan, "A Correspondence Journal of Paul Hamilton Hayne," *Georgia Historical Quarterly*, 26 (September-December 1942): 249-272;

McKeithan, "Paul Hamilton Hayne and *The Southern Bivouac*," *University of Texas Studies in English*, 17 (1937): 112-123;

Rayburn S. Moore, "'The Absurdest of Critics': Hayne on Howells," *Southern Literary Journal*, 12 (Fall 1979): 70-78;

Moore, "'A Great Poet and Original Genius': Hayne Champions Poe," *Southern Literary Journal*, 16 (Fall 1983): 105-112;

Moore, "Hayne the Poet: A New Look," *South Carolina Review*, 2 (November 1969): 4-13;

Moore, "'The Literary World Gone Mad': Hayne on Whitman," *Southern Literary Journal*, 10 (Fall 1977): 75-83;

Moore, "The Old South and the New: Paul Hamilton Hayne and Maurice Thompson," *Southern Literary Journal*, 5 (Fall 1972): 108-122;

Moore, "Paul Hamilton Hayne," *Georgia Review*, 22 (Spring 1968): 106-124;

Moore, *Paul Hamilton Hayne* (New York: Twayne, 1972);

Moore, "Paul Hamilton Hayne and Andrew Adgate Lipscomb: 'Sweet Converse' between

Poet and Preacher," *Georgia Historical Quarterly*, 66 (Spring 1982): 53-68;

Moore, "Paul Hamilton Hayne and Northern Magazines, 1866-1886," in *Essays Mostly on Periodical Publishing in America: A Collection in Honor of Clarence Gohdes*, edited by James Woodress and others (Durham, N.C.: Duke University Press, 1973), pp. 134-147;

Moore, "*Southern Bivouac*" and "*Southern Literary Gazette*," in *American Literary Magazines: The Eighteenth and Nineteenth Centuries*, edited by Edward Chielens (Westport, Conn.: Greenwood Press, 1986), pp. 375-385;

Edd W. Parks, *Ante-Bellum Southern Literary Critics* (Athens: University of Georgia Press, 1962), pp. 301-302, 329-344.

Papers:
The Paul Hamilton Hayne Papers, William R. Perkins Library, Duke University, is the chief collection of Hayne manuscripts, journals, letters, clippings, and memorabilia. There are also important Hayne letters and papers in the South Caroliniana Library, University of South Carolina, Columbia.

William Dean Howells
(1 March 1837-11 May 1920)

A. J. Kaul
University of Southern Mississippi

See also the Howells entries in *DLB 12: American Realists and Naturalists; DLB 64: American Literary Critics and Scholars, 1850-1880;* and *DLB 74: American Short Story Writers Before 1880*.

MAJOR POSITIONS HELD: Assistant editor (1866-1871), editor in chief (1871-1881), *Atlantic Monthly*; columnist, *Harper's New Monthly Magazine* (1886-1892); coeditor, *Cosmopolitan* (1892); columnist, *Harper's Monthly Magazine* (1900-1920).

BOOKS: *Poems of Two Friends*, by Howells and John J. Piatt (Columbus, Ohio: Follett, Foster, 1860);

Lives and Speeches of Abraham Lincoln and Hannibal Hamlin, life of Lincoln by Howells and life of Hamlin by J. L. Hayes (Columbus, Ohio: Follett, Foster, 1860);

Venetian Life (London: Trübner, 1866; New York: Hurd & Houghton, 1866; expanded, New York: Hurd & Houghton, 1867; London: Trübner, 1867; expanded again, Boston: Osgood, 1872; revised and expanded again, Boston & New York: Houghton, Mifflin, 1907; London: Constable, 1907);

Italian Journeys (New York: Hurd & Houghton, 1867; London: Low, 1868; enlarged, Boston: Osgood, 1872, revised, London: Heinemann, 1901; Boston & New York: Houghton, Mifflin, 1901);

No Love Lost: A Romance of Travel (New York: Putnam's, 1869);

Suburban Sketches (New York: Hurd & Houghton, 1871, London: Low, 1871; enlarged, Boston: Osgood, 1872);

Their Wedding Journey (Boston: Osgood, 1872; Edinburgh: Douglas, 1882);

A Chance Acquaintance (Boston: Osgood, 1873; Edinburgh: Douglas, 1882);

Poems (Boston: Osgood, 1873; enlarged, Boston: Ticknor, 1886);

A Foregone Conclusion (Boston: Osgood, 1875 [i.e., 1874]; London: Low, 1874);

Sketch of Life and Character of Rutherford B. Hayes . . . also a Biographical Sketch of William A. Wheeler (New York: Hurd & Houghton/ Boston: Houghton, 1876);

The Parlor Car: Farce (Boston: Osgood, 1876);

Out of the Question. A Comedy (Boston: Osgood, 1877; Edinburgh: Douglas, 1882);

A Counterfeit Presentment: Comedy (Boston: Osgood, 1877);

The Lady of the Aroostook (Boston: Houghton Osgood, 1879; Edinburgh: Douglas, 1882);

William Dean Howells

The Undiscovered Country (Boston: Houghton, Mifflin, 1880; London: Low, 1880);

A Fearful Responsibility and Other Stories (Boston: Osgood, 1881); republished as *A Fearful Responsibility and "Tonelli's Marriage"* (Edinburgh: Douglas, 1882);

Dr. Breen's Practice: A Novel (Boston: Osgood, 1881; London: Trübner, 1881);

A Day's Pleasure and Other Sketches (Boston: Houghton, Mifflin, 1881);

A Modern Instance: A Novel (1 volume, Boston: Osgood, 1882; 2 volumes, Edinburgh: Douglas, 1882);

The Sleeping Car: A Farce (Boston: Osgood, 1883);

A Woman's Reason: A Novel (Boston: Osgood, 1883; Edinburgh: Douglas, 1883);

A Little Girl among the Old Masters (Boston: Osgood, 1884);

The Register: Farce (Boston: Osgood, 1884);

Three Villages (Boston: Osgood, 1884);

The Elevator: Farce (Boston: Osgood, 1885);

The Rise of Silas Lapham (1 volume, Boston: Ticknor, 1885; 2 volumes, Edinburgh: Douglas, 1894);

Tuscan Cities (Boston: Ticknor, 1886; Edinburgh: Douglas, 1886);

Poems (Boston: Ticknor, 1886);

The Garroters: Farce (New York: Harper, 1886; Edinburgh: Douglas, 1887);

Indian Summer (Boston: Ticknor, 1886; Edinburgh:Douglas, 1886);

The Minister's Charge; or, The Apprenticeship of Lemuel Barker (Edinburgh: Douglas, 1886; Boston: Ticknor, 1887);

Modern Italian Poets: Essays and Versions (New York: Harper, 1887; Edinburgh: Douglas, 1887);

April Hopes: A Novel (Edinburgh: Douglas, 1887; New York: Harper, 1888);

A Sea-Change; or, Love's Stowaway: A Lyricated Farce in Two Acts and an Epilogue (Boston: Ticknor, 1888; London: Trübner, 1888);

Annie Kilburn: A Novel (Edinburgh: Douglas, 1888; New York: Harper, 1889);

The Mouse-Trap and Other Farces (New York: Harper, 1889; Edinburgh: Douglas, 1897);

A Hazard of New Fortunes (1 volume, New York: Harper, 1890, [i.e., 1889]; 2 volumes, Edinburgh: Douglas, 1889);

The Shadow of a Dream: A Novel (Edinburgh: Douglas, 1890; New York: Harper, 1890);

A Boy's Town Described for "Harper's Young People" (New York: Harper, 1890);

Criticism and Fiction (New York: Harper, 1891; London: Osgood, McIlvaine, 1891);

The Albany Depot: Farce (New York: Harper, 1891; Edinburgh: Douglas, 1897);

An Imperative Duty: A Novel (New York: Harper, 1892 [i.e., 1891]; Edinburgh: Douglas, 1891);

Mercy: A Novel (Edinburgh: Douglas, 1892); republished as *The Quality of Mercy* (New York: Harper, 1892);

A Letter of Introduction: Farce (New York: Harper, 1892; Edinburgh: Douglas, 1897);

A Little Swiss Sojourn (New York: Harper, 1892);

Christmas Every Day and Other Stories Told for Children (New York: Harper, 1893);

The World of Chance: A Novel (Edinburgh: Douglas, 1893; New York: Harper, 1893);

The Unexpected Guests: A Farce (New York: Harper, 1893; Edinburgh: Douglas, 1897);

My Year in a Log Cabin (New York: Harper, 1893);

Evening Dress: Farce (New York: Harper, 1893; Edinburgh: Douglas, 1893);

The Coast of Bohemia: A Novel (New York: Harper, 1893);

A Traveler from Altruria: Romance (New York: Harper, 1894; Edinburgh: Douglas, 1894);

My Literary Passions (New York: Harper, 1895);

Stops of Various Quills (New York: Harper, 1895);

The Day of Their Wedding: A Novel (New York: Harper, 1896); republished in *Idyls in Drab* (Edinburgh: Douglas, 1896);

A Parting and a Meeting: Story (New York: Harper, 1896); republished in *Idyls in Drab*;

Impressions and Experiences (New York: Harper, 1896; Edinburgh: Douglas, 1896);

A Previous Engagement: Comedy (New York: Harper, 1897);

The Landlord at Lion's Head (Edinburgh: Douglas, 1897; New York: Harper, 1897);

An Open-Eyed Conspiracy: An Idyl of Saratoga (New York & London: Harper, 1897; Edinburgh: Douglas, 1897);

Stories of Ohio (New York, Cincinnati & Chicago: American Book Company, 1897);

The Story of a Play: A Novel (New York & London: Harper, 1898);

Ragged Lady: A Novel (New York & London: Harper, 1899);

Their Silver Wedding Journey, 2 volumes (New York & London: Harper, 1899);

Bride Roses: A Scene (Boston & New York: Houghton, Mifflin, 1900);

Room Forty-Five: A Farce (Boston & New York: Houghton, Mifflin, 1900);

An Indian Giver: A Comedy (Boston & New York: Houghton, Mifflin, 1900);

The Smoking Car: A Farce (Boston & New York: Houghton, Mifflin, 1900);

Literary Friends and Acquaintance: A Personal Retrospect of American Authorship (New York & London: Harper, 1900);

A Pair of Patient Lovers (New York & London: Harper, 1901);

Heroines of Fiction, 2 volumes (New York & London: Harper, 1901);

The Kentons: A Novel (New York & London: Harper, 1902);

The Flight of Pony Baker: A Boy's Town Story (New York & London: Harper, 1902);

Literature and Life (New York & London: Harper, 1902);

Questionable Shapes (New York & London: Harper, 1903);

Letters Home (New York & London: Harper, 1903);

The Son of Royal Langbrith: A Novel (New York & London: Harper, 1904);

Miss Bellard's Inspiration: A Novel (New York & London: Harper, 1905);

London Films (New York & London: Harper, 1905);

Certain Delightful English Towns with Glimpses of the Pleasant Country Between (New York & London: Harper, 1906);

Through the Eye of the Needle: A Romance (New York & London: Harper, 1907);

Between the Dark and the Daylight: Romances (New York: Harper, 1907; London: Harper, 1912);

Fennel and Rue: A Novel (New York & London: Harper, 1908);

Roman Holidays and Others (New York & London: Harper, 1908);

The Mother and the Father: Dramatic Passages (New York & London: Harper, 1909);

Seven English Cities (New York & London: Harper, 1909);

My Mark Twain: Reminiscences and Criticisms (New York & London: Harper, 1910);

Imaginary Interviews (New York & London: Harper, 1910);

Parting Friends: A Farce (New York & London: Harper, 1911);

New Leaf Mills: A Chronicle (New York & London: Harper, 1913);

Familiar Spanish Travels (New York & London: Harper, 1913);

The Seen and Unseen at Stratford-On-Avon: A Fantasy (New York & London: Harper, 1914);

The Daughter of the Storage and Other Things in Prose and Verse (New York & London: Harper, 1916);

The Leatherwood God (New York: Century, 1916; London: Jenkins, 1917);

Years of My Youth (New York & London: Harper, 1916);

The Vacation of the Kelwyns: An Idyl of the Middle Eighteen-Seventies (New York & London: Harper, 1920);

Mrs. Farrell: A Novel (New York & London: Harper, 1921);

Prefaces to Contemporaries (1882-1920), edited by George Arms, William M. Gibson, and Frederic C. Marston, Jr. (Gainesville, Fla.: Scholars' Facsimiles & Reprints, 1957);

Criticism and Fiction and Other Essays, edited by Clara Marburg Kirk and Rudolf Kirk (New York: New York University Press, 1959);

The Complete Plays of W. D. Howells, edited by Walter J. Meserve (New York: New York University Press, 1960);

W. D. Howells as Critic, edited by Edwin H. Cady (London & Boston: Routledge, 1973);

Editor's Study: A Comprehensive Edition of W. D. Howells' Column edited by James W. Simpson (Troy, N.Y.: Whitson, 1983).

Collection: *A Selected Edition of W. D. Howells,* edited by Edwin H. Cady, Ronald Gottesman, Don L. Cook, and David Nordloh, 20 volumes to date (Bloomington: Indiana University Press/Boston: Twayne, 1968-).

William Dean Howells, on his odyssey from self-educated printer's devil to critic, novelist, and preeminent arbiter of American letters, passed through the offices of the *Atlantic Monthly* during the post-Civil War years. For fifteen years Howells and the *Atlantic* helped forge a new literary sensibility, shifting the ground of American literature from a New England Puritan romanticism to a more continental literature with a realistic and often "western" voice. He befriended, encouraged, and published many writers, notably Mark Twain and Henry James, who established a genuinely native American literary canon. Howells's columns in *Harper's New Monthly Magazine* advocated a new "realism"–which he defined as "the truthful treatment of material"–that broke with "fine literary airs" in favor of "the dialect, the language, that most Americans know."

A "westerner" himself, Howells was born to William Cooper and Mary Dean Howells at Martin's Ferry, Belmont County, Ohio, in 1837, the year Ralph Waldo Emerson's Phi Beta Kappa address, "The American Scholar" declared America's literary independence from England. His father moved the family to Hamilton, Ohio, in 1840, when he became editor of a Whig paper, the *Intelligencer.* By age seven Howells was setting type in his father's print shop and delivering the papers after they were pulled from the press. In 1849, Howells's father bought the *Dayton* (Ohio) *Transcript,* but the venture failed, and the family moved again. They spent 1850 in a log cabin near Xenia, Ohio, where Howells's father unsuccessfully tried to rebuild a paper mill and his meager resources. In *My Year in a Log Cabin* (1893) Howells would recall his father's reading aloud to the family from the literary classics and religious books.

Although his formal education ended with the move to Dayton, reading and writing were Howells's abiding passions. "I was always reading when I was not playing," he recalled in *Years of My Youth* (1916). Howells consumed Miguel de Cervantes, William Shakespeare, Charles Dickens, and William Makepeace Thackeray while teaching himself French, Spanish, Portuguese, Latin, and Italian. He spent hours imitating the classical authors, writing verses and sketches in their dictions, styles, and manners. His voracious after-hours reading was supplemented by the practical education he received at the type case.

When Howells's father became a ten-dollar-a-week clerk of the Ohio Legislature in Columbus in 1851, Howells supplemented the family income with the four dollars a week he earned as a compositor for the *Ohio State Journal.* A year later the elder Howells became editor of the *Ashtabula* (Ohio) *Sentinel,* which was moved after six months to Jefferson, Ohio, and renamed the *Gazette.* William Dean Howells contributed poems and sketches to the *Gazette,* and when his father returned to the state legislature as a clerk in 1856, he left his son in charge of the newspaper. In 1857 Howells joined his father in Columbus, where father and son produced a daily letter about legislative matters for the *Cincinnati Gazette* and the *Ohio State Journal.*

Howells accepted a position at the *Cincinnati Gazette* but quit after a few weeks and returned to the *Jefferson Gazette.* Next, a job offer came from the *Ohio State Journal,* and Howells, eager to return to Columbus, accepted. Soon after he joined the *Journal* he was appointed news editor. His duties included producing the column "News and Humors of the Mail," consisting of items gleaned from exchange newspapers to which Howells added his satirical editorial commentary.

"I do not know that my life differed outwardly from that of any other young journalist, who had begun as I had in a country printing-office, and might be supposed to be looking forward to advancement in his profession or in public affairs," Howells recalled in *Literary Friends and Acquaintance* (1900). "But inwardly it was altogether different with me. Inwardly I was a poet, with no wish to be anything else, unless in a moment of careless affluence I might so far forget myself as to be a novelist." In addition to poems, sketches, and criticism in the *Journal,* Howells's literary output had appeared in the *Saturday Press*

Howells being paid in gold by George Ticknor, publisher of the Atlantic Monthly, *for Howells's poem "The Pilot's Story"*

of New York, and the *Atlantic* had accepted five or six poems. The standards of literary excellence were established far from provincial Ohio. "We looked to England and the East largely for our literary opinions," Howells wrote. "We accepted the *Saturday Review* as law if we could not quite receive it as gospel."

With the $175 he realized from a campaign biography, *Lives and Speeches of Abraham Lincoln and Hannibal Hamlin* (1860), which he wrote with J. L. Hayes, Howells embarked on a tour of New England, ostensibly to gather material for a subscription book about the region's major industries. Quickly losing interest in that project, he turned the trip into a literary pilgrimage. In Cambridge, James Russell Lowell gave him a letter of introduction to Nathaniel Hawthorne, who sent him to Emerson. Lowell also arranged a dinner for Howells, during which Oliver Wendell Holmes leaned over to his host and, "with a laughing look at me," said, "Well, James, this is something like the apostolic succession; this is the laying on of hands."

In Boston Howells visited the offices of the *Atlantic* and its publishers, Ticknor & Fields. At the moment they met, James T. Fields, editor of the *Atlantic*, was reading proof sheets of Howells's narrative poem "The Pilot's Story," which the magazine had accepted for publication. Fields introduced Howells to the firm's senior partner, George Ticknor, who asked if Howells had been paid for the poem. "I confessed that I had not, and then he got out a chamois-leather bag, and took from it five half-eagles in gold and laid them on the green cloth top of the desk.... The publisher seemed aware of the poetic character of the transaction; he let the pieces lie a moment, before he gathered them up and put them into my hand, and said, 'I always think it is pleasant to have it in gold.'" Howells would say years later: "I have never since felt myself paid so lavishly for any literary work, though I have had more for a single piece than the twenty-five dollars that dazzled me in this constellation." Emboldened by his encounters with New England's literary luminaries, Howells proposed himself to Fields as assistant editor of the *Atlantic*, but no vacancy existed at that time. "It was to his recollection of this prompt ambition of mine that I suppose I may have owed my succession to a like vacancy some four years later," Howells would write.

A visit to the bohemian editors of the *Saturday Press* in New York City left Howells unimpressed. "I fancied a conspiracy among them to shock the literary pilgrim," Howells recalled, "and to minify the precious emotions he had experienced in visiting other shrines." At Pfaff's beer cellar, a gathering spot for New York's literary bohemians, he met Walt Whitman.

Using his Lincoln biography as an entrée, Howells sought appointment to a diplomatic post. The president's secretaries, John Nicolay and John Hay, secured for him an appointment as United States consul in Venice at a salary of fifteen hundred dollars; his major task was to report the presence of Confederate ships in Mediterranean waters. In September 1861 Howells set sail for Venice and "the beginning of the best luck I have had in the world." His few consular duties made a nearly full-time literary life possible. When not studying nineteenth-century Italian literature, he was writing verse. Howells sent his poems to "magazines in every part of the English-speaking world, but they came unerringly back." Turning to prose, he wrote a series of travel letters, later collected in *Venetian Life* (1866), which were rejected by the *Atlantic* but were published in the *Boston Advertiser* between March 1863 and May 1865. He also wrote a critical essay, "Recent Italian Comedy," which he sent to the *North American Review*, edited by Lowell and Charles Eliot Norton. Lowell wrote to Howells, informing him that the essay had been published, asking for another one, and praising his travel letters. The move from poetry to prose, Howells later recalled, was "the turning point of my life."

On 24 December 1862 in the American Embassy in Paris, Howells married Elinor Gertrude Mead of Brattleboro, Vermont, whom he had met in Ohio; they had two daughters and a son.

The Howells family returned to the United States in the late summer of 1865. Needing salaried employment to support his wife and first daughter, Howells briefly visited Ohio; finding nothing suitable, he returned to New York, "resolved to fight my way in, somewhere." He wrote editorials on "European and literary topics" for newspapers, including the *New-York Times*, but realized that journalism was not his forte. The *Nation*, which had printed some of his Venetian letters, offered him forty dollars a week to write criticism starting in November 1865.

Howells encountered Fields in New York on New Year's Eve 1865; a few days later, a letter from Fields arrived on Howells's desk at the *Nation*, asking if he would be the *Atlantic*'s assistant editor. Howells went to Boston to confer with

Cover for an issue of the magazine which, under Howells's editorship, became the arbiter of literary taste in the United States

Fields about the details. Howells would be paid fifty dollars a week; his duties were to read manuscripts and correspond with contributors, to do the literary proofreading, and to write four or five pages of book notices. With "unfailing tact and kindness," Fields let Howells know that "the qualification I had as practical printer for the work was most valued, if not the most valued, and that as proof-reader I was expected to make it avail on the side of economy." Howells began work at the *Atlantic Monthly* on his twenty-ninth birthday, 1 March 1866. Fields extended considerable freedom to his assistant editor; and in July 1871 he relinquished the editorship to Howells, whose salary was raised to five thousand dollars a year.

When Howells arrived, the *Atlantic* was a distinctively New England literary magazine; into "the company of those gods and half-gods and quarter-gods of New England" who had filled the *Atlantic*'s pages Howells placed the westerners Bret Harte and Mark Twain. The "transatlantic muse" that had given the *Atlantic* the work of Dickens, Alfred, Lord Tennyson and Robert Browning began to pale because, in Howells's judgment, "she had not anything so acceptable to give us as our own muse."

With the editorship, Howells inherited a "bushel" of manuscripts his predecessor had accepted but not yet published. The *Atlantic*'s custom was to pay contributors upon publication. "I will not pretend that I read them," he admitted. "For me the fact that they were accepted was enough, if they had any life in them. The test was very simple. If the author was still living, then his contribution was alive; if he was dead, then it was dead too; and I will never confess with what ghoulish glee I exulted in finding a manuscript exanimate." Howells published the early work of Mark Twain, Henry James, Edith Wharton, and Sarah Orne Jewett. He relinquished the *Atlantic* editorship, effective 1 March 1881, his forty-fourth birthday.

Free of his editorial burdens, Howells devoted himself to writing short stories, plays, and such novels as *A Modern Instance* (1882), *The Rise of Silas Lapham* (1885), and *Indian Summer* (1886). In 1885 Joseph W. Harper asked Howells to write for *Harper's New Monthly Magazine*. After negotiating through letters and a meeting with the publisher, an agreement was reached that for ten thousand dollars Howells would write one short novel a year for the magazine; for an additional three thousand dollars a year he agreed to write a monthly column of criticism called "The Editor's Study." Beginning in January 1886 this column was Howells's forum to indulge his "prejudices" and "grudges." He polemicized against literary sentimentalism and romanticism; any "work of the imagination" must meet this test, "Is it true?–true to the motives, the impulses, the principles that shape the life of actual men and women? This truth, which necessarily includes the highest morality and the highest artistry–this truth given, the book cannot be wicked and cannot be weak.... we know of no true picture of life–that is, of human nature–which is not also a masterpiece of literature, full of divine and natural beauty." For six years Howells introduced and defended in "The Editor's Study" writers who portrayed "men and women as they are." The columns were published in book form in 1983.

In 1891 John Brisben Walker, who had acquired the faltering *Cosmopolitan* magazine two years earlier, asked Howells to edit the periodical. Howells confided to his father that "the lifelong habit of being on a salary had something to do" with his return to magazine editing. Howells's editorial influence showed in the May 1892 issue of *Cosmopolitan*, which published works by James, Hamlin Garland, and Jewett. Howells severed the relationship with the *Cosmopolitan* after only two issues, citing "hopeless incompatibility" with the strong-willed publisher.

In the last two decades of his life Howells continued writing novels, reminiscences, and travel essays. He also wrote a monthly critical column, "The Editor's Easy Chair," for *Harper's New Monthly Magazine*, which had dropped the *New* from its title in 1900. Howells wrote to Thomas Bailey Aldrich, his successor at the *Atlantic Monthly*: "I hate criticism.... I never did a piece of it that satisfied me; and to write fiction, on the other hand, is a delight. Yet in my old age, I seem doomed (on a fat salary) to do criticism and essays. I am ending where I began, in a sort of journalism." Howells realized that the literary fashions that he had done so much to shape were changing. "I could not 'serialize' a story of mine now in any American magazine, thousands of them as they are," he wrote to James. "I am comparatively a dead cult with my statues cut down and the grass growing over them in the pale moonlight."

His wife of forty-eight years and his closest literary friend, Mark Twain, both died in 1910. His other great literary comrade, Henry James, died in 1916. Howells died in his New York apartment on 11 May 1920 at the age of eighty-three. His funeral the next day at the Church of the Ascension, New York, was attended by members of the American Academy of Arts and Letters, of which he had been serving as first president at the time of his death. Howells's ashes were buried in Cambridge Cemetery, near the grave of Henry James.

A "true picture of life" grounded the "New Journalism" of the 1960s, a style that fused novelists' techniques to a fidelity to "the actual life of men and women" in a language that "most Americans know." Thus the literary realism that had made William Dean Howells a "dead cult" was resurrected in the most important stylistic movement of twentieth-century journalism.

Letters:

Life in Letters of William Dean Howells, edited by Mildred Howells, 2 volumes (Garden City, N.Y.: Doran, 1928; London: Heinemann, 1929);

The Correspondence of Samuel L. Clemens and William D. Howells, 1872-1910, edited by Henry Nash Smith and William M. Gibson, 2 volumes (Cambridge, Mass.: Harvard University Press, 1960);

Selected Letters, 1852-1872, edited by George Arms and others (Boston: Twayne, 1979);

Selected Letters, 1873-1881, edited by Arms and Christof K. Lohmann (Boston: Twayne, 1979);

Selected Letters, 1882-1891, edited by Robert C. Leitz III (Boston: Twayne, 1980);

Selected Letters, 1892-1901, edited by Thomas Wortham (Boston: Twayne, 1981).

Interviews:

Ulrich Halfmann, ed., *Interviews with William Dean Howells* (Arlington, Tex.: American Literary Realism, 1974).

Bibliographies:

William M. Gibson and George Arms, *A Bibliography of William Dean Howells* (New York: New York Public Library, 1948);

John K. Reeves, "The Literary Manuscripts of W. D. Howells: A Descriptive Finding List," *Bulletin of the New York Public Library*, 62 (June 1958): 267-278; (July 1958): 350-363; supplement, 65 (September 1961): 465-476;

James L. Woodress and Stanley P. Anderson, *A Bibliography of Writings about William Dean Howells*, American Literary Realism, Special Number (1969);

Vito J. Brenni, *William Dean Howells: A Bibliography* (Metuchen, N.J.: Scarecrow Press, 1973).

Biographies:

Edwin H. Cady, *The Road to Realism: The Early Years, 1837-1885, of William Dean Howells* (Syracuse: Syracuse University Press, 1956);

Cady, *The Realist at War: The Mature Years, 1885-1920, of William Dean Howells* (Syracuse: Syracuse University Press, 1958);

Van Wyck Brooks, *Howells: His Life and World* (New York: Dutton, 1959);

Kenneth S. Lynn, *William Dean Howells: An American Life* (New York: Harcourt Brace Jovanovich, 1971).

References:

George N. Bennett, *The Realism of William Dean Howells: 1889-1920* (Nashville: Vanderbilt University Press, 1973);

Edwin H. Cady and David L. Frazier, eds., *The War of the Critics over William Dean Howells* (Evanston, Ill.: Row, Peterson, 1962);

Everett Carter, *Howells and the Age of Realism* (Philadelphia: Lippincott, 1954);

Delmar G. Cooke, *William Dean Howells* (New York: Dutton, 1922);

James L. Dean, *Howells' Travels toward Art* (Albuquerque: University of New Mexico Press, 1970);

Kenneth Eble, ed., *Howells: A Century of Criticism* (Dallas: Southern Methodist University Press, 1962);

Herbert Edwards, "Howells and the Controversy over Realism in American Fiction," *American Literature*, 3 (November 1931): 237-248;

Oscar Firkins, *William Dean Howells* (Cambridge: Harvard University Press, 1924);

William M. Gibson, *William D. Howells* (Minneapolis: University of Minnesota Press, 1967);

Henry Gifford, "W. D. Howells: His Moral Conservatism," *Kenyon Review*, 20 (Winter 1958): 124-133;

Robert L. Hough, *The Quiet Rebel: William Dean Howells as Social Commentator* (Lincoln: University of Nebraska Press, 1959);

Clara M. Kirk, *W. D. Howells and Art in His Time* (New Brunswick: Rutgers University Press, 1965);

Kirk, *W. D. Howells: Traveler from Altruria, 1889-1894* (New Brunswick: Rutgers University Press, 1962);

Kirk and Rudolf Kirk, *William Dean Howells* (New York: Twayne, 1962);

William McMurray, *The Literary Realism of William Dean Howells* (Carbondale: Southern Illinois University Press, 1967);

Alma J. Payne, "William Dean Howells and the Independent Woman," *Midwest Review*, 5 (Autumn 1963): 44-52;

Lionel Trilling, "William Dean Howells and the Roots of Modern Taste," *Partisan Review*, 18 (September-October 1951): 516-536;

Kermit Vanderbilt, *The Achievement of William Dean Howells* (Princeton: Princeton University Press, 1968);

Edward Wagenknecht, *William Dean Howells: The Friendly Eye* (New York: Oxford University Press, 1969).

Papers:
Harvard University has more than seven thousand letters to and from William Dean Howells, in addition to many manuscripts and journals. There are also significant collections at the Huntington Library in San Marino, California; the Library of Congress; Yale and Columbia Universities; and the Rutherford B. Hayes Library in Freemont, Ohio.

John Foster Kirk

(22 March 1824-21 September 1904)

Janet E. Ramsey
State University of New York, College at Buffalo

MAJOR POSITION HELD: Editor, *Lippincott's Magazine* (1870-1886).

BOOKS: *History of Charles the Bold, Duke of Burgundy*, 3 volumes (London: John Murray, 1863, 1868; Philadelphia: Lippincott, 1864, 1868);

A Supplement to Allibone's Critical Dictionary of English Literature and British and American Authors, 2 volumes (Philadelphia: Lippincott, 1891);

Charles Sumner (Philadelphia: Lippincott, 1892).

OTHER: William H. Prescott, *History of the Conquest of Mexico*, edited by Kirk (Philadelphia: Lippincott, 1873);

Prescott, *History of the Reign of Ferdinand and Isabella the Catholic*, edited by Kirk (Philadelphia: Lippincott, 1873);

Prescott, *History of the Conquest of Peru*, edited by Kirk (Philadelphia: Lippincott, 1874);

Prescott, *History of the Reign of Philip the Second, King of Spain*, edited by Kirk (Philadelphia: Lippincott, 1874);

Francis Palgrave, *The Golden Treasury of the Best Songs and Lyrical Poems in the English Language*, edited by Kirk (Philadelphia: Lippincott, 1895);

William Robertson, *The History of the Reign of the Emperor Charles the Fifth*, edited by Kirk (Philadelphia: Lippincott, 1902);

Prescott, *The Works of William H. Prescott*, edited by Kirk (Philadelphia: Lippincott, 1904).

Opening page from an issue of the literary magazine Kirk edited for sixteen years

PERIODICAL PUBLICATIONS: "Some Recollections of Thackeray," *Lippincott's Magazine*, 7 (January 1871): 106-110;
"Madam De Staël," *Lippincott's Magazine*, 27 (January 1881): 62-73;
"Shakespeare's Tragedies on the Stage," *Lippincott's Magazine*, 33 (May 1884): 501-510; 34 (June 1884): 604-616;
"An English Family in the Seventeenth Century," *Atlantic Monthly*, 71 (March 1893): 371-382;
"Macbeth," *Atlantic Monthly*, 75 (April 1895): 507-515;
"A Slender Sheaf of Memories," *Lippincott's Magazine*, 70 (November 1902): 605-617.

John Foster Kirk, editor of *Lippincott's Magazine* for sixteen years, was a man who did not influence his times so much as he enjoyed a tranquil and privileged position in them. Far removed from modern magazine hustle and promotion, Kirk was a scholarly editor who represented a literary stratum of society which had the leisure to consider the humanities and arts long before the explosion of pop culture. The post-Civil War nineteenth century had its share of strife, scandal, and social problems, but Kirk's life and journalistic work seem removed from all disturbance. The magazine he edited was dominated by a refined interest in the classical rather than the commonplace, in romance rather than impoverished reality.

By all reports Kirk was a scholar and a gentleman. Research yields little negative criticism of either the man or his work; everywhere Kirk is praised for his thorough scholarship, his intelligence and style, and his general affability. Research also yields almost no information about Kirk's personal life–indeed, he seems generally to have preferred anonymity in all that he did. This absence of information about personal psychology, about personal or professional conflict, creates a sense of distance and formality in all that Kirk accomplished and wrote.

John Foster Kirk was born in Fredericton, New Brunswick, the son of Mary Hamilton Kirk and Abdiel Kirk, a man whom Kirk's wife described in later correspondence as having "desultory occupations chiefly musical and literary." Kirk's ancestry was English. Soon after Kirk's birth his parents moved to Truro, Nova Scotia, where Kirk spent most of his youth and was taught by an English clergyman, the Reverend Mr. Burnyeat. Kirk was privately educated by tutors and never graduated from any accredited school; however, his education, a strongly classical one, was praised by many of his contemporaries, and his knowledge of classical and modern European languages was impressive.

In 1842 Kirk went to Quebec, and after a few months he traveled to the United States and settled in Boston. He spent the next five years studying in Boston, apparently unable to decide upon a career. Among his friends in those years was the famous actor William Charles MacCready, who believed that Kirk had a great natural talent and urged him to go into the theater. In an article titled "Shakespeare's Tragedies on the Stage," written for *Lippincott's* about forty years later (May 1884), Kirk describes his "first–and last–appearance on the stage," as the doctor in *Macbeth*. Of his short-lived stint as an actor, Kirk writes that it satisfied his intellectual curiosity: "I gained the object of the experiment, that of getting a glimpse of the matter from the actor's point of view, comprehending the different perspective, feeling the whirr and bustle of the scene instead of looking at and hearing it from a distance." In the same article he describes the theaters of that time in an undesirable light: "The stage appointments everywhere were shabby beyond description. Horrible melodramas, roaring farces, and ghastly pantomimes formed the staple entertainment in some of the largest and best 'patronized' houses, and the manners of the audiences were on a level with the performances." Kirk developed a permanent enthusiasm for drama, though he writes that the theater's "mimic presentations" never interested him as much as "that drama of history and actual life in which we are all performers as well as spectators."

Another friend of Kirk's at that time was Robert Carter, private literary secretary for a brief time to the great historian William Hickling Prescott. Carter decided to leave his position with Prescott and suggested that Kirk take the job. On 9 June 1848 Kirk signed a contract with the historian, who was blind, to "read and write for Mr. Prescott, for five hours a day, for five years, the hours to be selected by Mr. Prescott." For this work Kirk was to receive four hundred dollars a year with increments of fifty dollars to a maximum of five hundred dollars per annum, but had to pay his board "when the parties are out of Boston."

Kirk's decision to work for Prescott set a direction for his life which was to continue to its end. Through Prescott, Kirk expanded his interest in history, acquired a knowledge of the methods and materials of research, and was introduced to J. B. Lippincott Company, the firm that would eventually publish all Kirk's work and the magazine he edited.

Of Prescott's many secretaries, Kirk was the one who remained with him the longest, for eleven years from 1848 to 1859. George Ticknor, in his *Life of William Hickling Prescott* (1863), describes Kirk as Prescott's "ever-faithful" secretary, and Kirk's attachment to Prescott, who was highly regarded and warmly praised by his contemporaries, seems to have been a fairly pleasant one.

In 1850 Kirk accompanied Prescott to Europe, visiting France, Belgium, Holland, and Scotland and spending considerable time in London. The significant number of travel articles which Kirk included later in *Lippincott's Magazine* suggests that he found traveling on the Continent creatively stimulating and personally enjoyable. In a February 1905 *Lippincott's* article, "John Foster Kirk: An Appreciation," editor Harrison Morris writes that in London Kirk was able to meet many of the celebrities who flocked to see Prescott. In addition, as well as attending "informal gatherings of the pre-Raphaelite Brotherhood," Kirk was able to meet Thomas Carlyle, who invited him home to tea. Kirk recalls some of the time he spent with Carlyle in the April 1881 notice of Carlyle's death which appeared in the "Our Monthly Gossip" column of *Lippincott's*. Kirk recounts for his readers a highly memorable moment when the two men sat one on each side of the chimney, smoking clay pipes, and Carlyle pronounced on the conventional notion of heaven, saying, " 'My idea of heaven,'–here the eyes looked far away and the voice subsided into a soft lingering cadence–'and what I find to have been the idea of Moses and of Jesus, is that it is a rest,–just a rest.' "

In another *Lippincott's* article ("A Slender Sheaf of Memories," November 1902) Kirk describes his many pleasant evenings of conversation with young acquaintances in London, saying that his accidental meeting with James Hanney (later of the *Edinburgh Evening Courant*) led him to "a glimpse of the London literary Bohemia of that day which I should not otherwise have had." Kirk met Dante Gabriel Rossetti, then more an artist than a poet, and discussed with him Edgar Allan Poe, whom Rossetti admired profoundly. Kirk discussed Ralph Waldo Emerson with these young friends, mentioning as an aside in his article that he edited the 1847 edition of Emerson's poems, correcting the punctuation–"a matter which the author, professing his own ignorance, had left to the discretion of the printer."

The influence of the time Kirk spent in London is reflected in the literary discussions he included in *Lippincott's*–the many references to Carlyle, William Makepeace Thackeray, Charles Dickens, John Keats, and Rossetti. Kirk describes himself as a young man in London belonging "to that portion of our generation in whom a belief in Carlyle and Emerson was a mighty tide and trend in the whole being: who were ready to shatter conventions in defense of those prophets."

Kirk supplemented his secretarial work for Prescott by writing critical and historical papers for periodicals, particularly the *Atlantic Monthly*. In 1852 he married Mary Weed of North Andover, Massachusetts. Also at about this time he was elected to membership in the Massachusetts Historical Society.

Kirk remained with Prescott until the historian died in January 1859 and, in fact, was reading to Prescott on the day he died. Prescott, who was interested in the life of the renegade duke Charles the Bold, may have suggested that Kirk write a full-length book on the subject. In the preface to his first book publication, *History of Charles the Bold, Duke of Burgundy* (1863-1868), Kirk acknowledges his indebtedness to Prescott, who employed "all the facilities at his command for procuring the requisite materials" and displayed "generous interest" in a "doubtful enterprise."

The first two volumes of *Charles the Bold* were published in 1863 in London, followed by an American edition by Lippincott's in 1864; the third volume appeared in 1868 after Kirk returned to Europe. He spent many months there "exploring hitherto untouched manuscript sources, the German and Latin letter-books of the Government of Berne, all the despatches [sic] of the Venetian and Milanese agents, finally, with the utmost minuteness, going over the different battlefields," according to Morris.

The early volumes received positive reviews in Britain and the United States, with the *New York Times* critic stating that "a work has scarcely ever more clearly borne on each page the impress of sustained mental power" and the London *Saturday Review* writer asserting that Kirk's "extensive and minute knowledge is the learning of a man of vigorous thought, accustomed to bring his mind to consider men and things, not merely as they have been written about, but as they actually were, in the variety and complexity of their real existence." The *Times* review of the third volume was slightly more critical, offering negative comments about Kirk's style– "when he attempts a strain of philosophical moralizing ... he is very apt to become turgid, or feeble, or both, and his style becomes disfigured by a redundancy which makes it decidedly wearisome." Other reviewers occasionally echo this criticism of Kirk's writing style.

In 1864 Kirk became a member of the American Philosophical Society, and in 1870 his career took a new turn when he moved to Philadelphia to become editor of *Lippincott's Magazine*, a position he would hold from 1870 to 1886. Kirk was also engaged during the 1870s in editing new Lippincott editions of Prescott's histories.

In many ways *Lippincott's Magazine* reflected the personality of its editor. It was a distinguished and conservative publication with high-quality printing and few illustrations, though the illustrations that do appear are excellent. Because the magazine was offered by a publishing house, it did not have to be concerned excessively with profits; in fact, it refused to release its circulation figures. Particularly noted for the breadth of its literary contributions, *Lippincott's* offered a full range of national authors. All American regions were liberally represented, with George M. Towle, Harriet Prescott Spofford, Emma Lazarus, and Rebecca Harding Davis from the Northeast; Charles Warren Stoddard, Maurice Thompson, and Octave Thanet (Alice French) from the West; and William Gilmore Simms, John Esten Cooke, Sidney Lanier, and Margaret Preston from the South.

At first *Lippincott's* planned to publish only American serial novels, but in 1869 it published an Anthony Trollope novel; thereafter, under Kirk's editorship, it published widely from literature on both sides of the Atlantic, including some works in translation. Ouida's classic tale, "A Dog of Flanders: A Story of Noel," was published in January 1872 to considerable public acclaim.

Also under Kirk's editorship, the magazine offered an extensive number of travel articles concerning a wide variety of foreign countries. Articles covered such subjects as "The Diamond-Mines of South Africa" (March 1881), "Searching for the Quinine-Plant in Peru" (February 1873), and "A Glance at the Site and Antiquities of Athens" (February 1873). Prentice Mulford, Edward Nealy, and Robert M. Walsh were among the travel writers. On the other hand many articles turned on society and manners, such as "Country Life in Virginia Nowadays" (January 1872) and "An American Lady's Occupations Seventy Years Ago" (January 1875).

The magazine seldom devoted space to political or economic issues nor did it concern itself with racial or ethnic matters. Rare exceptions include an article on Negro spirituals and a single article in 1876 on trade unionism.

One strength of the publication lay in its numerous and excellent book reviews, critiquing George Eliot's *Middlemarch* (1871-1872), Henry Wadsworth Longfellow's *Three Books of Song* (1872), Victor Hugo's *L'Année terrible* (1872), and Nathaniel Hawthorne's posthumously published *Septimus Felton* (1871). After 1884 the number of book reviews rose significantly.

Poetry was *Lippincott's* least distinctive feature, but the magazine had many regular contributors: Margaret Preston, Kate Hilliard, R. H. Stoddard, Charles Warren Stoddard, Thomas Dunn English, and Paul Hamilton Hayne. Sidney Lanier's "Corn," "Symphony," and "Psalm of the West" appeared in 1875 and 1876.

Editor Kirk was unobtrusive in *Lippincott's Magazine*, though he was undoubtedly instrumental in maintaining the literary virtuosity of its articles and the quality of its book reviews. Even in the "Our Monthly Gossip" column, where he could have expressed personal views about current issues, he is largely silent or at least speaks anonymously. Many short entries are signed with initials or pseudonyms.

When Kirk wrote a brief reminiscence of Thackeray in January 1871, he signed the entry with the initials "A. Z." Other articles which he wrote for *Lippincott's* Kirk signed "a sexagenarian" or simply "*senex*." An uninformed reader would have no way of recognizing his authorship. Presumably, Kirk selected the entries included in "Our Monthly Gossip," and these reflect his learned, somewhat bland, interests. The March 1874 column, for example, discusses New Year's visits and winemakers of France, tells a "scientific yarn" about a laundress who swallowed a needle, describes a ball given at the Parthenon, and gives notice of a new edition of Benjamin Franklin's autobiography published by Lippincott's.

Kirk left the design of the magazine virtually unchanged from its conception in 1868. He added some personal "notes" to the "Our Monthly Gossip" column in 1872, but these gradually became fewer in number and ceased completely by 1884. The layout continued a neat and balanced two-column format throughout most of Kirk's editorship; nothing exotic or flashy in headlines or type forced the reader's attention. Some of the illustrations seem a bit melodramatic, like the literature they decorated, but many of them are scenic–arresting rather than shocking. The tone of the publication remained pleasant, serene, and intellectual.

In 1876-1877 *Lippincott's* published serially the first novel of a thiry-four-year-old writer from Connecticut, Ellen Warner Olney. *Love in Idleness* was written by the daughter of educator and geographer Jesse Olney, himself an author of many textbooks. Publication of her novel brought Ellen Warner Olney immediate fame, which continued throughout the prolific writing career which followed. Olney became Kirk's second wife in 1879; it was her only marriage. Writing under the pseudonym "Henry Hayes" as well as her own name, Olney produced twenty-nine full-length novels, as well as many stories and articles. Many of her books were best-sellers, and at least two, *The Story of Margaret of Kent* (1886) and *Queen Money* (1888), won both popular and critical acclaim.

The Kirks lived in the Chestnut Hill, Germantown, section of Philadelphia, and an anonymous article in *Lippincott's* titled "New Germantown and Chestnut Hill" (April 1884) was probably written by Kirk as a tribute to the lovely, quaint nature of his home community.

Kirk joined the faculty of the University of Pennsylvania in 1886, lecturing on European history until 1888. He was honored with an LL.D. degree by that university in 1889.

From 1886 to 1891 Kirk labored to produce a supplement to *Allibone's Dictionary*, which offered biographical, bibliographical, and critical material on the entire field of literature in the English language. Kirk's work covered American and British authors in the thirty years subsequent to Allibone's work, but despite the more abbreviated time span, Kirk published thirty-seven thousand entries in two volumes. His effort was prodigious, as reviewers of the text noted. Most critics expressed admiration for his labor and gratitude for the information it made available. A 17 January 1892 *New York Times* review asserted that "the honor that ... goes with the completion of this work is peculiar ... and distinctly high," and noted Kirk's "rare modesty" in "withholding, under his own name, all information except two lines."

In perhaps the only controversy of his career, Kirk reacted to a 21 January 1892 critical review of his *Supplement* in *Nation*. The damning review–and another in the *Critic* on 26 December 1891–listed errors in Kirk's text. In an exchange of published letters in *Nation*, Kirk defended his efforts: "The mistakes and oversights, real and imaginary, all of them comparatively trivial, which you have enumerated, do not amount to one-fiftieth of one percent in the whole number of my statements" (13 February 1892). The reviewer was quick to retort in the same issue, however, that since his examination of Kirk's text was not exhaustive, Kirk "should not plume himself" on the low percentage of discovered errors.

After publication of *A Supplement to Allibone's*, Kirk revisited Switzerland, Florence, Venice, and the Italian lakes. When he returned to the United States, he began working on Lippincott's *New Dictionary*.

Morris writes of Kirk in those years: "His sympathy and appreciation of life, people, and books, instead of deadening, seemed, indeed, to have grown more acute as old age lifted him into a region where he saw the facts of human existence with unimpaired vision.... Few men excelled him in wit, and his good things dropped from him like the ripe, dry fruit of a long experience." Kirk was apparently in good health until his death at his home in Chestnut Hill on 21 September 1904. He was survived by four children: Sophia, William Hamilton, John Foster, and Abby.

Any assessment of the life and work of John Foster Kirk must acknowledge that much of what he did was derivative. His was not an original, creative soul. Kirk seems to have been most comfortable following another's lead, but he demonstrates an honorable kind of imitation–an imitation that through continuing labor helps to reveal the original's essence and value. This is evident in his historical writing inspired by his mentor Prescott, in his assumption of the editorship of *Lippincott's Magazine*, and in work he did on the supplement to Allibone's dictionary. If we cannot admire Kirk's brilliance, we can respect his honest intelligence and his optimistic industriousness. Kirk himself seemed to understand the limits of different personalities and, from all accounts, to be at peace with the intentions and achievements of his own. He writes of Thackeray that he was not *l'homme de genie*, a man of genius, but a man of spirit, *l'homme d'esprit*–"meaning by that term not so much the witty man, or the man of talent or even of intellect, but rather the man whose powers, without being great or profound, are always at his service." Kirk could equally well have been describing himself.

Reference:
"John Foster Kirk: An Appreciation," *Lippincott's Magazine*, 75 (February 1905): 189-192.

Papers:
Correspondence concerning John Foster Kirk is at the archives of the University of Pennsylvania and the American Philosophical Society in Philadelphia.

Frank Leslie
(Henry Carter)
(29 March 1821-10 January 1880)

William E. Huntzicker

See also the Leslie entry in *DLB 43: American Newspaper Journalists, 1690-1872*, and the Frank Leslie Publishing House entry in *DLB 49: American Literary Publishing Houses, 1638-1899*.

MAJOR POSITIONS HELD: Engraver, *Illustrated London News* (1842-1848), *Gleason's Pictorial Drawing-Room Companion* (1851-1852); chief engraver, *Illustrated News* (1853); publisher, *Frank Leslie's Ladies' Gazette of Fashion and Fancy Needlework*, renamed *Frank Leslie's Ladies' Gazette of Fashion and the Beau Monde* in 1855, renamed *Frank Leslie's Gazette of Fashion and the Beau Monde* in 1856, renamed *Frank Leslie's New Family Magazine* in 1857, renamed *Frank Leslie's Monthly* in 1860, renamed *Frank Leslie's Lady's Magazine* in 1863 (1854-1880), *Frank Leslie's New York Journal of Romance, General Literature, Science and Art* (1855-1857), *Frank Leslie's Illustrated Newspaper* (1855-1880), *Frank Leslie's Illustrirte Zeitung* (1857-1880), *Frank Leslie's Budget of Fun* (1859-1878), *Stars and Stripes* (1859-1860), *Jolly Joker* (1862-1878), *Mr. Merryman's Monthly* (1863), *Frank Leslie's Ten Cent Monthly*, renamed *Frank Leslie's New Monthly* in 1865, renamed *Frank Leslie's Pleasant Hours* in 1866 (1863-1880), *Record of Fashion* (1864-1865), *Frank Leslie's Chimney Corner* (1865-1880), *Illustracion Americana de Frank Leslie* (1866-1870), *Frank Leslie's Children's Friend*, renamed *Frank Leslie's Boys' and Girls' Weekly* in 1866 (1866-1880), *Last Sensation*, renamed *Day's Doings* in 1870, renamed *New York Illustrated Times* in 1876 (1867-1880), *New World*, merged into *Frank's Leslie's Chimney Corner* (1869), *Frank Leslie's Modernwelt* (1870-1871), *Once a Week: The Lady's Own Journal*, renamed *Frank Leslie's Lady's Journal* in 1871 (1871-1880), *Champagne* (1871), *Brickbat* (1872), *Frank Leslie's Tag für Tag*, merged into *Frank Leslie's Illustrirte Zeitung* (1873), *Frank Leslie's Amerikanische Gartenlaube* (1873-1874), *Frank Leslie's Boys of America* (1873-1878), *Happy Home*, renamed *Young American* in 1874 (1874-1876), *Frank Leslie's Popular Monthly* (1876-1880), *Frank Leslie's Sunday Magazine* (1877-1880), *Idle Hour* (1877), *Some Other Folks* (1877), *Frank Leslie's Budget of Wit, Humor, Anecdote and Adventure*, renamed *Frank Leslie's Budget of Humorous and Sparkling Stories, Tales of Heroism, Adventure and Satire* in 1879 (1878-1880), *Frank Leslie's Chatterbox* (1879-1880).

BOOKS: *Incidents of the Civil War in America* (New York: F. Leslie, 1862);
Frank Leslie's Pictorial Life of Abraham Lincoln (New York: American News Co., 1865);
Report on the Fine Arts, Paris Universal Exposition, 1867: Reports of the Commissioners (Washington, D.C.: Government Printing Office, 1868);
Report on the Fine Arts Applied to the Useful Arts, Paris Universal Exposition, 1867: Reports of the Commissioners, by Leslie, Samuel F. B.

Frank Leslie

Morse, and Thomas W. Evans (Washington, D.C.: Government Printing Office, 1868);

Illustrated History of the National Peace Jubilee and Musical Festival: Held in Boston, June 15-19, 1869 (New York, 1869);

Frank Leslie's Historical Register of the United States Centennial Exposition, 1876, edited by Frank H. Norton (New York: Frank Leslie's Publishing House, 1877);

The American Soldier in the Civil War (New York: Bryan, Taylor, 1895).

Frank Leslie fathered pictorial journalism in the United States, developed the engraving process that made illustrated news a national medium, created specialized publications for different markets, and built a publishing empire. His colorful second wife legally took the name Frank Leslie after her husband's death and used it to rescue their business, which had become overextended.

Leslie was born Henry Carter in Ipswich, England, on 29 March 1821 to Joseph Leslie and Mary Elliston Carter. Joseph Carter expected his son to succeed him in the family's prosperous glove manufacturing business; to this end, the boy was provided a solid education and practical experience in the business. But he loved art, a pursuit which his father strongly discouraged. He would stop en route to school to watch the workmen in a turner's shop carving figures; at home, he created implements to construct imitations of what he had seen. At the age of thirteen he made a wood engraving of the coat of arms of the City of Ipswich which earned the praise of his schoolmaster. Eventually, he collected enough engraver's tools to teach himself the trade.

To get additional business training, Carter was sent to London to work in the large dry-goods store owned by his mother's family. While acquiring considerable business acumen at work, he spent his leisure time studying the theory and the practical aspects of the engraving trade he wanted to enter. Believing that he could draw as well as some of the artists and engravers whose work appeared in the books of the London publishers, he submitted some sketches; out of fear of discovery by his father, he signed them "Frank Leslie." To his pleasure they were published. In 1841 he married Sarah Ann Welham; they had three sons, Alfred, Henry, and Scipio.

Leslie deserted the family business to join the *Illustrated London News*, the pioneer pictorial news magazine, soon after it was founded in 1842, and quickly reached the position of superintendent of the engraving department. He learned every aspect of the business, including the method of controlling light-and-shade effects for making wood engravings for printing–a process he would later introduce to the United States.

Leslie absorbed from the *Illustrated London News* a strong sense of self-importance about pictorial journalism as an archive of contemporary culture and a conveyor of news in a popular new form. "The truth is," the *News* noted, "that our self-congratulation lies rather in the good we do and hope to continue, than in any glory of doing it. We are proud for the public. We know that the advent of an Illustrated Newspaper in this country *must* mark an epoch–give wealth to Literature and stores to History, and put, as it were milestones upon the travelled road of time."

He landed in New York in 1848 and set up an engraving business at 98 Broadway. In 1849 he convinced the showman P. T. Barnum to hire him to produce illustrated programs for the American tour of the singer Jenny Lind.

The first American publication to copy the *Illustrated London News* was founded in 1851 by Boston magazine publisher Frederick Gleason.

Gleason's Pictorial Drawing-Room Companion was a sixteen-page folio with many illustrations. Leslie, one of the few experienced wood engravers in the nation, was quickly hired by the new publication. Because of the time required to do the engravings, the pictures were confined to such subjects as travel, natural history, sculpture, ships, and military scenes; Gleason showed little interest in illustrated *news*, and Leslie remained with him for less than a year.

After Gleason started his magazine, the engraver T. W. Strong had founded the *Illustrated News* in New York using a similar formula. Its appeal, like that of Gleason's magazine, depended on cheap fiction, popular poetry, and many illustrations. The *Illustrated News* experimented with news pictures, but the delay was still too long between the events and the appearance of printed pages from the hand-engraved wood blocks. The paper failed after six months, and Barnum, H. D. Beach, and A. E. Beach revived it in 1853 with Leslie as head of the engraving department. Impressed with Leslie and frustrated with his own managers, Barnum offered Leslie twenty thousand dollars to take charge of the paper. When Leslie declined, Barnum sold the paper to Gleason, who merged it with the *Pictorial Drawing-Room Companion*.

Leslie did not accompany the *Illustrated News* when it was sold to Gleason; he wanted to start his own publication. Deciding that a fashion magazine would turn the quickest profit, he started the monthly *Frank Leslie's Ladies' Gazette of Fashion and Fancy Needlework* in January 1854. Its first editor was Ann Stephens, who later became a dime novelist. Typically, the sixteen quarto pages contained woodcuts by Leslie and others, one hand-colored fashion plate, piano music, short stories, book reviews, dress and embroidery patterns, and notices of the opera, theater, and art galleries.

By the end of the first year the magazine's success enabled Leslie to set up his own steam press. Four pages were added to each issue in 1855, when the magazine was renamed *Frank Leslie's Ladies' Gazette of Fashion and the Beau Monde;* the price was increased to thirty cents in 1856, and the name was changed to *Frank Leslie's Gazette of Fashion and the Beau Monde;* four more pages were added in 1857. The publication was renamed *Frank Leslie's New Family Magazine* in September 1857, *Frank Leslie's Monthly* in April 1860, and *Frank Leslie's Lady's Magazine* in February 1863.

Title page for an issue of the magazine Leslie bought in 1855, changing its name from the New York Journal of Romance

The early success of the *Gazette* enabled Leslie to put together enough capital to purchase the failing *New York Journal of Romance*, which specialized in fiction. Adding illustration and miscellany, he renamed the publication *Frank Leslie's New York Journal of Romance, General Literature, Science and Art*. The first issue of the monthly appeared in January 1855. Leslie's in-house engraving department and presses designed for pictorial work gave him an advantage over competitors in quality of illustrations and price.

The *Journal* did not place as much emphasis on illustration as Leslie's later publications would, but the early issues reveal the formula on which Leslie built his empire. Typically, the first page opened an installment of a long-running serial story. Throughout the magazine, contemporary and historical anecdotes defined morals, evoked chuckles, described exotic behavior, and conveyed simple nonsense. Stories of varied length told of timely rescues and chivalrous actions. Stories with foreign settings dominated, with such titles as "Story of the Young Italian," "Something about Norway," "Matrimony in Germany," "Bear-Hunting in Russia," "Spanish Bull Fight," and "Overland Mail Route to India." Leslie added much miscellaneous information to the fiction paper, and readers may have had difficulty separating fact from fiction. The *New York Journal* reflected nineteenth-century optimism in its promotion of science and technology. It praised the proposed transcontinental railroad as "a glorious project" and the "greatest material enterprise ever undertaken," and it quoted a British demand for advanced technology in the Crimean War to save "thousands of lives of our bravest men" and "millions of money." It offered chemistry lessons for young readers and described plants and animals in far parts of the world. It discussed telescopes, speculating about the possibility of other life in the universe; articles on microscopes described the art of drawing and engraving the magnified image. It carried articles such as "Practical Instructions in the Art of Photography" and "How to Make Home Tolerable" and tips on cooking, crocheting, knitting, and sewing; and it had a regular column on chess. A large nameplate across the top and an illustration across the bottom dominated the front page of the first issue, leaving a narrow strip of copy across three columns in the center of the page. Other pages contained no newspaper-style headlines, only labels over the first column giving the name of the article or story.

After six months the *Journal* reported that its success "has astonished even ourselves." The preface to the index to the first volume (Leslie always changed volume numbers of his magazines every six months, rather than annually) demonstrates that Leslie had acquired a sense of self-importance from the *Illustrated London News* and a penchant for overstatement from Barnum. "Since the NEW YORK JOURNAL passed into the hands of FRANK LESLIE, it has contained one-third more reading matter than it did before: increase of size and solid type has produced this effect; and at this moment the JOURNAL contains more reading matter, and of a higher class, than any work of the country, perhaps of the world. To this is added more engravings, and of a superior quality, than any work illustrated after a like fashion can give for the price, as the best artists are employed, always under the publisher's own supervision."

The *Journal* occasionally hinted at its publisher's real interests with a monthly news summary, and relief maps and street scenes took readers to the Crimean War. The *Journal* and *Gazette* had drawn together the literary, artistic, and mechanical talent to support a more important enterprise, and, despite a shortage of capital, Leslie embarked on an illustrated newspaper. "His plan," according to Richard Kimball, who wrote short stories for Leslie publications, "was to give exact illustrations of the current events of the day, and in this way to make them a prime agent in the instruction of the people." Leslie even told *Journal* readers that his forthcoming paper would be more important than the one they were reading. "If a perfect Journal in all its branches can be produced in America," Leslie told his readers, "we are certain that the one we shall have the honor of presenting in a few weeks will be all that our readers can desire."

Earlier attempts to establish illustrated newspapers had failed, Leslie thought, for several reasons: the time lag between events and published illustrations, high costs, a shortage of talented artists and wood engravers, lack of the proper wood for the blocks, dependence upon foreign suppliers of bolts and screws necessary to hold the engraved blocks together under pressure, and lack of the special kind of press necessary to print high-quality pictures. Leslie would succeed because he had created one of the largest establishments for wood engraving in the country, with an experienced staff and the proper equipment.

The first issue of *Frank Leslie's Illustrated Newspaper*, on 15 December 1855, portended what was to come. News and pictures came from around the world. The cover illustration depicted Elisha Kent Kane's expedition to the Arctic; future expeditions that would be chronicled included Matthew Perry's to the Orient, David Livingstone's to Africa, and several to the American West. Portraits and maps still tended to take the place of actual depictions of events, and what action pictures there were often emphasized the settings, such as large trees and mountains, ocean waves or buildings; yet even the first issue contained several dramatic illustrations.

Frank Leslie's Illustrated Newspaper, which initially sold for ten cents a copy or four dollars a year, was about the size of a modern tabloid. It was printed on a single sheet that was cut and folded to make sixteen pages. Illustrations appeared on only one side of the original sheet, and thus on pages 1, 4-5, 8-9, 12-13, and 16 of the newspaper.

Leslie's engraving department

The differences between the *Illustrated Newspaper* and Leslie's other periodicals, such as the *Journal*, were in the number and size of the illustrations and the emphasis on current events. It contained miscellaneous and foreign material similar to that which appeared in the *Journal*. Like the earlier magazines, the *Illustrated Newspaper* included serial fiction, and many of the illustrations related not to the news but to the home, natural history, fiction, or exotic scenes. As the paper's success grew, Leslie sent his own correspondents to the far reaches of the globe.

Leslie developed a mass-production process to allow his engraving department to complete illustrations of major events overnight. Previously, one or two engravers would do an entire scene–a process that could take a week or more. With Leslie's process, an illustration was drawn in reverse on a wood block the size of the final engraving. The block was then cut into as many as thirty-two squares for a full-page illustration, and thirty-two engravers would work on separate parts of the scene. When all were finished, the squares were bolted back together and printed. If some areas of a picture had greater detail than others, the squares would be cut in varying sizes, with the larger ones containing less detailed work. Occasionally, Leslie stretched the process to extremes, producing fold-out illustrations nearly two by three feet in size.

The *Illustrated Newspaper* became the flagship of the Leslie fleet, but it was so expensive to produce that it often teetered on the verge of bankruptcy. The large staff required to turn out timely stories and illustrations had to be maintained continuously, even though it was not needed for every issue. Leslie created many other publications to help support the paper, and economies of scale helped him keep prices low to reach the mass audience he needed.

Leslie had another means for ensuring the weekly's success: sensationalism. According to Kimball, the publisher awoke one morning in 1857 feeling financially desperate. "I . . . heard the newsboys crying a shocking murder," Leslie told Kimball. "It was that of Dr. Burdell, the Bond Street dentist, which, as you know, stirred all New York, and which, by the mystery surrounding it and the proceedings which followed, became a cause célèbre. So great was the excitement, that it required a force of policemen to keep the multitude from the house. I seized upon this incident. I caused exact illustrations to be made of the minutest detail, and to be published immediately. The sales of the *Illustrated Newspaper* rose enormously, and when the excitement subsided, enough new purchasers stuck by it to put the paper beyond any fear of failure."

Although the paper may have been saved from failure by one dramatic news event, its long-term success stemmed from its continuing effort to provide illustrated details of current events, such as the inauguration of President Buchanan and the execution of John Brown. Other innovations which drew readers were the illustrations of technology, such as the construction of railroads and the laying of the Atlantic cable, and of ordinary life, such as street scenes.

In 1857 Leslie sold the *Journal* at a profit and created *Frank Leslie's Illustrirte Zeitung*, a German-language version of his *Illustrated Newspaper*. The year also brought a national depression and the founding in January of Leslie's major rival, *Harper's Weekly*. In response Leslie lowered his price to six cents a copy, or two dollars a year, and reduced his staff. Another sign of hard times was the heavy amount of material his journals borrowed from foreign publications during the year. During the same year a special act of the New York legislature legally conferred on Frank Leslie the name he had been using since he submitted his first engravings to the London publishers.

With the appearance of *Frank Leslie's New Family Magazine* in September, "Frank Leslie's Gazette of Fashion" became a sixteen-page supplement at the end of the eighty-page, twenty-five-cent quarto. The supplement carried women's articles such as "What to Buy, and Where to Buy It," "Review of Fashions," "The Art of Making and Modeling Paper Flowers," "The Laws of Color Applied to Ladies' Dress," and tips on embroidery, needlework, and household ornaments. Serials begun in earlier issues were carried in the supplement. Although he was discarding the original *Gazette* formula in favor of a more diversified one, the publisher's explanation conveys the same lack of modesty that had accompanied the *Journal*. "We do not flatter ourselves when we say, that the MONTHLY GAZETTE OF FASHION has long been known and acknowledged as the highest and only reliable authority in matters of taste and artistic elegance known in the United States; and encouraged by this appreciation, we are determined that no effort shall be spared on our part to make it, in its new form, still more worthy of the high position it occupies, until it is considered not only a desideratum, but a necessity in every family with any pretensions to cultivation and refinement." The new and improved version would continue to be "an infallible guide not only in the art of dressing, but in the art of shopping." It would help those "who are not residents of the city, and prevent much of the embarrassment and loss of time frequently experienced by strangers who desire to make purchases in the metropolis. It will also be a lifelike panorama of the movements of fashionable society, exceedingly interesting and amusing for the moment, but still more valuable as a faithful daguerreotype and historical record to preserve for future reference."

The new publication opened with a nineteen-page article, "A Trip to Havana," by "Our Own Correspondent." Poems, stories, anecdotes, and illustrations explored the evils of alcohol, the purity of nature, the innocence of childhood, and the strange customs of exotic peoples. Curious facts were cited, such as a comment from an entomology book that a spider's web is not one strand but at least four thousand strands woven together like a rope. An article on animals discussed the reasoning abilities of elephants, dogs, monkeys, and the architectural science of ants. Like Leslie's *Journal* the publication contained humor, short anecdotes, and stories from abroad. One article celebrated the gazelle of India and Persia as an alternative to the "odious" and "revolting" modern house pets on which sensibilities were wasted. "If the ladies must go into ecstasies over anything, let them cherish cooing doves, little singing birds, or better still, let them caress gentle gazelles!"

Some subjects appeared in the magazine only because they made dramatic illustrations. For example, "The Antiquities of Strasbourg" provided an excuse to show two bizarre animal pictures: one of six large rats whose tails were hooked together and the other of five cats in the same predicament. The magazine claimed that the illustrations were exact copies of prints of strange visitations to the city in the year 1683. "These marvelous relics of the past combine the most exquisite art with the most revolting subjects." Another example of the use of a picture for its own sake was a full-page illustration titled "The Girl and Lamb," which was included because pictures of childhood "carry our thoughts back to days of innocence, when we were at least free from care, if not overflowing with enjoyment." This emphasis on illustration in all of Leslie's publications was underscored in 1883 by *Frank Leslie's Popular Monthly*, which was founded in 1876: "The stories required by Frank Leslie's should consist of from 2,500 to 3,500 words, and should be full of action and incident, so as to give opportunity for making effective pictures."

Leslie frequently used the same illustrations in different publications. The illustrations were saved in "cut rooms," which by 1883 contained more than 175,000 plates or woodcuts. A comprehensive index made it possible for an editor to retrieve any illustration at almost a moment's notice.

In the spring of 1858 Leslie became a pioneer muckraker with a series in the *Illustrated Newspaper* on "the swill-milk horrors" that affected the quality of milk and the health of children. Cows in the dairies that supplied New York City were being fed refuse from distilleries, and their milk continued to be sold even though the cows had sores all over their bodies and their tails had rotted off. "It is positively asserted," Leslie's reporter noted, "that cows have been propped up by machinery, being too weak to stand, milked while in dying condition, and the carcasses dragged out and carted off to the butchers–the diseased meat to be sold and the poisonous milk of the dying cows to be given to infants." Artists drew pictures of the revolting scenes. The newspaper hired detectives to follow the milk wagons, then published the addresses where the milk was left and warned the buyers that they were poisoning their children.

While the reporters, artists, and detectives supplied the facts, the newspaper editorialized against the political corruption that allowed the business to continue. "For the midnight assassin," it said, "we have the rope and the gallows, for the robber the penitentiary; but for those who murder our children by the thousands we have neither reprobation nor punishment. They are not penal villains, but licensed traders, and though their traffic is literally in human lives, the Government seems powerless or unwilling to interfere." Underestimating the power of illustrated journalism, the board of health and, later, the city issued reassuring reports. In response, the paper printed a cartoon which became symbolic of the campaign: three aldermen whitewashing a cow with no tail. Finally the mayor was forced to order a real investigation that found Leslie's charges justified. The committee's report was released in the spring of 1859, but it took two more years for the legislature to outlaw the sale of milk from cows fed on distillery waste. Leslie was presented a gold watch and chain with an inscription expressing the gratitude of the mothers and children of New York. The lid displayed an en-

Watch and chain presented to Leslie in 1859 after the success of the "swill-milk" campaign conducted by his Illustrated Newspaper

graving of his new press, the chain's links were in the shape of cows' tails, and the charm carried an engraving of the whitewashing cartoon.

One event for which Leslie spared no expense was the prizefight between Britain's Tom Sayers and John C. Heenan, a Troy, New York, native known as the Benicia Boy because he first boxed in Benicia, California. Staff writer Augustus Rawlings and artist Albert Berghaus went to England to witness the fight, which was held thirty miles from London; twenty-four hours later an extra edition of the *Illustrated Newspaper* appeared on the streets of London, impressing the British with American speed. The team quickly caught a boat to New York with the plates and 20,000 printed copies. The fight edition, dated 12 May 1860, sold a record 347,000 copies.

Berghaus, who also drew many of the swill-milk pictures, was a leading artist for the newspaper for more than a quarter of a century, beginning with its first issue. As was the case with his colleagues who dealt with the printed word, Berghaus's emphasis on speed required sacrifices in terms of quality. The special artists often witnessed the major events of the day but, like print reporters, they also reported on events they had not seen. They depended on photographs, sketches by others who were not artists, and verbal descriptions. Because Berghaus was better at drawing architecture than people, many of his illustrations emphasize the scene as much as the action or the actors. Artists generally favored settings because they could visit the scene before an event to take down details or to sketch background which they would not have time to record while an event was taking place. Even when they did not witness events, artists could draw settings from their own memories or earlier sketches of the same place.

Leslie hired many young and inexperienced artists and trained them for the peculiar needs of his illustrated newspaper. After receiving training from Berhgaus and Leslie, Thomas Nast went on to *Harper's*, where he gained international fame. "Mr. Leslie, who was himself a first-class engraver, was severe in his judgment of my work," recalled Joseph Becker, who directed the weekly's art department for twenty-five years. "I have to thank him, however, for the exacting standard he set up for me. It made me toil harder and more carefully."

The three major illustrated papers–*Leslie's*, *Harper's Weekly*, and the *New York Illustrated News*, founded in 1859–engaged in a lively competition for reports and pictures from the fronts during the Civil War. These publications were the first media to bring timely, realistic pictures of war into American homes. *Leslie's* and *Harper's* hired "special artists" who sent back both words and pictures from the field. These artist-reporters had to observe details and sketch them quickly. In New York, artists redrew the pictures on wood; engravers then cut away the wood around the artists' lines. The New York office could alter sketches from the scene to tone down violence and, with the many artists and engravers involved, some sketches looked like the work of committees by the time they were published. The New York artists and the special artists also worked from photographs, as well as from rough sketches and even descriptions of events by soldiers. *Leslie's* claimed to have twelve correspondents at the fronts and more than eighty artists in New York working on nearly three thousand Civil War pictures. *Leslie's* could appear on the New York streets one week after an event. (Leslie regularly advance-dated his papers, so that copies circulated about a week before the paper's printed date.) Extras were issued for some events, and many issues carried full- and double-page battle scenes. But the artists did their best work on scenes which could be drawn at leisure, such as daily camp life, a field hospital, or portraits. *Leslie's* and *Harper's* published books of their wartime illustrations that were blatantly partisan for the North; but Leslie tried to be impartial at the beginning of the war, providing illustrations and reports from both sides and soliciting sketches from soldiers in both armies.

The illustrated press reached its peak during the Civil War. At *Leslie's*, increased production costs brought the price back up to ten cents an issue and four dollars a year. Circulation reached 164,000 during the war, fell to 50,000 by 1865, and only went up to around 70,000 at the beginning of the 1870s.

In 1859 Leslie had created *Frank Leslie's Budget of Fun*, the longest running of the era's humor magazines; it lasted until 1878, when it was merged with the new *Frank Leslie's Budget of Wit, Humor, Anecdote, and Adventure*. A sixteen-page monthly quarto, the *Budget of Fun* usually featured a political cartoon on the front page. Like many other Leslie magazines, it came to be dominated by sentimental fiction. It sold for twenty cents at first and later for a dime. The *Jolly Joker*, created for less respectable humor, ran from September 1862 to May 1878, at first as a monthly and later as a semimonthly.

Leslie entered the low-cost general magazine market with *Frank Leslie's Ten Cent Monthly*, "devoted to useful and entertaining literature," in August 1863. The magazine became *Frank Leslie's New Monthly* in 1865 and *Frank Leslie's Pleasant Hours* in 1866. By then it sold for fifteen cents and was "devoted to light and entertaining literature." This magazine was one more development of the Leslie formula of mixing a variety of trivia with longer fictional pieces. The January 1865 issue, for example, opens with an illustration and part of the first paragraph of a story which runs for the first nine of the edition's seventy-six pages. The tenth page is devoted to a description of the home and tomb of President James K. Polk and short items on monkeys in Java, silkworms in South America, and a royal hunt in Italy. The magazine contains five poems, two pages of rhyming riddles with answers to follow the next month, two pages of fashion, four pages of "Fun for the Family" containing games, jokes, and limericks, and a one-page article titled "The Managing Woman." The three longer stories–nine to twenty-three pages–each carry two or three illustrations. The issue also contains a twenty-three-page installment of a serialized story by Leslie's son Henry. Several illustrations appear in one part of the magazine with short explanations elsewhere in the issue; some of these illustrations do not even include page references to the stories explaining them. Topics illustrated in this manner include gems found with gold, remains of a house at Pompeii, and a statue on exhibit at the National Academy of Design. The practice of separating the text from the pictures–a convenience for the printing process–was a common one in nineteenth-century illustrated magazines.

Miriam Florence Squier, the editor of *Frank Leslie's Lady's Magazine*, demonstrated her sensitivity to the mass market and her strong personal influence with the publisher when she planned, started, and edited *Frank Leslie's Chimney Corner*, whose first number appeared 3 June 1865. This magazine was Leslie's entry into a growing market for fiction for the entire family in one publication. It included domestic stories, romances, adventures, fairy tales, travel reports, and fashion news. It reached a circulation of eighty thousand, but, as was the case with many other Leslie publications, its circulation dropped in the late 1870s. The "Great Family Paper of America" lasted until 6 December 1884, when it was changed to *Leslie's Fact and Fiction for the Chimney Corner* with the addition of more serious articles. The revised publication survived only six months.

The market for juvenile magazines flourished after the Civil War. *Frank Leslie's Children's Friend* began in April 1866, but within the year its name was changed to *Frank Leslie's Boys' and Girls' Weekly*; it ran until 9 February 1884. *Frank Leslie's Boys of America* began in 1873 and folded during Leslie's financial difficulties in 1878.

In February 1867 Leslie went to Europe to represent the United States as a commissioner to the Paris Universal Exposition, which he had promoted in his publications. With Samuel F. B. Morse and Thomas W. Evans he judged the fine arts exhibit and wrote the *Report on the Fine Arts* (1868), published by the United States government. In August he was among the commissioners received by the emperor Napoleon III, who presented him with a medal for his service.

Leslie took with him to Europe Miriam Squier and her husband, Ephraim George Squier, an archaeologist who had edited the *Illustrated Newspaper* since 1861. Their boat landed at Liverpool, where Squier had an old debt outstanding, and upon the party's arrival he was arrested. Leslie–who had sent a dispatch to Squier's creditor from Queenstown, Ireland–borrowed fifteen hundred dollars from his sister to obtain Squier's release, but used the money only after he and Mrs. Squier had spent two weeks touring London and staying in a hotel not commonly frequented by Americans.

Leslie had separated from his wife in 1860; in 1863 he had discontinued his support of her because she refused to give him a divorce. Since the separation Leslie had been living in a room in the Squier home. In December 1866 he had tried to get a divorce in the New York Superior Court, but the suit was discontinued when he and the Squiers left for England. By 1871 Leslie was providing alimony of ten thousand dollars annually under the threat of imprisonment. In 1872 Sarah Leslie finally agreed to a divorce on grounds of adultery, in return for a payment of twenty-eight thousand dollars. Her lawyers charged that Leslie had been having an affair with Miriam Squier since 1 January 1867.

Leslie tried to compete with the *National Police Gazette* with his blatantly sensational *Last Sensation*, begun on 28 December 1867. This illustrated scandal sheet was renamed *Day's Doings* in 1870. It and *Champagne*, which ran from June to December 1871, were published under other imprints, using Leslie's business address. When attacked by the *New York Times* for sensationalism, Leslie said that he was merely illustrating stories from the *Times* police reports. The pictures, he said, only made the stories *seem* more sensational. In 1873 *Day's Doings* was toned down and given the Leslie imprint. It was renamed the *New York Illustrated Times* in 1876 and ran until 1881.

Once a Week, edited by Miriam Squier, was one of the few respectable publications to start without Frank Leslie's name in the masthead when it appeared on 4 March 1871. That development did not last long, however, because the publication was renamed *Frank Leslie's Lady's Journal* on 18 November. Each issue contained large woodcuts and a hand-colored fashion plate. The *Journal* gradually became the leading fashion magazine of the Leslie's house, letting the monthly *Lady's Magazine* handle general literature. Circulation of the weekly reached thirty thousand, but both it and the monthly, which had enjoyed a peak of fifty thousand after the Civil War, declined to under seven thousand by 1880.

Leslie and Miriam Squier used *Day's Doings* to push E. G. Squier into agreeing to a divorce. Leslie artists were present when an inebriated Squier, who had been led from one saloon to another by the artists themselves, appeared at a house of ill repute at an address Miriam had told him would be the site of a grand dinner. The artists captured some of the moments the unfortunate archaeologist spent with a woman named Gypsy in illustrations which could be used, if necessary, in *Day's Doings*. Publication was unnecessary: the Squiers' sixteen-year marriage ended quietly in May 1873. Miriam and Leslie were married the following year.

Frank Leslie's Popular Monthly began in January 1876 and continued after its sale to another publisher in 1905 as *American Magazine*. The quarto sold for $2.50 per year. It was lower in price and quality than *Harper's* and *Scribner's* in the monthly market, but it quickly lived up to its optimistic title and compensated for Leslie's failures of this period. Like all of Leslie's other publications, the *Popular Monthly* contained popular poetry, stories from exotic places, adventures, romances, animal stories, articles on political and natural history, and accounts of unusual events or places that lent themselves to interesting illustrations. Content and appearance were of somewhat higher quality than many other Leslie publications. The first issue opened with a color plate inside the cover depicting three women standing over a bassinet. Curiosities, foreign tidbits, natural history, and animal stories dominated the short items. For example, "A Chinese Surgeon-Barber's Hand" briefly explained an illustration of hands with very long fingernails–considered aristocratic in some circles–and "Curious Oak Tree at Baden-Baden" explained the illustration of a tree that grew in a circle, with the trunk dividing near the base and reuniting eight feet from the ground. A description of the picture "Frog Strategy" said that a naturalist had returned from Egypt telling of frogs that held sticks in their mouths, making them too wide for snakes to swallow them. An illustration with a short explanation showed children riding a bear in Bern, Switzerland. A discussion of vegetation in Chihuahua and a scene from the marketplace in Augsburg, Germany, also appeared. The magazine contained more serious items as well. A reproduction of the *Transfiguration* by Raphael, copied from the original in the Vatican; a brief biography of Henry Wadsworth Longfellow; an article on earthquake research; a story and pictures on southern life; and an anthropological article arguing that what separates men from beasts is not reason but the ability to use fire, with small sketches showing how men started fires in different parts of the world. The first number concluded with sections on science, scientific discoveries, recipes, beef carving, and entertaining tidbits.

The opening article in the first issue was on the national centennial celebration in Philadelphia, describing the site and defending the idea of the celebration, its finances, its location in Philadelphia, its public relations, and the centennial commission. The article contained two and a half pages of illustrations of exposition buildings. Leslie's emphasis on the centennial is hardly surprising; he was a commissioner for the State of New York to the American Centennial Commission. He sponsored a Frank Leslie Pavilion, displaying files of his periodicals, and produced *Frank Leslie's Historical Register of the United States Centennial Exposition, 1876* (1877), which he sold by subscription with souvenir lottery tickets.

In January 1877 he introduced *Frank Leslie's Sunday Magazine*, a family-oriented periodical emphasizing religion, primarily nondenominational Protestantism. The publication was usually edited by a minister, beginning with Charles F. Deems. It contained the typical Leslie miscellany, but emphasized the religious or moral overtones; many of the exotic foreign places described had religious significance. Instead of tidbits of trivia as filler items, the magazine used Bible verses and sentimental quotations. The magazine's first four pages were devoted to a column titled "Some Sundays in London," in which a minister provided an illustrated tour of churches there. The first number also contained a poem from an infant's tomb; the history of a hymn; "The Story of a Lapsed Christian"; and a reproduction and discussion of Leonardo Da Vinci's Last Supper. The conflict between science and religion was a common subject of both prose and poetry. The magazine usually opened with a color illustration of flowers and a message facing the first page, printed on strong paper stock so that it could be used as a small poster. The messages in the first three issues were "God Bless Our Home," "Love One Another," and "Be Faithful to the End." A typical issue carried a hymn on the back cover. "His idea in starting this publication," the *Sunday Magazine* said in its obituary of Leslie, "was to provide for

Cover for an issue of one of Leslie's longest-running periodicals. This issue was the first one published after his death.

the family a Magazine which should not only interest and entertain, but also instruct. To this end his constant energies were directed, and we feel and know that the *Sunday Magazine* gave him more thought than any other of his numerous publications."

Leslie started many other publications, most of which have been little noted nor long remembered; many lasted less than two years. For example, *Stars and Stripes* ran from 1859 to 1860; *Mr. Merryman's Monthly* began and ended in 1863; *Record of Fashion* ran in 1864 and 1865; *New World* was started in 1869 and merged into *Chimney Corner* after six months; *Frank Leslie's Modenwelt* appeared on 1 November 1870 and ended with the 28 October 1871 issue; *Brickbat*, one of many comic magazine begun during this era, lasted only a few months in 1872, even though it carried Matt Morgan's political cartoons from the *Illustrated Newspaper; Happy Home* ran for four months in 1874, was renamed *Young American*, and continued for another two years; both *Idle Hour* and *Some Other Folks* had their first and last issues in 1877.

With the success of *Frank Leslie's Illustrirte Zeitung*, Leslie decided to try his hand at other foreign-language publications. *Illustracíon Americana de Frank Leslie*, a Spanish translation of the *Illustrated Newspaper*, which ran from 1866 to 1870, was sold primarily in Cuba and Central America. *Frank Leslie's Tag für Tag* ran for six months in 1873 before it was merged into *Frank´ Leslie's Illustrirte Zeitung*. *Frank Leslie's Amerikanische Gartenlaube* lasted for a year in 1873 and 1874.

In 1877 Leslie decided to make a journey across the country by rail; in exchange for their promotion of railroad travel, the Leslies were given free transportation in a special car. They took two writers, three artists, a photographer, a business manager, other guests, and Miriam Leslie's terrier, Follette. Despite free railroad fare and possibly free hotel stays, the trip cost the Leslies fifteen thousand dollars. The two-month Leslie excursion yielded weekly articles in *Frank Leslie's Illustrated Newspaper* between 23 June 1877 and 25 May 1877, and many subsequent feature stories and illustrations. Mrs. Leslie's book about the trip, *California: A Pleasure Trip from Gotham to the Golden Gate*, was published in December 1877. Its perspective was that of an eastern aristocrat looking at the rough West. Mrs. Leslie called Virginia City, Nevada, a "God-forsaken place" and added: "The population is largely masculine, very few women, except of the worst class, and as few children." Defending the honor of its town, the *Virginia City Territorial Enterprise* responded with a blistering "Extra" on 14 July 1878, which it reprinted as a pamphlet. The newspaper had gathered juicy tidbits on Miriam Leslie's colorful past and the Leslies' premarital affair, and it served them up with bitter sarcasm.

The Leslies returned from their journey to find their business in a shambles. Among the creditors waiting to collect on more than $335,000 in bad debts was a paper firm whose staff included E. G. Squier's brother. A committee of creditors assigned control of the business to Isaac W. England, publisher of the *New York Sun*. Leslie was to become an employee of his own firm for three years, or until the debts were paid.

The firm's problems included acquisition of a new press and a move to a new building–the fifth move since the company was founded–during a period of declining magazine circulation (the *Illustrated Newspaper*'s circulation was down to thirty-three thousand); an overextended business with too many magazines and book publishing projects; the Leslies' lavish life-style that included diamonds, expensive gowns, a home on Fifth Avenue, and a country estate at Saratoga Springs; too many investments in real estate at a time when land values were falling; legal fees for a libel suit against Leslie by the commission agent for his centennial souvenirs and a legal action by Leslie to keep his son Henry from using the name Frank Leslie, Jr., for a competing business; and a significant loss on Leslie's *Historical Register of the Centennial*.

Leslie managed to get his creditors to agree to allow him to resume control of his business on payment of fifty percent of his debts. While putting together the money, Leslie learned in December 1879 that he had cancer in his neck. He asked his wife to "go to my office, sit in my place, and do my work until my debts are paid" and drew up a will leaving the business to her. On 10 January 1880, a judge ruled in his favor against his son Henry; the same day his wife, his son Alfred (his third son, Scipio, had died in 1879), and friends were at his bedside when he died.

Attendance at his funeral at the Church of the Holy Paternity included between one hundred and two hundred of his employees. "Frank Leslie," the clergyman said, "had devoted himself to the education of the people in the knowledge and appreciation of the refined, the beautiful and the true in art, in nature and in daily life." Leslie was buried in Woodham Cemetery.

Leslie could have been one of the characters in the popular fiction that filled his magazines. A self-made man, he was a benevolent individualist who maintained a superb physique and never used profanity. Kimball described him as always gracious and genial to employees, down to the "humblest of boys." At the same time, he was "open-hearted and outspoken, and I think more truly natural in his life than almost any one I ever knew." He freely granted medical leaves and even helped some employees with medical and other expenses. "He dearly loved his art-department," Kimball wrote, "and often after a rough skirmish in the great battle, he would repair to the artists' room, and there, pencil in hand, help the beginner, suggest to the experienced, and criticize the work of the expert."

Miriam Leslie adopted the name Frank Leslie, which was made legally hers by court order in 1882. To take control of the business, she had to win nineteen lawsuits, including an at-

Miriam Follin Leslie, who legally changed her name to Frank Leslie after her husband's death and ran his publishing empire until 1900

tempt to set aside her husband's will. Like her husband, she personally supervised every periodical. She read manuscripts being considered for publication and reorganized every department of the publishing house. She closed and consolidated failing magazines that her husband had refused to abandon. As her husband had used a murder, she used a single event to revive *Frank Leslie's Illustrated Newspaper*. When President Garfield was shot in July 1881, she stopped production on the issue about to go to press, broke up the forms, and started over with news and pictures of the assassination. Her motto was: "The public shall have the newest news." She changed the *Illustrated Newspaper* to a magazine format with a decorative cover and better paper, attracted new writers, and increased the circulation to fifty thousand. After putting the firm on a solid financial footing, she leased it in 1895 to a syndicate and made an extended European tour. When she returned three years later, she had to rebuild the company a second time. She was forced into retirement by her partners in 1900.

Miriam Leslie lived by many names. She worked at keeping her birthdate a mystery, but she was born Miriam Florence Folline—she later dropped the *e*–on 5 June 1836 in New Orleans. In 1857 she made a brief attempt at a stage career with the actress Lola Montez as her sister "Minnie Montez." She was married four times: briefly in 1854 to jeweler David Charles Peacock, in 1858 to Squier, in 1874 to Leslie, and in 1891 to William Charles Kingsbury Wilde, brother of Oscar Wilde, whom she divorced in 1893. In 1901 she took the title Baroness de Bazus, claiming that it had been conferred upon her French ancestors. She was the author of five books and a play and the translator of two books from the French. She continued to lead an active social life, enjoying the friendship of many notables, including William Gladstone, Alfred Tennyson, and Robert Browning, until her death in New York City on 18 September 1914. She left two million dollars–half of which was spent to ward off challengers to her will–to the woman suffrage movement.

The longest running Leslie publications were *Frank Leslie's Illustrated Newspaper* and *Frank Leslie's Popular Monthly*. Mrs. Leslie sold the former in 1889 to the publishers of *Judge*. Its name was changed to *Frank Leslie's Illustrated Weekly* in 1891 and, after undergoing several other name changes–all of them retaining *Leslie's* in the title–and enjoying a boom during World War I, it was merged into *Judge* in 1922. Under Mrs. Leslie the *Popular Monthly*'s circulation rose to 125,000 in 1887 but declined drastically during her three years in Europe. On her return she reorganized the magazine, and its circulation reached 200,000 in four months. Its name was changed to *Leslie's Monthly* in 1904 and to *American Illustrated Magazine* in 1905. In 1906 five writers for *McClure's Magazine*, after falling out with S. S. McClure, purchased the *American Magazine* as a muckraking and human-interest magazine. In 1915 the Crowell Company of Springfield, Ohio, changed it to a family magazine promoting domestic life and financial success, boosting its circulation from 400,000 to 2.3 million.

Frank Leslie's firm was influential by the sheer number of its publications and the number of people it reached. In her biography of Mrs. Leslie, Madeleine B. Stern compiled a list of thirty periodicals and eighty-six books, pictorials, and other works published by the firm between 1854 and 1905. *Frank Leslie's Illustrated Newspaper* and the other Leslie magazines took hundreds of thousands of Americans to places they could never visit, to witness events they could never see.

Throughout his career Frank Leslie introduced technological innovations for printing illustrations as fast as he learned them, but the technology for printing photographs in magazines and newspapers was not created until ten years after his death. From a television-dominated era, it is hard to imagine the impact of the first medium that emphasized large pictures with short, tightly written copy. Leslie and his imitators provided the most accessible, if not the most realistic, pictures available in the mass media of their day.

Bibliographies:

Madeleine B. Stern, "The Frank Leslie Publishing House," *Antiquarian Bookman*, 7 (16 June 1951): 1973-1975;

Stern, *Publishers for Mass Entertainment in Nineteenth Century America* (Boston: G. K. Hall, 1980), pp. 180-189.

References:

Joseph Becker, "An Artist's Interesting Recollections of *Leslie's Weekly*," *Leslie's Weekly*, 101 (14 December 1905): 570;

Walter Davenport and James C. Derieux, *Ladies, Gentlemen, and Editors* (Garden City, N.Y.: Doubleday, 1960), pp. 13-49;

"Frank Leslie," *Frank Leslie's Sunday Magazine*, 7 (March 1880): 369, 372-373;

"The Frank Leslie Publishing House," *Frank Leslie's Illustrated Newspaper*, 55 (24 March 1883): 81-84;

Budd Leslie Gambee, Jr., *Frank Leslie and His Illustrated Newspaper 1855-1860* (Ann Arbor: University of Michigan Department of Library Science, 1964);

"The Home of Illustrated Literature," *Frank Leslie's Popular Monthly*, 16 (August 1883): 129-138, 140, 141;

Richard B. Kimball, "Frank Leslie," *Frank Leslie's Popular Monthly*, 9 (March 1880): 258-263;

Mrs. Frank Leslie, *California: A Pleasure Trip from Gotham to the Golden Gate* (New York: Carleton/London: Low, 1877); facsimile edition, with introduction by Madeleine B. Stern (Nieuwkoop, Netherlands: DeGraff, 1972);

Fulton Oursler, "Frank Leslie," *American Mercury*, 20 (May 1930): 94-101;

Harriet Quimby, "How Frank Leslie Started the First Illustrated Weekly," *Leslie's Weekly*, 101 (14 December 1905): 568;

Stern, "The Leslies of Publishers' Row," *Publishers' Weekly*, 152 (11 October 1947): B233-B237;

Stern, *Purple Passage: The Life of Mrs. Frank Leslie* (Norman: University of Oklahoma Press, 1953);

W. Fletcher Thompson, Jr., *The Image of War: The Pictorial Reporting of the American Civil War* (New York: Yoseloff, 1960);

N. P. Willis, "Frank Leslie, a Life-Lengthener," *Frank Leslie's Illustrated Newspaper*, 10 (15 December, 1860): 53.

Eliakim Littell
(2 January 1797-17 May 1870)

and

Robert S. Littell
(5 May 1831-7 April 1896)

Cathy Packer
Boston College

Eliakim Littell

MAJOR POSITIONS HELD: editor and publisher (1819-1821, 1823-1834, 1836-1842, 1844), publisher (1822, 1835, 1843), *Philadelphia Register and National Recorder*, renamed *National Recorder* in 1819, renamed *Saturday Magazine* in 1821, renamed *Museum of Foreign Literature and Science* in 1822, renamed *Museum of Foreign Literature, Science, and Art* in 1833, renamed *Eclectic Museum of Foreign Literature, Science, and Art* in 1843; publisher, *Journal of Foreign Medical Science and Literature* (1821-1824), *Religious Magazine; Or, Spirit of the Foreign Theological Journals and Reviews* (1828-1830); editor (1844-1846), editor and publisher (1846-1870), *Littell's Living Age*; publisher, *Panorama of Life and Literature* (1855-1857).

Robert S. Littell

MAJOR POSITION HELD: editor and publisher, *Littell's Living Age* (1870-1896).

Eliakim and Robert S. Littell, father and son, were editors and publishers of several eclectic literary and scientific magazines that spread European thought in America throughout the nineteenth century. Rather than making original contributions to American magazine journalism, they reprinted foreign magazine articles for an American audience.

Eliakim Littell, the more famous of the two, was born in Burlington, New Jersey, to Stephen and Susan Gardiner Littell. He attended grammar school in Haddonfield, New Jersey, and began reading widely. His strong literary interests led him to serve several years as an apprentice in a bookstore and to acquire a depth of knowledge about English literature that would shape his later career.

Littell began his fifty-year career in publishing by launching the *Philadelphia Register and National Recorder* on 2 January 1819. He was editor and joint publisher with R. Norris Henry of the sixteen-page weekly. In July of that year the periodical was renamed the *National Recorder* and changed into a literary miscellany or eclectic. It contained reprints of American newspaper articles; selections from foreign magazines such as essays on politics, economics, science, and literature; papers read before the Agricultural Society of Philadelphia; and some original copy. Some earlier American magazines were eclectics because original contributions were not to be had. During the second half of the eighteenth century, about three-quarters of the contents of American magazines were extracted from other American and British publications. In 1819, however, magazines were eclectics due to the popularity of the format, not because of a shortage of literary work produced by American authors. This literary piracy, as it was regarded by some, was perfectly legal. International copyright laws were passed only at the end of the nineteenth century.

While in Philadelphia Littell also published religious and medical journals, and for several years in the 1820s and 1830s he had a bookstore with his brother, editor and author John Stockton Littell. From January 1821 to October 1824 he published the *Journal of Foreign Medical Science and Literature* as a continuation of the *Eclectic Repertory and Analytic Review, Medical and Philosophical*, a quarterly that had been edited by an association of physicians and published by T. Dobson and Son. In 1825 Littell's journal, which was edited by S. Emlen, Jr., and William Price, merged with the *American Medical Recorder*. Then in 1828 he began the *Religious Magazine; Or, Spirit of the Foreign Theological Journals and Reviews*, with the Reverend George Weller as editor.

On 7 July 1821 Littell's *National Recorder* was renamed the *Saturday Magazine*. Expanded to twenty-four pages, it primarily consisted of reprints from British magazines and scientific journals. The *Saturday Magazine* was the first American periodical to publish English essayist Thomas de Quincey's *Confessions of an English Opium-Eater*, which had been a sensation when it was first published in the *London Magazine*. It also introduced many Americans to the work of English essayist and poet Charles Lamb.

Littell found it inconvenient to continue long reprints from one week to the next, however, so in 1822 he expanded his struggling magazine, made it a monthly, and again changed its name. It became the ninety-six page *Museum of Foreign Literature and Science*, and "for twenty years it was the leading American eclectic," according to magazine historian Frank Luther Mott. In 1870 Littell's obituary said the *Museum* "included nearly everything that was really worthy of reproduction in the periodical literature of Great Britain. For twenty-one years it had a brilliant reputation, and held the foremost rank among publications of a similar character in this country." The *Museum* was edited in 1822 by Robert Walsh, who also was editor of the Philadelphia *National Gazette* and had been editor of the *American Review*, the first regular quarterly review in the United States. After Walsh departed, Littell became the editor, with occasional assistance from his brother, physician Dr. Squier Littell. Littell began using plates in 1827 and regularly used them from 1830. Before that year the *Museum*, which had a circulation of about two thousand, leaned toward belles lettres, but later it devoted a large portion of its space to serial fiction by Charles Dickens, William Thackeray, and other popular contemporary English novelists.

In 1843 Littell purchased the *American Eclectic*, a New York bimonthly, and combined it with the *Museum* as the *Eclectic Museum of Foreign Literature, Science, and Art*. The magazine's professed goal was to print the best foreign periodical literature. The *Eclectic Museum* was published in New York and Philadelphia and edited by John Holmes Agnew, a Presbyterian minister who had been an editor of the *American Eclectic* when Littell took it over.

In 1844 Littell sold his interest in the *Eclectic Museum* to Leavitt, Trow and Company. The new owners of the *Eclectic Museum* changed its title to the *Eclectic Magazine*, and it continued for sixty years.

Littell moved to Boston, where he was encouraged by some of the area's most prominent citizens to publish another eclectic. Among those who encouraged him were Joseph Story, a Massachusetts politician and associate justice of the United States Supreme Court; American historian William Hickling Prescott; and former president of the United States John Quincy Adams. Littell founded *Littell's Living Age*, a sixty-four-page weekly magazine that consisted mainly of reprints from the British press. Littell wrote in the magazine's first issue on 11 May 1844, "The steamship has brought Europe, Asia, and Africa into our neighborhood and will greatly multiply our connections as Merchants, Travelers, and Politicians with all parts of the world, so that much more than ever it now becomes every intelligent American to be informed of the condition and changes of foreign countries. And this not only because of their nearer connection with ourselves, but because the nations seem to be hastening, through a rapid process of change, to some new state of things, which the merely political prophet cannot compute or foresee." Mott observed, "There was a special effort made . . . to select material which would interest American readers; and nearly all the comment of British periodicals on American affairs appeared in the *Living Age*." It was serious material such as essays from the *Edinburgh Quarterly*, criticism of poetry and political commentary from *Blackwood's*, and works from the *Spectator*, the *Examiner*, the *Athenaeum*, and the *Literary Gazette* that gave *Littell's Living Age* its appeal. Weeklies and newspapers also were quoted. Littell wrote in the first issue of his magazine, "We do not consider it beneath our dignity to borrow wit and wisdom from *Punch*; and when we think it good enough, make use of the thunder of the *Times*." Much of the fiction reprinted in the magazine was second or third class because the more famous English novelists sold their advance sheets to other American periodicals. The periodical cost six dollars a year at fifteen cents a copy. It sold approximately five thousand copies a week early on, not reaching ten thousand until 1880. It prospered, in spite of lower circulation, because its contents cost only the price of subscriptions to English periodicals.

The first issue included twelve articles and nine poems. Included were an article by Ralph Waldo Emerson reprinted from the *Foreign Quarterly Review*, an article on French cookery from the *London Magazine*, and a history of the conquest of Mexico from *Do*. In the magazine's second issue, Littell noted that all the copies of the first issue had been sold within two days.

The *New York Times* used the ninetieth anniversary of *Littell's Living Age* in 1934 as an occasion to heap lavish praise on Littell and *Littell's Living Age*. On 20 May the paper editorialized, "No cultivated American home felt itself complete without at least one of the several magazines of Littell's indefatigable ventures, which began when he was barely of age and culminated in the one publication that for decades bore his name as a patronymic.... Such has been the record of this unique periodical that one may be excused for thinking that his given name, which meant, "whom God sets up," had some significance, though as a matter of fact he was named for his grandfather...."

In July 1855 in Boston Littell expanded his publishing business by launching the *Panorama of Life and Literature*, a 144-page monthly eclectic magazine that was lighter reading and less expensive than *Littell's Living Age*. The *Panorama* promised in its first issue, "Every month we shall offer to you articles of leading interest; grave and earnest, but not heavy; popular, and yet of abiding value. To these will be added, in profuse abundance and great variety, Tales, Poetry, Voyages, and Travels, and whatever, (within the bounds of sound taste and good principle) may be included under the large head of Light Reading.... It will be suited to the leisure of the prudent, old, and wise, and yet be eagerly sought by the young, the ardent, and progressive."

In addition to publishing, Littell was active in politics, and he was particularly interested in the nation's financial affairs. He was the author of the Compromise Tariff in 1833, which provided for a gradual reduction of tariffs on foreign imports. The tariff was advocated by Henry Clay and carried through Congress during the administration of President Jackson in an effort to avert a civil war by appeasing Southern politicians who objected to high tariffs they said put the South at the mercy of Northern manufacturers. Littell later supported the Union cause during the Civil War.

By some reports, Littell was an irritable man of brusque manners. However, he was said to have many friends. On 12 February 1828 he married Mary Frazee Smith. They had six children, two of whom died in infancy. Their son Robert Smith Littell, who was born in Philadelphia on 5 May 1831, was his father's partner in the publishing business for several years before Eliakim died in 1870 in Brookline, Massachusetts. Robert then assumed control of *Littell's Living Age*. Assisted by his sister, Susan Gardiner Littell, Robert remained the editor and manager of the magazine without changing its editorial policy until his death of heart disease in 1896 in Brookline, Massachusetts.

In 1874 the circulation list of *Every Saturday* was absorbed by *Littell's Living Age*, and *Littell's* became the only eclectic magazine in the country. After Robert Littell's death, the family sold the periodical to Frank Foxcroft, who dropped "Littell's" from the name and broadened its scope by adding sections on American books and authors. The *Living Age* was almost a century old when it died in 1941. It was the prototype for later eclectic magazines such as *Reader's Digest*. The Littell's literary heritage survived even longer through their descendants. Robert's son Philip (1868-1943) was an editor of the Milwaukee *Sentinel* and one of the original editors of the *New Republic*. Philip's son Robert (1896-1963) was a senior editor for *Reader's Digest* and a writer for the *New York World*.

Eliakim and Robert Littell are primarily remembered for contributing to the early development of American culture by importing foreign thought and spreading it through their eclectic magazines. In 1859 literary historiographer S. Austin Allibone called Eliakim Littell "an eminent literary benefactor to the public mind." He said, "Few men indeed have laboured so long and so successfully in the great cause of public education, and few, therefore, are so well entitled to the gratitude of their countrymen ... Many of them owe him their first introduction to the great minds of the past half-century, the commencement of that profitable acquaintance which hath soothed the pangs of sorrow, dispelled the gloomy shades of care, and made them wiser and better, happier and more contented, men."

References:

S. Austin Allibone, *Critical Dictionary of English Literature, and British and American Authors* (Philadelphia: Childs and Peterson, 1859; London: Trubner and Company, 1859);

A General Index to "The Eclectic Magazine," and to Vols. 37-148 of "The Living Age" (Bangor, Maine: Q.P. Index, 1881);

Albert H. Smyth, *The Philadelphia Magazines and Their Contributors, 1741-1850* (Philadelphia: R.M. Lindsay, 1892);

Algernon Tassin, *The Magazine in America* (New York: Dodd, Mead and Company, 1916).

Papers:

The Massachusetts Historical Society and the Historical Society of Pennsylvania hold letters by Eliakim Littell.

James Russell Lowell
(22 February 1819-12 August 1891)

Bert Hitchcock
Auburn University

See also the Lowell entries in *DLB 1: The American Renaissance in New England; DLB 11: American Humorists, 1800-1950;* and *DLB 64: American Literary Critics and Scholars, 1850-1880.*

MAJOR POSITIONS HELD: Coeditor, *Pioneer* (1843); editor, *Atlantic Monthly* (1857-1861); coeditor, *North American Review* (1863-1872).

BOOKS: *Class Poem* (Cambridge, Mass.: Metcalf, Torry & Ballou, 1838);

A Year's Life and Other Poems (Boston: Little & Brown, 1841);

Poems (Cambridge, Mass.: Owen, 1844; London: Mudie, 1844);

Conversations on Some of the Old Poets (Cambridge, Mass.: Owen, 1845; London: Clarke, 1845);

Poems: Second Series (Cambridge, Mass.: Nichols/ Boston: Mussey, 1848; London: Wiley, 1848);

A Fable for Critics (New York: Putnam's, 1848; London: Chapman, 1848);

The Biglow Papers (Cambridge, Mass.: Nichols/ New York: Putnam's, 1848; London: Chapman, 1849);

The Vision of Sir Launfal (Cambridge, Mass.: Nichols, 1848; London: Sampson & Low, 1876);

Poems, 2 volumes (Boston: Ticknor, Reed & Fields, 1849; London: Routledge, 1851-1852);

The Biglow Papers: Second Series (3 parts, London: Trubner, 1862; Boston: Ticknor & Fields, 1867);

Fireside Travels (Boston: Ticknor & Fields, 1864; London: Macmillan, 1864);

Ode Recited at the Commemoration of the Living and Dead Soldiers of Harvard University, July 21, 1865 (Cambridge, Mass.: Privately printed, 1865);

Under the Willows and Other Poems (Boston: Fields, Osgood, 1869);

The Cathedral (Boston: Fields, Osgood, 1870);

Among My Books (Boston: Fields, Osgood, 1870; London: Macmillan, 1870);

My Study Windows (Boston: Osgood, 1871; London: Sampson, Low, 1871);

Among My Books. Second Series (Boston: Osgood, 1876; London: Sampson, Low, 1876);

Three Memorial Poems (Boston: Osgood, 1877);

James Russell Lowell (crayon portrait by Charles Akers)

Democracy and Other Addresses (Boston & New York: Houghton, Mifflin, 1887; London: Macmillan, 1887);

Heartsease and Rue (Boston & New York: Houghton, Mifflin, 1888; London: Macmillan, 1888);

Political Essays (Boston & New York: Houghton, Mifflin, 1888; London: Macmillan, 1888);

Latest Literary Essays and Addresses, edited by Charles Eliot Norton (Boston & New York: Houghton, Mifflin, 1892; London: Macmillan, 1892);

The Old English Dramatists, edited by Norton (Boston & New York: Houghton, Mifflin, 1892; London: Macmillan, 1892);

Last Poems, edited by Norton (Boston & New York: Houghton, Mifflin, 1895);

Lectures on English Poets, edited by S. A. Jones (Cleveland: Rowfant Club, 1897);

Impressions of Spain, compiled by Joseph B. Gilder (Boston & New York: Houghton, Mifflin, 1899);

The Anti-Slavery Papers of James Russell Lowell, 2 volumes (Boston & New York: Houghton, Mifflin, 1902);

Early Prose Writings (London & New York: Lane, 1902);

Uncollected Poems, edited by Thelma M. Smith (Philadelphia: University of Pennsylvania Press, 1950).

Editions and Collections: *The Writings of James Russell Lowell*, Riverside Edition, 10 volumes (Boston & New York: Houghton, Mifflin, 1890);

The Complete Poetical Works, Cambridge Edition, edited by Horace Elisha Scudder (Boston & New York: Houghton, Mifflin, 1897);

The Complete Writings of James Russell Lowell, Elmwood Edition, edited by Charles Eliot Norton, 16 volumes (Boston: Houghton, Mifflin, 1904);

The Function of the Poet and Other Essays, edited by Albert Mordell (Boston & New York: Houghton Mifflin, 1920);

James Russell Lowell: Representative Selections, edited by Harry Hayden Clark and Norman Foerster (New York: American Book Company, 1947);

Lowell: Essays, Poems and Letters, edited by William Smith Clark II (New York: Odyssey, 1948);

Literary Criticism of James Russell Lowell, Regents Critics series, edited by Herbert F. Smith (Lincoln: University of Nebraska Press, 1969);

The Biglow Papers [First Series]: *A Critical Edition*, edited by Thomas Wortham (De Kalb: Northern Illinois University Press, 1977);

The Poetical Works of James Russell Lowell, Cambridge Edition Revised, edited by Marjorie Kaufman (Boston: Houghton Mifflin, 1978).

OTHER: *The Poetical Works of John Keats*, edited by Lowell (Boston: Little, Brown/New York: Evans & Dickerson/Philadelphia: Lippincott, Grambo, 1854);

The Poetical Works of John Dryden, 5 volumes, edited by Lowell (Boston: Little, Brown, 1854);

The Poetical Works of William Wordsworth, 7 volumes, edited by Lowell (Boston: Little, Brown/New York: Evans & Dickerson/Philadelphia: Lippincott, Grambo, 1854);

The Poetical Works of Percy Bysshe Shelley, edited by Mary Shelley, with a memoir by Lowell (Boston: Little, Brown/New York: Dickerson/Philadelphia: Lippincott, Grambo, 1855);

The Poetical Works of Dr. John Donne, with a Memoir, edited by Lowell (Boston: Little, Brown/ New York: Dickerson/Philadelphia: Lippincott, 1855);

The Poetical Works of Andrew Marvell, with a Memoir of the Author, edited by Lowell (Boston: Little, Brown, 1857);

Izaak Walton, *The Complete Angler; or The Contemplative Man's Recreation, of Izaak Walton and Charles Cotton,* 2 volumes, introduction by Lowell (Boston: Little, Brown, 1889).

Although he will never again command the status of literary giant accorded him in the last years of his life, Americans can relegate James Russell Lowell to the condition of unsampled historical curiosity only with injustice to him and loss to themselves. The absence of popular and scholarly attention to Lowell in the mid twentieth century indicates the precipitous decline in the reputation of one of the most important New England fathers of a distinctive and distinguished national literature. Perhaps he wrote and did too much in his long lifetime. He was lawyer, professor, social reformer and political activist, poet, essayist, critic, diplomat, and editor–but if his immense versatility was somehow his downfall, his essential vitality is undeniable. If he is too broadly and perfectly representative, the achievements as well as the very fact of that representativeness are remarkable. If he offers both successes and failures to public view, the offering is rich and enriching. Just as his poetry ranges from high philosophical seriousness to humorous local color and political satire in dialect, Lowell in his life and literature evidences a variety of accomplishments that deserve admiration. Creating American literature, he contributed to world literature; helping Americans discover themselves, he revealed important aspects of humanity. To answer the contention that his editorship of two of America's most prestigious magazines was the result of provincial social status or inflated contemporary reputation, one need only note the quality of what was published in the early, short-lived periodical of which he was a founding editor, or point to the development into a national institution that rested on his first, crucial editorship of the *Atlantic Monthly.*

Although he lived for brief periods elsewhere in the United States and in Europe, the geographical and spiritual center of Lowell's life was Cambridge, Massachusetts. There, in Elmwood, the Lowell family home, on 22 February 1819 he was born to Charles and Harriet Traill Spence Lowell. There he was educated, receiving– barely–a baccalaureate degree in 1838 and– unenthusiastically–a law degree in 1840 from Harvard University; in 1855 he was selected Henry Wadsworth Longfellow's successor as Harvard's Smith Professor of Modern Languages and Literature; he served as a member of the Harvard faculty for sixteen years thereafter, for several years after 1874, and again in 1885. Three of Lowell's children as well as his mother and his wife, Maria White Lowell, whom he married in 1844, died between 1847 and 1853, and three nephews died during the Civil War. In Cambridge in the early 1840s he struggled to become a writer, and as the years passed achieved popular success and international critical acclaim. He left Cambridge to serve as United States minister to Spain from 1877 to 1880 and Great Britain from 1880 to 1885. Frances Dunlap Lowell, whom he married in 1857, died in 1885 after six years of intermittent disability and insanity reminiscent of his mother's last years. He returned to Cambridge in 1889 to prepare a collected edition of his works. Two years later on 12 August 1891 he died in the house in which he had been born.

Periodicals, especially magazines, were integral to Lowell's aspirations and achievements. Selected an editor of the 1837-1838 college literary magazine *Harvardiana,* he also became one of its contributors. He began to have poems appear in more public periodicals as early as 1839. Once even paying him five dollars, the *Southern Literary Messenger* was almost an exclusive place of publication for him before he ventured a small book of poetry, *A Year's Life,* in 1841. By 1844, when a second volume, *Poems,* was released, Lowell's work had repeatedly appeared in *Graham's Magazine,* the *Boston Miscellany, Arcturus,* and the *United States Magazine and Democratic Review.* In 1848 he received a contract for five hundred dollars from the *National Anti-Slavery Standard* for one year's worth of weekly contributions either in prose or verse. The same year he published *Poems: Second Series* and his most widely admired long works: *The Biglow Papers* (First Series), which brilliantly attacked the United States role in the Mexican War; *A Fable for Critics,* which provided incisive characterizations of America's contemporary writers; and *The Vision of Sir Launfal,* whose moral message and memorable lines such as "And what is so rare as a day in June?" became familiar to generations of the nation's schoolchildren. Those last two, unlike *The Biglow Papers,* whose parts had appeared over a two-year period in the *Boston Courier* and *National Anti-Slavery Standard,* first came to the public as books. They signaled a new phase of Lowell's career, but not a phase that abandoned the publication pattern of the early years. Lowell's many personal and critical essays, collected in several volumes and editions, first appeared in the *Atlantic,* the *North American Review,* the *Nation, Graham's,* or *Putnam's,* and *Atlantic* publication preceded the appearance in book form of two other major poetical works, *The Biglow Papers: Second Series* (1867) and *The Cathedral* (1870). The *Nation, Atlantic,* and the *New York Ledger* were among the periodical outlets for Lowell's work at the very end of his life, and *Harper's, Scribner's,* and the *Century* carried Lowell essays and poems for as many years after his death.

These last three periodicals, along with the *Atlantic,* are the standard prime examples of the "golden age" of American magazines in the latter decades of the nineteenth century. To this achievement Lowell contributed significantly as a writer. His was also an important role as an editor, for at early, critical times he occupied three such posts. Contrary to Henry James's belief, these positions were, for Lowell and American literary history, more than merely "initiations of periodical editorship which, either as worries or as triumphs, may never perhaps be said to strike very deep."

In late 1842 the choice of the *Pioneer* as the name for a new literary magazine was quite deliberate, and most appropriate, for Lowell and his colleague Robert Carter. In a prospectus the editors claimed that each issue of their monthly publication would be "entirely original" and consist of "articles chiefly from American authors of the highest reputation." Their purpose in establishing the *Pioneer,* they wrote, was "to furnish the intelligent and reflecting portion of the Reading Public with a rational substitute for the enormous quantity of thrice-diluted trash, in the shape of namby-pamby love tales and sketches, which is monthly poured out to them by many of our popular magazines–and to offer instead thereof, a healthy and manly Periodical Literature, whose perusal will not necessarily involve a loss of time and a deterioration of every moral and intellectual faculty." The magazine was to be forty-eight pages long, handsomely printed, illustrated with fine engravings, and priced at twenty-five cents a copy or three dollars a year, "payable, in all cases, in advance." Unlike British periodicals it was to have no advertisements, and unlike American magazines, no women's fashion plates. Fired with literary enthusiasm but exhibiting little business sense, Lowell and Carter signed a distribution contract with the Boston firm of Leland & Whiting in which they gave away practically all profit prospects and made themselves liable to a five-hundred-dollar penalty if they were unable to furnish copies by the twentieth of each month.

The editorial promises of the prospectus proved less difficult to keep than the terms of the contract. The *Pioneer* existed for only three issues, January through March 1843, but they were impressive numbers, including contributions by Jones Very, W. W. Story, T. W. Parsons, John Greenleaf Whittier, Edgar Allan Poe ("The Tell-Tale Heart" and "Notes upon English Verse"), Nathaniel Hawthorne ("Hall of Fantasy" and "The Birthmark"), and Lowell himself.

Severe problems with his eyes forced Lowell to go to New York for extended treatment soon after the January issue was prepared, and his supervision of the magazine suffered to the point that no April issue could be printed. Legal actions were initiated by both Lowell and Carter and Leland & Whiting, the result being that Lowell assumed a heavy financial debt which burdened him for years. Later judgments of the *Pioneer* variously accused Lowell of irresponsible "misguided ambition" and praised him for "a high-souled adventure in magazinedom, garroted by the cord of a commercial contract."

Lowell's second effort at magazine editing was much more successful. Again he was the first editor of a new periodical, but this time he was not the publisher and therefore did not have financial responsibility for the venture. The opinion expressed by the editor and writer Nathaniel Parker Willis upon publication of the first number of the *Pioneer,* that a man like Lowell who is "merely a man of genius" is "a very unfit editor for a periodical," seems not to have deterred Phillips, Sampson & Company of Boston, founders of the *Atlantic Monthly* in 1857. Destined to become the nation's premier intellectual and literary magazine, the *Atlantic* was the brainchild of Francis H. Underwood, who had labored for the better part of a decade to bring his idea to reality. Underwood's role in the establishment and early operation of the monthly was vital, but he soon assumed a secondary position because of the enthusiastic support secured at the outset from some of the country's most honored writers: Ralph Waldo Emerson, Henry Wadsworth Longfellow, John Lothrop Motley, Oliver Wen-

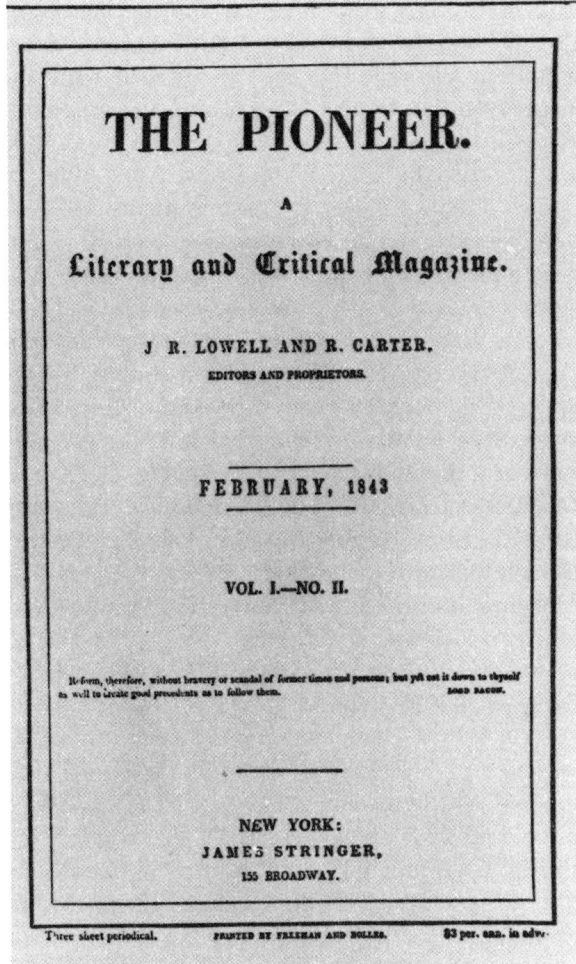

Title page for the second of the three issues of the literary periodical started in 1842 by Lowell and Robert Carter

dell Holmes, and Lowell. After initial perplexity about a name and an editor for the new magazine, Holmes's suggestion for a title and Emerson's urging of Lowell to be selected as editor won approval.

While the *Pioneer* had been descriptively subtitled *A Literary and Critical Magazine*, the subtitle of the *Atlantic* was *A Magazine of Literature, Art and Politics* (*Science* was added in 1865). Lowell provided strong, steady guidance for the two critical thrusts of the new periodical. First was the courageous and outspoken coverage of contemporary public affairs, the intellectual but unhesitant urging of moral positions in the political arena. Second was American nationalism, which, while it was also connected with politics, was particularly evident in the magazine's attitude toward literature. Good foreign contributors would be sought on the basis of their merit, but, the editor said, native American writers "will receive the most solid encouragement, and will be mainly relied upon to fill the pages of the *Atlantic*." This policy echoes the prospectus of the *Pioneer* that had appeared fourteen years earlier, and the *Atlantic* pursued the same end Lowell had set forth in the lead article of that magazine: the achievement of a distinguished national literature through creation of a distinctive *natural* literature.

The editorship of the *Atlantic* was for Lowell, by then a Harvard professor, an avocation that provided welcome additional income; clearly, however, it was also more. He showed, said Edward Everett Hale, "almost motherly care of the new-born magazine." One of the conditions on which Lowell accepted the editor's job was that the magazine would receive frequent contributions from Oliver Wendell Holmes; and Holmes's famous "Autocrat" papers were the consequence. During Lowell's editorship the pages of the *Atlantic* included the work of every American writer of repute except Melville and Thoreau, and often it was the writers' best work that appeared there. Twentieth-century critical opinion has not seconded all of Lowell's judgments as *Atlantic* editor, but it has confirmed many, including acceptance of forward-looking realistic fiction by such women as Rebecca Harding Davis.

Yet his tenure at the *Atlantic* was not without criticism. Lowell's editorial work seems to have been more deliberate than efficient, and despite his occasional fifteen-hour workdays, both his own work and that for the *Atlantic* suffered from delays. It appeared to snow manuscripts, he said, and he had to shovel and shovel to try to get out from under them. To the consternation of prospective contributors, he too often misplaced or lost submissions, and sometimes he was months behind in his correspondence. In preparing a piece for publication he often made changes or deletions that outraged the author. From competing periodicals and writers in other parts of the country came accusations that the *Atlantic* catered exclusively to New England writers, and from New England clergymen came condemnations of the theology advanced by various *Atlantic* pieces.

Amid the demands and frustrations of his second editorship, however, Lowell did not lose his sense of humor, his natural genial playfulness. Privately he referred to the *Atlantic* as the "Maga" and labeled a troublesome contributor a "pen-and-inkubus." To James T. Fields, who succeeded him as editor in 1861, he wrote that he wished to lay aside his "paper crown and feather sceptre," to abdicate "delusive royalty" with grace. Lowell advised Fields that the editorship would be "no bad apprenticeship or prelude for that warmer and more congenial world to which all successful booksellers are believed by devout authors to go." Still, said Lowell, he relinquished his *Atlantic* responsibilities with regret if only because of the reduced income and because "a bore, moreover, that is a periodical gets a friendly face at last, and we miss it on the whole." Following the four years of Lowell's guidance, Fields was taking over a magazine that had a stable circulation well into the thousands and that in intellectual tone and literary quality matched or surpassed the best periodicals published in Europe.

Lowell's final editorship offered little opportunity for pacemaking achievement. The *North American Review* had been founded in 1815 with the intent that it would rival the great British "quarterlies." Except in the minds of a few New England worthies, this goal was never realized, and by 1863 even proud Bostonians saw that revitalization of the periodical was a drastic necessity. Later scholarly descriptions of the *Review* at this point in its history range from "awfully proper" through "torpid and respectable" to "almost extinct"; standing for "elegant leisure and a somewhat remote criticism," the journal was conspicuous for its "dull dignity" and "prodigious gravity." Lowell assessed the matter similarly at the time. The *North American*, he said, was "an eminently safe periodical, and accordingly was in great danger of running aground.... Perhaps," he went on, "the day of the quarterlies is gone by, and these megatheria of letters may be in the mere course of nature withdrawing to their last swamps to die in peace. Anyhow, here we are with our megatherium on our hands, and we must strive to find what will fill his huge belly, and keep him alive a little longer."

The "we" to whom Lowell referred included his coeditor Charles Eliot Norton, but Lowell had firm ideas of his own of what was needed to rescue the *North American Review*. He saw as a major deficiency the lack of what he called a thorough loyalty, an unswerving, principled devotion to the ideal represented by the American nation. The two other chief deficiencies he recognized were that the magazine "wasn't lively" and "had no particular opinions on any particular subject." Cultivating opinion and loyalty Lowell thought easy; creating a lively style was another matter.

The editorship provided additional needed money for Lowell, but he made it clear from the beginning that he would serve only as a coeditor. Thus he shared the post with Norton from 1863 until 1868, with E. W. Gurney from 1868 to 1870, and with Henry Adams from 1870 to 1872–serving during this time more as a contributing than as a managing editor. Lowell's contributions were a series on contemporary political topics (the first of the articles was on Lincoln) and critical literary pieces on writers, including Shakespeare, Chaucer, Dryden, Pope, Dante, and Rousseau. Although its influence as an informed journal of opinion was enhanced during the almost ten years of Lowell's association with it, the *North American Review* remained rather heavy and essentially humorless, plainly a critical rather than a literary publication. Lowell's more imaginative literary productions during this time were placed elsewhere, such as with the still flourishing, more lively *Atlantic Monthly*.

" 'Tis the curse of an editor that he must always be right," Lowell wrote in 1867, and he looked eagerly toward the day when he would be out from under such demands and could "kick up my heels and be as ignorant as I please!" He left the *North American Review* in 1872, but such indulgences were not allowed a Harvard professor or a United States diplomat.

Lowell the man is revealed all too infrequently in his published works. In his literary production are only glimmers of the capacious, principled intellect and the congenitally playful personality so consistently evident in his correspondence and personal intercourse, including that occasioned by his magazine editorships. "I knew and felt his greatness somehow apart from the literary proofs of it," said William Dean Howells: "he ruled my fancy and held my allegiance as a character, as a man." He had "much of the boy in him to the last," thought Howells, and being around him one experienced a "constant glow" of "incandescent sense," the result of his boyishness and of his complete embodiment of that "literary aspiration which would not and could not part itself from the love of freedom and the hope of justice." Lowell, wrote Henry James, "was strong without narrowness, he was wide without bitterness and glad without fatuity." Such judgment is possible for few writers and editors, for few human beings.

Letters:

Letters of John Holmes to James Russell Lowell and Others, edited by William Roscoe Thayer (Boston: Houghton Mifflin, 1917);

New Letters of James Russell Lowell, edited by M. A. de Wolfe Howe (New York: Harper, 1932);

The Scholar-Friends: Letters of Francis James Child and James Russell Lowell, edited by Howe and G. W. Cottrell, Jr. (Cambridge, Mass.: Harvard University Press, 1952);

James C. Austin, *Fields of The Atlantic Monthly: Letters to an Editor, 1861-1870* (San Marino, Cal.: Huntington Library, 1953);

Browning to His American Friends: Letters Between the Brownings, the Storys and James Russell Lowell, edited by Gertrude Rees Hudson (London: James & Bowes, 1965);

Transatlantic Dialogue: Selected American Correspondence of Edmund Gosse, edited by Paul F. Mattheisen and Michael Millgate (Austin: University of Texas Press, 1965).

Bibliographies:

George Willis Cooke, *A Bibliography of James Russell Lowell* (Boston: Houghton, Mifflin, 1906);

Luther S. Livingston, *A Bibliography of the First Editions in Book Form of the Writings of James Russell Lowell* (New York: Privately printed, 1914).

Biographies:

Frances H. Underwood, *The Poet and the Man: Recollections and Appreciations of James Russell Lowell* (Boston: Lee & Shepard, 1893);

Edward Everett Hale, *James Russell Lowell and His Friends* (Boston: Houghton, Mifflin, 1899);

Horace Elisha Scudder, *James Russell Lowell: A Biography,* 2 volumes (Boston: Houghton, Mifflin, 1901);

Ferris Greenslet, *James Russell Lowell: His Life and Work* (Boston: Houghton, Mifflin, 1905);

Richmond Croom Beatty, *James Russell Lowell* (Nashville, Tenn.: Vanderbilt University Press, 1942);

Leon Howard, *Victorian Knight-Errant: A Study of the Early Literary Career of James Russell Lowell* (Berkeley: University of California Press, 1952);

Martin Duberman, *James Russell Lowell* (Boston: Houghton Mifflin, 1966);

Edward Wagenknecht, *James Russell Lowell: Portrait of a Many-Sided Man* (New York: Oxford University Press, 1971);

C. David Heymann, *American Aristocracy: The Lives and Times of James Russell, Amy and Robert Lowell* (New York: Dodd, Mead, 1980).

References:

George Arms, *The Fields Were Green* (Stanford: Stanford University Press, 1953);

William C. Brownell, "Lowell," in *American Prose Masters* (New York: Scribners, 1909), pp. 271-235;

William Dean Howells, *Literary Friends and Acquaintance* (New York: Harper, 1900);

Henry James, *Essays in London and Elsewhere* (New York: Harper, 1893);

Marjorie Kaufmann, "Introduction," in *The Poetical Works of James Russell Lowell,* Cambridge Edition Revised (Boston: Houghton, Mifflin, 1978);

Herbert F. Smith, "Introduction," in *Literary Criticism of James Russell Lowell* (Lincoln: University of Nebraska Press, 1969);

G. Thomas Tanselle, "The Craftsmanship of Lowell: Revisions in *The Cathedral,*" *Bulletin of the New York Public Library,* 70 (January 1966): 50-63;

Thomas Wortham, "Introduction," in *The Biglow Papers: A Critical Edition* (Dekalb: Northern Illinois University Press, 1977).

Papers:

With the James Russell Lowell Papers and holdings in a number of other collections, the Houghton Library of Harvard University is the single most important depository for Lowell materials. Collections at the New York Public Library also contain many important Lowell papers. Other American libraries with significant holdings include the Boston Public Library, Colby College Library, the Hispanic Society Library of New York, the Huntington Library, the Library of Congress, the Massachusetts Historical Society, the Morgan Library, the University of Pennsylvania Library, the University of Texas Library at Austin, the University of Virginia Library, and the Yale University Library.

John Ames Mitchell
(17 January 1845-29 June 1918)

Therese L. Lueck
Bowling Green State University

MAJOR POSITION HELD: Copublisher and editor, *Life* (1883-1918).

BOOKS: *The Summer School of Philosophy at Mt. Desert* (New York: Holt, 1881);
The Romance of the Moon (New York: Holt, 1886);
The Last American: A Fragment from the Journal of Khan-li, Prince of Dimph-yoo-chur and Admiral in the Persian Navy (New York: Stokes, 1889; London: Gay & Bird, 1894; revised, New York: Stokes, 1902);
Life's Fairy Tales (New York: Stokes, 1892; London: Gay & Bird, 1894);
Amos Judd (New York: Scribners, 1895; London: Dent, 1896);
That First Affair, and Other Sketches (New York: Scribners, 1896);
Gloria Victis (New York: Scribners, 1897; London: Nutt, 1898); revised as *Dr. Thorne's Idea* (New York: Life, 1910);
The Pines of Lory (New York: Life, 1901);
The Villa Claudia (New York: Life, 1904; London: Henderson, 1904);
The Silent War (New York: Life, 1906);
Pandora's Box (New York: Stokes, 1911);
Drowsy (New York: Stokes, 1917).

PERIODICAL PUBLICATIONS: "Contemporary American Caricature," *Scribner's Magazine*, 6 (July-December 1889): 729-745;
"Why *Pandora's Box* Was Written," *Book News Monthly*, 30 (1912): 476-478.

John Ames Mitchell (courtesy of Mr. Henry T. Rockwell of New York)

John Ames Mitchell left his mark as an artist, an author of fiction, and an architect. In 1883 he founded *Life*, and he devoted his last thirty-six years to editing the humor magazine which was at the forefront in assessing and molding the taste of modern America's middle class. Known as a "picture paper," *Life* lampooned society and social situations. Its highbrow humor of manners was spiced with reviews of cultural events and a dash of political commentary. During the 1890s, when its artwork was at a high point, Mitchell's *Life* helped establish the sophisticated attitudes that were America's answer to the Victorian era in England. For example, Charles Press said that Charles Dana Gibson, in developing his characteristically American Gibson girl for the magazine, "changed the way women dressed and even walked and set the upper-middle-class mood for a generation." *Life* continued production until 1936, when its name was bought by Time, Incorporated.

Mitchell was born on 17 January 1845 to Asa Mitchell and Harriet Ames Mitchell and spent his boyhood in the Plymouth region of Massachusetts. E. S. Martin, the first literary editor of *Life*, writing after Mitchell's death in 1918, attributed Mitchell's independence to his Ames Pilgrim heritage: "From that derivation may have come his shrewdness, his capacity to hold on and his mastership, as well as prudence in expenditure and ability to save money."

Mitchell received his early education at Phillips Academy, Exeter, New Hampshire, and attended Lawrence Scientific School at Harvard. He studied architecture in the office of Ware and Van Brunt in Boston for two years and at the Ecole des beaux-arts, Paris, from 1867 to 1870.

When he returned to America he married Mary Mott and practiced architecture in Boston. In 1876 he returned to Paris to study drawing and painting at the Atelier Julien. While in France, he produced a series of etchings, *Croquis de l'Exposition*, which was published in *L'Art*.

After exhibiting work at the Paris Salon in 1880, Mitchell returned to New York. Intending to work as an illustrator, he established a studio at 1155 Broadway. His friend, the publisher Henry Holt, had Mitchell illustrate an edition of vers de société. In 1881 Holt published a humorous picture book by Mitchell titled *The Summer School of Philosophy at Mt. Desert*.

Mitchell wanted to translate his interest in black-and-white drawings into work for an American audience, but he could not find a vehicle he considered suitable. The existing American humor magazines, *Puck* and *Judge*, catered to common taste and emphasized political humor; Mitchell's work was stylized and highbrow. He approached Holt about starting a magazine but received only advice against such a move.

Despite similar advice from others, Mitchell persisted. He asked Edward Sanford Martin, onetime editor of the *Harvard Lampoon*, to edit the literary side of the magazine. Martin agreed and put Mitchell in touch with another Harvard graduate, Andrew Miller, who became the business manager. In an age that was accustomed to the quick demise of budding periodicals, starting a magazine was a risky venture, and Mitchell's lack of experience was poor insurance against failure. Gillis Brothers were persuaded to become the magazine's printers by his appeal to their aesthetic sensibilities: "But this paper will be a very different thing from any of its predecessors—of a higher grade and far more artistic." Mitchell initially invested a legacy of ten thousand dollars in the venture. No one considered the amount adequate capital with which to start a magazine. One month later Mitchell invested another thousand dollars.

The first issue of *Life* was dated 4 January 1883. Since Mitchell had provided the initial inspiration and financial support, he was always considered the editor in chief. Writing in the 4 January 1923 issue of *Life*, Brander Matthews said, "*Life* was Mitchell's and his alone. He knew what he wanted it to be, even if he was not able to attain his ideal in the first number or in the twentieth.... When success came at last *Life* became what its founder had intended before it began."

Mitchell consciously set out to appeal to the middle class. By the second issue, the subhead of the magazine read, "A new, illustrated weekly, humorous, satirical, refined." In the 4 January 1923 issue Robert Bridges, a contributor who wrote book reviews under the byline Droch, recalled: "The very first number of *Life* made an appeal by its appearance, attitude, and associations to young college men. There was no periodical appealing to that spirit of gaiety, satire, and humor which the *Harvard Lampoon* had been first to cultivate." Amid much punning on the word *life*, the first issue announced in its editorial: "We wish to have some fun in this paper, and to have it as nearly of the right sort as may be. And while we do not pledge ourselves to invariable jocularity, we shall try to domesticate as much as possible of the casual cheerfulness that is drifting about in an unfriendly world." It continued, "We shall have something to say about religion, about politics, fashion, society, literature, the stage, the stock exchange, and the police station, and we will speak out what is in our mind as fairly, as truthfully, and as decently as we know how."

Although it seemed even to the optimistic Mitchell (called "the General" by his employees) that the best draftsmen and writers were monopolized by other publications, *Life* carried an admirable staff from the beginning. It drew particularly from the *Harvard Lampoon*, which had suspended publication by the early 1880s. With capable staffers on both sides, neither words nor artwork were sacrificed to the domination of the other; the mixture was important. One editor said, "Great stress was laid upon the right wording under the pictures." In a special issue of *Book News Monthly* dedicated to Mitchell, Thomas L. Masson, who became literary editor of *Life* in 1895, said: "We have a habit in the *Life* office of giving some of our best jokes (or the jokes we think best) to be illustrated by artists." By Septem-

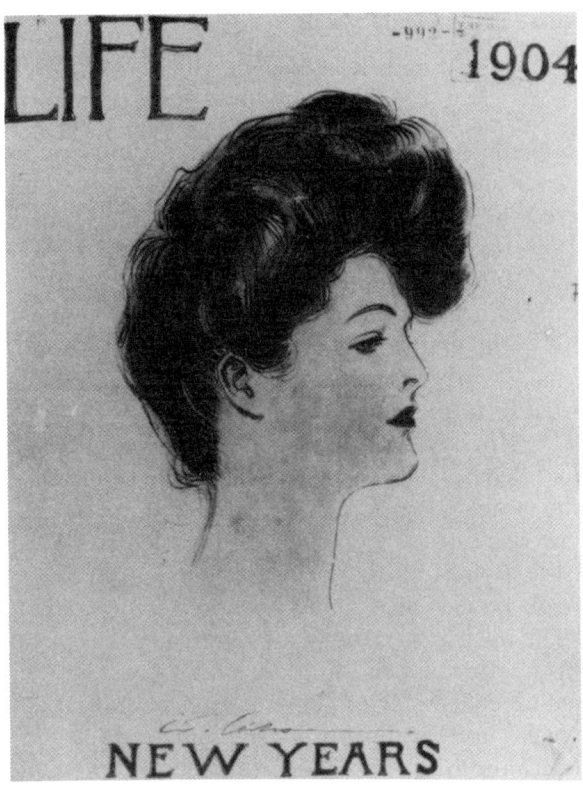

Cover by Charles Dana Gibson for an issue of the humor magazine founded by Mitchell in 1883

ber 1883 the magazine had broken even, and the trend continued upward. Early in its second year circulation rose above 20,000. Just as *Life* was showing signs of success, however, a relapse of malaria forced Martin to leave New York (he returned to the magazine in 1888). When he turned in the quarter-interest initially allotted him by Mitchell, Mitchell and Miller became partners. By 1890 circulation reached 50,000, and by 1916 there were 150,000 readers.

Mitchell the artist set the tone of *Life* by illustrating the early issues with drawings which attempted to promote what he saw as higher social values; they also show his empathy with France. Mitchell designed and drew the cover and the motif at the top of the editorial page, an allegory of life showing a knight, lance forward, chasing a devil, with the caption "While there is Life there's Hope." The first two-page illustrations in *Life*, an often-used format that began in the tenth issue, were drawn by Mitchell. His views in these spreads are easily discerned. For instance, in his two-page illustration for the sixteenth issue, he depicts the Statue of Liberty wearing a sandwich board. The sign reads, "Kind foreigner as you sail into this harbor please drop a few coppers in the box: This statue is the gift of a friendly nation to the city of New York but we can not raise the funds for a pedestal–Please help us!" The statue, a recent gift of France, stands towering, its skirts in the water of the harbor surrounded by small boats. The caption reads, "The Pearl and the Swine."

Empathy was not the only aspect of Mitchell's contact with France to emerge in the magazine. While abroad Mitchell had been introduced to innovative artistic techniques and printing processes, both of which he put to use. Since he intended the magazine as a vehicle for pen-and-ink line drawings, Mitchell was willing to use new processes, such as zinc etching, which could reproduce line drawings directly instead of having them engraved on a wood block. Engraving the drawings on wood was an expensive and laborious process to which some magazines adhered long after Mitchell had switched. The halftone, a black-and-white illustration in which light and dark shades are reproduced by means of small and large dots, was introduced during the 1880s, and Mitchell made use of the process by the Christmas issue of 1886. Although color was standard for later issues of *Life*, Mitchell used color only for holiday issues at first. For instance, with the Christmas number for the magazine's first year, December 1883, Mitchell's cover ran in blue and red.

Mitchell encouraged artists to provide line drawings, silhouettes, cartoons, and washes. Martin recalled, "When he started *Life* there was no considerable market for such drawings as he wanted, and they were not made. He had to develop that industry and did develop it. As soon as he established a market the merchants of drawings began to come to it, and he helped a great many of them to perfect themselves in the trade." In 1923 Mitchell described his ideals of illustration: "It was necessary that drawings representing scenes in high life should be of a style and quality unlike anything then published this side of the Atlantic.... For *Life*'s uses, such drawings, while being true to nature and clever artistically, must show a lightness of touch, an ease, brilliancy, and a force of expression which are not demanded in other work. Moreover, a sense of humor, a playfulness, and a gentle exaggeration are indispensable to the perfect work."

In its energy and variety *Life* reflected Mitchell's personality and taste. Masson said Mitchell was in "horror of anything that is vague

Cartoon by Gibson for a 1904 issue of Life

or decadent, either in literature or art." Both in pictures and words, *Life* also carried Mitchell's arguments against the practices of modern medicine and its code of ethics. He railed against vivisection, the performance of surgical experiments on living animals. Favorable images of children and animals abounded in the magazine. In an ode to *Life* in the fortieth anniversary issue, a poem by Arthur Guitarman was quoted partially:

> What multitudes of every known degree
>   Amid that throng the dazzled eye discovers!
> What beasts that never were on land or sea,
>   What hosts of pretty girls from painted covers,
> What packs of all the breeds of dog there be,
>   What troops of rich men, poor men, lawyers, lovers,
> And children–bless their hearts, the little stupids!
> And what a very avalanche of cupids!

Mitchell used *Life* to sponsor a Fresh Air fund which made possible the establishment of summer camps for underprivileged urban children. Later the magazine raised funds for French war orphans. Perhaps because of his upper-middle-class sense of values and ideas of individual worth, Mitchell laid great importance on personal involvement. He also provided others a platform, even if their views differed from his. In Martin's words, he "said what he thought was right, and if some one thought it was wrong, he tried to give him room in *Life* to say so."

In *Book News Monthly* Sinclair Lewis noted that Mitchell "began to write novels, as a pastime, and it is as a novelist that he is best known." His most popular works were *Amos Judd* (1895) and *The Pines of Lory* (1901). He illustrated his novels *The Summer School of Philosophy at Mt. Desert* (1881), *The Villa Claudia* (1904), and *Pandora's Box* (1911).

Mitchell supported the Spanish-American War in *Life* and, because of his love for France, was an early supporter of the involvement of the United States in World War I. He lived to see the United States join the war but did not live to see the outcome, dying of apoplexy at his summer home in Ridgefield, Connecticut, on 29 June 1918.

Although staffed with capable artists and employing notables such as Norman Rockwell, Robert Sherwood, Will Rogers, Dorothy Parker, and Dr. Seuss, *Life* lost its influence after Mitchell's death. None of the many editors who succeeded him used experimental processes to enhance its artwork or had the foresight that had enabled Mitchell to keep abreast of American social thought. Readers, like the returning veterans of World War I, increasingly turned to more innovative publications such as the *New Yorker*.

References:

Book News Monthly, special Mitchell issue, 30 (March 1912);

John Flautz, *Life, the Gentle Satirist* (Bowling Green, Ohio: Popular Press, 1972);

Life, special anniversary issue, 21 (January 1893);

Life, special anniversary issue, 81 (January 1923);

E. S. Martin, "John Ames Mitchell, 1845-1918," *Harvard Graduates' Magazine*, 27 (September 1918): 27-30;

Charles Press, *The Political Cartoon* (East Brunswick, N.J.: Associated University Presses, 1981).

Papers:

The library at Princeton University contains letters from Mitchell. The Beinecke Rare Book and Manuscript Library, Yale University, contains two of his manuscripts.

Charles Jacobs Peterson

(20 July 1819-4 March 1887)

Karen Nipps
Library Company of Philadelphia

MAJOR POSITIONS HELD: Coeditor, *Casket, and Philadelphia Monthly Magazine, Embracing Every Department of Literature: Embellished with Engravings, the Quarterly Fashions, and Music, Arranged for the Piano-Forte, Harp, and Guitar* (1839-1842), renamed *Graham's Lady's and Gentleman's Magazine (The Casket and Gentleman's United). Embracing Every Department of Literature: Embellished with Engravings, Fashions, and Music, Arranged for the Piano-Forte, Harp, and Guitar* in 1841; coeditor and copublisher, *Saturday Evening Post*, renamed *United States Saturday Post and Chronicle* in 1842 (1840-1843); coeditor and publisher (1842-1853), editor and publisher (1854-1887), *Lady's World*, renamed *Ladies' National Magazine* in 1842, renamed *Peterson's Magazine of Art, Literature and Fashion* in 1849, renamed *Peterson's Magazine* in 1851, renamed *Peterson's Ladies' National Magazine* in 1853, renamed *Peterson's Magazine* in 1855; editor and publisher, *Neal's Saturday Gazette* (1848-1849).

BOOKS: *The Algerine and Other Tales*, as Harry Danforth (Boston: Gleason, 1846);
Agnes Courtenay; A Tale of the Old Dominion (Amherst: Nims, 1847);
The Oath of Marion: A Story of the Revolution (Boston: Gleason, 1847);
The Military Heroes of the Revolution: With a Narrative of the War of Independence (Philadelphia: Leary, 1848); republished as *A History of the American Revolution, and Biographical Sketches of the Military Heroes of the War of Independence* (Philadelphia: Gihon, 1852); republished in *Peterson's American Wars: A History of the Wars of the United States, containing a History of the Revolution and of the Wars of 1812 and Mexico, with Biographical Sketches of All the Prominent American Military Heroes Engaged in Those Wars* (Philadelphia: J. B. Smith, 1857);
The Military Heroes of the War of 1812, with a Narrative of the War (Philadelphia: Leary, 1848); republished in *Peterson's American Wars* (1857);

Charles Jacobs Peterson (Dictionary of American Portraits, edited by Hayward and Blanche Cirker [New York: Dover, 1967])

The Military Heroes of the War with Mexico, with a Narrative of the War (Philadelphia: Leary, 1848); republished in *Peterson's American Wars* (1857);
Grace Dudley; Or, Arnold at Saratoga (Philadelphia: Peterson, 1849);
Cruising in the Last War (Philadelphia: Peterson, 1850);
The Valley Farm; Or, The Autobiography of an Orphan, as edited by Peterson (Philadelphia: Peterson, 1850);

General History of the World, from the Earliest Period to the Year 1840: Embracing an Account of the Origin and Manners and Customs of All the Nations of the Earth; the Rise and Progress of Judaism, Paganism, and Christianity: &c. &c. &c.; . . . With a Continuation, Containing an Account of the Various Revolutions and Wars in All Parts of the World, from 1840 to the Present Time. . . . Forming Together a Complete Narrative from the Creation to the Year 1850, by Peterson, Charles von Rotteck (Karl Wenzeslaus Rodecker von Rotteck), and Frederick Jones (Philadelphia: Leary, 1851);

The Cabin and the Parlor; or, Slaves and Masters, as J. Thornton Randolph (Philadelphia: Peterson, 1852); republished as *Courtenay Hall; Or, The Hospitality and Life in a Planter's Family: A True Tale of Virginia Life,* as Randolph (Philadelphia: Peterson, 185?);

A History of the United States Navy (Philadelphia: Gihon, 1852); republished as *The American Navy: Being an Authentic History of the United States Navy, and Biographical Sketches of American Naval Heroes, from the Formation of the Navy to the Close of the Mexican War* (Philadelphia: J. B. Smith, 1856);

Kate Aylesford: A Story of the Refugees (Philadelphia: Peterson/Boston: Phillips, Sampson, 1855); republished as *The Heiress of Sweetwater: A Love Story,* as Randolph (Philadelphia: Peterson, 1873);

Mabel; Or, Darkness and Dawn (Philadelphia: Peterson, 1857);

The Old Stone Mansion (Philadelphia: Peterson, 1859);

Rome (Philadelphia: Dreer, 1883).

PERIODICAL PUBLICATIONS: "The Persecutor's Daughter," *Graham's Lady's and Gentleman's Magazine,* 21 (December 1842): 320-325;

"The Roman Martyrs," *Graham's American Monthly Magazine of Literature, Art, and Fashion,* 28 (July 1845): 6-11; (August 1845): 75-81;

"The Young Dragoon," *Graham's American Monthly Magazine of Literature, Art, and Fashion,* 34 (June 1849): 379-382;

"George R. Graham," *Graham's American Monthly Magazine of Literature, Art, and Fashion,* 37 (July 1850): 43-44;

"John Randolph of Roanoke," *Graham's American Monthly Magazine of Literature, Art, and Fashion,* 38 (March 1851): 199-206;

"The Disguised Frigate," *Sartain's Union Magazine of Literature and Art,* 8 (April 1851): 245-248;

"The Heroine of the Border," *Peterson's Magazine,* 21 (January 1852): 70-74;

"Mormonism and the Mormons," *Graham's American Monthly Magazine of Literature, Art, and Fashion,* 42 (May 1853): 531-540;

"The Poetry of Read," *Peterson's Magazine,* 29 (February 1856): 204-208.

Charles Jacobs Peterson was the founder of *Ladies' National Magazine,* better known as *Peterson's National Magazine,* the most popular women's periodical in America during the mid-nineteenth century. As the owner, publisher, manager, editor, and major contributor for this magazine's first forty-five years, he helped create a new market in American publishing. Peterson also helped foster the growth of an immensely popular middlebrow American literature largely forgotten today, much of it written by his fellow Philadelphians. He was the author of many popular works of fiction, nonfiction, and poetry; a member of the most prestigious literary and social clubs in the city; and a close friend of such literary figures as Charles Kingsley, George Rex Graham, Louis A. Godey, Edgar Allan Poe, James Russell Lowell, and Frances Hodgson Burnett.

Peterson was born in Philadelphia on 20 July 1819, the eldest son of Thomas and Elizabeth Jacobs Peterson. Peterson's Swedish ancestors had immigrated to the Delaware Valley in the early seventeenth century. Peterson had four brothers; three of them (Theophilus B., Thomas, and George W.) went on to found the highly successful publishing firm of T. B. Peterson and Brothers. This firm published most of Charles Peterson's work and for many years occupied the same Chestnut Street building as his magazine. Two cousins, Henry and Robert Evans Peterson, were also active in literature and publishing in nineteenth century Philadelphia.

Peterson entered the University of Pennsylvania in 1838 to study law but remained there only a year. A fellow classmate was Graham, and for a time after Peterson left the university the two also studied in the same law offices. From 1838 to 1840 they are listed as coeditors of the *Daily Focus,* a small Philadelphia penny daily. In 1839 Peterson had been admitted to the bar; he listed himself as an attorney-at-law in the directories in the 1840s, but he seems never to have practiced.

Graham appears to have been a decisive force in shaping Peterson's early journalistic career. In 1839 Graham bought a local magazine called *Atkinson's Casket, or Gems of Literature, Wit, and Sentiment* (soon renamed *Graham's Lady's and Gentleman's Magazine*) and employed his friend Peterson as an assistant editor. This position was of a general managerial nature, but Peterson was also specifically responsible for the fashion-related aspects of the magazine. The same year, Graham bought a half-interest in another magazine, the *Saturday Evening Post*, and in March 1840 he arranged for Peterson to purchase the other half from John Du Solle.

Soon Graham suggested to Peterson that he start his own magazine. Graham felt that a cheap magazine devoted to fashion was a natural choice for Peterson and that it would probably fare well; he may also have hoped that such a magazine would cut into the business of his major rival, *Godey's Lady's Book*. Founded in 1830, *Godey's* had been a pioneer in the field of ladies' magazine publishing and was still by far the leader. Following Graham's advice, Peterson bought the *Lady's World of Fashion* from V. Quarre, a Frenchman, and published the first number in January 1842 under the name *Lady's World*; later that year he changed the title to *Ladies' National Magazine*.

The newly styled magazine won popular favor immediately. In 1843 Peterson sold his interest in the *Saturday Evening Post*–by then renamed the *United States Saturday Post and Chronicle*–to Samuel D. Patterson and immersed himself wholly in his new venture. He established himself first at 302 Chestnut Street in the heart of publishers' row. In 1855 he changed the magazine's name to *Peterson's Magazine*, the title by which it is generally known despite more than thirteen variations over the years.

Peterson's Magazine was modeled after the popular French fashion magazines which featured fashion talk and fashion plates. Like *Godey's*, *Peterson's* was a monthly with a large octavo format containing light fiction (in serial and short story form), poetry, short book reviews and critical essays, recipes, gardening tips, occasional sheet music, and knitting and sewing patterns. Both periodicals contained copious illustrations.

The number of similar magazines that quickly appeared (and often just as quickly disappeared) in the 1840s, 1850s and 1860s is indicative of the popularity of this sort of periodical. Besides *Godey's* and *Peterson's*, some of the more successful titles were T. S. Arthur's *Home Maga-*

Advertisement for the literary weekly coedited and copublished by Peterson from 1840 to 1843

zine, Eliza Leslie's *Miss Leslie's Magazine*, Joseph C. Neal's *Saturday Gazette*, William W. Snowden's *Ladies Companion*, and the *Lady's Wreath*. A contemptuous Poe wrote in 1845 that such magazines "are so nearly alike, that if the covers were changed, it would not be easy to distinguish one from the other. They nearly all have the same contributors and the same embellishers."

How did *Peterson's* compare with these competitors? In the early months of his magazine's publication, Peterson wrote to a friend that Graham was "verging into solid literature slowly, cutting the fashion plates . . . and indulging in more heavy prose" and that his own magazine "will slide into the position left by Graham–that is we will make it light, spicy, romantic, and lady-like, sprinkling into it, here and there, critical articles, etc., etc. It will be like the Lady's Book and Lady's Companion, though at a less price." The great success of *Peterson's Magazine* lies in the fact that its owner kept to his plan. While never claiming that his magazine was especially sophisticated, Peterson saw it as a true repository of culture, both amusing and instructive. Moreover, *Peterson's* annual subscription rate was two dollars while most of its competitors, including *Godey's*, charged three dollars. As Peterson reiterated time and again in his editorials, "Our aim is to combine cheapness with real merit."

One way that Peterson achieved his goal of cheapness and merit was through his choice of contributors. Graham and Godey paid such writers as Poe, Emerson, and Longfellow at a scale commensurate with their reputations. On the other hand, Peterson was keenly aware that the more one paid for a contribution the more one would have to charge the public for a magazine. As a result, he wrote much of the magazine himself and relied heavily on new talent and a group of regular contributors, most of them women.

Most notable of the regulars was Ann S. Stephens, who had worked with Graham and Peterson at *Graham's Magazine* and had joined Peterson when he left his friend's magazine to found his own. This was no little draw as Stephens had previously established a faithful following of her own through her earlier editorial work on the *Portland Magazine* and as the author of numerous historical romances. Through 1847 she was such a major contributor that she was named on the magazine's annual title page as editor, though Peterson always maintained primary editorial control. Stephens left her post at *Peterson's* in the mid 1850s but remained a frequent contributor until her death in 1886.

Peterson's was promoted as a magazine written primarily by and for women. As Peterson stated in a March 1845 editorial, "The plan we have chalked out for the conduct of this magazine will make it a complete treasure house for the production of female writers so that its volumes will hereafter be referred to as containing the best refutation of the mistaken opinion that the intellect of women is inferior to that of men...." Besides Stephens, regulars included many of the most popular women authors of the period: Emily H. May, Frances S. Osgood, Elizabeth Oakes Smith, Lydia Sigourney, Lydia Jane Pierson, and Mary V. Spencer. One notable female author whose talents Peterson recognized early on was Frances Hodgson Burnett. "Ethel's Sir Lancelot," Mrs. Burnett's first attributed story, appeared in the November 1868 issue of *Peterson's*, and the author remained a faithful contributor to the magazine throughout her life.

Male contributors to *Peterson's* were in a distinct minority. Among the more well-known of these were T. S. Arthur, Thomas Buchanan Read, Frank Lee Benedict, and Graham. Oddly enough, Peterson refused to accept James Russell Lowell's work for his periodical, though they had become friends while both were in their twenties. Peterson certainly recognized Lowell's gifts as a writer, but he encouraged him to place his work in more literary magazines than his own.

Peterson took special pride in his magazine's hand-colored engraved fashion plates. *Peterson's* and *Godey's* were the only two magazines of the time to feature these lavish plates every month, though other magazines occasionally ran engravings of a lesser quality. Accompanying "Les Modes Parisiennes" in each issue were one or two engraved plates, along with numerous uncolored wood engravings. He employed most of the illustrators and illustrative techniques of the time, though for financial reasons he steered away from the work of such prominent artists as John Sartain. The relief-cuts were sometimes called vulgar by contemporaries, but the mezzotints and other engravings were of the highest quality.

One major reason for *Peterson's* popularity was the lack of overt political and controversial content. Peterson disliked sensationalism and wanted to entertain his readers. Throughout the 1860s and 1870s the Civil War was never mentioned as a political reality in *Peterson's*. Critics were exasperated by this blandness. In 1849 John Tamlin wrote that the magazine was "tasty in the arrangements but weak in the matter" and that its intent, along with *Godey's* and *Graham's*, was to "ruin and vitiate the taste for strong and manly food.... Everything they send forth is so diluted that scarcely anything has the consistency of pap. Long stories about love ... surfeit the mind with the extreme silliness of each conceit."

During a period of the rapid expansion of this country's economic, social, and physical frontiers, Peterson worked conscientiously to make his magazine a truly national periodical. He wrote in the December 1850 issue: "We have arranged for a tale of New England, a novel of the Middle States, a story of the South, a fiction of the West, a legend of the Border, and a romance of the South-West." He was acutely aware of the

Cover for an issue of the magazine founded by Peterson in 1842 as the Lady's World. *It became the most popular women's periodical in America during the mid nineteenth century.*

differences in the tastes and values in the different regions and wanted to appeal to the women in each area. The greatest concentration of readers was in the South and West.

This combination of a feel for popular taste, a cheap price tag, and national marketing resulted in a soaring circulation for the magazine. By the start of the Civil War *Peterson's* rivaled *Godey's*, and in 1866 its editor proudly proclaimed "*Peterson's* has now, and has had for years the largest circulation of any ladies' periodical in the United States, or even in the world." In the early 1870s circulation reached its highest mark, over 165,000. Historians have considered *Godey's* the most significant of the nineteenth century ladies' periodicals. However, the consistently higher circulation figures of *Peterson's* cannot be ignored when assessing its significance to the Victorian American reader. Not until the late 1880s did the magazine's sales begin to decline.

Apart from his own publishing efforts, Peterson was also an editorial writer for the *Philadephia Bulletin* when it was begun in 1847 and a main editorial writer for the *Public Ledger* during most of his life. Like so many Victorian writers, Peterson wrote an almost endless stream of verse and prose. Much of this material appeared in either his own or associates' magazines; he wrote for both *Graham's* and Sartain's *Union Magazine*, just as Graham, Sartain, and other magazine publishers contributed to his magazine. A great deal of this appeared anonymously and is therefore impossible to attribute. All of Peterson's poetry was privately printed in limited quantity for friends and family and is today quite rare; this is also the case with some of his separately printed prose. He published roughly ten separately printed works of fiction from 1849 to 1859. Most are historical novels with a distinctly nostalgic tone, reminiscent of the works of fellow Philadelphians Stephens, Burnett, and Henry Peterson. The bygone South, particularly of the Revolutionary period, was a favorite setting. Most of his stories are centered upon the trials of a heroine who is lively, courageous, beautiful, poised, and extremely moral. The language is typically flowery and sentimental. His narratives rely heavily on dialogue, and he is unusually adept at capturing Negro dialect. All of these elements are exhibited in one of his better-known works, *The Cabin and the Parlor* (1852). With its portrayal of the virtuous whites and happy blacks on Southern plantations, this work was considered even by contemporaries as a pro-South antidote to Harriet Beecher Stowe's *Uncle Tom's Cabin* (1852). Although Peterson was a staunch member of the Republican Club, which supported Lincoln in 1860, and of the Union League, he was not an abolitionist ("... the greatest objection I have against Abolitionists is their wholesale damnation of every man who don't think as they think.... It takes a strong testimony to persuade me I am wiser than my fathers").

Peterson wrote four separately published works of nonfiction, all patriotic histories of American military and naval heroes, plus a continuation of Karl Wenzeslaus Rodecker von Rotteck and Frederick Jones's *General History of the World, from the Earliest Period to the Year 1840*. Peterson also wrote a great deal of periodical nonfiction, the most notable piece being a biographical sketch of his friend Graham (*Graham's Magazine*, July 1850) which is still used as a major biographical source. Peterson's nonfiction shared the weaknesses of his fiction. His prose was praised by the press of the time but holds little distinction today. His portraits of people and places–be they real or imagined–were bright and lively but at times so detailed that the coherence of the narrative was threatened.

Perhaps the most famous event of Peterson's life was his encounter with Poe, which took place while he was still assistant editor of *Graham's Magazine*. In 1841 Poe was hired as a literary editor at *Graham's*. He had previously worked at William E. Burton's *Gentleman's Magazine*, which Graham had purchased and merged with his own magazine in 1840. Many of Poe's short stories and poems including "Murders in the Rue Morgue" and "Masque of the Red Death" were published in *Graham's* both during and after his employment there. But he was never happy at the magazine, and in May 1842 he left *Graham's*, his place taken by another recently hired editor, Rufus Griswold. There are many versions of the story, none entirely reliable, but the gist seems to be that Peterson, Poe, and Griswold were competing for power and for Graham's regard. Graham, later in life, wrote that a brief office quarrel between Peterson and Poe ended with his firing Poe. Poe claimed that he quit; to a friend on 25 May 1842 he wrote, "My reason for resigning was disgust at the namby-pamby character of the magazine . . . the contemptible pictures, fashion-plates, music, and love-tales." Whatever happened in May 1842, Peterson always spoke highly of Poe and of his works and was among the many who gave him money. The worst he could say was that Poe was unstable, as indeed he must have been.

From contemporary accounts Peterson was a witty, sophisticated, intelligent, genial, and, above all, a warm and kind man. His magazine's history and popularity attest to his business sense, industriousness, and modest tastes. His generosity and conscientiousness can be seen in his personal relationships and his active civic life. Peterson was said to have loved history and astronomy. He was a member of many of the literary and social clubs of the time, the Press Club, the Philadelphia Club, and the Union League most notable among them. At a time when women's roles in society were diminishing, Peterson championed their rights as workers, individuals, and women.

Peterson and his wife, Sarah Powell Howard, whom he married in 1845, lived in extremely comfortable circumstances in Center City Philadelphia. Many of their summers were spent at their mansion in Newport, socializing with such luminaries as Julia Ward Howe, Bret Harte, and Alexander Agassiz. The family traveled to Europe in 1866-1867. His later life was saddened by the drowning of his only son. When Peterson died on 4 March 1887 his wife took over the management of the magazine. Its popularity was beginning to wane; but in his time Peterson knew what his colleagues were capable of and what the public wanted, and he encouraged and served both accordingly.

References:

Joseph Jackson, *Literary Landmarks of Philadelphia* (Philadelphia: McKay, 1930);

Ellis Paxson Oberholtzer, *Literary History of Philadelphia* (Philadelphia: Jacobs, 1906);

Arthur Peterson, "Members of the Peterson Family in the Publishing Business in Philadelphia between 1840 and 1890," *Pennsylvania Magazine of History and Biography*, 36, no. 1 (1912): 117-119;

Ann Prestwich, "Charles Jacobs Peterson, Editor and Friend of Lowell and Poe," M.A. thesis, Columbia University, 1938;

J. Albert Robbins, "George R. Graham, Philadelphia Publisher," *Pennsylvania Magazine of History and Biography*, 75 (July 1951): 279-294;

Edward Robins, "Some Philadelphia Men of Letters," *Pennsylvania Magazine of History and Biography*, 50, no. 4 (1926): 316-343;

Albert H. Smyth, *The Philadelphia Magazines and Their Contributors* (Philadelphia: Lindsay, 1892);

Bertha Monica Stearns, "Philadelphia Magazines for Ladies: 1830-1860," *Pennsylvania Magazine of History and Biography*, 69 (July 1945): 207-219;

University of Pennsylvania, *Biographical Catalogue of the Matriculates of the College* (Philadelphia, 1893);

Owen Wister, *The Philadelphia Club: 1834-1934* (Philadelphia, 1934).

William Sydney Porter
(O. Henry)
(11 September 1862-5 June 1910)

Carolyn Garrett Cline
University of Texas at Austin

See also the Porter entries in *DLB 12: American Realists and Naturalists* and *DLB 78: American Short-Story Writers, 1880-1910*.

MAJOR POSITION HELD: Editor and publisher, *Iconoclast*, renamed *Rolling Stone* (1894-1895).

BOOKS: *Cabbages and Kings* (New York: McClure, Phillips, 1904; London: Nash, 1904);
The Four Million (New York: McClure, Phillips, 1906; London: Nash, 1916);
The Trimmed Lamp (New York: McClure, Phillips, 1907; London: Hodder & Stoughton, 1916);
Heart of the West (New York: McClure, 1907; London: Nash, 1912);
The Voice of the City (New York: McClure, 1908; London: Nash, 1916);
The Gentle Grafter (New York: McClure, 1908; London: Nash, 1916);
Roads of Destiny (New York: Doubleday, Page, 1909; London: Nash, 1913);
Options (New York & London: Harper, 1909; London: Harper, 1910);
Strictly Business (New York: Doubleday, Page, 1910; London: Nash, 1916);
Whirligigs (New York: Doubleday, Page, 1910; London: Hodder & Stoughton, 1916);
Sixes and Sevens (Garden City, N.Y.: Doubleday, Page, 1911; London: Hodder & Stoughton, 1916);
Rolling Stones (Garden City, N.Y.: Doubleday, Page, 1912; London: Nash, 1916);
Waifs and Strays (Garden City, N.Y.: Doubleday, Page, 1917; London: Hodder & Stoughton, 1920);
O. Henryana (Garden City, N.Y.: Doubleday, Page, 1920);
Postscripts, edited by Florence Stratton (New York & London: Harper, 1923);
O. Henry Encore, edited by Mary S. Harrell (Dallas: Upshaw, 1936; New York: Doubleday,

William Sydney Porter

Doran, 1939; London: Hodder & Stoughton, 1939);
Stories of the Old Texas Land Office (Austin: Museums Committee of the Daughters of the Republic of Texas, 1964).

Collections: *The Complete Writings of O. Henry*, 14 volumes (Garden City, N.Y.: Doubleday, Page, 1917);
The Biographical Edition, 18 volumes (Garden City, N.Y.: Doubleday, Doran, 1929);

The Complete Works of O. Henry, 2 volumes (Garden City, N.Y.: Doubleday, 1953).

PLAY PRODUCTION: *Lo!, A Musical Comedy*, book and lyrics by Porter and Franklin P. Adams, music by A. Baldwin Sloane, Aurora, Illinois, 25 August 1909.

OTHER: J. W. Wilbarger, *Indian Depredations in Texas*, illustrated with woodcuts by Porter (Austin, Texas: Hutchings Printing House, 1889).

William Sydney Porter is best remembered as the prolific writer O. Henry, whose books and short stories earned him worldwide popularity. The self-styled "Caliph of Bagdad-on-the-Subway," the man beset by personal disasters, the driven, hard-drinking author was a far cry from the dashing young Will Porter who founded an audacious little magazine in Austin, Texas, in 1894. Most biographies tell little of this period in Porter's life, but during his years in Texas Porter developed the distinctive style which characterized his later writings; this was also his last period of unclouded happiness.

Porter's Texas years have been obscured by the author's own refusal to discuss the period, for he remained deeply ashamed of the prison term he served for the embezzlement of $854.08 from the First National Bank of Austin. In his only news interview, in the *New York Sunday Times* in 1909, the date of his birth is incorrect, and no mention is made of the wife he married in Austin or the two children who were born there. Porter's Austin period was memorable for many reasons, and several reliable accounts of the period have been reconstructed from contemporary sources and Porter's friends from that period.

Porter was born in Greensboro, North Carolina, on 11 September 1862 to Algernon Sydney Porter, a doctor, and Mary Jane Virginia Swain Porter. His family life was cultured and comfortable until Porter's mother died in 1865 after the birth of a third child. His grief-stricken father moved in with his own mother and lost interest in medicine, preferring to tinker with mechanical inventions such as a perpetual-motion waterwheel. Porter and his sister Shirley were supervised by their grandmother and by an aunt, Evelina Porter, who ran a private primary school.

As a youth Porter demonstrated a love of and talent for drawing. He was offered tuition and board at a boys' school in North Carolina in return for his drawings, but he declined because he was unable to pay for uniforms and books. At nineteen his health was poor, and Dr. and Mrs. James Hall of Greensboro invited him to accompany them on a visit to their three sons in Texas. Porter remained at the Hall ranch in LaSalle County enjoying the frontier life and continuing his drawing. He completed forty illustrations for a proposed book, but the author became discouraged and destroyed both the manuscript and Porter's drawings.

After two years Porter moved to Austin, where he stayed with another Greensboro family, the Harrells. Austin was still a young city, but it had a new university, the state capital, and an active social life which welcomed the handsome young man. Porter, then twenty-one, was short, slight, and well-mannered, with wide gray eyes and an attractive mustache. An early contemporary described Porter to biographer L. W. Payne as quiet, steady, and unassuming. "He had a wholesome, sweet, lovable disposition, like a woman–almost effeminate–quiet and demure. He never violated the conventions of ordinary social life. 'When in Rome,' he used to say, 'we must do as Romans do.' He was wonderfully adaptable. He read character and noticed every point about every person he met."

Porter seemed content to lead a rather aimless life. Shortly after arriving in Austin he got a job at the Morley Brothers Drug Company, but after a few weeks he tired of the routine and resigned. For a year he played the role of bachelor socialite, active in a city militia company, singing groups, and the choirs of at least three churches.

In 1885 the cornerstone of the new Texas Capitol was laid, and according to legend it was either at that ceremony or at the ball which followed when Porter met seventeen-year-old Athol Estes. He pursued her for two years, while she finished high school. His infatuation may have made him more concerned about finding a career, for in the autumn of 1885 he was hired as a bookkeeper for one hundred dollars a month, a substantial salary for the period. Two years later his friend Dick Hall became state land commissioner and hired Porter as an assistant compiling draftsman. On the night of 5 July 1887, after Athol had graduated from high school, the couple eloped, arriving by surprise at their minister's house. After rather gracelessly admitting that they were old enough to know what they were doing, the minister wed them. Athol's mother, who had preferred a richer suitor, flew into a fury; she refused to speak to the minister or even to attend church for several months.

The Porters settled into a small house and a happy life. Athol urged her husband to write, and his first publications appeared in 1887 in the *Detroit Free Press* and *Truth*. Their first child, born on 6 May 1888, was a son who was to have been named Will, but he died in infancy. Their second child, Margaret Worth Porter, was born on 30 September 1889. The Porters returned from a visit to North Carolina to find Porter's land office job a casualty of Hall's unsuccessful run for governor.

Porter again worked in a drugstore, then in February 1891 took a job which would forever mark his life: a position as a teller at the First National Bank. He was unsuited to the bank work, and customers reported that they discovered the teller sketching and writing while he was supposed to be counting money. In 1894 he began his venture into publishing.

Three years earlier, W. C. Brann had founded a radical newspaper called the *Iconoclast*, but the publication had lasted only a few months in conservative Austin. Porter heard that Brann's equipment was available, and with two cosigners he bought the press in March 1894. Two issues of Porter's *Iconoclast* appeared in April 1894, but Brann wanted to issue a paper under his old title, so Porter released his claim on it. The newly christened *Rolling Stone* appeared on 28 April 1894 as volume 1, number 3. Porter and his father-in-law were the publishers, and they set forth their goals in the first issue. "The *Rolling Stone* is a weekly newspaper published in Austin, Texas, every Saturday and will endeavor to fill a long-felt want, that does not appear by the way, to be altogether insatiable at present. The idea is to fill its pages with matter that will make a heartrending appeal to every lover of good literature, and every person who has a taste for print; and a dollar and a half for a year's subscription; six months, $1.00.... Each number will contain stories, humorous sketches, poems, jokes, properly labeled, side-splitting references to the mother-in-law, the goat, Governor Hogg, and the states of the weather and Texas."

Years later, in the *Times* interview, Porter gave a jumbled account of his *Rolling Stone* endeavor: "As a youngster I always had an intense desire to be an artist. It wasn't until I was 21 that I developed the idea that I'd like to write. After about a year on the Houston *Post* I got an opportunity to exercise both of these artistic yearnings.

Brann had been publishing his *Iconoclast* at Houston and failed. I bought out the whole plant, name and all, for $250, and started a ten-page weekly story paper. Being an editor, I of course resigned from the *Post*. The stories were mostly humorous. The editor did most of the writing and all the illustrating. Meanwhile Brann had gone to Waco. He wrote and asked if I wouldn't let him have his *Iconoclast* title back. I didn't think much of it and let him have it. My paper was accordingly christened *The Rolling Stone*. It rolled for about a year and then showed unmistakable signs of getting mossy. Moss and I were never friends, and so I said good-by to *The Rolling Stone*."

The confusion of cities and sequence of events (Porter again worked for the *Post* after the failure in Austin) was probably part of his continuing efforts to obscure his past, especially links to the banking scandal. According to a study of the paper by Paul Aubrey Tracy, a more accurate version of the events was given by Dixie Daniels in a 1912 interview with the *Dallas Morning News*: "It was the spring of 1894 that I floated into Austin, and I got a place in the State printing office. I had been working there for a short time when I heard that a man named Porter had bought out the old *Iconoclast* plant–known everywhere as Brann's *Iconoclast*–and was looking for a printer to go into the game with him. I went around to see him, and that was the first time I met O. Henry.... I talked things over with him, the proposition looked good, and we formed a partnership then and there. We christened the paper *The Rolling Stone* after a discussion, and in smaller type across the full-page head we printed 'Out for the Moss!' which is exactly what we were out for. Our idea was to run this weekly with a lot of current events treated in humorous fashion, and also to run short sketches, drawings and verse. I had also been doing a lot of chalk-plate work and the specimens I showed seemed to make a hit with Porter. Those chalk-plates were the way practically all of our cuts were printed. Porter was one of the most versatile men I had ever met. He ... could write remarkably clever stuff under all circumstances, and was a good hand at sketching.... Well ... we moved into the old *Iconoclast* plant, got out a few issues and moved into the Brueggerhoff Building. *The Rolling Stone* met with unusual success at the start."

Daniels's name does not appear on the paper until the eighteenth issue, and then as business manager. Earlier, Porter enlisted the help of his wife, and he had at least six assistants during

Front page for an issue of the humor journal edited by Porter in 1894 and 1895. The illustrations and most of the articles and poems were by Porter.

the year the paper lasted. Only one coeditor, Henry Ryder-Taylor, contributed copy; Porter relied on some syndicated materials, including a column by Bill Nye that he ran for about six months, until he could no longer afford it, and there was an occasional local contribution; but, as Tracy explained, "the overwhelmingly greater part of *The Rolling Stone*, week after week, was written by Porter himself. Several times he found himself scraping the bottom of his literary barrel, even to the extent to reprinting the same stories several times."

Although some of the charm and humor of Porter's work is lost to modern audiences unfamiliar with the local issues of his time, the *Rolling Stone* does reveal the talent which would explode forth under the pseudonym O. Henry. Only one of his major short stories, "Bexar Script No. 2692," appeared in the magazine, but Porter's genius still shines in the prose, poetry, and cartoons he contributed to the magazine. One of the publication's features during its last six months of existence was "The Plunkville Patriot," which, Daniels explained, "was a page gotten up in imitation of a backwoods country paper." Because of the intentional errors in type and illustrations, Daniels set the type himself for the page, and the result is a delightful parody of a small-town publication.

Rolling Stone maintained a long-running feud with the Germans in central Texas, and Porter's satires may have cost him some advertisers. The first anti-German article appeared in the third issue with Porter's account of a statewide gathering of German singing societies. Titled "A Full Report of the Twentieth Meeting Held at Houston–Between Drinks," it began: "Houston, Texas, May 8–The City is filling up with alarming quickness. Visitors are rapidly pouring in. Pouring in beer more than anything else. Turner Hall has been handsomely decorated with German mottoes that are familiar to the singers of every biergarten in America. Over the front door is the legend, 'Gruess Gott der Sangers Breuder von Fern und Mars,' which means, "Great God! the singers do not appear to be bringing anything to eat with them." Daniels recalled that the strongest reaction was to a sketch of a German music director, with a four-line verse printed below:

> With his baton the professor beats the bars.
>   And 'tis said he also beats them then when he treats.
> Upon the stage and off it he sees stars,
>   When the bouncer gets the cue to bar the beats.

This anti-German doggerel is not representative of Porter's surprising flair for poetry, mostly humorous, but including some dramatic monologues in the style of Robert Browning. Porter abandoned poetry after the success of his short stories, so the *Rolling Stone* offers rare glimpses of Porter as a poet. He scattered limericks throughout the issues; much of the short verse appeared in a column, "Loose Gravel," or under the pseudonym Ten Eyck White.

The *Rolling Stone* also offers a look at Porter the illustrator. His cartoons and illustrations were always humorous and were usually rough in their execution as a result of the constant deadline pressure. Many of the drawings were used as headings for stories or poems; some illustrated a joke; others stood alone.

While it was basically a forerunner of such humor magazines as *Life* and *Judge*, the *Rolling Stone* did tackle serious editorial issues. Viewing itself as a local reform paper, it ran campaigns against the city's dangerous swinging signs, the low wages of municipal workers, and the cluttered grounds of the Capitol. Porter also dealt with state and national issues, opposing legalized lotteries and attacking donations to foreign missions when help was needed at home. The editorial comment, always on page four, included an editor's column that contained serious paragraphs alternating with witticisms. The page also ran editorials on single topics. The general editorial policy was stated only once, in the 25 September 1894 issue, and then with Porter's serious concerns embedded in humor. In response to a question about the "politics and platform" of the paper, Porter wrote: "The politics of THE ROLLING STONE is Independent, with an inclination toward Presbyterianism, and the theory that the world is supported on the back of a mud turtle. Our platform might be stated in the following words: We believe in treating everybody square all around, backing the winning horse, and closing all open accounts with a note when hard pressed. We will hew to the line, provided the chips fall our way. We believe in personal liberty, but think it not right to drink forty-seven schooners of beer in a garden on Sunday and then shout 'Gotterdammerrungheinrichbringzwanzigmehrbeersdamkvikzuhellundplazesalready' in a strong barrel-tone voice in the back door of a man who is sincerely trying to figure out Moses' answer to Bob Ingersoll with the aid of a concordance and the Heavenly Twins. We believe that charity begins at home, but skips a powerful lot of want and misery before it strikes the ground again among the heathen. We believe that a man who borrows his neighbor's paper to read instead of subscribing is full of prunes and canal water, and it shall come to pass that he shall cry out for some one to moisten the tip of his tongue with an E. & W. on Lemps, but his name shall be mud, and even a draft that strikes him from the door shall be protested. We believe a good many other things, that we will communicate in good time. THE ROLLING STONE rolls on both sides of the fence, but knocks a few planks off every time it rolls."

As O. Henry, Porter later would portray the New York working class with sensitivity and concern, and this trait was already evident in Austin. Many of his editorials deal with the rights of the unemployed and the poverty-stricken; he particularly defended the municipal street workers, writing in May 1894 that "if the interest on the money that has been carried away from Austin by foreign contractors was added to the wages received by the working men now laying the new water pipes on the streets, they would not be forced to begin work at 5 o'clock in the morning in order to make a dollar a day." He editorialized against the brutal treatment of the horses which drew the city's express wagons and suggested shooting "about twenty-five of the big, fat, lazy" drivers as a benefit to the county. He lobbied for civic improvements, such as an opera house, more libraries, and street improvements, and chided police for not clearing out a section of town inhabited by opium smokers. He also editorialized about one of his pet peeves: "If the preachers would not preach so much about future punishment, and preach about thirty minutes instead, there would be less courting in the choir and more souls awakened—or kept awake."

The publication jumped into Texas politics, especially the gubernatorial race, running editorials, cartoons, political poems, and "interviews" with the candidates. Tracy described these "interviews" as "among the funniest pieces *The Rolling Stone* carried. They are more characteristic of his later work, perhaps, than anything else.... In each he creates a ludicrous setting for the imaginary talk, whips through a farcical interchange of sentences and cuts off the story suddenly and unexpectedly. He misquotes literary allusions, indulges in circumlocutions, and trips lightly as a clown into malapropisms—all O. Henry's familiar stocks in trade."

Porter established a San Antonio Department managed by Henry Ryder-Taylor, who wrote editorials about that city's politics. The editorials were controversial, but the magazine had few subscribers and no advertisers in San Antonio. Porter, however, enjoyed his overnight trips there, and some of his later stories were based on these visits.

If Porter had no success in attracting advertisers in San Antonio, he had only slightly more success in Austin; during its short career the *Rolling Stone* had only eighty-five advertisers, most of them on a sporadic basis. The lack of a solid advertising base seriously weakened the paper; the average issue carried eighteen advertisements, and one carried only six. Yet the quality of the ads is surprising; occasionally Porter wrote the copy, even running what appeared to be bona fide news stories with surprise endings typical of O. Henry as promotions for advertisers. One lengthy "news" story about the escape of Napoleon's Marshal Ney to the Carolinas was actually an ad for a local furniture dealer.

Porter tried desperately to build up advertising by opening the San Antonio bureau, by purging the subscription list of those who had not paid, and finally by cutting ad rates by fifty percent. The circulation figure of fifteen hundred that Porter quoted to advertisers may have been an exaggeration, for the popular city paper had a circulation of less than five thousand in 1894.

In the early issues the publication was a five-column sheet, thirteen by twenty inches, on inexpensive paper; after thirteen issues the page size was reduced, and it was printed on glossy stock. Two more format changes were made, and when it folded the *Rolling Stone* was back to quarto size on cheap paper. The large-size paper averaged eight pages; the smaller, twelve. It appears that there were forty-eight issues over the fifty-five-week life of the magazine; according to Daniels, issue numbers cannot be trusted because the staff had great difficulty keeping track of the proper numbers.

Porter explained on 30 March 1895 why he had missed two issues; at the same time he provided an insight into his own perception of his role on the magazine:

> The person who sweeps the office, translates letters from foreign countries, deciphers communi-

Regular one-page feature of the Rolling Stone, *intended as a parody of a country newspaper (Huntington Library)*

cations from graduates of business colleges, and does most the writing of this paper, has been confined for the past two weeks to the underside of a large red quilt with a joint case of la grippe and measles.

We have missed two issues of *The Rolling Stone*, and we are now slightly convalescent, for which we desire to apologize and express our regrets.

Everybody's term of subscription will be extended enough to cover all missed issues, and we hope soon to report that the goose remains suspended at a favorable altitude. People who have tried to run a funny paper and entertain a congregation of large piebald measles at the same time will understand something of the tact, finesse, and hot sassafras tea required to do so. We expect to get out the paper regularly from this time on, but are forced to be very careful, as improper treatment and deleterious after-effects of measles, combined with the high price of paper and press work, have been known to cause a relapse. Anyone not getting their paper regularly will please come down and see about it, bringing with them a ham or any little delicacy relished by invalids.

In October 1894 a federal bank examiner discovered irregularities in Porter's accounts. After his forced resignation from the bank the *Rolling Stone* was Porter's only source of income, and it proved to be a poor source indeed. Convinced that his attempts to build circulation and advertising were doomed, he began to look for another job. In a letter to an old colleague in Chicago he says: "I can worry along here and about live but it is not the place for one to get ahead in. You know that, don't you? See if you can't get me a job there, or if you think our paper would take and we could get some support, what about starting it up there?"

The stress was too much for Porter, and he fell ill with a relapse of measles. The *Rolling Stone* was so much a one-man operation that no one could take over from him, and after his recovery Porter made no effort to resume publication; the last issue appeared on 27 April 1895. Rollins was convinced that if Porter's personal and financial crises had been resolved, the weekly could have become a national success: "Though intended chiefly for local readers, *The Rolling Stone* is really delightful. Its crowning glory is the short stories written by Porter, and one can detect in them the touches and mannerisms that made O. Henry great. Had Porter continued to edit the paper and had the financial side been well managed, there can be no doubt that it would have become one of the leading humorous weeklies in the United States."

With the demise of the *Rolling Stone*, Porter's happiest period ended. His only means of support was an occasional free-lance piece. He was offered a job in Washington, but shortly before they were to depart Athol fell ill with tuberculosis, and Porter would not leave her. In his deep depression, he revisited the LaSalle County ranch to recall his happier days. Finally, in October 1895, the name W. S. Porter appeared on the payroll of the *Houston Post*. He was earning fifteen dollars a week, substantially less than in his Land Office job. Porter moved to Houston, and Athol's health had improved enough for her to join him there.

On 9 February 1896 Porter was indicted for embezzlement and summoned back to Austin to stand trial. The case against him was not particularly strong; the bank was known for loose management, and Porter had strong community support. But he fled to New Orleans, then to Honduras, only returning in 1897 when he learned that Athol was near death. He was arrested and released on bail; Athol soon died, and the following year Porter was convicted and sentenced to the federal penitentiary at Columbus, Ohio, for five years. He served three years and three months and left prison determined to put the humiliation and pain of the Texas years behind him. The writer who emerged from prison was far different from the bright young editor who had sung Gilbert and Sullivan choruses and wooed Athol on her porch swing. He had seen the darker side of life, yet those bright early days forever permeated the works of O. Henry; his writings were those of the eternal romantic, finding the glimmer of love and humor even in a New York tenement.

From prison Porter went to Pittsburgh, where he wrote for a variety of magazines. In 1902 he arrived in New York. In the few years he had left Porter lived lavishly, gambling, drinking heavily, and relying on overwork to sustain his life-style. He drove himself mercilessly, producing an exceptionally large body of short stories but destroying his health in the process. He collapsed on 3 June 1910 and died two days later of cirrhosis of the liver. He was survived by his second wife, Sarah Lindsay Coleman Porter, whom he had married in 1907.

His stories often drew on his adventures in the West, but the facts about those years were shrouded in mystery. He deliberately falsified chronologies, and as his fame grew so did the number of friends who claimed to know the "truth" about Porter; one even claimed to have escaped to Honduras with him, but the boast was a lie. For decades after Porter's premature death, reporters and scholars interviewed those who had known him in Austin and Houston, resulting in conflicting recollections but a consensus that Porter had not been guilty of the embezzlement after all. The confusion was compounded by the disappearance of most issues of the *Rolling Stone*; circulation had been limited, and it had never been taken seriously enough to save, so that it was unavailable for biographers until several private collections were consolidated at the University of Texas at Austin. Stories from the publication had been collected as *Rolling Stones* in 1912 by Doubleday, but the availability of the actual issues finally made possible a serious analysis of Porter's first literary venture. Rough as it is, the *Rolling Stone* not only foreshadows the unique style that characterized O. Henry's writings but shows the gifts for sketching and poetry he abandoned after prison. It offers a chance to experience the wit and spirit of Porter during the time when his own life seemed to promise the happy ending that never came to O. Henry.

Letters:
Letters to Lithopolis, from O. Henry to Mabel Wagnalls, edited by Mabel Wagnalls (Garden City, N.Y.: Doubleday, Page, 1922).

Bibliography:
Paul S. Clarkson, *A Bibliography of William Sydney Porter* (Caldwell, Idaho: Caxton, 1938).

Biographies:
Sara Lindsay Coleman, *Wind of Destiny* (New York: Doubleday, Page, 1916);
C. Alphonso Smith, *O. Henry Biography* (New York: Doubleday, Page, 1916); Reprinted with an introduction by Warner Berthoff, "American Men & Women of Letters Series" (New York: Chelsea House, 1980);
Al Jennings, *Through the Shadows with O. Henry* (New York: Fly, 1921; London: Duckwork, 1923);
Frances G. Maltby, *The Dimity Sweetheart: O. Henry's Own Love Story* (Richmond, Virginia: Dietz, 1930);
Robert H. Davis and Arthur B. Maurice, *The Caliph of Bagdad: Being Arabian Nights Flashes of the Life, Letters, and Work of O. Henry* (New York: Appleton, 1931);
William Wash Williams, *The Quiet Lodger of Irving Place* (New York: Dutton, 1936);
Lollie Cave Wilson, *Hard to Forget: The Young O. Henry* (Los Angeles: Lymanhouse, 1939);
E. Hudson Long, *O. Henry: The Man and His Work* (Philadelphia: University of Pennsylvania Press, 1949);
Dale Kramer, *The Heart of O. Henry* (New York: Rinehart, 1954);
Gerald Langford, *Alias O. Henry: A Biography of William Sydney Porter* (New York: Macmillan, 1957);
Ethel Stephens Arnett, *O. Henry from Polecat Creek* (Greensboro, North Carolina: Piedmont, 1962);
Richard O'Connor, *O. Henry: The Legendary Life of William S. Porter* (Garden City, N.Y.: Doubleday, 1970).

References:
Joseph Gallegly, *From Alamo Plaza to Jack Harris's Saloon: O. Henry and the Southwest He Knew* (The Hague: Mouton, 1970);
Mary Sunlocks Harrell, "O. Henry's Texas Contacts," M.A. thesis, University of Texas at Austin, 1935;
Richard C. Harris, *William Sydney Porter (O. Henry); A Reference Guide* (Boston: Hall, 1980);
O. Henry Papers: Containing Some Sketches of His Life Together with an Alphabetical Index to His Complete Works (Garden City, N.Y.: Doubleday, Page, 1924);
Trueman O'Quinn, "O. Henry in Austin," *Southwestern Historical Quarterly*, 43 (October 1939): 143-157;
L. W. Payne, Jr. "The Humor of O. Henry," *Texas Review*, 4 (October 1918-July 1919): 18-37;
Hyder E. Rollins, "News for Bibliophiles: *The Rolling Stone*," *Nation*, 99 (2 July 1914): 11-12;
Rollins, "O. Henry," *Sewanee Review*, 22 (April 1914): 213-232;
Rollins, "O. Henry's Texas Days," *Bookman*, 40 (October 1914): 154-156;
Paul Aubrey Tracy, "A Closer Look at O. Henry's *Rolling Stone*," M.A. thesis, University of Texas at Austin, 1949).

Papers:
The most complete collection of William Sydney Porter's papers is in the Greensboro, North Caro-

lina, Public Library. The most complete collection of Porter's Texas works, including woodcuts and illustrations, copies of the *Iconoclast* and the *Rolling Stone,* and documents from Porter's trial, are in the Barker Texas History Center at the University of Texas at Austin. The Austin History Center and O. Henry House in Austin contain collections of Porter ephemera.

George Palmer Putnam

(7 February 1814-20 December 1872)

Shirley M. Mundt
Louisiana State University

See also the Putnam entry on in *DLB 3: Antebellum Writers in New York and the South* and the G. P. Putnam's Sons entry in *DLB 49: American Literary Publishing Houses, 1638-1899.*

MAJOR POSITIONS HELD: Publisher and editor, *Booksellers' Advertiser and Monthly Register of New Publications* (1834-1836); publisher, *Putnam's Monthly Magazine of American Literature, Science, and Art* (1853-1857), renamed *Putnam's Magazine: Original Papers on Literature, Science, Art, and National Interests* (1868-1870).

BOOKS: *Chronology: or, An Introduction and Index to Universal History, Biography, and Useful Knowledge; Comprising a Chronological, Contemporary, and Alphabetical Record, of Important and Interesting Occurrence, from the Earliest Period to the Present Time* (New York: Leavitt/Boston: Crocker & Brewster, 1833); revised and enlarged as *The World's Progress: A Dictionary of Dates; With Tabular Views of General History* (New York: Putnam's, 1850; revised, 1851); republished as *Handbook of Chronology and History: The World's Progress, A Dictionary of Dates: with Tabular Views of General History* (New York: Putnam's, 1852); republished as *The World's Progress: A Dictionary of Dates, with a Tabular View of General History* (New York: Barnes/Cincinnati: Derby, 1854); republished as *The World's Progress: A Dictionary of Dates; With Tabular Views of General History and a Historical Chart* (New York: Putnam's, 1857); revised and enlarged as *Cyclopedia of Chronology; or, The World's Progress: A Dictionary of Dates, with Tabular Views of General History and an Historical Chart* (New York: Barnes & Burr, 1860); revised and enlarged as *The World's Progress; A Dictionary of Dates, Being a Chronological and Alphabetical Record of All Essential Facts in the Progress of Society, from the Creation of the World to the Inauguration of Lincoln* (New York: Putnam's, 1864); revised and enlarged as *The World's Progress: A Dictionary of Dates: Being a Chronological and Alphabetical Record of All Essential Facts in the Progress of Society, from the Creation of the World to August, 1867* (New York: Putnam's, 1867);

The Tourist in Europe; or, a Concise Summary of the Various Routes, Objects of Interest, &c in Great Britain, France, Switzerland, Italy, Germany, Belgium and Holland; with Hints on Time, Expenses, Hotels, Conveyances, Passports, Coins, &c; Memoranda During a Tour of Eight Months in Great Britain and on the Continent, in 1836 (New York: Wiley & Putnam, 1838);

American Facts: Notes and Statistics Relative to the Government, Resources, Engagements, Manufactures, Commerce, Religion, Education, Literature, Fine Arts, Manners and Customs of the United States of America (London: Wiley & Putnam, 1845);

Memorial of James Fenimore Cooper (New York: Putnam's, 1852);

Catalogue of A Private Collection of Autograph Letters, Documents, Portraits and Curiosities (New York: Putnam's, 1858);

Before and After the Battle: A Day and Night in "Dixie" (New York, 1861?);

George Palmer Putnam

Suggestions for Household Libraries of Essential and Standard Books (Exclusive of Scientific and Religious Works) (New York: Putnam's, 1870); revised as *The Best Reading: Hints on the Selection of Books; on the Formation of Libraries, Public and Private* (New York: Putnam's, 1873).

OTHER: *Popping the Question, and Other Tales; Embracing the Best Stories of the Best Authors; Now First Collected*, edited by Putnam (Philadelphia: Peck & Bliss, 1858);

Ten Years of the World's Progress, Being a Supplement to the Work of That Title, edited by Putnam (New York: Putnam's, 1861);

Letters from Europe Touching the American Contest, and Acknowledging the Receipt, from Citizens of New York, of Presentation Sets of the "Rebellion Record" and "Loyal Publication Society Publications," edited by Putnam (New York: Loyal Publication Society, 1864);

Haydn's Dictionary of Dates, edited by Benjamin Vincent with a supplement by Putnam (New York: Putnam's, 1867).

PERIODICAL PUBLICATIONS: "Recollections of Irving: By His Publisher," *Atlantic Monthly*, 6 (November 1860): 601-612;

"Some Things in London and Paris–1836-1869," *Putnam's Magazine: Original Papers on Literature, Science, Art, and National Interests*, 3 (June 1869): 733-743;

"Leaves from a Publisher's Letter-Book," *Putnam's Magazine: Original Papers on Literature, Science, Art, and National Interests*, 4 (October 1869): 467-474; (November 1869): 551-561; (December 1869): 675-682.

At a time when American writers were hardly appreciated at home and not at all in the rest of the world and when American publishers were pirating English and American works to make quick, easy money, George Palmer Putnam made a name and a career for himself and his descendants by promoting American writers at home and abroad. He paid them well for their manuscripts, sometimes at great personal financial risk, and he paid British and other foreign authors for rights to publish their works in the United States. In 1837 he began to draft letters to congressional committees, arguing for an international copyright law. He continued this pursuit through a number of organizations until his death in 1872. At fifteen he began collecting and arranging historical facts; in 1833 he published them in a four-hundred-page work which he revised, updated, and republished for the rest of his life. At thirty-four Putnam started his own business, collecting and publishing the works of American and British writers; at thirty-nine he solicited original articles from American authors and began publishing a literary magazine, which won international acclaim. He seemed to feel a moral obligation to make the study of history easy and accessible, to make literature attractive and affordable to the average person, and to prove to the world that American authors deserved recognition.

Putnam was born on 7 February 1814 in Brunswick, Maine, to Henry and Catherine Hunt Palmer Putnam. His father, educated at Harvard and admitted to the bar in Maine, was in poor health. Putnam's mother supported the family by running a small coeducational school which she opened in 1808 and continued after she moved to New York in 1829. George Putnam and his three sisters attended their mother's school. When Putnam was eleven, his parents sent him to Boston to live with his father's sister and her husband, John Gulliver, who needed a helper in his carpet business. Errands, cleaning duties, and carpet deliveries kept Putnam busy. He took a few short lessons in writing and studied French but had no formal education after he left his mother's school.

In 1829 Putnam took a schooner to New York City. He found a job as a clerk with bookseller George W. Bleeker, publisher of the *Enterpiad: An Album of Music, Poetry, and Prose*. Putnam lived with Bleeker's family above the store and made twenty-five dollars a year. Bleeker sometimes sent him to Hudson and Poughkeepsie, New York, to promote subscriptions to the *Enterpiad*. Putnam's experience with Bleeker introduced him to his life's work: publishing, promoting, and selling books. After two years Putnam left Bleeker and went to work as general clerk and messenger for bookseller and publisher Jonathan Leavitt and his assistant, Daniel Appleton. At Leavitt's he earned two dollars a week at first (he was later raised to four). Leavitt was expanding his stock in religious publications at this time, so Putnam probably worked hard at moving and cataloging books. When he finished his work about nine or ten each evening, he hurried to the New York Mercantile Library to pursue a self-organized course in history, often staying at the library until two in the morning. The notes and parallel tables, devised for his personal ease in learning history, he later put together in a four-hundred-page manual which he entitled *Chronology: or, An Introduction and Index to Universal History, Biography, and Useful Knowledge; Comprising a Chronological, Contemporary, and Alphabetical Record, of Important and Interesting Occurrence, from the Earliest Period to the Present Time* (1833). Leavitt said he would publish it if Putnam would get a scholar to examine and approve it. Putnam did so, and while he was getting his book ready for publication, Daniel Appleton left Leavitt's to open his own business. Both Appleton and Leavitt had invested in the printing of one thousand copies of Putnam's book, so they divided the stock. Putnam later wrote, "It was rather grand to have to say that two great publishing firms were required to produce my first work; for this little book of reference thus anonymously put forth by two (now rival) sponsors had been honestly compiled, originally for my own benefit alone, from some 150 different volumes of historical works." Both publishing houses soon sold all their copies. In the following years Putnam added more to this work and published it himself in 1850 under a new title: *The World's Progress: A Dictionary of Dates; With Tabular Views of General History*. In the preface Putnam says that the volume was planned "to facilitate access to the largest amount of useful information in the smallest compass." He devised a "tabular view," arranging the tables so that a reader could refer to any date on the chart and see at a glance what major events had occurred in major countries. It was a practical visual aid, since used in many reference works. The volume had gone through twenty editions by 1873, the year after Putnam's death. The last revision was in 1927.

Soon after the first appearance of his *Chronology* Putnam began another project–a list of newly published works, both foreign and American, with occasional reviews. He called it *Booksellers' Advertiser and Monthly Register of New Publications* and arranged for John T. West and John F. Trow to print it monthly until 1836. Years later Putnam marveled at his "audacity"–a twenty-year-old errand boy reviewing works like George Bancroft's *History of the United States*, William Gilmore Simms's *Guy Rivers*, and James Fenimore Cooper's *A Letter to His Countrymen*, all published in 1834. He believed the *Advertiser* was "the first attempt in this country to furnish a booksellers' journal with a statistical record of American publications" and called it "the grandfather" of the *American Publishers' Circular and Literary Gazette*, which was a forerunner of *Publishers' Weekly*. It was a timely but time-consuming project, and after a year he became too busy to continue it. He was still a clerk at Leavitt's when he wrote the "Valedictory" in the last issue and revealed his identity.

Around 1834 Putnam joined the publishing firm of John Wiley and George Long. He soon persuaded Wiley to let him go to London to investigate the possibility of setting up a branch house. The exact date of this first trip is unclear, but Putnam's travel guide, *The Tourist in Europe; or, a Concise Summary of the Various Routes, Objects of Interest, &c in Great Britain, France, Switzerland, Italy, Germany, Belgium and Holland; with Hints on Time, Expenses, Hotels, Conveyances, Passports, Coins, &c; Memoranda During a Tour of Eight Months in Great Britain and on the Continent, in 1836* (1838), suggests that he could have been looking for a location for a shop as early as 1836. In 1837 Putnam and several authors, among them William Cullen Bryant, Albert Matthews, James Fenimore Cooper, and Fitz-Greene Halleck, began the first

Opening page from an issue of the magazine Putnam published from 1853 until it was suspended during the financial panic of 1857

organization in America to appeal for a copyright law.

When George Long retired from Wiley and Long in 1840, Putnam moved up as Wiley's partner and shortly thereafter opened the first shop in London to promote sales of American books in Great Britain. Once established, Putnam also bought rights for publication of English books. In 1841 Putnam returned briefly to New York, and on 13 March 1841 he married sixteen-year-old Victorine Haven, one of his mother's students. Putnam and his bride returned to London where he continued selling books at the shop he had opened on Paternoster Row. In 1844 he moved the agency to Waterloo Place and arranged for space to display American books, paintings, newspapers, and magazines. The young couple entertained often in their modest home which they called Knickerbocker Cottage. Visitors included authors and, occasionally, diplomats from America; authors and publishers from England; and exiles from other European countries. Some of their more notable guests were Edward Moxon, Mary Cowden-Clarke, William Howitt, Washington Irving, Giuseppe Mazzini, and Louis Napoleon (later Napoleon III).

In his business and social contacts Putnam observed that Europeans knew little about America. He was frustrated with the shortsighted opinions he encountered, so he compiled three hundred pages of information which Wiley and Putnam published in 1845 as *American Facts: Notes and Statistics Relative to the Government, Resources, Engagements, Manufactures, Commerce, Religion, Education, Literature, Fine Arts, Manners and Customs of the United States of America*. It ran through three editions during the next three or four years—popular abroad and in America.

Despite Putnam's success at getting some American books to sell in England, he was not making enough money to make the venture practical. In February 1847 the Putnams began a ten-week European tour, returning to London in early May. In June they returned to the United States, and Putnam dissolved his partnership with Wiley, moving into quarters at 155 Broadway. One of Putnam's first acts as an independent publisher was to write to Irving and offer to republish his works which had gone out of print during the years Irving was serving as minister to Spain. Irving agreed to the offer, and between 1848 and 1855 Putnam published the 16-volume *The Works of Washington Irving*, comprising reprints and revisions of previously published works as well as new manuscripts as Irving wrote them. During his first year Putnam contracted to publish for Edgar Allan Poe, James Russell Lowell, Cooper, and other American authors just being recognized in the United States. He also obtained rights to publish British authors, including Thomas Hood, Leigh Hunt, Samuel Taylor Coleridge, and Thomas Carlyle. Putnam paid authors for the privilege of publishing their works, but he frequently ran into the problem of having works he had paid for reprinted by both British and American firms without permission and, of course, without payment, either to himself or to the author. The piracy cut deeply into Putnam's pride and into his profits, and he continued to argue for a copyright law.

By October 1852 Putnam's business was well established at 10 Park Place, to which he had moved in 1850. He was ready to begin a different venture–a periodical which he described in a letter requesting contributions as "essentially an organ of American thought." He called the new magazine *Putnam's Monthly Magazine of American Literature, Science, and Art* and employed Charles F. Briggs as editor. The first issue appeared in January 1853, bound in a pea green cover with a simple design of cornstalks forming an arch over the title. Putnam's policy was to publish only original material, to pay for every contribution, and to print everything anonymously. By giving well-established authors the same anonymity he gave unknown authors, Putnam hoped to increase readership of little-known American writers. He paid three, five, or ten dollars per page for prose and ten to twenty-five dollars for poems.

Each issue of *Putnam's Monthly Magazine* contained in its 120 pages a variety of literary forms on a wide range of topics. There were essays which sparked controversy, like "Cuba," in the first issue, which predicted that Cuba would be annexed to the United States; and "Have We a Bourbon Among Us?," in the second number, which attempted to prove that the Reverend Eleazar Williams was really Louis XVII of France. There were illustrated articles, like "New York Daguerreotyped," a series of illustrated articles on the architecture of New York City. Poems were generally undistinguished, but a few were written by notables such as Henry Wadsworth Longfellow, John Greenleaf Whittier, and James Russell Lowell. Since all contributions were unsigned, it is difficult to know who many of the minor poets were. Considerable space was devoted to fiction, the most famous of which were works by Herman Melville. "Bartleby, the Scrivener" was serialized in *Putnam's* in 1853, as was *Israel Potter, His Fifty Years of Exile* from 1854 to 1855. The final section of the magazine consisted of reviews of contemporary publications of American, British, French, and German literature; scientific news; and commentary on music and fine arts. Putnam, Briggs, and Curtis wrote for the magazine, but it is hard to know just how much Putnam himself contributed. Curtis named many of the authors in later years, but the average subscriber to the magazine probably had no idea of who wrote what he read. Among the contributors were Caroline Kirkland, Henry David Thoreau, John Pendleton Kennedy, Bayard Taylor, and Cooper.

In the May 1854 number Putnam published praiseworthy critical reviews of his magazine he had collected from numerous sources. He was probably proudest of words of acclaim from British publications like the *Exeter Gazette*, which said, "Among the numerous samples of American serial literature which have found their way to British readers, few, if any, possess those distinctive marks of excellence which adapt transatlantic monthlies to the taste of European critics in so eminent a degree as *Putnam's Magazine*." Circulation of the magazine ranged from twelve thousand to twenty thousand copies, but Putnam needed more subscriptions to pay for the original material he insisted upon using. Although *Putnam's* was well received, it was not a money-maker for its owner; and when Putnam's publishing company foundered in 1855, the magazine was sold. The last issue of *Putnam's Monthly* came out in December, 1857.

A series of financial losses, poor management on the part of a partner, and difficult economic conditions in 1857 forced Putnam to assign all his property to Mason Brothers, publishers. Fortunately for Putnam, his friend Irving bought his own plates from Mason. Then, learning of Putnam's dilemma, he presented the plates to Putnam to continue publication with the same royalty arrangement as they had had in the past. Because of Irving's faith in him, a few other authors came back to Putnam and he was able to rebuild business. By 1859, the year of Irving's death, Putnam had fully repaid him for the plates. Although his business was recovering, Putnam was not able to revive the magazine immediately. At first the publishing company required his full attention. Sales of Irving's works increased markedly after his death; Putnam produced several new editions. But the onset of the Civil War slowed business again. Libraries were not buying and booksellers were closing shop. Encouraged by friends, Putnam applied for the position of tax collector for the wealthy eighth district of New York. When he received the appointment, he arranged for Melancthon Hurd and Henry Houghton to print and sell Putnam publications.

Although Putnam's greatest contribution to the Union cause was probably his perseverance in collecting taxes to finance the war, he also helped by lending his publishing expertise to an organization called the Loyal Publication Society, which published tracts and pamphlets for distribution at home and abroad. Putnam made only one brief appearance at a battle. He volunteered to help with the wounded at Bull Run and de-

Opening page from an issue of the magazine Putnam published from 1868 until it was merged with Scribner's Monthly *in 1870*

scribed his experience in *Before and After the Battle: A Day and Night in "Dixie"* (1861).

In March 1866 Putnam was suddenly relieved of his duties as tax collector. Officeholders were being assessed to pay for the Republican convention held in Baltimore that spring; Putnam regarded the assessment as unfair and refused to pay. President Andrew Johnson immediately sent down a message of dismissal, giving Putnam twenty-four hours to turn in his books and money. Although a few days later Putnam received a letter from the secretary of the treasury commending him for his integrity and his success in collecting millions of dollars in taxes, his job was not restored.

Putnam retrieved his plates and publications from Hurd and Houghton and returned to the business of publishing. His son George Haven Putnam joined him, and the company name was changed to G. P. Putnam and Son. (The name changed again in 1871 when another son, Bishop Putnam, became a partner, and in 1872 when still another son, Irving Putnam, came into the business the name was changed to G. P. Putnam's Sons.) Finding the market for books slow in 1866, Putnam began preparations to revive his magazine. He again circulated letters asking for contributions and suggestions. The response was gratifying, with Longfellow, Melville, Bryant, and Reverend A. T. Fullerton offering testimonials. Putnam changed the name of his magazine to *Putnam's Magazine: Original Papers on Literature, Science, Art, and National Interests*, and the first issue came out in January 1868. Putnam announced in the January issue that every number of the new series would include discussion of public policy, religion, education, science, art, industrial pursuits, finance, sketches of travel, and fiction. In addition, each issue would include a monthly chronicle touching on "occurrences at home and abroad"; "literature–books of the Month; literary intelligence; statistics"; "fine arts"; "music"; and "Table Talk." Also added were twenty pages of "Putnam's Monthly Advertiser." The new magazine was also different in that contributors were named in the table of contents. The list included some of the same contributors from the first series with some notable additions: Grace Greenwood, William Dean Howells, Louisa May Alcott, Mrs. Nathaniel Hawthorne (Sophia Peabody), Julian Hawthorne, and Susan Fenimore Cooper.

Putnam himself contributed more to the new series. His trip abroad in 1869 prompted a lengthy piece which he called "Some Things in London and Paris–1836-1869." In October, November, and December of 1869 he published some of the many letters he had collected over the years under the title "Leaves from a Publisher's Letter-Book."

In the three years of the second series Putnam received 3,035 manuscripts–ten times more than he had room to publish. Apparently, Briggs returned as editor at first, although George Haven Putnam says that Putnam himself carried out most of the duties of editor in the first year. Frederick B. Perkins was editor during the second and most of the third year, and Parke Godwin, associate editor of the first series, took over the magazine in its final months. Circulation peaked at fifteen thousand–again not enough to keep the magazine solvent. Putnam was short of capital from the beginning of publication. Three new magazines, *Scribner's Monthly*, *Lippincott's*, and the *Galaxy*, had entered into competition for subscriptions as well as for contributors, and they had money to spend on illustrations, whereas Putnam did not. In the October 1870 issue Putnam announced that *Putnam's Magazine* would be consolidated with *Scribner's Monthly* at the end of the year. In describing Putnam's feelings about the sale of the magazine, his son wrote: "The closing of this second series of the magazine was a very keen personal disappointment to the publisher whose name it bore. It was, in fact, a shock that really added at once to my father's age. The feeling that he was no longer in touch with the reading public, that his literary judgment could not be depended upon as trustworthy, that his personal influence could not bring into his office in the face of the competition of other publishers, the best literary material of the day, the hampering restriction of want of adequate resources with which to carry out larger and more permanent literary plans—all these things weighed upon him...."

In 1870 Putnam published a work which helped to turn business around for him and his sons. His *Suggestions for Household Libraries of Essential and Standard Books* (*Exclusive of Scientific and Religious Works*) listed books appropriate for home and school libraries and, of course, promoted Putnam publications. Putnam was also busy at this time (between 1868 and 1872) with the organization of the Metropolitan Museum of Art. Although he had no money to contribute to the purchase of works of art, his secretarial duties in the organization led him to act as peacemaker among the members of the planning committee who had strong but different opinions on how the museum should be organized. His success was achieved by keeping the members of the committee together until the definite means of acquiring funds and a definite location for the first exhibit were agreed upon. He was made honorary secretary of the institution.

In November 1872 Putnam went to Washington as a representative of the copyright league and the Publisher's Association to argue for the passage of the Copyright Bill which had finally made its way up to the Judiciary Committee. He had helped to draft the bill as a member of the American Copyright Association. Unfortunately his argument was opposed at the committee hearing by his lifelong competitor, Harper and Brothers, and the bill failed to pass the committee.

Putnam went back to New York, disappointed and fatigued. A few weeks later, on the afternoon of December 20, he was working in the publishing office with his son George Haven Putnam when he fainted from exhaustion and fell into his son's arms. He never regained consciousness. His son said he died "in the midst of the books that he loved ... a fitting close to a life which had certainly in itself been ... thoroughly happy."

One might look at Putnam's accomplishments as minimal—his books were largely compilations of data and edited versions of the works of others; his magazine failed twice; his publishing company almost went bankrupt several times before his sons took over the business; and he was fired from his only political appointment. But Putnam's real influence came through his efforts to publish up-to-date historical and literary volumes which small American schools and libraries could afford; his behind-the-scenes encouragement to American authors, some of whom might never have been published if Putnam had not provided the opportunity; and his perseverance in keeping the copyright issue alive. Although his magazine failed because he insisted upon paying for what he printed, he set a precedent by publishing a magazine whose specialty was original American literature.

Biography:
George Haven Putnam, *A Memoir of George Palmer Putnam, Together with a Record of the Publishing House Founded by Him*, 2 volumes (New York: Putnam's, 1903); revised as *George Palmer Putnam: A Memoir* (New York & London: Putnam's, 1912).

References:
Scribner's Monthly, 5 (March 1873): 632-635;
John Tebbel, *A History of Book Publishing in the United States* (New York & London: Bowker, 1972).

Papers:
Three of Putnam's letters to Mellin Chamberlain are located in the Boston Public Library.

Henry J. Raymond
(24 January 1820-18 June 1869)

Nora Baker
Southern Illinois University at Edwardsville

See also the Raymond entry in *DLB 43: American Newspaper Journalists, 1690-1872.*

MAJOR POSITIONS HELD: Chief assistant, *New York Tribune* (1841-1843); editor, *Morning Courier and New York Enquirer* (1843-1851); managing editor, *Harper's New Monthly Magazine* (1850-1856); editor and publisher, *New-York Daily Times*, renamed *New-York Times* in 1857 (1851-1869).

BOOKS: *Association Discussed; or, The Socialism of the Tribune Examined: Being a Controversy between the New York Tribune and the Courier and Enquirer*, by Raymond and Horace Greeley (New York: Harper, 1847);

The Relations of the American Scholar to His Country and His Times: An Address Delivered before the Associate Alumni of the University of Vermont, at Burlington, Vt., August 6, 1850 (New York: Baker & Scribner, 1850);

An Oration Pronounced before the Young Men of Westchester County, on the Completion of a Monument, Erected by Them to the Captors of Major Andre, at Tarrytown, Oct. 7, 1853 (New York: Callahan, printer, 1853);

Political Lessons of the Revolution: An Address Delivered before the Citizens of Livingston County, at Geneseo, N.Y., July 4, 1854 (New York: Baker, Godwin, printers, 1854);

A State System of Education for New York: An Address Delivered before the Literary Societies of the Rochester University, at Rochester, N.Y., July 11, 1854 (New York: Baker, Godwin, & Co., 1854);

The Union Question: Mr. H. J. Raymond's Remarks at a Union Meeting in Albany, January 12, 1860 (Albany, N.Y., 1860);

Disunion and Slavery: A Series of Letters to Hon. W. L. Yancey, of Alabama, by Henry J. Raymond, of New York (New York?, 1861?);

The Financial Necessities and Policy of the National Government: Remarks by Mr. H. J. Raymond, of New York, in Committee of the Whole, on the Finance Resolutions Reported by the Committee of

Henry J. Raymond

Ways and Means, and in Reply to Mr. Hulburd. In Assembly, Tuesday Evening, Jan. 28, 1862 (New York?, 1862);

The Position and Duty of the Republican Party: Remarks of Hon. H. J. Raymond, at the Festival of the Republican General Committee in the City of New York, on the Celebration of Washington's Birthday, February 22d, 1862 (Albany, N.Y.: Weed, Parsons, printers, 1862);

The Rebellion and Our Foreign Relations: Remarks of Henry J. Raymond, Speaker of the Assembly on the Conduct of Our Foreign Affairs and the Action and Disposition of European Powers. In As-

sembly, State of New York, Mar. 5, 1862 (Albany: Weed, Parsons, 1862);

Governor Seymour and the War: Remarks of the Hon. H. J. Raymond, at Cooper Institute, New York City, October 16, 1863 (N.p., 1863?);

The Administration and the War: The Duty of Supporting the Government–Arbitrary Arrests–Object of the War to Save the Union–The Question of Reconstruction. Remarks of Mr. H. J. Raymond, of New York, at Wilmington, Delaware, November 6, 1863 (Wilmington, Del.?, 1863);

The Life of Abraham Lincoln, of Illinois; and the Life of Andrew Johnson, of Tennessee, life of Lincoln by Raymond, life of Johnson by John Savage (New York: Derby & Miller, 1864);

History of the Administration of President Lincoln: Including His Speeches, Letters, Addresses, Proclamations, and Messages. With a Preliminary Sketch of His Life (New York: Derby & Miller, 1864); enlarged as *The Life and Public Services of Abraham Lincoln, Sixteenth President of the United States: Together with His State Papers, Including His Speeches, Addresses, Messages, Letters, and Proclamations, and the Closing Scenes Connected with His Life and Death. To Which Are Added Anecdotes and Personal Reminiscences of President Lincoln, by Frank B. Carpenter* (New York: Derby & Miller, 1865; London: Stevens, 1865); republished as *Lincoln: His Life and Times,* 2 volumes (New York: Hurst, 1891);

The Issues of the Campaign: Speeches of Henry J. Raymond and Gen. J. H. Martindale, Delivered at the Union Meeting in Tweddle Hall, Albany, on the Evening of Wednesday, October 11, 1865 (Albany, N.Y.?, 1865?);

Peace and Restoration: Speech of Hon. H. J. Raymond . . . in Reply to Hon. T. Stevens . . . Delivered in the House of Representatives, December 21, 1865 (Washington, D.C.: Printed at the Congressional Globe Office, 1865);

Restoration and the President's Policy: Speech of Hon. H. J. Raymond, of New York, on Changing the Basis of Representation, and in Reply to Hon. S. Shellabarger, of Ohio; in the House of Representatives, January 29, 1866 (Washington, D.C.: Printed at the Congressional Globe Office, 1866);

The Civil Rights Bill: Mr. H. J. Raymond's Remarks in the House of Representatives, March, 8, 1866 (N.p., 1866);

The Principles of Taxation: Speech of Hon. H. J. Raymond, of New York, on the Internal Revenue Bill, May 7, 1866 (Washington, D.C.: Printed at the Congressional Globe Office, 1866);

Constitutional Amendments: Speech of Hon. Henry J. Raymond, of New York, on the Proposed Amendment of the Constitution; Delivered in the House of Representatives, May 9, 1866 (Washington, D.C.: Printed at the Congressional Globe Office, 1866);

Restoration and the Union Party: Speech of Hon. Henry J. Raymond, of New York, on the Conditional Admission of the States Lately in Rebellion to Representation in Congress. Delivered in the House of Representatives, June 18, 1866 (New York: Baker & Godwin, printers, 1866).

PERIODICAL PUBLICATION: "Extracts from the Journal of Henry J. Raymond," edited by Henry W. Raymond, *Scribner's Monthly,* 19 (November 1879): 57-61; (January 1880): 419-424; (March 1880): 703-710; 20 (June 1880): 275-280.

Henry J. Raymond was a voice of moderation in an era of journalistic sensationalism. A contemporary and rival of James Gordon Bennett and Horace Greeley, he was respected for his clear, concise writing; reasoned thinking; and astute political observation. Although these same attributes of moderation and reasoning hurt him in the political arena, Raymond remained a force in journalism until his death at age forty-nine. Best known as the founder and editor of the *New York Times* and tireless supporter of the infant Associated Press, he was also an author with a keen interest in literature and the first managing editor of *Harper's New Monthly Magazine.*

Henry Jarvis Raymond was born in 1820 near Lima, New York, to Jarvis and Lavinia Brockway Raymond, poor farmers with a reputation for industry and thrift. Raymond was the eldest of their six children; he and his brothers, Samuel and James, were the only ones to survive infancy. A precocious child who learned to read at age three, Raymond attended the nearby district school, followed by the village elementary school and three years at Genesee Wesleyan Seminary (later Syracuse University). When he finished the seminary he was only fifteen, "too young to go to college, for which I was better prepared than my father was to send me," he wrote later. For the next year he worked in a country store and taught in a district school at Wheatland, fifteen miles from Lima. Finally, in 1836 his father mortgaged the eighty-acre family farm for one thousand dollars, which, coupled with Raymond's savings, was enough for tuition at the University of Vermont in Burlington.

At the university Raymond began to develop his skill as an orator and also saw his words in print for the first time. On 30 September 1837 his poem "The Flower-Girl's Song" appeared in Horace Greeley's *New-Yorker*. The *New-Yorker* was soon publishing more of Raymond's poems as well as his book reviews and short news items from Burlington. The Junior Exhibition at the 1839 commencement established Raymond's reputation as an orator: Kentucky senator Henry Clay, on a political tour, was in the audience when Raymond gave an address titled "The Moral Influence of Reflection upon the Past." When the youth finished, Clay remarked to the person sitting next to him: "That young man will make his mark. Depend upon it, you will hear from him hereafter."

The president of the university was James Marsh, professor of moral and intellectual philosophy, whose keen intellect also embraced classical and modern literature and foreign languages. Raymond had always been a voracious reader, often staying up all night with a book, but under Marsh's tutelage he began reading the ancient classics, English classics, modern English and American poetry, and literary periodicals. Another early influence on Raymond was Rufus Wilmot Griswold, five years his senior and later to become a minor literary figure best remembered as the slanderer of Edgar Allan Poe. When they met in 1838 or 1839 Griswold was living about twenty-five miles south of Burlington and editing a newspaper. The friendship with Griswold apparently increased Raymond's interest in literary journalism.

In 1839 Raymond went to New York City to see about future employment. He asked Greeley for a job at the *New-Yorker*, but none was available; instead, Greeley offered to sell him the publication. Raymond, with neither capital nor experience, declined.

In 1840 Raymond graduated with highest honors and returned to Lima. He had reached his mature height of five feet, six inches, but his energy and enthusiasm belied his delicate stature. He joined the Whig campaign on behalf of William Henry Harrison, then tried to find a teaching position locally; none was available, nor was any other suitable work, and he headed for New York City.

Title page for the first issue of the magazine of which Raymond was the first managing editor

Raymond again applied for a job at the *New-Yorker*; Greeley had just hired an assistant–Raymond's friend Griswold–but agreed to allow Raymond to spend as much time in the office as he liked. The young man began to learn the business of journalism by tallying election returns, proofreading, and generally trying to make himself useful. When Griswold left without notice to edit the *Philadelphia Daily Standard* at a time when Greeley was also absent, Raymond attempted to put out an edition of the publication; it was not a success, and Greeley wrote to Griswold, blaming him for the fiasco: "Raymond is a good fellow, but utterly destitute of experience or knowledge.... He went to work as a novice would, shears in fist...."

Greeley eventually forgave Raymond; when the latter was offered a teaching position in North Carolina, Greeley matched the proffered salary of eight dollars per week. Raymond made the *New-Yorker* literary department his chief concern. He augmented his meager salary by acting as a correspondent for newspapers in other states, writing advertisements for patent medicines, and teaching Latin in a private school.

On 10 April 1841 Greeley launched a new Whig newspaper, the *New York Tribune*. Raymond was promoted to chief assistant on the paper, with no raise in pay. Later that year Raymond demanded and got a raise to twenty dollars per week. In October 1843 he accepted an offer of an editorship at James Watson Webb's *Morning Courier and New York Enquirer* at twenty-five dollars a week. On 24 October he married Juliette Weaver of Winooski, Vermont, his sweetheart from college days; they had seven children, two of whom died in early childhood. Raymond was given full editorial control of the *Courier and Enquirer* in 1848. He was elected to the New York State Assembly in November 1849; following his reelection in 1850, the Whig-dominated assembly named him speaker.

In addition to his journalistic and political duties, Raymond was reading manuscripts and scouting for new talent for the Harper and Brothers publishing firm. In 1850, at a salary of one hundred dollars per month, he became managing editor of a new publication, *Harper's New Monthly Magazine*, the brainchild of Fletcher Harper. Original plans had called for the first issue to usher in the new year of 1850, but it was not until spring that actual production began. The delay may have been because of Raymond's busy schedule: during the winter of 1849 he was in Albany, and he also had demanding editorial duties at the *Courier*. The Harper brothers, however, considered him to be the most qualified for the job, not only for his skill as an astute reader of manuscripts but because he was a writer who could compress the news objectively and clearly. From the start, Raymond wrote the "Monthly Record of Current Events" column, which concerned itself with American and European political and cultural news. At first the column was ten to twelve pages long; in later volumes it dropped to five or six pages as new columns were added to the magazine, requiring a reduction in space.

"A Word At The Start" was the introduction to volume 1, number 1 of *Harper's New Monthly Magazine*, published in June 1850. It promised readers 144 double-columned octavo pages for each issue. The editors also promised the periodical writings of the best authors in the world, including Charles Dickens and Edward Bulwer-Lytton. The magazine would offer literary criticism, reprints from leading British and American quarterly reviews, notices of scientific discoveries and mechanical inventions, travel articles, and transcriptions of important speeches. The first issue included the beginnings of two serials: *Maurice Tiernay, Soldier of Fortune* by Charles Lever and *Lettice Arnold* by Mrs. Anne Marsh; three short stories, two of them by Dickens; travel essays; biographical sketches; popular articles on science; and two pages of fashion plates. A book review section, "Literary Notices," was written by George Ripley, founder of the Brook Farm colony and the *Dial*. Columns added later included the "Editor's Drawer," written by Lewis Gaylord Clark of the *Knickerbocker* and based on amusing clippings from the desk drawer of Fletcher Harper; the "Editor's Table," dealing with political, social, and philosophical topics, by Tayler Lewis, a professor at Union College; and the "Editor's Easy Chair," by Donald G. Mitchell. Another later addition was "Comicalities, Original and Selected," a page or two of cartoons.

The magazine was an instant success, although it was criticized as being a slap in the face to American authors. Most of the contents consisted of the serialization of works by British authors and excerpts from Dickens's *Household Words* and other British publications. The monthly columns were written by American writers, but because of the prevailing vogue for anonymity, none of their bylines ever appeared. In fact, few bylines appeared anywhere unless the author had the stature of a Leigh Hunt, Samuel Coleridge, or Thomas Babington Macaulay.

Most of the readers quickly became hooked on the serial installments of such books as Dickens's *Bleak House*, William Makepeace Thackeray's *The Newcomes*, Bulwer-Lytton's *My Novel*, and George Eliot's *Romola*. The most successful of the serials in the early years, however, was John S. C. Abbott's *History of Napoleon Bonaparte*. It ran from volumes 3 to 10 and took the French rather than British point of view. Much of its appeal came from the woodcuts which illustrated it. *Harper's* had progressed from a few pages of pictures in the back of the first edition to a degree of illustration previously unknown in magazines.

Mindful of the competition from the approximately 685 other periodicals then being published, the Harper brothers printed only 7,500 copies of the first issue. By the end of the year they were printing 50,000 copies. In early 1853 the magazine boasted a circulation of 118,000.

Readers eagerly gobbled up a magazine that was larger than its competitors and, at twenty-five cents per issue or three dollars a year, cheaper.

The *International Weekly Miscellany,* edited by Raymond's old friend Griswold, began on 1 July 1850; it became a monthly in September and was renamed the *International Miscellany* in October and the *International Monthly Magazine* in December. The two magazines continuously battled over famous authors, but Griswold was no match for the wily Fletcher Harper. The last issue of Griswold's magazine was published in April 1852. Subscribers were informed that the publication was merging with *Harper's,* but no such announcement appeared in that magazine.

In 1851 Webb altered one of Raymond's editorials on the slavery issue, and the latter resigned from the *Courier.* With one of his former colleagues at the *Tribune,* George Jones, who was by then a banker in Albany, and Edward B. Wesley, another banker, Raymond started the *New-York Daily Times.* With Raymond as editor, the first issue came off the presses on 18 September 1851.

In 1853 Raymond and Greeley tangled in the pages of their respective newspapers over the international copyright treaty then pending in the United States Senate. It was common practice at this time for publishers in the United States and Great Britain to pirate manuscripts originally published in each other's countries. Greeley, a proponent of the treaty, knowing of Raymond's association with the Harper brothers, accused the city's wealthy publishers of profiteering. Raymond argued that, while authors should receive due recompense for their labors in their native land, the imposition of restrictions on foreign works would lead to their nonpublication in America, thus depriving the reading public of a source of great literature. When the *New York Evening Post* accused *Harper's* of pirating "Uncle Bernard's Story" from an American magazine, *Putnam's Monthly,* Raymond countered with an editorial in the *Times* on 6 September 1853 explaining that "the Editor of *Harper's Magazine,* who gave it into the printer's hands, happened to be in Europe when the June number of *Putnam's Monthly* was issued; and to this circumstance his ignorance of the fact of its having appeared in that work, is due." He also pointed out that *Putnam's* had, in fact, copied the work from *Eliza Cook's Journal,* a London weekly. Actually, although *Harper's* depended on pirated materials in its early days, the Harpers had begun to buy the American rights to British

Raymond's home at 12 West Ninth Street, New York. His unconscious body was placed inside the front door after midnight on 18 June 1869; he died a few hours later of a cerebral hemorrhage.

works in 1852 with *Bleak House.* Raymond realized, however, that appearances were against him. It did not help matters that Fletcher Harper's son had just bought into the *Times.*

On 10 December 1853 the Harper publishing establishment was destroyed by fire. Raymond later wrote that "the fire originated, strangely enough, in the excessive carefulness of a plumber, who had occasion to make some repairs of water-pipes in a press-room. Having lighted his lamp from a gas-burner, and not wishing to throw the paper which he had used upon the floor for fear of fire, he looked about for the means of extinguishing it; and seeing what he supposed to be a pan of water in a small room adjoining, devoted to cleaning the press-roller, he thrust the lighted paper into it." The pan contained highly inflammable camphine, which immediately caught fire, "and the flames spread with a rapidity, and blazed with a fury, which rendered it impossible to check them." The fire broke out when most employees were out to lunch; only one woman, who jumped out of a window and broke her leg, was seriously injured. Everything was lost in the fire except some contracts, business papers, and printing plates which had been stored underground. By the end of the day the Harpers had tallied their losses–more than one million dollars, only twenty percent of it covered by insurance–and decided to rebuild the business. The most vital concern was the January issue of *Harper's New Monthly*. Raymond was instructed to telegraph contributors to send replacement copy. By the next morning plans had been made to salvage the subterranean plates as soon as the ruins cooled sufficiently, to contract with other printers to print them, to order type, to see what use could be made of the two surviving buildings, and to order printing presses. Finally, an advertisement was drafted for the Monday morning newspapers, thanking the police and firemen who had helped and announcing that the firm would stay in business. When the meeting broke up, Raymond remarked: "This has been more like an evening of social festivity than a consultation over a great calamity." By 10 January 1854 the first postfire issue of the magazine was ready. Its 144 pages contained no illustrations; text could be quickly typeset, but pictures could not be engraved as rapidly. For the 135,000-copy edition Raymond wrote "A Word of Apology," a three-page history of the firm that was given the lead position in the issue. Raymond resigned from the magazine in 1856 because of the press of duties at the *Times* and in politics.

In 1857 Juliette Raymond and the children sailed for Europe, ostensibly for the purpose of the children's education. Although Raymond's absences due to work and politics were partially responsible for the separation, he was not totally to blame. Mrs. Raymond, beautiful and brilliant, was also puritanical, to the degree that she would not allow a deck of cards in her home; she also possessed a violent temper. Their socializing at home, which her husband so enjoyed, became rarer. The rift between them was never so deep as to cause total estrangement, but it was deep enough to effect long separations. Raymond made several trips to visit his family during their sojourn.

In 1859 Raymond and *Times* correspondent William Johnston made their way to Solferino, Italy, where a battle of the Franco-Austrian war was pending; they were the only American journalists present. After the battle they went to an inn in Castiglione and pieced together what had happened, partly from their own observations and partly through accounts from the wounded leaving the field; Raymond wrote the dispatch. At dawn Johnston rode to Brescia and passed the report to an imperial courier en route to Paris, where it was delivered to Mrs. Raymond with instructions to get it on the first steamer for New York. Although bulletins about Solferino had already appeared in the press, Raymond's account, published eighteen days after the battle, was the first eyewitness description printed in any American newspaper. In late summer Raymond and his family returned home.

At the 1860 Republican convention in Chicago Raymond hoped to see William Henry Seward named as the Republican presidential candidate, but Abraham Lincoln won the nomination. Raymond was a member of the committee that went to Springfield to congratulate the victor. He spent most of the Civil War years traveling to Albany; Washington, D.C.; and the various battlefields. As the war progressed, the *Times* offered more and more support to administration policies. In 1861 Raymond was again elected to the state assembly and named speaker. In 1864 he narrowly won election to the House of Representatives on the ticket of the Union party, a coalition of Republicans and disaffected Democrats.

When the war ended, Mrs. Raymond and the children–except for the oldest son–returned to Europe. Raymond turned to other women for companionship, particularly Rose Eytinge, an actress.

In his first major speech before Congress, in December 1865, Raymond urged the body "to act with those who seek to complete the restoration of the Union.... I would exact of them all needed and all just guarantees for their future loyalty to the Constitution and to the laws of the United States.... But I would seek to allay rather than stimulate the animosities and hatred, however just they may be, to which the war has given rise...." But the Radical Republicans in Congress steadily gained control. In March 1866 a Radical-sponsored civil rights bill forbidding racial discrimination was passed. Raymond voted against it because, although he agreed with its goals, he also believed in state sovereignty. Three months later, however, Raymond voted in favor of the Fourteenth Amendment, which would achieve the same purpose as the civil rights bill. Although he explained that he favored the amendment because it was constitutional whereas the civil rights bill was not, he was accused of "trimming," an accusation which would surface many times in the next few years. When Democrats moved into positions of power in his branch of the Union party, Raymond performed another about-face, and his newspaper supported the Radical candidate for governor against the Democratic candidate. During the second session of the House he voted against the military reconstruction act, arguing that military force was not needed in the South; when the act was altered by the Senate, Raymond turned about again and voted in its favor.

After adjournment Raymond returned home exhausted to his newspaper and his work with the growing Associated Press. In the summer of 1867, suffering from severe headaches, he went to Europe to visit his family. When he returned he announced in the *Times* that he was finished with politics and henceforth would devote all his energies to journalism. He went back to Europe in the summer of 1868. He was still having headaches and had developed a trembling in his right hand and a facial twitch, but he refused to see a doctor. When he returned to New York, Mrs. Raymond and the children–except for a daughter who was still in school on the Isle of Wight–came with him.

In February 1869 Raymond's fourteen-year-old son Walter died following an illness. Raymond was grief-stricken, particularly since his own father had died a few months previously. The melancholia which had plagued him for the past four years–he called it "soul weariness"–worsened. On 17 June Raymond and his daughter Mary drove to Greenwood Cemetery in Brooklyn to select a permanent gravesite for Walter. They returned to New York around six in the evening. Raymond stopped briefly at the *Times*, then went home for dinner and an evening with visitors. About ten o'clock he excused himself to go to a "political consultation," as the *Times* euphemistically described it later; actually, he visited Rose Eytinge. After midnight a carriage stopped in front of Raymond's house; two men deposited the unconscious Raymond on the floor inside his front door and fled. Mary discovered her father several hours later and summoned a doctor, but Raymond died of a stroke in the early dawn hours.

The newspapers hailed Raymond as "probably" the nation's greatest journalist, but there was less of a consensus about his political career. Some expressed admiration for the way he had put his country above his political party and always adhered to his convictions; most of the criticism centered on Raymond's dividing his energies between journalism and politics. As to his personal qualities, however, opinion was unanimous. *Harper's Weekly* summed it up: "No man in the editorial fraternity will be personally remembered for more friendly acts, for a more constant kindliness of nature."

Biographies:

Augustus Maverick, *Henry J. Raymond and the New York Press for Thirty Years* (Hartford, Conn.: Hale, 1870);

Francis Brown, *Raymond of the Times* (New York: Norton, 1951).

References:

Eugene Exman, *The Brothers Harper* (New York: Harper & Row, 1965), pp. 254-256, 314-315, 321-322;

Exman, *The House of Harper* (New York, Evanston & London: Harper & Row, 1967), pp. 71-72, 133, 147, 259.

Papers:

Papers of Henry J. Raymond are at the New York Public Library; the New York Historical Society; Widener Library, Harvard University; the Boston Public Library; and in the Abraham Lincoln Papers at the Library of Congress.

Josephine St. Pierre Ruffin

(31 August 1842-13 March 1924)

Nora Hall
University of Minnesota

MAJOR POSITION HELD: Editor and publisher, *Woman's Era* (1894-1898).

In 1894, when most black Americans were uneducated, struggling to make sure their families were provided for, and striving to obtain and keep jobs, Josephine St. Pierre Ruffin, a wealthy black Bostonian, began publishing the *Woman's Era*, a national magazine. The *Woman's Era* was established for educated black women and was an outlet for their writing. Black education, cultural pride, cultural advancement, and personal and community improvement were among topics covered in the publication. The magazine was not frivolous; its founding marked a distinctive political and literary period for black women.

Born in Boston, Massachusetts, 31 August 1842, Josephine St. Pierre was the sixth child of John and Eliza Matilda Mehenick St. Pierre. Her father was a free black of mixed Indian, English, and French ancestry. Her mother was a native of Cornwall, England. She began her early education in Salem, Massachusetts, elementary schools because her parents did not want her to be limited by segregated educational environments in Boston. In 1855 the school segregation ban was lifted in Boston, and she returned home to attend the Bowdoin School.

At age sixteen Josephine married Boston native George L. Ruffin. His family was one of the wealthiest Afro-American families in the country. Shortly after marriage the couple moved to Liverpool, England, hoping to escape discrimination. They returned to Boston in 1861, and George Ruffin began attending Harvard law school. He was one of its earliest black graduates when he completed degree requirements in 1869. George Ruffin later became a state legislator and a member of the Boston City Council. In 1883 he became the first black judge in Massachusetts. He held that post until his death in 1886.

Between 1861 and 1883 five children were born to the Ruffins. One son, Hubert St. Pierre, had a career in the field of law. George Lewis

Josephine St. Pierre Ruffin (courtesy of the Trustees of the Boston Public Library)

was in the manufacturing business, and their third son, Stanley, was an inventor. Florida, the only girl born to the family, was a Boston schoolteacher. One of their children, Robert, died when he was an infant.

Josephine Ruffin organized her home life, cared for the children, and also rose to prominence within Boston's black community as a club organizer and suffragist. As evidenced by her activities in many arenas during the Civil War, Ruffin enjoyed public affairs, actually recruiting for the Union army. In 1879 she was primarily responsible for organizing the Boston Kansas Relief Association, which sent clothing and money to large numbers of needy blacks who had migrated to Kansas. Ruffin was an active member of the New England Women's Club and served on the executive board of the Massachusetts School Suffrage Association. It was her affiliation with those organizations that introduced her to leading women activists Julia Ward Howe, Susan B. Anthony, Elizabeth Cady Stanton, and Lucy Stone.

In the early 1890s, before her club organizing began in earnest, Ruffin worked as a columnist for the weekly *Boston Courant*. The *Courant* was one of many black newspapers established during the nineteenth century to address the deplorable condition of black Americans. No records of her exact contributions to the *Courant* have been found. She joined the New England Women's Press Association during the early 1890s. She undoubtedly was one of the association's first black members.

In 1894 Ruffin organized the Woman's Era Club, one of the first clubs in the United States for black women. She became its president. That same year Ruffin founded, edited, and published the national *Woman's Era* magazine as a mouthpiece for club activities. The *Era* soon became a vehicle for literary articles on social and political issues affecting black women nationally. Poetry, short stories, and essays were also major features. Ruffin encouraged guest columns from women's club leaders throughout the country. Josephine's daughter, Florida, and Maria L. Baldwin assisted in coordinating club activities. Florida Ruffin was also one of the magazine's editors.

"The stumbling block in the way of even the most cultured colored woman is the narrowness of her environment," Ruffin wrote in the 1 June 1894 issue of the *Era*. "But let the fact be emphasized that in the work for the betterment of the world the claims for recognition of this class cannot be overlooked, it is a large and growing factor in the intellectual as well as industrial life of the country; and the strength of the chain of woman's advancement will be determined by the strength of this weak link. It is to help strengthen this link by hastening the day when a keener appreciation of the hindrances of this class and a better understanding between all classes shall exist that this little venture [the *Woman's Era*] is sent out on its mission." Some historians have referred to the *Woman's Era* as a newspaper. Its format, style, and content, however, are more like the magazines of the period.

A single issue of the *Woman's Era* sold for ten cents. Annual subscription to the magazine was one dollar, and clubs could purchase bulk orders of one hundred copies for an annual fee of seven dollars. In the November 1894 issue of the *Era* Ruffin called upon all club members to support the advertisers that purchased space in the magazine. The November issue carried retail store, candy shop, cosmetic, real estate, piano agent, and food store advertisements.

Ruffin's goal for *Woman's Era* was to highlight the professional contributions of Afro-American women and to promote cooperation among women (especially women of color) throughout the United States. There were regular reviews of literature, music, and drama. Topics examined in the periodical included the aesthetic value of domestic science and the shame of lynching. Gertrude Bustill Mossell, a well-known black historical writer, had a column in the *Era* called the "Open Court," which examined public opinion. Ruffin frequently featured in cover stories unusual black businesswomen like Nova Scotia ice merchant Georgianna Whetsel. Position papers prepared by various women's clubs were featured in nearly every issue. Ruffin's quest to promote cooperation among black women in the United States led her to organize the National Federation of Afro-American Women in 1895. It united thirty-six black women's clubs in twelve states. Among states represented in the first few months of the organization's formation were Alabama, California, Georgia, Illinois, Kansas, Louisiana, Massachusetts, Missouri, New York, Nebraska, North Carolina, Pennsylvania, Rhode Island, South Carolina, Tennessee, and Virginia. The *Era* became the symbol of the federation and always provided activity columns from club women in different states. Editors tried to feature a different state each month.

The purpose of the National Federation of Afro-American Women was to illustrate the intelligence of black women and disprove charges of immorality. Its first meeting was held in Boston 29-31 July 1895. Ruffin is best known for the speech that she made during that meeting calling for cooperation among Afro-American and white women's clubs. She also sought to clarify the role of black women: "All over America there is to be found a large and growing class of earnest, intelligent, progressive colored women who, if not leading full, useful lives, are only waiting for the op-

First page of an issue of the magazine for black women founded by Ruffin in 1894

portunity to do so, many of them still warped and cramped for lack of opportunity, not only to do more but to be more; and yet if an estimate of the colored women of America is called for, the inevitable reply, glibly given, is: 'For the most part, ignorant and immoral, some exceptions of course, but these don't count.'... it is ... our bounden duty to stand forth and declare ourselves and our principles, to teach an ignorant and suspicious world that our aims and interests are identical with those of all good, aspiring women."

Mrs. Booker T. Washington, the wife of the founder of Tuskegee Institute in Alabama, became the president of the National Federation of Afro-American Women. The federation did its work through departments at the national level. Club representatives carried those initiatives back to their local chapters and conducted needed community work based on the national agenda. The federation's major departments included: Woman Suffrage, Education, Patriotism, Health Care, Child Welfare, and Gainful Employment.

In July 1896 the federation became the National Association of Colored Women. It reportedly had three hundred thousand members, located in every state, as well as members in Liberia, Canada, Haiti, and Cuba. Mary Church Terrell was selected as its first president. Josephine Ruffin was elected one of the vice-presidents.

In November 1897, just three years after the magazine had begun, Ruffin announced that the *Woman's Era* had accomplished its mission. The magazine changed its focus and became an advocate for prison reform in the South; articles that appeared in the *Era* beginning with this issue contained information on the convict lease system and the imprisonment of young people for minor offenses. The magazine ceased publication in 1898.

From 1899 to 1902 Ruffin was an executive board member of the Massachusetts State Federation of Women's Clubs. She created quite a stir by constantly citing accusations that racism excluded black memberships in popular women's clubs. She worked toward cooperation with all women's clubs but often faced exclusion. At age fifty-eight Ruffin made one last attempt to dispel club memberships based on race by attempting to get the General Federation of Women's Clubs to accept the Women's Era Club as a member. The federation refused membership to the black club at its Milwaukee, Wisconsin, meeting in 1900. Josephine Ruffin attended the meeting as a representative.

Ruffin's journalism career ceased when the *Woman's Era* folded, but she continued to be active as a community leader. She helped develop the Association for the Promotion of Child Training in the South. She was one of the founders of the Boston branch of the National Association for the Advancement of Colored People and the League of Women for Community Service. She helped raise funds for the enlargement of Mrs. Jennie (Davis) Sharpe's school at Mount Coffee, Liberia, in 1902.

In 1924, at age eighty-one, Ruffin died of nephritis at her home in Boston. She was buried at Mount Auburn Cemetery, in Cambridge, Massachusetts.

References:
Hallie Q. Brown, *Homespun Heroines and Other Women of Distinction* (Xenia, Ohio: Aldine, 1926), pp. 151-153;

Penelope L. Bullock, *The Afro-American Periodical Press 1838-1909* (Baton Rouge: Louisiana State University Press, 1981), pp. 169-170, 189-194, 215, 276;

Elizabeth Lindsay Davis, ed., *Lifting As They Climb: An Historical Record of the National Association of Colored Women* (Washington, D.C.: National Association of Colored Women, 1933), pp. 17-19, 236-239;

Marianna W. Davis, ed., *Contributions of Black Women To America, Vol. 1* (Columbia, S.C.: Kenday, 1981), pp. 231-233;

Eleanor Flexner, *Century of Struggle: The Woman's Rights Movement in the United States* (Cambridge, Mass.: Belknap Press, 1979), pp. 193-195;

Paula Giddings, *When and Where I Enter* (New York: Bantam Books, 1984), pp. 30ff.;

Julia Ward Howe, ed., *Representative Women of New England* (Boston: New England Historical Publishing Company, 1904), pp. 335-339;

Gerda Lerner, *Black Women in White America: A Documentary History* (New York: Vintage Books, 1973), pp. 440-443.

Papers:
A few personal notes written by Ruffin can be found in the Mary Church Terrell Papers, Manuscript Division, Library of Congress, Washington, D.C.

Edward I. Sears

(1819?-7 December 1876)

Donna Ullrich-Eaton
University of Detroit

MAJOR POSITION HELD: Editor and publisher, *National Quarterly Review* (1860-1876).

TRANSLATION: Henri Emile Chevalier, *Legends of the Sea: 39 Men for One Woman* (New York: Bradburn, 1862).

PERIODICAL PUBLICATIONS: "Quackery of Insurance Companies," *National Quarterly Review*, 10 (September 1862): 72;
"Our Quack Doctors and Their Performances," *National Quarterly Review*, 16 (March 1864): 72;
"Kepler and His Discoveries," *National Quarterly Review*, 16 (March 1864): 335;
"Commencements of Colleges and Seminaries," *National Quarterly Review*, 18 (September 1864): 347;
"English Rule of Ireland," *National Quarterly Review*, 25 (June 1866): 358;
"Central Park under Ring-Leader Rule," *National Quarterly Review*, 44 (March 1871): 294.

Edward Isidore Sears is best known for his campaigns against the "quacks and scoundrels" of his time. His *National Quarterly Review* became an early champion of the same ideals Adolph Ochs would establish as he turned the failing *New York Times* into the most respected news publication of the twentieth century, printing "All the News That's Fit to Print." Sears was well versed on many subjects and was able to expound upon historical, scientific, political, educational, economic, and literary topics at length and with confidence. Considering his prolific contribution to nineteenth-century journalism, it is striking that so little has been recorded about the editor and publisher of the *National Quarterly Review*.

Sears did not aspire to fame through his writing, and instead dedicated himself to the publication of the review and to teaching. The few biographical accounts that exist list his birth year variously as 1819, 1820, and 1824. Most sources agree that Sears was born in 1819 in The Neale, County Mayo, Ireland, to a family of means. He was reared, with two brothers and one sister, as a member of the gentry, receiving a superior education and training in the manners of the upper class. While he loved fishing, hunting, and the equestrian sports, he viewed them only as forms of relaxation.

He earned an A.B. from Trinity College of Dublin in 1839. Prior to his move to the United States in 1848, he wrote for the *Impartial Reporter* of Enniskillen, Ireland, and there married Catherine Irvine.

At the age of twenty-nine he moved with Catherine to New York City, and immediately he began reporting duties at the *New York Herald* under James Gordon Bennett. Later he transferred to Horace Greeley's *New York Tribune* before beginning his review and a teaching career. Sears made a respectable living by his pen, contributing to the *Dublin University Magazine*, *Fraser's Magazine*, *Holden's Magazine*, *North American Review*, *American Journal of Education*, *Westminster Review*, *Edinburgh Review*, and *Boston Post*, among others.

However well received his writings might have been during this period, Sears viewed these free-lance efforts and the general reporting assignments as beneath his intelligence and talents. It was his frustration that led Sears to conceive of his quarterly periodical, modeled after British reviews which he greatly admired. He felt it should represent the entire country, unlike the *North American Review*, which was published in and for the Boston area. Hoping that it would attract the scholarship of the nation, he named it the *National Quarterly Review*. By 1860 he was ready to distribute his prospectus announcing the new periodical which would "be American in the broadest, and most legitimate acceptation of the term." The *National Quarterly Review*, "although devoted mainly to Literature, Art, Education and general Culture," would "contain occasional articles on the prominent political questions of the day." The prospectus ended with Sears's assurance that "no pains nor expense will be spared to render it in fact, as well as in name, THE NATIONAL QUARTERLY of the United States."

In June 1860, as Sears had promised, the first issue appeared. Shortly thereafter he added a slogan to its cover, "Pulchrum est bene facere reipublicae, etiam bene dicere haud absurdum est" (It is beautiful to do well for your country, also to speak well of your country is not absurd).

Readers were entertained with lengthy discussions of national and New York City politics, arts, economics, literature, and critical reviews. In the tradition of English journals of this kind, Sears and his contributors provided the reader with background information to explain the timeliness of the subject. For this reason, each issue, which sold for one dollar, regularly ranged from two hundred to four hundred pages.

Although the publication was announced and treated as a quarterly, and the review's own catalog of issues and articles makes it appear as if it did publish quarterly, this was not always true. Particularly in the early years, two quarters would be combined for publication, and in later years the publication would appear randomly. While libraries have tried to catalog the magazine by volumes, Sears and his successor, David A. Gorton, preferred to identify them only by issue numbers. In twenty years the *National Quarterly Review* published seventy-nine issues.

By December 1861 Sears had added advertising to the *National Quarterly Review*, and full-page advertisements appeared at the beginning and end of each issue until its demise. Advertisements for colleges outweighed any other offering. Manhattan College regularly enjoyed a page's promotion, as did the Supplee Institute, Poughkeepsie Female Academy, and the Ursuline Academy, to name a few. Other publications, whose editors' praise of this review could be found in the issue, were also included. Interestingly enough, insurance, one of the main targets of Sears's campaign against "quacks and scoundrels," was also a service regularly advertised in the *National Quarterly Review*. Very few insurance companies were included, but those that did advertise included detailed charts of their assets and breakdowns of the financial investment expected from the consumer. Sears wrote article after article with titles like "Insurance Companies, Good, Bad and Indifferent" and "The Quacks of Insurance," upbraiding insurance companies for their scams. Considering his active literary crusades against fraud in insurance, it is likely that he played a major role in determining the content of insurance advertisements in his publication.

It was only in these sections, opening and closing each issue, that graphics of any kind appeared. Within the text of the issue, the gray of unrelieved print followed the lead of other traditional journals and reviews.

Although the prospectus assured readers that this "new Periodical will not be the organ of any clique or party," Sears's conservative nature showed in his lack of support for Abraham Lincoln.

Sears, who never became an American citizen, wrote with hostility of English rule in Ireland. Gorton wrote, "One should remember that Dr. Sears was an Irishman. And what kind of an Irishman, pray, must he be who could love England?" And so, objectivity and fair play as suggested in the prospectus sometimes gave way to the influences and convictions of the publisher.

His disdain for what he called "immoral" literature, in particular translations of French writers, drew attention in the *National Quarterly Review*, as did his love for classical literature and languages. Often he would discuss the works of writers and philosophers like Dante, Horace, Chaucer, Plato, and Fichte, quoting from Latin and Greek texts without translation.

Sears was not a religious man, "preferring to leave theology to the theologians," but he welcomed discussion of various religious sects in the *National Quarterly Review* without offering discussion or criticism himself. Gorton wrote, "while he may not have feared God, his respect for man forbade him to speak lightly of man's noblest sentiment–Religion." Here his beliefs did not influence the review's content.

Some regular contributors to the *National Quarterly Review* included Karl Blind on European politics, Dr. R. S. Mackenzie on European politics and literature, John T. Morse, Jr., on history, David Trowbridge on astronomy, John Pyne on history and comparative theology, Professor Charles Morris on archaeology, and Henry Giles on moral and literary topics. Contributors respected Sears and counted on 'him to improve upon their work with his keen editing skills and guidance. Mrs. A. Lincoln Phelps, in her contribution to a lengthy discussion of Sears after his death (published in the January 1877 issue of *National Quarterly Review*) explained Sears's effect on her writing and perspective: "To Dr. Sears I am indebted for thus putting me into a new school, where, to some extent, I learned the beautiful art of journalism and reviewing; to take the cream from both, and to mold this into new forms."

Articles were uniformly unsigned, as was the policy of such reviews as late as 1879 when other American reviews had begun to abandon the tradition of contributor anonymity. In fact, the first article printed with a byline opened the March issue of 1879 and was stolen from the *Democratic Review* of 1846, an unfortunate occurrence for the already failing publication.

Gorton, a medical doctor and close friend of Sears, took control of the *National Quarterly Review* just prior to Sears's death. Sears, according to Gorton, worked on the December 1876 issue right up to his death, editing copy and proofreading printer's galleys. Under Gorton the publication followed its original format with very few changes, though more literary and arts reviews were added and the size of the publication increased slightly. But even Gorton admitted that the review lost character when it lost Sears. The *National Quarterly Review* continued under Gorton's charge through 1879, when he turned it over to associate editor C. H. Woodman, who published the final year. In October 1880 the last issue of the *National Quarterly Review* rolled off the presses.

In its prime the *National Quarterly Review* earned the esteem of its competitors in Great Britain and Canada as well as in the United States. The *London Spectator* considered it the finest American periodical of its time, and the *Toronto Leader* urged that it "receive encouragement in this province." In addition to praise for the high literary quality of his publication, Sears was applauded for his "courage to unmask false pretensions" by the *Edinburg Scotsman* and by the *Boston Journal* for his "fearless utterance" against corruption and dishonesty.

The *National Quarterly Review* and Edward I. Sears were synonymous. The publication could barely exist without its founder, as proved by its decline and ultimate demise after his death. Sears had been advised that he might recover from what was to be his final battle with angina if he took a vacation to a warmer climate. He chose instead to stay and continue publishing the review. So consuming was the *National Quarterly Review* to Sears that its demands would force him to give up his chair at Manhattan College in 1866 after only four years of teaching.

The tone of the *National Quarterly Review* was dictated by Sears's writings. He had two general styles in which to present his subjects, the classical essay and literary composition. He employed the first when discussing topics of historical or educational direction, but he preferred a more literary style when he intended to employ wit and sarcasm. Gorton points out, however, that Sears was an interpreter of other men's ideas, rather than an originator of ideas himself: "he did not wander in unbeaten paths, nor rack his brain over some new conception of the Infinite."

For Sears, education was a never-ending process. As he traveled, he challenged himself to learn the details of artists, writers, and musicians of the cultures he visited, as well as the customs and politics of the ethnic groups he encountered.

Fluent in Latin, Greek, French, German, Italian, and Spanish, he wrote at length about the contributions of writers and philosophers of these cultures. He was especially partial to classical Latin and Greek. He was equally versed in mathematics, chemistry, history, physics, literature, art, music, and jurisprudence. In 1864 he was awarded an honorary doctorate of law from the University of New York, because of his expertise in the field. "Many a time has he tripped up and confused an unwary medical counselor whom he called to attend his family," Gorton wrote of Sears's knowledge of the science.

His explosive temper, which even his most devout followers recognized as his worst attribute, coupled with his well-rounded educational base and an intense desire for truth led him to regularly wage battle within the pages of the *National Quarterly Review* with those "charlatans, scams and quacks" of his time. He took on the medical profession, insurance companies, educational institutions, and political systems, attacking the offending parties vehemently. He was no less kind to authors. According to Sears there were no weak books, only good books or bad books. Therefore, in his reviews weak books were bad books.

Exposing fraudulent insurance companies, Sears spent a great deal of time working out charts to calculate the true assets of the companies he was investigating. He explained at length the definitions of such terms as "premium notes," "deferred premiums," "interest due and accrued," and others as they pertained to the consumer's investment.

He was especially remembered for his mockery of New York City politics of the 1870s. His "Central Park under Ring-Leader Rule" article caused quite a stir during the period and was so popular that it drew a written response from the city's political machine. That response Sears chose to run in the following issue under the title "The 'Spiteful' National Quarterly and Innocent Ring-Leader Rule."

So effectively could Sears incite anger from those he criticized that he regularly experienced threats to the publication's well-being and his own life. Abusive and insulting letters, libel suits, and blackmail were also the norm, but nothing seemed to succeed in stopping Sears's critical pen or in damaging the reputation of the *National Quarterly Review*. It is to his credit that he never argued an issue without evidence.

Sears joined Manhattan College in 1862 as a professor of Latin and English literature. According to the Reverend Brother Paulian, Sears had a "multilateral and acquisitive rather than an analytical and exhaustive mind." Paulian, making a contribution to the remembrance of Sears in the *National Quarterly Review*, described him as a practical teacher expecting students to account for the knowledge they gained. To do this, Sears regularly challenged his students with questions in class.

His love for the classic languages fit naturally into his teaching scheme. He promoted the languages and their conversational usage by conducting conversation classes and encouraging students to practice extemporaneous speaking as often as possible to insure eloquence of style and substantial quality of message. Paulian observed that Sears would not simply award general approval or disapproval of a student's work, but would analyze each sentence. Even Paulian agreed that when he was incited, Sears's pen could be "dipped in vinegar."

By 1866 the *National Quarterly Review* required so much of Sears's time that he was forced to leave his teaching post and devote his full attention to the publication, but only with great regret. He continued to support the college with the profits of the *National Quarterly Review*, establishing a professorship in Latin and directing additional funds for other uses by the college.

Though he and Catherine never had any children of their own, he maintained a special interest in children. He is credited with financing the education of many young men and women. At the time of his death he was financing the piano lessons of a little girl who learned of his death only after she wrote to inquire why payments for her lessons had ceased. He was known to spend a great deal of time listening to and talking with children, taking their views on subjects seriously. He was also fond of his dog, Dash, who was always at his side. So indispensable was Dash that Sears claimed he could not write well without him nearby.

His friends consisted mainly of scholars, many of whom he had never met but with whom he corresponded. He felt more comfortable in his writings than in discussions which called for "a certain amount of light conversation," something he admitted he had "only a small fund of."

Apart from his teaching and his work at the *National Quarterly Review*, Sears was recognized for his contributions to journals and reviews both abroad and in the states. He was also known for his work in translating *Legends of the Sea: 39 Men for One Woman* (1862) by the French author Henri Emile Chevalier. In Sears's preface to the book he assures readers that it is not an immoral book, as might be inferred from the title.

Whether waging battles with or about words, Sears filled his life and the pages of his review with character, conviction, and commitment. In announcing Sears's death to the readers of the *National Quarterly Review*, his editors and contributors used exclamation points to proclaim their despair and loss. One described him as "sans peur et sans reproche" (without fear and without reproach). He dedicated his life to journalism, but it brought him little lasting attention or fame.

References:

David A. Gorton, "The Death of the Editor of the National Quarterly Review," *National Quarterly Review*, 67 (December 1876): 7-10;

Gorton, "Impressions and Reminiscences of Edward I. Sears, LL.D.," *National Quarterly Review*, 68 (March 1877): 197-246;

Gorton, "Note to Volume XXXIV," *National Quarterly Review*, 68 (March 1877): 5-6;

D. J. O'Donoghue, *The Poets of Ireland* (Dublin: Hodges Figgis, 1912), p. 418.

Roswell Smith

(30 March 1829-19 April 1892)

Frederic B. Farrar
Temple University

MAJOR POSITIONS HELD: Business manager, *Scribner's Monthly Magazine* (1870-1881), *St. Nicholas: Scribner's Illustrated Magazine for Girls and Boys* (1873-1880); president, *Century Illustrated Monthly Magazine* (1881-1890); *St. Nicholas: An Illustrated Magazine for Young Folks* (1881-1890).

Roswell Smith was an archetypal publisher. He was the president of the *Century Illustrated Monthly Magazine* when that publication was regarded as America's best periodical. He originated *St. Nicholas: Scribner's Illustrated Magazine for Girls and Boys*, considered the finest magazine published for children. He also published *The Century Dictionary and Cyclopedia* (1884-1891), the authoritative work until the *Oxford Dictionary*. Smith's motto was: "Work hard and hold your promise," to which he added business practices based on a faith in man and God. Smith was one of the first publishers to establish employee stock options and profit-sharing plans. His pioneer advertising and distribution ideas helped create the modern magazine. Smith maintained a low profile during his life and continues to be virtually unknown, forgotten by biographers, despite his major contributions to American magazines.

Roswell Chamberlain Smith was born in Lebanon, Connecticut, on 30 March 1829 to Asher Ladd and Wealthy Pratt Smith. Named for his uncle, he rarely used his full name. His father and uncle were teachers who disliked the available textbooks, so they published their own. After being immersed in this educational atmosphere for fourteen years, Smith was shipped off to New York to learn the book publishing trade at Paine and Burgess, who published books written by Smith's family.

In 1847 Smith entered Brown University's two-year liberal arts program, which he completed with high grades. He then studied law in Thomas C. Perkins's Hartford office. In Connecticut Smith met Henry L. Ellsworth, a well-known lawyer and the first patents commissioner. When Ellsworth moved to Lafayette, Indiana, he asked

Roswell Smith (Dictionary of American Portraits, *edited by Hayward and Blanche Cirker [New York: Dover, 1967]*)

Smith to join his law practice and land office. In 1852, shortly after settling in Indiana, Roswell Smith married Ellsworth's daughter Annie.

Although he became a leading citizen of Lafayette, Smith never felt quite at home in the West. In 1868 the Smiths decided to leave Indiana. Ellsworth had died and left his extensive real estate holdings to the Smiths, and coal was found on the land. With this inheritance and the fruits of a sixteen-year law practice, the Smiths fulfilled a long-standing ambition to see Europe.

In Indiana, as chairman of the Lafayette Lyceum, Smith had met the noted author and journalist Dr. Josiah Gilbert Holland when the latter was on a lecture tour. Coincidentally, both men found 1868 to be a year of career transition and planned to meet in Europe. In Geneva Smith's desire to start a new publication and Holland's offer from Charles Scribner to edit a magazine resulted in a prospectus for a new publication. Holland would be the editor and Smith would be the business manager, while Scribner would back the enterprise. In 1869, after a few meetings with Smith, Scribner agreed with Holland that the magazine could succeed with the lawyer's acumen.

Holland returned to New York in the spring of 1870, and the first issue of *Scribner's Monthly* appeared in November. In the first issue the prolific English writer and cleric George MacDonald began a long novel, "Wilfrid Cumbermede." Popular throughout Victorian England, MacDonald, known today only for his children's tales, wrote over fifty novels plus the strange story "Phantastes." Hans Christian Andersen began "Lucky Peer" in January 1871. Early *Scribner's* authors included William Cullen Bryant, Christina G. Rossetti, Bayard Taylor, Joaquin Miller, and Frank R. Stockton, who wrote the famous short story "The Lady or the Tiger?"

Scribner's Monthly was successful from the start. Readers were promised the finest illustrations, and these were provided by Alexander W. Drake, who had perfected a method of transferring photographs onto wood blocks. This process gave *Scribner's* a fine edge in illustrations until the photoengraving method became common in the next decade. Smith selected Theodore De Vinne, whose press set new standards for typographic beauty and artistic illustrations, to print the magazine. As a result the physical appearance of *Scribner's* easily surpassed that of its rivals, *Harper's Monthly* and the *Atlantic Monthly*.

In 1871 Smith began to seek advertising, a practice which was virtually unheard of at that time. Advertising historian Frank S. Presbrey credits *Scribner's* with helping to "give commercial publicity dignity at a time when it sorely needed it." Within its first year *Scribner's Monthly* carried almost four times as much advertising as *Harper's Monthly*, although the new magazine's circulation was much smaller. Twenty years later, when Smith retired, his magazine was running over seventy advertising columns per issue.

In 1873 *Scribner's Monthly* became the first American magazine to establish an English edition. Smith engaged the author and critic Edmund Gosse to represent his interests in Great Britain. Also in 1873, despite a financial depression that ruined many businesses, Smith launched another project. Dissatisfied with the quality of current publications for young people, he founded *St. Nicholas: Scribner's Illustrated Magazine for Girls and Boys*. The business manager used the production and distribution facilities of *Scribner's Monthly* for the new publication, but the decisive move was the appointment of Mary Mapes Dodge as editor. Dodge directed *St. Nicholas* for over thirty-two years. Leading critics acclaimed the magazine as "the best of all periodicals published for children," "one of the phenomenal successes of juvenile literature," and "the acknowledged leader of all periodicals for boys and girls not only in America, but in the world." Dodge wanted to produce "the cheeriest, prettiest, jolliest, welcomest magazine that boys and girls, or their parents either, have ever beheld . . ." and asserted that "a child's magazine is its leisure-ground." During Dodge's editorship contributors included Mark Twain, Bret Harte, Louisa May Alcott, Theodore Roosevelt, Howard Pyle, Emily Dickinson, Kate Douglas Wiggin, Robert Louis Stevenson, and Arthur Rackham. "Little Lord Fauntleroy" by Frances Hodgson Burnett appeared first in *St. Nicholas*, as did some of the animal stories of Rudyard Kipling. Despite the literary accolades, what many young readers remembered for years were the Palmer Cox "Brownies" who cavorted wisely in each issue. President William H. Taft said: "It is a source of pleasure, edification, and inspiration for the older as well as the younger members of the family." Once again, Smith's judgment had paid off. Later he bought and merged several children's magazines, including *Our Young Folks*, the *Little Corporal*, the *Schoolday Magazine*, and the *Children's Hour*, into *St. Nicholas*.

Growing revenues permitted Smith to explore new, exciting editorial serials. Before *St. Nicholas* was launched and the British market invaded, Smith felt the company should invest in a series to help the South get back on its feet. Amid a national depression the optimistic business manager spent the tremendous sum of thirty thousand dollars to gather material and pictures for a series titled "The Great South." He sent an expedition to investigate and report on conditions at a time when federal troops still held Southern cities. "The Great South" was an early attempt to bridge the chasm that divided the country.

As Smith continued to investigate new ventures, he began to consider book publishing. Con-

Cover for an issue of the magazine Smith published from 1881 until 1890. Prior to 1881 the magazine was titled Scribner's Monthly.

cerned about competition for his firm, Scribner sold his interest in the magazine and insisted that his name be removed from the company and the magazine. Thus in 1881 the Century Company was born and *Scribner's Monthly* became *Century Illustrated Monthly Magazine*. The first *Century* appeared in November. Holland died before the magazine was distributed, and Smith suddenly had sole control. Smith paid a lasting compliment to his friend: the only name on *Scribner's Monthly* had been "Conducted by J. G. Holland" on the cover; a December *Century* editorial said: "When Doctor Holland's name disappears from the cover, no other will take its place there." Holland and Smith had surrounded themselves with young, ambitious people, and from this enterprising group Smith chose Richard Watson Gilder, Holland's former assistant, as the new editor.

From the beginning of their association Holland and Smith had wanted to treat deserving employees with consideration. Smith established stock options and profit-sharing for employees at a time when so-called robber barons were dominating industry and labor unions were beginning to win support.

Smith continued to generate progressive publishing ideas, some of which still benefit today's periodicals. For example, formerly publishers had to keep a separate account for each subscriber if postage was prepaid or if the subscriber paid. Smith suggested to the Post Office that publications be weighed in bulk and that the publisher pay all the postage, thus eliminating unnecessary costs to publishers and their subscribers.

Smith's wife, Annie Ellsworth Smith

Now with his own publishing house, Smith turned to publishing books on sports and religion. He tried to organize the best biblical scholars to publish a revised American Bible, but the project was dropped when Smith became ill. He was able to see one ambitious publishing project through to completion–*The Century Dictionary and Cyclopedia*. Originally planned as a revision of *The Imperial Dictionary* designed to meet the needs of American readers, this educational enterprise cost over six hundred thousand dollars before a single copy was sold. *The Century Dictionary and Cyclopedia* was hailed as the best work of its kind.

Smith wrote little except business letters. One sixteen-line poem, "What the Devil Said to the Young Man," discouraged sin. Two Horatio Alger-type stories in *St. Nicholas*, "The Boy Who Worked" and "Little Holdfast," completed his literary accomplishments.

One project overseen by Smith made a lasting contribution to American history: *Battles and Leaders of the Civil War* (1887-1888), a collection of eyewitness accounts initially written for the *Century* and published regularly from 1883 to 1885. What made the war series unique were the hundreds of stories that depicted the impressions and emotions of the men who actually fought the battles. Smith had agreed to invest in the series, but he doubted that there was a continuing interest in the war. He was wrong. Circulation doubled almost overnight to 250,000, and the Century Company made nearly one million dollars on the war series, a staggering sum at that time and twice the worth of the entire company when Holland and Smith bought out Scribner.

Smith's final series project involved his hero, Abraham Lincoln. To capitalize on the national sentiment aroused by the war series, Smith persuaded John G. Nicolay and John Hay, Lincoln's two war secretaries, to write a biography of the president, the ten-volume *Abraham Lincoln: A History* (1890).

During the 1890s the *Century Magazine* hit its peak in popularity. One historian has pointed to the February 1885 issue as the greatest twenty-five-cent value in American reading. That issue contained chapters from William Dean Howells's *The Rise of Silas Lapham* (1885), Henry James's *The Bostonians* (1886), Mark Twain's *Huckleberry Finn* (1884), and Ulysses S. Grant's *Personal Memoirs* (1885). Although the *Century* continued to publish until the depression of the 1930s, the magazine never regained its overwhelming popularity of the 1880s.

In 1890 Roswell Smith abandoned his *Century* duties, resigned from all his activities, and began to fight the Bright's disease that would end his life within two years. He died on 19 April 1892, just as the magazine world was changing drastically and just before muckraking became synonymous with investigative reporting. He was eulogized by editor Gilder as a "powerful personality" who came closest to "realizing the strictest editorial idea of what a publisher ... should be." Roswell Smith, the archetypal publisher, belongs in the company of such magazine greats as Cyrus K. Curtis, Harold Ross, and Henry Luce; and in terms of his personal qualities, he leads such figures.

References:

George Washington Cable, *A Memory of Roswell Smith* (New York: Privately printed, 1892);

James C. Derby, *Fifty Years among Authors, Books and Publishers* (New York: Carleton, 1884), pp. 704-708;

Arthur John, *The Best Years of The Century* (New York: Century, 1910), pp. 9-12;

Peter Lyon, *Success Story: Life and Times of S. S. McClure* (De Land, Fla.: Everett/Edwards, 1967), pp. 46-47;

Memorials to Roswell Smith, *Century Magazine* (June 1892): 309-317;

Frank Presbrey, *The History and Development of Advertising* (Garden City, N.Y.: Doubleday, Doran, 1929), pp. 464-469;

George Presbury Rowell, *Forty Years an Advertising Agent, 1865-1905* (New York: Printers' Ink Publishing Co., 1906), pp. 413-415;

Algernon Tassin, *The Magazine in America* (New York: Dodd, Mead, 1916), pp. 287-311;

L. Frank Tooker, *The Joys and Tribulations of an Editor* (New York & London: Century, 1924).

Elizabeth Cady Stanton
(12 November 1815-26 October 1902)

Beth M. Waggenspack
Virginia Polytechnic Institute and State University

MAJOR POSITION HELD: Editor, *Revolution* (1868-1870).

SELECTED BOOKS: *Letter to the Woman's Rights Convention, Held at Worcester Oct. 1850* [and] *Letter to the Woman's Rights Convention, Held at Syracuse, Sept. 1852* (Syracuse, N.Y.: Master's Print, 1852?);

Address to the Legislature of New-York, Adopted by the State Woman's Rights Convention, Held at Albany, Tuesday and Wednesday, February 14 and 15, 1854 (Albany, N.Y.: Printed by Weed, Parsons, 1854);

The Slave's Appeal (Albany, N.Y.: Printed by Weed, Parsons and Company, 1860);

Free Speech: By Elizabeth Cady Stanton, at the Fourth Annual N.Y. State Anti-Slavery Convention at Association Hall, Albany, N.Y., February 4th and 5th, 1861 (Albany?, N.Y., 1861);

Address of Elizabeth Cady Stanton, on the Divorce Bill, before the Judiciary Committee of the New York Senate . . . Feb. 8, 1861 (Albany, N.Y.: Printed by Weed, Parsons and Company, 1861);

Address in Favor of Universal Suffrage, for the Election of Delegates to the Constitutional Convention Before the Judiciary Committee of the Legislature of New York, in the Assembly Chamber, January 23, 1867, in Behalf of the American Equal Rights Association (Albany, N.Y.: Printed by Weed, Parsons and Company, 1867);

Address of Mrs. Elizabeth Cady Stanton, Delivered at Seneca Falls & Rochester, N.Y. July 19th & Au-

Elizabeth Cady Stanton (Gale International Portrait Gallery)

gust 2d, 1848 (New York: Printed by Robert J. Johnston, 1870);

Memorial of Elizabeth Cady Stanton, Isabella Beecher Hooker, Elizabeth L. Bladen, Olympia Brown, Susan B. Anthony, and Josephine L. Griffing, to the Congress of the United States, and the Arguments Thereon before the Judiciary Committee of the U.S. Senate, by Isabella Beecher Hooker, Elizabeth Cady Stanton, and Susan B. Anthony, Washington, January 12, 1872* (Washington, D.C.: Chronicle Publishing Company, 1872);

The Pleasures of Age: An Address Delivered by Elizabeth Cady Stanton on Her Seventieth Birthday (N.p., 1885?);

Bible and Church Degrade Women (Chicago: H. L. Green, 189?)–comprises *The Effects of Woman Suffrage on Questions of Morals and Religion, The Degraded Status of Woman in the Bible,* and *The Christian Church and Woman;*

Woman Suffrage: Hearing before the Judiciary Committee of the House of Representatives . . . February 11, 1890 (Washington, D.C.: U.S. Government Printing Office, 1890);

Suffrage a Natural Right (Chicago: Open Court Publishing Company, 1894);

The Woman's Bible, 2 volumes (New York: European Publishing Company, 1895, 1898);

Eighty Years and More (1815-1897): Reminiscences of Elizabeth Cady Stanton (New York: European Publishing Company, 1898; London: Unwin, 1898);

Elizabeth Cady Stanton to Her Life-long Friend and Co-worker Susan B. Anthony on Her Eightieth Birthday, February 15, 1900 (N.p., 1900);

Solitude of Self: An Address Delivered by Elizabeth Cady Stanton, Before the United States Congressional Committee on the Judiciary, Monday, January 18, 1892, edited by Harriot Stanton Blatch (New York?, 1910?);

Elizabeth Cady Stanton as Revealed in Her Letters, Diary and Reminiscences, edited by Blatch and Theodore Stanton (New York & London: Harper, 1922);

Elizabeth Cady Stanton/Susan B. Anthony: Correspondence, Writings, Speeches, edited by Ellen Dubois (New York: Schocken, 1981).

OTHER: *History of Woman Suffrage,* volumes 1-3, edited by Stanton, Susan B. Anthony, and Matilda Joslyn Gage (New York: Fowler & Wells, 1881-1886).

Elizabeth Cady Stanton lived in an era when the law placed a "burden of sex" on women, denying them property ownership, employment, and suffrage, as well as rights in marriage and over their children. For much of her adult life, she led the woman's movement in America, advocating woman's rights issues; she set the movement's agenda, developed and presented its philosophy, and articulated its demands. Cady Stanton believed that women had been placed in a subordinate position by a society based upon Judeo-Christian traditions, English common law, and a patriarchal social system–all of which were wrong in their basic tenets. Her rhetoric was marked by impassioned zeal, innovative thinking, and advocacy for change.

Born in Johnstown, New York, Elizabeth Cady was the daughter of Margaret Livingston Cady and Daniel Cady, a distinguished lawyer, state judge, and congressman. Of her birth she wrote later, "With several generations of vigorous, enterprising ancestors behind me, I commenced the struggle of life under favorable circumstances . . . the same year that my father, Daniel Cady, was elected to Congress. Perhaps the excitement of a political campaign, in which my mother took the deepest interest, may have had an influence on my life and given me the strong desire that I have always felt to participate in the rights and duties of government." Her early years were influenced by two men: her father, who felt that her sex limited her worth yet who allowed her to attain unusual academic credentials; and her next-door neighbor, Simon Hosack, a Presbyterian minister and her intellectual mentor, who encouraged her probing mind.

When she was eleven, her only brother, Eleazer, who had just graduated from Union College, died as a result of an accident. Elizabeth Cady went to her father's study to comfort him, and they sat in companionable silence. Then her father made a remark which he would repeat several times during her maturing years: "Oh, my daughter, would that you were a boy!" It was at this point that Elizabeth Cady pledged her life to study so that she could earn her father's esteem even though she was of the incorrect sex.

Since their gardens shared common boundaries, Elizabeth Cady was Hosack's frequent visitor and companion on his parish rounds. She later called his habit of using adult expressions and then explaining them the earliest influence on her intellectual development, awakening in her young brain a taste for rhetoric. Hosack also instilled self-confidence in Elizabeth Cady, telling her that it was her mission to help mold society. He taught her to express her opinions in a forthright manner, to be true to herself.

Her education was superior to that given most girls of her time. Until age fifteen Elizabeth

Cady was schooled at the Johnstown Academy, where she studied Latin, Greek, and mathematics in a coed atmosphere. Since her father's law office adjoined the house, she spent much of her time there, hearing the pitiful stories of women who had lost property or legal control over their children and becoming familiar with laws affecting women. This experience was the foundation for most of her lifelong efforts to change statutes unfair to women. In 1830 Elizabeth Cady was enrolled at Emma Willard's Troy Female Seminary, which was considered an intellectual mecca for young women because of its advanced educational standards. Here she studied physiology, geography, higher mathematics, Greek, Latin, French, music, and elocution. After two or three years at Troy she returned to her family in Johnstown.

The Cady family paid yearly visits to a cousin, Gerrit Smith, a leading reformer and orator whose home served as a forum for discussions of politics, temperance, religion, slavery, and woman's rights. There Elizabeth Cady met Henry Brewster Stanton, an Abolitionist speaker (later a lawyer and journalist), to whom she became engaged in 1839. Despite family objections, the two were wed on 10 May 1840. The tone of their marriage, which lasted nearly half a century, was set when Cady persuaded the clergyman to eliminate the word *obey* from the wedding vows; she also declared that she wished to be known as Elizabeth Cady Stanton, noting: "There is a great deal in a name. It often signifies much and may involve a great principle. Why are slaves nameless unless they take that of their master? Simply because they have no independent existence; even so with women. The custom of calling women Mrs. John This or Mrs. Tom That is founded on the principle that white men are lords of us all."

The newlyweds' honeymoon took them to London, where the World's Anti-Slavery Convention was meeting. American women delegates were banned; Cady Stanton spent time with Lucretia Mott, a Quaker liberal whose seat had been denied. The two discussed improving the legal and traditional social status of women and promised that upon returning to America, they would form a society and hold a convention to advocate the rights of women.

Upon her return to Johnstown Cady Stanton soon found much of her time occupied by her rapidly growing family. Over a period of seventeen years she had seven children: Daniel Cady (1842-1891), Henry B. (1844-1903), Gerrit S. (1845-1927), Theodore W. (1851-1925), Margaret L. (1852-1938), Harriot E. (1856-1940), and Robert L. (1859-1920). In autumn 1843 the family moved to Boston, where Cady Stanton met writers and intellectuals such as Theodore Parker, Ralph Waldo Emerson, Bronson Alcott, Nathaniel Hawthorne, John Greenleaf Whittier, Parker Pillsbury, and Lydia Maria Child. Their time in Boston was intellectually stimulating, and the young woman lived an activity-filled life of reform conventions and lectures. Henry Stanton's delicate health necessitated a drier climate, however, and the family moved to Seneca Falls, New York, in 1847.

The First Woman's Rights Convention was held in Seneca Falls on 19-20 July 1848. Cady Stanton, Lucretia Mott, Mary Ann McClintock, Jane Hunt, and Martha C. Wright called the convention, planned the agenda, resolutions, and a "Declaration of Sentiments," patterned after the Declaration of Independence and setting out a list of eighteen grievances women had against tradition and law. The resulting document, first published in the 14 July 1848 issue of the *Seneca County Courier*, declared that "men and women are created equal," called attention to women's limited educational and economic rights, and protested the double standards of the times. Several resolutions concerning rights to property and children were drafted. Cady Stanton, despite the opposition of her husband and Lucretia Mott, proposed a resolution advocating suffrage for women; this first public demand by women for the vote was adopted after Frederick Douglass seconded it in an impassioned plea.

The convention became the object of ridicule and denunciation from the press and pulpit; yet other conventions devoted to the same purpose soon followed. Cady Stanton played a major role in many of them, writing letters and lecturing. In addition, she began writing letters on woman's rights to Horace Greeley's *New York Tribune*, which had been the only influential newspaper to give the woman's rights conventions any serious notice. Under the pseudonym Sun Flower, she also wrote articles for Amelia Bloomer's temperance paper, the *Lily*. Cady Stanton spoke before legislative bodies, presenting petitions and protests on temperance and Abolition, but as the years progressed she devoted more time to issues related to woman's equality.

In 1851 Elizabeth Cady Stanton met Susan B. Anthony, whom she enlisted in the woman's rights crusade. This historic partnership was marked by a half-century of collaboration which ended only with Cady Stanton's death. Their association was complementary. Where Anthony was severe, single-minded, and intense, Cady Stanton was good-natured and philosophical. Cady Stanton was an eloquent, forceful speaker and writer, while Anthony was an able organizer and researcher. Together they planned campaigns, speeches, and legislation, and appeared on convention platforms and before legislative committees to plead for woman's rights. One of their greatest collaborations was the *Revolution*, the first major national weekly concerned with woman's rights. Because Cady Stanton had antagonized Greeley as well as another ally, Wendell Phillips of the *Anti-Slavery Standard*, with letters and speeches opposing enfranchisement of blacks, woman's issues were no longer given serious coverage in their newspapers.

From January 1868 until May 1870 the *Revolution* served as a voice for women's demands as well as a major catalyst for events that would split the movement for three decades. The goal of the *Revolution* was to create a public agenda that would give forceful direction to women's issues and activities; but there was an almost immediate rift in the movement. Cady Stanton and Anthony accepted the financial backing of George Francis Train (1829-1904), a merchant, promoter, and eccentric Democrat, and many feminists were uncomfortable with the Train-Cady Stanton-Anthony alliance.

The first issue of the *Revolution* appeared on 8 January 1868, with Cady Stanton as senior editor and primary author of most columns and Parker Pillsbury, former editor of the *Anti-Slavery Standard*, as coeditor. (He was the only member of the staff with previous editorial experience.) Anthony was office manager, accountant, and taskmaster. Train's name did not appear on the masthead, but he wrote columns for the *Revolution* in which he stated his unorthodox financial views. Train's friend Davis Melliss, financial editor of the *New York World*, also contributed financial news and Wall Street gossip. Cady Stanton and Anthony felt this financial section was of little importance, but some of the public saw its presence in the *Revolution* as proof that suffragists preached financial heresy.

The organ of the National Party of New America, the *Revolution* was probably given its title by Cady Stanton, who often used the word *revolution* in speeches and articles. In a 28 December 1869 letter to Anthony she defended the name: "The establishing of woman on her rightful throne is the greatest revolution the world has ever known or ever will know. A journal called the *Rosebud* might answer for those who come with kid gloves and perfumes to lay immortal wreaths on the monuments which in sweat and tears others have hewn and built; but for us . . . there is no name like the *Revolution*."

Ten thousand copies of the sixteen-page first issue were printed; the subscription price was two dollars. With the motto "Principle, not Policy; Justice, not Favors; Men, their rights & nothing more; Women, their rights & nothing less" on its masthead, the *Revolution* included Pillsbury's coverage of political affairs such as Andrew Johnson's impeachment trial, but Cady Stanton's advocacy of woman's rights dominated the magazine. Its primary purpose was to advance the woman suffrage cause, focusing on the inequality fostered by the Fourteenth and Fifteenth Amendments, which enumerated the rights of male citizens. In a 22 July 1869 editorial, Cady Stanton said the fifteenth amendment, which upheld the rights of black males, was "invidious to their [the female] sex . . . a trick of a corrupt and unprincipled school of politicians to save themselves and their party." Cady Stanton proposed a sixteenth amendment granting suffrage to all educated citizens. The *Revolution* served as a clearinghouse for information on suffrage lectures, meetings, and conventions. By mobilizing arguments against the opposition's stands on the suffragists' religious, political, and social ideals, the *Revolution* informed other woman's rights activists and helped them to marshal their thoughts.

The problems and concerns of working women received much notice; the *Revolution* called for equal pay, deplored long hours, highlighted the need for unions, and frequently published information on the strikes and other activities of the Working Women's Association, which Anthony had founded. In a November 1868 article on the Working Women's Association Cady Stanton discussed its purposes and goals, concluding that "of course, no changes will be granted until women secure the ballot." Every issue included informative sketches about women doctors, clerks, inventors, and jurors–Cady Stanton's attempts to demonstrate the ever-expanding sphere of women beyond the home.

Among other concerns addressed in the *Revolution* were social problems such as abortion, prostitution, conditions of prisons and tenement houses, and the plight of American Indians. The amount of hard liquor being consumed in the United States came under Cady Stanton's scrutiny on 14 May 1868, when she presented statistics on the money spent on liquor consumption and showed that the sum was equal to that needed to erase the national debt. Marriage, in Cady Stanton's eyes "an institution of legalized slavery and prostitution," was often assailed; a 28 October 1869 article called for a change in the marriage contract which would favor divorce. Civil service and politics also came under her notice; on 2 December 1869 she stated: "This corruption at every level is further evidence of the fact that men alone cannot run the government." The diversity of the *Revolution* is apparent in the 18 June 1868 issue, which contained articles on funeral customs, corporal punishment, individualism, Tammany Hall, religious interpretations of scripture, conventions, women in the civil service, an excerpt from Mary Wollstonecraft's *Vindication of the Rights of Women* (1792), correspondence, poems, and a progress report of the Union Pacific Railroad.

The *Revolution* received mixed reviews, which it printed for its readers. The *Troy* [New York] *Daily Times* called the *Revolution* "readable, well-edited, and instructive." Greeley's *New York Tribune* and Phillips's *Anti-Slavery Standard* both ignored its publication–a typical conservative reaction. Theodore Tilton, editor of the *Independent* (and also a close friend of Cady Stanton's), predicted in January 1868 that "the *Revolution* will arouse, thrill, edify, amuse, vex, and nonplus its friends. But it will compel attention." At the same time the *New York Times* said that the motto of the *Revolution* was meaningless and that the paper was a victim of illogical thinking, while the *Northampton* [Massachusetts] *Free Press* said, "when they get all these [reforms], which naturally they won't get for some scores of years yet, we suppose they will find out some other reforms that are needed. But they have good courage, and the *Revolution* will be spicy and readable."

Several events led to the untimely end of the *Revolution*. It had barely been in existence for one month when Train sailed for England, leaving Anthony with six hundred dollars and instructions that Melliss would supply columns and any needed funds. Unfortunately, Train's support of the Irish national movement caused his arrest and imprisonment in a Dublin hotel; he sent lively correspondence detailing his arrest back to the *Revolution*. The letters did not help the periodical's reputation; but, more important, Train's arrest stopped its monetary support, once Melliss's funds were exhausted. The Train alliance, unpopular editorials, and Cady Stanton's strict stand against patent medicines had reduced advertising and circulation revenues. With few advertisers and subscriptions peaking at three thousand (with few renewals), the *Revolution* drew near bankruptcy. Train returned and withdrew his support, hoping to bring in new subscribers; but the paper was primarily circulated to women, who were not major moneyholders. Its subscription price (later raised to three dollars), was not enough to support a weekly periodical. Anthony borrowed money and pleaded for contributors. An 1869 stock-company plan, which would have relieved Anthony from all financial liability if the editors agreed to change the paper's name, fell through when Cady Stanton refused to compromise.

Another cause for the demise of the *Revolution* was the split in the woman's movement over issues. Cady Stanton and Anthony's differences with conservative members of the American Equal Rights Association, begun with the Train alliance and carried on with the liberal stands of the *Revolution*, culminated at the May 1869 convention. Frederick Douglass called for support of the Fifteenth Amendment; Cady Stanton argued for its defeat because it did not give voting rights to women. Her vehemence stunned former allies. Also, Anthony was accused of using American Equal Rights Association funds to finance the *Revolution*; although her accounting was eventually accepted, resentment and suspicion remained.

In 1868 Cady Stanton began her national lecturing career for the New York Lyceum Bureau in order to help finance her children's education. She spoke about family life and the training of children in speeches with titles such as "Our Girls," "Our Boys," "Marriage and Divorce," and "Coeducation." She lectured throughout the country for eight months every year and was one of the tour's most popular speakers for twelve years. With her rosy cheeks and stylish dress, she created a good impression, and her natural oratorical powers endeared her to her audiences.

In May 1869 a disgruntled Elizabeth Cady Stanton formed the National Woman Suffrage Association, which refused male members and promoted her liberal views, including federal woman suffrage. In November 1869 the conservative American Woman Suffrage Association was formed, dedicating itself to achieving suffrage state-by-state. The American Woman Suffrage Association also published the *Woman's Journal*, which was well financed, respectable, conservative, and very successful, becoming the official publication of the reunited suffrage group, the National American Woman Suffrage Association in 1890.

After two and one-half years of operation, the *Revolution* failed, leaving Anthony with a ten-thousand-dollar personal debt. In May 1870 it was sold to Laura C. Ballard, who refocused it into a literary society journal, abandoning most of its liberal and controversial policies. Eighteen months later, the *Revolution* was merged with the *New York Christian Enquirer*.

During the early 1880s Cady Stanton, Anthony, and Matilda Joslyn Gage edited the first three volumes of *History of Woman Suffrage*, which compiled the documents and letters of the suffrage movement for the years 1848-1885. The history is an in-house documentary, a collection of minutes, speeches, clippings, and recollections; while there is little clearcut order or analysis, the volumes are invaluable as a historical record.

After her husband's death in 1887 Cady Stanton made her home in New York City. She served as president of the American Woman Suffrage Association for the first two years. Much of her time was devoted to writing for various newspapers and magazines, including the *New York Journal*, *American*, *Westminster Review*, *Arena*, *Forum*, and the *North American Review*. The *Omaha Republican* syndicated her column on women. The *Woman's Tribune* serialized her reminiscences, which she later developed into her autobiography, *Eighty Years and More* (1898). Cady Stanton claimed that the book was merely a private history; it was actually carefully shaped to present her life as a series of minor challenges which were easily overcome by self-confidence and intelligence. She did not depict incidents in which she appeared radical, arrogant, or self-centered, nor did she say much about her marriage or mention any scandals. The flawed autobiography depicts her as self-sufficient and heroic, the public image she wanted to project. In October 1902 she began revising the book. This version was published as part of *Elizabeth Cady Stanton as Revealed in Her Letters, Diary and Reminiscences* (1922), edited by two of her children, Theodore Stanton and Harriot Stanton Blatch.

Cady Stanton's *The Woman's Bible* (1895, 1898) was her attempt to challenge religious teachings which preached woman's inferiority. The two volumes presented Cady Stanton's commentaries on sections of the Old and New Testaments that relegated women to subordinate status. While Cady Stanton did not condemn the Bible completely, she claimed that it reflected male bias. *The Woman's Bible*, with its sarcasm and animosity, developed conclusions about biblical interpretation that are commonly accepted today, but in her time the book served as another example of Cady Stanton's radical disrespect for tradition. The book received sensational publicity. It became a best-seller, went through seven printings in six months, and was translated into several languages. Yet, bowing to the storm of criticism, many libraries refused to circulate it, and the National American Woman Suffrage Association censured both the book and author.

Perhaps Elizabeth Cady Stanton's greatest legacy was her concept of "self-sovereignty" for women. In her effort to free women's minds from self-imposed bonds, she argued that people should be treated as individuals, without regard to social traditions or custom. She was a philosopher, a liberal thinker, and a courageous advocate who felt that breaking down the barriers that held women back was essential for the improvement of society.

Biographies:
Alma Lutz, *Created Equal: A Biography of Elizabeth Cady Stanton 1815-1902* (New York: Day, 1940);

Lois W. Banner, *Elizabeth Cady Stanton: A Radical for Woman's Rights* (Boston: Little, Brown, 1980);

Elisabeth Griffith, *In Her Own Right: The Life of Elizabeth Cady Stanton* (Oxford & New York: Oxford University Press, 1984).

References:
Karlyn Kohrs Campbell, "Stanton's 'The Solitude of Self': A Rationale for Feminism," *Quarterly Journal of Speech*, 66 (October 1980): 304-312;

Miriam Gurko, *The Ladies of Seneca Falls: The Birth of the Woman's Rights Movement* (New York: Macmillan, 1974);

Ida Usted Harper, *The Life and Work of Susan B. Anthony*, 3 volumes (Indianapolis & Kansas City: Bowen-Merrill/Indianapolis: Hollenbeck Press, 1898-1908).

Papers:
Most of Elizabeth Cady Stanton's papers are at the Library of Congress and the Vassar College Library. Some letters are also held at the Henry E. Huntington Library, New York Public Library, the Sophia Smith Collection at Smith College, and the Schlesinger Library at Radcliffe College. Susan B. Anthony's scrapbooks, which contain notes and press comments about Cady Stanton, are at the Library of Congress.

Lucy Stone

(13 August 1818-18 October 1893)

Lee Jolliffe
Ohio University

MAJOR POSITION HELD: Editor, *Woman's Journal* (1870-1893).

PERIODICAL PUBLICATIONS: "The Protest," by Stone and Henry B. Blackwell, *Worcester Spy* (May 1855);

"Obedience of Wives," *Woman's Journal*, 8 (3 February 1877): 36;

"Rights of Husbands," *Woman's Journal*, 8 (10 March 1877): 36;

"What a Connecticut Wife May Own," *Woman's Journal*, 8 (31 March 1877): 100;

"Twelve New Lady Physicians," *Woman's Journal*, 8 (28 April 1877): 129;

"Crimes against Women," *Woman's Journal*, 8 (16 June 1877): 188;

"Notes along the Way to Colorado," *Woman's Journal*, 8 (8 September 1877): 281;

"The Remonstrants' Hearing," *Woman's Journal*, 15 (9 February 1884): 48;

"Suffrage Convention at Rock Island [Illinois]," *Woman's Journal*, 15 (28 June 1884): 208;

"Miss Muller and Her Taxes," *Woman's Journal*, 15 (12 July 1884): 224;

"Black Gowns vs. Blue-Stockings," *Woman's Journal*, 15 (19 July 1884): 232;

"The Convention and the Colored Man," *Woman's Journal*, 15 (26 July 1884): 240;

"All Honor to Farmers," *Woman's Journal*, 24 (21 January 1893): 20;

"Women Wage-Earners," *Woman's Journal*, 24 (11 February 1893): 44.

OTHER: *History of Woman Suffrage*, volumes 1-3 edited by Elizabeth Cady Stanton, Susan B. Anthony, and Matilda Joslyn Gage (New York: Fowler & Wells, 1881-1887); volume 4 edited by Anthony and Ida H. Harper (Indianapolis: Hollenbeck Press, 1902)–contains sixteen speeches by Stone;

"The Progress of Fifty Years," in *World's Congress of Representative Women*, edited by May Wright Sewall (Chicago & New York: Rand McNally, 1894).

Lucy Stone

Lucy Stone founded the longest-lived woman suffrage publication, Woman's Journal, in 1870 and, with her husband, edited it from 1872 until her death in 1893. She also traveled widely and spoke persuasively for the suffrage cause, earning the sobriquet "the morning star of the woman's rights movement."

Stone was born in West Brookfield, Massachusetts, on 13 August 1818 to Francis and Hannah Matthews Stone. Stone began teaching at sixteen, studying at nearby seminaries and saving money for college. In 1843 she enrolled at Oberlin College, one of the few institutions that accepted women and blacks. Oberlin was a stop on the Underground Railway and strongly abolitionist, but even in this progressive atmosphere Stone's radicalism proved troublesome. Chosen to write a speech for commencement, she was asked to compose it so that a man might read it for her. Stone angrily resigned, as did the other students who were to share the platform with her. Thirty-six years later she spoke at Oberlin's semicentennial.

After her graduation in 1847 Stone became a lecturer for the American Anti-Slavery Society, but friction soon developed between Stone and William Lloyd Garrison, her sponsor, because Stone mixed talk of woman's rights into her lectures on the abolition of slavery. A compromise was reached; Stone agreed to lecture on Saturday nights and Sundays for the Garrisonians and was free the rest of the week to lecture for woman's rights. Both occupations were arduous, not only because they demanded constant travel, but because speakers with unpopular ideas were often doused with cold water, pelted with rotten fruit, or smoked out of their lecture halls with burned pepper. Stone persevered, though. She participated in the First National Woman's Rights Convention (held two years after the better-known Seneca Falls Convention) at Worcester, Massachusetts, on 23 October 1850, and her speech there was reported in both the United States and Great Britain.

Although she had resolved not to marry because of the great disabilities current law placed upon married women, Stone did marry Henry Browne Blackwell on 1 May 1855 after a long courtship, much of it recorded in letters. Blackwell came from a forward-thinking family; two of his sisters were pioneer physicians, one a newspaper correspondent, and another a biographer. Blackwell's brother Samuel married Antoinette Brown, the first ordained woman minister and

Stone in the 1880s, holding a copy of her Woman's Journal

Stone's closest friend from her Oberlin days.

At their wedding Blackwell and Stone read a protest against the marriage laws of the time, which was published in the *Worcester Spy* and widely reported throughout the country. Stone was the first of many feminists who did not adopt her husband's last name; as the woman's movement grew, others who followed her example became known as "Lucy Stoners." Stone retired briefly from public life after the birth of her daughter Alice Stone Blackwell in 1857, returning to found, organize, and support numerous woman's rights organizations, among them the Women's Loyal National League, the American Equal Rights Association, the New Jersey Woman Suffrage Association, and the New England Woman Suffrage Association.

In 1869 a major schism occurred in the woman's movement. Susan B. Anthony and Elizabeth Cady Stanton, formerly allies of Stone, expanded their reform interests to include such causes as socialism and free love and extended

Stone's husband, Henry B. Blackwell

their circle of supporters to include George Francis Train, a wealthy dilettante, and the notorious Victoria Woodhull, a spiritualist, medium, and free-love advocate. Stone, along with Julia Ward Howe and other New England feminists, favored concentrating on a single issue, the franchise for women, and felt that other reforms would follow from the vote. Stanton and Anthony formed the National Woman Suffrage Association in May 1869; Stone and Howe formed the American Woman Suffrage Association in November 1869.

Stone then launched the *Woman's Journal* in 1870. Stone's publication was aimed at an audience of well-educated club women, professionals, and writers. Stone published editorials that discussed in rational tones and great detail the political issues of the day as they related to woman's rights, and Henry Blackwell contributed analyses of legal proceedings and political events. From its inception, the journal was supported by the written contributions of woman's rights advocates from all over the United States, as well as France and England. Stone also reprinted many articles from other magazines, such as *Harper's Bazar*, and newspapers, such as the *New York World* and the *Chicago Times*, choosing those that related to women's issues, but not exclusively those that were pro-woman's rights. A regular column, "Concerning Women," ran on the front page of each issue, highlighting professional activities and praiseworthy deeds by women.

Subscribers could not finance all the production costs of the journal, and advertising was not easy to sell. Stone wrote in 1874 to a friend, "I wish I could rest. I have been trying to get advertisements for the *Woman's Journal* to eke out its expenses. Yesterday I walked miles; to picture stores, to crockery stores, to special sales, going up flight after flight of stairs only to find the men out, or not ready to advertise. And for all my day's toil I did not get a cent. . . ."

The schism in the woman's rights movement was healed in 1890, in part through Alice Blackwell's efforts, and Stone became the chairman of the executive board of the National American Woman Suffrage Association formed when the two groups merged. She continued to travel and speak for the cause to which she had devoted her life. Her last talks on woman suffrage were given at the World's Columbian Exposition in Chicago in 1893. She died at Dorchester, Massachusetts, on 18 October 1893. The *Woman's Journal* was edited by Alice Blackwell until 1917.

Letters:
Loving Warriors: Selected Letters of Lucy Stone and Henry B. Blackwell, 1853 to 1893, edited by Leslie Wheeler (New York: Dial, 1981).

Biographies:
Alice Stone Blackwell, *Lucy Stone: A Pioneer of Woman's Rights* (Boston: Little, Brown, 1930);
Elinor Rice Hays, *Morning Star: A Biography of Lucy Stone 1818-1893* (New York: Harcourt, Brace & World, 1961).

Papers:
Lucy Stone's papers are at the Boston Public Library and at the Schlesinger Library at Radcliffe College. The Blackwell Family Papers at the Library of Congress, Manuscript Division, also include many of Stone's letters and records.

Albion W. Tourgée

(2 May 1838-21 May 1905)

Kate Esary Russell
University of Georgia

MAJOR POSITIONS HELD: Publisher and editor, *Our Continent*, renamed *Continent* in 1883 (1882-1884); editor, *Basis: A Journal of Good Citizenship* (1895-1896).

BOOKS: *A Plan for the Organization of the Judiciary Department, Proposed by A. W. Tourgée, of Guilford, as a Section of the Constitution* (Raleigh, N.C.: Privately printed, 1868);

Toinette: A Novel, as Henry Churton (New York: Ford, 1874); revised as *A Royal Gentleman*, republished in *A Royal Gentleman and 'Zouri's Christmas* (New York: Fords, Howard & Hulbert, 1881);

The "C" Letters, as Published in "The North State," anonymous (Greensboro, N.C.: North State Book & Job Printing Office, 1878);

Figs and Thistles: A Western Story (New York: Fords, Howard & Hulbert, 1879);

A Fool's Errand: By One of the Fools, anonymous (New York: Fords, Howard & Hulbert, 1879; London: Low, 1880); revised and enlarged as *A Fool's Errand, by One of the Fools; the Famous Romance of American History . . . To Which is Added, by the Same Author, Part II: The Invisible Empire: A Concise Review of the Epoch on Which the Tale is Based*, as Tourgée (New York: Fords, Howard & Hulbert, 1880);

Bricks without Straw: A Novel (New York: Fords, Howard & Hulbert / London: Low / Montreal: Dawson, 1880; London: Low, 1881);

John Eax and Mamelon: or, The South without the Shadow (New York: Fords, Howard & Hulbert, 1882);

Hot Plowshares: A Novel (New York: Fords, Howard & Hulbert, 1883);

An Appeal to Caesar (New York: Fords, Howard & Hulbert, 1884);

A Man of Destiny, as Siva (Chicago: Belford, Clarke, 1885);

The Veteran and His Pipe, anonymous (Chicago & New York: Belford, Clarke, 1886);

Button's Inn (Boston: Roberts, 1887);

Albion W. Tourgée

Black Ice (New York: Fords, Howard & Hulbert, 1888);

Eighty Nine; or, The Grand Master's Secret, as Edgar Henry (New York: Cassell, 1888);

Letters to a King (Cincinnati: Cranston & Stowe / New York: Phillips & Hunt, 1888);

With Gauge & Swallow, Attorneys (Philadelphia: Lippincott, 1889);

Pactolus Prime (New York: Cassell, 1890);

Murvale Eastman, Christian Socialist (New York: Fords, Howard & Hulbert / London: Low, Marston, Searle & Rivington, 1890);

A Son of Old Harry: A Novel (New York: Bonner, 1891);

Out of the Sunset Sea (New York: Merrill & Baker, 1893);

An Outing with the Queen of Hearts (New York: Merrill & Baker, 1894);

Historical Souvenir of the 105th Regiment of Ohio Volunteers, Prepared for the Nineteenth Annual Reunion (Buffalo: McGerald, 1894);

To the People of the 34th Congressional District (Brocton, N.Y.: Grape Belt Print, 1894);

The Mortgage on the Hip-Roof House (Cincinnati: Curts & Jennings, 1896);

The Story of a Thousand: Being a History of the Service of the 105th Ohio Volunteer Infantry, in the War for the Union from August 21, 1862 to June 6, 1865 (Buffalo: McGerald, 1896);

A Memorial of Frederick Douglass from the City of Boston (Boston: By Order of the City Council, 1896);

The War of the Standards: Coin and Credit Versus Coin without Credit (New York: Putnam's, 1896);

The Man Who Outlived Himself (New York: Fords, Howard & Hulbert, 1898);

A Fools Errand [play], by Tourgée and Steele MacKaye, edited by Dean H. Keller (Metuchen, N.J.: Scarecrow, 1969).

PLAY PRODUCTION: *A Fool's Errand*, by Tourgée and Steele MacKaye, Philadelphia, Arch Street Theater, 26 October 1881.

OTHER: *Book of Forms*, prepared by North Carolina Commissioners of the Code: Tourgée, Victor C. Barringer, and William B. Rodman (Raleigh, N.C., 1868);

The Code of Civil Procedure of North Carolina, to Special Proceedings, prepared by Tourgée, Barringer, and Rodman (Raleigh, N.C.: Paige, 1868);

The Code of Civil Procedure of North Carolina, with Notes and Decisions, compiled by Tourgée (Raleigh, N.C.: Nichols, 1878);

A Digest of Cited Cases in the North Carolina Reports, compiled by Tourgée (Raleigh, N.C.: Williams, 1879);

Statutory Adjudications in the North Carolina Reports, compiled by Tourgée (Raleigh, N.C.: Williams, 1879).

PERIODICAL PUBLICATIONS: "The Lagby Papers," *Greensboro Union Register*, January 1867;

"Aaron's Rod in Politics," *North American Review*, 132 (February 1881): 139-162;

"A Veteran and His Pipe," *Chicago Inter Ocean*, 25 April-19 September 1885;

"Letters to a Mugwump," as Trueman Joyce, *Chicago Inter Ocean*, 26 September-12 December 1885;

"A Child of Luck," *Chicago Inter Ocean*, 20 March-4 December 1886;

"The Renaissance of Nationalism," *North American Review*, 144 (January 1887): 1-11;

"A Bystander's Notes," *Chicago Inter Ocean*, 21 April 1888-12 August 1893, 5 May 1894-5 January 1895, 21 November 1896-2 October 1898;

"The South as a Field for Fiction," *Forum*, 6 (December 1888): 404-413;

"The Claim of Realism," *North American Review*, 148 (March 1889): 386-388;

"Shall White Minorities Rule?," *Forum*, 7 (April 1889): 143-155;

"Our Consular System," *Independent*, 54 (23 January 1902): 208-210.

Albion W. Tourgée's career as a magazinist grew out of his success as a writer. Tourgée's first periodical, *Our Continent* (1882-1884), began on the heels of *A Fool's Errand: By One of the Fools* (1879) and *Bricks without Straw: A Novel* (1880), his popular novels fictionalizing Southern Reconstruction. Similarly, his second periodical, the *Basis: A Journal of Citizenship* (1895-1896), was an outgrowth of Tourgée's popular column "A Bystander's Notes" which appeared in the *Chicago Inter Ocean*. Although Tourgée is remembered primarily as a novelist, his brief experiences in magazine editing marked important stages in his varied and colorful career.

Throughout his life, Tourgée was a man of causes. His experiences in North Carolina as a judge and radical Republican from 1865 until 1879 molded both his thinking and his career. Labeled a carpetbagger early on, Tourgée was an outspoken critic of Southern attitudes and politics, particularly as they concerned the Negro. Tourgée suffered much in the South, where he came to understand many of the differences that separated the North and South following the war. He was one of the first advocates for providing a federal education program for the South and one of the earliest writers to document the activities of the Ku Klux Klan. His views, gained from firsthand knowledge, were expressed in his fiction and nonfiction, including his writings for his magazines.

Tourgée's wife, Emma. It was reported in the press that her hair turned white overnight after a Ku Klux Klan raid on their home in North Carolina (Tourgée Papers, Westfield, New York)

Albion Winegar Tourgée, the only surviving son of Valentine and Louisa Winegar Tourgée, was born 2 May 1838 in Williamsfield, Ohio. His mother died when he was six years old, and the family moved to a farm near Kingsville, Ohio, where he spent his boyhood. Tourgée's quick mind and outgoing personality made him popular, but he was fiercely independent and became even more so after he lost the sight in his right eye in a boyhood accident. His values were shaped by the Republican sentiments of Western Reserve reformism and the idealism expressed by writers such as Milton, Scott, Byron, and Burns. He excelled in his studies at Kingsville Academy and entered Rochester University as a sophomore in 1859. The war interrupted his education, but he received the A.B. degree from the university in 1862 on the merits of his military service.

Tourgée had been a Union soldier for two months when he received a serious spinal injury in July 1861, following the Battle of Bull Run. He recovered enough to return to active service, but the injury continued to plague him throughout the war and for the rest of his life. Tourgée was wounded slightly at Perryville, Kentucky, in October 1862 and later spent four months of 1863 in a Confederate prison. On furlough following his release from prison, he married his hometown sweetheart, Emma L. Kilbourne, in Columbus, Ohio, on 14 May 1863. Tourgée remained with the army until complications from his spinal injury forced his resignation in December of that year.

Back in Ohio, Tourgée read law during his convalescence and was admitted to the bar in 1864. Finding clients scarce, he taught school and worked as a newspaper reporter to support himself. Dissatisfied with his work, he decided to seek his fortune as a Yankee entrepreneur in the war-torn South. Tourgée embarked on his "southern scheme" in the summer of 1865 and settled in Guilford County near Greensboro, North Carolina, that same year.

Tourgée's wartime experiences reinforced his abhorrence of slavery and intensified his desire to see the South become a viable part of the Union. To the horror of his new neighbors he accepted the Negro freedmen as social and political equals without hesitation. Tourgée's willingness to accept Negroes as law clients and employ them in a nursery business he had begun brought even sharper criticism. Because of his convictions, he soon became involved in the political chaos that was sweeping the state. Initially he aligned himself with the Southern Unionists, who had opposed the Confederacy but did not support Negro equality. Tourgée's involvement with the Unionists led him to establish and edit the *Greensboro Union Register* in 1866. For this newspaper Tourgée wrote his first fictional account of Reconstruction, "The Lagby Papers," modeled after James Russell Lowell's *The Biglow Papers* (1848). The *Register* was short-lived, partly because Tourgée was increasingly critical of what he saw as the party's unwillingness to take a firm stand on controversial issues. By 1867 he had joined the Republicans in the state and was forever branded a carpetbagger.

As a delegate to the North Carolina constitutional convention of 1868, Tourgée was an outspoken proponent of humanitarian reform. He was one of three attorneys appointed to recodify the law and legal procedure of North Carolina. In 1868, just as the Ku Klux Klan was becoming active in the state, Tourgée was elected a state superior court judge. He took his judicial duties seriously and was a vociferous critic of the Klan's attempts to circumvent justice. Although he was later recognized, even by his enemies, as a judge of unusual ability, Tourgée and his wife were ostracized, slandered, and forced to endure constant threats to their personal safety.

Unseated from his judicial position in 1874, Tourgée began his literary career in earnest. *Toinette: A Novel* (1874), fictionalizing Southern Reconstruction, appeared under the pseudonym Henry Churton. The short story "Mamelon" appeared in 1876, and his infamous *The "C" Letters, as Published in "The North State"* (1878), written to a Greensboro newspaper, caused a furor in the state's Democratic party. Although Tourgée remained active in politics until 1879, when he left the South, he turned to writing as an outlet for his views concerning Reconstruction, the South, and the Negro.

Tourgée's second novel, *Figs and Thistles: A Western Story* (1879), appeared shortly after he left North Carolina. It was followed closely by *A Fool's Errand: By One of the Fools*, which became an overnight success. Within a year, the novel had sold 150,000 copies, and Tourgée found himself a celebrity. Hailed by both northern and southern critics, *A Fool's Errand* is in many ways an autobiographical account of Tourgée's trials as a carpetbagger. It was his egalitarian view of the issues and individuals caught up in Reconstruction, however, that marked the novel as unique. His fourth novel, *Bricks without Straw*, which appeared in the fall of 1880, focuses on similar issues and further advanced Tourgée's growing reputation.

A Fool's Errand and *Bricks without Straw* made Tourgée a rich man. In 1881 he purchased a large home in Mayville, New York, which he named Thorheim. There he continued to write new novels, revise existing ones, and bask in the privileges of success. The energetic Tourgée was soon seeking a new outlet for his writing talent, however, one that he hoped would further increase his wealth and influence. In the fall of 1881 Tourgée, Robert S. Davis of Philadelphia, and Daniel G. Brinton, editor of the Philadelphia *Medical and Surgical Reporter*, invested more than $150,000 to form Our Continent Publishing Company for the purpose of producing *Our Continent*, an illustrated weekly magazine. Shares were sold to other investors, including former president Ulysses S. Grant, who invested $1,000.

As editor of the weekly, Tourgée touted the magazine on 18 October 1882 as "the first serious attempt ever made to put into a weekly the attractions and excellences of our great monthlies." He also adopted an editorial policy which he termed "independent journalism" and declared

Drawing by William Sydney Porter of Tourgée, carrying his carpetbag, leaving Greensboro

that *Our Continent* was "not . . . intended to be the vehicle of any particular ideas." Nonetheless, he maintained on 15 March 1882 that the editors and writers would "not be deterred from the discussion of any question affecting our political, social, or religious welfare, because it may be the subject-matter of partisan or factional difference." Tourgée admitted that "The CONTINENT was organized upon a plan somewhat peculiar," but insisted (19 April 1882) that it was "for the purpose of filling a special niche in American journalism." Variety was to be the governing policy as long, he said (15 February 1882), as "Americanism in literature and art" was exhibited in all aspects of the magazine.

Modeled after the monthly periodicals of the day, *Our Continent* was an illustrated ten-cent large-format magazine of sixteen pages, filled with short stories, poems, serials, and articles. A diverse staff was assembled to head the various departments: "The Household" by Helen Campbell offered tips on homemaking; "In Lighter Vein" by Max Adeler contained humorous anecdotes; "The Still Hour" by J. L. Russell presented religious items; "Our Society" by Louise Chandler Moulton offered advice on etiquette; and "The Art of Adornment" by Kate Field was a dressmaking column. "Home Horticulture" by F. A. Benson appeared in later issues. The magazine was justifiably proud of its art department headed by Donald G. Mitchell. Superb illustrations adorned the magazine's logos, articles, fiction, and poetry. A number of well-known artists worked on the staff at various times, including Joseph Pennell, Howard Pyle, Kenyon Cox, H. F. Farney, and Henry Wolf. Louis Tiffany did the rendering of the Aztec Calendar Stone that was used on the magazine's cover.

All early indications were that the magazine would be a success. In the issue of 29 March 1882 Tourgée boasted that "no literary venture was ever more warmly welcomed and generally commended by the press" and claimed that fifty-eight thousand copies of the first issue had been sold in three days. Tourgée's assertion (12 April 1882) that nothing was "too good for 'the masses' of American readers" was most evident in the magazine's lavish expenditures. For the first issue (15 February 1882) Oscar Wilde, for example, was paid twenty-four guineas for two poems, "Le Jardin" and "La Mer." Reportedly, George Washington Cable was offered (but did not accept) seventy-five hundred dollars for a single serial. In addition the magazine had a policy of returning all declined manuscripts at its own expense. When circulation figures failed to rise above thirteen thousand copies by the summer of 1882, Davis and Brinton panicked and withdrew their support before the end of the first volume. The ever-optimistic Tourgée bought their shares and assumed full control of the magazine, changing the name to the *Continent*, adopting a thirty-two-page smaller format, and making other minor adjustments.

The contents of the *Continent* were in keeping with the most popular monthlies of the day, and Tourgée published serials by well-known authors–sometimes as many as three concurrently. Tourgée's *Hot Plowshares: A Novel* (1883) was serialized from 12 July 1882 to 23 May 1883 with only occasional interruption. Other popular serials included Julian Hawthorne's *Dust*, Harriet P. Spofford's *The Marquis of Carabas*, Helen Campbell's *Under Green Apple Blossoms*, Marion Harland's *Judith: A Chronicle of Old Virginia*, and Orpheus C. Kerr's *Once There Was a Man*. In the magazine's later issues Tourgée introduced an innovative alternative to the serial. The "Too True for Fiction" series contained anonymously published stories by significant writers, including Charles Bernard, Edgar Fawcett, James R. Gilmore, Anna K. Green, Edward Everett Hale, Sarah Orne Jewett, Philip B. Marston, Harriet Beecher Stowe, and, naturally, Tourgée. The readers who matched ten, twenty, or thirty stories with their correct authors were to be awarded prizes–novels by Tourgée or subscriptions to the *Continent*. The magazine, however, folded before any prizes could be awarded.

Tourgée's preference for sentimentalized writing was apparent in his choices of both fiction and poetry. Local colorists such as Jewett, Rose Terry Cooke, Constance Fenimore Woolson, and Joel Chandler Harris were frequent contributors. Poetry in the *Continent* was highly sentimental and second-rate at best, with the exception of poems by Harris, Sidney Lanier, John Greenleaf Whittier, and John T. Trowbridge.

Tourgée included a wide variety of nonfiction in his magazine as well. Nonfiction such as "The House that Jill Built After Jack Had Proved a Failure" (by architect Eugene C. Gardner) and "From Lobby to Peak" (by Donald G. Mitchell) ran as series. Other articles included "The Sign Language of the Central American Indians," "Training a Canary," "The Sister of Edgar Allan Poe," and "Pottery in the Dining Room." Many of these articles were lavishly illustrated, sometimes with full-page sketches.

Tourgée wrote several columns for the magazine. The unsigned "Literary News and Notes" eventually became "The Bookshelf," and "Current Events" was replaced by the "Reference Column." "Migma," Tourgée's most important column, appeared in the early issues and was eventually expanded to include all his editorial writing. One of Tourgée's most innovative additions to the *Continent* appeared first in the 25 April 1883 issue as "Notes and Queries." Sometimes called "Notedum et Inquiredum," the column solicited questions of general interest from readers, and the editor or other readers supplied the answers. Again, variety was the key. Questions included the meaning and proper pronunciation of "dude" and "sanitary engineer," how to ebonize wood, whether or not William Wordsworth had a sister, and the proper Latin quotation for a seventieth-birthday celebration.

Tourgée's editorials in the *Continent* made interesting reading, particularly in light of his editorial policy. Although he claimed from the beginning (15 March 1882) that he had "no axes to grind nor hobbies to ride," he clearly took advantage of his "independent journalism" policy, particularly in the "Migma" column. Tourgée prided himself on being fearless and outspoken, and his editorials were filled with his candid opinions on politics, current events, religion, and literature. He continued to write on his favorite topics, namely the South, the Negro, the Republican party, and federal educational aid; however, as Otto Olsen points out, Tourgée's editorials soon "began to define a newer reformism that he would champion throughout his life." Tourgée saw the new federal constitutional amendments ratified between 1865 and 1870 as guaranteeing equality to all men without regard to race. Through the *Continent* he hoped to encourage, as he said on 17 May 1882, "a public sentiment that would not only permit but demand their [the amendments'] enforcement." Tourgée further violated his nonpartisan policy by expressing his views on the 1884 presidential election and roundly criticizing the Republican party.

Yet Tourgée's editorials were not all politics and vendettas. Tourgée openly catered to the interests of his readers and discoursed frequently on topics such as history, travel, foreign languages, domestic issues, science, nature, and literature. Still, he could not refrain from moralizing on certain subjects, such as his aversion to tobacco and alcohol. What Olsen terms Tourgée's "puritanical code" led Tourgée to ban the advertisement of these products in his magazine.

Tourgée's comments on literature, particularly those concerning literary realism, are of interest. As evidenced by his own novels and the fiction chosen for the *Continent*, the idealistic Tourgée disliked realism, especially as represented by William Dean Howells and Henry James. On 14 March 1883 Tourgée openly criticized all works falling under the "taint of the realistic school." He later said (1 August 1883) that Howells and James were "novelists of first-rate abilities, writing with second-rate purposes on second or third-rate materials." Realism, Tourgée believed, focused primarily on the "unpleasant,

Cover of the weekly Tourgée edited for two years (Library of Congress)

petty and debasing elements in human nature" rather than "its better side and nobler aspects" (22 August 1883). He charged that Howells's method in *A Modern Instance* (1882) was that of an "anatomist" who approached his subject as one would approach a dissecting table (22 December 1882). Nor did he approve of James's psychological approach to characterization. As he said on 18 April 1883, "whatever his art may represent, it has not fellowship with the noblest and deepest facts of life. Till some gleam of spirituality is added he must remain artist, but can never become creator."

Tourgée was convinced that romanticism revealed a more accurate picture of life. For him (1 March 1882), "the *human heart*, its pains and passions, its strength and weaknesses, its longings and more than all its love" were the true elements of literature. As evidenced by the pages of the *Continent*, Tourgée favored works by well-known sentimentalists such as E. P. Roe and Francis Marion Crawford, who wrote historical fiction. Tourgée saw no discrepancy between "a true fiction" and fiction portrayed in romantic terms. Asked by a *Continent* reader if his novels were "really fair exponents of Southern life" or "merely fictitious," Tourgée responded defensively in the 5 December 1883 issue: "The obligation which rests upon the novelist in the depiction of sentiment and motive is precisely the same as rests upon the historian in the narration of mere facts." Apparently, Tourgée either did not recognize or chose to ignore the elements of realism in his own fiction.

Like many magazines of the era the *Continent* was doomed to failure by lack of capital. In late 1883 Tourgée moved the magazine to New York hoping to gain more subscribers and advertisers. The magazine finally collapsed in the summer of 1884 when Charles H. Blair, the corporation's largest stockholder, demanded immediate payment of his loan. According to Tourgée's sworn statement regarding the magazine's finances, monthly receipts from subscriptions amounted to only $1,426, hardly enough to repay the debt. The last issue of the *Continent* appeared on 13 August 1884. Tourgée's version of these unfortunate events is recorded by his biographers: "A very rich man induced me in 1881 to engage with him in publishing the *Continent* magazine. When his extravagance and pretense had swamped what ought to have been a success, he dug out and I very foolishly undertook to resuscitate the corpse. Had I been brave enough to cut expenses down to bed-rock, I should have succeeded. But I was not.... It was a bad break–took everything and a lot more."

Following the collapse of the *Continent*, Tourgée retired to Thorheim. With half the profits from his book sales diverted to pay debts and with his house mortgaged he struggled for the next twelve years to provide a living for his family. He continued to write novels, but none achieved the success of *A Fool's Errand*. For a time his chief source of income came from his lectures on the lyceum circuit. But as early as December 1884 Tourgée was working to reestablish himself as a journalist. Remembering the controversial reception of his "C" letters, Tourgée penned a series of similar letters for the *Chicago Inter Ocean*. These anonymous letters, signed Siva, were highly critical of President-elect Grover Cleveland and, as Tourgée had hoped, created something of a stir. A series of columns–"A Veteran and His Pipe" (25 April-19 September 1885), "Letters to a Mugwump" (26 September-12 December 1885), and "A Child of Luck" (20 March-4 December 1886)–followed, and in spring 1888 Tourgée's column "A Bystander's Notes" became a regular feature in the newspaper.

Tourgée continued to espouse his favorite causes in "A Bystander's Notes," which gradually became a forum for his views on Negro civil rights. Repeatedly he defended the Negro's constitutional rights and mocked the false logic used to support Jim Crow laws. The column quickly gained the attention of Negro activists and journalists such as Harry C. Smith, Ida Wells-Barnett, Charles W. Chesnutt, Robert Pelham, Jr., F. J. Loudin, and Louis A. Martinet. Along with Martinet and other Negro leaders, Tourgée helped establish the biracial Citizens Equal Rights League in 1890. Through his column, Tourgée organized the National Citizens Rights Association (N.C.R.A.) in 1891 with the goal of involving more southern Negroes in the civil-rights struggle. As a leader in this organization Tourgée was instrumental in planning nonviolent protests to test the legality of the Jim Crow laws. As an attorney for the N.C.R.A., Tourgée was directly involved in the best-known test case–*Plessy* v. *Ferguson*. Although Tourgée carried the case of Homer Adolph Plessy to the United States Supreme Court, the appeal was unsuccessful and "separate but equal" became the law of the land for nearly sixty-five years.

In the winter of 1894 the *Inter Ocean* discontinued Tourgée's column, leaving him with no outlet in which to voice his support for the N.C.R.A. Early in 1895 several New York businessmen and civic leaders approached him with a proposal that he begin a new magazine dedicated to citizenship. Tourgée was cautious. As much as he wanted editorial control of a magazine, he had scarcely recovered from the financial disaster brought on by the *Continent*. Tourgée agreed to edit the new magazine but made careful arrangements to insure that he would not be personally responsible for any debts incurred. In March 1895 the first issue of the *Basis: A Journal of Good Citizenship* appeared; but before it was published, several of the investors withdrew their support, and Tourgée once again found himself in control of a magazine with lofty goals but shaky capital.

Tourgée established editorial offices in Buffalo, New York, but ran much of the magazine's business from Thorheim. The early issues employed a two-column format with illustrations, and each thirty-two-page issue sold for five cents a copy or $1.50 a year. The first issue indicated that the *Basis* was to be "devoted to Good Citizen-

columns in the *Continent*. Tourgée's daughter, Aimée, contributed "In Lighter Vein," and Tourgée's own "Migma" appeared occasionally. Tourgée also reused the title of his *Inter Ocean* column "A Bystander's Notes" in his new magazine. Other regular columns included the "Good Government Club Department" by Thomas R. Slicer, "Boy and Girl Citizens" by William K. Wickes, and "Our Women Citizens" by Ada C. Sweet.

The magazine was frequently filled with articles of a political or historical nature with occasional series such as portions of Tourgée's *The Story of a Thousand* (1896). Aimée Tourgée contributed fiction, poetry, and an occasional feature article. One feature, entitled "Some Uncollected Autographs," consisted of letters written to her father by such notables as Arthur Conan Doyle, Kate Field, James A. Garfield, Oliver Wendell Holmes, Julia Ward Howe, and Edmund Clarence Stedman. Other contributors to the *Basis* included Edward L. Keys, Rose Baker Howe, John Cunningham More, J. W. Ritner, James Edwin Campbell, Marian Darwin, W. H. Anderson, and W. H. Stowers.

As he had done in the *Continent*, Tourgée continued to criticize realists such as Howells, Thomas Hardy, and James in his literary notes and reviews. Book reviews were a regular feature, and a column called "Today's Thought–Literature and Art" appeared infrequently. A literary column by J. W. R. March, "Modern Literary Conditions," appeared in the last two issues.

Tourgée in the late 1890s (Tourgée Papers, Westfield, New York)

ship, Good Government, [and] Good Literature." As editor of the *Basis*, Tourgée made no attempt to downplay his partisan views as he had done in the *Continent*. "What will The Basis represent?" he asked, and he answered in the first issue: "The Convictions of the editor. No man or set of men will have any power to restrict or modify the expression of his views. Whatever he believes to be for the welfare of the American people . . . that he will advocate."

The *Basis* became the new mouthpiece of the N.C.R.A., and, predictably, Tourgée expounded frequently on civil-rights issues. One of his more startling innovations was a regular column, "The Mob Record," which was a nationwide report on the murders and lynchings of Negroes. When he was not championing civil rights, Tourgée editorialized on his favorite subjects–the Republican party, Christian Socialism, education reform, the South, and voting issues.

A few of the regular "departments" in the *Basis* were fashioned after the most successful

Tourgée did everything in his power to sustain the *Basis*. As early as the first issue, he launched a series of prize contests for the best short stories, essays, poems, and sermons, but no prizes were ever awarded. Advertisements were encouraged, and subscribers were solicited through various promotions. The magazine was run almost entirely by Tourgée, his wife, and his daughter, even after Slicer became an associate editor in September 1895. In December 1895 the magazine became a monthly with no illustrations, and its price was increased to fifteen cents per issue. In addition Tourgée closed the Buffalo editorial offices and moved the entire operation into his home. Despite these measures, the magazine failed. Tourgée's career as a magazine editor ended in April 1896 with the last issue of the *Basis*.

The final phase of Tourgée's eventful life was his appointment as consul to Bordeaux, France, in 1897. Although he continued to write, his consular duties and poor health greatly hindered his efforts. He died in Bordeaux on 21 May 1905. Following a funeral service in Bordeaux, his body was cremated and his ashes sent to Thorheim for burial.

Tourgée's reputation as a novelist and magazinist has been slowly revived as a new generation of scholars examines his work. His early novels are now recognized as realistic and perceptive accounts of the Reconstruction South. His contributions to the early Negro civil-rights movement have attracted notice in the last twenty years. *The Continent*, despite its short life, was one of the finest illustrated weeklies published prior to the great magazine boom of the late nineteenth century. Yet throughout his brilliant successes and devastating failures, Tourgée remained something of the idealistic fool he had portrayed in novels. "The life of the Fool proper," he wrote, "is full of the poetry of faith. He may run after a will-o'-the-wisp, while the Wise deride; but to him it is a veritable star of hope."

Bibliographies:

Dean H. Keller, "A Checklist of the Writings of Albion W. Tourgée (1838-1905)," *Studies in Bibliography*, 18 (1965): 269-279;

Marguerite Ealy and Sanford Marovitz, "Albion Winegar Tourgée," *American Literary Realism*, 8 (Winter 1975): 53-80.

Biographies:

Roy F. Dibble, *Albion W. Tourgée* (New York: Lemcke & Buechner, 1921);

Otto H. Olsen, *Carpetbagger's Crusade: The Life of Albion Winegar Tourgée* (Baltimore: Johns Hopkins Press, 1965).

References:

Theodore L. Gross, *Albion W. Tourgée* (New York: Twayne, 1963);

Gross, "Albion W. Tourgée: 'Reporter of the Reconstruction,'" *Mississippi Quarterly*, 16 (Spring 1963): 111-127;

Dean H. Keller, "Albion W. Tourgée as Editor of The Basis," *Niagara Frontier*, 12 (Spring 1965): 24-28;

E. Bruce Kirkham, "The Continent," in *American Literary Magazines: The Eighteenth and Nineteenth Centuries*, edited by Edward E. Chielens (New York: Greenwood Press, 1986), pp. 116-121;

Otto H. Olsen, "Albion W. Tourgée: Carpetbagger," *North Carolina Historical Review*, 40 (1963): 434-454.

Papers:

The majority of Albion W. Tourgée's papers are held at the Chautauqua County Historical Society in Westfield, New York. An index to the holdings is Dean H. Keller's *An Index to the Albion W. Tourgée Papers in the Chautauqua County Historical Society, Westfield, New York*, Research Series, vol. 7, *Kent State University Bulletin*, no. 52 (May 1964).

Joseph Addison Turner

(23 September 1826-29 February 1868)

Wallace B. Eberhard
University of Georgia

MAJOR POSITIONS HELD: Editor, *Turner's Monthly* (1848); editor and publisher, *Eatonton (Georgia) Independent* (1854); editor, *Plantation* (1860); editor and publisher, *Countryman* (1862-1866).

BOOKS: *A Letter to Hon. N. G. Foster, candidate for Congress in the 7th Congressional District of Ga., in reply to a speech delivered by him against the Democratic Party and in favor of the doctrine of the Know-Nothings, in Eatonton, on Thursday, 16th August, 1855* (Milledgeville, Ga.: Federal Union Power Press, 1855);

The Cotton Planter's Manual: Being a compilation of facts from the best authorities on the culture of cotton; its natural history, chemical analysis, trade, and consumption; and embracing a history of cotton and the cotton gin (New York: Saxton, 1857);

The Discovery of Sir John Franklin and Other Poems (Mobile, Ala. & New York: Goetzel & White, 1858);

The Old Plantation: A Poem by The Wanderer (Turnwold, Ga.: Countryman Print., 1862);

Autobiography of "The Countryman," 1866, edited by Thomas H. English (Atlanta: Emory University Library, 1943).

"Ever since I have had a wish, I have wished to be a writer of articles, the perusal of which would not be confined to a few partial friends, but which would be conned over by everybody that took up the book or paper or magazines in which I wrote." Thus wrote Joseph Addison Turner, then thirty-three years old, as he launched one of the several editorial ventures which earned him a place in Southern literary history. His life was short, but most of his adult years were devoted to the written word, either by contributing to established journals or by starting new ones which provided platforms for his varied literary and editorial visions. Not only did he pursue publication vigorously, but he did it with a fierce independence of thought. He was proslavery, antisecession, anti-Yankee, and passionately devoted to the development of a truly Southern literary tradition.

Turner was born on 23 September 1826 near Eatonton, in Putnam County, Georgia, on the plantation where his father, William Turner, was also born. Struck by a bone infection at age seven, he was left permanently lame. Because he was essentially homebound as a boy, his father tutored him at home, where he had access to a four-thousand-volume library until he was able to attend nearby Phoenix Academy. After seven years there, he moved to Emory College at Oxford, Georgia, for a semester before returning to Eatonton to teach for a year. He read law in Eatonton and in 1847 passed the Georgia Bar exam. He seemed on the verge of a successful life as attorney and son of a prominent landowner, but for the next twenty years his career moved between lawyering and farming and the real loves of his life, writing and publishing.

Turner's success as editor and publisher was built on a foundation of experience from previous literary efforts and publishing ventures, most of which did not survive long. In 1847, when Turner was twenty-one, he was involved with the production of a volume of poetry, which collected early verse under the pseudonym "Frank Kemble." The book was apparently printed in Augusta, but there are no surviving copies available for study. Within two years he had been involved in another dozen or so publishing ventures, including three issues of *Turner's Monthly*, an 1848 literary publication, and in 1849, at least one issue of the *Red Lion*. In the first issue of his *Monthly* Turner admitted that periodical literature of higher quality was available but went on to ask, "But is it to be found in Georgia? Have you no *State pride* which will prompt you to support a home literature in its incipiency . . .?"

On 28 November 1850 he married Louisa Jane Dennis, the daughter of a merchant and planter from Eatonton. Within the year he bought a plantation near his father's, about nine miles from Eatonton. Soon he dropped its name–Merry Dale–and merged it with the original family household, then owned and occupied by his brother William, under the title of Turnwold.

He continued to pursue a dual career as plantation owner and writer-editor, and in 1853 an acrimonious exchange with New York publisher Charles B. Norton ensued over publication of a long, satirical poem, "The Times." "He has acted as a scoundrel," wrote Turner of Norton, "as completely as ever a man did, and there is a correspondence now going on between us relative to the matter." Ultimately Norton refused to promote the sale of the poem because of its alleged libelous nature; the copies were sent to Turner for sale through a Macon bookseller. Another collection of verse, *The Discovery of Sir John Franklin and Other Poems*, was published in 1858. Many of the poems are amateurish, though ambitious and reflective of a thoughtful talent. All of this literary effort was prologue to an innovative publishing venture which in 1860 pitted a lively Southern mind against the backdrop of growing antislavery sentiment in one of the centers of American publishing, New York City. Turner boldly set out to create a vehicle for the Southern viewpoint and to promote a unique Southern literary heritage. Behind the *Plantation* was not only the desire to advance Southern writing and viewpoints, but his basic disdain for things Northern. As he later wrote, "From my youth up I have hated yankees and yankee literature."

The *Plantation*, which first appeared in March 1860, was a quarterly of substantial proportions. Its 220 pages contained both prose and poetry, and it was praised for its quality in the *Southern Literary Messenger*, whose editor said, "We shall take great pleasure in exchanging with [this] first-class journal." While this support might be predictable from another Southern publication, the new magazine also was praised by the pro-Republican *New York Evening Post*: "The PLANTATION is a pro-slavery organ, and most of the articles have a direct bearing on this theme.... [It] is neatly printed on smooth elegant paper, and Southerners now have another opportunity of showing whether they can support a Magazine, which, however much we may differ from its politics, we must confess, possesses considerable literary merit."

Turner's plan for Northern publication of a Southern journal was not merely confrontational–it was practical. He recognized New York as a center of efficient, state-of-the-art printing technology, and having a New York printer took the production problem out of his hands. Although he was anti-Yankee, he wanted his journal to have the best potential for circulation in the North and South. Publishers in New York, he wrote, "have the machinery in operation to force out a book or journal into a circulation that exists nowhere in the South." The first issue included poetry; essays on such topics as John Brown's raid, slavery in "the territories," and cotton; and "the Goose-Quill Essays," articles about plantation life. It is likely that most of the prose in the *Plantation* came from Turner's own pen, though his brother William is credited as author of at least one piece in a later issue. In addition, there were a number of articles reprinted from other journals, American and foreign, centering on politics and the slavery issue.

The *Plantation* survived for four issues; the date on the last was December 1860, and prophetic of the gathering storm that led to the bloody schism a few months later. The magazine seemed to be thriving but the Civil War marked an end to the venture. Turner wrote in the last issue: "We know not whether we shall be in the Union the coming year or out of it; but whether in or out, the purposes of this Journal will be the same, and we shall work with renewed energy for their accomplishment." The times, not a lack of skill and inventiveness of the editor, ended the short, lively life of the *Plantation*, and its four issues represent what magazine historian Bertram H. Flanders calls "one of the most ambitious journalistic undertakings made by any man in the Old South."

Although he had been successfully juggling other interests, including farming and politics, Turner had not abandoned his editorial ventures. Elected to the Georgia Senate in 1859, he worked faithfully at his duties despite occasional ill health and wrote a major revision in the state's common school law. The journalistic and literary achievement for which Turner is most noted and remembered could not have been launched at a worse moment in American history. The war was well into its first year when, on 4 March 1862, one hundred copies of the *Countryman* came off an aging Washington handpress which Turner had purchased and moved from the town of Greensboro, Georgia, some twenty miles away. The possibility of a journal published "at home" was not new to Turner. As early as 25 January 1857 he had written in his journal, "Am becoming afflicted with the idea of issuing a small journal from this place," but the coming of the war that shut down the more ambitious New York-based magazine turned his energy to what seemed a more modest venture. The *Countryman* would, he said, be a country paper devoted to the people who lived in the country. This was a bit disarming, in that he had elsewhere written of his interest in "indulging a quixotic freak to publish a Essayist–not a newspaper–on my plantation, to be devoted to–everything generally." This personal kind of journal would need his close attention, and hence the purchase of a press and hiring of an experienced printer. "I would not have the newspaper printed away from my supervision, so that I could not read the proof. I would not trust Faust himself to do that."

Within three months of the first issue, the publication had wide readership in the Confederacy and was an apparent success, both financially and journalistically. Critics are universal in their praise of the *Countryman* (a pseudonym Turner used first in writing articles for the Milledgeville newspapers). One writer said this about it: "Freshness, aliveness and variety characterized its contents. Its columns contained useful items of information for country people during the war such as substitutes for salt and quinine, instructions on how to make tallow candles, and lists of prices current in the Augusta market." Beyond these stories useful to readers was a varied potpourri: casualty lists, articles on hunting, Turner editorials on virtually everything, and items from newspapers outside Georgia. "Through the four years of its publication there was not one dull or conventional issue," according to one scholar. To label the *Countryman* an "amazing success" is clichéd, but it was just that, with circulation estimated at two thousand from Virginia to Texas. It was, despite inflation, shortages of supplies, and a host of wartime difficulties, a financial success as well. Although Turner was proslavery and pro-Confederacy, he was known as one who treated his own slaves fairly and generously, and was open-minded in ways that many of his contemporaries were not. For instance, he saw no practicality in a state law against teaching slaves to read, and saw no practical reason not to teach them. "The negro is either capable of education, or he is not.... If he is capable of education it is a sin to withhold it from him. If he is incapable of it and created by his Maker, it may be folly to say, by law, he shall not have an education, but it is neither wickedness, nor sin."

Sherman's march through Georgia eventually brought Union troops to Turnwold, and Turner's witness to war is recorded in his newspaper and journals. The *Countryman* continued publication after Union occupation and the end of the war, although it was interrupted for six months when Turner tried the patience of military authority. In June 1865 he published an editorial which supported state sovereignty in domestic matters to include the right to secession, as well as no punishment for those who served the Confederacy under sanction of state governments. The same editorial appeared in four issues, whereupon Union soldiers escorted him before Gen. James Wilson in Macon. There, Turner said, he was "subjected to very rough TALK, amounting to grossest insult." Turner halted publication for six months, claiming that the military government had imposed such stringent restrictions on what he could say as to be unacceptable. His newspaper's motto changed from "Independent in Everything, Neutral in Nothing" to "Independent in Nothing, Neutral in Everything." In February 1866 he resumed publication, but the *Countryman* lasted only until 8 May of that year. In his valedictory editorial he wrote that his newspaper was "a representative of independent country life, and of the home of the planter. These are gone, and the *Countryman* goes with them." The first issue of the *Countryman* carried an advertisement from Turner seeking a boy to learn the printer's trade. Joel Chandler Harris, then fourteen, picked up a copy of that issue at the Eatonton post office, responded, and was hired. His printer's apprenticeship was also an editorial tutorial under a demanding but supportive editor. Turnwold with its slaves, the turmoil of the Civil War, and the twilight of plantation life fed his memory with material for both a successful editorial career at the *Atlanta Constitution* and the writing of the Uncle Remus stories, which brought him lasting recognition in American literature.

Turner's own life, which ended on 29 February 1868, survived that of the *Countryman* by only two years, but his plantation newspaper had earned him contemporary success and a place in American journalism history, not just for its unique publishing locus but for its lively journalistic and literary content. Although Turner's *Countryman* bought him a historical niche on its own merits, it would have been worth at least a footnote in history for producing a journalist-author familiar to the public at large.

References:

Paul M. Cousins, *Joel Chandler Harris* (Baton Rouge: Louisiana State University Press, 1968), pp. 19-86;

Bertram H. Flanders, *Early Georgia Magazines* (Athens: University of Georgia Press, 1944), pp. 93-95, 150-156, 164-176;

Lawrence Huff, "Joseph Addison Turner and his Quarterly, the *Plantation*," *Georgia Historical Quarterly*, 54 (Winter 1970): 493-506;

Huff, "Joseph Addison Turner: A Study in the Culture of Ante-Bellum Middle Georgia," Ph.D. dissertation, Vanderbilt University, 1958;

Huff, "The Literary Publications of Joseph Addison Turner," *Georgia Historical Quarterly*, 46 (September 1962): 223-236.

John Brisben Walker
(10 September 1847-7 July 1931)

Erwin K. Thomas
Norfolk State University

MAJOR POSITIONS HELD: Special writer, *Cincinnati Commercial Gazette* (1873-1876); managing editor, *Pittsburgh Telegraph* (1876); editor, *Washington Daily Chronicle* (1876-1879); editor and publisher, *Cosmopolitan* (1889-1905), *Twentieth Century Home* (1904-1905).

BOOKS: *The History of the World's Largest Corporation* (New York: Aldine, 1904?);

Report of Mr. Walker, on the Condition of the Chicago Packing House and Stock Yard; Embracing the Result of a Twelve Days' Study. An Analysis of the Business of Buying, Slaughtering and Packing Cattle (New York, 1906);

Woodrow Wilson; Has He Been for "America First"? Has He Been for the Great Mass of the American People, or Has His Administration Stood in with the Special Interests? Address by John Brisben Walker, at Cooper Union, on Thursday, November 18th, 1915 (New York?, 1915).

PERIODICAL PUBLICATIONS: "A Modern City's Factors of Growth," *Cosmopolitan*, 9 (May 1890): 62-75;

"Public Baths for the Poor," *Cosmopolitan*, 9 (August 1890): 414-422;

"Alfalfa Farming," *Cosmopolitan*, 12 (November 1891): 85-94;

"The Problem of Aerial Navigation," *Cosmopolitan*, 12 (March 1892): 624-630;

"Some Speculation Regarding Rapid Transit," *Cosmopolitan*, 20 (November 1895): 26-33;

"Men and Events–Henry George and Charles A. Dana," *Cosmopolitan*, 24 (December 1897): 199-204;

"Some Difficulties of Modern Journalism," *Cosmopolitan*, 24 (January 1898): 328;

"Studies of Our Government," *Cosmopolitan*, 24 (April 1898): 630-636;

"Mohammed: The Building of An Empire," *Cosmopolitan*, 26 (March 1899): 475-482;

"The Wonders of New York, 1903 and 1909," *Cosmopolitan*, 36 (December 1903): 143-160;

"The Conquest of Asia By Russia," *Cosmopolitan*, 36 (February 1904): 381-386;

"The Final Conquest of the Air," *Cosmopolitan*, 36 (March 1904): 501-516;

"If Europe Goes To War," *Cosmopolitan*, 36 (April 1904): 621-632.

John Brisben Walker, editor and publisher of the *Cosmopolitan* from 1889 until 1905, brought respectability and popularity to the failing magazine. In five years he built the magazine's circulation from twenty thousand to four hundred thousand. His many interests–iron mining, growing alfalfa, automobiles, and aviation–are reflected in the diversity of articles (some of which he wrote) in *Cosmopolitan*. The magazine was also notable for its articles on current affairs and for its poetry, fiction, and literary essays.

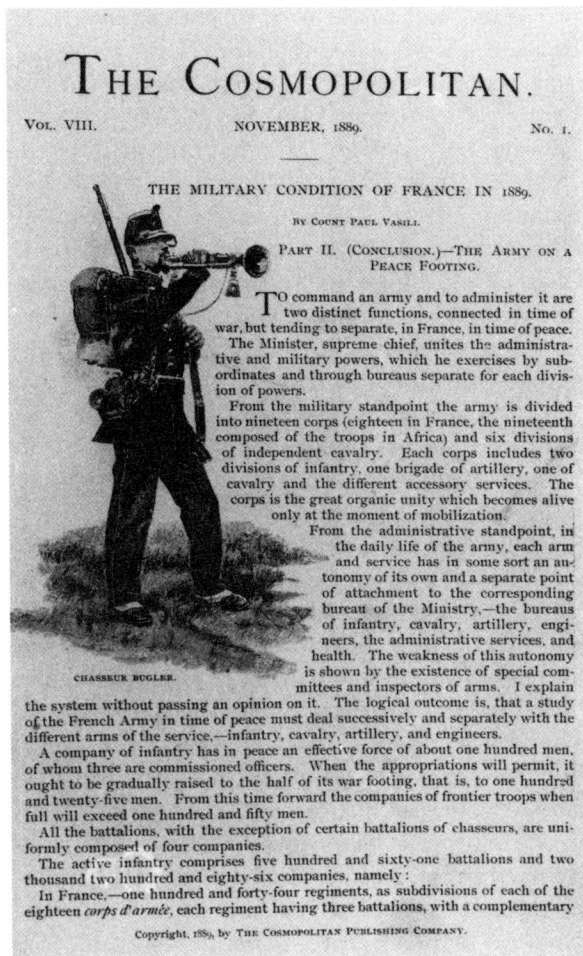

Opening page from an issue of the magazine Walker owned and edited from 1889 to 1905

Walker was born on 10 September 1847 at his parents' country house on the Monogahela River, near Pittsburgh, Pennsylvania. The son of John and Anna Krepps Walker, Walker attended Gonzaga College in Washington, D.C., and Georgetown College. He left Georgetown in 1865 to accept an appointment to the United States Military Academy at West Point. Before completing his degree he resigned from the academy and went to China to serve as an adviser during the reorganization of the Chinese military system.

On his return to the United States in 1870 Walker became involved in manufacturing iron in the Kanawha Valley, West Virginia. In 1872 he ran for Congress as a Republican and was defeated. He prospered in the iron business but lost his holdings after the economic panic of 1873.

In 1873 Walker wrote a series of articles on the mineral industry for Murat Halstead's *Cincinnati Commercial Gazette,* and he continued as a special writer for that paper until 1876, when–through Halstead's recommendation–he was appointed managing editor of the *Pittsburgh Telegraph.* Within a few months he had become editor of the *Washington [State] Daily Chronicle.* After the *Chronicle* was discontinued, Walker developed a successful alfalfa ranch in Denver, Colorado, where he reclaimed a wide tract of flood land on the Platte River.

In 1889 Walker bought *Cosmopolitan* from Joseph N. Hallock. That same year he became president of the Stanley Automobile Company of America and built a factory to manufacture Locomobile steam cars at Philipse Manor, New York. In addition to *Cosmopolitan,* Walker briefly edited *Twentieth Century Home* (later the *Twentieth Century*), a women's monthly, and *Your Affairs,* a pacifist monthly. In 1905 he sold *Cosmopolitan* to William Randolph Hearst. During World War I he became active in the Friends of Peace and Justice, an isolationist group.

Walker was married three times. He had eight children by his first wife, Emily Strother, from whom he was divorced, and four children by his second, Ethel Richmond. At the time of his death, on 7 July 1931, he was married to Iris Calderhead.

The decade of the 1890s was a colorful period in American magazine history, and the *Cosmopolitan,* like many other magazines of that time, underwent considerable growth. Walker filled his magazine with illustrated articles on diverse subjects, as well as poetry and fiction.

The May and June 1890 issues contained such articles as "Artists and Art Life in Munich," "At The Home of A Corean Nobleman," "The Rise of The Tall Hat," "The South and Its Colored Citizens," "Fashion in Literature," "Farm Life and Irrigating In Persia," "Soft Crabs, Canvasbacks, and Terrapin," "The Coaching Era," "A Study of The Half-Breed Races In the West Indies," "The Romance of Versailles, Part I," "Side Glances At American Beauty," "Some Curious Prophecies," "Fragments of the Stars (Meteorites)," and "Leading Writers of Modern Spain." For the May and August issues, Walker himself wrote "A Modern City's Factors of Growth" and "Public Baths For the Poor."

Other 1890 issues included–in addition to poetry and fiction–stories on Persia, the West Indies, Sweden, and Guatemala; articles on beauty and fashion, education, courtly life, fishing and hunting, religion, literature, business, current events, travel, and social issues such as club life and suffrage. One year later *Cosmopolitan* was also publishing articles on emigration from the cities, music, South Africa's diamond fields, Russian women, artists, charities, the military, mining, and the press. All were vital ingredients to the Walker formula for making *Cosmopolitan* appealing. The magazine's early attention to women was apparent. In the September and October 1891 issues there were five stories on women, one, "Society Women as Authors," written by a woman and illustrated with portraits of some of the writers discussed.

In 1892 *Cosmopolitan* carried information on "aerial navigation," and offered prizes for the best essays on the subject. Walker was committed to supporting the development of the airplane. Thomas A. Edison became a consultant, serving the cause without pay. Notable professors also became advisers. The March 1892 issue featured an article by Walker titled "The Problem of Aerial Navigation." Though he transferred some of his enthusiasm to the automobile, Walker continued to follow developments in aeronautics, as is evident in his "The Final Conquest of the Air" (*Cosmopolitan*, March 1904), which followed the Wright brothers' first successful flight at Kitty Hawk on 17 December 1903.

In 1891 Walker decided to make *Cosmopolitan* more literary, and hired William Dean Howells as joint editor. Howells began work in March 1892 but worked only on the May and June issues before resigning. The July through October issues also contained much fiction and poetry, however.

Among the stories in 1892 issues were "Evening Dress" by Howells, "Social Strugglers" by H. H. Boyesen, "The Passing of Sister Barsett" by Sarah Orne Jewett, and "Jersey Villas" by Henry James. In the same year the *Cosmopolitan* published poems by James Russell Lowell, Edmund Clarence Stedman, and John Hay. Other contributors during Walker's ownership were Richard Malcolm Johnston, Gertrude Atherton, John Esten Cooke, Octave Thanet (Alice French), Richard Henry Stoddard, Albion W. Tourgée, Harold Frederic, Richard LeGallienne, H. G. Wells, Israel Zangwill, James Lane Allen, Rudyard Kipling, Robert Louis Stevenson, Mark Twain, Jack London, and Edith Wharton. In 1893 novelist Arthur Sherburne Hardy became joint editor of the *Cosmopolitan*, remaining with the magazine for two years, and at the turn of the century H. H. Boyesen was an assistant editor.

Murat Halstead, formerly of the *Cincinnati Commercial Gazette*, worked for Walker, editing a "Review of Current Events" department in 1890-1892 and writing articles on national and international issues. Walker's interest in foreign affairs led in 1895 to his sending Hobart C. Chatfield-Taylor to Spain to negotiate with Spanish officials on buying Cuba's freedom for one hundred million dollars. The Spanish would not discuss the offer with him.

Cosmopolitan was reported to have been produced on presses designed for the finest quality of printing and capable of turning out twenty thousand magazines per day. In 1893 the circulation of *Cosmopolitan* was one hundred fifty thousand. Most copies were distributed in the United States and Canada, but some went to South America, Turkey, Italy, Spain, Russia, China, Australia, France, England, and Germany. It was estimated that some three-quarter million people would examine these one hundred fifty thousand copies.

In July 1893, hoping to reach a wider audience, Walker cut his magazines's price from fifteen cents to twelve and a half cents, but he changed the price back to fifteen cents in December. In 1895 he lowered the price again, this time to ten cents per issue to compete with *Munsey's* and *McClure's*.

By 1894 Walker had moved his magazine's headquarters from New York to the newly completed Cosmopolitan Center at Irvington-on-the-Hudson, about fifty minutes from New York City at that time. The building, designed by the architectural firm of McKim, Mead and White, was planned to accommodate the growing staff of the *Cosmopolitan*, which by this time had a circulation of four hundred thousand.

The copies of each issue of the *Cosmopolitan* filled ten mail cars. While most of the staff was moved to Irvington-on-the-Hudson, the magazine also kept editorial and business offices in New York.

Modern education was one of Walker's major concerns. He was a pioneer in offering college scholarships to successful salesmen of *Cosmopolitan* subscriptions, giving one thousand of these rewards in 1893. In the August 1897 issue Walker announced the foundation of Cosmopolitan University, a free correspondence school, asking: "Why should not provision be made for a liberal education for the many who, while forced to work, are yet willing and anxious to study and require only wise direction?"

Walker appointed E. Benjamin Andrews, who had just left the presidency of Brown University, as the first president of Cosmopolitan University. Andrews returned to his former position after a few weeks, and Walker named Eliphalet Nott Potter, who had been president of Union College, as Andrew's successor.

In October Walker announced that 5,856 people had applied to the university; by November the number had risen to 9,491; and in January 1898, the magazine announced that more than 12,000 had applied. Walker had planned to spend one hundred fifty thousand dollars on the university over the next five years, and the enormous response to his offer not only took him by surprise but also found him financially unprepared. The magazine asked students to pay five dollars per quarter voluntarily and most complied, but Cosmopolitan University was largely disbanded after two years, due to problems in finding instructors as well as funding. Walker continued to maintain a much smaller correspondence school for several years and to speak out against the elitism he saw in higher education, urging Congress to establish and fund a national correspondence university.

Walker's most significant achievement was his ability to make the *Cosmopolitan* a magazine that reflected his many interests while appealing to a general readership with high-quality literature and articles on the important events of the day–all presented in an attractive, well-illustrated format.

References:

Sister Mary Damascene Brocki, CSSF, "A Study of *Cosmopolitan* Magazine, 1890-1900: Its Relation to the Literature of the Decade," Ph.D. dissertation, University of Notre Dame, 1958;

"The Napoleon of the Mags," *New York Herald*, 3 September 1893;

Flora Mai Holly, "Notes on Some American Mag Editors," *Bookman*, 12 (December 1900): 357-368;

Charles Hanson Towne, *Adventures in Editing* (New York: Appleton, 1926), pp. 21-52, 66-67.

George Wilkes

(1817-23 September 1885)

Sam G. Riley
Virginia Polytechnic Institute and State University

MAJOR POSITIONS HELD: Editor, publisher, *Subterranean* (1844); cofounder, editor, and publisher, *National Police Gazette* (1845-1866); associate editor, *Porter's Spirit of the Times* (1856-1858); editor (1859-1875) and publisher (1859-1885), *Wilkes' Spirit of the Times*, renamed *Spirit of the Times* in 1875.

BOOKS: *Review of Miss Martineau's Work on 'Society in America'* (Boston: Marsh, Capen & Lyon, 1837);
The Mysteries of the Tombs: A Journal of Thirty Days Imprisonment in the New York City Prison; For Libel (New York, 1844);
The History of Oregon, Geographical and Political (New York: Colyer, 1845);
An Account and History of the Oregon Territory: Together with a Journal of an Emigrating Party across the Western Prairies of America, and to the Mouth of the Columbia River (London: Lott, 1846);
The Lives of Helen Jewett, and Richard Robinson (New York, 1847);
Europe in a Hurry (New York: Long, 1853);
The Great Battle, Fought at Manassas, between the Federal Forces, under General McDowell, and the Rebels, under Gen. Beauregard, Sunday, July 21, 1861 (New York: Brown & Ryan, 1861);
McClellan: Who He Is and What He Has Done (New York: Tousey, 1862); enlarged as *McClellan: From Ball's Bluff to Antietam* (New York: Tousey, 1863);
Shakespeare, from an American Point of View; Including an Inquiry as to His Religious Faith, and His Knowledge of Law: With the Baconian Theory Considered (New York: Appleton, 1877; London: Low, Marston, Searle & Rivington, 1877; revised, New York: Appleton, 1882).

OTHER: *Rules and Regulations for the Government of Racing, Trotting & Betting as Adopted by the Principal Turf Assoc. throughout the U.S. & Canada*, compiled by Wilkes (New York: Brown, 1866).

George Wilkes

George Wilkes was founder of the rough-and-tumble *National Police Gazette*, which attained a large circulation under his leadership but became larger still under Richard Kyle Fox, who bought it in 1876. Wilkes made a far bigger name for himself as owner of *Wilkes' Spirit of the Times*, which has been called the first comprehensive sports magazine in America.

Little has been recorded about Wilkes's early life. He was born in New York City in 1817. His formal education was limited to an unknown number of years in that city's public schools. Wilkes later determined that a legal career might suit him and worked for some time in a law office. Literary interests took his attention away from the law, however, and he began selling articles, mostly to the city's more sensational periodicals and newspapers.

At age twenty Wilkes published a modest fifty-four-page pamphlet in which he reviewed Harriet Martineau's *Society in America* (1837). Martineau, who was English, had traveled in America for two years, and her often critical comments drew sharp attacks in the American press. No admirer of the newspapers of his day, Wilkes defended Martineau as "a lady of unblemished moral reputation," and as possessing a literary character "beyond the reach of all the denunciation that our press can utter." He agreed with Martineau's contention that the American newspaper press was servile to politicians, going so far as to say, "It cannot be denied that, with few exceptions, our newspaper editors are the most contemptible, time-serving, unworthy and vulgar set of men in the whole community." He agreed also that the American public was apathetic regarding many vital issues.

In 1844 Wilkes edited and published a short-lived four-page New York periodical called the *Subterranean*. Crime, police corruption, and vice were his abundant targets. During the year of the journal's existence Wilkes was shot twice and arrested six times. The last of these arrests, on a libel charge, resulted in thirty days' imprisonment in the Tombs. Upon his release he rushed to press with a second pamphlet, which described the awful conditions in the jail and helped unseat the mayor, Robert Morris, in the next election. Meanwhile, the *Subterranean* had expired for lack of funds, and Wilkes went into partnership with lawyer and former journalist Enoch E. Camp, launching on 13 September 1845 a new crusading weekly periodical, the *National Police Gazette*. Camp bankrolled the venture, then pulled out in 1847. Police records provided material for a series called "Lives of the Felons," which detailed the unsavory exploits of the city's criminal element. At various times the thieves and brawlers, so described, descended on the *Gazette*'s basement offices on Centre Street bent on preventing any further publicity. Wilkes and his two bodyguards, "Sergeant" Belcher and Tim "Keel-Layer" Mooney, assisted by other staffers, had to fight for their lives; and on one such occasion *Gazette* reporter Andrew Frost was killed.

By displaying the names of Mexican War deserters, Wilkes persuaded the government to place a large subscription to his magazine for its military bases to discourage further desertions. Thus buoyed, Wilkes waged war on political corruption, prizefighting, rent inflation, mistreatment and robbery of newly arrived immigrants (known as immigrant-shaving), and blue laws.

In the same year as the founding of the *National Police Gazette* Wilkes published *The History of Oregon, Geographical and Political*, the second section of which depended heavily on a series of letters written, he claimed, by a gentleman then living in Oregon. This gentleman was not named but appears to have been Peter H. Burnett, a Tennessee-born lawyer who later served Oregon as governor and as a state supreme court justice. The book is a curious mixture of fiction and accurate facts about roads, fords, distances, and other information of real value to persons wishing to emigrate there.

In this work Wilkes suggested that a government-owned railroad be built to connect the Atlantic and Pacific coasts. This early proposal for a transcontinental railroad was criticized and satirized, for Wilkes's plan was viewed at this time as nothing more than a grandiose pipe dream. Twenty-four years later, however, the rail project he had proposed was a reality, complete with the scandals Wilkes predicted would occur if the railroad were built privately with government subsidies.

Still lacking the respectability he desired, Wilkes used his spicy *National Police Gazette* to cover a succession of scandals. One of the biggest took place in the winter of 1846 when, acting on a tip, Wilkes went to a bordello on New York's Walker Street. There he found John B. Gough, prominent temperance advocate, drunk and in the company of two prostitutes. On the following Saturday the *Gazette* broke the story. Gough claimed that he had been drugged and threatened to sue the journal for libel. When he failed to file suit, Wilkes sued Gough for slander, though he later dropped the case.

Wilkes crusaded against grave robbers, pickpockets, river pirates, and the city's more dangerous and disreputable alleys. The Robinson-Jewett murder loomed large in the *National Police Gazette*, and in 1847 Wilkes authored a book about the misadventures and murder of Helen Jewett, whose real name was Dorcas Doyen. It was a tale of lost virtue, written in the form of politely worded titillation–the story of a young girl cast out, literally, into the snow, and of vile seducers who "made merchandise of her young charms." Other stories involved swindler Robert "Bob the Wheeler" Sutton; the loose-moraled Virginia Myers of Richmond, Virginia; the murder of Mrs. Emeline Houseman and her infant child by

Front page of an early issue of the magazine Wilkes cofounded in 1845

Polly Bodine; and the furious altercations between pugilists Bill Poole and John Morrissey. A story that lasted, off and on, from 1846 until the 1870s–after the *Gazette* had come into the possession of Richard Kyle Fox–involved Philadelphia's infamous abortionist Ann Lohman, better known as Madame Restell.

In 1849 Wilkes traveled to the California gold fields with his close friend David C. Broderick, who later became a United States senator. It is likely that Wilkes acted as Broderick's publicist. Wilkes's obituary in the *New York Times* says that he returned to New York in 1851, though it is possible that he returned much sooner, and began writing sports news for the *Spirit of the Times* under editor William T. Porter. Wilkes also traveled to Europe and in 1853 wrote a travel book titled *Europe in a Hurry*, tracing his route from London to Paris and Brussels, through Germany and Switzerland to Italy. The influence of the *National Police Gazette* shows clearly in his choice of topics. In London he wrote gleefully about the hard-bitten denizens of Seven Dials, Thieves Kitchen, and other London dens of iniquity, and commented with sober interest on London's Pentonville, Millbank, and Newgate prisons. He was fascinated by the mummies of Kreutzberg, the torture chamber of a castle at Baden-Baden, and other such tourist sights.

Back in New York, he continued his association with Porter at the *Spirit of the Times*, a periodical modeled after *Bell's Life in London* and devoted to sports, humor, entertainment, and light literature. Porter died in 1858, and Wilkes continued the *Spirit*, changing its title to *Wilkes' Spirit of the Times*. Wilkes was a recognized authority on horses and racing and made his periodical the leading sports journal of the time, addressing not only racing but field sports and the stage. Competitors in the city were Frank Queen's *New York Clipper* and Ed James's *Sportsman*.

Broderick died from wounds suffered in a duel with Judge David S. Terry that took place on 13 September 1859, leaving an estate of three hundred thousand dollars. It at first appeared that he had died intestate, but Wilkes produced a will in which he was named beneficiary of the entire amount with the exception of a ten-thousand-dollar bequest to another party. The California attorney general contested this will, and in the trial court, judgment was entered for the state. Wilkes appealed and won a reversal; after legal fees he received a reported one hundred thousand dollars from the estate.

During the Civil War Wilkes gave his *Spirit* a more political slant, editorializing regularly on the war effort. His forceful editorials praising Ulysses Grant and attacking George McClellan were widely reprinted, and he became one of Secretary of War Edwin Stanton's favorite journalists. Wilkes went to the front to report the Battle of Manassas for the *Spirit* and published a pamphlet on the conflict and a book on General McClellan.

In 1868 Wilkes dropped his name from the title of the *Spirit* and resolved to live a life of greater leisure, as he by then enjoyed a more than ample income. He officially retired in 1875, installing E. A. Buck as editor and half-owner. His *National Police Gazette* had declined in circulation and had been sold in 1866 to an old foe, George W. Matsell, former New York police chief.

Still striving for respectability, Wilkes ran unsuccessfully for Congress on the Republican ticket. He hoped to be appointed minister to Mexico in the first Grant administration, and when this position was not offered to him he lived abroad for several years, then returned to New York in the fall of 1884. Another disappointment was the lack of attention paid his last book, *Shakespeare, from an American Point of View* (1877). An honor that did come to him, however, was the grand cross of the Order of St. Stanislas, which he received from Czar Aleksandr II in 1870 for his suggestion of a railroad route from China, across Russia, to India. Wilkes died of kidney disease on 23 September 1885 at his home at 352 W. Sixty-first Street in New York. He had married twice but died a widower, leaving a daughter by his second wife and an adopted son. He was buried in Greenwood Cemetery. The *Spirit of the Times* was published until 1902, when it merged into Chicago's *Horseman* as *Horseman and Spirit of the Times*.

George Wilkes, flamboyant, frequently caustic magazine journalist of the mid 1800s, has been largely passed over by modern media historians, yet he edited and published two long-lived and widely circulated New York periodicals. The *National Police Gazette* was one of America's earliest successful men's magazines devoted to entertainment. *Wilkes's Spirit of the Times*, was one of the nineteenth century's best sporting journals, and probably the first general sports magazine published in the United States. Though financially successful, Wilkes never attained the respectability to which he so long aspired.

References:

Clarence B. Bagley, "George Wilkes," *Washington Historical Quarterly*, 5 (January 1914): 3-11;

Walter Davenport, "The Nickel Shocker," *Collier's*, 81 (10 March 1928): 26-28, 38, 40;

Edward Van Every, *Sins of New York as "Exposed" by the Police Gazette* (New York: Stokes, 1930).

Victoria C. Woodhull

(23 September 1838-10 June 1927)

John A. Lent
Temple University

MAJOR POSITIONS HELD: Columnist, *New York Herald* (1870); publisher and editor, *Woodhull and Claflin's Weekly* (1870-1876); editor, *Humanitarian* (1892-1901).

SELECTED BOOKS: *A Page of American History: Constitution of the United States of the World* (Washington, D.C.: Cheltenham, Norman, Sawyer, 1870);

A Lecture on Constitutional Equality, Delivered at Lincoln Hall, Washington, D.C., Thursday, February 16, 1871 (New York: Journeymen Printers' Cooperative Association, 1871);

A Speech on the Great Social Problem of Labor & Capital Delivered at Cooper Institute, New York City . . . May 8, 1871, Before the Labor Reform League (New York: Journeymen Printers' Cooperative Association, 1871);

A Speech on the Principles of Finance, . . . Delivered at Cooper Institute, New York City, Thursday, August 3, 1871 (New York: Woodhull, Claflin, 1871);

"And the Truth Shall Make You Free": Being A Speech on the Principles of Social Freedom, Delivered in Steinway Hall . . . Nov. 20, 1871 (New York: Woodhull, Claflin, 1871; London: Blackfriars, 1894);

The Origins, Tendencies and Principles of Government; or, A Review of the Rise and Fall of Nations from Early Historic Times to the Present (New York: Woodhull, Claflin, 1871);

Freedom! Equality!! Justice!!! These Three; but the Greatest of These is Justice. A Speech on the Impending Revolution, Delivered in Music Hall, Boston, Thursday, Feb. 1, 1872, and the Academy of Music, New York, Feb. 20, 1872 (New York: Woodhull, Claflin, 1872);

Reformation or Revolution, Which? or, Behind the Political Scenes: A Speech Delivered in Cooper Institute, October 17, 1873 (New York: Woodhull, Claflin, 1873);

The Scare-Crows of Sexual Slavery, an Oration Delivered . . . at Silver Lake, Mass., Camp Meeting,

Victoria C. Woodhull

on Sunday, Aug. 17, 1873 (New York: Woodhull, Claflin, 1874);

Tried as by Fire; or, The True and the False Society: An Oration Delivered 150 Consecutive Nights (New York: Woodhull, Claflin, 1874);

Breaking the Seals; or, The Key to the Hidden Mystery. An Oration Delivered . . . August 20, 1875 (New York: Woodhull, Claflin, 1875);

A Speech on the Garden of Eden; or, Paradise Lost and Found, Delivered at Cooper Institute, New York, December 30, 1875 (New York: Woodhull, Claflin, 1876; revised edition, London, 1890);

A Fragmentary Record of Public Work Done in America, 1871-72 (London, 1887);

The Arguments for Woman's Electoral Rights, a Review of my Work at Washington, D.C., 1870-1 (London: Norman, 1887);

Stirpiculture; or, The Scientific Propagation of the Human Race (London, 1888);

Humanitarian Government (London, 1890);

The Human Body, the Temple of God; or, The Philosophy of Sociology, by Woodhull and Tennessee C. Claflin (London, 1890);

The Talebearer: How Scandals Are Spread; How Press Libels are Written (London, 1890);

The Rapid Multiplication of the Unfit (London & New York, 1891);

Humanitarian Money: The Unsolved Riddle (London, 1892).

Victoria C. Woodhull was one of the most flamboyant and controversial figures in nineteenth-century letters. Thomas Nast caricatured her in *Harper's Weekly* as "Mrs. Satan"; a story in the *New York Herald* described her and her sister Tennessee Claflin as "queens of finance" and "bewitching brokers"; an English reporter said she was "the United States mother of woman's suffrage"; and the Reverend Henry Ward Beecher, whom she accused of an illicit love affair, labeled her a "prostitute."

Her unconventional and jolting reformist antics made her the subject of many book-length biographical treatments, as well as the object of ridicule by cartoonists and novelists of her day. Novels by Harriett Beecher Stowe, by Henry James, and by Mark Twain and Charles Dudley Warner included characters believed to be depictions of Woodhull. Stowe presented her as the phony, publicity-seeking Dacia Dangyereyes in *My Wife and I* (1871), while James used a character named Mrs. Headway to deal with Woodhull's later siege of London society. Twain and Warner's *The Gilded Age* (1874) includes a character named Laura said to be modeled partly on Woodhull.

Victoria Claflin Woodhull was born in Homer, Ohio, 23 September 1838, the seventh child of Reuben Buckman Claflin, a miller, and Roxanna Hummel Claflin. She was an aggressive achiever in a society dominated by men. By the time she reached fifty-five she had announced her candidacy for president of the United States three times, first for the 1872 election; she had also opened the first woman's brokerage house; established two periodicals, one a radical weekly that espoused unpopular causes; helped define the woman suffrage movement, along with Susan B. Anthony and Elizabeth Cady Stanton; and presided over the National Association of Spiritualists.

Additionally, she was a captivating orator who had given hundreds of lectures across the United States and England on topics as diverse as spiritualism, the Bible, prostitution, free love, good marriages, workers' rights, woman's rights, and menstruation. Her lectures, writings, and lifestyle landed her in jail occasionally, had her evicted from her homes, barred from speaking in various places, and boycotted in business matters.

Through much of her career in the United States, Woodhull was surrounded by an entourage that included her parents; her husband, Col. James H. Blood, whom she married in 1865; for a time her former husband, Canning Woodhull, whom she had married in 1853; her two children by her first marriage; siblings, including Tennessee Claflin; and hangers-on at either her brokerage firm or weekly periodical. Her frequent lecture tours may have been necessary as an escape and as a means to provide for such a brood, as well as to finance her newspaper. Gratitude for her efforts often eluded the clan; in fact, some members of the family, including her mother, lambasted Woodhull in the press while still living under her roof.

The Claflins were always quarrelsome and, at various times, prone to unethical and often illegal activities. Buck and Roxanna Claflin dabbled in spiritualism, mesmerism, table tippings and rappings, and quack medicine as they shunted the family (seven of the ten children survived to adulthood) from town to town. Neighbors in Homer, Ohio, forced Buck Claflin to leave town after the suspicious burning of his recently insured grist mill and held a benefit bazaar to provide the family with the means to relocate. After several temporary stopovers in nearby towns, the family went on the road as a vagabond medicine show. Tennessee, a teenager, appeared as the chief fortune-teller and healer. At one stopover, in Ottawa, Illinois, they established an "infirmary" for the cure of cancer. The death of one of the patients and Tennessee's indictment for manslaughter sent them tramping again.

Woodhull had her own specialty–spiritualism. In 1868, according to her own statement, she had a vision of the Greek orator Demosthenes, who told her that fortune and fame awaited her in New York. There, both the

Woodhull's sister, Tennessee Claflin (courtesy New-York Historical Society)

fortune and fame were embodied in the physical being of Commodore Cornelius Vanderbilt, with whom her father had finagled a meeting for flirtatious and round-heeled Tennessee. The railroad tycoon, recently widowed and ailing, had a bent for spiritualism and was attracted to Tennessee's type of "magic healing." He was also amused by Victoria's high-principled antics against snobbery, pretension, and prejudice. In return for the "cure" and amusement, Vanderbilt gave Woodhull and Claflin sound financial advice and needed funds, with which they established themselves as the first "lady brokers" on Wall Street.

With their quick success and exotic backgrounds the sisters immediately became darlings of the New York press. Their obsession with filling scrapbooks was a prelude to the publicity they sought the rest of their long lives. Also, the financial success of the brokerage house, Woodhull, Claflin and Co., allowed the Claflins and party to move into a large and plush mansion.

The hypnotic and adventuresome personalities of the two women snared others besides Vanderbilt. In describing Woodhull, Frank Luther Mott writes that she never failed "to impress those whom she met by her beauty, her intelligence, and her very extraordinary personal magnetism. She had boundless ambition, no scruples, and unusual histrionic ability." Those qualities were appealing to Colonel Blood, who, after his marriage to Woodhull, became a partner in the brokerage, and to Stephen Pearl Andrews, who, in the twilight of his life, was a linguist, spiritualist, advocate of free love, and anarchist.

With Blood's and Andrews's encouragement, the confidence gained while capturing the business world, and a belief in women's competence, Woodhull decided to enter politics, announcing her candidacy for president of the United States in 1870, at age thirty-two. The leap into the political arena came while she was starting a writing career. Anxious to promote many of Andrews's ideas, Woodhull wrote a series of articles under the title "The Origins, Tendencies and Principles of Government," first published in the *New York Herald* in 1870, and as a book the following year. A key point of this series was Andrews's notion of the Pantarchy, where children, property, and economic matters were governed by the state, adults were in charge of their own nature, and free love reigned.

Besides giving Woodhull space for a regular column, "Petticoat Politician," *New York Herald* publisher James Gordon Bennett also editorialized favorably upon her candidacy. In one editorial he proclaimed, "Now there can certainly be no objection to such a competition as this; . . . Now for Victory for Victoria in 1872!" In still another, he described her as, "A woman and a smart and handsome woman, she is the proper person to stand forth against the field as the woman's right candidate for the White House."

However, the conservative *New York Times* was particularly galled by her views on capitalism, communism, and woman suffrage. The *Times* only gave Woodhull's candidacy 10 articles (contender Horace Greeley was the subject of 329) and in their only editorial on her presidential bid, compared her to the Jewish virgins of the parables who believed it not necessary to fill their lamps with oil on their wedding day. In an unnecessary aside, and in an accusatory tone, the *Times* said it might be "inappropriate to style her a foolish virgin," because she had been "married rather extensively." On her presidential capabilities, the *Times* wrote that Woodhull "fancies she is capable of illuminating the dark places of politics and social ethics without the light of reason."

On 14 May 1870 Woodhull and Claflin themselves entered the publishing business with *Woodhull and Claflin's Weekly*. Designed mainly as a campaign organ, the weekly espoused numerous causes, especially those of Andrews and Blood, who apparently wrote much of the copy. Yet, the periodical's inaugural edition stated its purpose as being "primarily devoted to the vital interests of the people.... it will support Victoria C. Woodhull for President with its whole strength; otherwise it will be untrammeled by party or personal considerations, free from all affiliations with political or social creeds, and will advocate Suffrage without distinction of sex." Ambitious in format and content, *Woodhull and Claflin's Weekly* included lively articles and features, including a serialized novel by George Sand and pieces on legal tender and Egypt's role in history, probably written by Andrews, who had several unpublished essays on hand. Also included were discussions of women achievers in various fields, book and theater reviews, fashion and financial columns, sports scores, and many advertisements.

The editors showed restraint in the first number of the magazine, but Andrews's plans for a Pantarchy, and other taboo subjects, soon began to fill the pages. The editorial page proclaimed a set of "fundamental propositions," among which were "A United States of the World–the Pantarchy; the Universal Church; Universal Home; Universal Science, based on the Nature of Things and the Philosophy of Integration; the Universal Language, Alwato; A Universal Canon of Art; Reconciliation–Harmony of the Race through the Cooperation of the Spirit World, and the Inauguration of the Millenium." Forthright essays on sexual hypocrisy, similar to Woodhull's lectures, targeted prostitution, calling for licensing of the houses and women, weekly medical checks, and the abandonment of police shakedown raids. By September, another Andrews idea was advocated, that being stirpiculture, the breeding of special stocks and races to bring together the best blood. On other occasions, *Woodhull and Claflin's Weekly* took a strong stand on free love, especially after Woodhull's speech in November 1871, when she departed from the script to say: "I have an inalienable, constitutional, and natural right to love whom I may, to love as long or as short a period as I can, to change that love every day if I please!"

Free love eventually was tied to other *Woodhull and Claflin's Weekly* issues, including woman's rights and stirpiculture. In the 2 November 1872 issue Woodhull intertwined free love and stirpiculture, saying the "scientific propagation and cultivation of the human animal, demands free love or freedom of the varied union of the sexes."

The more radical nature of the weekly was evidenced in the October 1871 issue when the motto "Upward and Onward" gave way to "Progress! Free Thought! Untrammeled Lives! Breaking the Way for Future Generations." Made up of sixteen pages, four columns to a page, the weekly called for less rigid divorce laws, organized labor, dietary and housing reform, and birth control; it also attacked abortion. The front page always used announcements paid for by reputable financiers, while advertisements for liquor and wine dealers, billiard parlor operators, and cure-alls were tucked inside. Also kept to inside pages were personals for mates, such as the following: "A lady in good standing having no acquaintances among gentlemen, would like to meet with one of liberal tendencies, worth from $15,000 to $20,000 . . . [he] should be mature in years of genial nature."

Priced at five cents a copy (later raised to ten), the weekly initially was supported by advertisements which sold at the high rate of $1.00 to $2.50 a line; a circulation of twenty thousand to forty thousand; Wall Street earnings from Woodhull, Claflin and Co.; and financial angels, most notably Vanderbilt. When she was particularly outspoken on sensitive issues, and the financiers pulled back, Woodhull attempted to raise funds by launching another lecture tour or by resorting to blackmail. Her biographers claim Woodhull was not above showing people stories in galley form with the threat to publish if donations were not volunteered. The blackmail threats were more prevalent, or open, at about the time of the Beecher-Tilton exposé, when Tennie C. (as Tennessee Claflin began to sign her name) claimed to have the "moral biographies" of about five hundred prominent New York males. The paper also threatened to publish the contents of a ledger kept for years by a madam. Blackmail, a fact of life in the Claflin family, was even defended in *Woodhull and Claflin's Weekly* with the statement: "If the laws will not protect women, they must protect themselves by the same crude justice that invented the blackmail system."

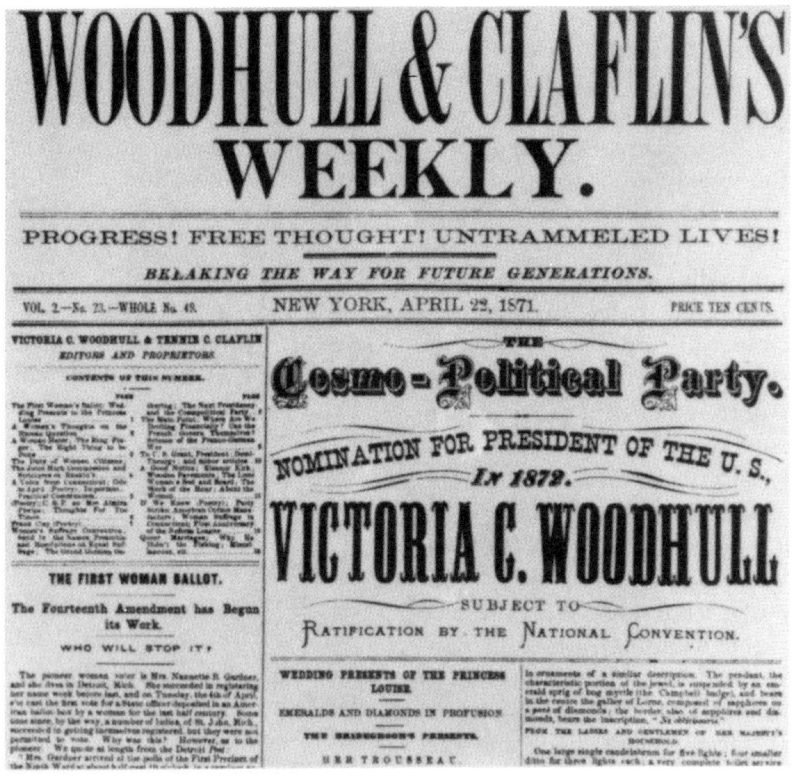

Front page of an issue of the weekly Woodhull and Claflin published in the 1870s (courtesy New-York Historical Society)

Woodhull and Claflin's Weekly served to provide Woodhull an importance she never felt while hustled throughout the Midwest as a child. Most issues contained her radical views, as well as rejoinders to critics and a few notes of adoration, presumably from readers. In a November 1870 issue of the weekly she presented an important argument for woman suffrage–that the Fourteenth and Fifteenth Amendments, written to enfranchise the Negro, also gave women the vote. The following month she went to Washington to offer Congress a memorial which, it was said, was inspired by the vision of Demosthenes, encouraged by Andrews and Blood, and most likely written by Congressman Benjamin Butler. When, on 11 January 1871, she delivered her speech before the Judiciary Committee of the House of Representatives, urging woman suffrage under the already enacted amendments, she had a hearing that Susan B. Anthony, Elizabeth Cady Stanton, and others had not been able to obtain. That very day she was invited by the suffragists to address their convention, which, by no coincidence, happened to be meeting in Washington. Her charm and persuasive oratory skills won over the group, some of whose members, listening to scandalmongers, had strong negative feelings about Woodhull's morals.

At the 1871 meeting of the National Woman Suffrage Association Woodhull delivered a rousing, revolutionary speech, saying in part, "We mean treason; we mean secession.... We are plotting revolution." The following year she published a manifesto in *Woodhull and Claflin's Weekly* seeking the support of the association in forming a People's party to enter the presidential race. When Anthony balked at the idea, Woodhull held her own convention, from which she obtained an endorsement for president of the United States on the Equal Rights party ticket, with Frederick Douglass, who supported Ulysses S. Grant in the election, nominated in absentia as her running mate.

Woodhull was at the zenith of her career at this point. However, the family feuds and the strain of maintaining her lecture schedule were beginning to sap her energy. Vanderbilt remarried and was either unwilling or unable to continue financial support; the suffragists, primarily concerned with uniting the two main factions of the movement, abandoned her as not very useful to the cause; and financial problems forced her to give up the mansion and, in June 1872, to fold *Woodhull and Claflin's Weekly*.

The accelerated radicalness of her writing and speaking had turned away financial backers and periodicals that at one time had helped her. By 1872 she attacked bastions of capitalism–the Astors and Vanderbilt himself. She came out against monopolization and accumulated wealth, exposed the corruption of politicians and the unethical practices of insurance companies, and campaigned against the revered rich, especially local landlords. On 24 February 1872, for example, the weekly reported: "An Astor may sit in his sumptuous apartments and watch the property bequeathed to him rise in value from one to fifty millions, and everybody bows low before his power. But if a tenant of his whose employer had discharged him because he did not vote the Republican ticket, fails to pay his month's rent to Mr. [William Blackhouse] Astor, the law sets him and his family into the street." Attacking the owner of New York's largest department store, Woodhull wrote: "Mr. [A. T.] Stewart . . . succeeds in twenty years in obtaining from the customers, whom he entraps into purchasing from him, fifty million dollars . . . and builds costly public beneficiaries, and straightaway the world makes him a philanthropist. But a poor man who should come along with a bolt of cloth which he smuggled into the country and which consequently he would sell at a lower price than Mr. Stewart . . . would be cast into prison."

In the eyes of capitalists who either had supported or tolerated the journal, by late 1871 and 1872 *Woodhull and Claflin's Weekly* had stepped over the fine line dividing eccentricity and madness. There was little outcry when it became the first periodical in the United States to print the *Communist Manifesto*.

Perhaps lost in all of this, however, was that Woodhull was practicing in 1872 what Theodore Roosevelt, thirty years later, termed muckraking. Mott described the journal's investigative reporting thus: "It discussed the strike in the anthracite coal region of Pennsylvania, defending the strikers. It exposed scandals in insurance companies and bond deals; it was a really valuable muckraker. It printed items about women in industry and business gleaned from here and there."

Part of the mystique surrounding Woodhull was related to her unpredictable and contradictory nature. She was capable of conducting serious investigative reporting, but also of indulging in sensationalism. Her involvement in the Beecher-Tilton adultery affair, the biggest scandal of the century, was a mixture of both. Woodhull had

Thomas Nast cartoon depicting Woodhull as "(Mrs.) Satan" in Harper's Weekly, *17 February 1872 (courtesy New-York Historical Society)*

known for some time about the relationship between America's most sacrosanct minister, the Reverend Henry Ward Beecher, and a parishioner, Elizabeth Tilton. Elizabeth Cady Stanton had reported the affair to Woodhull in confidence. More important, however, was the role of the victimized and vengeance-prone husband, Theodore Tilton, editor of the religious periodical the *Independent*, author of a flattering biography of Woodhull, and, for a time, her lover.

When Woodhull revealed Beecher's shenanigans in a speech before the National Association of Spiritualists, the dailies stayed mute, sparking Woodhull's resolve to get a wider audience for the exposé. On 2 November 1872 *Woodhull and Claflin's Weekly* was revived for the purpose of publicizing the Beecher-Tilton adultery case. The issue was planned with much deliberation. The "Great Universal Washing Day" had arrived, according to Woodhull, who mentioned the five hundred other biographies in her possession. She also told of the persecution the weekly had faced during that summer. The Beecher-Tilton story, Woodhull said, was the "commencement of a series of aggressive moral warfare on the social question." She intended for the revelation to "burst like a bombshell into the ranks of the moralistic social camp." Although she detailed the scandal, her bigger concern was to promote free love, reveal the follies of marriage, and denounce hypocrisy in high places.

The American News Company refused to distribute the issue, but it nevertheless sold out quickly and was resold at prices as high as ten to forty dollars a copy. The long-term consequences of the publication were not as fortuitous, because of a second exposé done by Tennie C. In a story spiced with lurid details, a wealthy broker, Luther C. Challis, was accused of seducing two young girls. Challis sued for libel. Far more important, however, was that Anthony Comstock, who was just beginning his activities with the New York Society for the Suppression of Vice, decided to make this a cause célèbre. When the copy of *Woodhull and Claflin's Weekly* which he had ordered arrived by post, he obtained a warrant for the arrest of Woodhull and associates under the newly enacted legislation preventing the mailing of obscene literature. Thus, the day before the national election, contender Woodhull and her sister began what became a thirty-one-day stay in Ludlow Street Jail. Woodhull received no votes.

Upon her release from jail, Woodhull planned to lecture in Boston on the experience, but the governor of Massachusetts prevented the speech. She revived the weekly once again on 28 December in order to publish the suppressed speech, entitled "Moral Cowardice and Modern Hypocrisy; or, Four Weeks in Ludlow Street Jail."

She was arrested again, which helped strengthen her case that she was being persecuted. The public reacted positively, and resolutions were passed against the "persecution." The paper now had a peak circulation, and Woodhull found renewed popular support through "Victoria Leagues" and spiritualist societies. Eventually, Challis lost his libel suit, and the sisters were acquitted of publishing obscene articles, the judge ruling in the latter case that the statute dealt with books, not newspapers.

In the 15 February 1873 issue Woodhull reproduced *New York Herald* advertisements for contraceptives, abortionists, venereal disease doctors, and madams, and challenged Comstock to act. On 17 May the entire Beecher-Tilton story was reprinted. But, gradually the paper appeared less frequently, partly because of a serious illness suffered by Woodhull, but also because of the demands of her regular lecture tours and arrests and trials. Tennie C. retired from her part of the editorship in May 1873, and increasingly, *Woodhull and Claflin's Weekly* was edited by Woodhull's brother-in-law, George Blood, and by Robert W. Hume.

Woodhull had extensive lecture tours in 1873-1874, acquiring money to sustain the family and the weekly. To a large degree, *Woodhull and Claflin's Weekly* now served as a promotion organ for the lectures. Barely surviving, it carried begging editorials that asked, "What will become of the *Weekly*?," and after 5 December 1874 its sixteen pages were cut by half to save money.

Subscribers, and writers such as Andrews, had deserted to the still radical *Crucible* by 1875, when Woodhull did a complete about-face in her thinking. Woodhull adopted Roman Catholicism and changed her lectures and articles to topics such as Biblical symbolism, "Newly Discovered Truth about Society," "Sexual Purity and Impurity," the body as a "holy temple," and menstruation. Dismayed, her readers called her "Mrs. Judas" as she tried to disassociate herself from causes of the past. She severed all ties with spiritualism and free love and sued James Blood for divorce. In the last issue of *Woodhull and Claflin's Weekly*, 10 June 1876, Woodhull claimed she had been misinterpreted on the subject of free love and that others had advocated it in her name.

Woodhull and Claflin ended up in England, where both married wealthy husbands. Before becoming Mrs. John Biddulph Martin on 21 October 1883, however, Woodhull spent a tremendous amount of energy, time, and money attempting to erase and reconstitute her past feats and antics. Later, with her sister (now the wife of Sir Francis Cook) and financial help from her new husband, Woodhull issued pamphlets and wrote numerous letters to New York and London dailies in an effort to create a past respectable in British eyes. She even sued the British Museum for possessing Beecher materials that termed her a blackmailer.

On 29 January 1881 Woodhull published one number of her famous periodical in London, retitled *Woodhull and Claflin's Journal*, to attack Blood and Andrews. She said she had been the "ostensible editor of a New York journal" whose main purpose was the "elevation of women, politically, morally and religiously," but that while she lectured, Blood and Andrews printed free love articles without her knowledge. She continued the same refrain in an evening paper, the *Cuckoo*, to which some people believed she donated some of Martin's money so that she could have a voice.

She returned to New York occasionally to fight old battles, announce another bid for the United States presidency, or to check on the New York edition of the *Humanitarian*, a magazine she had started in July 1892. Partly edited by her daughter, Zulu Maud, and mostly written by Dr. Charles Stuart Welles, a nephew by marriage, the *Humanitarian* promoted what Mott called an "unusually unscientific kind of eugenics." It also was packed with pseudophilosophical ideas and materials to help Woodhull defend herself and achieve respectability, including reprints of her many pamphlets, old New York newspaper clippings complimentary to her, and photographs of her in younger and more beautiful days. Biographer Johanna Johnston notes that the *Humanitarian* lasted one year longer than *Woodhull and Claflin's Weekly* "without making even a ripple to compare to the *Weekly*'s tidal wave." Another biographer, M. M. Marberry, states that the *Humanitarian* died in December 1901, a "nine-year-old stillborn child."

Woodhull lived another twenty-six years, to the age of eighty-eight. In later years, her obsession with gaining British-style respectability was fulfilled, and she assumed the role of a grand lady in her manor house at Bredon's Norton.

According to biographer Emanie Sachs, Woodhull was "on the way to sociological significance when she took the turning that led to fortune instead of fame" and, as a result, became an "interesting phenomenon instead of a heroine of history." The same indecision on which path to take seemed to plague the *Weekly*. Edward H. G. Clark, in the May 1873 *Thunderbolt*, already recognized it, describing the *Weekly* as having "voices from the 'seventh heaven,' and gabblings from a frog pond . . . yet the amazing journal is crowded with thought, and needed information that can be got nowhere else." Mott characterized the *Weekly* as being "by turns . . . the propagandist of grandiose schemes for human betterment, and an advocate of confused absurdities–a ringing voice in behalf of the downtrodden, and a shrill scream raised against the decencies–a banner lifted high for liberty and equality, and a blackmailing sheet."

Victoria Claflin Woodhull did, however, contribute to the literary and journalistic scenes by daring to expose corruption, injustice, hypocrisy, and pretension, much in the muckraking vein. Most important, however, she introduced and fought for causes that represented advanced thought, laying the groundwork for social advances in later decades.

Biographies:
Theodore Tilton, *Life of Victoria Claflin Woodhull* (New York: Golden Age, 1871);

G. S. Darewin, *Synopsis of the Lives of Victoria Woodhull and Tennessee Claflin* (London: J. H. Corthesy, 1891);

Madeleine Legge, *Two Noble Women, Nobly Planned* (London: Phelps Brothers, 1893);

Emanie Sachs, *"The Terrible Siren": Victoria Woodhull* (New York: Harper, 1928);

Johanna Johnston, *Mrs. Satan. The Incredible Saga of Victoria C. Woodhull* (New York: Putnam's, 1967);

M. M. Marberry, *Vicky. A Biography of Victoria C. Woodhull* (New York: Funk & Wagnalls, 1967);

Marion Meade, *Free Woman: The Life and Times of Victoria Woodhull* (New York: Knopf, 1976).

References:
Anonymous, *The Beecher-Tilton Scandal, a Complete History of the Case, with Mrs. Woodhull's Original Statement* (Brooklyn, 1874);

Ernest Earnest, *The American Eve in Fact and Fiction, 1775-1914* (Urbana: University of Illinois Press, 1974);

Gerald W. Johnson, "Dynamic Victoria Woodhull," *American Heritage*, 7 (June 1956): 44-47;

Frank Luther Mott, *A History of American Magazines 1865-1885* (Cambridge, Mass.: Harvard University Press, 1938-1968), pp. 443-453;

Louise R. Noun, *Strong-Minded Women* (Ames: Iowa State University Press, 1969);

Irving Wallace, *The Square Pegs* (New York: Knopf, 1957).

Papers:
A large collection of Woodhull's papers is held at Southern Illinois University, Carbondale.

Checklist of Further Readings

Alden, Henry Mills. *Magazine Writing and the New Literature*. New York: Harper, 1908.

Allen, Frederick Lewis, William L. Chenery, and Fulton Oursler. "American Magazines, 1741-1941," *Bulletin of the New York Public Library*, 45 (June 1941): 439-456.

Arndt, Karl J. R., and May E. Olson. *German-American Newspapers and Periodicals, 1732-1955*. Heidelberg: Quelle & Meyer, 1961.

Atchison, Ray M. "*The Land We Love*: A Southern Post-Bellum Magazine of Agriculture, Literature, and Military History," *North Carolina Historical Review*, 37 (October 1960): 506-515.

Atchison. "*Our Living and Our Dead*: A Post-Bellum North Carolina Magazine of Literature and History," *North Carolina Historical Review*, 40 (October 1963): 423-433.

Atchison. "*Scott's Monthly Magazine*: A Georgia Post-Bellum Periodical of Literature and Military History," *Georgia Historical Quarterly*, 49 (September 1965): 294-305.

Brainerd, Marion. "Historical Sketch of American Legal Periodicals," *Law Library Journal*, 14 (October 1921): 63-69.

Bullock, Penelope L. *The Anglo-American Periodical Press, 1838-1909*. Baton Rouge: Louisiana State University Press, 1981.

Calhoun, Richard J. "The Ante-Bellum Literary Twilight: *Russell's Magazine*," *Southern Literary Journal*, 3 (Fall 1970): 89-110.

Cardwell, Guy A. "Charleston Periodicals, 1795-1860: A Study in Literary Influence, with a Descriptive Check List of Seventy-Five Magazines," Ph.D. dissertation, University of North Carolina, 1936.

Cardwell. "The Influence of Addison on Charleston Periodicals, 1795-1860," *Studies in Philology*, 35 (July 1938): 456-470.

Carson, Betty Farley. "Richmond Renascence: The Virginia Writers' Club of the 1920s and *The Reviewer*," *Cabellian*, 2 (Spring 1970): 39-47.

Chenery, William L. "American Magazines, 1741-1941," *Bulletin of the New York Public Library*, 45 (June 1941): 445-448.

Chielens, Edward E. *American Literary Magazines: The Eighteenth and Nineteenth Centuries*. Westport, Conn.: Greenwood Press, 1986.

Chielens. *The Literary Journal In America to 1900*. Detroit: Gale Research Company, 1975.

Clark, Charles Hopkins. "Newspapers and Periodicals of Connecticut," in *History of Connecticut in Monographic Form*, edited by Norris Galpin Osborn. New York: States History Company, 1925, II: 57-188.

Cohen, Sidney J. *Three Notable Ante-Bellum Magazines of South Carolina*. Columbia: University of South Carolina Press, 1915.

Cox, Leland. "Realistic and Humorous Writings in Ante-Bellum Charleston Magazines," in *South Carolina Journals and Journalists*, edited by James B. Meriwether. Spartanburg, S.C.: Reprint Co., 1975, pp. 177-205.

Daniel, Walter C. *Black Journals of the United States*. Westport, Conn.: Greenwood Press, 1982.

Davis, Sheldon Emmor. *Educational Periodicals During the Nineteenth Century*. U.S. Department of the Interior, Bureau of Education, Bulletin no. 28. Washington, D.C.: U.S. Government Printing Office, 1919.

Demaree, Albert Lowther. *The American Agricultural Press, 1819-1860*. New York: Columbia University Press, 1941.

Ditzion, Sidney. "History of Periodical Literature in the United States," *Bulletin of Bibliography*, 15 (January/April 1935): 110; (May/August 1935): 129-133.

Drewry, John Eldridge. *Some Magazines and Magazine Makers*. Boston: Stradford, 1924.

Ellison, Rhoda Coleman. *Early American Publications: A Study in Literary Interests*. University: University of Alabama Press, 1947.

Endres, Fred F. "The Pre-Muckraking Days of *McClure's Magazine*, 1893-1901," *Journalism Quarterly*, 55 (Spring 1878): 154-157.

Felker, Clay S. "Life Cycles in the Age of Magazines," *Antioch Review*, 29 (Spring 1969): 7-13.

Ferguson, Marjorie. *Forever Feminine: Women's Magazines and the Cult of Feminity*. Portsmouth, N.H.: Heinemann, 1983.

Flanders, Bertram H. "*Bugle-Horn of Liberty*: A Confederate Humorous Magazine," *Emory University Quarterly*, 9 (June 1953): 78-85;

Flanders, Bertram H. *Early Georgia Magazines: Literary Periodicals to 1865*. Athens: University of Georgia Press, 1944.

Flanders, Ralph B. "Newspapers and Periodicals in the Washington Memorial Library, Macon, Georgia," *North Carolina Historical Review*, 7 (April 1930): 220-223.

Forsyth, David P. *The Business Press in America, 1750-1865*. Philadelphia: Chilton, 1964.

Garwood, Irving. "American Periodicals From 1850 to 1860," *Western Illinois State Teachers College Quarterly*, 9 (December 1929): 1-50; (March 1930): 53-85.

Gilmer, Gertrude. *Checklist of Southern Periodicals to 1861*. Boston: F. W. Faxon, 1934.

Gilmer. "A Critique of Certain Georgia Ante-Bellum Literary Magazines Arranged Chronologically, and a Checklist," *Georgia Historical Quarterly*, 18 (December 1934): 293-334.

Graybar, Lloyd J. "Albert Shaw and the Founding of the *Review of Reviews*, 1891-1897," *Journalism Quarterly*, 49 (Winter 1972): 692-697, 716.

Greene, Theodore P. *America's Heroes: The Changing Models of Success in American Magazines*. New York: Oxford University Press, 1970.

Griffin, Max L. "A Bibliography of New Orleans Magazines," *Louisiana Historical Quarterly*, 18 (July 1935): 491-556.

Hammond, Otis Grant. *Bibliography of the Newspapers and Periodicals of Concord, New Hampshire, 1790-1898*. Concord: Printed by Ira C. Evans, 1902.

Holland, Dorothy Garesche. *An Annotated Checklist of Magazines Published in St. Louis Before 1900*. Washington University Library Studies, no. 2. St. Louis: Washington University Press, 1951.

Hoole, William Stanley. *A Check-List and Finding-List of Charleston Periodicals 1732-1864*. Durham, N.C.: Duke University Press, 1936.

Hubbell, Jay B. "Southern Magazines," in *Culture in the South*, edited by W. T. Couch. Chapel Hill: University of North Carolina Press, 1934, pp. 159-182.

Ingraham, Charles A. "American Magazines, Past and Present," *Americana*, 15 (October 1921): 325-333.

Jackson, David K. "An Estimate of the Influence of *The Southern Literary Messenger*, 1834-1864," *Southern Literary Messenger*, new series 1 (August 1939): 508-514.

Jillson, Willard Rouse. *The Newspapers and Periodicals of Frankfort, Kentucky, 1795-1945*. Frankfort: Kentucky State Historical Society, 1945.

Johnson, Charles S. "The Rise of the Negro Magazine," *Journal of Negro History*, 13 (January 1928): 7-21.

Kelly, R. Gordon, ed. *Children's Periodicals of the United States*. Westport, Conn.: Greenwood Press, 1984.

Klingberg, Frank J. "The Value of Regional Literature," *Historical Magazine of the Protestant Episcopal Church*, 10 (December 1941): 399-401.

Linneman, William R. "*Southern Punch: A Draught of Confederate Wit*," *Southern Folklore Quarterly*, 26 (June 1962): 131-136.

Littlefield, Daniel F., and James W. Parins. *American Indian and Alaskan Native Newspapers and Periodicals, 1826-1924*. Westport, Conn.: Greenwood Press, 1984.

McDowell, Tremaine. "Bryant and *The North American Review*," *American Literature*, 1 (March 1929): 14-26.

McKeithan, Daniel M. "Paul Hamilton Hayne and *The Southern Bivouac*," *University of Texas Studies in English*, 17 (8 July 1937): 112-113.

McLean, Frank. "Periodicals Published in the South before 1880," Ph.D. dissertation, University of Virginia, 1928.

Matthews, Brander. "American Magazines," *Bookman*, 49 (July 1919): 533-541.

Meyer, S. E. *America's Great Illustrators*. New York: Abrams, 1978.

Moore, L. Hugh. "*The Sunny South* and Its Literature," *Georgia Review*, 19 (Summer 1965): 176-185.

Moore, Rayburn S. "A Distinctly Southern Magazine: *The Southern Bivouac*," *Southern Literary Journal*, 2 (Spring 1970): 51-65.

Moore, Rayburn S. "Southern Writers and Northern Literary Magazines, 1865-1890," Ph.D. dissertation, Duke University, 1956.

Mott, Frank Luther. *A History of American Magazines*, 5 volumes. Cambridge, Mass.: Harvard University Press, 1938-1968.

Oberholtzer, Ellis Paxson. *The Literary History of Philadelphia*. Philadelphia: George W. Jacobs, 1906.

Oursler, Fulton. "American Magazines, 1741-1941," *Bulletin of the New York Public Library*, 45 (June 1941): 448-456.

Paskoff, Paul, and Daniel J. Wilson, eds. *The Cause of the South: Selections from DeBow's Review*. Baton Rouge: Louisiana State University Press, 1982.

Polk, Noel E. "W. W. Hicks and *The XIX Century*, 1869-1871," in *South Carolina Journals and Journalists*, edited by James B. Meriwether. Spartanburg, S.C.: Reprint Co., 1975, pp. 121-131.

Pullar, Elizabeth. "Illustrated Magazines of the 19th Century," *Antiques Journal*, 34 (November 1979): 25-27, 46-47.

Rawings, Kenneth W. "Trial List of Kentucky Newspapers and Periodicals Before 1860," *Kentucky Register*, 36 (July 1938): 263-287.

Repplier, Agnes. "American Magazines," *Yale Review*, 16 (January 1927): 261-274.

Riley, Sam G. *Index to Southern Periodicals*. Westport, Conn.: Greenwood Press, 1986.

Riley, Sam G. *Magazines of the American South*. Westport, Conn.: Greenwood Press, 1986.

Riley, Susan B. "The Hazards of Periodical Publishing in the South During the Nineteenth Century," *Tennessee Historical Quarterly*, 21 (1962): 365-376.

Riley, Susan B. "The Southern Literary Magazine of the Mid-Nineteenth Century," *Tennessee Historical Quarterly*, 23 (September 1964): 221-236.

Rivers, William L. "William Cowper Brann and His 'Iconoclast,' " *Journalism Quarterly*, 35 (Fall 1958): 433-438.

Rollins, Hyder E. "O. Henry's Texas Days," *Bookman*, 40 (October 1914): 154-165.

Rusk, Ralph Leslie. *The Literature of the Middle Western Frontier*, 2 volumes. New York: Columbia University Press, 1925.

Savory, Jerold, and Patricia Marks. *The Smiling Muse: Victoriana in the Comic Press*. Philadelphia: Art Alliance Press, 1985.

Schacht, J. H. *A Bibliography for the Study of Magazines*, fourth edition. Urbana, Ill.: College of Communications, 1979.

Severance, Frank Hayward. "The Periodical Press of Buffalo, 1811-1915," *Buffalo Historical Society Publications*, 19 (1915): 177-280.

Shearer, Augustus Hunt. "American Historical Periodicals," *Mississippi Valley Historical Review*, 4 (March 1918): 484-491.

Singerman, Robert. *Jewish Serials of the World: A Research Bibliography of Secondary Sources*. Westport, Conn.: Greenwood Press, 1986.

Stearns, Bertha Monica. "Early New England Magazines for Ladies," *New England Quarterly*, 2 (July 1929): 420-457.

Stearns. "Southern Magazines for Ladies," *South Atlantic Quarterly*, 31 (January 1932): 70-87.

Steinberg, S. H. *Reformer in the Marketplace: Edward W. Bok and the Ladies' Home Journal*. Baton Rouge: Louisiana State University Press, 1979.

Steiner, Linda. "Finding Community in Nineteenth-Century Suffrage Periodicals," *American Journalism*, 1 (Summer 1983): 1-15.

Stephens, Ethel. *American Popular Magazines, A Bibliography*. Bulletin of Bibliography Pamphlets, no. 23 (1916).

Stuntz, Stephen Conrad. *List of Agricultural Periodicals of the United States and Canada Published During the Century July 1810 to July 1910*. U.S. Department of Agriculture, Miscellaneous Publication, no. 398. Washington, D.C.: U.S. Government Printing Office, 1941.

Tassin, Algernon de Vivier. *The Magazine in America*. New York: Dodd, Mead, 1916.

Tebbel, John. *The American Magazine: A Compact History*. New York: Hawthorn Books, 1969.

Terwilliger, W. Bird. "A History of Literary Periodicals in Baltimore," Ph.D. dissertation, University of Maryland, 1941.

Thomas, Dana. *The Media Moguls*. New York: Putnam, 1981.

Venable, William Henry. "Early Periodical Literature of the Ohio Valley," *Magazine of Western History*, 8 (June 1888): 101-110; (July 1888): 197-203.

Wish, Harvey. "George Frederick Holmes and Southern Periodical Literature of the Mid-Nineteenth Century," *Journal of Southern History*, 7 (1941): 343-356.

Wolseley, Roland E. *The Changing Magazine*. New York: Hastings House, 1983.

Wood, James Playsted. *Magazines in the United States, Their Social and Economic Influence*. New York: Ronald Press, 1971.

Contributors

Nora Baker	*Southern Illinois University at Edwardsville*
Maurine H. Beasley	*University of Maryland*
James Boylan	*University of Massachusetts, Amherst*
John C. Bromley	*University of Northern Colorado*
Douglas S. Campbell	*Lock Haven University*
Philip B. Dematteis	*Columbia, South Carolina*
Lloyd E. Chiasson	*The University of Southwestern Louisiana*
Carolyn Garrett Cline	*University of Texas–Austin*
Thomas B. Connery	*College of Saint Thomas*
Wallace B. Eberhard	*University of Georgia*
Charles Egleston	*Columbia, South Carolina*
Kathleen L. Endres	*Bowling Green State University*
George Everett	*University of Tennessee, Knoxville*
Frederic B. Farrar	*Temple University*
Charles A. Fleming	*Oklahoma State University*
Ralph Frasca	*University of Iowa*
Lloyd J. Graybar	*Eastern Kentucky University*
Nora Hall	*University of Minnesota*
Bert Hitchcock	*Auburn University*
W. J. Hug	*Auburn University*
William E. Huntzicker	*Minneapolis, Minnesota*
Terry Hynes	*California State University, Fullerton*
Lee Jolliffe	*Ohio University*
A. J. Kaul	*University of Southern Mississippi*
Kathleen Kearney Keeshen	*Morgan Hill, California*
John A. Lent	*Temple University*
Roger Cameron Lips	*University of Minnesota at Duluth*
Therese L. Lueck	*Bowling Green State University*
Rayburn S. Moore	*University of Georgia*
Shirley M. Mundt	*Louisiana State University*
Whitney R. Mundt	*Louisiana State University*
Jack A. Nelson	*Brigham Young University*
Karen Nipps	*Library Company of Philadelphia*
Cathy Packer	*Boston College*
Janet E. Ramsey	*State University College at Buffalo*
Paula Cozort Renfro	*Southwest Texas State University*
Sam G. Riley	*Virginia Polytechnic Institute and State University*
Patt Foster Roberson	*Southern University*
Kate Esary Russell	*University of Georgia*
Gary W. Selnow	*Virginia Polytechnic Institute and State University*
Linda Steiner	*Governors State University*
James Glen Stovall	*University of Alabama*
J. Douglas Tarpley	*CBN University*
Erwin K. Thomas	*Norfolk State University*
Donna Ullrich-Eaton	*University of Detroit*
Beth M. Waggenspack	*Virginia Polytechnic Institute and State University*

ISBN 0-8103-4557-9

90000

(Continued from front endsheets)

120 *American Poets Since World War II, Third Series*, edited by R. S. Gwynn (1992)

121 *Seventeenth-Century British Nondramatic Poets*, First Series, edited by M. Thomas Hester (1992)

122 *Chicano Writers*, Second Series, edited by Francisco A. Lomelí and Carl R. Shirley (1992)

123 *Nineteenth-Century French Fiction Writers: Naturalism and Beyond, 1860-1900*, edited by Catharine Savage Brosman (1992)

124 *Twentieth-Century German Dramatists, 1919-1992*, edited by Wolfgang D. Elfe and James Hardin (1992)

125 *Twentieth-Century Caribbean and Black African Writers*, Second Series, edited by Bernth Lindfors and Reinhard Sander (1993)

Documentary Series

1 *Sherwood Anderson, Willa Cather, John Dos Passos, Theodore Dreiser, F. Scott Fitzgerald, Ernest Hemingway, Sinclair Lewis*, edited by Margaret A. Van Antwerp (1982)

2 *James Gould Cozzens, James T. Farrell, William Faulkner, John O'Hara, John Steinbeck, Thomas Wolfe, Richard Wright*, edited by Margaret A. Van Antwerp (1982)

3 *Saul Bellow, Jack Kerouac, Norman Mailer, Vladimir Nabokov, John Updike, Kurt Vonnegut*, edited by Mary Bruccoli (1983)

4 *Tennessee Williams*, edited by Margaret A. Van Antwerp and Sally Johns (1984)

5 *American Transcendentalists*, edited by Joel Myerson (1988)

6 *Hardboiled Mystery Writers: Raymond Chandler, Dashiell Hammett, Ross Macdonald*, edited by Matthew J. Bruccoli and Richard Layman (1989)

7 *Modern American Poets: James Dickey, Robert Frost, Marianne Moore*, edited by Karen L. Rood (1989)

8 *The Black Aesthetic Movement*, edited by Jeffrey Louis Decker (1991)

9 *American Writers of the Vietnam War: W. D. Ehrhart, Larry Heinemann, Tim O'Brien, Walter McDonald, John M. Del Vecchio*, edited by Ronald Baughman (1991)

10 *The Bloomsbury Group*, edited by Edward L. Bishop (1992)

Yearbooks

1980 edited by Karen L. Rood, Jean W. Ross, and Richard Ziegfeld (1981)

1981 edited by Karen L. Rood, Jean W. Ross, and Richard Ziegfeld (1982)

1982 edited by Richard Ziegfeld; associate editors: Jean W. Ross and Lynne C. Zeigler (1983)

1983 edited by Mary Bruccoli and Jean W. Ross; associate editor: Richard Ziegfeld (1984)

1984 edited by Jean W. Ross (1985)

1985 edited by Jean W. Ross (1986)

1986 edited by J. M. Brook (1987)

1987 edited by J. M. Brook (1988)

1988 edited by J. M. Brook (1989)

1989 edited by J. M. Brook (1990)

1990 edited by James W. Hipp (1991)

1991 edited by James W. Hipp (1992)

Concise Series

Concise Dictionary of American Literary Biography, 6 volumes (1988-1989): *The New Consciousness, 1941-1968; Colonization to the American Renaissance, 1640-1865; Realism, Naturalism, and Local Color, 1865-1917; The Twenties, 1917-1929; The Age of Maturity, 1929-1941; Broadening Views, 1968-1988.*

Concise Dictionary of British Literary Biography, 8 volumes (1991-1992): *Writers of the Middle Ages and Renaissance Before 1660; Writers of the Restoration and Eighteenth Century, 1660-1789; Writers of the Romantic Period, 1789-1832; Victorian Writers, 1832-1890; Late Victorian and Edwardian Writers, 1890-1914; Modern Writers, 1914-1945; Writers After World War II, 1945-1960; Contemporary Writers, 1960 to Present.*